THE PAPERS OF ALEXANDER HAMILTON

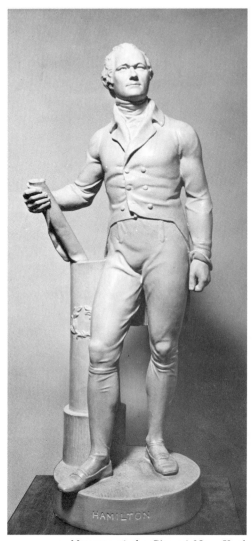

Alexander Hamilton
Model for statue made in 1831
by Robert Ball Hughes

THE PAPERS OF

Alexander Hamilton

VOLUME XXI

APRIL 1797–JULY 1798

HAROLD C. SYRETT, EDITOR

Associate Editors

BRIGID ALLEN

BARBARA A. CHERNOW   PATRICIA SYRETT

 COLUMBIA UNIVERSITY PRESS

NEW YORK AND LONDON, 1974

FROM THE PUBLISHER

The preparation of this edition of the papers of
Alexander Hamilton has been made possible by the
support received for the work of the editorial and
research staff from the generous grants of the Rocke-
feller Foundation, Time Inc., and the Ford Foundation, and by the far-sighted cooperation of the
National Historical Publications Commission. To
these organizations, the publisher expresses gratitude
on behalf of all who are concerned about making
available the record of the founding of the United
States.

A generous gift from Mr. Thomas S. Brush and
the balance of a grant from the Charles E. Merrill
Trust have enabled the Press to publish this volume.

PREFACE

THIS EDITION of Alexander Hamilton's papers contains letters and other documents written by Hamilton, letters to Hamilton, and some documents (commissions, certificates, etc.) that directly concern Hamilton but were written neither by him nor to him. All letters and other documents have been printed in chronological order. Two volumes of Hamilton's legal papers, entitled *The Law Practice of Alexander Hamilton*, have been published by the Columbia University Press under the editorial direction of the late Julius Goebel, Jr. The third and last volume of this distinguished work is being completed by Professor Joseph H. Smith, George Welwood Murray Professor of Legal History of the School of Law, Columbia University.

Many letters and documents have been calendared. Such calendared items include routine letters and documents by Hamilton, routine letters to Hamilton, some of the letters or documents written by Hamilton for someone else, letters or documents which have not been found but which are known to have existed, letters or documents which have been erroneously attributed to Hamilton, and letters to or by Hamilton that deal exclusively with his legal practice.

Because all of Hamilton's significant legal opinions appear in *The Law Practice of Alexander Hamilton* they have been omitted from these volumes.

The notes in these volumes are designed to provide information concerning the nature and location of each document, to identify Hamilton's correspondents and the individuals mentioned in the text, to explain events or ideas referred to in the text, and to point out textual variations or mistakes. Occasional departures from these standards can be attributed to a variety of reasons. In many cases the desired information has been supplied in an earlier note and can be found through the use of the index. Notes have not been added when in the opinion of the editors the material in the text was either self-explanatory or common knowledge. The editors, moreover, have not thought it desirable or necessary to provide full annotation for Hamilton's legal correspondence. Finally, the editors on some occasions have been unable to find the desired information, and on other occasions the editors have been remiss.

GUIDE TO EDITORIAL APPARATUS

I. SYMBOLS USED TO DESCRIBE MANUSCRIPTS

AD	Autograph Document
ADS	Autograph Document Signed
ADf	Autograph Draft
ADfS	Autograph Draft Signed
AL	Autograph Letter
ALS	Autograph Letter Signed
D	Document
DS	Document Signed
Df	Draft
DfS	Draft Signed
LS	Letter Signed
LC	Letter Book Copy
[S]	[S] is used with other symbols (AD[S], ADf[S], AL[S], D[S], Df[S], L[S]) to indicate that the signature on the document has been cropped or clipped.

II. MONETARY SYMBOLS AND ABBREVIATIONS

bf	Banco florin
V	Ecu
f	Florin
₶	Livre Tournois
medes	Maravedis (also md and mde)
d.	Penny or denier
ps	Piece of eight

£	Pound sterling or livre
Ry	Real
rs vn	Reals de vellon
rdr	Rix daller
s	Shilling, sou or sol (also expressed as /)
sti	Stiver

III. SHORT TITLES AND ABBREVIATIONS

Adams, *Works of John Adams*

Charles Francis Adams, *The Works of John Adams* (Boston, 1850–1856).

Annals of Congress

The Debates and Proceedings in the Congress of the United States; with an Appendix, Containing Important State Papers and Public Documents, and All the Laws of a Public Nature (Washington, 1834–1849).

Archivo, Miranda, XV

Archivo del General Miranda: Negociaciones 1770–1810 (Caracas, 1938), XV.

ASP

American State Papers, Documents, Legislative and Executive, of the Congress of the United States (Washington, 1832–1861).

Boyd, *Papers of Thomas Jefferson*

Julian P. Boyd, ed., *The Papers of Thomas Jefferson* (Princeton, 1950–).

Callender, *History*

James Thompson Callender, *The History of the United States for 1796; Including a Variety of Interesting Particulars Relative to the Federal Government Previous to That Period* (Philadelphia: Snowden and McCorkle, 1797).

Debrett, *A Collection of State Papers*

John Debrett, *A Collection of State Papers, Relative to the War against France Now carrying on by Great-Britain and the several other European Powers, Con-*

taining Authentic Copies of Treaties, Conventions, Proclamations, Manifestoes, Declarations, Memorials, Remonstrances, Official Letters, Parliamentary Papers, London Gazette Accounts of the War, &c. &c. &c. Many of which have never before been published in England (London: Printed for J. Debrett, opposite Burlington House, Piccadilly, 1794–1797).

Dropmore Papers *The Manuscripts of J. B. Fortescue, Esq., Preserved at Dropmore* (Historical Manuscripts Commission, Vol. 30), I–IV (London, 1892–1905).

Duvergier, *Lois* J. B. Duvergier, *Collection Complète des Lois, Décrets, Ordonnances, Réglemens, et Avis du Conseil-d'Etat, Publiée sur les Editions Officielles du Louvre; de L'Imprimerie Nationale, Par Baudouin; et Du Bulletin des Lois* (Paris, 1824–1825).

Executive Journal, I *Journal of the Executive Proceedings of the Senate* (Washington, 1828), I.

Ford, *Writings of Jefferson* Paul Leicester Ford, ed., *The Writings of Thomas Jefferson* (New York, 1892–1899).

Goebel, *Law Practice* Julius Goebel, Jr., ed., *The Law Practice of Alexander Hamilton: Documents and Commentary* (New York and London, 1964–).

GW John C. Fitzpatrick, ed., *The Writings of George Washington* (Washington, 1931–1944).

Hamilton, *Intimate Life* Allan McLane Hamilton, *The Intimate Life of Alexander Hamilton* (New York, 1910).

Hamilton, *James Monroe* Stanislaus Murray Hamilton, ed., *The Writings of James Monroe Including a Collection of His*

	Public and Private Papers and Correspondence Now for the First Time Printed (New York, 1898–1903).
Hamilton, *Reminiscences*	James A. Hamilton, *Reminiscences of James A. Hamilton* (New York, 1869).
HCLW	Henry Cabot Lodge, ed., *The Works of Alexander Hamilton* (New York, 1904).
House List of Private Claims	*Digested Summary and Alphabetical List of Private Claims Which Have Been Presented to the House of Representatives From the First to the Thirty-First Congress, Exhibiting the Action of Congress on Each Claim, With References to the Journals, Reports, Bills, &c., Elucidating Its Progress. Compiled by Order of the House of Representatives* (Washington, 1853).
Isambert, *Recueil Général des Anciennes Lois Françaises*	*Recueil Général des Anciennes Lois Françaises, Depuis L'An 420 Jusqu'à La Révolution de 1789, par MM. Jourdan, Docteur en droit, Avocat à la Cour royale de Paris; Isambert, Avocat aux Conseils du Roi et à la Cour de Cassation; Decrusy, ancien Avocat à la Cour royale de Paris* (Paris, 1821–1833).
JCC	*Journals of the Continental Congress, 1774–1789* (Washington, 1904–1937).
JCH Transcripts	John C. Hamilton Transcripts, Columbia University Libraries.
JCHW	John C. Hamilton, ed., *The Works of Alexander Hamilton* (New York, 1851–1856).
Journal of the House, I, II	*Journal of the House of Representatives of the United States* (Washington, 1826), I, II.
JPP	"Journal of the Proceedings of the President," George Washington Papers, Library of Congress.

King, *The Life and Correspondence of Rufus King*

Charles R. King, ed., *The Life and Correspondence of Rufus King* (New York, 1894–1900).

Martens, *Recûeil*, III, V, VI

Georg Friedrich von Martens, *Recûeil des principaux Traités d'Alliance, de Paix, de Trêve, de Neutralité, de Commerce, de Limites, d'Echange etc. conclus par les puissances de l'Europe tant entre elles qu'avec les puissances et etats dans d'autres parties du monde depuis 1761 jusqu'à présent*, 2nd edition (Göttingen, 1817–1829), III, V, VI.

Mayo, *Instructions to British Ministers*

Bernard Mayo, ed., "Instructions to the British Ministers to the United States," *Annual Report of the American Historical Association for the Year 1936* (Washington, 1941), III.

Miller, *Treaties*, II

Hunter Miller, ed., *Treaties and Other International Acts of the United States of America* (Washington, 1931), II.

Minutes of the Common Council

Minutes of the Common Council of the City of New York, 1784–1831 (New York, 1917).

"Minutes of the S.U.M."

MS minutes of the Society for Establishing Useful Manufactures, City of Paterson, New Jersey, Plant Management Commission, Successors to the Society for Establishing Useful Manufactures.

Mitchell, *Hamilton*

Broadus Mitchell, *Alexander Hamilton* (New York, 1957–1962).

Mix, *Catalogue: Maps and Surveys*

David E. E. Mix, ed., *Catalogue: Maps and Surveys, in the Offices of the Secretary of State, State Engineer and Surveyor, and Comptroller, and the New York State Library* (Albany, 1859).

Monroe, *A View of the Conduct of the Executive*

James Monroe, *A View of the Conduct of the Executive, in the Foreign Affairs of the United*

States, Connected with the Mission to the French Republic, During the Years 1794, 5 & 6 (Philadelphia: Printed by and for Benjamin Franklin Bache, 1797).

Moore, *International Adjudications*   John Bassett Moore, ed., *International Adjudications; Ancient and Modern, History and Documents, Together with Mediatorial Reports, Advisory Opinions, and the Decisions of Domestic Commissions, on International Claims* (New York, 1929–1936).

Morris, *In the Account of Property*   Robert Morris, *In the Account of Property* (King & Baird, Printers, No. 9 Sansom Street [Philadelphia], n.d.).

Naval Documents, Quasi-War, February, 1797–October, 1798   *Naval Documents Related to the Quasi-War Between the United States and France: Naval Operations from February 1797 to October 1798* (Washington, D.C., 1935).

N.Y. Colonial Manuscripts   *Calendar of N.Y. Colonial Manuscripts: Indorsed Land Papers; in the Office of the Secretary of State of New York. 1643–1803* (Albany, 1864).

PRO: Adm or PRO: F.O.   Public Record Office of Great Britain.

Réimpression de L'Ancien Moniteur   *Réimpression de L'Ancien Moniteur, Seule Histoire Authentique et Inaltérée de la Révolution Française* (Paris, 1847).

"Reynolds Pamphlet"   Alexander Hamilton, *Observations on Certain Documents Contained in No. V and VI of "The History of the United States for the Year 1796," in which the Charge of Speculation against Alexander Hamilton, Late Secretary of the Treasury, is Fully Refuted. Written by Himself* (Philadelphia: Printed for John Fenno, by John Bioren, 1797).

1 *Stat.*	*The Public Statutes at Large of the United States of America* (Boston, 1845).
6 *Stat.*	*The Public Statutes at Large of the United States of America* [Private Statutes] (Boston, 1846).
Werner, *New York Civil List*	Edgar A. Werner, ed., *Civil List and Constitutional History of the Colony and State of New York* (Albany, 1891).
Wharton, *Revolutionary Diplomatic Correspondence*	Francis Wharton, ed., *The Revolutionary Diplomatic Correspondence of the United States* (Washington, 1889).

IV. INDECIPHERABLE WORDS

Words or parts of words which could not be deciphered because of the illegibility of the writing or the multilation of the manuscript have been indicated as follows:

1. ⟨– – – – –⟩ indicates illegible words with the number of dashes indicating the estimated number of illegible words.
2. Words or letters in broken brackets indicate a guess as to what the words or letters in question may be. If the source of the words or letters within the broken brackets is known, it has been given a note.

V. CROSSED-OUT MATERIAL IN MANUSCRIPTS

Words or sentences crossed out by a writer in a manuscript have been handled in one of the three following ways:

1. They have been ignored, and the document or letter has been printed in its final version.
2. Crossed-out words and insertions for the crossed-out words have been described in the notes.
3. When the significance of a manuscript seems to warrant it, the crossed-out words have been retained, and the document has been printed as it was written.

VI. TEXTUAL CHANGES AND INSERTIONS

The following changes or insertions have been made in the letters and documents printed in these volumes:

1. Words or letters written above the line of print (for example, 9ᵗʰ) have been made even with the line of print (9th).
2. Punctuation and capitalization have been changed in those instances where it seemed necessary to make clear the sense of the writer. A special effort has been made to eliminate the dash, which was such a popular eighteenth-century device.
3. When the place or date, or both, of a letter or document does not appear at the head of that letter or document, it has been inserted in the text in brackets. If either the place or date at the head of a letter or document is incomplete, the necessary additional material has been added in the text in brackets. For all but the best known localities or places, the name of the colony, state, or territory has been added in brackets at the head of a document or letter.
4. In calendared documents, place and date have been uniformly written out in full without the use of brackets. Thus "N. York, Octr. 8, '99" becomes "New York, October 8, 1799." If, however, substantive material is added to the place or date in a calendared document, such material is placed in brackets. Thus "Oxford, Jan. 6" becomes "Oxford [Massachusetts] January 6 [1788]."
5. When a writer made an unintentional slip comparable to a typographical error, one of the four following devices has been used:
   a. It has been allowed to stand as written.
   b. It has been corrected by inserting either one or more letters in brackets.
   c. It has been corrected without indicating the change.
   d. It has been explained in a note.
6. Because the symbol for the thorn was archaic even in Hamilton's day, the editors have used the letter "y" to represent it. In doing this they are conforming to eighteenth-century manuscript usage.

THE PAPERS OF ALEXANDER HAMILTON

1797

From Francisco de Miranda [1]

a Paris ce 1. avril 1797.

Mon cher et respectable ami,

C'est depuis quatre ans que je reprends la plume [2] pour vous dire que je suis encore au Nombre des vivans qui restent en france depuis la tyrannie. Voici *un Livre* qui vient de paraitre sur la Révolution française pas *Desodoards*.[3] Il contient tous les faits principaux, et indique les Causes, avec Connaissances, Impartialité, et modération à

ALS, Hamilton Papers, Library of Congress; ALS (duplicate), Hamilton Papers, Library of Congress.

1. Miranda, a native of Venezuela, was a Spanish-American revolutionist who during the American Revolution had served with the Spanish forces in attacks on Pensacola and British colonies in the Caribbean. Miranda traveled in the United States from June, 1783, until December, 1784, and he met H during his visit to New York from January to July, 1784. In 1785 he went to Europe and toured the Continent with William S. Smith, John Adams's son-in-law. He visited England in 1789 in an attempt to interest the British ministry in aiding his plans for a revolution in Spain's Latin American colonies. Although he received some encouragement from the British government during the Nootka Sound controversy, British interest waned with the settlement of that dispute. In 1792 Miranda went to France, where his plans attracted the attention of Pierre Henri Hélène Marie Lebrun-Tondu, Minister of Foreign Affairs during the first months of the Convention, and Jean Pierre Brissot de Warville, leader of the Girondins. He was again unsuccessful, but he did secure an appointment as a lieutenant general in the French army. Miranda was charged with the responsibility for the French defeat at Neerwinden in 1793, but he was acquitted by the Revolutionary Tribunal. He was, however, again arrested and imprisoned. Set free in 1795, he remained in France for three years. Although he had been banished on September 4, 1797, he managed to remain in France until January, 1798, when he went to England to attempt to interest England and the United States in his plans for the liberation of Latin America.

For a discussion of Miranda's plans and his earlier efforts to secure H's aid, see the introductory note to H to Miranda, November 23, 1784. See also H to Miranda, January–July, 1784; Miranda to H, April 5, 1791, November 4, 1792.

2. Miranda to H, November 4, 1792.

3. Antoine Etienne Nicolas Fantin des Odoards, *Histoire philosophique de la révolution de France, depuis la convocation des notables, par Louis XVI, jusqu'a là séparation de la convention nationale*, 2 vols. (Paris, 1796).

mon avis. Et tous Ceux qui Connaissent à fonds la révolution, m'ont confirmé dans cette opinion que j'avais formée d'abord en le lisant. Ne manquer pas de le lire immédiatement, et de le faire passer après au nouveau président, s'il ne l'a pas lu encore. Mrs Paine et M——e, qui sont déja partis d'ici pour se rendre ches Vous,⁴ ne seront pas peutetre du mème-avis; mais je crois qu'ils ont mieux Connu le système des *Jacobins,* que celui de la révolution française. Enfin il est certain, mon ami, que l'ex-President Washington fit une faute bien grave en envoyant ici pour ambassadeurs Mr Morris,⁵ et Mr. Monroe, tous deux exagerés dans *un sens* Contraire. Il est vrai que le premier est un homme infiniment plus instruit, et bien moins extravagant que l'autre. P——e est devenu un Marat tout à fait—Dieu veuille qu'il ne fasse pas plus de mal au nouveau monde, que l'autre n'en a fait à la france.

Adieu, mon cher ami, continuer à soutenir avec Courage la Cause de *la Liberté,* que tant de *brigands* et *d'ignorants* deshonorent depuis cinq ans, tout en prétendant de l'aimer et de la défendre. Je suis réuni ici (et pour cela persécuté encore) avec le petit nombre de ceux qui la connaissent et qui la défendent Sincérement; Veuille la Providence nous accorder du Succès pour le bonheur de ces pays ci ainsi que pour la tranquillité des autres, au moins. Donnez moi des nouvelles de nos amis communs Knox, et W. Duer.⁶ Faites leur bien des Complimens de ma part, en leur Communiquant la partie de cette lettre—si que Vous jugerez à propos, aussi bien que le livre. Je Vous prie de présenter mes respectueux Complimens au gl. Washington—ainsi qu'à tous mes amis à New York &c. &c.

Yours most sincerely   F. Miranda.

4. Miranda was mistaken, for Thomas Paine did not return to the United States until 1802.

James Monroe was United States Minister Plenipotentiary to France from 1794 to 1796. On January 1, 1797, Monroe "took leave of the Executive Directory of France, in an audience specially assigned me for the purpose . . ." (Monroe, *A View of the Conduct of the Executive,* liii). Monroe then decided "to leave France and to proceed to Holland, to remain there during the winter, which he accordingly did. In the spring he returned and passed hastily through Paris to Bordeaux, from where he sailed on the 20th of April 1797 . . ." (Stuart Gerry Brown, ed., *The Autobiography of James Monroe* [Syracuse, 1959], 142).

5. Gouverneur Morris was United States Minister Plenipotentiary to France from 1792 to 1794, when he was succeeded by Monroe.

6. On his visit to the United States in 1783 and 1784, Miranda became acquainted with Henry Knox and William Duer.

P.S. Je viens de Recevoir dans le moment une Lettre de Mr. Monroe, par son Secretaire Mr. Prevost.[7] Le contenue de cette Lettre me fait soupçoner quelque cabale ou intrigue des Mess. Paine, et M——e (avec qui je n'ai jamais eû aucume liaison) ainsi je m'empresse de vous envoier Copie de cette petite Correspondence, pour vous mettre à même de pouvoire Repondre aux Calomnies qui sont les armes de la Secte *Jacobitte*.

Alex: Hamilton, Esqe. at Newyork.

[ENCLOSURE]

John B. Prevost to Francisco de Miranda [8]

[Paris, March 27, 1797]

Sir,

I have called several times at your lodgings in the rue florentin, but have hitherto been so unfortunate as to find you abroad, may I therefore request you to name Some moment when your leisure will permit you to See me in Paris.

I am, Sir,   your humble servant   J. B. Prevost
of New York.

Septedi.

[ENCLOSURE]

Francisco de Miranda to John B. Prevost [9]

Réponse.   a Paris ce 8 Germinal an 5.

Le General Miranda fait bien des Complimens à M. Prevost. Il a reçu Sa note d'hier, et ne trouvant pas Sur celle ci aucun motif qui

7. John B. Prevost was Monroe's secretary of legation. Prevost was a member of the New York Assembly in 1798 and 1799, and he became recorder of New York City in 1801. In 1804, during the recess of the Senate, Thomas Jefferson appointed Prevost a judge of the Superior Court for the Territory of Orleans. His nomination was sent to the Senate on November 30, 1804, and confirmed on December 11 (*Executive Journal*, I, 476, 477).

8. Two copies, in Miranda's handwriting, Hamilton Papers, Library of Congress.

9. Two copies, in Miranda's handwriting, Hamilton Papers, Library of Congress.

exige une Entrevue particuliére, Se trouvant d'ailleurs fort occupé, et ne se rappellant pas d'avoir eu l'avantage de Connaitre M. Prevost de New York, il le prie de vouloir bien remettre la Conférence à des mom⟨ents⟩ plus tranquilles.

[ENCLOSURE]

John B. Prevost to Francisco de Miranda [10]

[Paris, April 1, 1797]

M. Prevost does not conceive a conference to be absolutely necessary and has therefore adopted this mode of Communication as the one most agreable to M. Miranda. The papers alluded to in the within note are those which respect a Negotiation with M. Pitt confided to M. Miranda some time Since by Messieurs hamilton and Knox, the object of which was to adopt Some effectual Measure to liberate south America. M. Prevost will call at any moment M. Miranda may appoint to take charge of Such Documents relative thereto as may remain in the hands of M. Miranda.

Duodi 12 Germinal.

[ENCLOSURE]

James Monroe to Francisco de Miranda [11]

Paris March 17. 1797.

Sir,

I was informed by M. Paine that you had some papers of Importance to our governement which you Sometime Since expressed a wish to deposit in my hands. Being on the point of departing for the U. States, I have thought proper to notify you of it, and to assure you that I Shall be happy to take charge of Such papers. M. Prevost who will have the pleasure to deliver you this, will explain to you the nature of M. Paines communication and take charge of such

10. Two copies, in Miranda's handwriting, Hamilton Papers, Library of Congress.
11. Two copies, in Miranda's handwriting, Hamilton Papers, Library of Congress.

papers as you are pleased to deliver him. With great Respect I have
the honor to be your very humble servant   Ja Monroe.

[ENCLOSURE]

Francisco de Miranda to John B. Prevost [12]

Réponse.   A Paris ce 2 avril 1797.

Le général Miranda S'empresse d'envoyer à monsieur Prevost la
résponse à la lettre de M. Monroe, que M. Prevost lui a adressée—en
le priant de vouloir bien la lui faire parvenir.

[ENCLOSURE]

Francisco de Miranda to James Monroe [13]

a Paris Ce 2 avril 1797.

Monsieur,

Ce n'est que dans le moment que je reçois Votre lettre du 17 mars.
Mr. Prévost qui me l'envoie m'explique ainsi l'objet de Votre sol-
licitude: "the papers alluded to in the within note (votre lettre) are
those which respect a negotiation with Mr. Pitt; confided to Mr.
Miranda Some time Since by Messieurs hamilton and Knox,[14] the
object of which was to adopt Some effectual measure to liberate
South America." Je puis Vous assurer, monsieur, qu'il n'y a pas *un
mot* de vrai dans tout ce rapport. Mr. Paine,[15] duquel Vous dites le

12. Two copies, in Miranda's handwriting, Hamilton Papers, Library of
Congress.
13. Two copies, in Miranda's handwriting, Hamilton Papers, Library of
Congress.
14. No evidence has been found that either Knox or H recommended that
Miranda carry on negotiations with William Pitt for the liberation of South
America.
15. In a letter dated March 20, 1806, Paine described his relationship with
Miranda as follows: ". . . I met Miranda at the house of [John] Turnbull and
[John] Forbes, merchants, Devonshire Square, London. He had been a little
before this in the employ of Mr. Pitt, with respect to the affair of Nootka
Sound, but I did not at that time know it.
". . . I was elected a member of the French Convention, in September . . .
[1792]; and went from London to Paris to take my seat in the Convention,
which was to meet the 20th of that month. . . . After the Convention met,
Miranda came to Paris, and was appointed general of the French army, under

tenir, S'est assurément trompé en prenant pour des *négociations* quelques notes peut-ètre qu'il a vues à ma Compagne de minilmontant, faites dans le tems de mes Voyages dans les Etats Unis, et qui m'ont été données par ces deux respectables amis quand ils n'etaient que de Simples Citoyens, bien antérieurement à leur ministére. C'est la seule fois que M Paine ait été chez moi, et que nous aions parlé (autant que je puis m'en Souvenir) de la situation politique de l'amérique du Sud, ma patrie. Et certes, Vous conceves d'abord que si j'eusse eu le Desir, depuis deux ans, de remetre des papiers entre Vos mains, ou de les faire passer en Amérique, je n'aurais pas manqué de Vous en prévenir, dans les deux seules occasions que j'ai eu l'honneur de Vous voir, en nous rendant des Visites d'honnèteté, à ma Sortie des prisons de la tyrannie.

Je Vous Souhaite un tres heureux Voyage, et voulant profiter de Votre offre généreuse, je Vous prie de Vouloir bien Vous charger de présenter mes Complimens respectueux, aux général washington— le C. A. hamilton, et le général knox. Je suis avec parfaite Consideration,

Monsieur   Votre très humble et très obeissant Serviteur

f. Miranda.

James Monroe Esqe.

General [Charles François] Dumouriez. But as the affairs of that army went wrong in the beginning of the year 1793, Miranda was suspected, and was brought under arrest to Paris to take his trial. He summoned me to appear to his character. . . .

"A few days after his acquittal he came to see me, and in a few days afterwards I returned his visit. He seemed desirous of satisfying me that he was independent, and that he had money in the hands of Turnbull and Forbes. . . . But he entered into conversation with respect to Nootka Sound, and put into my hands several letters of Mr. Pitt's to him on that subject. . . .

"Now if it be true that Miranda brought with him a credit upon certain persons in New York for sixty thousand pounds sterling, it is not difficult to suppose from what quarter the money came; for the opening of any proposals between Pitt and Miranda was already made by the affair of Nootka Sound. Miranda was in Paris when Mr. Monroe arrived there as Minister; and as Miranda wanted to get acquainted with him, I cautioned Mr. Monroe against him, and told him of the affair of Nootka Sound. . . ." (Philip S. Foner, ed., *The Complete Writings of Thomas Paine* [Reprinted: New York, 1969], II, 1481–82.)

To Timothy Pickering

[New York, April 1, 1797]

My Dear Sir

I have received your letter of the 30th. with the statement inclosed. I do not believe that its publication would have any influence upon the question of a rupture with France; but yet, as it seems that those who surround the President are not agreed in the matter— as an opinion is industriously circulated that too much fuel has been added by the publications of the Government—as it is important to disarm a certain party of the weapons of calumny—as it is in general best to avoid inofficial publications of Official matter—as it may be even useful for the sake of *impression* to reserve the disclosure till the Meeting of Congress, when the accumulation of insult may be the instrument of giving a strong impulse—I rather advise the withholding of the statement. When Congress meet it will be very useful to have a statement of this kind ready as the abstract of the communications to present to the people a summary view.

Such, My Dear Sir, is the infatuation of a great part of our Community that it will be policy in our Government to do a great deal too much to make the idea palpable that Rupture was inevitable.

Adieu Yrs. truly   A Hamilton

April 1. 1797

If the statement is published, I would close with the words "January last" in the last Paragrap[h]. The residue will make a good separate news Paper Paragraph. Pray who is the Emigrant alluded to? [1]

T Pickering Esq

ALS, Massachusetts Historical Society, Boston.
1. Charles Maurice de Talleyrand-Périgord. See Pickering to H, March 30, 1797, note 12.

To Uriah Tracy [1]

[*New York, April 1, 1797.* On April 6, 1797, Tracy wrote to Hamilton: "I thank you for your Letter of the 1st. inst." *Letter not found.*]

1. Tracy was United States Senator from Connecticut and the state's attorney for Litchfield County.

From Rufus King [1]

London Ap. 2. 1797

Dear Sir,

As Mr. Church [2] is the bearer, I refer you to him for what it would take many Pages to relate, and will only say that notwithstanding the injuries we continue to receive from France I still hope, the same policy that has hitherto kept us out of the war, will continue to influence and decide our Government.

How the new President will conduct himself in a situation thorny and embarrassing remains to be seen; the first Step is very important, and therefore shd. be deeply and extensively considered.

Every thing looks like an active, and to a certain degree, a vigourous campaign: yet with all these appearances of the continuance of the war, Peace may be near: But what will be the consequence of such a Peace as alone can be had at this Time? A late Arret of the Directory [3] gives notice to all french Citizens, that the Treaty of Feb. 1778 between France and the UStates of Amer. has been (of full right,) in virtue of the 2d. article thereof, modified so as to conform to the stipulations contained in the treaty of 1794 between the UStates & G Britain [4]—the arret then proceeds to specify the modification:

ALS, Hamilton Papers, Library of Congress.
1. A former United State Senator from New York, King was United States Minister Plenipotentiary to Great Britain.
2. John B. Church was married to Elizabeth Hamilton's sister, Angelica.
3. King is referring to a decree issued by the Directory on March 2, 1797 (Duvergier, *Lois*, IX, 358–61). An English translation is printed in *ASP, Foreign Relations*, II, 30–31.
4. King is referring to that part of the introduction to the decree which

1. all Enemy Goods, and all merchandize "non suffisament con-statée neutre," on board Amer. Vessels shall be lawful Prize; but the vessel shall be released &c.[5]

2. to the articles of Contraband specified in the treaty of Feby. 1778 shall be added "les bois de construction" &c enumerating the additional articles of Contraband contained in the treaty between the US. & G. Br.[6]

---

reads: ". . . qu'il importe, par conséquent, à l'instruction tant des commandans de la force armée de la République et des bâtimens commissionnés par elle, que des tribunaux chargés de prononcer sur la validité des prises, de prendre des mesures pour empêcher, ou qu'on ne suppose existans des traités qui n'ont jamais eu lieu, ou qu'on ne regarde comme étant encore en vigueur des traités conclus pour un temps déterminé qui est expiré, ou comme devant être encore exécutés à la lettre des traités qui ont été modifiés depuis leur conclusion; qu'à cette dernière espèce appartient singulièrement le traité d'amitié et de commerce conclu, le 6 février 1778, entre la France et les Etats-Unis de l'Amérique, qu'en effet, par l'art. 2 de ce traité, la France et les Etats-Unis de l'Amérique *s'engagent mutuellement à n'accorder aucune faveur particulière à d'autres nations, en fait de commerce et de navigation, qui ne devienne aussitôt commune à l'autre partie;* et qu'il est ajouté par le même article, que celle-ci *jouira de cette faveur gratuitement si la concession est gratuite ou en accordant la même compensation si la concession est conditionnelle;* qu'ainsi les dispositions stipulées en faveur de l'Angleterre par le traité d'amitié, de commerce et de navigation passé à Londres le 19 novembre 1794 entre cette puissance et les Etats-Unis d'Amérique, sont censées l'avoir été en faveur de la République française elle-même, et par suite modifient, dans les points qui y sont contraires, le traité conclu le 6 février 1778; que c'est d'après ces dispositions que le Gouvernement français a déclaré par ses arrêtés des 14 et 28 messidor an 4, comme il est encore forcé de le faire aujourd'hui, qu'il usera des justes mesures de réciprocité qu'il était en droit d'exercer à cet égard, en tout ce qui tient aux circonstances de la querre ainsi qu'aux intérèts politiques, commerciaux et maritimes de la République française; que conséquemment, il est nécessaire de fixer, par le rapprochement des traités du 6 février 1778 et du 19 novembre 1794, toute incertitude sur les cas où doit s'exercer ce droit de réciprocité" (Duvergier, *Lois,* IX, 359).

For the decree of July 2, 1796, see H to George Washington, January 19, 1797, note 4. No evidence has been found that a new decree was issued on July 16, 1796.

5. Article 3, Section 1, of the decree of March 2, 1797, reads: "D'après l'article 17 du traité de Londres du 19 novembre 1794, . . . toute marchandise ennemie ou non suffisamment constatée neutre, chargée sous pavillon américain, sera confisquée; mais le bâtiment à bord duquel elle aura été trouvée, sera relâché et rendu au propriétaire. Il est enjoint aux commissaires du Directoire exécutif de faire accelerer, par tous les moyens qui sont en leur pouvoir, le jugement des contestations qui pourront s'élever, soit sur la validité des prises de cargaison, soit sur les frets et surestaries" (Duvergier, *Lois,* IX, 360).

For Article 17 of the Jay Treaty, see "Remarks on the Treaty . . . between the United States and Great Britain," July 9–11, 1795, note 59.

6. Article 3, Section 2, of the French decree of March 2, 1797, reads: "D'après l'article 18 du traité de Londres du 19 novembre 1794, . . . aux objets déclarés

3. "D'apres l'article 21 du traité de Londres de 19. Nov. 1794, tout individu reconnu Américain, porteur d'une commission donnée par les Ennemis de la france, ainsi que tout marin de cette nation faisant partie des Equipages des Navires ou Vaisseaux ennemis, sera ce seul fait, declaré pirate, et traité comme tel, sans qu'il puisse aucun cas, alleguer qu'il y a été forcé par violence, menace ou autrement." [7]

4. According to the Law of 14. feb. 1793, the Regulations of that of ye 21. Octr. 1744, and of that of 26 July 1778, concerning the Trial of neutral Ships & Cargos, shall be observed; and in Consequence thereof, every american Ship shall be a *good Prize*, on board whereof there shall not be found, *un Rôle d'equipage en bonne forme* such as is required by the Form annexed to the Treaty of the 6. feb. 1778, the execution of which is hereby required.[8]

5. respects certain causes of Forfeiture by reason of misconduct in destroying papers, possessing double Papers &c &c.[9]

----

contrebande par l'article 24 du traité du 6 février 1778, sont ajoutés les objets suivans:
"Les bois de construction;
"Les brais, goudrons et résines;
"Le cuivre en feuilles;
"Les voiles, chanvres et cordages,
"Et tout ce qui sert directement ou indirectement à l'armement et à l'équipement des vaisseaux, excepté le fer brut et le sapin en planches. Ces divers articles seront confisqué toutes les fois qu'ils seront destinés ou qu'on essaiera de les porter à l'ennemi." (Duvergier, *Lois*, IX, 360.)
  For the text of Article 18 of the Jay Treaty, see "Remarks on the Treaty . . . between the United States and Great Britain," July 9–11, 1795, note 63.
  7. This is a quotation of Article 3, Section 3, of the French decree of March 2, 1797 (Duvergier, *Lois*, IX, 360–61).
  For the text of Article 21 of the Jay Treaty, see "Remarks on the Treaty . . . between the United States and Great Britain," July 9–11, 1795, note 68.
  8. Article 3, Section 4, of the French decree of March 2, 1797, reads: "Conformément à la loi du 14 fevrier 1793, les dispositions des réglemens du 21 octobre 1744 et du 26 juillet 1778, concernant la manière de constater la propriété des navires et des marchandises neutres, seront exécutées selon leur forme et teneur:
"Sera en conséquence de bonne prise,
"Tout navire américain qui n'aura pas à bord un rôle d'équipage en bonne forme, tel qu'il est prescrit par le modele annexé au traité du 6 février 1778, dont l'exécution est ordonnée par les articles 25 et 27 du même traite." (Duvergier, *Lois*, IX, 361.)
  For the decree of February 19 (not 14), 1793, see Duvergier, *Lois*, V, 200. The regulation of October 21, 1744, is printed in Isambert, *Recueil Général des Anciennes Lois Françaises*, XXII, 173–77. The regulation of July 26, 1778, is printed in Martens, *Recûeil*, III, 18–25.
  9. Article 3, Section 5, of the French decree of March 2, 1797, reads: "Il est enjoint aux commissaires du Directoire exécutif d'appeler la séverité des tribunaux sur les manœuvres frauduleuses de tout armateur se disant neutre,

6. repeals certain former Regulations.[10]

7. directs the insertion of the arret in the Bulletin of the Laws &c The third article is a false construction, for obvious purposes, of the analogous article in our Treaty with Engd—the fourth will render *all our Ships* liable to Capture and if acted upon to condemnation, since no American Vessel has on board her the Document required. In our printed Laws, are also the treaties; and among them those we formed with France—to the coml. Treaty, though the 25. & 27 articles refer to it,[11] there is no model or Form of a Passport. Mr.

---

américain ou autre, à bord du bâtiment duquel il sera trouvé, ainsi qu'il a déjà été fait plusieurs fois dans la querre actuelle, soit des papiers de mer en blanc, quoique signés et scellés, soit des papiers en forme de lettres contenant des signatures de particuliers en blanc, soit de doubles passeports ou lettres de mer qui indiquent différentes destinations au bâtiment, soit de doubles factures, connaissemens ou pappiers de mer quelconques qui assignent à tout ou partie de la même marchandise des propriétaires différens ou différentes destinations" (Duvergier, *Lois*, IX, 361).

10. Article 6 of the decree of March 2, 1797, reads: "Au moyen des dispositions du présent arrêté, celui du 9 frimaire dernier, concernant les frets et surestaries, est rapporté en ce qui concerne les surestaries seulement" (Duvergier, *Lois*, IX, 361).

For the regulations of November 29, 1796, see Duvergier, *Lois*, IX, 275–76.

11. King is referring to the Treaty of Amity and Commerce between the United States and France, which was signed at Paris on February 6, 1778 (Miller, *Treaties*, II, 3–29). Article 23 (originally 25) of the treaty reads: "It shall be lawful for all and singular the Subjects of the most Christian King and the Citizens People and Inhabitants of the said United States to sail with their Ships with all manner of Liberty and Security; no distinction being made, who are the Proprietors of the Merchandizes laden thereon, from any Port to the places of those who now are or hereafter shall be at Enmity with the most Christian King or the United States. It shall likewise be Lawful for the Subjects and Inhabitants aforesaid to sail with the Ships and Merchandizes aforementioned and to trade with the same Liberty and security from the Places, Ports and Havens of those who are Enemies of both or either Party without any Opposition or disturbance whatsoever, not only directly from the Places of the Enemy afore mentioned to neutral Places; but also from one Place belonging to an Enemy to another place belonging to an Enemy, whether they be under the Jurisdiction of the same Prince or under several; And it is hereby stipulated that free Ships shall also give a freedom to Goods, and that every thing shall be deemed to be free and exempt, which shall be found on board the Ships belonging to the Subjects of either of the Confederates, although the whole lading or any Part thereof should appertain to the Enemies of either, contraband Goods being always excepted. It is also agreed in like manner that the same Liberty be extended to Persons, who are on board a free Ship, with this Effect, that although they be Enemies to both or either Party, they are not to be taken out of that free Ship, unless they are Soldiers and in actual Service of the Enemies" (Miller, *Treaties*, II, 20–21).

Article 25 (originally 27) of the treaty reads: "To the End that all manner of Dissentions and Quarrels may be avoided and prevented on one Side and the other, it is agreed, that in case either of the Parties hereto should be engaged in War, the Ships and Vessels belonging to the Subjects or People

Jefferson has certified that Treaty to be correct, and a perfect copy, as you will see by his printed certificate in the Law Book.

I have a copy of the coml. Treaty with France printed in London in 1783, wh. has the Form of a Passport, Role d'Equipage &c annexed.[12] A copy of it I have given to Mr. Church who will shew it to you; by wh. you will see that none of our Vessels are exempt from Capture if this Copy is that referred to in the late Arret—indeed it seems too absurd in some things to be genuine, yet I suspect it is the model or Form referred to & required by the 4th Art. of the arret.[13]

farewel yrs &c   Rufus King

---

of the other Ally must be furnished with Sea Letters or Passports expressing the name, Property and Bulk of the Ship as also the name and Place of habitation of the Master or Commander of the said Ship, that it may appear thereby, that the Ship really & truely belongs to the Subjects of one of the Parties, which Passport shall be made out and granted according to the Form annexed to this Treaty; they shall likewise be recalled every Year, that is if the Ship happens to return home within the Space of a Year. It is likewise agreed, that such Ships being laden are to be provided not only with Passports as above mentioned, but also with Certificates containing the several Particulars of the Cargo, the Place whence the Ship sailed and whither she is bound, that so it may be known, whether any forbidden or contraband Goods be on the board the same: which Certificates shall be made out by the Officers of the Place, whence the Ship set sail, in the accustomed Form. And if any one shall think it fit or adviseable to express in the said Certificates the Person to whom the Goods on board belong, he may freely do so" (Miller, *Treaties*, II, 23–24).

12. For the "Form of the Passports and Letters, which are to be given to the Ships and Barks, according to the twenty seventh Article of this Treaty," see Miller, *Treaties*, II, 28–29.

13. See note 8.

From William Loughton Smith [1]

[*Philadelphia, April 2, 1797.* On April 5, 1797, Hamilton wrote to Smith: "I have received . . . Your letter of the 2d April (97)." *Letter not found.*]

1. Smith was a Federalist member of the House of Representatives from South Carolina, a close friend of H, and one of the leading advocates in the House of the policies which H had introduced as Secretary of the Treasury.

From Philip Schuyler [1]

Albany April 3d 1797

My Dear Sir

I took my leave of the senate [2] on friday, And as Mr. Abm. V. Vechten has consented to be nominated a candidate for a seat in senate and will probably be Elected,[3] I am more at ease than I should have been, If a less able man than he had been proposed, for Spencer, Gold and Tillotson [4] have already combined to divest Mr. Jones of his seal under pretence that the comptroller ought not to be of the Legislature,[5] a resolution for that purpose was to have been brought forward on Saturday but finding a majority averse, they would not venture, the fact is that three I have mentioned wish to govern the senate, as L hommedieu [6] would stand alone in opposition to them. If V Vechten should not be elected, L'hommedieu and Tillotson are at variance, and the former most sincerely hates Spencer and Goold, all our friends are therefore Anxious that he should be re-elected, and I believe It will be proper that he should.

Pray when you come up bring the contract between Hogeboem and me with you, new propositions have been made me relative to the Claverack estate and that paper may be wanted.[7]

I am not in good health, my wounds are opened afresh, I hope however to be able to go to Philadelphia.

We are extremely anxious that our Eliza and the Children should Accompany you hither, pray urge her to it. Let all participate with you in our love.

Yours most affectionately   Ph: Schuyler

Alexander Hamilton Esqr

ALS, Hamilton Papers, Library of Congress.
1. Schuyler was H's father-in-law.
2. See Schuyler to H, March 19, 1797.
3. Abraham Van Vechten was an Albany lawyer and Federalist politician. He was elected to the New York Senate in 1798 and served until 1805.
4. Ambrose Spencer, Thomas R. Gold, and Thomas Tillotson were members of the New York Senate.
5. By an act of February 17, 1797, the New York legislature created the office of comptroller (*New York Laws*, 20th Sess., Ch. XXI). Samuel Jones,

a state senator from Oyster Bay, was reported "to have been the principal author of the measure" (Jabez D. Hammond, *The History of Political Parties in the State of New York* [Albany, 1842], I, 104). On March 15, 1797, Jones became the state's first comptroller (Werner, *New York Civil List*, 216). As Schuyler indicates, the efforts to prevent Jones from holding two offices simultaneously failed.

6. Ezra L'Hommedieu was a Federalist and a member of the New York Senate from 1783 to 1809 (except for the year 1792–1793). In addition, he had been a member of the New York Provincial Congress, the state Assembly, the Continental Congress, and the New York Council of Appointments.

7. The "Claverack estate" was a tract of land which extended eastward from the Hudson River for twenty-four miles in the southern part of what is now Columbia County, New York. In 1755, when Schuyler married Catharine Van Rensselaer, this tract of land belonged to her father, John (or Johannes) Van Rensselaer. Van Rensselaer had repeated disputes with both squatters from Massachusetts and tenants, who maintained that they held freeholds in Claverack and were therefore under no obligation to Van Rensselaer. Following Van Rensselaer's death in 1783, Schuyler represented the interests in Claverack of his wife and the other devisees, and H in turn acted as Schuyler's legal adviser in the series of disputes over the right to various pieces of property in Claverack. For a discussion of the disputes and controversies over the lands in Claverack, see forthcoming Goebel, *Law Practice*, III.

The contract between Peter Hogeboom, a Hudson, New York, merchant, and Schuyler is dated November 5, 1795. In this contract Schuyler attempted to sell Catharine Schuyler's portion of the Claverack estate (DS, Schuyler Papers, Box 17, New York Public Library).

Deed from Peter Goelet, Robert Morris, and William Popham [1]

[New York, April 4, 1797]

Peter Goelet Robert Morris & William Popham Trustees for all the Creditors of Peter Hassenclever and others under an Attachment &c To Alexander Hamilton

Deed dated the fourth day of April An: Dom 1797. in Consideration of two thousand four hundred and twenty two pounds thirteen shillings and ten pence for a Tract of Land situate lying and being in the Manor

of Cosby, on the North side of the Mohawk river, containing Lots from No. 22 to 50 inclusive, contai[n]ing Six thousand seven hundred and fifty five Acres as described in a Map of that part of the Manor of Cosby which lies on the North side of the Mohawk river.

D, Miscellaneous Chancery Papers, American Iron Company, Clerk of the Court of Appeals, Albany, on deposit at Queens College, New York City.
    1. For an explanation of the contents of this document, see the introductory note to Philip Schuyler to H, August 31, 1795. See also H to Phineas Bond, September 1, 1795; H to Morris, September 1, 1795; H to Barent Bleecker, March 20, 1796; Peter Goelet to H, June 25, 27, 1796; "Receipt from Peter Goelet," October 4, 1796.

To Barent Bleecker [1]

[New York, April 5, 1797]

Sir

The fourth & last installment of the purchase money of the Cosby Manor Lands [2] has become due. It is 1655 Dollars & 50 Cents of which your ¼ is 413. Dollars & 87 Cents. I beg the favour of you to lose no time in forwarding this Sum to me.

With esteem   Yr very hum ser   A Hamilton
                                                      April 5. 1797

Blecker Esqr.
Albany

ALS, Detroit Public Library.
    1. For an explanation of the contents of this letter, see the introductory note to Philip Schuyler to H, August 31, 1795. See also H to Phineas Bond, September 1, 1795; H to Robert Morris, September 1, 1795; H to Bleecker, March 20, 1796; Peter Goelet to H, June 25, 27, 1796; "Receipt from Peter Goelet," October 4, 1796; "Deed from Peter Goelet, Robert Morris, and William Popham," April 4, 1797.
    2. Under the date of April 14, 1797, H made the following entry in his Cash Book, 1795–1804: "Cash Dr. to Barent Bleeker for this sum received toward Payt. of Cosby Manor Lands 414" (AD, Hamilton Papers, Library of Congress).

From Timothy Pickering

Philadelphia April 5. 1797

Dear Sir,

I received your letter of the   [1] and accord with your opinion that the proposed publication of the intelligence from Genl. Pinckney should be omitted. The "emigrant" we conclude to be Perigord, formerly bishop of Autun.[2] Sometime since, I was informed that he left this country with signs of enmity towards it; and the Directory would naturally place great confidence in his opinion: and yet it is so extravagant we may wonder that it should gain any credit.[3] But, as Barras said to Monroe, "They will not stoop to calculate the consequences of our condescension to our ancient tyrants;" [4] nor, it would seem, of their own atrocities. They are giddy with their successes, and stick at no means which promise to promote their views of domination & plunder.

I have omitted to answer your letter of Feby. 10. To-day, I have examined Chancellor Livingston's letter books. On the 25th of March 1783, he wrote to the American Commrs Adams, Franklin, Jay & Laurens,[5] acknowledging the rect. of their letter with the "preliminary articles." He tells them that "the steadiness manifested in not treating without an express acknowledgement of our independence,

ALS, Hamilton Papers, Library of Congress; ALS, letterpress copy, Massachusetts Historical Society, Boston.
   1. Space left blank in MS. Pickering is referring to H's letter of April 1, 1797.
   2. Charles Maurice de Talleyrand-Périgord. See Pickering to H, March 30, 1797, note 12.
   3. On July 24, 1797, Mme Maulde de Blacons wrote to Théophile Cazenove: "vous desirer Savoir, Monsieur, S'il est vrai que j'aye dit a mon arivée à philadelphie que M de talleyrand avait écrit en france contre l'amérique et fomenté de tout Son pouvoir la mésintelligence qui reignait entre les deux pays. je puis, monsieur, vous Satisfaire d'un seul mot le propos qu'on me prête est de toute fausseté . . ." (ALS, Hamilton Papers, Library of Congress). Mme Maulde de Blacons and her husband, Henri-François-Lucrecius-Armand de Forest, marquis de Blacons, were French exiles.
   4. Pickering is referring to a speech made by Paul François Jean Nicolas Barras, President of the Directory, on December 30, 1797, to James Monroe, when Monroe presented his letter of recall. For this speech, see Uriah Tracy to H, March 23, 1797, note 4.
   5. Wharton, *Revolutionary Diplomatic Correspondence*, VI, 338–40.

previous to a treaty, is approved, and it is not doubted but it accelerated that declaration." Yet you will recollect (as I have stated in my printed letter to Genl. Pinckney) [6] that Count de Vergennes urged Mr. Jay's negociating with Mr. Oswald without insisting on that previous acknowledgement; and this concurring with other facts inspired Mr. Jay with the suspicions which the Chancellor censures.[7] The grounds of those suspicions were detailed in Mr. Jay's letter of Septr. 18.[8] of Which the Chancellor acknowledged the receipt on the 30th of December 1782.[9]

In the same letter of March 25th 1783, to the Comrs, after informing them that the preliminary articles had been laid before Congress —"that they had met with their warmest approbation, & been gen-

6. Pickering to Charles Cotesworth Pinckney, January 16, 1797 (LC, RG 59, Diplomatic and Consular Instructions of the Department of State, 1791–1801, Vol. 3, June 5, 1795–January 21, 1797, National Archives).

7. In his letter to Pinckney on January 16, 1797, Pickering wrote: "In 1781, with the assistance of a French army by land and a powerful fleet by sea, a second British army was captured.

"This event made even the British Government dispair of bringing the united States again under her subjection. The ministry was changed: and the Parliament passed an act to authorize the King to make peace. In the summer of 1782 an agent on the part of Great Britain repaired to Paris to negotiate with the Commissioners of the united States. For some time Dr. Franklin and mr. Jay were alone at Paris. The commission to mr. [Richard] Oswald (the British negotiator) authorized him to treat of and conclude a peace or truce with any Commissioner or Commissioners named or to be named by the *Colonies* or *Plantations* of New Hampshire, &c. (naming the thirteen) or with any of them separately, with parts of them, or with any persons whatsoever. Mr. Jay was not satisfied with this Commission to Mr. Oswald: the independence of the thirteen States was no w[h]ere intimated. Agreeably to their instructions from Congress to take advice of the court of France, the Commissioners communicated Mr. Oswald's commission to the Prime Minister, the Count de Vergennes. The Count expressed his opinion that the Commission was sufficient; that it was such an one as we might have expected it would be; 'That an acknowledgment of our independence, instead of *preceding*, must, in the natural course of things be the *effect* of the treaty.' This opinion the Count continued from time to time to repeat. In short, 'it was evident the Count did not wish to see our independence acknowledged by Britain until they had made all their uses of us.' Mr. Jay still continued unmoved. He conferred with mr. Oswald, and 'urged, in the strongest terms, the great impropriety, and consequently the utter impossibility of our ever treating with Great Britain on any other than an *equal footing;* and told him plainly that he (Mr. Jay) would have no concern in any negotiation in which we were not considered as an independent people.'" (LC, RG 59, Diplomatic and Consular Instructions of the Department of State, 1791–1801, Vol. 3, June 5, 1795–January 21, 1797, National Archives.)

8. John Jay to Robert R. Livingston, September 18, 1782 (Wharton, *Revolutionary Diplomatic Correspondence*, V, 740).

9. Wharton, *Revolutionary Diplomatic Correspondence*, VI, 173–76.

erally seen by the people in the most favourable point of view; and made some comments on the subject; and noticed the British debts which, says he, "no honest man could wish to withhold"—he adds— "But, gentlemen, tho' the issue of your treaty has been successful, tho' I am satisfied that we are much indebted to your firmness & perseverance, to your accurate knowledge of our situation & of our wants for this success, yet I feel no little pain at the distrust manifested in the management of it, particularly in signing the treaty without communicating it to the court of Versailles, till after the signature, and in concealing the separate article from it even when signed. I have examined with the most minute attention all the reasons assigned in your several letters to justify these suspicions. I confess they do not appear to strike me so forcibly as they have done you; and it gives me pain that the character for candor & fidelity to its engagements which should always characterize a great people should have been impeached thereby. The concealment was in my opinion absolutely unnecessary. For had the court of France disapproved the terms you had made after they had been agreed upon, they could not have acted so absurdly as to counteract you at that late day, & thereby put themselves in the power of an enemy who would certainly betray them, & perhaps justify you in making terms for yourselves. The secret article is no otherwise important than as it carries in it the seeds of enmity to the court of Spain, and shews a marked preference for an open enemy." The Chancellor continues his remarks on the secret article, and expresses his opinion that the same boundary for West Florida should have been stipulated, into whose hands soever it might fall at the conclusion of the war. "I feel (says he) for the embarrassment explanations on this subject must subject you to, when this secret is known to your allies." He incloses to them his report (or letter) to congress [10] on the manner in which the negociation had been conducted, in regard to the concealment from the Court of Versailles, and the secret article, and the motions to which the communication gave rise in Congress. But while under consideration, letters arrived from Count D'Estaing & the Marquis de la Fayette,[11] containing accounts that preliminaries

10. Livingston to the President of Congress, March 18, 1783 (Wharton, *Revolutionary Diplomatic Correspondence*, VI, 313-16).
11. Lafayette sent two letters on February 5, 1783—one to the President of

(I suppose of a general peace) were signed; and the whole affair went over without any decision.

In his report to Congress, he reminds them of their reiterated expressions of Confidence in France, and quotes their *public* resolution of the 4th of Octr. 1782, "That Congress will not enter into the discussion of any overtures for pacification but in confidence and in concert with his most Christian Majesty." "Yet (says he) it has unfortunately so happened that the ministers of these states have imagined they had sufficient grounds to suspect the sincerity & the court of France, & have not only thought it prudent to agree upon & sign preliminaries with Great Britain, without communicating them till after the signature to the ministers of his most Christian Majesty, but have permitted a separate article to be inserted in their treaty which they still conceal from the court of France." This he considers as reducing Congress to a most embarrassing situation, either of contradicting all their former professions of confidence in their ally, or of exposing their ministers at the court of France, and too when those ministers have obtained such terms from the court of London as does great honor to them, & at least equals our highest expectations." The preamble to the provisional articles he supposes to have been *framed in England;* and all his observations manifest this suspicions of insidious designs in that power. Finally he submits the following resolutions.

"That the secretary for foreign affairs be directed to communicate the separate article in the provisional preliminary treaty with Great Britain, to the minister of his most Christian Majesty, in such manner as will best tend to remove any unfavourable impression it may make on the court of France of the sincerity of those states or their ministers."

"That the ministers for negociating peace be informed of this communication, and of the reasons which influenced Congress to

Congress and the other to Livingston (Wharton, *Revolutionary Diplomatic Correspondence,* VI, 237–40). Lafayette's letters arrived "on . . . a Sloop of War . . . dispatched by [Charles Henri Hector] the Comte d'Estaing and the Marquis Lafayette from Cadiz" (Elias Boudinot to George Washington, March 23, 1783 [Edmund C. Burnett, ed., *Letters of Members of the Continental Congress* (Washington, 1921–1938), VII, 93]). The vessel also carried a copy sent by d'Estaing of "the heads of the preliminaries of peace, signed the 20th of January . . ." (Burnett, *Letters,* VII, 94n).

make it. That they be instructed to agree that in whatsoever hands West Florida may remain at the conclusion of the war, the United States will be satisfied that the line of north boundary be as described in the said separate article."

"That it is the sense of the U. States in Congress, that the articles agreed upon between the ministers of these states and those of his Britannic Majesty, are not to take place until a peace shall have been *actually signed* between their most Christian & Britannic Majesties."

Actually signed—If you turn to the preamble of the provisional articles, you will see that it was declared that the treaty of peace, which the articles were to constitute, was not to be concluded "until terms of a peace shall be *agreed* upon between G.B. & France; and his B.M. shall be *ready* to conclude such treaty accordingly." Now, says the Chancellor, "this preamble is so expressed as to render it very doubtful whether our treaty does not take place the moment France & England have agreed on the terms of their treaty, tho' France should refuse to sign till her allies were satisfied."

As you have not mentioned the object of your enquiry on this subject, this detail may perhaps be deficient or redundant. In either case you will advise me; and particularly I must request you to acknowledge the receipt of this letter, that I may be sure of its having reached your hands.

I am dear sir   very truly yours   T. Pickering

To William Loughton Smith

New York, April 5th 97 [1]

I have received My Dear Sir Your letter of the   [2] with your little work [3] accompanying it, which I shall read with the interest I take in the author, the first leisure hour. I have cast my eye over it and like very much the plan.

Our affairs are indeed very critical. But I am sorry to find that I do not agree with several of my friends.[4] I am clearly of opinion for an extraordinary mission and as clearly that it should embrace *Madison.* I do not think we ought to construe the declaration of the Directory against receiving a Minister Plenipotentiary as extending to an *extraordinary* mission *pro hac vice*. And if it does, it would be no reason with me against it. I would accumulate the proofs of French Violence & demonstrate to all our Citizens that nothing possible has been omitted. That a certain party desires it is with me a strong reason for it—since I would disarm them of all plea that we have not made every possible effort for peace. The idea is a plausible one that as we sent an Envoy Extraordinary to Britain so ought we to send one to France. And plausible ideas are always enough for the multitude.

These and other reasons (and principally to avoid Rupture with a political monster which seems destined soon to have no Competitor but England) make me even *anxious* for an extraordinary mission.

And to produce the desired effect, it seems to me essential that it shall embrace a *distinguished* character agreeable to France & having the confidence of the adverse party. Hence I think of Madison—but I think of him only as *one*, because I would not trust him alone. I would unite with him *Pinckney* & some strong Man from the North, say *Cabot*, and two of the three should rule.

We should then be safe. I need not tell you that I am disposed to make no sacrifices to France. I had rather perish myself and Family than see the Country disgraced. But I would try hard to avoid Rupture & if that cannot be to unite the opinions of all good Citizens of whatever political denomination. This is with me a mighty object.

I will give you hereafter my ideas of what ought to be done when Congress meet. My plan ever is to combine *energy* with *moderation*.

Yrs. Affectly   A Hamilton

Wm. Smith Esq

ALS, William Loughton Smith Papers, Library of Congress.
1. The date is not in H's handwriting.
2. Space left blank in MS. Letter not found.
In an unknown handwriting the blank space has been filled with "2d April (97)."
3. William Loughton Smith, *Comparative View of the Constitutions of the Several States with each other, and with that of the United States: Exhibited in Tables the Prominent Features of each Constitution, and Classing together their most important Provisions under the Several Heads of Administration: with Notes and Observations* (Philadelphia, 1796).
4. See Timothy Pickering to H, March 26, 1797; Oliver Wolcott, Jr., to H, March 31, 1797.

To Oliver Wolcott, Junior

[New York, April 5, 1797]

Dear Sir

I have received your letter of March 31. I hope nothing in my last [1] was misunderstood. Could it be necessary I would assure you that no one has a stronger convinction than myself of the purity of the motives which direct your public Conduct or of the good sense and judgment by which it is guided. If I have a fear (you will excuse my frankness), it is lest the *strength* of your feelings, the companions of energy of character, should prevent that pliancy to circumstances which is sometimes indispensable. I beg you only to watch yourself on this score & the public will always find in you an able as well as faithful servant.

The situation of our Country My Dear Sir, is singularly Critical. The map of Europe is every way discouraging. There is too much reason to apprehend that the Emperor of Germany in danger from Russia & Prussia, perhaps the Porte, as well as France may be compelled to yield to the views of the latter. England standing alone may be driven to a similar issue. It is certain that great consternation in Court and Country attended the intelligence of Buonapartes last victories. Either to be in rupture with France united with England alone or singly as is possible would be a most unwelcome situation. Divided as we are who can say what would be hazarded by it?

In such a situation it appears to me we should rather err on the side of condescention than on the opposite side. We ought to do every thing to avoid rupture, without unworthy sacrifices, and to keep in view as a primary object union at home.

No measure can tend more to this than an extraordinary Mission. And it is certain to fulfil the ends proposed it ought to embrace a character in whom France and the Opposition have full Credit. What risk can attend sending *Madison* if combined as I propose with Pinckney & Cabot or such a man (two deciding). Depend on it *Pinckney* is a man of honor & loves his Country. Cabot we both know. Besides there ought to be certain leading instructions from which they may not deviate.

I agree with you that we have nothing to retract—that we ought to risk every thing before we submit to any dishonorable terms. But we may remould our Treaties. We may agree to put France on the same footing as Great Britain by our Treaty with her. We may also liquidate with a view to *future wars* the import of the mutual gurantee in the Treaty of alliance substituting specific succours & defining the casus fœderis.[2] But this last may or may not be done, though with me it is a favourite object.

Ingersol [3] will not fulfil the object but I had rather have him than do nothing.

I am clearly of Opinion with You that the President shall come forward to Congress in a manly tone & that Congress shall adopt vigourous defensive measures. Those you propose are proper & some others on which I may write hereafter.

If Madison is well couplied I do not think his intrigues can operate as you imagine. Should he advocate dishonorable concessions to France the public opinion will not support. His colleages by address & shewing a disposition to do enough may easily defeat his policy & maintain the public Confidence. Besides that it is possible too much may be taken for granted with regard to Mr. Madison.

Yrs. very truly   A H

April 5. 1797

After reading Return me the inclosed.[4]

Oliver Wolcott Jun Esq

ALS, Connecticut Historical Society, Hartford; copy, Hamilton Papers, Library of Congress.

1. H to Wolcott, March 20, 1797.
2. See H to George Washington, January 25–31, 1797; H to Theodore Sedgwick, February 26, 1797.
3. Jared Ingersoll. See Wolcott to H, March 31, 1797.
4. Rufus King to H, February 6, 1797. See Wolcott to H, April 12, 1797.

From Uriah Tracy

Philada. 6th. April '97

Sir

I thank you for your Letter of the 1st inst.[1]—but as Johnson of Salisbury [2] teazes to purchase for him the Land, which lies in that Town, in your care, I will thank you to write me or him, whether you mean he should have it.

Your plan you say respecting our public affairs is to move together till common danger rouse to common Action. I am perfectly in sentiment with you—provided we can rouse before all is lost—*And to exhaust attempts at negociation.* In this, I agree, if it has not been done already; I have no objection to clothing with full powers, to Treat with France, either of our foreign Ministers, or even keeping Mr Pinckney at Amsterdam, or any other convenient place, for the purpose, as he has all the ordinary & extraordinary powers of the plenipotentiary & Envoy—& let France & the world know we are ready to negociate on any terms of accomodations—the moment the French Governmt are willing to treat us with civility & propriety, but Sir, I am not willing to send an Envoy Extraordinary to France, nor to retract a syllable of our Governmental Acts, nor a single step of the administration; sending an Envoy now would do all this, and more, it would commit the whole of our national dignity, to be trampled upon by that haughty & accursed Nation, & rivet their infamous disorganizing chains on us, beyond even our present disgraceful situation.

Every nerve ought to be exerted to induce a preparation for War; This preparation is not only proper, but necessary to our existence as an independent Nation—& if such a Vote cannot be obtained in the House of Representatives, (the Senators there seem to be yet a doubt of) what will be the condition of our Country? We shall be much worse than Colonies to France, we shall be like the little Sister Republics in Europe—oppressed with spoliations & then taxed for the very fraternal piracy. If the Country can be roused to a proper sense of their wrongs, & their National dignity, if we are not so far benumbed with French principles as to have lost a sense of all propriety we shall undoubtedly arm in self defence, & let the French Nation & the World know, we have the discernment & spirit to discover & resent injuries of the most flagrant nature.

But if the House of Reps as I much fear they will not only vote to do nothing, but add to this their opinion by a public Vote, that the Governmt has injured France, & we deserve all this, as many of them now talk—Then it is, & in that case only, that I urge a separation.

The Southern part of the Union is increasing by frequent importations of foreign scoundrels as well as by those of home manufacture, their country is large & capable of such increase both in population & number of States—that in both houses of Congress, the Northern States will soon be swallowed up, & the name & real character of an American soon be known only as a thing of tradition; add to this the explosion which must sooner or later derive itself from their Slaves, & which must be hastened by such a step of the Government, drawing closer the bands of Amity with the French; all these, & many more painful facts induce me to believe a separation absolutely necessary to preserve an independence in a part, which could not be done united. We are really so different in manners in opinion and in activity & exertion, that the Northern States have been a number of years carrying the Southern on their backs—as the living subjects of Mezentius [3] were doomed each to carry a corpse. In this view of the subject, I cannot be brought to regret a separation; if we must altogether become Colonies or worse to France or Separate, I am for a Separation—if we are, in the Northern States, to be Colonies to France or England, I choose the latter; but I really see no danger of any connection, beyond that of Commerce & Navigation, such as we now have with G Britain, with some additions of a similar kind. An influence of a political kind, cannot be established by the British Nation, and as to the French with the South combating the North in Connection with Britain; allow the worst it is only subjugation to one power, or another, and is that any worse than the situation we shall be in, if my fears are verified, as to the conduct of the House of Reps? French influence must not be increased, it must be diminished. I cannot hesitate a moment between the increase of French influence, & a division of the Union. I can conceive of no possible situation so terrible to this Country, as to admit the French to impose such *friendship* upon us as they are determined to, unless timely resistance is given. I cannot fear British influence, but had rather risk it, than not to knock off the chains of French fraternity; which are literally the primal curse of Heaven. Pardon me, my Dear Sir, I will not be obstinate, but I must be convinced of my Error, & I will retract. I know the sensible part of our Southern Brethren fear a separation, & I really think a measure, would tend to hinder it. I am Sir, Yrs sincerely, Uriah T⟨racy⟩

Col⟨o⟩ Hamilt⟨on⟩

ALS, Hamilton Papers, Library of Congress.
1. Letter not found.
2. See Tracy to H, March 23–24, 1797.
3. In Roman mythology Mezentius was an Etruscan king who bound living persons face to face with dead ones, leaving them to starve.

To Rufus King

[New York, April 8, 1797]

I thank you, My Dear Sir, for your letter of the 6th. of February. The intelligence that the Directory have ordered away our Minister is every way unpleasant. It portends too much a formal Rupture as the only alternative to an ignominious submission. Much public feeling has been excited. But the Government, I trust and believe, will continue prudent and do every thing that honor permits towards accommodation. Tis however to be feared that France successful will be too violent and imperious to meet on any admissible ground.

Congress are called to gether. I can give you no conjecture as to what will be done. Opinions are afloat. My idea is another attempt to pacify by negotiation, vigorous preparation for war, and *defensive* measures with regard to our Trade. But there never was a period of our affairs in which I could less foresee the course of things.

I believe there is no danger of want of firmness in the Executive. If he is not ill-advised he will not want prudence. I mean that I believe that he is himself disposed to a prudently firm course.

You know the map of our Senate. That of our house of Representatives is not ascertained. A small majority on the right side is counted
upon. In Virginia it is understood that *Morgan* comes in place of
Rutherford & *Evans* in place of Page.[1] The whole result of the Virginia election is not known.[2]

The conduct of France has been a very powerful medicine for the
political disease of this Country. I think the Community improves
in soundness.

Adieu God bless you   A Hamilton
                                                        April 8. 1797

R King Esq

ALS, New-York Historical Society, New York City.
    1. This proved to be correct, for Daniel Morgan supplanted Robert Ruther-
ford, and Thomas Evans supplanted John Page. Morgan and Evans were
Federalists; Rutherford and Page were Republicans.
    2. In 1797, elections in Virginia were held on the third Monday in March
(*Virginia Laws*, October, 1792, Sess., Ch. I [December 26, 1792]), which was
March 20.

From Elisha Boudinot [1]

New Ark [*New Jersey*] *April 10, 1797.* "I have considered your
propositions in the business of Col. Fays [2] and reflected on the situation of his partner, and would rather sacrifice what is my right—
then bare hard on him. . . . If he will take up two Notes which I
have given, and are lodged in Mr. Seatons [3] hands the one for two
hundred & thirty four dollars payble 10 May—the other for seven
hundred & fifty dollars payble 1st. July I will give him a discharge.
In making this offer be kind enough to do it, so as no use is to be
made of it in case of his declining it—which if he should do please to
issue the writ, without the least delay and then let the law determine
between us. . . ."

ALS, Hamilton Papers, Library of Congress.
    1. Boudinot, a lawyer and businessman in Newark, was involved in various
transportation and banking enterprises in New Jersey.
    2. Colonel Joseph Fay, a land speculator from Bennington, Vermont, had
been secretary to the Council of Safety and of the State Council from September, 1777, to 1784, and secretary of state from 1778 to 1781. He was an

emissary of Ethan and Ira Allen in the Haldemand negotiations of 1780–1781. See "New York Assembly. Remarks on an Act Acknowledging the Independence of Vermont," March 28, 1787. Fay moved to New York City in 1794, and he retained H as his attorney on several occasions. See the entries in H's Cash Book, 1795–1804, under the dates of February 18, August 1, 1797 (AD, Hamilton Papers, Library of Congress). Fay died of yellow fever in New York City in October, 1803.

Fay's son, Joseph Dewey Fay, was one of H's law clerks. On May 28, 1798, H wrote in his Cash Book, 1795–1804: "received of Col Fay for part of fee with his son 125" (AD, Hamilton Papers, Library of Congress). On July 15, 1800, the New York Supreme Court read and filed "A Certificate of Alexander Hamilton bearing date the 15th July 1800 . . . by which it appears that Joseph D. Fay has served a regular Clerkship in his Office, and that he is of good Moral Character—Ordered that he be examined with respect to his learning & ability to practice as an Attorney of this Court." Fay was admitted to practice in the New York Supreme Court on July 23, 1800 (MS Minutes of the New York Supreme Court, 1796–1800 [Hall of Records, New York City]).

3. William Seton, former cashier of the Bank of New York, was a partner with David Maitland in the New York City mercantile firm of Seton, Maitland, and Company.

From Philip Schuyler

Albany Monday April 10th 1797

My Dear Sir

The Governor left this on the day of the date of your letter covering one for him [1]—which as it is now useless I do not return to you.

I am so much in disposed that I apprehend I shall not be able to attend Congress at the opening of the session,[2] If it all.

In the present posture of our affairs, France seems to have left us no Alternative but a mean and Ignominous submission to her despotic caprice or a dignified resentment, under my present feelings I am for the latter, even at the risk of an open rupture, for I believe It better manfully to meet a war than to degrade the national Character by a pussilanimous Acquiescence In Insult and injury. Our Commerce will suffer, but It suffers already as much or nearly as much as It would were war actually proclaimed. Our seaports too will be exposed to insult they are so Already—and we have no means of protecting them, unless we seek aid where only It is to be found as well for the protection of our commerce as of our ports, I mean by an Alliance with Britain. It is not now, and I believe never will be the interest of that nation to see france domineer over us. It cannot be the interest of the former ever to Attempt to annex those states to her diminions, I believe we are more valuable to her, Mutual good will subsisting, as independant states than we could be as colonies. Indeed the Attempt by either nation to subjugate us appears to me must most certainly fail.

I hope to have the pleasure of seeing you My Dear Eliza and the Children here at the Close of this or early in next week.

God bless you all   Yours most affectionately   Ph: Schuyler

ALS, Lloyd W. Smith Collection, Morristown National Historical Park, Morristown, New Jersey.
    1. Neither H's letter to Schuyler nor his letter to John Jay has been found.
    On the day Schuyler wrote this letter to H, Jay was in New York City where he issued the following commission: "Whereas by an Act of the Legislature of this State 'to render the Funds of this State more productive of Revenue' it is enacted & provided, that no Obligation or Covenant concerning the Premises shall be passed or Executed between the Treasurer of this State and the Corporation of the Bank of New York, until the same shall have been approved by the Person administering the Government of this State for the Time being—or by the Attorney General thereof, together with one or more of such Counsel learned in the Law, as the Person administering the Government of this State shall for that purpose appoint—Now Know Ye that for the Purpose aforesaid, I have appointed & hereby do appoint Samuel Jones Esqr., the Comptroller of this State and Alex Hamilton Esqr both of them Counsellors learned in the Law" (copy, from the original in the New York State Library, Albany). Under the terms of this act, which was passed on February 17, 1797 (*New York Laws*, 20th Sess., Ch. XXIII), the Bank of New York purchased United States six percent stock and deferred stock from the State of New York and also agreed to advance the state money from time to time as should be required.
    2. See Schuyler to H, March 19, 1797, note 1.

To William Loughton Smith

[New York, April 10, 1797]

Dr Sir

Since my last to you [1] I have perused with great satisfaction your little work on our Governments.[2] I like the execution no less than the plan. If my health & leisure should permit, I would make some

ALS, William Loughton Smith Papers, Library of Congress.
    1. H to Smith, April 5, 1797.
    2. See H to Smith, April 5, 1797, note 3.

notes, but you cannot depend on it, as I am not only extremely occupied but in feeble health.

I send you My ideas of the course of Conduct proper in our present situation. It is unpleasant to me to know that I have for some
time differed materially from many of my friends on public subjects; [3] and I particularly regret that at the present critical juncture
there is in my apprehension much danger that *sensibility* will be an
overmatch for *policy*. We seem not to feel & reason as the *Jacobins*
did when Great Britain insulted and injured us, though certainly we
have at least as much need of a temperate conduct now as we had
then. I only say, God Grant, that the public interest may not be
sacrificed at the shrine of irritation & mistaken pride. Farewell

Affectly Yrs.   A H

April 10. 1797

Wm. Smith Esq

[ENCLOSURE] [4]

It must be acknowleged by all who can comprehend the subject
that the present situation of the UStates is in an extreme degree critical, demanding in our public councils a union of the greatest prudence with the greatest firmness. To appreciate rightly the course
which ought to be pursued it is an essential preliminary to take an accurate view of the situation.

That the preservation of peace is a leading article in the policy of
this country has been peculiarly the tenet of the friends of the Government. It is a tenet supported by conclusive reasons. In addition to
the general motives to peace which are common to other nations—it
is of the utmost consequence to us that our progress to that degree
of maturity which puts humanly speaking our fortunes absolutely
in our hands shall not be retarded by a premature war.

But the state of affairs externally and internally suggests the
strongest imaginable auxiliary motives to avoid, if possible, at this

3. See Timothy Pickering to H, March 26, 1797; Oliver Wolcott, Jr., to
H, March 31, 1797; Uriah Tracy to H, April 6, 1797.
4. AD, William Loughton Smith Papers, Library of Congress.

time a rupture with France. Externally we behold France most formidably successful—extending too her connections and influence, while the affairs of her remaining enemies decline. The late events in Italy have for the present put that Country intirely in the power of France with all its resources. It was evident that the Emperor had made a violent exertion for the relief of Mantua.[5] The issue has been to him a terrible one. He will probably be able to bring forward new and powerful forces but it is likely to be attended with great difficulty and embarrassment—and there is too much reason to suspect that these new forces will be under the disadvantage, of *raw-troops* contending with Veterans led by a General who seems to have chained Victory to his cha[i]r. It would seem too that France has awed or seduced Naples into her alliance.[6] And who can say what she may not do as to Venice? Does not every thing seem to promise her the intire command of Italy and its cooperation against the Emperor?

What is the situation of Great Britain? Triumphant at sea but deeply, if not mortally wounded in her vital part, in that which is the vital energy of the Opposition to France—I mean in her pecuniary system. The late measures with regard to the Bank, however vieled, amount to nothing less than a stoppage of payment and an act of bankruptcy in that Institution.[7] The magic which surrounded it, and gave it its principal force exists no longer. Opinion must be injured and with it credit. The consequences are incalculable. An incapacity to afford further subsidies or loans to the Emperor may be inferred with almost moral certainty. Though the great national resources of England and the universal interest in public Credit may arrest and abrige the extent of the evil yet it is scarcely possible that it shall not very much enervate the future efforts against France & it may be expected to fortify extremely the desire of peace in the Nation.

The conduct of the present Emperor of Russia is at best equivocal. Having departed from the engagements of his predecessor towards

5. See Rufus King to H, February 6, 1797, note 6.
6. On October 10, 1796, the Kingdom of the Two Sicilies concluded a treaty of peace with France (Martens, *Recûeil*, VI, 235–38).
7. See King to H, March 8, 1797, note 1.

the Emperor it is in the course of calculation that he may be thrown into the opposite scale.[8] What is the King of Prussia about? Nothing friendly to the Emperor of Germany, if we may reason from his conduct for sometime past—though if we were to reason from his solid interest we ought to conclude that he would not be willing to have France for a contiguous neighbour commanding Holland, and the Emperor of Germany so weakened as to be a counterpoise neither to *France* nor *Russia*.[9] Yet a crooked policy pursuing some immediate interest seems most likely to be his governing motive.

According to appearances then there is great danger that the Emperor and England may be compelled to subscribe to the conditions of France, or to continue the contest on unequal and ruinous terms. It is true in the shifting scenes of Europe the political hemisphere may quickly wear a totally different aspect, but such as it is, it exhibits every evil omen to the enemies of France.

To be involved in a contest with France at this time and under such circumstances would be in the highest degree inauspicious. If the war continues between her and her present enemies the contest can still promise nothing but evil to us without a possibility of Gain. If a sudden peace in Europe takes place and we are left to contend alone the prospect is a most uncomfortable one. France will have large bodies of troops that she will be glad to get rid of and it cannot be doubted that she will be governed by a spirit of *domination* and *Revenge*.

Internally, though our situation in this respect, mends, it is certain that there is a very large party infatuated by a blind devotion to France. Who will guarantee that in a contest so dangerous these men on considerations of ambition fear interest and predilection

8. See H to Pickering, March 22, 1797, note 3.
9. Prussia had made peace with France with the Treaty of Basel, April 5, 1795 (Martens, *Recûeil*, VI, 45–48). On August 5, 1796, the two countries agreed to a secret supplement to that treaty which provided for certain territorial adjustments in the event of a European peace (Martens, *Recûeil*, VI, 59–62). Although Frederick William II of Prussia and his minister of state, Christian August Heinrich Kurt, Count von Haugwitz, were both committed to neutrality and opposed to France's objectives in Germany, they were not in a position to oppose openly French interests. Accordingly, in the winter of 1797, Haugwitz and the French ambassador, Antoine-Bernard Caillard, discussed a French proposal for a Franco-Prussian alliance against Austria. In the end, however, Frederick William rejected this proposal.

would not absolutely join France? There is at least enough of danger of this to furnish a strong reason for avoiding if possible rupture.

In the South we have a vast body of blacks. We know how successful the French have been in innoculating this description of men and we ought to consider them as the probable auxiliaries of France. Let us add that we may have to contend on the South & West with Spain & all the Savage tribes they can influence.

The aggregate of these considerations is little less than awful.

In such a state of things large and dispassionate views are indispensible. Neither the suggestion of pride nor timidity ought to guide. There ought to be much cool calculation united with much *calm* fortitude. The Government ought to be all intellect while the people ought to be all feeling.

The result is in my mind that there ought to be 1 a further attempt to negotiate & 2 vigorous preparation for war with an intermediate embargo.

As to a further attempt to negotiate—let a Commission extraordinary consisting of three persons be sent to France, and let *Jefferson* or *Madison* be at the head of this Commission, perhaps as the Ostensible Minister, but obliged to cooperate with his Colleagues & to conform to the Major opinion. Let General *Pinckney* be one of the Commission, and let Mr. King or Mr. Cabot or some other able man of the Northern Region be the third. If thought expedient the Com~. May go to Amsterdam & announce their mission by a Courier asking for passports &c.

Let two leading principles of action be prescribed to these Commissioners. They must not directly or indirectly acknowlege any fault or culpability in the U States—they must not stipulate any succour to France of any kind or in any shape in the present War—they must stipulate nothing inconsistent with any existing treaty with another Power.

What may they do? They may now modify our Treaties with France so as to assimilate the Commercial one [10] with that with Great Britain and so as mutually to *do away*, or liquidate with an eye to future *defensive* wars the guarantee contained in the Treaty of al-

10. H is referring to the Treaty of Amity and Commerce between the United States and France signed at Paris on February 6, 1778 (Miller, *Treaties*, II, 1–34).

liance, substituting specific succours in defined cases to the *general guarantee*.[11]

This measure will keep open the door of accommodation and give us the chance of favorable events. It will furnish a bridge to the pride of France to retreat. It will give her the motive of endeavouring to strengthen her party by appearing to yield peace to a leader of that party. It will convince the people completely that the Government is at least as solicitous to avoid War with France as it was to avoid it with Great Britain. It will take from the partisans of France the argument that as much has not been done in her case as in that of Great Britain & thus it will contribute, if the measure fails, to the all important end of uniting Opinion at home.

Let us see the objections to this measure and the answers they admit.

Objection 1. The conduct of France has been so violent & insulting towards us that we cannot without disgrace make a further Overture for negotiation.

Answer. This was the opinion of many with regard to Great Britain when Mr. Jay was sent & in all appearance her conduct was very outrageous. Yet our moderation on that occasion not only averted war but raised the character of the Country abroad. It is true France has gone much further than Great Britain ever did. But on the other hand the state of things, and of opinion, requires greater circumspection in the case of France, than was necessary in that of Great Britain. If we couple this measure with others which will evince that we are in earnest about defending ourselves and repelling aggression, our honor will be saved and our moderation only will be displayed. When also it shall be known that our ministers were prohibited from unworthy concessions, it will be demonstrated that we did nothing more than wave *punctilio* in favour of peace. It is often too wise by some early *condescension* to avoid the danger of future *humiliation*. Our Country is not a military one. Our people are divided. France may present herself to their imaginations as the

11. This is a reference to the Treaty of Alliance between the United States and France signed at Paris on February 6, 1778 (Miller, *Treaties*, II, 35-44). See H to George Washington, January 25-31, 1797; H to Theodore Sedgwick, February 26, 1797.

In the margin opposite the end of this paragraph H wrote: "indemnification."

terrible and invincible conqueror of Europe. Who will answer for their fortitude and exertion under such circumstances? Will it not be prudent to avoid if we can the Experiment by a little condescention now?

But this is not all. The measure will tend to *unite* and *fortify* & this may ensure that very fortitude which in a different state of things might be wanting. It may beget the noble resolution to die in the last ditch.

2 Object: The sending of a man unfriendly to the course of our Government & devoted to France may give an opportunity to play into the hands of France & leave greater odium upon the Government for not acceding to inadmissible terms of accommodation. He may be a medium of Cabal between France and the party rather than the Negotiator of accommodation.

Answer. There is perhaps more weight in this than in any other Objection which can be made. But it seems to admit of a satisfactory answer. First. It goes further in ascribing *Turpitude* to the character in question than perhaps is warrantable. It is far from certain that he would be disposed to make an absolute sacrifice of his country and it is to be remembered that in accepting the appointment with known restrictions he agrees to their reasonableness & engages his reputation upon the issue of success. Considerable securities result from these considerations. But admit the disposition to do what is feared, If he is coupled with men of address a counter game may be played & such a complexion may be given to the thing as may put both him and France intirely in the wrong. All will depend on the characters combined. Pinckney, it may be depended on, is a man of honor & loves his Country. Unite with him a man of *skill* and an effectual counteraction is provided. Such a man can certainly be found in a case where the Government may command any of its citizens.

3 Objection. If the measure succeeds under such a man it will strengthen his hands and through him increase the influence of France from which it is of the utmost importance to emancipate the Country.

Answer. There will be some evil of this sort. But this must be weighed against the good obtained. That will be the preservation of peace in the most dangerous crisis that can well be imagined. Besides the credit of the measure will at least be divided between the Authors & the Agent. The President and the Government will have a large share. And the poison will carry with it its antidote. Moreover it is morally certain that the course of things in France will furnish every day some new cure to a moral and orderly people like the people of this Country. But this objection such as it is lies against the *person* not the *measure*.

4th Objection. The conduct of France has been such as to free us from the shakles of Treaties which present only nominal advantages to us or such as in future will be real to her (alluding chiefly to the mutual guarantee).

Answer. This may be true, but the consequence can only take place in a final Rupture. And this would be to stake perhaps our political existence against a partial incumbrance. Surely it could not be wise to attempt to disengage ourselves from our connection with France by a War with her at such a juncture. It might happen that in the end we might be obliged to consent to be fettered in a much greater degree, and increase rather than diminish the evil for which the rupture was hazarded. Expediency is so clearly against it that it is unnecessary to examine the morality of such a policy.

Objection 5   The conduct of France leaves no hope that such a measure will be useful or even that the mission will be heared. There will then be pure disgrace without any advantage.

Answer. The course of things in France does not authorise us to expect any very steady plan there. Events within and without will govern—and there may exist when the Minister arrives a good disposition to receive and hear him. The refusal to receive a minister Plenipotentiary may mean only *an ordinary one to reside* & may not extend to an extraordinary one *pro hac vice*. But suppose the worst, it will tend to the most precious of all things *Union* at home. The repetition of effort to avoid war and of Insult from France will have the most happy influence upon the Temper of our Country.

Object 6. The policy of remodifying our Treaty of Alliance is very questionable. It converts a vague into a specific contract, and substitutes precise obligations to such as each party may interpret according to its convenience.

Answer. This is not an essential part of the plan & may be rejected if thought inexpedient.

But considering the Treaty of alliance as the *price*, no less than the instrument of the assistance from France, morality, which is most consistent with good policy, requires it should be paid. The genuine meaning of that alliance, as to the obligation of the U States, seems to be that when France is *really* & *truly* engaged in a *defensive* war & her West India possessions are attacked the U States ought to assist in their defence with their whole force. In future the U States will not have the excuse of *inability*. They are becoming dayly a powerful nation. They must then either evade their obligation, or as often as France is engaged in a defensive war with a maritime power, take part with her with their whole force. Hence they may be exposed to frequent wars. The denial of their duty besides the guilt & disgrace of broken faith may not avoid that consequence, for as it would be a just so it might be the actual cause of War with the ally.

The vagueness of the Obligation as a source of reciprocal Controversy is in itself an evil which it would be important to get rid of.

Specific succours by either party to the other would not necessarily have the effect of involving the Giver in War. It is settled that such succours in consequence of a Treaty antecedent to the War are not a cause of War.

It would therefore seem to be a great point to the UStates to convert its obligation into that of a specific succour to be defined & thus lessen the danger of a quarrel either with France or its enemies and likewise the evils of a general War.

It is bad to be under obligations which it will be a violation of good faith not to perform & which it will certainly compromit the peace of the Country to perform.

In addition to the reasons already given for pacificatory measures are these cogent ones. The plan of the Government and of the Fœderal party has been to avoid becoming a party in the present War. If any measure it has taken is either the cause or pretext of a War with France, the end will be lost. The credit of preserving peace will not exist. The wisdom of the plan pursued will be questionned. The confidence in the Government will be shaken. The adverse party will acquire the Reputation & the influence of superior foresight. The evil avoided will be forgotten. The evil incurred will be felt. The doubt entertained by many of the justifiableness of the Treaty with G B in respect to France may increase with suffering and danger—& the management of Affairs may be thrown into the hands of the opposite party by the Voice of the people & the Government & the Country sacrificed to France.

Hence it is all important to avoid War if we can—if we cannot to strengthen as much as possible the Opinion that it proceeds from the *Unreasonableness* of France.

As to preparation for War they ought in my opinion to consist of these particulars.[12]

I REVENUE, which ought to go as far as not to be really oppressive. A large sum may be raised within this limit. The objects may be hereafter designated.

II A loan of five Millions of Dollars on the basis of that Revenue.

12. On June 5, 1797, Smith informed the House of Representatives that "he wished to lay upon the table a number of resolutions, which it appeared, if it should not be found advisable to carry the whole of them into effect, were at least worthy of discussion. He did not, however, at present, pledge himself to support the whole. . . ." Smith's resolutions, which closely followed those which H proposed in this document, read: "I. *Resolved,* That further provision ought to be made by law, for fortifying the ports and harbors of the United States.

"2. *Resolved,* That further provision be made by law, for completing and manning the frigates United States, Constitution, and Constellation.

"3. *Resolved,* That provision be made by law, for procuring by purchase a further naval force, to consist of ——— frigates of ——— guns, and ——— sloops of war of ——— guns.

"4. *Resolved,* That provision be made by law, for empowering the President to employ the naval force of the United States, as convoys to protect the trade thereof.

"5. *Resolved,* That provision be made by law, for regulating the arming of the merchant vessels of the United States.

"6. *Resolved,* That the existing Military Establishment ought to be augmented by an addition of one regiment or corps of artillerists and engineers, and ——— companies of dragoons.

"7. *Resolved,* That provision be made by law, for empowering the President to raise a provisional army, to consist of ——— regiments of infantry, one regiment of artillery, and one regiment of dragoons, by commissioning the officers, and by volunteers or enlistments, whenever the circumstances of the country shall, in his opinion, render the said army necessary for the protection and defence of the United States: *Provided,* That neither officers nor soldiers shall receive any pay or emoluments until called into actual service.

"8. *Resolved,* That provision be made by law, to authorize the President to borrow, on the credit of the United States, a sum not exceeding ——— dollars, to defray the expense which may arise in providing for the defence and security of the United States.

"9. *Resolved,* That provision be made by law, to raise a revenue adequate to the reimbursement, within ——— years, of such sum as may be borrowed, as aforesaid.

"10. *Resolved,* That provision be made by law, to prohibit, for a limited time, the exportation of arms, ammunition, and military and naval stores." (*Annals of Congress,* VII, 239.)

This may be put on a footing which will ensure its gradual, yet timely success.

III The completion of the three frigates [13] with all possible speed & the purchase of *Twenty* ships the most fit to be armed and equipped as Cutters & Sloops of War. These will serve to guard our Trade against the Pickeroons of France in the West Indies which are chiefly dangerous. They are to be used in the first instance merely as convoys with instructions purely defensive—prohibitted from cruising for prizes or from attacking, or from *capturing except when attacked.*

IV Instructions to our Minister in Great Britain, if the Negotiation fails, to endeavour to purchase from Great Britain or obtain on a loan Two ships of the line & three frigates. It will be her interest to do this as she has more ships than she can well man & our men employed in them will increase the force to be employed against the common enemy. This may be the most expeditious mode to augment our navy.

V To grant Commissions to such of our Merchantmen as choose to take them authorising them to arm and defend themselves but not to cruise and not to capture unless attacked.

VI To lay a general Embargo with authority to The President to grant licenses to sail, if the Vessels go themselves armed or with Convoys either of our own or of any foreign Nation. This will serve our Vessels and our seamen without arresting our Trade. In a short time, it will go on as usual under protection.

VI To raise upon the *Establishment* some additional Artillery and Two thousand additional Cavalry. These will be useful guards against the Insurrection of the Southern Negroes—and they will be a most precious arm in case of Invasion. Cavalry will be of infinite importance as auxiliary to *new* against *veteran* Troops.

VII The establishment of a provisional army of Twenty thousand infantry. They may be engaged to serve if a War breaks out with any foreign power, and may receive *certain* emoluments in the

13. The construction of the *United States, Constitution,* and *Constellation* had been authorized by Congress in 1794 ("An Act to provide a Naval Armament" [1 *Stat.* 350 (March 27, 1794)]), but in 1797 the ships were still not completed. On March 3, 1797, Congress appropriated one hundred and seventy-two thousand dollars for their completion ("An Act making appropriations for the Military and Naval establishments for the year one thousand seven hundred and ninety-seven" [1 *Stat.* 508–09]). See H to Sedgwick, January 20, 1797, note 4.

mean time—cloaths, full wages when they assemble to exercise, a dollar ℔ Month at other times. This corps must be regularly organised & officered by the United States. The Officers to take rank with those of the establishment. Its advantage will be to have a body of men at a small expence ready for emergencies. The chance of not being employed will facilitate the obtaining of the men on moderate terms.

There may be a disposition to rely wholly on the Militia on three grounds—the supposed improbability of an Invasion—the belief that Militia are sufficient—the Expence in the first instance.

Those who may think an Invasion improbable ought to remember that it is not long since there was a general Opinion the U States was in no danger of War. They see how difficult it has been and is to avoid one. They ought to suspect that the present opinion that there is no danger of invasion may be as chimerical as that other which experience proves to be false.

If France can transport her troops here what is to hinder an invasion? Will she not be very likely to imagine that numerous partisans will join her standard so as to enable her to effect a Revolution & place us more completely under her influence? What if the corps destined to this service be lost? Will it not be to get rid of an incumbrance rather than to sustain a loss? While the War with Great Britain continues it will be difficult though not impossible to throw any considerable Corps into our Country. But if the War with G Britain should end there is no longer any thing to hinder. It is then an event so much in the compass of possibility that it ought to enter seriously into our calculations by anticipation. The situation of Europe is so extraordinary that the most improbable enterprizes in ordinary times become now probable.

Should an invasion take place, though the Militia & after raised troops may finally rescue us, yet there will be no comparison in the expence and evils with or without such a corps prepared beforehand as the *trunk* of our Military force.

VIII Fortification of our Principal Ports.[14] This ought seriously to be attended to but it is a source of expence not requited beyond the utility to embrace more than the principal port in each state.

14. On March 20, 1794, Congress passed "An Act to provide for the Defence of certain Ports and Harbors in the United States" (1 *Stat.* 345–46). For the

In addition to these measures it may be proper by some religious solemnity to impress seriously the minds of the People. A philosopher may regard the present course of things in Europe as some great providential dispensation. A Christian can hardly view it in any other light. Both these descriptions of persons must approve a national appeal to Heaven for protection. The politician will consider this as an important mean of influencing Opinion, and will think it a valuable resource in a contest with France to set the Religious Ideas of his Countrymen in active Competition with the Atheistical tenets of their enemies. This is an advantage which we shall be very unskilful, if we do not improve to the utmost. And the impulse cannot be too early given. I am persuaded a day of humiliation and prayer besides being very proper would be extremely useful.

Perhaps attempts to engage the *good offices*, not the *mediation*, of some other foreign powers may be useful. In this light Spain Holland & Prussia present themselves. This however is a very delicate point.

But we have a further object in the Mission—to obtain compensation and redress for the Spoliations on our Trade. This is an object which our Government ought not to lose sight of. Here however it may be expedient to facilitate the matter by allowing as an offset to France some of her gratuities during the late War. It is useful to get rid of obligations as fast and as fully as we can; for we see the compensation hitherto claimed is nothing less than the sacrifice of our Independence.

---

implementation of this act, see Henry Knox to H, March 29, 1794. On February 23, 1795, the House of Representatives resolved that an additional fifty thousand dollars be appropriated for the completion of the fortifications of ports and harbors (*Journal of the House*, II, 338), and Congress authorized this appropriation in Section 1 of "An Act making further appropriations for the Military and Naval establishments, and for the support of Government" (1 *Stat.* 438 [March 3, 1795]). Timothy Pickering's report on the state of these fortifications, dated January 16, 1796, and his statement of the sums appropriated for fortifying the harbors in 1794 and 1795, dated February 17, 1796, are printed in *ASP, Military Affairs*, I, 110–11, 115–16. Congress provided an additional twenty thousand dollars for "the completion of the fortifications, magazines, store houses and barracks at West Point" in Section 1 of "An Act making appropriations for the support of the Military and Naval Establishments for the year one thousand seven hundred and ninety-six" (1 *Stat.* 493–94 [June 1, 1796]). On June 23, 1797, Congress passed "An Act to provide for the further Defence of the Ports and Harbors of the United States," which appropriated one hundred and fifteen thousand dollars for the fortifications of certain ports and harbors (1 *Stat.* 521–22).

From Oliver Wolcott, Junior

Phila. Apl. 12. 1797.

Dear Sir

I thank you for your Letter of April 5th. & enclose Mr. Kings Letter.[1] I presume that the British Comrs. under the 6th. Article (for Debts) [2] will contend for a similar construction [3] respecting cases determined in our Courts. Is there any ground on which the principle can be opposed?

Are we to consider the British Credit as at an end,[4] if so what effects, will it probably produce here?

Your further opinions respecting the course to be pursued by France, will be very acceptable.

Sincerely yours   Oliv Wolcott Jr

A Hamilton Esq

ALS, Hamilton Papers, Library of Congress.
    1. Rufus King to H, February 6, 1797.
    2. In Article 6 of the Jay Treaty, the United States guaranteed the payment to Great Britain of bona fide private debts contracted before the peace treaty of 1783. The amount of the debts was to be determined by a mixed commission of five members (Miller, *Treaties*, II, 249–51). The British commissioners were delayed in leaving England, and the first meeting of the commission, held in Philadelphia, did not take place until May, 1797.
    3. This is a reference to the British interpretation of Article 7 of the Jay Treaty. See King to H, February 6, 1797.
    4. This is a reference to the suspension of specie payments by the Bank of England. See King to H, March 8, 1797, note 1.

From Nicholas Romayne [1]

[New York, April 13, 1797]

I enclose you, my dear Sir, the letter I mentioned to you last evening that I had recd. from the other side of the Ocean on the subject of

ALS, Hamilton Papers, Library of Congress.
    1. Romayne was a New York City physician and professor of medicine who had attended King's College when H was there ("Matricula of King's

our conversation. I presume it may eventually be necessary for me to go over, but there is much reason to apprehend that I hazard more in going than most ordinary persons, and which merits some consideration on my part as well as my friends.

I know what I have said to you rests with you as a sacred deposit. If I come into town tomorrow evening I will not fail to call upon you.

Yours sincerely   Nichs. Romayne
                                                     April 13. 1797

[ENCLOSURE]

William Pulteney to Nicholas Romayne [2]

Weymouth [England] 20 Jany 1797

Dear Sir

I received with great pleasure your letter of 20 Nov. I acknowledge that I was disappointed at not hearing from you sooner, as I learnt however that the Hope had arrived Safe on the 5 Oct & all passengers well, I was the less uneasy. It was unlucky that my letter to Mr Williamson [3] sent to Genesee by Mr Johnston [4] & had not

---

College," 1774) and received the M.D. degree at Edinburgh in 1780. In the seventeen-eighties he taught private classes in medicine and was a member of the faculty of the Medical School of Columbia College. He then formed his own medical school, the College of Physicians and Surgeons. When the Columbia authorities objected, Romayne abandoned his school, and in 1792–1793 he worked out an agreement by which his students would receive degrees from Queen's (later Rutgers) College in New Jersey. He subsequently became a licentiate and a fellow of the Royal College of Physicians in London.

By the mid-nineties, Romayne was disgusted with the practice of medicine in the United States, and he decided that he could make his fortune in western land speculation. In this venture he became associated with Robert Troup, who was investing heavily in lands in western New York and was an attorney for the Pulteney Associates. It was Troup's plan that Romayne go to Europe and raise money for the purchase of lands in western New York. The principal person that Romayne was to approach was Sir William Pulteney, the head of a group of English associates who had invested heavily in the Genesee country in western New York. For information on the Pulteney Associates, see Troup to H, March 31, 1795.

2. ALS, Hamilton Papers, Library of Congress.

3. Charles Williamson was Pulteney's American agent in the Genesee country. See Troup to H, March 31, 1795.

4. John Johnstone, who served as Williamson's assistant in the Genesee country, was returning to the United States after a visit to England.

returned from thence, when your letter was wrote, as it was of importance that he should have received it much sooner, but tho the delay has had unlucky consequences there is no help for it now.

It gives me great pleasure to hear from so good authority as yours, that every thing goes on well in America, & that the dispositions are favorable to this country. I will make the best use I can of your suggestions, when I go back to London, but I think it right to hint to you, that it would be of great service, if the Ideas you suggest, were communicated in confidence to Mr Liston,[5] because what comes from him will have very great weight here, He is by all accounts, a most excellent & honorable man, & I am glad he has found favor, on your side of the Water, he will make no improper use, of any communications which are made to him, & I am well asured is extremely well disposed to the U.S. It is appears to me that what you propose to be done on our part, is extremely proper, & when I mention Mr Liston, I do not mean to omit any thing which I can do to forward your Ideas, but I know, that what comes from a Minister abroad, has a different effect in the Cabinet than what comes in any other Chanel.[6]

5. Robert Liston, who succeeded George Hammond as British Minister to the United States, arrived in the United States on May 9, 1796, and presented his credentials to President Washington on May 16, 1796.

6. Despite the fact that Liston and Romayne were both involved in the Blount conspiracy (although in quite different ways), this paragraph does not concern that matter, for William Blount did not reveal his plans to Romayne until late January or early February, 1797 (*Annals of Congress*, VIII, 2340–45, 2356–58; Liston to Lord Grenville, January 25, 1797, in F. J. Turner, ed., "Documents on the Blount Conspiracy, 1795–1797," *American Historical Review*, X [April, 1905], 576–77; Mayo, *Instructions to British Ministers*, 132–33, 141–42). Under the circumstances, Pulteney could not have known of the conspiracy when he wrote this letter to Romayne on January 20, 1797. It therefore seems likely that Pulteney in this paragraph was referring to a proposed land speculation which Romayne had discussed with him when Romayne was in England. In a deposition before the House committee preparing articles of impeachment against Blount, Romayne stated: "That he [Romayne] had been acquainted with William Blount since the year 1782, when he first came to this city as a member of Congress. Some time after, he had occasion to correspond with him respecting some property belonging to the deponent in North Carolina. Upon that and various other subjects the correspondence between them had continued till very lately. While Mr. Blount was Governor of the Territory of the United States South of the Ohio, the deponent was requested by a friend to write to him, and to propose the solution of certain queries respecting the military lands on Cumberland, in that Territory, for the purchase of which it was contemplated to form a company, and to propose to Mr. Blount to become a party. This proposition was accordingly made

I remember you foretold, what was likely to happen, with regard to the French. Their conduct has not the Marks of Wisdom in the particular you mention, more than in many other instances; some great change seems likely to take place soon, if one can judge of Events from Causes. There seems to me no abatement of the Spirit of this Country, & I think highly of our Resources, tho something is wanting to give them their full effect, which I trust will be adopted.

I am extremely glad that Mr Jay enjoys now that good opinion of his countrymen, which he always deserved. Indeed it was to be expected, as truth will always at last prevail. I admire the Conduct of Genl Washington in nothing more than in his Resignation. The Election of a President, is that point of your Constitution, which exposes it to most danger, & it Showed great Wisdom & love of his

---

to him. Mr. Blount's answer to these queries and propositions was communicated by Captain [John] Chisholm, at that time an entire stranger to the deponent, but whom Mr. Blount recommended as a proper person to be employed by the company as a purchasing agent. The plan, however, was wholly dropped, on account of the person who proposed it going to Europe. Some time afterwards the deponent formed a resolution of paying a visit to Europe; which being known to Mr. Blount, a proposition originated between them that an attempt should be made there to form a company on the principles and for the purposes formerly mentioned, and to include Governor Blount and Captain Chisholm as partners. This happened previous to the 12th July, 1795, on which day the deponent sailed for England. An agreement to this effect was made and formally executed; but from motives of delicacy, and apprehensions of the fall of lands on account of the political events in Europe, no direct attempts were made to carry it into effect. The deponent, however, left maps and papers on the subject with certain persons of consideration in England, and was requested by them and some others to procure from the State of Tennessee a law for enabling them, as aliens, to hold lands. These persons contemplated to purchase lands as the price, circumstances, and their own convenience, should dictate. In case of their becoming purchasers, it was understood that Governor Blount and the deponent might be interested in the purchases, upon terms, however, which were not settled; and the propriety of the purchases was to depend, in a great measure, upon his opinion. On his arrival in this country, he was to keep up a correspondence with them, which he has done.

"In October last the deponent arrived in America. He has not been out of the State of New York since, till he was summoned to this place. Soon after his arrival he wrote to Governor Blount, informing him that he had done nothing in their business, more than has been before mentioned. To this letter he never received any answer; but, about the beginning of February last, Governor Blount came to New York on business of his own. . . ." (*Annals of Congress*, VIII, 2356–57.)

In reply to questions asked by the House committee, Romayne stated categorically that he never spoke or wrote to Pulteney about the Blount conspiracy (*Annals of Congress*, VIII, 2360–65).

Country in Genl Washington, to contrive, that a New Election Should be made in his lifetime, whilst his Weight & Character could contribute to make it pass over without convulsion. It is perhaps lucky too, that this Election came on when the Situation of America with regard to other Powers, was in some degree critical, which must contribute to prevent in all partys too much disunion.

I Shall be glad if you will express to Mr Hamilton, the late Secretary of the Treasury, my high respect for him from his Writings & his Character. His retiring from a Public office of such Consequence, & returning to the Bar, Marks in my Mind, an Elevation of Character, equal to any thing we read of in History. I am particularly desirous, to possess a full colection of all he has Written, & to know what of the papers in this Federalist came from his Pen.

I beg you also to remember me to Mr Troupe, from whose letters I received much information, & cannot but entertain a great Respect for the author. I hope he will favor me with his opinion upon a matter I Suggested to him in my letter.

I trust you will believe, that I Shall always be much gratified when you indulge me with the pleasure of hearing from you and am

Dear Sir Your most obedt & very humble Servant

William Pulteney

To Oliver Wolcott, Junior

[New York, April 13, 1797]

My Dear Sir

The post of today brought me a letter from you.[1] I am just informed that an order is come to the Custom House not to clear out any Vessel if *armed*, unless destined for the East Indies.[2] Under the present circumstances I very much doubt the expediency of this measure. The excesses of France justify passiveness in the Government and its inability to protect the Merchants required that it should leave them to protect themselves. Nor do I fear that it would tend to Rupture with France, if such be not her determination otherwise.

The *legality* of the prohibition cannot be defended. It must stand on its necessity. It would I think have been enough to require security that the vessel is not to be employed to cruise against any of the belligerent powers. Perhaps even now where vessels have been armed previous to the receipt of the prohibition, it is just and adviseable to except them on the condition of such security. Think of this promptly. The general measure may be further considered at leisure. Nor am I prepared to say that *having been* taken it ought to be revoked.

I will send you shortly some remarks in reply to Questions you propose.[3] Adieu. Yrs   A H

April 13. 1797

Ol Wolcott Jun Esq

ALS, Connecticut Historical Society, Hartford.
  1. Wolcott to H, April 12, 1797.
  2. H is referring to a Treasury Department circular to the collectors of customs, which was signed by Wolcott and dated April 8, 1797. The circular reads: "The depredations, to which the commerce of the United States is at present exposed, have given rise to a question which being of general concern, is therefore made the subject of a circular communication.

"The question is, *Whether it be lawful to arm the merchant vessels of the United States for their protection and defence, while engaged in regular commerce?*

"It is answered—that no doubt is entertained, that defence, by means of military force, against mere pirates and sea rovers, is lawful; the arming of vessels, *bona fide* engaged in trade to the East Indies, is therefore on account of the danger from pirates to be permitted as heretofore; but as the arming of vessels destined for European or West India commerce raises a presumption, that it is done with hostile intentions against some one of the belligerent nations and may cover collusive practices inconsistent with the act of Congress of June, 1794, unless guarded by provisions more effectual than have been hitherto established; it is directed that the sailing of armed vessels, not *bona fide* destined to the East Indies, be restrained, until otherwise ordained by Congress.

"Information has been received that some vessels are arming by strangers for the purpose of capturing the vessels of the United States. The utmost vigilance on the part of the Collectors to prevent the progress of this evil is enjoined; where there is reasonable ground to believe that vessels are equipped for the purpose of being employed against the commerce of this country, they are to be arrested, and the circumstances stated to this Department." (DS, RG 36, Records of the Bureau of Customs, Letters from the Treasury, 1789–1807, Vol. 4, National Archives.)

Section 3 of "An Act in addition to the act for the punishment of certain crimes against the United States" stated "That if any person shall within any of the ports, harbors, bays, rivers or other waters of the United States, fit out and arm . . . any ship or vessel with intent that such ship or vessel shall be employed in the service of any foreign prince or state to cruise or commit hostilities upon the subjects, citizens or property of another foreign prince or state with whom the United States are at peace . . . , every such person so offending shall upon conviction be adjudged guilty of a high misdemeanor, and shall be fined and imprisoned . . ." (1 *Stat.* 383 [June 5, 1794]).

3. See Wolcott to H, April 12, 1797.

From James McHenry

Philad. 14 April 1797 [1]

My dear Hamilton

The letter you sent me [2] has been confined to myself; but the other letters you have written on the same subject, has in your successor at least created some unpleasant feelings.[3] Where opinions clash, and where superiority is made too apparent something a little like envy will come into play especially should a suspicion take place that pains are used to gain proselites.

I have this moment received the inclosed paper,[4] and I must intreat you to consider yourself on the ground you once occupied, and to give me your answer at length that I may avail myself of your experience knowledge and judgement. I have not time to go into all the detail and research which is necessary. You have all at your fingers ends. I shall rely upon your friendship & patriotism for a sound opinion as soon as your avocations will permit, and that you will not communicate to any person what I now communicate to you or what you may write me. Send me with what you do for me the inclosed of which I have no time to make a copy.

ADf, James McHenry Papers, Library of Congress.

1. McHenry mistakenly dated this letter March 14, 1797.

2. H to McHenry, March, 1797.

3. See H to Oliver Wolcott, Jr., March 30, 1797; Wolcott to H, March 31, 1797.

4. The enclosure, a letter which John Adams sent to the heads of departments on April 14, reads: "The President of the United States requests the Secretary of State, The Secretary of the Treasury, The Secretary of War and the Attorney General of the United States to take into their Consideration and Make reports of their opinions in writing Viz

"1st. Whether the refusal to receive Mr. Pinckney and the rude orders to quit Paris, and the territory of the republic, with such Circumstances of Indignity, insult & Hostility, as we have been informed of are Bars to all further measures of Negotiation? or in other words will a fresh Mission to Paris be too great an Humiliation to the american People in their own sense and that of the world?

"2. If another Mission be admissible can any part and what parts as Articles of the Treaty of Amity and Commerce with Great Britain be offered to France, or ultimately conceded to that power in Case of necessity if demanded by her?

"3 What Articles of the Treaty of Alliance and of the Treaty of Commerce with France should be proposed to be abolished.

"4. Whether it will be prudent to say any thing concerning the Consular Convention with that Power, and if it will what alterations in it should be proposed?

"5 Whether any new articles, such as are not contained in either of our Treaties with France or England, Shall be proposed or Can be agreed to if proposed by the French Government?

"6. What Documents shall be prepared to send to France as Evidence of Insults and Injuries committed against the Commerce of the United States by French Ships of War or Privateers or by French Commissioners, agents, officers or Citizens?

"7 In what Terms Shall remonstrances against Spoliations of Property, Capture of Vessels, Imprisonment of Masters and Mariners, Cruelties, Insults and abuses of Every Kind to our Citizens be made?

"8. In what Terms Shall be restitution Reparation Compensation & Satisfaction be demanded for such Insults and Injuries?

"9. Shall demand be Made of payment to our Citizens for property purchased by the French Government in Europe, or in the East or West Indies?

"10. Shall demand be made of the French Government of payment for Vessels and Cargoes captured and Seized whether by Ships of War or private ships?

"11 Shall any Commission of Inquiry and Examination like that with England be agreed to?

"12 What articles in the British Treaty can be offered to France without compensation and with compensation and what Compensation shall be demanded?

"13 Shall a project of a new Treaty abolishing the Old Treaties and Consular Convention be proposed to France?

"14. Shall such a Project with a Project of Instructions to the Minister be proposed and laid before the Senate for their advice and Consent before they be sent to Europe?" (LC, Adams Family Papers, deposited in the Massachusetts Historical Society, Boston.)

To Elizabeth Hamilton

[Peekskill, New York, April 16, 1797]

My Dear Eliza

We arrived here last Evening well and shall proceed immediately on our journey.[1]

I forgot my brief in the cause of Le Guen against Gouverneur which is in a bundle of papers in my armed Chair in the Office. Request one of the Gentlemen to look for it and send it up to me by

the post of Tuesday. Beg them not to fail. Adieu My beloved. Kiss
all the Children for me.

Yrs.   AH

Peeks Kill April

16th 1797

Mrs. Hamilton

ALS, Mr. George T. Bowdoin, New York City.
    1. H was en route to Albany to appear before the New York Supreme Court
as attorney for the complainant in *Louis Le Guen* v *Isaac Gouverneur and
Peter Kemble.* For information on this case, see Goebel, *Law Practice,* II, 48–
164. In the course of this trip, H also appeared before the New York Court of
Chancery. See H to Timothy Pickering, May 11, 1797.

From John Girard [1]

Philadelphia, April 17, 1797. "As I wish to have the Suit against
Armstrong & Barnwall [2] Brought to an end, I wrote to Capn Briggs [3]
at New London to be ready for this next court. I received: Last
saturday his answer was that tho', he was just from Sea, that he was
forced to Sett off immediately for Jeremie. . . . Pray what and
how Shall I do? It is indispensable for you to take the properest
means So as to get said Capn or his new deposition for the Court in
Jully, I cannot Loss such a Sum my ciricumstances dont allow me
to make an abandon of it, But my generosity will make the greatest
acknowlegement for your Troubles; and if a commission of 10 ₱
Ct. is not Adequate with or to your time, I Shall add great deal
more. The capital is 48 or 4900 Drs. but the damages & interests
Brings that sum to above 8000 Drs. . . ."

ALS, Hamilton Papers, Library of Congress.
    1. John (or Jean) Girard was the brother of Stephen Girard, the Philadel-
phia merchant. Like Stephen, he was born in France. He migrated to Santo
Domingo, where by 1779 he was established in business as a commission agent.
Because of the slave revolt in Santo Domingo in 1791, John Girard came to
the United States, and in 1793 he became a citizen. After working briefly for
his brother (see Stephen Girard to H, February 26, 1794), he went into business for himself. He died at St. Vincent in November, 1803, leaving his family
destitute.
    2. *John Girard* v *William Armstrong and George Barnwall.* For a discus-
sion of this case, see Goebel, *Law Practice,* II, 191–98.
    3. William Briggs, captain of Girard's ship *Adolphe.*

To Elizabeth Hamilton [1]

[Albany, April 19, 1797] [2]

I informed you My Darling by a letter which will go by post [3] of my arrival here in good health and finding your family well. But this morning your papa has an attack of the Gout, *not* particularly severe, one indeed which in a different situation would give no uneasiness—but as his strength has been of late somewhat diminished, it is impossible not to feel anxiety about him. On the whole I advise Cornelia [4] and you to come up. He will be very glad to see you & I hope you will find him better. I pray you, don't alarm yourself for you know how dangerous it will be in your situation [5] and how much it is a duty should his case ever take a worse turn than we now apprehend to arm ourselves with Christian fortitude and resignation

God bless You My Beloved   AH

April 19. 1797

Mrs. E Hamilton

ALS, Mr. George T. Bowdoin, New York City.
  1. On the back of this letter, H wrote: "Mrs. Wendell will particularly oblige Col Hamilton by sending this letter with a particular charge by the Stage. Mrs. Hamilton will pay the bearer a Dollar."
  Mrs. Wendell was the wife of John H. Wendell, an Albany lawyer and a member of the New York Assembly from 1796 to 1798.
  2. H was in Albany to appear as an attorney before the New York Supreme Court and the New York Court of Chancery. See H to Elizabeth Hamilton, April 16, 1797.
  3. Letter not found.
  4. Cornelia was Elizabeth Hamilton's sister and the wife of Washington Morton.
  5. Elizabeth Hamilton was pregnant with her fifth child. William Stephen Hamilton was born on August 4, 1797.

From James McHenry

[Philadelphia] 19 April 1797.

My dear H.

I enclose you a further request on the subject of the paper communicated to you in my last,[1] that you may have the whole before you and that you may aid me with your talents and experience.

It strikes me that, it will be proper for the Pres. to state to Congress the species of defensive force necessary for the occasion, and consider it an essential attribute of negociations I had given him in writing the kind & the quantity & expence of the force I conceived indispensably requisite [2] and am very happy to find that I have met in every thing but quantity your ideas.

Would it be disadvantagious to the U.S. to propose to France a new commercial treaty considering the exist. com. treaty as null which should comprise in it every article of the B. treaty that can be made applicable to the Trade of the two countries. Would not this serve to silence Amer. clamours whether adopted or refused.

ADf, James McHenry Papers, Library of Congress.
    1. McHenry to H, April 14, 1797.
    McHenry's "further request" was for advice in replying to a letter which John Adams had written to him on April 15, 1797. Although Adams's letter to McHenry of April 15 has not been found, a notation in his letter book which follows the copy of a letter sent to Oliver Wolcott, Jr., on that date states: "A Similar Letter mutatis mutandis was sent to the Secretary of State, the Secretary at War and the Attorney General on the Same day." Adams's letter to Wolcott reads: "The President of the United States requests the Secretary of the Treasury, to commit to writing in detail, and report to the President in Writing, as early as may be convenient Such particulars as the Secretary may think necessary or expedient to be inserted in the President's Speech at the opening of the ensuing Congress under the heads of:
    "1. Such Things as ought to be communicated to Congress concerning the State of the Union.
    "2. Such Measures as ought to be recommended to Congress for their Adoption.
    "And the Presidents desire is that the Secretary would not confine himself to matters merely within the Treasury Department, but give himself a liberal Latitude, both in relation to the other departments, and to the illustrations and Reasonings in Support of his opinions.
    "The President also requests the Secretary to report to him his opinion of the Articles which ought to be inserted in the Instructions of an Ambassador, Envoy ordinary or Extraordinary or Minister Plenipotentiary to be sent to France upon Supposition it should be deemed consistent with the Dignity, Honour and Interest of the United States to Send another mission to that Power." (LC, Adams Family Papers, deposited in the Massachusetts Historical Society, Boston.)
    2. McHenry is referring to a letter which he sent to Adams on April 8, 1797. The letter was a report on the "quantum and kind of *defensive* force necessary at this juncture, and which it appears to the Secy. of War, Congress ought to make immediate provision for. . . ." McHenry proposed: "the following *actual and contingent force.* Of *actual force,* which ought to be raised as soon as possible vz. One Regiment or corps of Artillerists and Engineers; One Regt. of Infantry; two companies of Dragoons; *three* Frigates of 32 guns and six sloops of war of 16 guns. Of *contingent force* vz. 10,000 regulars to be raised only as wanted at the discretion of the President . . ." (AL, Adams Family Papers, deposited in the Massachusetts Historical Society, Boston).

From Elisha Boudinot

New Ark [*New Jersey*] *April 20, 1797.* "I wrote you a few days ago [1] relative to my business with F.[2] . . . and as I have not heard any thing from you on the subject, I take it for granted they have shuffled as usual, if so, please to order the writ to be issued at once—and in order to give you no further trouble of negociating with persons so little disposed to the common rules of equity—I have authorized Timothy Green [3] Esqr as my agent in fact—to accomodate the suit if they should be disposed to settle it previous to the trial, but they must not expect the lenient offers that have been made thru' you."

ALS, Hamilton Papers, Library of Congress.
  1. Boudinot to H, April 10, 1797.
  2. Joseph Fay.
  3. Green was a New York City attorney.

From Philip Hamilton [1]

[New York] April 21, 1797.

Dear Papa:

I just now received the enclosed letter from grandpapa,[2] in answer to a letter I wrote to him, in which he has enclosed to me three receipts for shares in the Tontine Tavern,[3] amounting to £100. I have given the receipts to mama.

I delivered my speech to Dr. Johnson [4] to examine. He has no objection to my speaking; but he has blotted out that sentence which appears to be the best and most animated in it; which is, you may recollect it

"*Americans, you have fought the battles of mankind; you have enkindled that sacred fire of freedom which is now,*" &c. Dear Papa, will you be so good as to give my thanks to grandpapa for the present he made me, but above all for the good advice his letter contains —which I am very sensible of its being extremely necessary for me to pay particular attention to in order to be a good man. I remain your most affectionate son

P.S. You will oblige me very much by sending back the letter I have enclosed to you.

Hamilton, *Reminiscences,* 15; Hamilton,, *Intimate Life,* 216–17.
    1. Philip Hamilton, H's oldest child, was a student at Columbia College.
    2. Philip Schuyler.
    3. The Tontine Plan, which was named for a Neapolitan banker, Lorenzo Tonti, provided its members with the essential features of a lottery and a program for old-age security. In 1791 a group of New York City merchants organized the Tontine Association and erected a building on the corner of Wall and Water streets. In 1793 this building became the headquarters for the stock exchange.
    4. William Samuel Johnson was president of Columbia College from 1787 to 1800.

To Oliver Wolcott, Junior [1]

[Albany, April 22, 1797]

The *consideration* for the candidates in the better part of the community stands nearly thus. *Clarkeson,*[2] *ver Plank,*[3] *Fish*[4] = *Walker,*[5] *Burrall,*[6] *Giles,*[7] *Watson.*[8]

I have thought it better to give you the map of the characters for the information of the President than to draw myself any definitive conclusion. It is not easy to err much in a choice among them.

I should have mentioned Col Smith[9] among the most prominent but for the late unfortunate circumstances[10] which attend him and which would render his appointment ineligible to such an Office at this time.

Yrs. truly   A Hamilton

                                                   April 22. 1797

Ol Wolcott Jun Esq

ALS, RG 59, General Records of the Department of State, Applications and Recommendations, 1792–1801, National Archives.
    1. On the back of this letter Wolcott wrote: "Alexr. Hamilton Esq re Collectorship N York Apl. 22d. 1797. arrived after the appointment took place."
    John Lamb, who had served as collector of customs at New York City since 1789, had been dismissed because of a shortage of funds in his accounts. On April 25, 1797, John Adams ". . . determined to make the following appoint-

ment for which a commission is to issue, Viz Joshua Sands, Collector of New york Vice Mr. Lamb dismissed" (LC, Adams Family Papers, deposited in the Massachusetts Historical Society, Boston). On May 20, 1797, the Senate consented to Sands's appointment (*Executive Journal*, I, 240).

2. Matthew Clarkson, a veteran of the American Revolution and a resident of New York City, had served in both the New York Assembly and Senate and had been United States marshal for the District of New York in 1791 and 1792. In February, 1795, he was appointed commissioner of loans for New York (*Executive Journal*, I, 170–71).

3. Daniel C. Verplanck was a New York City lawyer and banker.

4. Nicholas Fish, a veteran of the American Revolution and a close friend of H, had been appointed supervisor of the revenue for the District of New York by George Washington on December 30, 1793 (*Executive Journal*, I, 143–44).

5. Benjamin Walker. See H to Washington, January 31, 1797.

6. Jonathan Burrall. See H to Oliver Wolcott, Jr., December 21, 1796; H to Washington, January 31, 1797.

7. Aquila Giles was marshal for the District of New York.

8. James Watson, a veteran of the American Revolution, was a New York City lawyer and merchant. He had served in the New York Assembly, and from 1796 to 1798 he was a member of the state Senate.

9. William S. Smith, a veteran of the American Revolution, was John Adams's son-in-law. He was appointed secretary of the American legation in London in 1785. From 1789 to 1791 he was marshal of the District of New York, and from 1791 to 1792 he was supervisor of the revenue in the District of New York. He was heavily involved in land speculation in western New York.

10. H is referring to one or to both of two lawsuits in which Smith was involved. The first case concerned Smith's financial transactions with William Ward Burrows. As security for debts which he owed Burrows, Smith in 1796 pledged property which he previously had conveyed to William Constable. Since he failed to notify Burrows of this previous conveyance, Burrows, through his lawyer Robert Troup, instituted a suit against Smith for $194,000. For Smith's detailed defense of his conduct, see Southern History Association, *Publications* (1907), Vol. 11, 38–43. The second case concerned debts which Smith owed to Sir William Pulteney and William Hornby. These debts are described in Benjamin Walker to H, October 4, 1796. See also Robert Morris to H, May 10, 1796; H to Charles Williamson, May 17–30, 1796. The suit which Walker, who was agent for the Pulteney Associates, instituted against Smith for non-payment of these debts was referred to arbitrators (Walker to H, July 6, 1797), before whom a hearing was pending when this letter was written.

To Elizabeth Hamilton [1]

[Albany, April 23, 1797]

Lest my Dear Eliza any circumstance should have prevented your departure before this reaches you, I conclude to drop you a line to tell you your Father is considerably *better* at the same time considering the delicate state of his health generally I am very desirous you should come up as he is.

Yrs. Most Affec   AH
                                                      April 23. 1797
Mrs. Hamilton

ALS, Hamilton Papers, Library of Congress.
     1. For background to this letter, see H to Elizabeth Hamilton, April 16, 19, 1797.

From Louis Le Guen [1]

[Albany, April 24, 1797]

Monsieur

Les Evênements inatandue qui ont Empeschés Mr. Burr [2] de se réndre issy à temps de Vous Seconder dans mon Affaire, ont Parue Vous désobliger, sa présance est peu m'estre favorable. Néamoints, Monsieur, Vos talens, Votre Zélle, et L'integrités de Ceux qui doivent Estre mes Juges, ne me Laisse pas le Moindre doute que Vos Efforts ne me feront Obtenir un Jugement favorable. Enconcequ'ence Sy Vous n'avés aucu'unes objections, Veuillés bien demain pléder Ma Cause. Je my trouveraie Sy Vous le Jugés Convenable, et En tout disposés á mè diriger d'après Vos Sages Conseils

J'ay L'honneur d'Estre avec un Entier Devoûment   Votre trés humble et trés obéissant serviteur   L. Le Guen

Albany 24 avril 1797.
Colonel hamilton

ALS, Hamilton Papers, Library of Congress.
     1. For background to this letter, see H to Elizabeth Hamilton, April 16, 1797. For information on the case of *Louis Le Guen* v *Isaac Gouverneur and Peter Kemble*, see Goebel, *Law Practice*, II, 48–164.
     2. Aaron Burr was one of the lawyers, H among them, representing Louis Le Guen in his suit against Gouverneur and Kemble.

Petition to the Mayor, Aldermen, and Commonalty of the City of New York [1]

[New York, April 24, 1797] "The Memorial of Sundry Inhabitants of the City of New York and the vicinity thereof Respectfully Sheweth That your Memorialists have learnt . . . that the Corporation of the City of New York have purchased a lot of Ground situate in the Seventh Ward . . . which they intend to Convert into a Potters Field for the interment of the bodies of such persons as may die of infectious disorders. Your Memorialists seriously Alarmd at the consequence, . . . take the liberty to address to their consideration the following reasons and objections against the forming of a burial ground in the place aforementioned. In the first place they would state that the field designd for this purpose is situated so near the city and is so contiguous to the publick roads leading from the East to the West part of the Town that it cannot but produce the most unpleasant and fearfull sensations in all those who may have occasion to pass the ways and roads leading near and along the same. . . . Secondly—that the field referrd to lies in the neighbourhood of a number of Citizens who have at great expence erected dwellings on the adjacent lots for the health and accomodation of their families during the Summer Season. . . . And your memorialists would further suggest that from the rapid Increase of Building that is daily taking place both in the suburbs of the city and on the Ground surrounding the field alluded to it is certain that in the course of a few years the aforementioned field will be drawn within the precincts of the city and long remain a subject of nuisance and inconvenience to the Community. . . . And your memorialists further state that provided the Corporation from motives of regard towards them and their Fellow Citizens in General shall be inclind to forego the measure they are about to execute your memorialists do hereby make Assurance that to prevent the corporation from sustaining any loss or damage by reason thereof a Number of the Undersign'd are willing and ready to purchase of them the ground in question and to make them full and ample compensation for the same. . . ." [2]

DS, Municipal Archives and Records Center, New York City.
1. H was one of fifty-seven individuals who signed this petition.

2. On April 24, 1797, the petition was read and referred to a committee. On May 15, 1797, the committee reported that the ". . . Piece of Ground which the Petitioners will purchase . . . is well calculated for the purpose so far as that is removed a convenient Distance from the Greenwich and Albany Roads . . . But . . . to get to this Ground, the Hearse, a great subject of Complaint must travel either of the Roads above mentioned. . . .

". . . The Ground they offer is certainly an eligible Place . . . except the one mentioned.

"Whereupon the Question was raised that the Potters field be continued as the Burying Ground and it was carried in the Negative. . . ." (*Minutes of the Common Council,* II, 339, 348.)

To Brockholst Livingston

[*Albany*] *April 28* [*1797*]. "The situation of General Schuyler [1] & other family circumstances do not permit me to attend Court this day. Will you do me the favour to argue the motion for setting aside the Non suit & granting a new trial on the inclosed case? . . ." [2]

ALS, Hamilton Papers, Library of Congress.

1. Philip Schuyler, H's father-in-law, was ill. See H to Elizabeth Hamilton, April 19, 23, 1797.

2. The case in question was *Thomas Gilbert and Francis Farquharson* v *Jeremiah Hallett* (or Hallet). See Goebel, *Law Practice,* II, 25, note 94.

The following entry appears in the minutes of the New York Supreme Court for April 28, 1797:

"Gilbert & Ferguson vs. Hallett — Argument. On Motion to set aside the nonsuit in this cause, Mr Hamilton for the Plaintiff and Mr Riggs for Defendant— Curia Adversari vult."

(MS Minutes of the New York Supreme Court, 1797–1802 [Court of Appeals, Albany]).

From Rufus King

London Ap. 29. 1797

Dear Sir

Unless greater attention is given to the procuring of the requisite evidence in the Cases of Capture than has yet been done,[1] we shall ultimately meet with serious Losses, and give occasion to much Complaint.

The Sufferers depend on the Government, and the Government

on the Sufferers, and thus that wh. shd. be done is omitted. I inclose
to you a copy of notes wh. Mr. Gore [2] & I made this morning upon
this subject—he has sent a Copy to the Secy. of State—perhaps some
Public Notice shd. be given on this subject.

Yrs. &c   Rufus King

Col. Hamilton

P.S. We are anxious to hear from Vienna—the last post brings intelligence to the 12. The armistice expired on the next day—if no
treaty was concluded, a serious & decisive Battle must have been
fought before this Date. Some people Suppose Buona Parte's situation was critical, and very dangerous. The Check recd. by the
French in the Tyrol has enabled a corps of Austrian to gain the Rear
of Buona Parte's Army.[3]

ALS, Hamilton Papers, Library of Congress.
    1. King is referring to evidence presented to the mixed commission which
was authorized by Article 7 of the Jay Treaty and which was at this time
meeting in London. The commission was assigned the task of arbitrating United
States claims growing out of the violation of neutral rights. For information
on the members of the commission and its initial difficulties, see King to H,
February 6, 1797.
    2. Christopher Gore of Massachusetts was one of the American commission-
ers appointed to carry out the provisions of Article 7 of the Jay Treaty. On
April 30, 1797, Gore and William Pinkney, also an American commissioner,
wrote to Timothy Pickering that they had "conferred with Mr King on the
subject" of these cases (LS, RG 76, Records of the Boundary and Claims Commissions and Arbitrations, National Archives), and they enclosed notes on the
procedures to be followed in presenting claims to the board (copy, RG 76,
Records of the Boundary and Claims Commissions and Arbitrations, National
Archives). These may be the notes to which King is referring in the letter to
H printed above. On April 29, 1797, King wrote to Pickering: "Mess. Gore
and Pinckney will write to you on a subject on which I have had, and still
suffer, much anxiety—unless a more systematic attention is given to the procuring of the seasonable and requisite Evidence in cases of Capture, I see little
prospect in obtaining the reasonable satisfaction for our Losses, which with
proper diligence & skill in the Agency, and with present views of this Government, we might rationally expect to receive" (King, The Life and Correspondence of Rufus King, II, 177). As a result of the commissioners' complaints,
the Department of State issued the following notice on September 7, 1797:
"A Detail of the Proofs necessary to be exhibited before the Board of Commissioners appointed, under the 7th article of the Treaty of Amity, Commerce
and Navigation, between the United States and Great Britain, to adjust the
Claims of the Citizens of the United States on Account of illegal Captures and
Condemnations of their vessels, or other Property.
    "In all cases the proceess, that is, copies of the proceedings in the vice ad-
miralty courts, or at least so much as is considered necessary before the Lords

Commissioners, should be brought forward to accompany the claim preferred to the Board.

"It is advisable, that in all cases the affidavit of the party, his clerks and others knowing the transaction, also copies and extracts of entries in the books of the party, made at the time of and relating to the transaction, the truth of which should be sworn to by his clerks, should be furnished to show that the voyage and property were as the ship's papers declare them to be.

"In many cases the party may hold letters and documents from the shippers and others, written at the time of and concerning the voyage, vessel and cargo, or either, which may be in question, and which letters may serve to confirm or elucidate other evidence. Should such be sent, accompanied by the testimony of the party and his clerks, that they are true, or if from any cause it may be inexpedient to send the originals, let the attestation be to the truth of the copy, and that the original contains nothing more as to that particular voyage or property. It will also be well to state the reason why the original is not sent.

"The foregoing will be highly useful in all cases, even in those cases where there was no act done by the master or by others to impair or lessen the force and weight of papers found on board at the time of capture, and where the papers were complete and genuine and the transaction on the face of it perfectly fair.

"In all cases where the ship's papers were incomplete, where the transaction was in any degree suspicious from the want of papers ordinarily used and found on board vessels, or from any act of the master or others in destroying or concealing papers, or attempting to secrete property of the enemy, such extracts, correspondence and affidavits, as aforementioned, will be indispensable to show fully and clearly to whom the property belonged and to remove all suspicions and doubts as to the truth and fairness of the transaction.

"There are several classes of cases in which a charge may be brought forward of wilful omission and neglect, and which charge it will be necessary to remove.

"It should be understood in the United States, that in some cases the party captured neglected to make a claim for his property in the vice admiralty courts; that in some, after having made such claim there, he abandoned it; that in some after having prosecuted in the vice admiralty, he failed to claim an appeal there, or give security for prosecuting his appeal; in some, the party neglected to claim or enter his appeal in the courts of appeal within the time limited by law, which time, in cases where there was a claim filed in the vice admiralty court, is limited to nine months from the date of the sentence of the vice admiralty, and in cases where there was no claim in the vice admiralty, the time is limited to one year from the date of the sentence. There was at the request of Mr. Jay, a prolongation of the ordinary time for claiming appeals by special order of his Britannic Majesty. There are others where the party after having made his appeal neglected to take out the usual process or to serve the same on the captors; and others where the party did not bring forward copies of the proceedings in the court of vice admiralty.

"Testimony should be furnished satisfactorily accounting for the neglect or abandonment in the particular case, where it happened, and such as will remove the presumption of 'wilful omission and neglect'; where there has been an omission to claim in the vice admiralty, or an abandonment of the claim after being duly preferred, or a neglect to claim an appeal in due season of law, or within the time allowed under the particular order of his Britannic Majesty, or to prosecute such an appeal by not taking out and serving the usual process on the captors, or by not bringing forward copies of the proceedings in the court of vice admiralty.

"In cases where money has been expended in prosecuting for the property in the vice admiralty courts in the West Indies or elsewhere, it is necessary that evidence should be furnished, showing the amount expended and that it was of necessity. The affidavit of the person paying or receiving the money, or of those who were present at the payment, or knew of its being paid, would be satisfactory. In cases where the vessel has been hypothecated or property sold to provide the security demanded for prosecuting appeals from the vice admiralty courts, evidence should be furnished that such hypothecation or sale was necessary, the amount sold, the loss and damage which accrued to the party from such sale or hypothecation. Evidence of the price at which the property was sold, and that at which it would have sold at the place of destination, when the vessel would have probably arrived, had she not been stopped, will show the loss sustained by the sale.

"In cases of demurrage, the loss may be proved by showing what that vessel, or such a vessel, could have earned during the detention. This may be the testimony of those who hired or let vessels at the time, by the expenses incurred in victualling the crew, by the hazard to the vessel from the nature and waters of the harbor or ports where she was detained.

"In cases where a claim is preferred to the Board for compensation, for a loss sustained by capture and condemnation, the value of the property at the place of destination at the probable time of its arrival, had it not been prevented by capture, may be proved by the affidavits of auctioneers, brokers and others disinterested in the particular case, or in any cases under the commission: prices current published at such times and places, will afford very satisfactory evidence as to value. Evidence should be obtained from all the considerable seaports in the United States of the premium paid for insurance from the various foreign ports, especially in the West Indies or other foreign ports; and where the party has insured his property, he should prove the rate of premium at which he insured it." (Moore, *International Adjudications*, IV, 93–95.)

3. At the Battle of Rivoli on January 13–14, 1797, Napoleon overwhelmingly defeated the Austrians, who retreated into the Alps. On February 2, Mantua capitulated. Napoleon then marched into the Alps on a campaign which resulted in the collapse of the Austrian defense and which brought Austria to the verge of military disaster .On April 7, Napoleon and the Austrians agreed to an armistice which was to expire on April 13 (*Réimpression de L'Ancien Moniteur*, XXVIII, 669–70). On April 18 the preliminaries of peace were signed near Leoben (Martens, *Recûeil*, VI, 385–90). Napoleon was willing to agree to the preliminaries of peace because of the widespread rising of the Tyrolese, increased opposition by the Venetians, and his fear that he would soon be confronted by a much larger force of Austrians.

To James McHenry

[Albany] April 29. 1797

Dr Sir

I now send you a cursory answer to certain questions.[1] They are imperfect & probably will come too late. But court avocations and

ALS (photostat), James McHenry Papers, Library of Congress.

1. For the "certain questions," which John Adams had submitted to the members of the cabinet on April 14, 1797, see McHenry to H, April 14, 1797, note 4.

distress in the family have prevented any thing better. General
Schuyler has been critically ill though now as I hope out of danger.[2]
My Brother in law Mr. Rensselaer has just lost a favourite Daughter [3]
one & the Eldest of two Children without a prospect of more. The
whole has thrown a gloom upon the family & my health is not the
stoutest.

I shall answer your last by the next post.

Adieu   A H

[ENCLOSURE] [4]

Answer to Questions proposed by the President of the U States.

To The first.   It is difficult to fix the precise point at which indignity or affront from one state to another ceases to be negotiable
without absolute humiliation and disgrace. It is for the most part a
relative question—relative to the comparitive strength of the parties
—the motives for peace or war—the antecedent relations—the circumstances of the moment as well with regard to other nations as to
those between whom the question arises. The conduct of France
exclusive of the refusal of Mr. Pinckney is no doubt very violent
insulting and injurious. The treatment of Mr. Pinckney if it does not
pass certainly touches upon the utmost limit of what is tolerable.
Yet it is conceived that under all the singular and very extraordinary
circumstances of the case further negotiation may be admitted without the absolute humiliation and disgrace which ought perhaps never
to be incurred—to avoid which it is probably always wise to put
even the political existence of a Nation upon the hazard of the die.

In replying to the President's questions, McHenry followed closely the suggested answers which H gave in the letter printed above. McHenry's reply
to the President's questions is dated April 29, 1797 (ADS, Adams Family Papers, deposited in the Massachusetts Historical Society, Boston), and was enclosed in McHenry to Adams, May 5, 1797 (ALS, Adams Family Papers,
deposited in the Massachusetts Historical Society, Boston).

2. See H to Elizabeth Hamilton, April 19, 23, 1797.

3. Stephen Van Rennselaer, the eighth patroon, was lieutenant governor of
New York from 1795 to 1801. He was married to Elizabeth Hamilton's sister
Margaret (Margarita). Catherine Schuyler Van Rennselaer, who was seven
years old, died on April 26, 179·

4. AD, Columbia University Libraries; AD (photostat), James McHenry
Papers, Library of Congress.

The triumphs of France have been such as to confound and astonish mankind. Several of the principal powers of Europe even England herself have found it necessary or expedient in greater or less degrees to submit to some humiliation from France. At the present juncture the course of her affairs & the situation of her enemies more than ever admonishes those who are in danger of becoming so and who are not able to oppose barriers to her progress to temporise. The mind of mankind tired with the suffering, or spectacle, of a war, fatal beyond example, is prepared to see more than usual forbearance in powers not yet parties to it who may be in danger of being involved. It is prepared to view as only prudent what in other circumstances would be deemed dishonorable submission.

The U States have the strongest motives to avoid war. They may lose a great deal; they can gain nothing. They may be annoyed much and can annoy comparatively little. Tis even a possible event *that they may be left alone to contend with the Conquerors of Europe.* When interests so great invite and dangers so great menace, delicacy is called upon to yield a great deal to prudence. And a considerable degree of humiliation may, without *ignominy*, be encountered to avoid the possibility of much greater and a train of incalculable evils.

The former relations of the U States to France—the agency of that power in promoting our revolution—are reasons in the nature of things for not lightly running into a quarrel with—even for bearing and forbearing to a considerable extent. There is perhaps in such a case peculiar dignity in moderation.

France in declining to receive Mr Pinckney has not gone to the *ne plus ultra.* She has declined to receive a minister till grievances, of which she complains, are redressed. She has not absolutely ordered away a minister as the preliminary to war. She has mingled some qualifications. It is not even clear that she means to say she will not receive an *extraordinary* minister. This leaves some vacant ground between her act and *rupture.* The U States may occupy it by a further attempt at negotiation. This further attempt seems to be that which must carry us to the point beyond which we cannot go.

Besides the object of *explanation* to satisfy *France,* we have the most serious grievances *to complain of* and of which to *seek redress.* This last will be a principal object of an extraordinary mission. It will not be to make *submissions* but to *explain* and to demand *repara-*

tion. This double object contains a great *salvo* for the national honor.

We have just seen in the case of Sweden the negotiation in some way or other of a similar insult.[5] Though the refusal of our minister, as being more pretextless is more offensive, yet the forbearance of Sweden is a precedent of some force for us.

As to our own Country—There is a general and strong desire of peace—and with a considerable party still a particular repugnance to war with France. The state of public opinion is not likely to consider a farther attempt at negotiation as too humiliating. It may be safely taken for granted that it will approve such an attempt as prudent—& that at home it will have no other effect than to lay the foundation for great *Union* and *Constancy*, in case of failure.

But to preserve character abroad—and esteem for the Government at home, it is essential that the idea of further negotiation be accompanied by measures that shall demonstrate a spirit of resistance in case of failure—that shall yield present protection—and promise future security.

With this *adjunct*, it is believed that the Government in pursuing the plan for further negotiation will raise rather than depress the character of the Nation abroad & will preserve the dignity of the American mind & the esteem of the American people.

The enunciation of one measure by the Executive ought therefore to be accompanied with a decisive recommendation of the other course. In doing this however it will be wise to avoid all expressions that may look like menacing France with what we intend to do. The attempt to negotiate must be put upon the foot of an *appeal* to her *justice* and *friendship*. The recommendation of preparatory & defensive precautions must be put on the foot of *present necessity* in reference to the actual & ruinous depredations on our Trade and

5. Gustavus IV Adolphus of Sweden assumed power from the Regent, Karl, Duke of Södermanland, on November 1, 1796. On November 29, 1796, Carl Gustav König was appointed Swedish chargé d'affaires in Paris. König had been secretary at The Hague legation in 1793 and was transferred to the Paris embassy as secretary in 1796. On January 6, 1796, König presented himself to the Directory to replace the former ambassador, Erik Magnus, Baron Staël von Holstein. See "The Warning No. I," January 27, 1797, note 10. The Directory, however, refused to receive König on the ground that it could not accept a chargé d'affaires as a permanent substitute for an ambassador, but only as a deputy for one who was temporarily absent.

The information on König has been supplied by Mr. Olof von Feilitzen, Assistant Librarian, Kungliga Biblioteket, Stockholm, Sweden.

the possibility of *future dangers* which it may not be *in our power to avert.*

To the second—It will be expedient to declare to France that if there be any thing in the Treaty with G Britain which France is desirous of incorporating in the Treaty with her—The U States are ready to do so—having no wish to give to any other power privileges which France may not equally enjoy *on the same terms.* This general offer seems the most unexceptionable & will stop as well the mouth of France as of her partisans among ourselves. The duration of privileges should also be in both cases the same.

To the third.   It does not occur that it will be expedient to *propose* the abolition of any of the articles of our Treaties with France further than may be implied in the above general offer. To propose the abolition of things inconvenient to us would confirm the suspicion that we were disposed to narrow the privileges of France and would do harm there and here. The defining of some of the stipulations according to our practice upon them would be desireable if obtainable, but it is better to leave them as they are than define the other way. And the probability is that the definition would end in the last way which might compromit us with other powers. The only thing that can be done with advantage is to propose to liquidate the meaning and effect of the mutual Guarantee in the Treaty of Alliance.[6] That Guarantee is now general. The obligation it imposes on France towards us is essentially nominal in future, because our *sovereignty* and independence can hardly again come in question. That which it lays upon us would expose us to general war with the enemy of France as often as in a purely *defensive* war her West India posessions should be attacked. This is a great evil. The alternative in such a case is to chicane our engagements and risk war with France for not performing them—or to perform them, if called upon, and encounter war with her enemies. It would be a great point gained to reduce this general guarantee to a treaty of mutual *specific* definite succour,* excluding the present war and definining the *casus*

---

* A definite succour is not a cause of War, if previously stipulated.

6. H is referring to the mutual guarantees in Article 11 of the Treaty of Alliance concluded in 1778 between the United States and France. The United States guaranteed the present and future "Possessions of the Crown of france in America," and France guaranteed the "liberty, Sovereignty, and Independence" of the United States (Miller, *Treaties,* II, 39–40).

fœderis [7] to be that case in which the first *act* of *actual* hostility by sea or land is committed against the ally—without reference to antecedent motives and causes which are ever vague & complicated.

To the Fourth—If an amicable course of negotiation should take place modifications in this Convention may be proposed. Not having it by me the desireable alterations do not occur further than the restraining the mutual right of jurisdiction in questions between the citizens of either power to cases between the Officers & Crews of Vessels. Beyond this it works ill—establishes an *imperium* in imperio, extends foreign influence & indirectly injures our own Citizens & preventing efficacious justice between French Citizens who are often their debtors &c. Particularly it is ill to insert foreign jurisdiction in our country.

To the fifth—It does not appear expedient to propose or agree to such new articles. In general it is wisest neither to *give* nor *take* peculiar privileges—but equalize our commercial system with all nations. Indeed it will be very difficult to adjust such new articles without interference with other Treaties. The only method of favouring France is to stipulate that certain articles *if her production* or *manufacture* not common to Great Britain which enter largely into our supplies should be admitted without duty or on light duties to be specified. This applies principally to her *brandies* and *wines*; but even then they must lie on the same footing if coming through G Britain as if coming directly from France. Yet the essential & ultimate benefit would accrue to France as favouring the vent and consumption in our country of her peculiar commodities. But all this is far better avoided. The diminution of our Revenue and jealousies in other powers will be certain evils for which France will & can give no real equivalent.

To the 6th. What was done in the case of Great Britain will be a good precedent for this case.

To the seventh. The terms of the remonstrances against spoliations should be *mild* and *calm* without offensive epithets, but *serious* and depicting strongly the extent of the evil. They should *suppose* the West India constructions to be abuses of the Orders of the directory; but they should notice that these were so vague and indefinite in themselves as to be naturally liable to abuse. They should urge a

7. See H to George Washington, January 25-31, 1797, note 9.

revocation of these orders and compensation for the injuries they have produced as due from the *good faith Justice* and *Friendship* of France to the violated rights of the U States and their Citizens—and to restoration of cordial harmony between the two nations, which must otherwise suffer a deep and perhaps incurable wound.

To the 8th.　This is answered in the answer to the seventh.

To the 9th.　This claim of our Citizens ought to be noticed and urged as a great and serious one having from the motives of the individuals in the greatest number of cases a title to peculiar attention. Yet the whole ought to be managed as not to compromit the Government for the *ultimate vindication* of this claim. It is very questionable whether it be not such a one (as far as credit was voluntary) as that those who gave it ought finally to be left to the honor of the Government to which they trusted.

To the 10th.　This is answered in the Affirmative in the answer to the seventh Question. There is no solid distinction between captures and seizures by private vessels or public Vessels. The Government which gave the Commission to cruise is liable in both cases. This observation has reference to those depredations which result from *vague* orders of the Government or the abusive constructions of its Agents intrusted with local jurisdictions as Governors Commissioners &c.

To the 11th.　A Commission like that with England ought to be agreed to as a very happy issue out of the embarrassment.

To the 12th.　This is answered in the answer to the second question. The equivalent privileges in the French East India Trade will be the analogous compensation though not of equal extent. But situated as we are with France, it seems proper to be content with less. If privileges in her West India Trade could be obtained it would be desireable. But this ought not to be a *sine qua non*. A limitation of the duration of a new Treaty if made is a great desideratum.[8]

To the 13th.　It scarcely seems adviseable to offer the project of such a new Treaty. It opens at once all the *cards*. It is better to deal in generals. This will leave less in the power of France or her partisans.

To the 14.　It is conceived most adviseable to follow former precedent in this respect, which may avoid much delay and embarrass-

8. In the space between this and the following paragraph McHenry wrote: "Bridge for both."

ment. In the exercise of this branch of Executive Power, it will be found the best course to reduce the Cooperation of the Senate to the appointment of the Negotiator and the ultimate *fiat* or *Negative*. Much has been done to this end & it will not be expedient to relinquish the ground which has been gained.

From Timothy Pickering [1]

Philadelphia April 29. 1797.

Dear Sir,

In contemplating the idea suggested by you, of arming the merchant vessels of the United States for *Defence only*, a difficulty at once presented. This measure is incompatible with the right of a belligerent power to visit and examine neutral vessels, to ascertain whether they have on board contraband goods—&, where a treaty does not alter the law of nations, whether they are laden with enemies' goods—to see, indeed, whether under neutral colours, they are such, or enemies. The answer suggested to myself is this—That the power at war who has discarded treaties & the laws of nations, avowedly & practically, is not entitled to corresponding rights— rights relating to the same subject, under such treaties and laws; and consequently that American vessels, if allowed to be defensively armed, are not to submit to any such visits. Vessels of a neutral nation under convoy of the armed ships of such nation, I take it are not subject to such visits: and our armed merchant vessels *would be their own convoy*. I do not know where this question is treated of in books; you probably can inform me. The arming our merchant vessels, tho' only for *defence*, will be zealously opposed in the House of Representatives, on the above ground, that, as well by treaty as the law of nations, the French have a right to visit our vessels; and because of the danger of its leading to open war.

On the subject of a Commission Extraordinary to the French Republic, much difficulty occurs. To give a better prospect of success

ALS, Hamilton Papers, Library of Congress; ALS, letterpress copy, Massachusetts Historical Society, Boston.
1. This letter was written in reply to H to Pickering, March 22, 1797.

to this measure, you observe that a man agreeable to them should go; and you name two persons, either of whom you would advise to be joined with Mr. Pinckney & another on whose attachment to the system of our government, as established & administered, perfect reliance may be placed. But in the first place, would either of the two you name consent to go? You certainly reckon on Genl. Pinckney's inviolable integrity and federal attachments. Will not the man whom you name as agreeable to the French see that his hands will be tied? If you place any confidence in either of the two, that if commissioned he will faithfully consult and firmly persist in measures which the rights and neutral condition of our country demand without suffering his choice, his passions or his prejudices in favour of France and from hatred to G.B. to sacrifice any of our rights or interest to the former, why name a third Commissioner, of principles directly opposed, to check and effectually controul him? I should be inclined to think that neither of the two would under such a view of the case, accept the appointment; and one of them perhaps would from his present station deem it improper.

Would not the Directory also see such a commission constituted as you propose, in the same point of view? And would they not say that ostensibly there was an intention to manifest a particular respect and attention to them, while in reality we meant no such thing? Or do you consider Genl. Pinckney as a neutral character, in the politics of our country? And by appointing two associates of opposite characters, enable him to hold the balance? This is the most favourable light in which I can view the proposition. But when we consider the asperity of the parties here, and that the two characters named have been considered among the leaders—that probably neither has a confidence in the other—that your friend in particular will perhaps fear to disclose his sentiments on the most interesting questions lest they should be betrayed to the French; is there a well grounded hope that the mission would be successful?

On the organization of a provisional army, to receive certain compensations but not full pay, I shoud be glad to receive your ideas a little in detail. The propriety of increasing our artillery establishment is clear, & I should imagine not difficult to obtain. I have my doubts of the cavalry. The militia corps of horse are already composed, generally speaking, of the best man and best horses in the

country. But they need discipline. I much doubt, unless the danger
of a war should appear more certain than at present, whether even a
provisional army will be granted: if not, perhaps a much larger
army of select militia might be agreed to; the corps to be composed
of volunteers or draughts of young men, from the general militia,
and completely organized. The militia system to be improved.

On these several subjects and any others relating to our French
connections, I shall be happy to receive your communications, as
early as your leisure will admit.

I am most sincerely & respectfully yours.   T. Pickering

P.S. What if General Pinckney were to be appointed *Envoy Extraordinary*, or even *Ambassador*, with fresh instructions relative to the
subjects of complaint? The Directory have said they will not receive another *Minister Plenipotentiary*, until &c.[2] They refused to
receive the Chargé d'Affaires of Sweden,[3] sent to announce the
young King's ascending the throne, because at other courts the same
thing had been done by accredited *ministers*.[4] And they have made
it a subject of serious complaint (as J.Q. Adams was well informed
at the Hague) against Denmark, because that court omitted to announce to the Directory *the death of the old Queen Dowager!*[5] He

2. See Pickering to H, March 26, 30, 1797.
3. See H to James McHenry, April 29, 1797, note 5.
4. On February 17, 1797, John Quincy Adams wrote to Pickering:
". . . Their [the French] refusal to admit the chargé des affairs from Sweden
last Summer was mentioned in my letters at that time. The reason then
given was that they had personal objections against the man. Another has
since been appointed to notify the accession of the young king to the throne.
They have in the same manner refused to receive him not that they have any
personal objection (they say) against him for they know his *attachment to
the interests of France*, but because the king of Sweden had announced his
accession to other Governments by accredited Ministers, and they saw no
reason why he should not do the same to the French Republic" (LC, RG 59,
Despatches from United States Ministers to the Netherlands, 1794–1801, Vol.
2, November 16, 1796–July 1 ,1797, National Archives).
5. On February 17, 1797, John Quincy Adams wrote to Pickering: "The
neutrality of every other nation is as little respected by the French-Government
as that of the United States. They have recently proposed to Denmark to
shut up the mouth of the Elbe against all British vessels, and upon a refusal
of compliance have been equally industrious and equally uncivil in hunting
up pretences of complaint against the Danish Government. For such purposes,
they conceive any thing will answer: and they have made it a formal ground
of complaint that the Danish cabinet did not officially notify to the Directory
the recent death of the Queen Dowager, an old lady who had not the remotest concern with the public affairs of that Court and Nation" (LC, RG
59, Despatches from United States Ministers to the Netherlands, 1794–1801,
Vol. 2, November 16, 1796–July 1, 1797, National Archives).

remarks that they are seeking for pretences of quarrel with all the neutral commercial nations: their great object being to insist on measures to be adopted by neutrals, to injure or destroy the commerce of Britain.[6] If a commission extraordinary should be appointed, what should you think of Mr. Barlow [7] for a member? He has managed the negociations with Algiers with great ability, address, and zeal for the interest of his country. Having been formerly elected a member of the French Convention,[8] he may be deemed of sufficient respectability. He is even admitted, I take it, to French citizenship. His talents are unquestionable. *I* should sooner confide in him than in Mr. M.[9] The other person named by you,[10] I consider as out of the question, because of his station. Mr. Barlow has no personal antipathies & resentments to gratify, resentments engendered in the collision of parties at home.

Alexander Hamilton Esqr.

6. On February 17, 1797, John Quincy Adams wrote to Pickering: ". . . there remains little doubt upon my mind, but that the design to intercept by capture and perhaps by confiscation all the American Navigation to or from the ports under the dominion of Great-Britain. . . . With the declaration that the Directory will treat neutral vessels as their Governments suffer Great Britain to treat them, it can leave very little doubt as to their real design.

"The principal object of this measure doubtless is to operate as a hostility against Great Britain, it is one of the branches of the systems which I have frequently intimated heretofore of excluding the british commerce from all its markets. . . ." (LC, RG 59, Despatches from United States Ministers to the Netherlands, 1794–1801, Vol. 2, November 16, 1796–July 1, 1797, National Archives.)

7. After winning fame with the publication of *The Vision of Columbus, A Poem In Nine Books* (Hartford: Hudson and Goodwin, 1787), Joel Barlow went to Europe in 1788 as agent for the Scioto Company. In 1792 he published *A Letter To The National Convention Of France, On The Defects In The Constitution of 1791, And The Extent of The Amendments Which Ought To Be Applied. To Which Is Added The Conspiracy Of Kings, A Poem* (New York: Thomas Greenleaf, for J. Fellows, 1793), and in return the French government made him a citizen of that country. In 1795 David Humphreys, the United States Minister Resident to Portugal, was appointed "Commissioner Plenipotentiary for negotiating & concluding a Treaty of Peace with the Dey and Governors of Algiers" (Miller, *Treaties*, II, 303). As "Commissioner Plenipotentiary," he named Barlow consul to Algiers (Power of Agency, August 30, 1795 [copy, in Humphreys's handwriting, enclosed in Humphreys to Timothy Pickering, September 11, 1795 (ALS, RG 59, Despatches from United States Ministers to Spain, 1792–1825, Vol. 3, January 28, 1795–October 17, 1797, National Archives)]).

8. This statement is incorrect. Barlow stood for election as Savoy's deputy to the Convention, but he was defeated.

9. James Madison. See H to Pickering, March 22, 1797.

10. Thomas Jefferson. See H to Pickering, March 22, 1797.

To James McHenry [1]

[Albany, April, 1797]

Dr Sir

Situated as I am at this moment I am obliged to confine myself to very general hints respecting the paper of the 15 of April.[2]

As to the first head—I think it will be adviseable that the Speech should be confined to the *foreign Affairs* of the Country giving the primary & prominent place to those with France. This will make the main business the more striking. Domestic matters may follow in messages &c.

As to the second head—Announcing his intention to have recourse to the measure of an extraordinary mission—to endeavour by an earnest and amicable appeal to the justice candour and friendship of the french government to rectify misapprehensions, to satisfy them of the good faith and friendly sentiments which have always directed the U States, to endeavour, by a revision and readjustment of the Treaties between the two Nations, as far as shall consist with the engagements of the UStates towards other nations and the duties which their neutral position enjoins, to obviate causes of discontent and restore and confirm cordial harmony, to discuss and settle amicably the topics of mutual complaint and thereby to obtain a revocation of those acts on the part of France and of her Agents in her colonies which have oppressed our Trade and injured our Citizens and with it retribution for the losses which they have suffered from depredations contrary alike to the laws of Nations and the faith of Treaties.

ALS, Hamilton Papers, Library of Congress.

1. This letter was written in reply to McHenry to H, April 19, 1797, in which McHenry asked H for assistance in replying to a request from President John Adams for information and advice.

The letter printed above should be compared to McHenry's answer to the President's questions. In an undated letter to Adams, McHenry wrote what is essentially a verbatim copy of H's letter, for he made only a few minor changes in wording and inserted five brief paragraphs that are not in H's letter (ALS, Adams Family Papers, deposited in the Massachusetts Historical Society, Boston).

2. For this "paper," see McHenry to H, April 19, 1797, note 1.

The Speech should proceed to say that inasmuch as depredations by the cruisers of France continue to go on of a nature to destroy the mercantile capital ruin the Commerce of the Country and depress its agriculture & industry generally, and inasmuch as it is impossible to foresee the issue of the attempt by negotiation to avert the consequences of the serious misunderstandings which exist—it is matter of necessity, with regard to the interest honor present and future security of the UStates to adopt and carry into execution without delay vigorous measures of defensive precaution.

These measures to consist of the prompt equipment of a naval force sufficient to serve as convoys to our Trade and protect it against the spoliations of petty cruisers.

Permission to our vessels to arm for their own defence under proper guards and restrictions to prevent their cruising and acting offensively.

The intermediate passing of an embargo till these measures can be matured—with a discretion vested somewhere to grant licenses to sail to such ports & under such circumstances as may be deemed safe.

Arrangements which in case of emergency will give the Government the prompt command of an efficacious force with a particular view to Artillery and Cavalry; corps which require considerable time for forming them and which in case of need will be of the most peculiar and essential Utility.

The more complete & effectual fortification of our seaports especially the principal ones.

The increase of our Revenue, as far as shall be practicable without overburthening our Citizens to an extent which shall be equal to the additional expence of these provisions avoid an increase of the national debt and prepare the Country for the exigencies which may arise.

Whether it will be expedient for the President to go into detail or deal with energy in generals embracing the great points is a serious question. The inclination of my opinion is towards the fence dealing in *generals* in Speeches & having reports from departments either to be communicated afterwards or to be transmitted with the Speech by a general reference.

As to Instructions to the extraordinary Minister or Ministers they should embrace the following objects:

I Explanation of the real views & intentions of the Government of the U States during the present War so as to satisfy France that they have aimed at a sincere neutrality and have been influenced by no spirit partial to her enemies or inimical to her.

II The Discussion, if necessary, of the constructions of the Treaties between the two countries in the points which have been litigated, insisting upon our own, but not refusing to agree to any measures consistent with our constitution for avoiding an inconvenient or abusive application of them.

III The remodification of the Guarantee in our Treaty of alliance [3] into a stipulation of specific succours having reference to future wars and defining the *casus foederis* [4] to be that where the War has begun by the commission upon the ally of some *actual military hostility*, by sea or land. The succours on our part may in the next fifteen years be five sail of the line to be furnished *once for all*, or an equivalent sum of money to be defined with option to pay in provisions or military stores—after the fifteen years ten sail of the line, or an equivalent sum of money. The remaining Vessels to return at the Conclusion of the War.

IV The remodification of our Treaty of Commerce so as to accomodate it to that with G Britain having regard to duration as well as other things.

V Reparation for spoliations and other damages & the Payment of sums due by Contract. A Commission or Commissions may be agreed to but carefully restricted *to compensation to Individuals* on either side. For

VI There should in no event be admitted the idea of compensation from the Government of the U States to that of France Nor

VII Any admission directly or indirectly that they are Aggressors with regard to France.

VIII To avoid every stipulation in any shape inconsistent with our other Treaties or that may compromit our neutrality in the present War.

IX To steer clear of particular or exclusive privileges or preferences in Trade which are always precarious & embarrassing; occasioning disatisfaction at home & jealousy abroad.

3. See H to McHenry, April 29, 1797, note 6.
4. See H to George Washington, January 25–31, 1797, note 9.

X   To consent if desired by France to the annulling of the Treaties between the two Countries—altogether.

This last idea is a delicate one & it is only if at all to be so suggested as that Our Minister may in no case appear to contend for the continuance of these Treaties as a favour to the U States—as France may consider her *guarantee* of our *sovereignty* and independence as a thing of importance to us.

Yrs truly   AH

From William Loughton Smith

Philad. May 1. 97.

Dear sir

I shod. sooner have acknowledged the receipt of your interesting communication,¹ had I not been informed of your Journey to Albany.²

I coincide perfectly in opinion with you as to the expediency of measures of defence, & an extraordy. mission. But I see very considerable difficulty in the measure of a Commission, & still greater in its' including Jefferson & Madison. From the former plan I foresee embarassment & encreased expence, without any benefit. If the majority of the Commrs. be *anti*-gallicans, the party will not be gratified; we shall place an enemy in the Commission, without acquiring their support. If the majority be gallicans, we give up the Game. There are serious constitutional objections against Jefferson, as Commisr.—& Madison has done so much to prostrate this Country at the feet of France, that I fear his appointmt. would appear humiliating & give disgust to our Friends. I doubt also whether either of them would go on this business, unless as Sole Envoy; certainly not, unless as Senior Commissr. & this would be harsh to Pinckney, who has conducted himself well. From these considerations I have been induced to think the most dignified & safe mode of doing this business would be to Send *Pinckney* a new Commission either as Envoy or Ambassador Extraordy.: he is near at hand, he is unexcept[iona]ble. to all parties, the French have no personal objections to him, the Jacobins of most of the Southern states have great confidence in him, & he has made great sacrifices to go on a mission which has hitherto been attended with nothing but mortification. He is waiting at Amsterdam the orders of the Executive, probably expecting the Commission of Envoy Extraordy.—it is not improbable too that any thing like Slight to him may alienate more friends than would be acquired by adding to the mission one of the other party. I have lately met with a Report of the Comrs. of public safety in April 95, which was adopted by the Convention, on the subject of the different grades of Ministers, wherein it is Stated "that the Sending of an *Ambassador* is peculiarly agreable to Republics & a particular mark of respect." [3] This report preceded the reception of *De Stael* as *Ambassador Extraordy.* from Sweden: [4] I have shewn the Secy. of state the Report, & the Commission of De Stael: Perhaps it may be thought expedient to send a Com. of *Am. Extra.* to Gl. Pinckney, & to give weight & importance to the Mission to add, in the Character of Secretary to the Embassy, some character, above the common class of private Secretaries; this last point is however only a suggestion of my own; this practise is generally followd. in Europe.

I have shewn your letter to Tracy [5] & to Wolcott & McHenry, all of whom applied for the perusal of it & were much pleased with every part, except the Commission: this idea does not seem to coincide with the opinions of any of our friends here.

I leave town tomorrow for a Jaunt of a few days to Lancaster York &ca on my return I hope to hear from you & remain

Dear Sir   Very sincerely Yours   Wm Smith

ALS, Hamilton Papers, Library of Congress.
    1. H to Smith, April 10, 1797.
    2. See H to Elizabeth Hamilton, April 16, 1797.
    3. This is a reference to the speech made by Philippe Antoine Merlin of Douai to the National Convention, April 23, 1795 (Debrett, *A Collection of State Papers,* III, 302–03).
    4. For the reception of Erik Magnus, Baron Staël von Holstein, on April 21, 1795, see Debrett, *A Collection of State Papers,* III, 303–06; *Réimpression de L'Ancien Moniteur,* XXIV, 278. See also "The Warning No. I," January 27, 1797, note 10.
    5. Senator Uriah Tracy of Connecticut.

To William Hamilton [1]

Duplicate   Albany State of New York
                                          May the 2d. 1797

My Dear Sir

Some days since I received with great pleasure your letter of the
10th. of March.[2] The mark, it affords, of your kind attention, and
the particular account it gives me of so many relations in Scotland
are extremely gratifying to me. You no doubt have understood that
my fathers affairs at a very early day went to wreck; so as to have
rendered his situation during the greatest part of his life far from
eligible. This state of things occasionned a separation between him
and me, when I was very young, and threw me upon the bounty of
my mothers relations, some of whom were then wealthy, though
by vicissitudes to which human affairs are so liable, they have been
since much reduced and broken up. Myself at about sixteen came to
this Country. Having always had a strong propensity to literary
pursuits, by a course of steady and laborious exertion, I was able,
by the age of Ninteen to qualify myself for the degree of Batchelor
of Arts in the College of New York,[3] and to lay a foundation, by
preparatory study, for the future profession of the law.

The American Revolution supervened. My principles led me to
take part in it. At nineteen I entered into the American army as
Captain of Artillery. Shortly after, I became by his invitation Aide
De Camp to General Washington, in which station, I served till the
commencement of that Campaign which ended with the seige of
York, in Virginia, and the Capture of Cornwallis's Army. This Campaign I made at the head of a corps of light infantry, with which I
was present at the seige of York and engaged in some interesting
operations.

At the period of the peace with Great Britain, I found myself a
member of Congress by appointment of the legislature of this state.

After the peace, I settled in the City of New York in the practice
of the law; and was in a very lucrative course of practice, when the
derangement of our public affairs, by the feebleness of the general

confederation, drew me again reluctantly into public life. I became a member of the Convention which framed the present Constitution of the U States; and having taken part in this measure, I conceived myself to be under an obligation to lend my aid towards putting the machine in some regular motion. Hence I did not hesitate to accept the offer of President Washington to undertake the office of Secretary of the Treasury.

In that office, I met with many intrinsic difficulties, and many artificial ones proceeding from passions, not very worthy, common to human nature, and which act with peculiar force in republics. The object, however, was effected, of establishing public credit and introducing order into the finances.

Public Office in this Country has few attractions. The pecuniary emolument is so inconsiderable as too amount to a sacrifice to any man who can employ his time with advantage in any liberal profession. The opportunity of doing good, from the jealousy of power and the spirit of faction, is too small in any station to warrant a long continuance of private sacrifices. The enterprises of party had so far succeeded as materially to weaken the necessary influence and energy of the Executive Authority, and so far diminish the power of doing good in that department as greatly to take the motives which a virtuous man might have for making sacrifices. The prospect was even bad for gratifying in future the love of Fame, if that passion was to be the spring of action.

The Union of these motives, with the reflections of prudence in relation to a growing family, determined me as soon as my plan had attained a certain maturity to withdraw from Office. This I did by a resignation about two years since; when I resumed the profession of the law in the City of New York under every advantage I could desire.

It is a pleasing reflection to me that since the commencement of my connection with General Washington to the present time, I have possessed a flattering share of his confidence and friendship.

Having given you a brief sketch of my political career, I proceed to some further family details.

In the year 1780 I married the second daughter of General Schuyler, a Gentleman of one of the best families of this Country; of large fortune and no less personal and public consequence. It is impossible to be happier than I am in a wife and I have five Children, four sons and a daughter, the eldest a son somewhat passed fifteen, who all promise well, as far as their years permit and yield me much satisfaction. Though I have been too much in public life to be wealthy, my situation is extremely comfortable and leaves me nothing to wish but a continuance of health. With this blessing, the profits of my profession and other prospects authorise an expectation of such addition to my resources as will render the eve of life, easy and agreeable; so far as may depend on this consideration.

It is now several months since I have heared from my father who continued at the Island of St Vincents.[4] My anxiety at this silence would be greater than it is, were it not for the considerable interruption and precariousness of intercourse, which is produced by the War.

I have strongly pressed the old Gentleman to come to reside with me, which would afford him every enjoyment of which his advanced age is capable. But he has declined it on the ground that the advice of his Physicians leads him to fear that the change of Climate would be fatal to him. The next thing for me is, in proportion to my means to endeavour to increase his comforts where he is.

It will give me the greatest pleasure to receive your son Robert at my house in New York and still more to be of use to him; to which end my recommendation and interest will not be wanting, and, I hope, not unavailing.[5] It is my intention to embrace the Opening which your letter affords me to extend intercourse with my relations in your Country, which will be a new source of satisfaction to me.

AL, Hamilton Papers, Library of Congress; copy (incomplete), Hamilton Papers, Library of Congress.

1. William Hamilton was H's uncle and Laird of Grange, Ayrshire, Scotland.

2. Letter not found.

3. H may have qualified himself (as he put it) for such a degree from King's College, but there is no record that he received it. See "Matricula of King's College," 1774, note 1.

4. Letter not found. See James Hamilton to H, June 12, 1793.

H made the following entries in his Cash Book, 1795–1804: on November 29, 1796, "Account of Donations   pd draft my father   300"; on May 26, 1798, "Account of Donations—Dr to Cash   this sum paid Bill of my father   100"; on July 17, 1798, "Donations paid draft of my father   225"; and on December 24, 1798, "Donation paid draft of my father   16.25" (AD, Hamilton Papers, Library of Congress).

5. This is a reference to Robert W. Hamilton's desire to become an officer in the United States Navy. On August 8, 1798, H wrote to Secretary of the Navy Benjamin Stoddert recommending Robert W. Hamilton. During the Senate recess in 1798, President John Adams appointed several officers to the Navy, including Robert W. Hamilton as a lieutenant to serve on the *Constitution*. On January 29, 1799, Adams submitted these appointments to the Senate; on February 5, 1799, they were approved by the Senate (*Executive Journal*, I, 308, 310).

From William Constable [1]

[New York] *May 3, 1797*. "I forward to you . . . a Deed to Marvil Ellis for a tract of Land sold to him under a Contract[2] (which I believe was enclosed as I cannot lay my hands on it). This Instrument was executed at the time that I was extremely ill & the mortgage & Bonds for the payment of 3/4 s. the value of the Land were all perfected. . . . Mr Ellis expressing great anxiety to have the Writings completed as he was about to make sales to Settlers which he could not do without having the Title. . . . Not hearing from Mr. Ellis agreeably to his promise I began to feel some degree of solicitude least there might be some loop hole in the business . . . & I write the enclosed letter to afford you an opportunity of having any errors rectified which may have arisen."

LC, MS Division, New York Public Library.
1. Constable was a New York merchant and speculator in, among other things, lands in western New York State.
2. This is a reference to the sale of lands in Jefferson County, New York, made by Constable to Marvel (not Marvil) Ellis of Pittstown, New York. The lands in question constitute the site of the present town of Ellisburg. The first settlers arrived at Ellisburg in 1797.
In an enclosure to the letter printed above, Constable described his transaction with Ellis as follows: "Original sale 88,446 Dlrs for 46000 Acres with allowances recd. Cash *20,000*—66,335 Ballance on original Contract—Surplus Land agreed for 25th March as *expressed in Deed* the whole payable in 5 installments as ℔ Bonds executed in New York remaining in the hands of Mr. Ellis to be delivered on the rect. of the Deed" (LC, MS Division, New York Public Library).
On the same day that Constable wrote the above letter to H, he wrote to Ellis: "I have requested Colo. Hamilton to deliver you the Conveyance for the Township & to receive the Mortgage with the addition of Mrs Ellis signature & the 5 Bonds. He will transmit you this letter from Albany where he is attending the Court" (LC, MS Division, New York Public Library).

From Oliver Mann and Isaac Parker [1]

[*Boston, May 6, 1797.* On June 28, 1797, Hamilton wrote to Mann and Parker: "Your letter of the 6th of May last by making a circuit to Albany did not reach me in due time." *Letter not found.*]

1. Mann was a Boston physician. Parker, a lawyer in Castine, District of Maine, was a member of the House of Representatives from 1797 to 1799.

To Timothy Pickering

[New York, May 11, 1797]

My Dear Sir

On my return here I found your letter of the 29th   .[1] The sitting of a Court of Chancery and important business there have unavoidably delayed a reply. Now, it must be much more cursory than I could wish.

As to the mission, in some shape or other, the more I have reflected upon it, the more has it appeared to me indispensable. To accomplish, with certainty, a principal object of it—the silencing of Jacobin criticism and promoting union among ourselves—it is *very material* to engage in it a person who will have the Jacobin confidence. Else, if France should still refuse to receive, or if receiving, the mission should prove unsuccessful—it will be said that this was because a suitable Agent was not employed. Hence my mind was led to Jefferson or Madison. But as it would be unsafe to trust either alone, the idea of associates occurs as an essential part of the plan. This likewise is an expedient for saving Mr. Pinckneys feelings.

But will either of them go on this footing? If offered and they refuse, they will put themselves in the wrong. For on so great an emergency they cannot justifiably decline the service without a good reason & it would not be a good reason for refusal that there was to be a *commission*. The refusal too if it happened would furnish a reply to Jacobin clamour. It was offered to your leaders and they would not act.

I confide in Pinckneys integrity & foederal attachments. Why then name a third? Because 1 two may disagree and there may be *inaction* 2 Though I have the confidence I mention—I think Pinckney has had too much French *leaning* to consider him in conjunction with Jefferson or Madison as perfectly safe. A third on whom perfect reliance could be placed would secure Pinckney's cooperation. I do consider him as in some sort a *middle* character.

As to the two Gentlemen named (Jefferson & Madison) it may be fairly observed to either of them that the combination of characters is essential to combine the confidence of the Country & to render the result whatever it may be acceptable. It may also be observed that delicacy to Mr. Pinckney dictates this course—not to exclude him after what has happened. To Mr. Pinckney the state of parties here may also be pleaded.

The French Directory may also be made to understand indirectly that the association has proceeded from a desire in the Executive to unit Confidence in the mission and secure its success at home.

I should not despair that in such a crisis men of opposite politics might agree. I verily believe that Jefferson *Pinckney* & *King* would agree. There might be a *joint* commission for action, and a separate Commission to Jefferson as Envoy or Ambassador extraordinary for *representation*. I miscalculate if Jefferson will not be anxious for peace. I only fear that alone he would give too much for it.

If this plan is thought liable to too strong objections, the next best thing is to send the Commission of *Ambassador Extraordinary to Pinckney* & send him also some *clever fellow* as secretary of embassy.

But I repeat it with extreme solicitude—another mission is absolutely indispensable.

On the subject of permitting our vessels to arm there is some difficulty. You are right in the idea that Merchant vessels under the convoy of Ships of War are exempt from search. But I know no book where it is to be found. Yet I have so constantly understood it to be the usage that I venture to rely upon it. But I believe the privilege is confined to *Public ships* of war & could not according to usage be transferred to private armed Vessels. The measure must therefore be justified by the extremity.

Moreover—I understand no other consequence as resulting from the being armed than that it exposes the vessel to confiscation for resisting a search. It is no breach of neutrality to permit the being armed.

But I would avoid the *formation* of a Commission and would substitute some *Permit*, perhaps to be signed by the head of a department. This should be united with great precautions to prevent *abuse* by *cruising* by d[r]*iving contraband trade* by *transfer* to foreigners.

At all events our Trade must have protection. For our whole mercantile Capital will else be destroyed our seamen lost & our country involved in extreme distress.

As to a provisional army—I reason thus. No plan of a militia, which is not the equivalent, in other words which is not under a positive engagement to constitute *a permanent army in case of invasion* will be worth any thing. For we want a *stable* force created beforehand to oppose to the first torrent, which with mere militia, would involve incalculable dangers and calamities. Hence as a substitute for a standing army I offer a provisional one. It would be composed thus. The *Officers* to be *appointed by the United States* & rank with those of the establishment—to receive some pay till called into actual service say half a third or a fourth. Those employed to *recruit* to be fully paid.

The men to be regularly *inlisted* upon condition not to be called into actual service *except in case of Invasion* & then to serve during the war. To receive a *uniform* coat, & a *dollar* perhaps *two dollars* per Month when not in the field—to be obliged to assemble for exercise so may days in the year & then to have full pay and rations. When called into actual service to have the same compensations &c with the establishment, in short to become part of it. To be armed by the U States To be liable from the beginning to the articles of War.

I think such a corps from the *certainty of advantage* & the *uncertainty of service* might be engaged sooner than a standing force & with precautions in the enlistment would be a solid resource in case of need.

I am much attached to the idea of a large corps of *efficient Cavalry;* & I cannot allow this character to Militia. It is all important to an undisciplined against a disciplined army. It is a species of force not easy to be brought by an invader—by which his supplies may be cut off & his activity extremely checked. Were I to command an undisciplined army, I should prefer half the force with a good corps of cavalry to twice the force without one.

Yrs. truly   A H

                                                              May 11.

T Pickering Esq

ALS, Massachusetts Historical Society, Boston.
    1. Space left blank in MS, but see Pickering to H, April 29, 1797.

To Timothy Pickering

[New York] Saturday May 13. 97

My Dear Sir

Mr. Goodhue [1] takes on with him a Boston paper, the printer of which states that he has obtained by a Ship just arrived, a London Paper of March 24th; mentionning in positive terms an account just received from the Emperor that in consequence of a combination between Prussia & France [2] he is driven to the necessity of making an *immediate peace for the safety of the Empire*—that in consequence of this the King who was at Windsor had been sent for &c &c.[3]

The manner of announcing it is too positive to allow much doubt that the thing is substantially true.

This intelligence confirms the expediency of a further attempt to *negotiate*—but I hope it will not carry us too far. A firm and erect countenance must be maintained and the vigour of preparation increased. Safety can only be found in uniting energy with moderation. Honor certainly is only to be found there, and either as a *man* or *citizen*, I for one had rather perish than submit to disgrace.

Yrs.   A Hamilton

ALS, Massachusetts Historical Society, Boston.
    1. Senator Benjamin Goodhue of Massachusetts.
    2. See William Loughton Smith to H, April 10, 1797, note 9.
    3. The following report appeared in the [Boston] *Columbian Centinel*, May 10, 1797: "Since our last the *Galen*, Mackay; *Merchant*, Bates and *Eliza*, Davis; have arrived here from *London*. By the latter we have received a *Portsmouth* paper as late as April 3, containing London news to Saturday evening, April 1. By this last, it is rendered certain, that the article in the *London Oracle* of March 24th, announcing the promulgation of a Message from the EMPEROR to the *King* of *Great-Britain*, declaring that '*He was reduced to the fatal necessity of suing for an* IMMEDIATE PEACE, *to save the remaining part of his Do-*

minions,' in consequence of a new treaty of alliance between *Prussia* and *France,* is at least premature. . . ."

From Jeremiah Wadsworth [1]

Hartford, May 13, 1797. "A Mr Johnston who holds Mr Churches Land shewed me a letter from Mr Tracy dated last April in which he says. 'Col Hamilton says Col Wadsworth has the sole disposal of the Land in Salisbury:' Mr Johnston came to me to finish the business. . . . I believe Johnston would take a quit claim & risk the Title & secure the payment according to the inclosed appraisement."

ALS, Hamilton Papers, Library of Congress.
  1. Wadsworth, a friend of H for many years, was a Federalist member of the House of Representatives from Connecticut from 1789 to 1795 and a member of the Connecticut Executive Council from 1795 to 1801.
  For background to this letter, see Uriah Tracy to H, March 23, April 6, 1797.

From James McHenry

Philadelphia 14th May 1797.

My dear H.

I received your letters and papers.[1] I added to them, but changed nothing, for the train of ideas in both ran in the same channel and embraced the same objects.

The speech [2] extenuates nought—recommends proper measures —promises a fresh attempt at negotiation—and declares the principles by which administration mean to be governed, in other words that the President will follow the principles of the late administration.

It is not perhaps precisely such a speech as you would have written —a little too plain. It may however be better fitted on that account for the occasion.

Your affectionate   James McHenry

ALS, Hamilton Papers, Library of Congress.
  1. See H to McHenry, April 29 and April, 1797.
  2. This is a reference to President John Adams's speech on May 16, 1797, to the special session of Congress (*Annals of Congress,* VII, 54–59).

From Tench Coxe [1]

Philada. May 15 1797

Sir,

Mr. Robert Wescott who recd the title of the Land sold Messrs. Whelen Miller & Co. has reconveyed to me 36½ tracts thereof & I have replaced with them 3200 Drs. being the difference between their retained half of 73 tracts, and what they had paid. It proves the wisest measure for Whelen & Millers Notes are under Protest at all the Banks, and they have seperated. They have sold some parcels of 1800 Acres & 3600 Acres to some English Emigrants, who are going to improve. The above 36½ tracts are in the undivided moiety of 73, which they held immediately before and measures must be taken to divide them so that you can have Mr Church's 17¾ tracts, when desired.

I am Sir Your most obedient Servant   Tench Coxe

Alexr Hamilton Esq.
Atty. of J B. Church Esq.

Copy, RG 21, Records of the United States Circuit Court for the Eastern District of Pennsylvania, Equity Records, Case Files, 1790–1911, National Archives.
1. Coxe, who had been first a Loyalist and then a Patriot during the American Revolution, was a member of the Continental Congress in 1787 and 1788, Assistant Secretary of the Treasury from 1790 until the abolition of that office in 1792, and commissioner of the revenue from 1792 until his dismissal by President John Adams in December, 1797.
For an explanation of the contents of this letter, see the introductory note to Coxe to H, February 13, 1795. See also Coxe to H, February 17–18, 22, May 10, August 4, 1795, May 31, November 12, 1796; H to Joseph Anthony, March 11, 1795; Anthony to H, May 16, 1795.

From James McHenry

Philad. 15 May 1797

My dear H.

I wrote you a line yesterday acknowleging the receipt of your late letters from Albany.

I expect that there will be a quorum of both branches to-day.[1]

It appears that the news of the Emp. of Germ. having signified his intention to make peace was unfounded.[2] Had it even been so, it ought to have augmented our endeavours to meet hostility.

It is probable that a new character will be given Pinckney and a Secry to the Mission.

Yours

J McH

ALS, Hamilton Papers, Library of Congress.
  1. On March 25, 1797, President John Adams had called a special session of Congress to meet in Philadelphia on May 15 (*Annals of Congress*, VII, 49).
  2. See H to Timothy Pickering, May 13, 1797, note 3.

From John Scott [1]

St. Mildred's Court, Mansion House [*London*], *May 16, 1797.*
". . . I beg leave to trouble you with Power of Atty[2] from Mr. Hodgson to you accompanied with a Letter by Invoice of Goods to enable you to recover £247.15 of Mr. Bn. Bakewell of your Town who I understand is a very honest man. . . . I am trustee of Hodgson the Constituent who has also failed. . . ."[3]

ALS, Hamilton Papers, Library of Congress.
  1. Scott was an attorney of St. Mildred's Court, Poultry Street, London.
  This letter concerns a suit instituted by Benjamin Hodgson, a London bookseller, against Benjamin Bakewell, a New York City merchant. Bakewell owed Hodgson for a consignment of books and stationery. As the letter indicates, both men were bankrupt.
  2. The power of attorney is dated April 15, 1797 (DS, Hamilton Papers, Library of Congress). The invoice lists two shipments, dated March 24, 1795, and March 5, 1796, which together amounted to £247.15 (AD, Hamilton Papers, Library of Congress).
  3. In his Cash Book, 1795–1804, under the date of January 8, 1798, H wrote: "received of J Scott for Opinion   25" (AD, Hamilton Papers, Library of Congress).

From Robert Morris [1]

Philada. May 20th. 1797

Dear Sir

I cannot account for the little notice that has been taken of some of my latest letters to you, but I hope the present will obtain your favourable attention. When Capt. Williamson[2] agreed to give up

the Lien which my Deed gave to Colo Smith, it was expressly mention'd by me & agreed by him that the Suit which had been Commenced in the Court of Chancerry by Colo Walker should be withdrawn & the injunction that had been issued & served on me was to
be removed, otherwise I could not make use of the remaining property. Mr Sterett [3] to whom I have Conveyed 175 M Acres in search-
ing the Public Offices & obtaining Certificates got out of the Chancerry Court those which you will find inclosed herein, which as
they now stand would be an effectual Bar to any thing been done
with the Lands. I pray therefore that you will obtain a discharge of
the injunction & let a proper Certificate thereof be added to these
& then the whole be returned to me & let this be done with all possible expedition as these Papers are to be sent immediately to Europe. I wro⟨te⟩ also to Colo Walker for the Deed I gave to Colo
Smith.[4] He did not think it worth while to Answer my letter. I have
known the time when he would have thought differently & perhaps
I may notwithstanding present appearances, See that time again. I
ought to have had that Deed with the others & this Chancerry business should have been finished. As I cannot think that you mean to
Neglect me, I shall be thankfull if you will have these things done
for Dr Sir

Your faithfull Friend & Servant   Robt Morris

PS Mr Sterett told me that you had an Idea that the Land Conveyed to him was the same that is mortgaged to you.[5] I do not know
but their may be ⟨some⟩ [6] interference in a part & ⟨there⟩fore a
Conditional ⟨ad⟩dition was made to the Deed.   RM

Alexr Hamilton Esqr
New York

ALS, Hamilton Papers, Library of Congress; LC, Robert Morris Papers, Library of Congress.
    1. Morris, who had been a partner in the Philadelphia mercantile firm of
Willing, Morris, and Company, had served in the Continental Congress from
1775 to 1778, in the Provincial Assembly from 1775 to 1776, in the Pennsylvania
legislature from 1778 to 1779, 1780 to 1781, and 1785 to 1787. From July, 1781,
to November, 1784, he held the office of Superintendent of Finance. He was
a delegate to the Constitutional Convention in 1787 and a United States Senator
from 1789 to 1795. By 1795 he was involved in numerous and complicated land
speculations which led to his imprisonment for debt in February, 1798.

This letter concerns a debt which Morris owed to William Pulteney and William Hornby and which had been negotiated by William S. Smith acting as their representative. When this letter was written, Benjamin Walker, acting on behalf of Pulteney and Hornby, was trying to collect this debt, and he had instituted a Chancery suit against Morris. For an account of this debt and Walker's efforts to collect it, see the introductory note to Morris to H, April 27, 1796. See also Morris to H, May 3, 10, 17, 31, 1796, January 7, 23, February 9, 27, March 3, 8, 9, 27, 1797; H to Charles Williamson, May 17–30, 1796.

2. Charles Williamson was the agent for Pulteney and Hornby in the United States.

3. For Samuel Sterett, see H to Morris, March 18, 1795, note 10. See also Willink, Van Staphorst, and Hubbard to H, May 1, 1794, note 2.

4. Morris to Walker, April 14, 1797 (LC, Robert Morris Papers, Library of Congress).

5. This is a reference to one hundred thousand acres of land in the Genesee country which Morris had mortgaged to H to secure a debt which Morris owed to John B. Church. For an account of this debt and Morris's efforts to pay it, see the introductory note to Morris to H, June 7, 1795. See also Morris to H, March 31, July 20, November 16, December 18, 1795, January 15, March 6, 12, 14, 30, April 27, May 3, 10, 17, 18, 31, 1796, March 3, 27, 1797; William Lewis to H, May 4, 1796; H to Williamson, May 17–30, 1796.

6. Material within broken brackets has been taken from the letter book copy.

To Robert Morris

[*New York, May 22, 1797.* On May 23, 1797, Morris wrote to Hamilton: "Your letter of yesterday is arrived." *Letter not found.*]

From Robert Morris [1]

Philada. May 23d. 1797

Dear Sir

Your letter of yesterday [2] is arrived and the Contents are very Acceptable, I hope the business in the Chancerry Court will soon be dismissed and the Certificate returned to me with that addition.[3]

Accept my Congratulations on the arrival of Mr Church & his Family [4] and I will thank you to present Mrs Morris's & mine to Mr & Mrs. Church with the Assurance of the pleasure it will give us to See them here. I find by a letter from Mr Marshall [5] that Mr Church would not Treat with him for the purchase of the 100,000 Acres of Genesee Lands Mortgaged to you, but he has found another Person that will and therefore He desires me to forward a Copy of the Mortgage I gave to you, with a declaration that there are no other Incumbrances & that you will assign or release the Mortgage upon receiving the principal & interest of the debt for which it was given. Thus you see my Dear Sir I am obliged to give you trouble, altho I wish to spare it & in order to take it off of you personally I should be glad that you would get an Authenticated Copy from the Office where it is recorded with a Certificate that there are no other incumbrances upon record, and have a declaration drawn & endorsed on the said Copy to be signed by you purporting that you promise & bind yourself to assign or release the Original Mortgage upon receipt of the principal Sum & interest for which it was given, all this except the signing your Name may be done by a person employed for the purpose & I will chearfully pay the Cost. Expedition is necessary as I have an opportunity of sending the Papers by a Gentln whom I wish to be the bearer and he will soon depart. I must also request that you will examine to see that the Certificates & declaration are such as will be likely to give satisfaction to an European purchasor. I am not in a situation to answer offhand as was formerly the case, every claim on my justice, I ought most certainly to pay that which you call for and I will immediately cast about to see how it can be accomplished; respecting which you shall Soon hear again from Dr Sir

Your Obedt & faithfull Friend & Servant   Robt Morris

Alexr Hamilton Esqr
New York

ALS, Hamilton Papers, Library of Congress; LC, Robert Morris Papers, Library of Congress; copy, Hamilton Papers, Library of Congress.

1. Except for the first paragraph, this letter deals with a debt which Morris owed to John B. Church and which he had secured by mortgaging to H one hundred thousand acres of land in the Genesee country. For this debt and Morris's efforts to pay it, see the introductory note to Morris to H, June 7, 1795. See also Morris to H, July 20, November 16, December 18, 1795, January 15, March 6, 12, 14, 30, April 27, May 3, 10, 17, 18, 31, 1796, March 3, 27, 1797; William Lewis to H, May 4, 1796; H to Charles Williamson, May 17–30, 1796.

2. Letter not found.

3. This paragraph concerns a suit in Chancery instituted by Benjamin Walker to obtain payment of a debt which Morris owed to William Pulteney and William Hornby. See the introductory note to Morris to H, April 27, 1796. See also Morris to H, May 3, 10, 17, 31, 1796, January 7, 23, February 9, 27, March 3, 8, 9, May 20, 1797; H to Williamson May 17–30, 1796.

4. On May 22, 1797, The [New York] Minerva, & Mercantile Evening Ad-

vertiser reported: "In the Fair American, Capt. Duplex, from London, came passenger John B. Church, Esq. (Late member of the English Parliament) his lady and family.

"Mr. Church has taken his Excellency the Governor's private mansion house in Broadway; and we understand intends making this city his permanent place of residence." The *Fair American* arrived in New York on May 20 (*The* [New York] *Minerva, & Mercantile Evening Advertiser,* May 20, 1797).

5. James Marshall, Morris's son-in-law, was at this time in Europe as Morris's business representative. See Morris to H, June 7, 1795, note 10.

From John Evans [1]

New York, May 24, 1797. "The many inconveniencies resulting from the delay and expence of my continuance in this City, strike so powerfully at the prosperity of my views and business; as to reduce me to the absolute necessity of entreeting your opinion of the Case, submitted to you by me, at as early an Hour, as you possibly and conveniently can. . . ."

LS, Hamilton Papers, Library of Congress.
1. Presumably, a Philadelphia merchant by the name of John Evans.

Théophile Cazenove to Egbert Benson and Alexander Hamilton [1]

Philadelphia, May 29, 1797. "The enclosed extract of a Letter lately received from General Schuyler [2] will create much uneasiness amongst the Dutch proprietors who have obtained the faculty to hold their Lands in the state of New York 'till the 11th. April 1803. A Law passed in the last Session extends that faculty 'till 1816. provided the Dutch Proprietors shall interest themselves as stockholders or money lenders in the Western Canal Company for an amount of 250,000, Dollars. [3] I send herewith also a copy of the letter from the managers of the Western Canal Company to Mr. Busti. [4] It would be needless to observe how hard & disadvantageous to my friends the conditions offered to them, are. If as Moneylenders at the low rate of 3 ₱ ct. the mortgage offered is of a nature which will make an execution, most impossible & certainly fruitless—If as Stockholders, they will be only so to appearance—in short the meaning of the proposals translated in plain words is, 'You shall loose the 250/m Dollars if the undertaking of the Company does not Succeed. And if they Succeed, You shall have 3 ℔ ct. of Your money.' . . . I hope the Indian title for the Genesee Lands will be obtained this Year, but for more than a part cannot be expected.[5] In the actual state of things both here & in Europe it is not only possible but it is probable that neither exertions nor moderate prices will procure the Sale of all the Lands in the possession of our Dutch friends, at least not at a price equal to the risks, cares & casualties to which the proprietors are Submitted nor proportioned to the long credit the Sale of such a quantity of acres of Land will require. . . ."

LS, Hamilton Papers, Library of Congress; copy, Gemeentearchief Amsterdam, Holland Land Company. The Holland Land Company documents were transferred in 1964 from the Nederlandsch Economisch-Historisch Archief, Amsterdam.

1. The copy of this letter was enclosed in Cazenove to Benson and H, July 5, 1797.

This letter was written to H and Benson in their capacities as attorneys to the six Dutch banking firms which formed the Holland Land Company on February 13, 1796. For the full text of this document and other relevant documents, see forthcoming Goebel, *Law Practice*, III.

2. The extract from Philip Schuyler's letter reads: "It is my opinion & an opinion founded on an axtensive investigation of the views, which prevailed with no inconsiderable portion of the Legislature who had opposed the Law of last Session in every shape, and who only waited the expiration of the term afforded by that Law, to divest the Dutch Gentlemen of this property & that I seriously believed if the Lands were not bona fide Sold to Citizens of this & the United states before the expiration of the Seven Years, attempts would be made, & probably with Success, to deprive the present proprietors thereof that *a Sale in trust for Aliens would not stand the test of Law.* That I Knew *there were many who wished to Speculate on those Lands and whose influence, altho' they might not be members of the Legislature, was to be dreatet.* That only Six Years of the term granted by the Law of last Session remained unexpired. That the Indian title was not Yet extinguished, and *Some Years might elapse before that could be accomplished.* That if a Sale must be made under such various unfavorable circumstances it would only be considered as a forced Sale and consequently attended with all the disadvantages incident to such Sales. That an extension of the term to 20 or 25 Years would operate nearly as beneficial as the fee Simple if it was the intention to Sell the Lands. That if Such was not their intention the fee would be worth nothing unless they or Some of them Should actually come & reside in this Country, as free booters would take possession, and the expence of ejecting them would go beyond the value of the Land. That if any of the Dutch Gentlemen Should within the extended term find it convenient to reside in this Country the fee for *the part that Should be owned by Such residents* would immediately thereafter be granted, as that had been the invariable practice of the Legislature. That as the improvements in the internal navigation would be so accellerated by the proposed aid of money as to insure *the completion* thereof *in all the extent* to Lake Ontario certainly within the time limitated by the Act of in-

corporation the Value of the property in question would be so greatly enhanced as far to exceed the Sum to be contributed &caa" (copy, Hamilton Papers, Library of Congress).

3. For the efforts of the Holland Land Company to secure legislation enabling aliens to hold land in New York State, see H to Cazenove, January 22, 1796, notes 2 and 3. See also Robert Morris to H, June 7, 1795, note 37.

The name of this corporation was the Western Inland Lock Navigation Company. In 1792 the legislature of New York passed an act incorporating this company along with the Northern Inland Lock Navigation Company. The Western Company was incorporated to make possible water transportation from the Hudson River to Lake Ontario and Lake Seneca by the improvement of existing waterways, the construction of a few small canals, and the building of locks (Joseph Stancliffe Davis, *Essays in the Earlier History of American Corporations*, "Harvard Economic Studies," XVI [Cambridge, 1917], II, 160–67).

4. Gerard Walton to Paul Busti, May, 1797 (copy, Hamilton Papers, Library of Congress).

Busti, an Italian, had lived in Holland before coming to the United States. In 1796 the Holland Land Company had hired him to assist Cazenove in representing the company's interests in the United States. When Cazenove returned to Holland in 1799, Busti was placed in charge of all the company's interests in the United States.

5. For the negotiations with the Seneca Indians, see H to Herman LeRoy, William Bayard, and James McEvers, December 16, 1796; March 4–July 19, 1797.

Jacob Mark and Company to John B. Church, Alexander Hamilton, and John Laurance [1]

New York 30 May 1797

Gentlemen,

We are sorry to find that owing to the embarrassed situation of the Land You purchased from us last Year [2] so great an inconvenience and loss shou'd arise to You as well as ourselves in being retarded in the settlement; and as we are particularly anxious to remove the most distant hard thought from You towards us, we think it proper to make You such proposals as are not only founded on fair and honorable principals but which will certainly be for Your Particular interest to accept. Should You not think proper to come into the measures proposed, then be kind enough to set a price on Your Part of the Land at which You will sell, as the persons to whom we may Sell it, will not take short of the whole.

Do neither of the proposed measures meet Your ideas we then

beg You will not take it amiss in us to act in Such manner as circumstances may require.

We propose

1. To sell You our one fourth undivided Interest in Townships No.
21 & 15 which according to the surveyors return (together 42314¼
acres) contains 10578½ acres at 2 dollars and 25 cents per acre.

2. The Amount thereof being Drs. 23801. 62/100 to be given in endorsed Notes payable on the 1st. July next D   8000

1st. October   "   8500

1st. December "   7301.62

3. The two Notes which we hold Signed by Messrs. Laurance &
Hamilton payable in December 1797 & 1798 to be made payable to
J Mark & Co. or order.

4. The notes not to be delivered to us till a discharge of the mortgage on the two townships is fully produced.

You will oblige us by signifying to us Your decision on the above
as speedily as possible.

We are with the greatest esteem   Gentlemen   Your most obedt.
servts   J. Mark & Co.

Alexr. Hamilton ⎤
John Lawrance ⎬   Esqrs
J: B. Church ⎦

ALS, Hamilton Papers, Library of Congress.

1. Jacob Mark and Company was a firm of New York City merchants.
Church was Elizabeth Hamilton's brother-in-law. Laurance, a New York City
attorney, had served as an aide-de-camp to George Washington during the
American Revolution. He was a member of the House of Representatives from
New York from 1789 to 1793 and United States judge for the District of New
York from 1794 to 1796. He was a member of the first board of directors of
the Bank of the United States and in 1796 became a director of the New York
branch of the Bank of the United States. From 1796 to 1800 he was United
States Senator from New York.

2. The lands purchased by Church, Laurance, and H were located in Scriba's
patent in upstate New York. In 1794 George Scriba, a New York City merchant, purchased from John and Nicholas J. Roosevelt 490,136 acres in Oswego
and Oneida counties for £77,917 6s (N.Y. Colonial Manuscripts, 980; see also
Mix, Catalogue: Maps and Surveys, 19). On January 6, 1795, Scriba sold part
of this tract to Jacob Mark and Company (Indenture: John Laurance, John B.
Church, and Alexander Hamilton, June 28, 1804 [copy, Oneida County Clerk's
Office, Deeds, Vol. X, 499–502, Utica, New York]). On January 20, 1796, H
made the following entry in his Cash Book, 1795–1804: "John Laurance Dr to
Cash   for this sum dld John Laurance towards my share of two Townships of

Land No. 21 & No. 15 in Rosevelts purchase, purchased of Mr. Mark 1000"
(AD, Hamilton Papers, Library of Congress). See also H to Robert Troup,
July 25, 1795, note 17. H recorded additional payments for this land of
$5,000 on January 21, 1796; $88.90 on March 30, 1796; and $5,326.65 on Decem-
ber 12, 1796 (AD, Hamilton Papers, Library of Congress). H also paid
$226 on June 24, 1796, and $150 on October 11, 1796, for surveying the land
(AD, Hamilton Papers, Library of Congress). On August 21, 1802, H, Church,
and Laurance mortgaged a portion of this land to Robert Gilchrist of Westchester County, New York, to secure payment of $7,255 each (copy, Oneida
County Clerk's Office, Mortgages, Vol. III, 500–01, Utica, New York). In his
"Statement of my property and Debts July 1. 1804" H wrote: "My share of
Townships No. 9. 10. 15. 17 and 21 in Scribas Patent in connection with J B
Church and John Laurence viz
"⅙ of the first purchase of the whole being 31528 acres & ¼ of an acre &
one third of the residuary purchase upon the suit in chancery being together
nearly 20000 acres which now stand me in about 33000." (AD, New-York
Historical Society, New York City.)

To John Laurance

[*New York, June 1, 1797.* On June 3, 1797, Laurance wrote to
Hamilton: "I have received your letter of the first Instant." *Letter
not found.*]

To Robert Morris

[*New York, June 1, 1797.* On June 2, 1797, Morris wrote to
Hamilton: "Your letter of yesterday is this moment recd." *Letter
not found.*]

From Robert Morris

Philada. June 2d. 1797

Dear Sir

Your letter of yesterday [1] is this moment recd and I take my pen
upon the first impulse to tell you not to be uneasy, I will pay you
every farthing principal & interest,[2] have patience for my measures
to operate & rely yourself with Confidence. The Nature of your
debt ties me at all events & it shall be paid. As to Mr Church's Se-

curity[3] how can it be doubted. I told you before that Mr Marshall is in treaty for the Land at Two Dollrs ℔ Acre[4] & writes for the Papers I wrote to you for.[5] I beg you to send them as Speedily as possible. I think they will enab⟨le⟩ me to pay him off long before the time stipulated.

I am to be sure disagreeably situated, but my affairs are retrievable if I could get the Common aid of Common times and I will struggle hard. Keep All this to Yourself. I will address you again by & by. But send me the Papers written for.

Yours Sincerely   Robt Morris

Alexr. Hamilton Esqr

ALS, Hamilton Papers, Library of Congress; LC, Robert Morris Papers, Library of Congress.
  1. Letter not found.
  2. This refers to Morris's efforts to pay the balance of a debt which he owed to H. For an account of this debt, see the introductory note to H to Morris, March 18, 1795. See also Morris to H, March 31, June 2, 23, 30, July 18, 20, 1795; June 17, 27–30, November 19, December 8, 1796.
  3. This is a reference to security for a debt which Morris owed to John B. Church. For this debt, see the introductory note to Morris to H, June 7, 1795. See also Morris to H, July 20, November 16, December 18, 1795, January 15, March 6, 12, 14, 30, April 27, May 3, 10, 17, 18, 31, 1796, March 3, 27, May 20, 23, 1797; William Lewis to H, May 4, 1796; H to Charles Williamson, May 17–30, 1796.
  4. See Morris to H, May 23, 1797.
  5. Morris to H, May 23, 1797.

From John Laurance [1]

Philadelphia June 3d 1797

My dear Sir

I have received your letter of the first Instant,[2] with a Copy of a Letter from J Mark & Co. We gave for the Land about one dollar and seventy eight Cents per acre, since which, we have paid for surveying it, into Lots, near 2 Cents per Acre, to these sums must be added the Interest on the Money we have paid, which, I suppose, will make the price, at present, near 2 dollars per acre.

Township No 21, exclusive of its situation for large compact settlements, is a very valuable tract of Land, with regard to its Soil and Timbers, and must command a very good Price, whenever we deem it adviseable to commence Settlements. The Country about it, is settling very fast, and it must soon be, much in demand. The other Township, although the quality, in general, is not so good as the first, is well situated, for Settlement, and the great road to Oswego, will pass through it, in the course of this Summer.

What they mean by acting as Circumstances may require I know not, but I should be on my guard respecting them—J Mark at least. I cannot buy at present, and I am not willing to sell, but should I be induced to sell the money must be paid, immediately, and the price greater than they mention. If J Mark had made his payment on the Mortgage to Mr. Gilchrist,[3] at the time he was to have done it, We should not have been embarrassed; but it is difficult to go on and settle, when we are liable to be disturbed by the proprietors of the Mortgage. It may be well to converse with them to know what their Views are. I conjecture part of the Money, they ought to have paid Gilchrist in December last, comes due, in this Month, and the residue in November next and they must raise money to meet those new Engagements, being negotiable ones—That the offer to us is to obtain our Notes for this purpose.

This is a Letter on business. For Intelligence I refer you to the public Prints. They detail what has passed in the Legislature.

Yours, very sincerely   John Laurance

Colonel A Hamilton

ALS, Yale University Library.
    1. For background to this letter, see Jacob Mark and Company to John B. Church, H, and Laurance, May 30, 1797.
    2. Letter not found.
    3. Robert Gilchrist of Westchester County, New York. See Jacob Mark and Company to Church, H, and Laurance, May 30, 1797, note 2.

From William North [1]

Duanesburg [New York] June 4, 1797. "The necessary papers respecting our Contest with Voght,[2] will I hope be forwarded to you. . . . Our situation with respect to this business is not pleasant, As it is Our firm belief that the farms in dispute are our property, it is disagreeable to see them in a situation from which we can neither derive benefit, nor prevent Waste & Spoil. . . . We rely on your friendship to finish the Vexatious business as soon as possible, it is not on the friendship of an Atty or Councillor, but on that of Colonel Hammilton we rely."

ALS, New-York Historical Society, New York City.

1. North, a veteran of the American Revolution who had served as Baron von Steuben's aide-de-camp, was a member of the New York Assembly in 1792 and again from 1794 to 1796. He was speaker of the Assembly in 1795 and 1796. In 1798 he was appointed United States Senator to fill the vacancy caused by the resignation of John Sloss Hobart, and he served in that capacity from May 5 to August 17, 1798.

This letter concerns lands owned by James Duane, whose daughter North had married in 1787. Duane had died in February, 1797.

2. See Abraham Van Vechten to H, September 16, 1796.

From Oliver Wolcott, Junior

[*Philadelphia, June 6, 1797.* On June 8, 1797, Hamilton wrote to Wolcott: "I have received your two letters of the 6th and 7." *Letter of June 6 not found.*]

To Oliver Wolcott, Junior

[New York] June 6 [1797]

My Dear Sir

You some time ago put a question to me,[1] which through hurry, I never answered—*viz* whether there can be any distinction between the provision in the Treaty with Great Britain respecting *British debts* and that respecting *spoliations*,[2] *as to the power* of the Commissioners to rejudge the decisions of the *Courts*.[3] I answer that I can *discover none*.

I am of opinion however that in the exercise of this power two principles ought to be strenuously insisted upon. One, that The Commissioners ought not to intermeddle but where it is unequivocally ascertained, that justice cannot *now* be obtained through our Courts—the *other* that there ought to be no revision of the question of Interest where abatements were made by juries undirected by any special statutes. For it is certain that *interest* is capable of being affected by circumstances and that the law leaves a considerable discretion on this point with Juries. I take it for granted also that where compromises were made between *Creditor* & *Debtor* without the intervention of Courts or the injunctions of positive law, there will be no revision. This is all a very delicate subject one upon which great moderation on the part of the B Commissions is very important to future harmony.

I like very well the course of Executive Conduct in regard to the Controversy with France, and I like the answer of the Senate to the Presidents speech.[4] But I confess I have not been well satisfied with the answer reported in the house.[5] It contains too many hard expressions; and *hard words* are very rarely useful in public proceedings. Mr. *Jay* & other friends here have been struck in the same manner with myself. We shall not regret to see the answer softened down. *Real firmness* is good for every thing—*Strut* is good for nothing.

Last session, I sent *Sedgwick*, with request to communicate it to you, my project of a *building* tax. Inclosed is the rough *Sketch*.[6] I do not know whether there was any alteration in the copy sent to him.

But the more I reflect the more I become convinced that some such plan ought to be adopted & the idea of *valuation* dropped [7]— and I have also become convinced that the idea of a tax on *lands* ought to be deferred.[8]

The building tax can be accommodated to the *Quota*-Rule. For what were intended as *rates* may be considered as *ratios* only of each individual's tax. And then: as the *aggregate* of these *ratios* within a state is to the *sum* of the ratios on a particular building—so will the sum to be raised in the State be to the sum to be paid by the Owner of that building. And so the very bad business of *valuations* may be avoided—in general. In regard to *stores, if they are comprehended,* rents or valuations may be adopted & these rents may also be represented by *ratios* equivalent to the proportion of the specific *ratios* to the rents of houses to be estimated in the law.

If these ideas are not clear I will on your desire give a further explanation.

My plan of *ways* and *means* then for the present would be

			Dollars
A tax on buildings equal to			1000000

on *Stamps* including

a small percentage on policies of Insurance

> a per Centage on *collateral successions*
> a duty on *perfumeries*
> a duty on hats say 5/ Cents for the commonest kind 10/ for the middle & 20 for the best to be described by the materials.

500.000

on Saddle Horses *dollars* ℔ *horse*		150.000
on Salt so much as will make the *whole*		
duty 25 Cents	suppose	350.000
	Dollars	2000000

I should like also a remodification of the duties on licenses to sell *spiritous* liquors by multiplying *discriminations*.

I would then open a loan for 5000000 of Dollars to be repaid absolutely within *five years* upon which I would allow a high interest say 8 per Cent payable quarterly & redeemable *at pleasure* by paying off, and I would accept subscriptions as low as 100 Dollars. In case of pressure Treasury Bills bearing a like interest may be used.

If Unfortunately *War breaks* then every practicable object of Taxation should at once, so as to carry our revenue in the first instance to the extent of our ability. Nor is the field narrow.

I give you my ideas full *gallop* & without management of expression. I hope you always understand me aright and receive my communications as they are intended in the spirit of *friendly* frankness.

Yrs. very truly   A H

Oliver Wolcott Esq

ALS, Connecticut Historical Society, Hartford; copy, Hamilton Papers, Library of Congress.
1. See Wolcott to H, April 12, 1797.
2. H is referring to Articles 6 and 7 of the Jay Treaty. In Article 6 the United States guaranteed the payment of bona fide private debts owed to British subjects which were contracted before the peace treaty of 1783. Article 7 provided for compensation by Great Britain for spoliations of American commerce. In each case the amount due was to be determined by a mixed commission (Miller, *Treaties*, II, 249–53).
3. This question arose early in the meetings of the commission sitting in

London to determine the validity of American claims for compensation under Article 7 of the Jay Treaty. See Moore, *International Adjudications*, IV, 81–90. See also Rufus King to H, February 6, 1797.

4. H is referring to the Senate's answer of May 23, 1797 (*Annals of Congress*, VII, 12–14) to President John Adams's message to Congress of May 16, 1797 (*Annals of Congress*, VII, 54–59).

5. For the answer on June 3, 1793, of the House of Representatives to Adams's message to Congress, see *Annals of Congress*, VII, 236–37.

6. For this enclosure, see H to Theodore Sedgwick, January, 1797.

7. H is referring to Wolcott's recommendations for a tax on houses. See H to Sedgwick, January, 1797, note 4.

8. On December 14, 1796, Wolcott recommended to Congress a tax on lands (*ASP, Finance*, I, 439).

From John Williams [1]

Philadelphia 7th June 1797

Sr.

We shall be this day be engaged on the Subject of Regulating the Arming of Merchantmen.[2] A dificualty ariseth with me respecting the Construction of our Treaty with France.[3] Our Vessels will Claim a right as the Treaty with France expresseth. The French will exact the Decree of 2d March last [4]—hence both will be Authorized by their respective Nations and which will be diametrically Oposite each other.

Again: Victor Hughs has declared all American Vessels Taken Armed shall be treated as Pirates.[5]

Thus while on the One hand our Commerce Suffers—and on the other its Susceptible of commencing a misunderstanding which will probably lead to a War—which ought to be avoided. No talk of Embargo—only giving the Executive the Power in case of Emergency.

We shall direct the completion of Fortification but believe will only order the Frigates finished and probably Manned.

Do not believe we shall purchase Vessels for War or Order Convoys.

As it (in my Opinion) behoves us to Act with caution til we learn the Event of the Negociation, I am at present for pursuing the same measures as in the year 1794. Should the Negociation fail and France not be Satisfied with being put on an Equal footing with Other Nations—We shall be Unanimous in our Opposition.

Any remarks on these subjects or any other will be thankfully received   By Your Humble Servt   John Williams

Colo. Hamilton.

I am told the Lt. Governor [6] is in New York and Mrs. Van Rensselaer is very unwell if so please make my Complts. respectful to them.

ALS, Hamilton Papers, Library of Congress.

1. Williams, a native of England, emigrated to America in 1773 and settled in what is now Washington County, New York. A veteran of the American Revolution, he served in the New York Assembly in 1781 and 1782 and in the state Senate in 1777 and 1778 and again from 1782 to 1785. He was a member of the New York Ratifying Convention in 1788 and of the Council of Appointment in 1789. He was elected to the House of Representatives in 1795 and served until March 3, 1799.

2. On June 5, 1797, William Loughton Smith introduced in the House of Representatives ten resolutions designed to strengthen the defense of the United States. See H to Smith, April 10, 1797, note 12. The fifth of these resolutions, stating "that provision be made by law, for regulating the arming of the merchant vessels of the United States," came up for debate in the House on June 7, 1797 (*Annals of Congress*, VII, 239, 253).

3. This is a reference to Article 23 (originally 25) of the Treaty of Amity and Commerce of 1778 between the United States and France, which stipulated that "free Ships shall also give a freedom to Goods" (Miller, *Treaties*, II, 21).

4. This decree stated, among other things, that enemy property in neutral vessels was liable to capture. See Rufus King to H, April 2, 1797.

5. For this decree, dated February 1, 1797, see "The Warning No. VI," March 27, 1797, note 9.

6. Stephen Van Rensselaer.

From Oliver Wolcott, Junior

[*Philadelphia, June 7, 1797.* On June 8, 1797, Hamilton wrote to Wolcott: "I have received your two letters of the 6th and 7." *Letter of June 7 not found.*]

To Rufus King

[New York, June 8, 1797] [1]

I thank, you My Dear Sir, for two letters lately received from you [2] the last by Mr. Church. I feel very guilty for my negligence. But how can I help it?

The public prints will inform you of the course of public proceedings hitherto. You will perceive that the general plan is analogous to what was done in the case of Great Britain, though there
are faults in the detail. Some people cannot learn that the only force
which befits a Government is in the *thought* and *action* not in the
words and many reverse this golden rule. I fear we shall do ourselves no honor in the result and we shall remain at the mercy of
events without those efficient preparations which are demanded by
so precarious a situation and which not provoking war would put us
in condition to meet it. All the consolation I can give is that the
public temper of this Country mends dayly & that there is no final
danger of our submitting tamely to the yoke of France

    Yrs. Affecly

                                                A. H.

                                    June 8. 1797

The bearer of this is Mr. *Fleming* [3] a young American of good connection & as far as I have learnt good character.

R King Esq

ALS, New-York Historical Society, New York City.
   1. In *JCHW*, VI, 252, and *HCLW*, X, 266, this letter is dated June 6, 1797.
   2. The most recent letters which King had sent to H are dated March 8,
April 2, 1797.
   3. This is probably a reference to William Fleming of Virginia.

To Oliver Wolcott, Junior

                                  [New York, June 8, 1797]

Dr. Sir

I have received your two letters of the 6th & 7.[1] The last announces to me no more than I feared. Nor do I believe any sufficient
external impulse can be given to save us from *disgrace*. This however will be thought of.

I regret that you appear remote from the idea of a house tax
simply without combining the land.[2] I do not differ from your general principle. The truth is a solid one, that the sound state of the
political œconomy depends in a great degree on a general repartition

of taxes on taxable property by some equal rule. But it is very important to relax in theory so as to accomplish as much as may be practicable. I despair of a general land tax without actual war. I fear the idea of it keeps men back from the augmentation of revenue by other means which they might be willing to adopt. The idea of a house tax alone is not so formidable. If placed upon a footing which would evince practicability & moderation in the sum I think it might succeed. Now 1000000 of Dollars computing the number of houses at 600 000 would be an average of about a dollar & a half. The tax would be very *low* on the worst houses & could not be *high* on the best. This idea would smooth a great deal.

As to the circumstance of the habitations of the Southern negroes, I see no insuperable difficulty in applying ratios to them which would tend to individual Equity. As between the states the quota-principle would make this point unimportance.

As to the inequality in certain states, I believe on the plan suggested there could be no general tax which in fact would operate more equally. The idea of equalization by embracing lands does not much engage my confidence. Besides that this may be an after object & we are to gain points successively.

As to the productiveness of the stamp tax with the items I suggest it is difficult in the first instance to judge. But I am persuaded it would go far towards the point aimed. There cannot be much fewer than 3000000 of hats consumed in a Year in this Country; at an average of 8 Cents ℔ hat this would be 240 000 Dollars—a large proportion of the 500 000. If law proceedings can be included directly or indirectly the produce will be very considerable. I think you mistake when you say these taxes in England are inconsiderable in proportion.[3] According to my recollection the reverse is the truth.

Adieu Yrs.   A H

ALS, Connecticut Historical Society, Hartford; copy, Hamilton Papers, Library of Congress.
    1. Neither letter has been found.
    2. See H to Wolcott, June 6, 1797.
    3. This is a reference to "An Act for granting to his Majesty certain Duties on Licences, to be taken out by Persons vending Hats by Retail; and also certain Duties on Hats sold under such Licences; and for laying additional Duties on all Hats and Caps imported into this Kingdom" (24 Geo. III, C. 51 [1784]).

From Robert Morris [1]

Alexander Hamilton Esqre n york   Philada. June 10 1797

Dear Sir

I hold ten Shares in the Western Canal Navigation of new york [2] on which there has been paid $1070, and a Call of $25 ℔ Share was due the 1st May last & remains to be paid with 6 ℔ Ct Interest from that time. I don't know what State of Credit these Shares stand at present, but am confident they will be a most productive property hereafter. If you will take these Shares credit me for the amot I have paid & you make the Payment now due & answer such other Calls as the managers may make, you shall have them in part Payment of what I owe you. Mr Church begins already to threaten me with harsh measures [3] but I hope to disarm him.

With great Esteem   I am Dr Sir   Yrs   RM

LC, Robert Morris Papers, Library of Congress.

1. Except for the last sentence, this letter deals with Morris's efforts to pay the balance of a debt which he owed to H. For an account of this debt, see the introductory note to H to Morris, March 18, 1795. See also Morris to H, March 31, June 2, 23, 30, July 18, 20, 1795; June 17, 27–30, November 19, December 8, 1796; June 2, 1797.

2. See Ledger C, 157, Robert Morris Account Books, Historical Society of Pennsylvania, Philadelphia.

The name of this corporation was the Western Inland Lock Navigation Company. See Théophile Cazenove to Egbert Benson and H, May 29, 1797, note 4.

3. John B. Church had recently instituted proceedings in Chancery for the payment of the interest on a debt which Morris owed to Church. On July 5, 1797, Morris wrote to Richard Harison, who was his attorney in New York City: "You will see by the annexed copy of a letter from Mr. [Daniel] McKinnen of your city, that he has filed a bill in chancery against me for Mr. Church who wants I suppose to foreclose the mortgage mentioned, in order to get the Land for less than its value. I pray you to enter an appearance for me immediately and I will hereafter give you the heads of the defense to be made, altho' I expect the bill in chancery will be withdrawn or discharged upon payment of the interest due on my bond & this I expect soon to accomplish. You will observe there is not a moment to be lost in entering the appearance" (LC, Robert Morris Papers, Library of Congress).

For background on this suit and the debt Church was seeking to have paid by Morris, see the introductory note to Morris to H, June 7, 1795. See also Morris to H, July 20, November 16, December 18, 1795; January 15, March 6, 12, 14, 30, April 27, May 3, 10, 17, 18, 31, 1796, March 3, 27, May 20, 23, June 2, 1797; William Lewis to H, May 4, 1796; H to Charles Williamson, May 17–30, 1796.

To William Loughton Smith

[New York, June 10, 1797] [1]

My Dear Sir

I received your letter of the ———.[2] Though I do not like in some respects the answer of the house to the Speech;[3] yet I frankly own I had no objection to see it softened down. For I think there is no use in *hard words* & in public proceedings would almost always unite the suaviter in modo with the *fortiter in re*.

But I much regret that there is no prospect of the *fortiter in re*. I perceive clearly that your measures will wear upon the whole the aspect of *resentment*, without means or energy sufficient to repel injury. Our country will be first ruined and then we shall begin to think of defending ourselves.

I will not enter much into detail but I will observe that instead of three frigates of 32 I would prefer an increase of the number of the Cutters.[4] Surely 20 of these cannot embarrass the most squeamish and less than this number will be useless.

But from all I can see you will have no Revenue. Over-driven theory everywhere palsies the operations of our Government and renders all rational *practice* impossible.

My ideas of Revenue would be

A tax on buildings	1000,000
Stamp Tax including perfumeries a percentage on policies of insurance on collateral successions to real & personal estate *on hats* say 5 Cents for the worst 10 for the middling & 20 for the best	500 000
Saddles horses	150 000
Salt (so as make the whole 25 ⅌ Cent	350 000
	2 000 000

I have explained My ideas of the house tax to Wolcott & Sedgwick.[5]

It is to take certain *criteria* of different buildings & annex to them *ratios* not *rates*. (What I gave to Sedgwick as *rates* may serve as *ratios*).

Then apportion the tax among the States and distribute the quota of each among the Individuals according to ratios. The aggregate of the ratios will represent the quota of the State—then as that aggregate is to the sum of the quota so will be the sum of the ratios of each building to the tax to be paid by each individual.

I am told an objection will arise from the *negro houses* in the South.[6] Surely there is no impracticability in annexing *ratios* to them [which] [7] will be proportional to their taxable value. This plan will avoid the worst of all inconveniences *the arbitrary* of *valuations* & will avoid the embarrassment for the present of a land tax—will be also consistent with expedition. I entertain no doubt it can be adjusted so as to be free from any material objection. The smallness of the tax will render any material inequality impossible. You cannot compute fewer than 600 000 houses which at an average would be about a Dollar and a half a house. The proportions of the better houses on the proposed plan would make the tax fall light on the inferior & country houses which is desireable for recommending the first essay—nor would any house I am persuaded have to pay 10 Dollars. What room for serious objection. You then lay a foundation for an annual million on real property which will become a permanent accession to your revenue. Whereas you will feel an endless embarrassment about agreeing upon any tax on lands.

Yrs. truly   A H

Wm Smith Esq

ALS, William Loughton Smith Papers, Library of Congress.
    1. In *HCLW*, X, 224, his letter is dated "1797."
    2. Space left blank in MS. The most recent letter H had received from Smith is dated May 1, 1797.
    3. John Adams delivered his message to Congress on May 16, 1797 (*Annals of Congress*, VII, 54–59). The House replied on June 3, 1797 (*Annals of Congress*, VII, 236–37).
    4. On June 5, 1797, Smith recommended to the House of Representatives ten measures to strengthen the defenses of the country (H to Smith, April 10, 1797, note 12). The third of these reads: "*Resolved*, That provision be made by law, for procuring by purchase a further naval force, to consist of ——— frigates of ——— guns, and ——— sloops of war of ——— guns." In the debate that followed on this resolution, Smith suggested that the numbers for the blanks might be "three frigates of 32 guns, and six sloops of war of 16 guns" (*Annals of Congress*, VII, 239, 246).
    5. See H to Wolcott, June 6, 1797; H to Theodore Sedgwick, January, 1797.
    6. See H to Wolcott, June 8, 1797.
    7. In MS, "will."

From Elihu Chauncey Goodrich [1]

Claverack [*New York*] *June 12, 1797.* "Scarcity of Money (at this time) is such that I cannot without a very material Injury to my property and Credit raise the amount which you as attorney for Mr. James Bryson have received against Me as Endorser of a Note. . . . However previous to the first day of November next it will undoubtedly be in my power without much inconvenience to make the full payment—request you therefore to delay issuing any Execution untill the said 1st day of November. . . ."

LS, Hamilton Papers, Library of Congress.
    1. This letter concerns the efforts of James Bryson, a naturalized citizen, to obtain $3,051.14, which was owed to him by Goodrich, an attorney in Claverack. In 1796 Bryson retained H as his attorney, and the case went to the Supreme Court of New York, which in 1798 decided in favor of Bryson. See H's Law Register, 1795–1804 (D, partially in H's handwriting, New York Law Institute, New York City), and Goebel, *Law Practice*, I, 158.

Account with *John Barker Church* [1]

[New York, June 15, 1797]

John B Church Esquire in Account with Alexander Hamilton

Dr.

1796			
June	6	To Cash paid expences of my Clerk to Philadelphia to attend to execution of your Mortgage by Robert Morris [2]	10. 16 —
	20	To paid J Laurance your proportion of expence of surveys [3]	113. 8 —
July	7	To your half the purchase money of Eight lots in the City of N York bought of I. Riley Dolls. 1000	
		half expence of searching records for mortgages and Judgments	8. 12 —
			403. 5 — [4]
			1008. 12 =
August	8	To paid City tax on your lot broad Way	4. 16. 8 [5]
1797		To paid for cleaning white-washing & painting your house	34. 5. 6 [6]
March	7.	To paid Robinson Carpenter for fencing your lot	11. 11 — [7]

Cr.

1796			
April	8	By Ballance of Account rendered this day	£570. 2. 8
Aug	22	By this sum received of A Woodruff [14] on account of Carney's debt [15]	420 ——
October	11	By this sum received on account of Kinlocks Bond [16]	340. 4. 6
Nov.	26	By this sum received of Doctor Romayne [17]	354. 8. 10
Decr.	13	By this sum received of R Morris	400 ——
1797		By this sum received of Wm Cooper [18] in two payments on account of Holkers Debt [19]	600 ——

Dr.   Cr.

May	17	To Cash paid yourself	200——— [8]
	29	To ditto paid price of Negro Woman	90——— [9]
June	5	To paid for coal per Order	120——— [10]
	7	To Cash paid yourself	200——— [11]
		Ballance due J: B Church	1496. 13. 10
			£2684. 16———

£2684. 16———

From the above Ballance deductions are to be made on two Accounts

House Rent paid more than received about   300 [12]

Interest creditted from the supposition of a ballance which did not exist owing to a double credit of a sum received from Wadsworth,[13] whole sum creditted   300

                      600———

£329,9,04—excess about

E. E New York June 15. 1797
A Hamilton

ALS, Lloyd W. Smith Collection, Morristown National Historical Park, Morristown, New Jersey.

1. H prepared this account to give to Church on his arrival in the United States on May 20. See Robert Morris to H, May 23, 1797, note 4.

2. See the introductory note to Morris to H, June 7, 1795; Morris to H, May 31, 1796. An entry in H's Cash Book, 1795–1804, under the date of June 2, 1796, reads: "Account of Expences Dr. to Cash John B. Church for expence of Clk sent to Philadelphia for Mortgage R. Morris. . . . [$] 27" (AD, Hamilton Papers, Library of Congress).

3. See Jacob Mark and Company to Church, H, and John Laurance, May 30, 1797; Laurance to H, June 3, 1797.

4. See "Conveyance from Isaac and Hannah Riley," July 7, 1796.

5. See "Receipt from Morgan Lewis," March 18, 1796, note 2.

6. Church's house was at 52 Broadway, probably on one of the lots near Marketfield Street which H secured for him in 1796 (David Longworth, *Longworth's Almanack, New-York Register, and City Directory, for the Twentysecond Year of American Independence* . . . [New York: Printed for the Editor, by T. & J. Swords, No. 99 Pearl-street, 1797]; "Receipt from Morgan Lewis," March 18, 1796, note 2). An entry in H's Cash Book, 1795–1804, for February 1, 1797, breaks down the cost as follows: "John B. Church Dr. to Cash paid by Mrs. Hamilton for Washing cleaning & white washing house hired for him

20.18

paid Sherrard painter his account ℔ Rect   13. 7. 6.

34. 5. 6   86.94"

(AD, Hamilton Papers, Library of Congress).

7. See "Bill from James Robinson," March 7, 1797.

8. On May 22, 1797, H recorded in his Cash Book, 1795–1804: "John B. Church Dr. to Cash paid him this day 500" (AD, Hamilton Papers, Library of Congress).

9. An entry in H's Cash Book, 1795–1804, for May 29, 1797, reads: "John B. Church Dr. to Cash paid for negro woman & child 225" (AD, Hamilton Papers, Library of Congress).

10. On June 5, 1797, the following entry appears in H's Cash Book, 1795–1804: "John B. Church Dr. to cash for this sum pd. Wm. Dodge for Coal 300" (AD, Hamilton Papers, Library of Congress).

11. In his Cash Book, 1795–1804, H recorded the payment of five hundred dollars to Church on June 7, 1797 (AD, Hamilton Papers, Library of Congress).

12. An entry in H's Cash Book, 1795–1804, for March 14, 1797, reads: "John B. Church Dr. to Cash for this sum paid a quarters Rent of his house 312.50" (AD, Hamilton Papers, Library of Congress).

13. During the American Revolution, Jeremiah Wadsworth and Church had been partners in a firm supplying the French forces in America. They continued their business partnership until July, 1785.

14. Aaron D. Woodruff was a Trenton, New Jersey, lawyer.

15. See Woodruff to H, January 13, 1790, in which the name appears correctly as Kearney. An entry in H's Cash Book, 1795–1804, for August 22, 1796, reads: "Cash Dr. to John B. Church Esqr. for this sum received of A. D. Woodruff on account of money recovered by him from Carney [$]1050" (AD, Hamilton Papers, Library of Congress). The Kearneys were a large and prosperous clan. It cannot be stated definitely, but it seems likely that the individual in question was Stephen Kearney, a wine merchant from Newark who subsequently moved to New York. During the American Revolution his estates were confiscated because of his Loyalist activities.

16. Francis Kinloch was a South Carolina planter. For Church's transactions with Kinloch, see Cleland Kinloch to H, September 20, 1785; Charles Cotesworth Pinckney to H, June 5, 1796; H to Pinckney, September 12, 1796.

17. Dr. Nicholas Romayne. See Romayne to H, April 13, 1797. An entry in H's Cash Book, 1795–1804, for November 29, 1796, reads: "Cash Dr. to John B. Church Cost & Fees . . . for this sum received of Doctor Romayne [$]886.10" (AD, Hamilton Papers, Library of Congress).

18. William Cooper, the founder of Cooperstown, was one of the largest landholders in New York State. H served as his attorney in many of Cooper's land transactions (see forthcoming Goebel, *Law Practice*, III). In 1791 Cooper became a judge of Otsego County. From 1795 to 1797 and from 1799 to 1801 he was a Federalist member of the House of Representatives.

19. From 1778 to 1780 John Holker had been French consul in Philadelphia and agent for supplying the French navy. After the war he was a leading Philadelphia merchant and speculator. For Holker's debt to Church and for Holker's connection with Cooper, see H to John Chaloner, June 11, 1793, note 1. See also Thomas FitzSimons to H, March 21, July 14, December 17, 1795; H to William Cooper, December 16, 1796. In H's Cash Book, 1795–1804, an entry for March 10, 1797, reads: "Cash Dr. to John B. Church for this sum received of Wm Cooper acct. *Holker* 500" (AD, Hamilton Papers, Library of Congress.

To Jeremiah Wadsworth

New York June 16. 1797

My Dear Sir

This will be delivered to you by Mr. John Lytton [1] a kinsman of mine. He was born to a handsome fortune—but adversity in Trade has ruined him, insomuch that he is under the necessity of endeavouring to protect himself from too severe creditors by taking whatever benefit the laws of Connecticut will allow him. As he is a worthy man (besides being my relation) I recommend him to your advice and good offices. He will be glad to find employment as a Clerk, till he can obtain a discharge, and as he has been regularly bred to business and writes a good hand I have no doubt he would give satisfaction. If you can recommend him to employment you will oblige me. I am under obligations to a part of his family [2] which interest me the more in his affairs. When discharged I must endeavour to bring him forward into some line of business to which he is adapted.

Yrs. truly   A Hamilton

ALS, The Sol Feinstone Collection, Library of the American Philosophical Society, Philadelphia.

1. John W. Lytton was H's first cousin once removed. H's maternal grand-father, John Fawcett, had two daughters: Rachel, who married John Michael Lavien and was H's mother, and Ann, who married James Kirwan Lytton. One of the Lyttons' children was James Lytton, Jr., who in turn had a son named John W. Lytton (Holger Utke Ramsing, "Alexander Hamilton og hans mødrene staegt Tidsbilleder fra Dansk Vestindiens barndom," *Personalhistorisk tidsckrift*, 24 cm., 10 Raekke, 6 bd. [Copenhagen, 1939], 226–28, 240, 252). An entry in H's Cash Book, 1795–1804, for November 9, 1797, reads: "John W Lytton   Dr to Cash lent him   50" (AD, Hamilton Papers, Library of Congress).

2. This is a reference to Ann Lytton Mitchell (formerly Ann Lytton Venton), who was the daughter of James and Ann Lytton, as well as H's favorite cousin. See Ann Mitchell to H, 1796.

From Barbara Moland [1]

St. Vincent [*Windward Islands*] *June 19, 1797*. "I hope you will excuse the liberty I take in addressing this to you, but . . . your former attention to the late M Joseph Moland in the business be-tween Mr John Stephens and him on a Bond Sent by Sir John St Clair to Mr Moland—Induces me to hope you will let me know; if by the last treaty with Great Britain, whether I can get the lands that was made Over to Mr Moland by his Nephew Sir John St Clair, Situated on the East Side of Lake Champlain in the County of Albany granted to Sir J: St Clairs Father . . .[2] As Mr Moland has left a Son and two Daughters and I being nearest of Kin to them I would esteem it a very great favor if you Sir woud Act for them and See if you could get Possession of this land or Even a Compensa-tion for them. . . ."

ALS, Hamilton Papers, Library of Congress.

1. This letter concerns the estate of Sir John St. Clair, who was deputy quartermaster general in America from 1755 to 1767. In 1762 he married Betsey Moland, the oldest daughter of John Moland, a lawyer in Philadelphia. St. Clair purchased a country seat near Elizabeth, New Jersey, where he lived until his death in 1767. He was survived by one son, who became Sir John St. Clair, fourth Baronet. See Charles R. Hildeburn, "Sir John St. Clair, Baronet, Quarter-Master General in America, 1755 to 1767," *Pennsylvania Magazine of History and Biography*, IX (1885), 12–13.

2. The land in question consisted of two tracts—one of five thousand acres and the other of ten thousand acres—in what is now Addison County, Vermont. The statement made by Barbara Moland that the property was in "the County of Albany" arose from the fact that when the grants were made before the American Revolution, the land east of Lake Champlain was claimed by the province of New York. See *N.Y. Colonial Manuscripts*, 334, 393, 402, 527, 529.

From James Thompson [1]

[Bombay, June 22, 1797]

Dear Sir

Neither remoteness of Situation, nor lapse of time can efface from my Recollection the Obligations which I was under to you in the earlier part of my Life.[2] That I have not before acknowledged them you are freely at liberty to attribute to any Cause—but want of Gratitude—for whatever may be my Vices Ingratitude cannot be included in the Catalogue. You may believe me when I assure you that wherever I have been Situated or whatever had been my prospects I have uniformly entertained the same grateful Sense of your liberality.

No Occurrence in life could afford me a more sensible pleasure than that of having it in my power to make you a suitable Return. This however I can never expect, as the most I can hope for is to have an opportunity of Reimbursing you such pecuniary Advances as you have made or ought to have received on my Account. To effect this Object I have anxiously looked for an opportunity from this side of India, but without Success; there being little intercourse with America direct from hence and the Communication via China has been by the diabolical Treaty of Commerce put an end to,[3] and the ignorance of your Correspondent in England has prevented me from availing myself of that Channel.

I have embraced the present opportunity of Addressing you, as I am led to hope the Ship may again return to Bombay; but even if she should not, you will particularly oblige me by informing me of the Amount which I am in your Debt—Upon the Receipt of which I will find means of making an adequate Remittance. It matters not to what part of India the Ship is bound by which you write. If the Captain sends the letter to the Post Office, it will come safe to hand if address'd to me in Bombay.

I am   Sir   with profound Respect   Your most Obedt. Humble Servant   James Thompson

Bombay
22d. June 1797.
Alexander Hamilton Esqr:

ALS, Hamilton Papers, Library of Congress.

1. Thompson, a New York City merchant and the father-in-law of Elbridge Gerry, had been a Tory during the American Revolution and had traded with the British forces in occupied New York.

2. The nature of Thompson's obligations to H has not been discovered, but for Thompson's account with H in the seventeen-eighties, see H's Cash Book, March 1, 1782–1791.

3. This is a reference to Article 13 of the Jay Treaty, which stated that the United States could carry on only a direct trade with India (Miller, *Treaties*, II, 255–56).

From Rufus King

London June 27. 1797

Dear sir

Lord Malmesbury will leave London in three or four Days for Lille where the conferences between this Country and France are to be held.[1] Opinions fluctuate concerning the Probability of peace. A Struggle evidently exists in France between the Directory & the Legislature, in the latter of which Bodies it is supposed there is a sincere desire of Peace.

Some late proceedings in the Legislature, or rather in the Council of 500, give Occasion to hope that our Affairs are in train to assume a more friendly appearance.

If as many assert the public Opinion is friendly to America, it will be employed by the Legislature agt. the Directory wh. at this moment is viewed as a rival Power. We have just recd. the Presidents Speech;[2] it has arrived at a critical hour.

You will perceive by the News Papers that all Italy will be overturned—Venice is no more;[3] and Genoa has been completely revolutionized by Citizen Faypoult the Minister of France.[4] Portugal sees, but seems unable to escape, her Fate.[5]

Tho' these are days of wonder, still one dares not believe all we hear—the march already made by France has astonished, and confounded almost every Beholder. And we are told that she meditates and will attempt Projects still more gigantic than those She has executed—Plans which will operate a Change in the whole face of Europe, and which extend to every other Quarter of the Globe. Russia may be able to preserve her Dominions from the fire that is passing over the neighbouring Countries: this Nation has lately

renewed her commercial Treaty with Russia [6]—and by an arrangement of their mutual Intts. may strengthen their common Defence.
It may be worth remarking that during the negotiation Russia
never even proposed the project of the armed neutrality. so that
the omission of the requisite provisions on that subject may be
considered as an abandonment of the System by Russia.

Russia is to be treated in the Brit: Ports upon the same footing
as the most favored *European* Nation.[7]

Farewell yrs &c   R. King

Colo. Hamilton.

ALS, Hamilton Papers, Library of Congress.
    1. For the efforts of James Harris, first Earl of Malmesbury, to negotiate
a treaty with France in 1796, see King to H, November 30, 1796, note 3. The
negotiations to which King is referring in the letter printed above began at
Lille on July 7, 1797.
    2. John Adams's message to the special session of Congress was delivered on
May 16, 1797 (*Annals of Congress*, VII, 54–59).
    3. The treaty of peace between France and the Venetian Republic, signed
at Milan on May 16, 1797, abolished the Grand Council and hereditary aristocracy, established popular government, and provided for the occupation of
Venice by a French garrison. In return, the Venetians agreed to provide the
French with six million livres tournois, half in cash and half in the form of
supplies (Martens, *Recûeil*, VI, 391–93).
    4. On June 6, 1797, the Republic of Genoa concluded a convention with
Napoleon and Guillaume Charles Faipoult de Maisoncelle, the French Minister
at Genoa, dividing the Republic into communes and municipalities and establishing government by legislative and executive councils under the authority
of a doge (Martens, *Recûeil*, VI, 394–96).
    5. Portugal and Great Britain had been allies since the Treaty of London,
September 26, 1793. This treaty provided that both parties should receive one
another's ships in their ports, while the Queen of Portugal agreed to exclude
French warships and privateers from Portuguese ports for the duration of the
war (Debrett, *A Collection of State Papers*, I, 25–27). After August 19, 1796,
when France signed a treaty of alliance with Spain, Portugal was placed in a
position where it might become involved in a war between Spain and Great
Britain. On September 17, 1796, the Queen of Portugal published a decree
proclaiming Portugal's neutrality and prohibiting in the event of an outbreak
of war the entry into Portuguese ports of warships or privateers except in
cases of emergency (Martens, *Recûeil*, V, 609–10). The Portuguese ambassador
at Paris, Antonio D'Araujo D'Azevedo, disregarding opposition from Great
Britain, soon began negotiations for a treaty of peace and friendship with
France. The treaty was signed on August 10, 1797 (Martens, *Recûeil*, VI,
413–19).
    6. On March 25, 1793, Great Britain and Russia had signed a commercial
convention renewing their treaty of 1766 (Martens, *Recûeil*, V, 433–37). The
two countries made a defensive alliance on February 18, 1795, and on February 21, 1797, they signed a treaty of navigation and commerce at St. Petersburg (Martens, *Recûeil*, VI, 11–23, 357–67).

7. Article 3 of the Treaty of Navigation and Commerce between Great Britain and Russia stated: "L'on est convenu à cet effet, que les sujets des hautes parties contractantes seront admis avec leurs vaisseaux, bâtimens et transports de terre, dans tous les ports, places et villes dont l'entrée est permise aux sujets de toute autre puissance, qu'ils pourront y faire le commerce et y demeurer; et les matelots, voyageurs et navires . . . seront accueillis et traités comme la nation la plus favorisée . . ." (Martens, *Recûeil*, VI, 358–59).

To Simeon DeWitt [1]

New York, June 28, 1797. "I am applied to, to examine the Title to a tract of land described in the extract A, which is inclosed. It appears from the papers put into my hands, that a *Map* of the intire tract patented to John W Watkins the 25 of June 1794 [2] as surveyed is on file in your office. By the extract from the patent, which is also herewith, it is found that a number of tracts comprehended within the exterior lines of the tract patented to Watkins are *excepted* and *reserved*. The Question is whether the *North West* quarter or section of township No. 8 is wholly free from these exceptions and reservations or is affected by them. It is presumed that the map and survey in your Office will enable you to answer it. . . . Give me leave also to trouble you with an Inquiry concerning the Class rights described in the Extract B. These class rights appear to have been conveyed by John Carpenter of Goshen to one Benjamin Barton and by the latter to Elisha Boudinot of New Ark, but the Evidences of the Class rights, whatever they are, do not accompany the Conveyances.[3] You will perhaps be able to inform me from the files of your Office how the matter is situated. . . ."

ALS, MS Division, New York Public Library; ALS (photostat), Rutgers University Library, The State University of New Jersey, New Brunswick, New Jersey.

1. DeWitt was surveyor general of New York State.
2. This is a reference to the purchase made by Watkins and Royal Flint of a tract in what at the time was Tioga County. (New counties were formed from the original Tioga County in 1798, 1806, and 1836.) The grant to Watkins and Flint was for 336,880 acres (*N.Y. Colonial Manuscripts*, 929–30).
3. This is a reference to the case of *Elisha Boudinot* v *John Carpenter & Benjamin Barton*, in which H served as Boudinot's attorney and Caleb S. Riggs as Carpenter's attorney. Carpenter owned six hundred acres of land in Montgomery County, which on May 20, 1789, Carpenter sold to Benjamin Barton. Carpenter agreed to pay the patent fees for the land after the survey had been completed. Although Barton conveyed the land to Boudinot on April 10, 1796, Carpenter, having obtained the patents, refused to execute to Boudinot a conveyance of legal estate in the land (Bill, October 12, 1797, *Elisha Boudinot*

v *John Carpenter & Benjamin Barton* [Chancery Decrees Before 1800, B-160, Historical Documents Collection, Queens College, New York City]). Carpenter argued that before he had made his sale to Barton he had obtained a judgment against Barton in the New York Supreme Court for more than £1900, which was still unsatisfied. According to Carpenter, Boudinot and Barton were attempting by pretended conveyances to compel Carpenter to convey the land to Boudinot and thereby deprive Carpenter of the remedy he would have against the lands by means of the unsatisfied judgment if the legal title were made to Barton (Answer, December 5, 1797, *Elisha Boudinot* v *John Carpenter & Benjamin Barton* [Chancery Decrees Before 1800, B-160, Historical Documents Collection, Queens College, New York City]).

For a description of "class rights," see "An Act to raise Troops for the Defence of the Frontiers" (*New York Laws*, 3rd Sess., Ch. LIII [March 11, 1780]) and "An Act for raising Troops to complete the Line of this State, in the Service of the United States, and the two Regiments to be raised on Bounties of unappropriated Lands, and for the further Defence of the Frontiers of this State" (*New York Laws*, 5th Sess., Ch. XXII [March 23, 1782]).

To Oliver Mann and Isaac Parker

New York, June 28, 1797. "Your letter of the 6th of May [1] last by making a circuit to Albany did not reach me in due time—which is the principal cause of this late reply. The idea of there having been property lodged in my hands towards satisfaction of the notes surprized me, as nothing of the kind ever took place, nor do I recollect or believe that the expectation of it was ever suggested to me. My memory of what passed with Mr. Isaac Parker amounts simply to this—that *he desired me to stay proceedings until further order* and such further order I never received. Mr. Lowel, who sent me the notes, some time after this direction had been given me by Mr. Parker passed through this City. I mentioned to him the direction received and how the affair then stood; but he gave no further direction. . . . Since the receipt of your last I have inquired concerning Messrs Edward & Elias Parker. The answer I get is that one of those Gentleman is dead and that the other some time since quitted this City having left no property behind. Concluding that all further pursuit here would be useless I shall send this letter with the Notes under cover to Mr. Lowel who will do with them as he finds right."

ALS, Hamilton Papers, Library of Congress.
    1. For background to this letter, see John Lowell, Jr., to H, December 19, 1795.

Tract Granted by Robert Morris
Within the Genesee Lands [1]

[New York, June, 1797]

A   27 February 1793   Deed from R Morris & Wife to *Herman LeRoy* & others *called* 1000000 (but *by bounds*)

A2   20 of July 1793   Ditto to ditto (*called* 800000 as *before*)

A3   24 Decr. 1792   Do. to do   Two adjoining Tracts
No.   1000⎤ The most Western
                                                500⎦ & bounding on the
                                               lakes with a meridian line
                                               for the Eastern boundary

A6   28 Decr. 1796   do. to do   40000
        Mortgage   Eastern & extendg Westward to the point
                                of triangle of Le Roy & Bayard

A7   31 of Decr. 1796   Mortgage of same tract for a further purpose

        20 of July 1793   for three Tracts the one the SouthEastern
                                Corner of the whole Dutch tracts—
                                another   for 54.000 acres
        called   another   for 46 000

        500 000   100 000 acres
B   11 Jan 1793   From R M to Le Roy & Bayard
                                their own   80 000

        5 of April 1797   From Cottringer to R Morris
                                adjoining to Watson

                                               33 750.
        6 of April 1797—   From Morris to Craigie
                                Same tract except the *Genessee flats*
        1 May 1796—   From Morris to S Ogden
                                adjoining the lake (granted or to be
                                granted) 50000 acres except Genessee
                                Flats with covenant to give equal quan-
                                tity of upland.

From
May 31. 1796   to *A Hamilton* 100 000
                        May 4, 1797
May 4. 1797   from *Morris to Harrison*

AD, Columbia University Libraries, New York City.
  1. H endorsed this document: "*Tract,* granted by R Morris within the
Genesee *Lands,* Judgment on which purchase was June 1797."
  For background to this document and the individuals mentioned in it, see
the introductory note to H to Morris, March 18, 1795; Morris to H, June 7,
1795.

From Robert Morris

Philada July 2d. 1797

Dear Sir

I cannot account for your not having Answered the letter of
which the preceeding is a Copy,[1] in any other way than by supposing it did not get to your hands, it was written so long since as
the 23d of May last & sent by Post, and is of so important a nature
that I waited with Anxiety supposing however that the papers were
preparing and that you delayed writing untill they were ready. I
am become more Anxious now from the rigour of Mr Church.[2] I
pray of you for that Justice to which I am on this occasion entitled,
& beg that you will comply with the requests contained in that letter.
As I suppose it would not be agreable to you to appear against Mr
Church I must apply to other Counsel to oppose his proceedings
untill I can pay him the interests which I will do as soon as possible.

I am Dr Sir   Your Obedt Servt   Robt Morris

Alexr Hamilton Esqr
New York

ALS, Hamilton Papers, Library of Congress; LC, Robert Morris Papers, Library of Congress.
  1. Morris to H, May 23, 1797.
  2. This is a reference to proceedings in Chancery by John B. Church to
secure the payment of interest on a debt which Morris owed to Church. See
Morris to H, June 10, 1793, note 3. For an account of the debt and Morris's
efforts to pay it, see the introductory note to Morris to H, June 7, 1795. See

also Morris to H, July 20, November 16, December 18, 1795, January 15, March 6, 12, 14, 30, April 27, May 3, 10, 17, 18, 31, 1796, March 3, 27, May 20, 23, June 2, 10, 1797; William Lewis to H, May 4, 1796; H to Charles Williamson, May 17-30, 1796.

From Oliver Wolcott, Junior

[Philadelphia, July 3, 1797]

Introductory Note

The events described in this letter precipitated the final phase of what has come to be known as the "Reynolds Affair." In pamphlets appearing in June and July, 1797, James Thomson Callender stated that Hamilton, while Secretary of the Treasury, had joined with James Reynolds in a series of speculative ventures that were at best improper and at worst illegal.[1] Two months later Hamilton published the so-called "Reynolds

ALS, Hamilton Papers, Library of Congress.
    1. Callender, a native of Scotland, fled to the United States after he was indicted for sedition in January, 1793, because of his pamphlet *The political progress of Britain; or, An impartial account of the principal abuses in the government of the Country, From the Revolution in 1688; the whole tending to prove the ruinous consequences of the popular system of war and conquest* . . . Part I (London: Printed for T. Kay, 1792). Until the spring of 1796, he reported on congressional debates for *The Philadelphia Gazette and Universal Daily Advertiser*.
    Callender's charges against H appeared in pamphlets numbered V and VI, which were part of a series of tracts that were subsequently published in book form under the title *The History of the United States for 1796; Including a Variety of Interesting Particulars Relative to the Federal Government Previous to That Period* (Philadelphia: Snowden and McCorkle, 1797). The preface to Callender's *History* is dated July 19, and the charges against H are in chapters VI and VII.
    It should perhaps also be pointed out that on January 19, 1797, Callender had published the *American Annual Register, or Historical Memoirs of the United States, for the Year 1796* (Philadelphia: Bioren and Madan). This earlier version of Callender's history does not include any references to the "Reynolds Affair."
    Callender's series of pamphlets present several problems which historians either have ignored or have been unable to solve. In the first place, no copies of these pamphlets have been found, and scholars who have written about the "Reynolds Affair" have without exception used Callender's *History*, rather than his pamphlets, as their source for Callender's charges against H. See, for example, Mitchell, *Hamilton*, II, 706, note 24; Boyd, *Papers of Thomas Jefferson*, XVIII, 631, note 62, 646; Harry Ammon, *James Monroe: The Quest for National Identity* (New York, 1971), 606, note 7; Nathan Schachner, *Alexander Hamilton* (New York, 1946), 369; Jonathan Daniels, *Ordeal of Ambition: Jefferson, Hamilton, Burr* (New York, 1970), 164; W. P. Cresson, *James Monroe* (Chapel Hill, 1946), 161.
    Because no copies of Callender's pamphlets have been found, it is impos-

Pamphlet," [2] in which he wrote: "The charge against me is a connection with one James Reynolds for purposes of improper pecuniary speculation. My real crime is an amorous connection with his wife [Maria], for a considerable time with his privity and connivance, if not originally brought on by a combination between the husband and wife with the design to extort money from me." According to Hamilton, Reynolds had blackmailed him throughout 1792 under the threat of making the affair public.[3]

---

sible to determine with certainty either the number of pamphlets in the series or the dates on which they were published. Mitchell states that "the tracts first appeared in eight weekly numbers" and that pamphlet "V came out June 26, VI, July 4" (Mitchell, *Hamilton*, II, 706, note 24). Mitchell's source for this information is Charles Evans, ed., *American Bibliography: A Chronological Dictionary of All Books, Pamphlets and Periodical Publications Printed in the United States from the Genesis of Printing in 1639 down to and Including the Year 1820* (Chicago, 1931), XI, 159. Evans, however, does not give dates for the publication of each pamphlet, and the evidence is clear that he never saw the pamphlets in question. Boyd, without giving a source, asserts that "No. V . . . appeared late in June, 1797" and No. VI on July 4 (*Papers of Thomas Jefferson*, XVIII, 646).

Pamphlet No. V can be dated by an advertisement in the [Philadelphia] *Aurora. General Advertiser,* June 24, 1797, which reads: "On Monday next [June 26] will be published . . . No. V, *of the History of the United States for 1796 &c.*" All that can be said with certainty concerning the publication date of pamphlet No. VI is that it appeared before July 7, for on that date Wolcott wrote to H: "I send you the residue of the pamph[l]et."

Finally, the confusion concerning Callender's pamphlets is compounded by the fact that the chapters in Callender's *History* were not divided in the same fashion as his pamphlets had been. On July 8, 1797, H wrote to James Monroe: "I request to be informed whether the paper numbered V [i.e., document No. V in Callender's *History* and not to be confused with Callender's pamphlet No. V mentioned above] dated Philadelphia the 15 of December 1792 published partly in the fifth and partly in the sixth number of 'The History of the United States for 1796' . . . is the copy of a genuine original." In Callender's *History* all of document No. V appears in chapter VI. Without the original pamphlets, it is impossible to determine if there are any other significant differences between the pamphlets and the *History.*

2. The "Reynolds Pamphlet" was published on August 25, 1797, under the title of *Observations on Certain Documents Contained in No. V & VI of "The History of the United States for the Year 1796," In Which the Charge of Speculation Against Alexander Hamilton, Late Secretary of the Treasury, is Fully Refuted. Written by Himself* (Philadelphia: Printed for John Fenno, by John Bioren, 1797).

There is also a draft of this pamphlet in the Hamilton Papers, Library of Congress. Both the draft and the printed version of this document are printed below under the date of August 25, 1797.

Immediately following the publication of the "Reynolds Pamphlet," Callender publicly challenged the authenticity of H's defense in *Sketches of the History of America* (Philadelphia: Snowden and McCorkle, 1798).

3. For information of this phase of the "Reynolds Affair," see James Reynolds to H, December 15, 17, 19, 22, 1791, January 3, 17, March 24, April 3, 7, 17, 23, May 2, June 3–22, 23, 24, August 24, November 13–15, December 12,

The pamphlets by Callender and Hamilton are more akin to trial briefs than factual reports, and at several critical points they present evidence that is flatly contradictory. Although it is possible in a general fashion to reconcile the major contentions of Callender and Hamilton (that is, that Hamilton was guilty of official misconduct and of having an affair with Maria Reynolds), most historians and biographers, including those hostile to the first Secretary of the Treasury, have accepted Hamilton's version of his involvement with the Reynoldses. Of those scholars who have more or less taken Hamilton at his word, Broadus Mitchell not only presents the most balanced summary of what he thinks happened but also acknowledges that there remain several key questions to which he has found no satisfactory answers. Recently, however, Julian P. Boyd in a lengthy essay concludes that Hamilton's account may well be a fabrication and that at the very least the Secretary of the Treasury knowingly permitted certain individuals to use inside information to speculate in Government securities.

Despite the fact that the role of both James and Maria Reynolds is central to any interpretation of Hamilton's lapses in official or personal morality, until recently surprisingly little has been known about the background of either of them. Some historians have accused Maria Reynolds of lying about her past, but she accurately described herself to Hamilton as the "daughter of a Mr. Lewis . . . [and] sister to a Mrs. G—— Livingston of the State of New York." [4] She was equally accurate in reporting to Jeremiah Wadsworth that she was the "sister of Col DuBois." [5] Born on March 30, 1768, she was the daughter of Susanna (or Susannah) Van Der Burgh and her second husband, Richard Lewis, both of whom were residents of Dutchess County, New York. Maria's sister, Susannah, married Gilbert Livingston, while her half-brother was Lewis DuBois, the son of Susanna (or Susannah) Van Der Burgh and her first husband, Elias DuBois. On July 28, 1783, Maria married James Reynolds, and on August 18, 1785, their daughter Susan was born.[6]

1792; H to James Reynolds, December 15, 1791, April 7, June 3–22, 24, 1792; Maria Reynolds to H, December 15, 1791, January 23–March 18 (three letters), March 24, June 2, 1792; H to Maria Reynolds, December 6, 1792; H to ——, December 18, 1791.

4. "Draft of the Reynolds Pamphlet," August 25, 1797. In the printed version of the "Reynolds Pamphlet," August 25, 1797, Maria Reynolds is identified as the "sister of Mr. G. Livingston," which is also correct as the word "sister" in the seventeen-nineties could also mean "sister-in-law."

5. Wadsworth to H, August 2, 1797. Lewis DuBois was a colonel in the Fifth New York Regiment during the American Revolution, and from 1787 to 1793 he was brigadier general of the Dutchess County militia. He was sheriff of Dutchess County from 1781 to 1785 and represented the county in the state Assembly in 1786 and 1787.

6. See "Lewis Family Bible," *Dutchess County Historical Society Year Book*, XXIX (1944), 93; J. Wilson Poucher, "Dutchess County Men of the Revolutionary Period: Colonel Lewis DuBois—Captain Henry DuBois," *Dutchess County Historical Society Year Book*, XX (1935), 71–85; Florence Van Rensselaer, ed., *The Livingston Family in America and Its Scottish Origins* (New York, 1949), 107. For information on the later life of Susan Reynolds,

Whatever else may be said about Maria Reynolds—and, of course, both contemporaries and historians have said a great deal about her—she had what in a more genteel age was called respectable family connections.

James Reynolds was the oldest child of David and Mary Reynolds of Orange County, New York.[7] Both the father and son appear to have been dedicated to the principle that public policy provided the greatest opportunity for private gain. Both, moreover, were singularly unsuccessful in their endeavors. During the American Revolution, David Reynolds, as an assistant commissary of purchases under Jeremiah Wadsworth, procured supplies for the army in Orange County.[8] But by 1780 "his credit [had] fail'd," and three years later he was in prison for "publick Debts." [9]

---

see the MS "Memoir of Peter A. Grotjan, written late in life" in the Historical Society of Pennsylvania, Philadelphia.

7. David and Mary Reynolds had six children: James, Joseph, Elizabeth, Henry, Reuben, and Sarah (Draft Deposition of William W. Thompson, March 27, 1802 [Chancery Papers, BM-474-R, Hall of Records, New York City]; Draft Deposition of Isaac Van Duzor, Jr., December 18, 1802 [Chancery Papers, BM-474-R, Hall of Records, New York City]). Thompson, who was a farmer in Goshen, Orange County, New York, had been sheriff of Orange County from 1781 to 1785. Van Duzor was a farmer in Cornwall, Orange County.

8. See Royal Flint, an assistant commissary of purchases, to David Reynolds, July 30, August 22, September 8, 1778 (LC, Connecticut Historical Society, Hartford); Reynolds to James Monell, an assistant commissary of purchases, August 28, 1779 (ALS, Connecticut Historical Society, Hartford); Reynolds to Wadsworth, June 19, November 7, 1779 (ALS, Connecticut Historical Society, Hartford); Reynolds to Wadsworth, July 19, 1780 (LS, Connecticut Historical Society, Hartford); Wadsworth to Reynolds, September 26, November 21, December 4, 1779 (LC, Connecticut Historical Society, Hartford); Affidavit of James Mathews, October 23, 1779 (DS, Connecticut Historical Society, Hartford); Reynolds to Flint, January 13, 1780 (LS, Connecticut Historical Society, Hartford).

9. David Reynolds to Wadsworth, April 7, 1783 (ALS, Connecticut Historical Society, Hartford). The MS Minutes of the New York Supreme Court for 1781, 1782, and 1783 contain numerous entries for suits involving Reynolds and his creditors (Hall of Records, New York City).

On April 4, 1786, the Continental Congress received the following memorial from David Reynolds: "That your Memorialist in the year 1777 was appointed one of the Commissary's of Purchases for the Continental Army.

"That your Memorialist continued in said office purchasing 'till 1779 & 1780 when his credit fail'd as Assist. Commy. of purchases in behalf of the United States arising from a want of Cash which renderd him unable to discharge the debts he had contracted with sundry persons who had lost their confidence in public credit.

"That your Memorialist humbly begs leave to inform that in consequence of the most pressing exigencies of the Troops and the repeated Assurances of receiving Cash (daily in expectation) sufficient to discharge the Amount of such Contracts for provisions &c as he unavoidable must procure; was induced to give his own private notes of hand for such supplies as there was no other means whereby they cou'd be obtain'd.

"That your Memorialist being disappointed in the arrival (or rect.) of Cash for discharging of said notes of hand, Suits were in consequence brought against him in the Supreme Court of said state, for said notes respectively.

"That your Memorialist employ'd an Attorney to defend the said Suits,

Like his father, James Reynolds worked in the Commissary Department, for on June 26, 1789, when he was attempting to secure an appointment as a "Tide or Land Waiter," he wrote that he had been "employed in

---

but as he had no real defence to make final Judgments were enter'd in the said suits, and thereupon Executions were Issued against all the real and personal estate of your memorialist which was shortly afterwards sold at public Vendue very much below its real value, and the neat proceeds of the said sale were wholly apply'd to satisfy the said Judgments.

"That your Memorialist further begs leave to inform that he has obtained a final settlement with the Commissioners upon which there is due him a sum sufficient (if realised) to enable him to redeem a part of the lands which was sold by Executions as aforesaid.

"That your Memorialist has produced the most satisfactory voucher upon settlement to the Commissioners to shew that the Articles (for which his lands and tenements were sold by Execution) was deliver'd for the use of the Army.

"That your Memorialist by the sale of his real and personal Estate as aforesaid finds himself with a Wife and numerous family of Children reduced to the greatest distress and indigence." (DS, Papers of the Continental Congress, National Archives; JCC, XXX, 151, note 1.) The memorial was referred to the Board of Treasury, which on May 10, 1787, reported that Reynolds's memorial "cannot be complied with" (JCC, XXX, 250). For the subsequent efforts of Jacob Cuyler, deputy commissary general of purchases during the American Revolution, "to be relieved from a demand brought against him by David Reynolds . . . for one hundred and fourteen head of Cattle said to have been delivered by said Reynolds for the use of the Army and not charged in his accounts against the United States," see JCC, XXXI, 736–37; XXXIV, 526.

In 1796 H was retained by one of the Cunninghams (Abner, Obadiah, Andrew, or Charles) in a suit initiated by Reuben Reynolds, James Reynolds's brother. Reuben wished to regain possession of a tract of land in Cornwall which his deceased father had mortgaged in 1776 for a debt to Sheffield Howard (Bill, filed February 7, 1801 [Chancery Papers, BM-452-R, Hall of Records, New York City]). In 1783 David Currie, as the New York representative of the Connecticut mercantile firm of Barnabas Deane and Jeremiah Wadsworth, successfully brought suits against David and James Reynolds for nonpayment of debts (Judgment Roll, filed February 14, 1783 [Parchment 95-A-1, Hall of Records, New York City]; Judgment Roll, filed September 15, 1783 [Parchment 94-K-5, Hall of Records, New York City]; Judgment Roll, September 15, 1783 [Parchment 105-E-3, Hall of Records, New York City]). On May 20, 1796, Wadsworth, as the sole surviving partner of the firm of Deane and Wadsworth, transferred to Reuben Reynolds the balance due on these debts, and Margaret Currie, David Currie's widow, then "transferred . . . to the said Reuben all and singular the Monies Still due on the aforesaid Judgments" (Bill, filed February 7, 1801 [Chancery Papers, BM-452-R, Hall of Records, New York City]). After Margaret Currie revived the two suits against David and James Reynolds (Judgment, February 28, 1797 [Parchment 94-E-4, Hall of Records, New York City]), Reuben "caused a Certain Writ of Fieri Facias to be issued upon the said Judgment directed to the Sheriff of the County of Orange, for the purpose of levying on and selling the Lands and Tenements of the said David Reynolds and Whereof he died seized, for the purpose of Satisfying the said Judgment" (Bill, filed February 7, 1801 [Chancery Papers, BM-452-R, Hall of Records, New York City]). In the meantime, Samuel Sands had bought the land in Cornwall from the legal representatives of the now deceased Sheffield Howard, and Sands sold the land to Abner Cunningham in 1792. The Cunninghams conveyed the land in 1795 to George

the Service of the United States in the late War with his Sloop in the
North River upwards of two years, that he afterwards was employ'd in
the Commissarys Department to the close of the war, which duty he
discharged to the entire approbation of his employers." [10]

Brown, who, in turn, conveyed it to Isaac Tobias in 1799 (Answer, filed May
14, 1801 [Chancery Papers, BM-452-R, Hall of Records, New York City]). In
connection with this case, H made the following entries in his Law Register,
1795–1804:

"James Reynolds �️ Scire Facias
  Adsm | [Nicholas] Evertson for Plaintiff
Margaret Currie } Retained by one
Administratrix of | Cunningham
David Currie   ⎦ 15 Ds

November 3 Notice of appearance
  Abner Cunningham ⎫
  Obadiah Cunningham |
  Andrew Cunningham | Same parties
  Charles Cunningham ⎬ as above
    Adsm |
  George Brown" ⎭

(AD, partially in H's handwriting, New York Law Institute, New York City).
See also "Narrative of Margaret Currie, Administratrix of David Currie vs.
George Brown," October 29, 1796 (DS, Hamilton Papers, Library of Con-
gress).

In 1801 the suit was taken to the New York Court of Chancery as *Reuben
Reynolds* v *Isaac Tobias,* and H entered in his Law Register, 1795–1804:

"Tobias ⎫ of Counsel
 Adsm ⎬ with [Samuel] Jones
Reynolds ⎭ in Chancery

retainer 35 Ds" (AD, partially in H's handwriting, New York Law Institute,
New York City).

The editors are indebted to Miss Betty J. Thomas, associate editor of *The
Law Practice of Alexander Hamilton,* for the above information.

On January 20, 1842, the following entry appears in the *Journal of the House:*
"Mr. [James G.] Clinton presented a memorial of David Reynolds, late assistant commissary of purchases for the United States army, setting forth that
he did, during the revolutionary war, furnish supplies to the army of the United
States, for which he has never received any compensation; and that he was subsequently arrested by each of the persons of whom he purchased such supplies,
and judgment obtained against him, almost to his total ruin. He now prays relief in the premises." This memorial was referred to the Committee on Revolutionary Claims (*Journal of the House,* 27th Cong., 2nd Sess. [Washington,
1841], 236–37). On May 29, 1844, Joseph Vance of Ohio presented "a petition
of the heirs of David Reynolds, deceased, of the State of New York, an officer
in the war of the Revolution, for the payment of their claim for his services."
This petition was also referred to the Committee on Revolutionary Claims
(*Journal of the House,* 28th Cong., 1st Sess. [Washington, 1844], 983).

10. Copy, RG 59, Miscellaneous Letters, January 1–December 29, 1789, National Archives. The petition included a postscript in William Malcom's handwriting which reads: "We are well acquainted with the petitioner and recommend him as an honest industrious man, well Qualifyed for the office which
he Sollicits." This testimonial is signed by Malcom, Hendrick Wyckoff, and

In 1790 James Reynolds turned to speculation, for in that year he was hired by William J. Vredenburgh, a New York City merchant, as an agent to buy up the claims to arrears of pay from soldiers and officers in Virginia and North Carolina. In the same year Theodorick Bland of Virginia introduced in the House of Representatives a series of resolutions that were designed to protect the interests of the veterans.[11] Following the adoption of these resolutions, Hamilton made an unsuccessful effort to have them vetoed by George Washington.[12] Hamilton's opposition to these resolutions, which stands in marked contrast to the support given them by Thomas Jefferson, lends credence to the charge that the Secretary of the Treasury supplied speculators with the names of veterans and the amounts of the arrearages to which each veteran was entitled.[13]

Reynolds's difficulties with the United States Government—difficulties that would eventually land him in jail—arose not from his activities in Virginia and North Carolina but from an entirely different speculative venture. On November 16, 1792, Oliver Wolcott, Jr., who was then comptroller of the Treasury, initiated two suits against Reynolds and Jacob Clingman, who had been the clerk of Frederick A. C. Muhlenberg, a Pennsylvania Republican and Speaker of the House of Representatives in the First Congress. Reynolds and Clingman were charged with subornation of perjury and attempting to defraud the United States Government. Specifically they were accused of persuading John Delabar to commit perjury so that they could pose as the executors of the estate of Ephraim Goodenough of Massachusetts, an allegedly deceased soldier, who was a claimant against the United States.[14] On November 13, 1792—

John Blagge, New York City merchants; Robert Troup, a New York City attorney and close friend of H; and Robert Boyd, the sheriff of New York City and County.

Boyd reads Malcom's name as "Alwen" (*Papers of Thomas Jefferson*, XVIII, 627, note 53).

11. *Journal of the House*, I, 217–18. For these resolutions, see H to Washington, May 28, 1790, note 2.

12. See H to Washington, May 28, 1790.

13. For a detailed analysis of this controversy, see Boyd, *Papers of Thomas Jefferson*, XVI, 455–70; XVIII, 211–25. Boyd also states that in the Glaubeck affair H failed to understand "the impropriety of acting officially for friends . . ." (*Papers of Thomas Jefferson*, XVIII, 686–87, note 203). For information on Baron de Glaubeck and Andrew G. Fraunces, see the introductory note to Fraunces to H, May 16, 1793.

14. *Commonwealth* v *James Reynolds and Jacob Clingman*. Reynolds and Clingman were "Charged with having Employed, Aided and abbetted a certain John Delabar to defraud the United States of a Sum of money value near Four hundred Dollars, and having Suborned the said Delabar to commit a wilful and corrupt Perjury before George Campbell Esq register for the probate of wills and Granting Letters of Administration &Ca." (Mayor's Court Docket, 1792–1796, 71, Philadelphia City Archives; Inspectors of the County Prison, Prisoners for Trial Docket, 1790–1797, 113, Philadelphia City Archives). On November 16, 1792, Clingman was released on bail (Inspectors of the County Prison, Prisoners for Trial Docket, 1790–1797, 113, Philadelphia City Archives).

or three days before the Government's suit against Reynolds and Clingman—Wolcott had initiated proceedings against Delabar for perjury and
fraud.[15]

Clingman secured his release on bail on the same day on which he had
been arrested, but both Reynolds and Delabar went to jail in Philadelphia. During his imprisonment Reynolds "threatened to make disclosures
injurious to the character of some head of a Department." [16] Hamilton
then advised Wolcott "to take no step towards a liberation of Reynolds,
while such a report existed and remained unexplained." [17] Shortly after
Reynolds's imprisonment, Maria Reynolds appealed to Governor Thomas
Mifflin of Pennsylvania for assistance in securing her husband's release.
At the direction of Mifflin, Alexander J. Dallas, secretary of the Commonwealth of Pennsylvania, on December 12, 1792, wrote to Jared
Ingersoll, attorney general of Pennsylvania, "that in the case of Clingman
and Reynolds the Governor leaves it entirely in his [Ingersoll's] discretion to enter a Nolle Prosequi should the secretary of the treasury concur in thinking it proper." [18] Hamilton apparently concurred. In any
event, on the same day on which Dallas wrote to Ingersoll, the suits
against Reynolds and Clingman were dismissed.[19] In return for a promise by Wolcott to drop the prosecution against them, Reynolds and
Clingman turned over to him a list of the creditors of the United States
which they had obtained from the Treasury Department. In describing
these negotiations almost five years after they had taken place, Wolcott

15. *Commonwealth* v *John Delabar*. Delabar was "Charged with having been
Guilty of willful and Corrupt Perjury, and having defrauded the United States
of a Sum of Money of near Four Hundred Dollars" (Mayor's Court Docket,
1792–1796, 71, Philadelphia City Archives; Inspectors of the County Prison,
Prisoners for Trial Docket, 1790–1797, 113, Philadelphia City Archives).

Delabar's trial, which was originally set for December 17, 1792, was resched-
uled for the next session of the Mayor's Court (Inspectors of the County Prison,
Prisoners for Trial Docket, 1790–1797, 113, Philadelphia City Archives). On
November 19, Wolcott wrote to Samuel Emery, Goodenough's agent, "to take
measures for producing the said Goodenough and some person to whom he is
known" (copy, Connecticut Historical Society, Hartford). On March 7, 1793,
Levi Holden received payment "for his and Ephraim Goodenough's expences
coming from Boston to Philadelphia, at the request of the Comptroller of the
Treasury as witnesses in a suit instituted by the United States against Delabar
and returning" (RG 217, Miscellaneous Treasury Accounts, 1790–1894, Account
No. 3946, National Archives). Although the suits against Reynolds and Clingman were dismissed on December 12, 1792, Reynolds was "to be sent to the
Debtors Jail when discharged from this Suit 13/0 pd.," and Delabar remained
in prison until April 1, 1793 (Inspectors of the County Prison, Prisoners for
Trial Docket, 1790–1797, 113, Philadelphia City Archives).

16. See Wolcott's deposition, July 12, 1797, which is document No. XXIV in
the appendix to the printed version of the "Reynolds Pamphlet," August 25,
1797.

17. See Wolcott's deposition, July 12, 1797, which is document No. XXIV in
the appendix to the printed version of the "Reynolds Pamphlet," August 25,
1797.

18. *Pennsylvania Archives*, 9th Sess., I (n.p., 1931), 491.

19. Inspectors of the County Prison, Prisoners for Trial Docket, 1790–1797,
113, Philadelphia City Archives.

wrote that Clingman and Reynolds agreed "to surrender the lists, to restore the balance which had been fraudulently obtained, and to reveal the name of the person, by whom they had been furnished." Wolcott then informed Ingersoll "that an important discovery had been made, and the condition by which it could be rendered useful to the public in preventing future frauds; in consequence of which, the prosecutions against Clingman and Reynolds were dismissed." [20]

Among the many unanswered questions concerning the "Reynolds Affair" is the identity of the individual who made the list of creditors available to Reynolds and Clingman. Reynolds insisted that William Duer, who had been Assistant Secretary of the Treasury from September, 1789, to the spring of the following year, was the culprit.[21] But Wolcott, again writing some years after the event, stated: ". . . nothing occurred at any time to my knowledge, which could give colour to a suspicion, that Mr. Duer, was in any manner directly or indirectly concerned with or privy to the transaction. The infidelity was committed by a clerk in the office of the Register. Mr. Duer resigned his office in March, 1790 while the Treasury was at New-York—the Clerk who furnished the lists was first employed in Philadelphia in January 1791. The Accounts from which the lists were taken, were all settled at the Treasury subsequent to the time last mentioned; on the discovery above stated the Clerk was dismissed, and has not since been employed in the public offices." [22] Wolcott refused to divulge the name of the clerk, but Callender suspected that the lists had been furnished by Andrew G. Fraunces, who had been dismissed from the Treasury Department in March, 1793.[23] Recently Boyd has argued—and argued convincingly—that the dismissed clerk was Simeon Reynolds, "who was almost certainly a kinsman of James Reynolds" and who worked in 1791 and 1792 in the office of Joseph Nourse, the register of the Treasury.[24]

In the interval between his arrest and the dismissal of his case, Clingman turned to Muhlenberg, as a friend and former employee, for assist-

20. See Wolcott's deposition, July 12, 1797, which is document No. XXIV in the appendix to the printed version of the "Reynolds Pamphlet," August 25, 1797. See also Reynolds to H, November 13–15, 1792.

21. See "Reynolds Pamphlet," August 25, 1797; Callender, *History*, 213, 216, 218.

Duer, a prominent New York City businessman and speculator, was a director of the Society for Establishing Useful Manufactures from its inception in 1791 until the collapse of his financial affairs in 1792. On March 23, 1792, Duer was imprisoned for debt, and except for a brief period in 1797, he remained in prison until his death on May 7, 1799.

Although Duer may have supplied Vredenburgh with lists of arrears of pay due to soldiers and officers in Virginia and North Carolina in 1790, the clerk who supplied Reynolds and Clingman with the lists of creditors of the United States was probably Simeon Reynolds. See note 24.

22. Wolcott's deposition, July 12, 1797, which is document No. XXIV in the appendix to the printed version of the "Reynolds Pamphlet," August 25, 1797.

23. Callender, *Sketches*, 101.

24. *Papers of Thomas Jefferson*, XVIII, 656–57. Simeon Reynolds was a clerk in the office of Joseph Nourse, the register of the Treasury, from January 1, 1791, to December 17, 1792 (RG 217, Miscellaneous Treasury Accounts, 1790–1894, Account Nos. 1129, 3420, National Archives).

ance. According to Muhlenberg, "Clingman, unasked, frequently dropped hints to me, that Reynolds had it in his power, very materially to injure the secretary of the treasury, and that Reynolds knew several very improper transactions of his." [25] On December 12, 1792, Muhlenberg shared his suspicions about Hamilton's conduct with two Virginians, Senator James Monroe and Representative Abraham B. Venable.[26] Monroe and Venable immediately visited Reynolds in prison, where he repeated the accusations against Hamilton. Monroe and Venable agreed to meet Reynolds again on the morning of December 13, but at that time they were told that "he had absconded, or concealed himself." [27] On the evening of December 12, 1792, in a meeting with Monroe and Muhlenberg, Mrs. Reynolds corroborated her husband's story. According to the account of this meeting made by Monroe and Muhlenberg, Mrs. Reynolds "also mentioned, that Mr. Clingman had several anonymous notes addressed to her husband, which, she believed, were from Mr. Hamilton (which we have) with an endorsement 'from secretary Hamilton, Esq.' in Mr. Reynolds's hand writing. . . ." [28]

On December 15, 1792 (three days after the cases against Reynolds and Clingman had been dismissed), Muhlenberg, Monroe, and Venable called on Hamilton and, in Hamilton's words, explained that "information had been given them of an improper pecuniary connection between Mr. Reynolds and myself; that they had thought it their duty to pursue it and had become possessed of some documents of a suspicious complexion—that they had contemplated the laying the matter before the President,[29] but before they did this, they thought it right to apprise

25. See Muhlenberg's statement of December 13, 1792, which is document No. I (a) in the appendix to the printed version of the "Reynolds Pamphlet," August 25, 1797.

26. See Muhlenberg's statement of December 13, 1792, which is document No. I (a) in the appendix to the printed version of the "Reynolds Pamphlet," August 25, 1797.

27. For an account of this meeting, see the statement by Monroe and Venable, dated December 13, 1792, which is document No. II (a) in the appendix to the printed version of the "Reynolds Pamphlet," August 25, 1797.

28. See the statement by Monroe and Muhlenberg, dated December 13, 1792, which is document No. III (a) in the appendix to the printed version of the "Reynolds Pamphlet," August 25, 1797. See also Clingman's statement of December 13, 1792, which is document No. IV (a) in the appendix to the printed version of the "Reynolds Pamphlet," August 25, 1797.

29. Muhlenberg, Monroe, and Venable prepared the following letter to George Washington, dated December 13, 1792: "We think proper to lay before you, some documents respecting the conduct of Colo. Hamilton, in the Office of Secretary of the Treasury. The inclosed will explain to you the particulars, and likewise how they came to our knowledge. They appeared to us to be of such importance, as to merit our attention, and in further pursuit of the object, that the proper course was, to submit the whole to your inspection.

"What we have stated of our own knowledge, we are willing to depose on oath. We think proper, however, to observe, that we do not consider ourselves, as prosecutors, but as only communicating, for his information, to the Chief Magistrate, intelligence, it highly imports him to know. We were, however, unwilling to take this step without communicating it to the Gentleman, whom it

me of the affair and to afford an opportunity of explanation. . . ." After Muhlenberg, Monroe, and Venable had shown Hamilton the documents in their possession, the four men agreed to meet again that evening at Hamilton's house.[30] At the evening meeting, which Wolcott attended at Hamilton's request,[31] Hamilton defended himself by stating that he had had an affair with Maria Reynolds and had paid blackmail to her husband. As evidence, he presented several letters and receipts, which he subsequently published in the appendix to the "Reynolds Pamphlet." Hamilton requested and was granted permission to make copies of the incriminating documents which Muhlenberg, Monroe, and Venable had shown him earlier in the day.[32] Monroe retained the originals.[33]

At the conclusion of his meeting with Muhlenberg, Monroe, and Venable on the evening of December 15, 1792, Hamilton had reason to be-

---

concerns, that he might make the explanation, he has it in his power to give; we, therefore, informed Mr. Hamilton of the step we now take.

"You will readily perceive, that light might have been thrown on this subject, by the several public officers, who have had any part in the transactions of the prosecution and enlargement of Reynolds. But as we apprehended, an application to these parties might contribute to make the subject public, which, in tenderness to the person interested, we wished to avoid, on that account, we declined it." (Copy, The Library, Lehigh University, Bethlehem, Pennsylvania.) No evidence has been found that this letter was ever sent to Washington.

30. "Reynolds Pamphlet," August 25, 1797.

31. Clingman stated that at a meeting with H and Wolcott on December 14 "he was strictly examined by both, respecting the persons, who were enquiring into the matter, and their object; that he told Mr. Hamilton, he had been possessed of his notes to Reynolds, and had given them up to these gentlemen . . ." (Clingman's statement, December 15, 1792 [copy, The Library, Lehigh University, Bethlehem, Pennsylvania]). H, however, wrote that after his first interview with Muhlenberg, Monroe, and Venable on December 15, 1792, he met with Wolcott "and for the first time informed him of the affair and of the interview just had; and delivering into his hands for perusal ,the documents of which I was possessed, I engaged him to be present at the intended explanation in the evening" ("Reynolds Pamphlet," August 25, 1797).

Unless H meant that December 15 was the first time he informed Wolcott of his relationship with Maria Reynolds, his statement cannot be reconciled with Clingman's.

32. The "incriminating documents" were H to James Reynolds, April 7, June 3–22, 24, 1792; Reynolds to Clingman, December 13, 1792; Wolcott to Clingman, December 13, 1792; and two undated letters (Callender, History, 218–23). The first undated letter, which is from H to James Reynolds, reads: "My dear Sir, I expected to have heard the day after I had the pleasure of seeing you" ("Reynolds Pamphlet," August 25, 1797). The second undated letter, which is from H to Maria Reynolds, reads: "That person Mr. Reynolds inquired for on Friday waited for him all the evening at his house from a little after seven. Mr. R. may see him at any time to-day or to-morrow between the hours of two and three" ("Reynolds Pamphlet," August 25, 1797). H also received copies of the four depositions which form documents 1 (a)–IV (a) in the appendix to the printed version of the "Reynolds Pamphlet," August 25, 1797 (Callender, History, 209–18).

33. See H to Muhlenberg, Monroe, and Venable, December 17, 1792; Muhlenberg to H, December 18, 1792; Monroe to H, December 20, 1792.

lieve that he had convinced them that their suspicions concerning his public conduct were groundless.[34] He also thought that they had agreed not to reveal either their original charges against him or his own account of his less than exemplary behavior as a husband. On the other hand, it is difficult to imagine that he could have seriously thought that his secret —whatever it was—could have been kept indefinitely. Certainly Hamilton's friends and enemies suspected, if they did not know, that he had been charged with official misconduct. On May 6, 1793, Henry Lee wrote to Hamilton from Richmond, Virginia: "Was I with you I would talk an hour with doors bolted & windows shut, as my heart is much afflicted by some whispers which I have heard." Far more explicit—and from Hamilton's point of view, far more threatening—than whispers was a letter "From a Correspondent," which was printed in the [Philadelphia] *Aurora. General Advertiser*, October 23, 1795. The "Correspondent" wrote: "Quere—Whether a certain head of a department was not in the month of December 1792, privy and party in the circumstances of a certain enquiry of a very suspicious aspect, respecting real mal-conduct on the part of his friend, patron and predecessor in office, which ought to make him extremely circumspect on the subject of investigation and enquiry into supposed guilt?

"Would a publication of the circumstances of that transaction redound to the honor or reputation of the parties, and why has the subject been so long and carefully smothered up?"

The rumors concerning Hamilton became public knowledge in June and July of 1797, when Callender revived and published James Reynolds's earlier charges against Hamilton.[35] Stating that Federalist criticism of Monroe's ministry to France had motivated his publication, Callender wrote: "Attacks on Mr. Monroe have been frequently repeated from the stock-holding presses. They are cowardly, because he is absent. They are unjust, because his conduct will bear the strictest enquiry. They are ungrateful, because he displayed, on an occasion that will be mentioned immediately, the greatest lenity to Mr. Alexander Hamilton, the prime mover of the federal party." [36] In chapter VI Callender hinted that Hamilton's relationship with the Reynoldses involved more than a "volunteer acknowledgement of seduction" and implied that the Secretary of the Treasury had speculated in public funds.[37] In chapter VII Callender charged that Hamilton, fearful of the disclosures which James and Maria Reynolds might have made, had "packed them off." [38] In the same chapter Callender stated that if Reynolds "was *one* agent for the purchase of certificates, it may well be conceived, though it cannot *yet* be proved, that our secretary had twenty others. . . ." [39] In both chapters Callender included documents to support his accusations against

34. "Reynolds Pamphlet," August 25, 1797. See also Wolcott's deposition, July 12, 1797, which is document No. XXIV in the appendix to the printed version of the "Reynolds Pamphlet," August 25, 1797.
35. For Callender's publications, see note 1.
36. Callender, *History*, 204–05.
37. Callender, *History*, 206.
38. Callender, *History*, 228.
39. Callender, *History*, 231.

Hamilton.[40] In a letter dated July 6, 1797, to John Fenno, which was printed in Fenno's *Gazette of the United States, and Philadelphia Daily Advertiser* on July 8, 1797, Hamilton denied the accusations made by Callender in pamphlet "No. V."

Like almost every other aspect of the "Reynolds Affair," the authorship of Callender's public charges against Hamilton was—and remains—a subject of controversy. Theodore Sedgwick was certain that the author was John Beckley of Virginia, clerk of the House of Representatives and the individual usually given major credit for organizing the Republican party in Pennsylvania, and on June 24, 1797, he wrote to Rufus King: "The House of Representatives did not re-elect Mr. Beckley as their Clerk. This was resented not only by himself but the whole party, and they were rendered furious by it. To revenge, Beckley has been writing a pamphlet mentioned in the enclosed advertisement. The 'authentic papers' there mentioned are those of which you perfectly know the history, formerly in the possession of Messrs. Monroe, Muhlenberg & Venable. The conduct is mean, base and infamous. It may destroy the peace of a respectable family, and so gratify the diabolical malice of a detestable faction, but I trust it cannot produce the intended effect of injuring the cause of government." [41] But in the preface to his *History*, Callender wrote: "A report has been circulated, that Mr. John Beckley is the author of this volume. He did not frame a single sentence of it. He is unacquainted with my hand writing, and I could not be sure to distinguish his." [42] This disclaimer does not, however, preclude the possibility that Beckley had supplied Callender with copies of the James Reynolds correspondence, and Monroe, for one, thought that Beckley had done just that. On December 1, 1797, Monroe wrote to Aaron Burr: "You know I presume that Beckley published the papers in question. By his clerk they were copied for us. It was his clerk who carried a copy to H. who asked (as B. says) whether others were privy to the affr. The clerk replied that B. was, upon wh. H. desired him to tell B. he considered him bound not to disclose it. B. replied by the same clerk that he considered himself under no injunction whatever—that if H. had any thing to say to him it must be in writing. This from B.—most certain however it is that after our interviews with H. I requested B. to say nothing abt. it & keep it secret—& most certain it is that I never heard of it afterwards till my arrival when it was published. This if necessary will be declared by all.

"It was also intended by Muhlenberg & Venable to take copies, & copies were by them requested of B. If they omitted taking them it was their fault. This however is not material. I mention it for yr. own information." [43]

40. Callender printed all the documents cited in notes 32, 50, and 51. He also printed H to Monroe, Muhlenberg, and Venable, December [17], 1792 (Callender, *History*, 209–24).

41. King, *The Life and Correspondence of Rufus King*, II, 193.

42. Callender, *History*, viii.

43. ADfS, Historical Society of Pennsylvania, Philadelphia; ADf, Lloyd W. Smith Collection, Morristown National Historical Park, Morristown, New Jersey. The unsigned draft does not include the postscript quoted above.

Both Venable and Muhlenberg insisted that they had never made copies of any documents used by Callender and that they therefore could not have given these materials to him.[44] On July 11, 1797, Monroe stated that after the meeting on the evening of December 15, 1792, he had "sealed up his copy of the papers mentioned and sent or delivered them to his Friend in Virginia. . . ."[45] Then on July 17 Monroe and Muhlenberg informed Hamilton that the original papers were placed "in the hands of a respectable character in Virga. soon after the transaction took place," and on July 21 Monroe wrote to Hamilton that he "deposited the papers with a friend when I left my country, in whose hands they still are." Richard Hildreth, in *The History of the United States of America*, suggests that this "respectable character" was Thomas Jefferson,[46] and W. P. Cresson, in his biography of Monroe, states that Monroe's "friend" was "almost certainly Jefferson."[47] This view is supported by Callender's assertion in 1798 that "Mr. Jefferson had received a copy of these documents," but Callender also insisted that Jefferson "never shewed them, nor ever spoke of them, to any person."[48] Jefferson did indeed know of the charges against Hamilton, for on December 17, 1792 (which was two days after Hamilton's two meetings with Monroe, Muhlenberg, and Venable), Jefferson wrote the following memorandum: "The affair of Reynolds and his wife.—Clingham Muhlenb's clerk, testifies to F. A. Muhl. Monroe Venable.—also Wolcott at (and?) Wadsworth. Known to J(ames) M(adison). E(dmund) R(andolph). (John) Beckley and (Bernard) Webb.

"Reynolds was speculating agent in the speculations of Govt. arrearages. He was furnished by Duer with a list of the claims of arreages due to the Virga. and Carola. lines and brought them up, against which the Resolutions of Congress of June 4. 1790. were levelled. Hamilton advised the President to give his negative to those resolutions."[49]

44. On July 9, 1797, Venable wrote to H: "I had nothing to do with the transaction since the interview with you, I do not possess a copy of the papers at present, nor have I at any time had the possession of any of them, I avoided taking a copy because I feared that the greatest care which I could exercise in keeping them safely might be defeated by some accident and that some person or other might improperly obtain an inspection of them." The next day, Muhlenberg wrote to H in a similar fashion: ". . . I lament the publication of the papers respecting the Affair of Reynolds (of which I hope I need not assure you that I had neither Knowledge or Agency, for I never saw them since the Affair took place, nor was I ever furnished with a copy). . . ."

45. See "David Gelston's Account of an Interview between Alexander Hamilton and James Monroe," July 11, 1797.

46. Richard Hildreth, *The History of the United States of America* (Reprinted: New York, 1969), V, 111.

47. W. P. Cresson, *James Monroe* (Chapel Hill, 1946), 162.

48. Callender, *Sketches*, 102.

49. Boyd, *Papers of Thomas Jefferson*, XVIII, 649, and note 104.

After Jefferson became President, he told William A. Burwell, his private secretary, that "the affair [between Jefferson and Betsey Moore Walker] had long been known, & that Hamilton about the time he was attackd for his con-

Far more important to Hamilton than the way in which Callender had obtained the material for his pamphlets was the need to convince Monroe, Muhlenberg, and Venable that they should state publicly that they had believed—and that they still believed—the story which he had told them on the evening of December 15, 1792. On July 5, 1797, he accordingly wrote to Monroe and asked him for "a declaration equivalent to that which was made to me at the time in the presence of Mr. Wolcott by yourself and the two other Gentlemen." To refresh Monroe's memory, he enclosed a document which he described as a "copy of a memorandum of the substance of your declaration made by me the morning after our Interview." According to this document, Monroe, Muhlenberg, and Venable "regretted the trouble and uneasiness which they had occassionned to me in consequence of the Representations made to them . . . they were perfectly satisfied with the explanation I had given and . . . there was nothing in the transaction which ought to affect my character as a public Officer or lessen the public Confidence in my Integrity."

When Hamilton wrote to Monroe, he had not seen Callender's second pamphlet. He therefore did not know that it included a memorandum by Monroe, Muhlenberg, and Venable, dated December 16, 1792, which stated: ". . . We left him [on the evening of December 15, 1792] under an impression our suspicions were removed." [50] Nor did he know that the same pamphlet contained a note by Monroe recounting a meeting he had had with Clingman on January 2, 1793. According to Monroe's account of this meeting, "Mr. Clingman called on me this evening and

niction with Mrs. Reynolds had threatend him—with a public disclosure" (MS Memoir of William A. Burwell, Library of Congress).

50. D, in Monroe's handwriting, The Library, Lehigh University, Bethlehem, Pennsylvania. See also James Reynolds to H, November 13–15, 1792, note 1.

The memorandum of December 16 reads in full: "16th. Last night we waited on Colo. H when he informed us of a particular connection with Mrs. R—— the period of its commencement & circumstances attending it, his visiting her at Inskeep's—the frequent supplies of money to her & her husband on that acct.—his duress by them from the fear of a disclosure & his anxiety to be relieved from it and them. To support this, he shewed a great number of letters from Reynolds & herself—commencing early in 1791. He acknowledged all the letters in a disguised hand, in our possession, to be his. We left him under an impression our suspicions were removed. He acknowledged our conduct toward him had been fair & liberal—he could not complain of it. We brot. back all the papers even his own notes, nor did he ask their destruction.

"He said, the dismission of the prosecution agnst. the parties Reynolds & Mr. Clingman had been in consideration of the surrender of a list of pay improperly obtaind from his office, and by means of a person who had it not in his power now to injure the department—intimating he meant Mr. Duer—That he obtained this information from Reynolds.

"Owned that he had recd a note from Reynolds in the night at the time stated in Mr Clingmans paper, & that he had likewise seen him in the morning following.

"Sd. he never had seen Reynolds before he came to this place—& that the statement in Mr. Clingman's paper, in that respect, was correct."

mentioned that he had been apprized of Mr Hamilton's vindication by
Mr. Wolcott the day or two after our interview with him. He further
observed to me that he communicated the same to Mrs. Reynolds, who
appeared much shocked at it & wept immoderately. That she denied the
Imputation & declared that it had been a fabrication of Colonel Hamilton
and that her Husband had joined in it, who had told her so, & that he had
given him rects. for Money & written letters, so as to give countenance to
the pretence—that he was with Colo. H. the day after he left the jail when
we supposed he was in Jersey. He was of opinion she was innocent and
that the defense was an imposition." [51]

The publication of Monroe's version of his conversation with Clingman made it more imperative than ever for Hamilton to secure from
Monroe a clear-cut avowal of the Virginian's belief in the explanation
which Hamilton had given on the evening of December 15, 1792. With
this in mind Hamilton arranged a meeting with Monroe, and on July 11,
1797, he and John Barker Church called on Monroe, who was visiting
relatives in New York.[52] David Gelston, a New York City merchant and
Republican politician, was also present, and his detailed account of the
proceedings makes it clear how unsatisfactory the conference was to
Hamilton.[53] Monroe's estimate of the interview was much the same, for
on July 12 he wrote to Jefferson: ". . . *Here* I have had an interview
with the friend of Mr. & Mrs R. each of us having a friend present &
wh. furnished no result, the business being adjourned over to Phila.
where we meet the day after my return, there in compy. with the other
gentn. Muhg. & Venable. The details of this interview are reserved till
I see you. You may have some idea of them however when you recollect the previous good disposition of some of the parties for each other.

---

51. AD, The Library, Lehigh University, Bethlehem, Pennsylvania. This
manuscript is the third part of a document which Callender printed in full as
document No. V in his *History*. The first part was the statement of December
15, 1792, which Clingman made to Muhlenberg, Monroe, and Venable and
which is in the handwriting of Beckley's clerk, Bernard Webb. The second
is the document cited in note 50. In discussing these documents, Boyd wrote:
". . . It is important to note that Callender's text appended the names of the
three Congressmen to the second part and that of Monroe alone to the third
part, a clerical insertion that almost led to a duel because it gave Hamilton
the opportunity to focus his attack on Monroe. *There are neither signatures
nor initials appended to any part of the original manuscript of No. 5.* Hamilton may have been shown the first part of No. 5 in 1792, but he did not
see the second and third parts until Callender published them in 1797" (*Papers of Thomas Jefferson*, XVIII, 631, note 62). Monroe, however, clearly
states in part two that "Last night we waited on Colo. H," while in part three
he wrote: "Mr. Clingman called on me this evening." Clingman's meeting of
January 2, 1793, was clearly with Monroe alone.

52. Monroe, who had been United States Minister Plenipotentiary to France,
had been recalled on August 22, 1796 (Timothy Pickering to Monroe, August
22, 1796 [copy, Massachusetts Historical Society, Boston]). He arrived in Philadelphia on June 27, 1797.

53. See "David Gelston's Account of an Interview between Alexander Hamilton and James Monroe," July 11, 1797.

The issue is quite uncertain as to the mode of adjusting what is personal in the business."[54]

Following the July 11 meeting, Hamilton began what proved to be a protracted correspondence with Monroe, who repeatedly refused to make the kind of categorical statement that Hamilton demanded. On July 22, 1797, in a letter that was tantamount to a challenge, Hamilton wrote to Monroe: "On the contrary by the affected reference of the matter to a defence which I am to make, and by which you profess your opinion is to be decided—you imply that your suspicions are still alive. And as nothing appears to have shaken your original conviction but the wretched tale of Clingman, which you have thought fit to record it follows that you are pleased to attach a degree of weight to that communication which cannot be accounted for on any fair principle. The result in my mind is that you have been and are actuated by motives towards me malignant and dishonorable; nor can I doubt that this will be the universal opinion when the publication of the whole affair which I am about to make shall be seen." On July 31, 1797, Monroe accepted Hamilton's challenge in a letter in which he wrote: "I have always stated to you that I had no wish to do you a personal injury. The several explanations wh. I have made accorded with truth & my ideas of propriety. Therefore I need not repeat them. If these do not yield you satisfaction I can give no other unless called on in a way which always for the illustration of truth, I wish to avoid, but which I am ever ready to meet." The duel, however, was averted on August 9, when Hamilton wrote to Monroe: "The intention of my letter of the 4th instant, as itself imports, was to meet and close with an advance towards a personal interview, which it appeared to me had been made by you. From the tenor of your reply of the 6th, which disavows the inference I had drawn, any further step on my part, as being inconsistent with the ground I have heretofore taken, would be improper." Still the matter was not settled, for the letters continued to go back and forth between the two antagonists. Monroe with considerable justification complained that he did not know whether Hamilton did or did not want a duel, and finally, in early December, 1797, Monroe asked Aaron Burr and John Dawson either to conclude the arrangements for the duel or, if the dispute had been amicably settled, to publish an item in the newspapers to that effect.[55] In a letter to Monroe, which presumably was never sent, Hamilton accepted the challenge.[56] Although no evidence exists concerning how this

54. AL, James Madison Papers, Library of Congress.
55. See Monroe to H, December 2, 1797.
Burr, who had been United States Senator from New York from March 4, 1791, to March 3, 1797, had been elected in the spring of 1797 to the New York Assembly, which met in January, 1798.
Dawson, a graduate of Harvard, had been a member of the Continental Congress in 1788 and 1789 and a delegate to the Virginia Ratifying Convention; he was a Democratic-Republican member of the House of Representatives from Virginia from March 4, 1797, until his death in 1814.
56. H to Monroe, January, 1798.
For the correspondence relating to the dispute between H and Monroe, see Monroe to H, July 10, 16, 17, 18, 21, 25, 31, August 6, 1797; H to Mon-

dispute was settled, the fact remains that Hamilton and Monroe never did fight a duel.

Soon after the publication of Callender's charges and long before the conclusion of his correspondence with Monroe, Hamilton decided that he had no alternative but to "place before the public an exact detail of the affair in all its circumstances." [57] Although Muhlenberg and Venable indicated a willingness to accept the explanation given by Hamilton on the evening of December 15, 1792,[58] Monroe remained what can at best be called equivocal. Monroe's view of the entire matter is perhaps best exemplified by his statement to Hamilton on July 21, 1797, that "Whether the imputations against you as to speculation, are well or ill founded, depends upon the facts & circumstances which appear agnst you & upon yr. defense." Hamilton replied to Monroe on July 22: ". . . there appears a design at all events to drive me to the necessity of a formal defence—while you know that the extreme delicacy of its nature might be very disagreeable to me."

For several weeks Hamilton worked at preparing his defense and collecting the documents he needed to support it.[59] Finally, an advertisement dated August 25, 1797, in a Philadelphia newspaper announced: "This day published . . . Observations on certain Documents Contained in No. V and VI of 'The History of the United States for the year 1796,' In which the charge of speculation against Alexander Hamilton, Late Secretary of the Treasury, is FULLY REFUTED. WRITTEN BY HIMSELF." [60]

---

roe, July 10, 17, 18, 20, 22, 28, August 4, 9, 1797; William Jackson to H, July 24, 25, 31, August 5, 7 (two letters), 11, 1797; James McHenry to H, August 7, 1797; "David Gelston's Account of an Interview between Alexander Hamilton and James Monroe," July 11, 1797; "Certificate by James Monroe," August 16, 1797.

57. See H to Fenno, July 17–22, 1797.

Although no evidence has been found that this letter was ever sent to Fenno, on July 31, 1797, the following advertisement, dated July 25, appeared in Fenno's paper, the *Gazette of the United States, and Philadelphia Daily Advertiser:* "*Now in the press, and soon will be published,* Observations on certain documents contained in the Vth and VIth numbers of 'The History of the United States for the year 1796,' in which the charge of speculation against Alexander Hamilton, late Secretary of the Treasury, is fully refuted.

"WRITTEN BY HIMSELF.

"This publication will present a concise statement of the base means practised by the Jacobins of the United States to asperse the characters of those persons who are considered as hostile to their disorganizing schemes. It will also contain the correspondence between Mr. Hamilton and Messrs. Monroe, Muhlenburgh and Venable, on the subject of the documents aforesaid, and a a series of letters from James Reynolds and his wife to Mr. Hamilton, proving beyond the possibility of a doubt, that the connection between him and Reynolds, was the result of a daring conspiracy on the part of the latter and his associates to extort money."

58. See Venable to H, July 9, 10, 1797; Muhlenberg to H, July 10, 1797.

59. See H to Wadsworth, July 28, 1797; Wadsworth to H, August 2, 1797; Edward Jones to H, July 30, 1797; William Jackson to H, August 11, 1797.

60. *Gazette of the United States, and Philadelphia Daily Advertiser,* August 27, 1797.

Republicans greeted the "Reynolds Pamphlet" with understandable joy and wonderment, for it seemed to them that Hamilton had gone to extreme lengths to document a sordid affair while at the same time he had done nothing to discredit the charges of official misconduct. John Barnes, a Philadelphia merchant, wrote to Jefferson on October 3, 1797: "Very fortunately the inclosed pamphlett (which you request) was some few days since, left with me—in the state you find it. Mr H—— has assuredly, reduced his Consequence, to the most degrading & Contemptable point of view; And I am much pleased to find Mr Monroe would not, humour his restless, unreasonable & foolish Vanity, for under all circumstances, the several Gentlemens treatment towards him was, thro: polite, & respectfull. Such another piece of ridiculous folly: sure, never Man was guilty of—first, in Committing himself via his Dear (dear indeed,) Maria; and then, to publish it, himself: as if, it were possible—by that means to justify his public Conduct, by a *simple* confession of his private ridiculous Amour, at the expence of both—his Reputation and future peace of mind: how it must on Reflection, torture him, on poor Mrs. H. Accot: whose feelings on the Occasion must be severely injured. if not expressed: how you came (innocently) to be luged in—at the latter end of the fray, is yet to be explained; it seems, this poor Frauncis—to whom you addressed the two letters in question—was met by Mr H. on the Battery NewYork. and questioned respecting his situation & Circumstances—and withal asked, who was his friend, and if he stood in Need of Assistance—his look, and condition plainly evinced the supposition— and Mr H. afforded him a present relief, in the course of conversation F informed Mr H. he had waited upon you—in Philada—and to confirm it, produced your two letters. & withal added your promise of employmt. (at least so he expressed himself to me). Mr H—— immediately requested the perusal of them, with promise of returning them. imprudently F. Assented—and they still rest, with Mr H. And by *this sorry means* made Use of to *Grace*—as he supposes, his *ingracious* defence—in pity to F——s immediate wants (rather than his Merits) I could not but Assist him; After a short breakft. he left me, and I have not seen him since, nothing but his extreme want, & expectation of seeing a worthless Brother of his Here (Absent) brought him at this Crisis to Town and it is more than probable he will pay you another Visit on your Return to Philada. I intimated too him the improbability of your employing him— and added, the very imprudent disclosure of your letter to *Mr H.* could not but displease you." [61]

On October 20, 1797, James Madison wrote to Jefferson: ". . . The publication under all its characters is a curious specimen of the ingenious folly of its author. Next to the error of publishing at all, is that of forgetting that simplicity & candor are the only dress which prudence would put on innocence. Here we see every rhetorical artifice employed to excite the spirit of party to prop up his sinking reputation and whilst the most exaggerated complaints are uttered agst. the unfair & virulent persecution of himself, he deals out in every page the most malignant insinuations agst. others. The one agst. you is a masterpiece of folly, be-

61. From a Xerox copy supplied by Mr. Julian P. Boyd.

cause its importance is in exact proportion to its venom." [62] After reading the "Reynolds Pamphlet," Callender also wrote to Jefferson: ". . . If you have not seen it, no anticipation can equal the infamy of this piece. It is worth all that fifty of the best pens in America could have said agt. him, and the most pitiful part of the whole is his notice of you." [63]

The Republican charges against Hamilton were made more plausible by his refusal to make public the originals of the documents that he had printed in the appendix to the "Reynolds Pamphlet." When Callender wrote to him on October 29, 1797, asking for permission to "inspect" these documents, Hamilton did not reply and endorsed Callender's letter: "Impudent Experiment *NO Notice.*" Callender concluded that at least some of the documents in question did not exist and never had existed. In his *Sketches*, published in 1798, he wrote: ". . . Clingman and the lady [Maria Reynolds] have been married. They reside now at Alexandria [Virginia]. Reynolds himself lives, it is said, in New-York. If the letters published by Mr. Hamilton in the name of Maria are genuine, it would be very easy to obtain her attestation of the fact. A justice of the peace, at Alexandria, could dispatch the business in half an hour. She could be directed to give a sample of her hand; and, by comparing this with the letters, it would be ascertained whether or not they really came from her pen. But Camillus dares not to meet this test.

"Instead of such an obvious and decisive elucidation, Mr. Hamilton brings forward Mary Williams, keeper of a boarding house in Philadelphia. This woman swears, that she is well acquainted with the hand writing of Mrs. Reynolds, and that she is *well satisfied* of the letters being genuine.[64] She gives no particulars of her acquaintance with Mrs. Reynolds, except the declining to admit of her as a lodger. This is as lame a kind of evidence as can well be conceived. Why not appeal to the lady herself, in place of such a circuitous method?

". . . Send for the lady, or pay her a visit. Take her before a magistrate, and let us hear what she has to say. Your avoiding a public meeting with her, holds out a strong presumption of her innocence. Try, also, to find out Reynolds. Never pretend that you scorn to confront accusers. The world will believe that you dare not." [65]

Callender was correct in his assertion that both Maria and James Reynolds were available for questioning in the years after 1792. On May 14, 1793, Maria Reynolds filed a bill in the New York Court of Chancery requesting a divorce from her husband on the ground that he

62. ALS, James Madison Papers, Library of Congress.

63. September 28, 1797 (ALS, Papers of Thomas Jefferson, Library of Congress).

64. See the statement of Mary Williams, July 21, 1797, which is document No. XLI in the appendix to the printed version of the "Reynolds Pamphlet," August 25, 1797. According to William Loughton Smith, H ". . . lodged with me at Williams's when he was writing his Vindication & I left him in the midst of his corresponde. with Monroe in July last" (Smith to Rufus King, December 14, 1797 [ALS, Mr. Hall Park McCullough, North Bennington, Vermont]). Mary Williams's boardinghouse was at 104 Spruce Street (Cornelius William Stafford, *The Philadelphia Directory for 1797* [Philadelphia: William W. Woodward, 1797], 196).

65. Callender, *Sketches*, 98–99, 107.

had committed adultery with Eliza Flavinier,[66] and almost two years later the court issued the final decree granting the divorce.[67] In the early stages of the divorce proceedings John Beckley wrote to an unnamed correspondent: "Clingman . . . informs me, that Mrs. Reynolds has obtained a divorce from her husband, in consequence of his intrigue with Hamilton to her prejudice, and that Colonel Burr obtained it for her: he adds too, that she is thoroughly disposed to attest all she knows of the connection between Hamilton and Reynolds. . . ." [68] There is no record, however, that she ever attested to "all she knows." On the other hand, it may or may not be significant that she and Clingman were subsequently married, that they were living in Virginia in 1798, and that at a later time they moved to England.[69]

James Reynolds, like his wife, returned to the obscurity from which he had emerged. Before doing so, however, he did write a note to Hamilton on the night of his release from prison, and he visited the Secretary of the Treasury on the following morning.[70] Boyd suggests that Reynolds subsequently became a sea captain, but the evidence to support this conclusion is at best tenuous.[71] On the other hand, in 1798 in the course of a suit to recover two hundred dollars Reynolds described himself as a New York City grocer,[72] and in another case in 1803 he stated that he was forty-four years old and a laborer in Harlem in the Seventh Ward of New York City.[73] These facts tend to deepen rather than dis-

66. Bill, filed May 14, 1793, *Mary Reynolds* v *James W. Reynolds* (Chancery Decrees Before 1800, R-112, Clerk of the Court of Appeals, Albany, on deposit at Queens College, New York City).

On August 6 the case was brought up in the New York Supreme Court where "The Jury without going from the Bar Say that they find for the plaintiff Three hundred pounds damages and Six pence Costs" (MS Minutes of the New York Supreme Court, July–October, 1793 [Hall of Records, New York City]).

67. Decree, February 13, 1795, *Mary Reynolds* v *James W. Reynolds* (Chancery Decrees Before 1800, R-12, Clerk of the Court of Appeals, Albany, on deposit at Queens College, New York City).

68. Beckley to ———, June 22, 1793 (copy, Mr. Pierce W. Gaines, Fairfield, Connecticut). This letter is also printed in the introductory note to Andrew G. Fraunces to H, May 16, 1793. For the possibility that the unnamed addressee was James Monroe, see Boyd, *Papers of Thomas Jefferson*, XVIII, 629, note 57.

69. See the statement of Richard Folwell, which is printed as note 6 to Edward Jones to H, July 30, 1797. For evidence that the Clingmans moved to England, see Dorothy and Edmund Berkeley, *John Beckley, Zealous Partisan in a Nation Divided* (Philadelphia: Published by the American Philosophical Society, 1973), 171.

70. See the memorandum by Monroe, Venable, and Muhlenberg, December 16, 1792, which is printed in note 50. See also Clingman's deposition, December 13, 1792, which is document No. IV (a) in the appendix to the printed version of the "Reynolds Pamphlet," August 25, 1797.

71. *Papers of Thomas Jefferson*, XVIII, 642–43, note 89.

72. Narrative and Oyer, filed October 16, 1798 (Parchment 134-K-7, Hall of Records, New York City); Warrant of Attorney, filed October 16, 1798 (Parchment 134-K-7, Hall of Records, New York City).

73. Draft Deposition, May 30, 1803, *Reuben Reynolds* v *Isaac Tobias* (Chancery Papers, BM-474-R, Hall of Records, New York City). For the case of *Reuben Reynolds* v *Isaac Tobias*, see note 9.

pel one of the many mysteries surrounding the "Reynolds Affair," for they indicate that although Reynolds was available for questioning, either he was not asked or he did not wish to state for the record his version of what had happened.

In his attack on Hamilton's veracity in his *Sketches,* Callender also maintained that internal evidence indicated that the letters ascribed to Maria Reynolds in the "Reynolds Pamphlet" were in fact written by Hamilton. "These letters from Mrs. Reynolds," Callender wrote, "are badly spelt and pointed. Capitals, also, occur even in the midst of words. But waving such excrescences, the stile is pathetic and even elegant. It does not bear the marks of an illiterate writer. The construction of the periods disagrees with this apparent incapacity of spelling. The officer who can marshall a regiment, must know how to level a musket. A few gross blunders are interspersed, and these could readily be devised; but, when stript of such a veil, the body of the composition is pure and correct. In the literary world, fabrications of this nature have been frequent. Our ex-secretary admits that he has been in the habit of writing to this family in a feigned character. The transition was easy to the writing in a feigned stile." Callender then addressed himself directly to Hamilton: "You speak as if it was impossible to invent a few letters." [74]

In his recent reassessment of the "Reynolds Affair," Boyd agrees with Callender's conclusion and flatly asserts that the letters are fabrications: ". . . They are the palpably contrived documents of a brilliant and daring man who, writing under much stress in the two or three days available to him in 1792, tried to imitate what he conceived to be the style of less literate persons. The result was inexpert to the point of naivete, but its character is beyond doubt. The purported letters of James and Maria Reynolds as published in Hamilton's *Observations* cannot be accepted as genuine." [75]

74. Callender, *Sketches,* 99, 107.
75. *Papers of Thomas Jefferson,* XVIII, 682.
The awkward and incorrect spelling of words in the Reynolds letters is not necessarily proof that H forged the letters. Boyd argues that the "idiosyn-cratic spellings" of the letters from James Reynolds to H do not appear in either Reynolds's application for office in 1789 (see note 10) or in Reynolds's letter to Clingman on December 13, 1792 (*Papers of Thomas Jefferson,* XVIII, 681, 682). Boyd, however, is contradicting his earlier statement concerning the 1789 application: "Reynolds' addressing the petition as he did suggests that Troup, a lawyer aware of the constitutional role of the Senate in appointments to office, may have advised him as to form. He may have even drafted it for Reynolds to copy in his own hand . . ." (*Papers of Thomas Jefferson,* XVIII, 627, note 53). In fact, Reynolds's petition for office in 1789 is a copy in an unknown handwriting. The signature is not the same as Reynolds's sig-nature on a draft deposition, dated May 30, 1803, prepared for the case of *Reuben Reynolds* v *Isaac Tobias* (Chancery Papers, BM-474-R [Hall of Rec-ords, New York City]). For the case of *Reynolds* v. *Tobias,* see notes 9 and 73.
The other letter mentioned by Boyd (Reynolds to Clingman, December 13, 1792) presents a somewhat different problem. The original manuscript of this letter, which H saw (H to Muhlenberg, Monroe, and Venable, December 17, 1792; Muhlenberg to H, December 18, 1792; Monroe to H, December 20, 1792), has not been found. Boyd in effect concedes this point, for in using

If one assumes, as most historians have, that the documents used by Hamilton in the appendix to the "Reynolds Pamphlet" were authentic, the question of the final disposition of the originals of these documents has remained—and seems likely to remain—unanswered. On the one hand, Wolcott stated on July 12, 1797, that he had retained "certain letters and documents" pertaining to the "Reynolds Affair," but generations of scholars have been unable to find them in Wolcott's extant papers.[76] On the other hand, in the "Reynolds Pamphlet" Hamilton wrote that he had deposited the original papers with William Bingham,[77] and at the conclusion of the appendix he referred to "the gentleman with whom the papers are deposited." [78] But on November 18, 1799, James McHenry wrote to Hamilton: "I recd two hours ago your letter of the 14th, begging me to call upon and send you certain papers you had lodged with Mr Bingham. As he has not returned to this City I dispatched my servant with a note to which I have received the following answer inclosed. I do not remember to have seen the papers aluded to." In the enclosure mentioned by McHenry, Bingham wrote: "It Surely must have escaped Genl Hamilton's recollection that the Papers he alluded to, never were deposited with me.

"After reading the publication in which he mentioned this deposit being made, I was Surprized at the omission of which in Case I had been applied to for a View of them, I Should certainly have reminded him— under any other Circumstances, it would not have been delicate to have addressed him on the Subject." [79]

It is, however, difficult, if not impossible, to reconcile Bingham's disclaimer in 1799 with the following statement he made to Hamilton in a letter dated July 21, 1801: "Having a Packet of Papers which by your Desire, were deposited with me, & which have long lain dormant in my Possession, & being about embarking in a Short time for Europe, permit me to return them to you."

If Bingham did return the originals of the Reynolds-Hamilton correspondence, no evidence has been found that Hamilton subsequently showed the documents in question to even his closest associates. In 1795, when Hamilton thought that he was going to fight a duel with James Nicholson, he entrusted the disposition of his estate to Robert Troup. At the time he wrote to Troup: "In my leather Trunk . . . is also a bundle inscribed thus—J R *To be forwarded to Oliver Wolcott Junr. Esq.* I entreat that this may be early done by a careful hand." Hamilton

---

this letter to buttress his argument he gives as its source the printed version in Callender's *History*, 220–21 (Boyd, *Papers of Thomas Jefferson*, XVIII, 681, note 190).

76. Wolcott's deposition is document No. XXIV in the appendix to the printed version of the "Reynolds Pamphlet," August 25, 1797.

77. "Reynolds Pamphlet," August 25, 1797.

78. "Reynolds Pamphlet," August 25, 1797.
For Boyd's reading of this as " 'the gentlemen' with whom the papers had been deposited," see Boyd, *Papers of Thomas Jefferson*, XVIII, 677, note 180.

79. Bingham to McHenry, November 18, 1799, which is printed as an enclosure to McHenry to H, November 18, 1799.

then added: "This trunk contains all my interesting papers." [80] In going
through her husband's papers after his death, Elizabeth Hamilton wrote
under Hamilton's letter to Troup: "to be retained by myself." If Broadus
Mitchell is correct in assuming that the initials "J R" refer to the Reynolds correspondence,[81] it may not be too wild a leap of the imagination
to conclude that Elizabeth Hamilton inherited and then destroyed the
documents describing her husband's affair with Maria Reynolds. In this
connection it may be relevant to point out that Joseph Sabin states that
Hamilton's edition of the "Reynolds Pamphlet" was bought up and destroyed by Hamilton's family.[82]

Many historians like to view themselves as experts, and as such they
are reluctant to admit that at times they encounter questions for which
they can find no satisfactory answers. But such questions exist, and the
"Reynolds Affair" poses not one such question but a host of them.
Despite the most rigorous scholarship and the best intentions, historians
have been forced to leave the "Reynolds Affair" in essentially the same
enigmatic state in which they have found it. Over the years they have
discovered bits and pieces of new information, but no one has as yet
devised a way to put together an account that not only answers all
the questions that have been asked but also even meets the standards that
are usually required for research papers submitted by college seniors. In
this respect historians, both past and present, are little better than Hamilton's contemporaries, for what they have been wont to call conclusions
are in reality little more than acts of faith. Perhaps those who in the
future wish to analyze the "Reynolds Affair" should be advised to read
Frank R. Stockton's short story *The Lady or the Tiger?*

                                        Phila. July 3d. 1797

Dear Sir

I inclose you the pamphlet. You will see that the subject is but
partially represented with a design to establish an opinion that you
was concerned in speculations in the public funds. As my name is
mentioned I have been repeatedly called on for explanations. What
I have said is substantially as follows. That I was informed at the
time, of the whole transaction, & that though Munroe Muhlenburgh
& Venable at first represented the affair as connected with Specula-

80. H to Troup, July 25, 1795.
81. Mitchell, *Hamilton*, II, 713–14, note 93.
82. Joseph Sabin *et al.*, eds., *Bibliotheca Americana: A Dictionary of Books
Relating to America, from Its Discovery to the Present Time* (Reprinted:
Amsterdam, 1961), VIII, 28.

tion in the funds, yet an explanation took place in my presence when each of the Gentlemen acknowledged themselves perfectly satisfied, & that there was nothing in the affair which could or ought to affect your character as a public Officer or impair the public confidence in your integrity. I have also mentioned that no publication could have been made without a breach of confidence pledged in my presence by the Gentlemen above named. Mr. Venable I am told speaks of the publication as false & dishonourable.

I have good reason to believe that Beckley is the real author, though it is attributed to Calender.

You will judge for yourself, but in my opinion it will be best to write nothing at least for the present.

It is false that Duer had any hand in the transaction—the Lists are in my hands, with a Letter from Clingman & Reynolds, the Clerk who furnished the Lists was notified of the discovery by me & dismissed—his name has been hitherto concealed: I think you may be certain that your character is not affected, in point of integrity & official conduct. The indignation against those who have basely published this scandal, is I believe universal. If you determine to notice the affair, & I can assist you you may command me, but I doubt the expediency.

The faction is organized, public business is at a stand, and a crisis is approaching.

Yrs truly

Oliv Wolcott Jr

A Hamilton Esq

Théophile Cazenove to Egbert Benson and Alexander Hamilton [1]

Philadelphia, July 5, 1797. States: "Mr. Benson's absence retarding the answer upon my letter of the 29 May, which answer I have sollicited from your friendship, permit me to add to that letter some observations relative to the same Subject." Asks if the Holland Land Company "is allowed to sell at 10 & 12 years credit; . . . will

She be allowed to hold the mortgage upon the Land as a pledge for the payment?" Also asks: "What will be the consequences if the purchasers are not able to pay at the expiration of 10 or 12 years— and if then, the mortgaged lands, Sold under execution, does not produce the amount due? Will the Holland Compy. in such a case, be authorised to retake the land, & to hold that property—or must the land be sold at cash for any price and the Holld. Compy. loose the defficit, having only for that defficit, a claim against a purchaser not able to fulfill his engagements?"

ALS, Hamilton Papers, Library of Congress; copy, Gemeentearchief Amsterdam, Holland Land Company. The Holland Land Company documents were transferred in 1964 from the Nederlandsch Economisch-Historisch Archief, Amsterdam.

1. This letter was addressed to Benson and H in their capacities as attorneys for the Holland Land Company. For the full text of this letter and other relevant documents, see forthcoming Goebel, *Law Practice*, III.

For background to this letter, see H to Cazenove, January 22, 1796, notes 2 and 3; Cazenove to Benson and H, May 29, 1797. See also Robert Morris to H, June 7, 1795, note 37.

To James Monroe [1]

New York July 5th 1797

Sir

In a pamphlet lately published entitled "No V of the History of the United States for 1796 &c" are sundry papers respecting the affair of *Reynolds*, in which you once had an agency, accompanied with these among other comments—"They (certain attacks on Mr Monroe) are ungrateful, because he displayed on an occasion that will be mentioned immediately, the greatest lenity to Mr. Alexander Hamilton, the prime mover of the Federal Party. When some of the Papers which are now to be laid before the world were submitted to the Secretary; when he was informed that they were to be communicated to President Washington, he entreated in the most anxious tone of deprecation, that the measure might be suspended. Mr Monroe was one of the three Gentlemen who agreed to this delay. They gave their consent to it on his express promise of a guarded behaviour in future, and because he attached to the suppression of these papers a mysterious degree of solicitude which they feeling no personal resentment against the Individual, were unwilling to augment" (Page 204 & 205). It is also suggested (Page 206) that I made "a volunteer acknowledgement of *Seduction*" and it must be understood from the context that this acknowlegement was made to the same three Gentlemen.

The peculiar nature of this transaction renders it impossible that you should not recollect it in all its parts and that your own declarations to me at the time contradicts absolutely the construction which the Editor of the Pamphlet puts upon the affair.

I think myself entitled to ask from your candour and justice a declaration equivalent to that which was made me at the time in the presence of Mr Wolcott by yourself and the two other Gentlemen, accompanied by a contradiction of the Representations in the comments cited above. And I shall rely upon your delicacy that the manner of doing it will be such as one Gentleman has a right to expect from another—especially as you must be sensible that the present appearance of the Papers is contrary to the course which was understood between us to be proper and includes a dishonourable infidelity somewhere. I am far from attributing it to either of the three Gentlemen; yet the suspicion naturally falls on some Agent made use of by them.

I send you the copy of a memorandum of the substance of your declaration made by me the morning after our Interview.

With consideration I have the honour to be   Sir   Your very obed
serv   A Hamilton

P.s. I must beg the favour of expedition in your reply.

[ENCLOSURE]

Memorandum of Substance of Declaration of Messrs. Monroe Mughlenburgh & Venable concerning the affair of James Reynolds.[2]

"That they regretted the trouble and uneasiness which they had occasionned to me in consequence of the Representations made to them—That they were perfectly satisfied with the explanation I had given and that there was nothing in the transaction which ought

to affect my character as a public Officer or lessen the public Confidence in my Integrity."

LS, The Library, Lehigh University, Bethlehem, Pennsylvania; ADf, Hamilton
Papers, Library of Congress.
    1. This letter is document No. XXV in the appendix to the printed version
of the "Reynolds Pamphlet," August 25, 1797. H sent the same letter to
Abraham B. Venable and Frederick A. C. Muhlenberg, but these letters have
not been found.
    For background to this letter, see the introductory note to Oliver Wolcott,
Jr., to H, July 3, 1797.
    2. AD, The Library, Lehigh University, Bethlehem, Pennsylvania; ADf,
Hamilton Papers, Library of Congress.

To Frederick A. C. Muhlenberg

[*Philadelphia, July 5, 1797.* On July 10, 1797, Muhlenberg wrote
to Hamilton: "Your letter of the 5th inst did not reach me time
enough." *Letter not found.*]

To Nicholas Olive [1]

New York, July 5, 1797. Acknowledges receipt of papers sent by
Olive which "relate to transactions with Mr. Constable." [2] States that
he is already "generally engaged for Mr. Constable, and would not
in case of controversy act adversely to him for another. . . . But
perhaps it may be most advisable for you as an *Agent* to confide the
interest of your friend to some person free from any engagement to
Mr. Constable. . . ."

ALS, Mr. L. McCormick-Goodhart, Alexandria, Virginia.
    1. Olive was a New York City merchant who had emigrated from France
to the United States in 1793. He became interested in the Castorland project
to establish a French colony on land formerly owned by Alexander Macomb
on the Black River in northern New York. The prospectus for this project
was published in Paris in 1792.
    2. William Constable was a New York City merchant and speculator.

To Abraham B. Venable

[*Philadelphia, July 5, 1797.* On July 9, 1797, Venable wrote to Hamilton: "I have received your letter of the fifth instant by the hands of Mr. Wolcott." *Letter not found.*]

To John Fenno [1]

[New York, July 6, 1797]

Mr. Fenno,

I have seen in your paper of 27th June past, the advertisement of a new publication, being No. V of the History of the United States for 1796, and containing these paragraphs:

"This number likewise contains some singular and authentic papers relative to Mr. Alexander Hamilton, late Secretary of the Treasury. No greater proof can be given of the value which is attached to their *suppression* than the following anecdote:"

"During the late canvas for the election of a President, Webster in his Minerva [2] gave a hint that Mr. Hamilton would be an adviseable candidate. A person in this city who chanced to see this newspaper, wrote immediately to a correspondent in New-York. The letter desired him to put himself in Mr. Hamilton's way, and inform him that if Webster should in future print a single paragraph on that head, the papers referred to were instantly to be laid before the world. *The message was delivered to Mr. Hamilton and the Minerva became silent.*" [3]

I have also, since, seen the pamphlet, No. V. mentioned in the advertisement.

I think it proper to take an early opportunity to declare, that the anecdote stated in the above paragraph is wholly false, and that I never received any such intimation as is thereby pretended from any person whatever. As to the papers contained in the pamphlet, from a cursory perusal, I take them to be authentic. But the solution of them is simply this—They were the contrivance of two of the most profligate men in the world to obtain their liberation from imprisonment for a serious crime by the *favor of party spirit*. For this purpose recourse was had to Messrs *James Monroe,* Senator, *Frederick A. Muhlenbergh,* Speaker, and *Abraham Venable,* a Member of the House of Representatives, two of these gentlemen my *known political opponents*. A full explanation took place between them and myself in the presence of *Oliver Wolcott,* jun. Esq. the present Secretary of the Treasury, in which by *written documents* I convinced them of the falshood of the accusation. They declared themselves perfectly satisfied with the explanation, and expressed their regret at the necessity which had been occasioned to me of making it. It is my intention shortly to place the subject more precisely before the public.   ALEXANDER HAMILTON.

New-York, July 6, 1797

Gazette of the United States, and Philadelphia Daily Advertiser, July 8, 1797.
    1. Fenno was editor of the *Gazette of the United States, and Philadelphia Daily Advertiser.*
    For background to this letter, see the introductory note to Oliver Wolcott, Jr., to H, July 3, 1797.
    2. Noah Webster, Jr., was editor of *The* [New York] *Minerva, & Mercantile Evening Advertiser.*
    3. For Webster's refutation of this account, see document No. XLIII in the appendix to the printed version of the "Reynolds Pamphlet," August 25, 1797.

From Benjamin Walker [1]

Fort Schuyler [*New York*] *July 6, 1797.* "I will thank to advise what is best to be done to bring the business with Colo Smith [2] to a conclusion—it was referred to Judge Lewis [3] and John Murray [4] as Arbitrators. The former kept the papers a long time and then, Mr Murray informed me, he declined Acting. The arbitration bonds expired and Mr James Smith got a new one executed by his brother extending the time to October. Still Mr Lewis was inserted as the Arbitrator tho' I informed Mr Smith what Mr Murray had told me of his having declined. As Colo Smith was then gone no one knew where the matter rested. Now, they say Mr Lewis will be in Town the 20th of this month. I will attend to it—or if not that they will appoint Mr Lawrance [5] or Mr Harrison.[6] I have no objection to any man of character but such as are Creditors or connected in the affairs of Colo Smith these must certainly be objected to the Arbitrators must be perfectly indifferent as to the event. Mr Lawrence I am pretty sure is a Creditor. I dont know if Mr Harrison is or not but I think he declined once before from their whole proceeding. Refusing to appoint such Men as will attend to it &c. . . ."

ALS, Hamilton Papers, Library of Congress.
1. This is a reference to Walker's efforts to collect money which William S. Smith owed to William Pulteney and William Hornby. For this debt and H's part in the attempts to collect it, see Walker to H, September 15, 1793, October 4, 1796 (two letters); the introductory note to Robert Morris to H, April 27, 1796, note 6; H to Walker, October 15, 1796.
2. William S. Smith.
3. Morgan Lewis was a justice of the New York Supreme Court.
4. John Murray was a New York City merchant.
5. John Laurance.
6. Richard Harison was United States attorney for the District of New York.

From Oliver Wolcott, Junior [1]

Phila. July 7th. 1797

Dr. Sir

I send you the residue of the pamph[l]et.[2] I am astonished at the villany of Munroe—a more base, false, & malignant suggestion than is contained in his Note of Jany 2d 1793.[3] was never uttered.

I am yrs   Oliv Wolcott Jr

A Hamilton Esq

ALS, Hamilton Papers, Library of Congress.
1. For background to this letter, see the introductory note to Wolcott to H, July 3, 1797.
2. Wolcott enclosed pamphlet No. VI by James Thomson Callender.
3. James Monroe's note of January 2, 1793, is printed in the introductory note to Wolcott to H, July 3, 1797.

From Oliver Wolcott, Junior [1]

Phila. July 7th. 1797

My Dr. Sir.

I have recd. your Letter with the enclosures.[2] By what I last sent you,[3] you will see the perfidy of at least Munroe.

I will attend to your request as soon as possible, but all my time this day will be taken up, and perhaps tomorrow.

yrs.   Oliv Wolcott Jr

ALS, Hamilton Papers, Library of Congress.
    1. For background to this letter, see the introductory note to Wolcott to H, July 3, 1797.
    2. Letter not found. The enclosures were the letters which H wrote to James Monroe, Frederick A. C. Muhlenberg, and Abraham B. Venable on July 5, 1797 (see H to Monroe, July 5, 1797; Venable to H, July 9, 1797; Muhlenberg to H, July 10, 1797).
    3. Wolcott to H, July 7, 1797.

To James Monroe [1]

New York July 8 1797

Sir

I request to be informed whether the paper numbered V dated Philadelphia the 15 of December 1792 published partly in the fifth and partly in the sixth number of "The History of the United States for 1796" and having the signatures of *James Monroe, Abraham Venable* and *F A Mughlenberg* is the copy of a genuine original.[2]

I am Sir   Yr. humble servt   A Hamilton
                                                       July 8 1797

James Monroe Esq

ALS, Hamilton Papers, Library of Congress.
    1. For background to this letter, see the introductory note to Oliver Wolcott, Jr., to H, July 3, 1797; Wolcott to H, July 7, 1797.
    This letter is endorsed in H's handwriting: "James Monroe &c." A copy of

the same letter was presumably sent to Frederick A. C. Muhlenberg and Abraham B. Venable.

2. For document No. V, printed by James Thomson Callender, see Wolcott to H, July 3, 1797, notes 1, 50, and 51.

From Abraham B. Venable [1]

Philadelphia July 9th. 1797

Sir

I have received your letter of the fifth instant [2] by the hands of Mr Wolcott.

I had heard of the pamphlet you mentioned some days before, but had not read it. I am intirely ignorant of the Editor, and of the means by which he procured the papers alluded to.

I have had nothing to do with the transaction since the interview with you, I do not possess a copy of the papers at present, nor have I at any time had the possession of any of them, I avoided taking a copy because I feared that the greatest care which I could exercise in keeping them safely, might be defeated by some accident and that some person or other might improperly obtain an inspection of them. I have indeavoured to recollect what passed at the close of the interview which took place with respect to this transaction, it was said I believe by us in general terms, that we were Satisfyed with the explanation that had been given, that we regreted the necessity we had been Subjected to in being obliged to make the enquiry, as well as the trouble and anxiety it had occasioned you, and on your part you admitted in general terms that the business as presented to us bore such a doubtful aspect as to justify the inquiry, and that the manner had been satisfactory to you.

I have now to express my Surprise at the contents of a letter published yesterday in Fennos paper,[3] in which you indeavour to impute to party motives, the part which I have had in this business, and indeavour to connect me with the releasement of persons, *committed as you say for serious crimes*. Clingman had been released before I heard of the business, and Reynolds on the very day I received the first intimation of it, arrangements having been previously made for that purpose, by those who had interested themselves to bring it

about. So that no application was made to me on that subject, either
directly or indirectly the object being intirely accomplished by other
means, and before I was informed of their confinement; If you will
take the trouble to examine the transaction you will find this statement correct, and you cannot be insensible of the injury you do me
when you say, this was an attempt to release themselves from imprisonment by favor of party spirit, and that I was one of the persons resorted to on that ground. I appeal to your candour, and ask
you if any part of my conduct in this whole business has justifyed
such an imputation.

This having been a joint business & Mr Monroe being now in New
York, I must avoid Saying any thing more on this Subject untill I
can see him and Mr Mughlenberg together, which I hope will be
in the present week.

I am Sir   Hble Sert   Abm B. Venable

ALS, Hamilton Papers, Library of Congress.
  1. This letter is document No. XXX in the appendix to the printed version
of the "Reynolds Pamphlet," August 25, 1797. For background to this letter,
see the introductory note to Oliver Wolcott, Jr., to H, July 3, 1797.
  2. Letter not found. This was presumably the same as the letter that H
wrote to James Monroe on July 5, 1797.
  3. H to John Fenno, July 6, 1797.

From James Thomson Callender [1]

[Philadelphia, July 10, 1797]

Sir,

I have seen your letter of the 6th inst. in Mr. Fenno's Gazette. An
answer seems requisite. It shall be as concise as possible.

With regard to the anecdote of the Minerva, you affirm it to be
WHOLLY FALSE. Information, which I sincerely credit, states it as
being strictly true. There the story may rest. As for what you say
of the papers signed by Messrs. Muhlenberg, Venable, and Munroe,
I shall quote the whole as an act of justice to you, and shall insert intermediate remarks in justice to the public.

"They (the papers) were the contrivance of two of the most
profligate men in the world, to obtain THEIR liberation from imprisonment, for a serious crime, by the FAVOUR OF PARTY SPIRIT."

(You will observe that Clingman was not in jail, during any part of the time to which these papers refer. This appears upon the face of them. Hence it is an entire mistake when you say that TWO MEN contrived them to obtain their liberation. Reynolds was the only person imprisoned. The papers were not of his contrivance. He never saw nor heard one line of them, nor does it appear from any part of their contents that he knew of their having been written. They were not drawn up, till after he had been discharged from prison by our intercession with mr. Wolcot. It is amazingly absurd in you to say that he or they contrived them to get out of prison, when it is plain to any one who looks at the papers, that they did not exist until AFTER REYNOLDS HAD BEEN ENLARGED.) "For this purpose recourse was had to Messrs. James Munroe, Senator, Frederick A. Muhlenberg, speaker, and Abraham Venable, a member of the House of Representatives, two of them my KNOWN POLITICAL OPPONENTS." (The words FAVOUR OF PARTY SPIRIT, in the end of the former extract, have no meaning that I can conceive. As to the RECOURSE, Mr. Muhlenberg, in his narrative [2] has distinctly told in what way he got the story from Clingman. Reynolds, when the three gentlemen went to him in prison, was far from expecting that they could give him assistance nor did he stand in need of it. He was so far from telling them any thing in order THAT THEY MIGHT GET HIM OUT, that on the contrary, he refused to give them information until AFTER HE SHOULD GET A DISCHARGE FROM JAIL. This discharge he expected and actually received by your assistance. He told them that if he gave any intelligence, while in prison, this measure might hinder him from obtaining his liberty. Your insinuation as to RECOURSE, &c. stands in stupendous contradiction to the clear matter of fact. Reynolds had no RECOURSE to the three members of Congress. They came to him UNASKED. He was even afraid of speaking to them.)

"A full explanation took place between them and myself in the presence of Oliver Wolcott, jun. Esq. the present secretary of the Treasury, in which by WRITTEN DOCUMENTS I convinced them of the falsehood of the accusation." (According to my information, these WRITTEN DOCUMENTS consisted of a series of letters pretended to be written relative to your alledged connection with Mrs. Reynolds. You told the members a confused and absurd story about her, of which they did not believe a single word, and which, if they had been true, did not give a proper explanation as to your correspondence with her husband.)

Pardon me for adding that Mr. Wolcott and the other gentlemen must have found it hard to help laughing in each other's faces, when you told your penitential tale of your depravity at the George.[3] A more ridiculous scene cannot be conceived. Your entreating that the papers might be concealed from the President was another curious part of the affair. Your letter of last week to Mr. Munroe regarding that and other precious confessions have come to hand.[4] He is since gone to New-York, where you can see him personally.[5]

"They declared themselves perfectly satisfied with the explanation, and expressed their regret at the necessity which had been occasioned to me of making it." (The best and only way to vindicate yourself will be to get a written certificate from the three members, that they were satisfied with your explanation). "It is my intention, shortly to place the matter more precisely before the public." You are in the right, for they have at present some unlucky doubts. They have long known you as an eminent and able statesman. They will be highly gratified by seeing you exhibited in the novel character of a lover.

I am,   with great respect,   Sir,   Your most obedient servant,

JAMES THOMSON CALLENDER

Philadelphia, July 10th, 1797.

P. S. As a preliminary to fair explanation, it might be advisable for you to reprint the whole original papers on which the suspicion is grounded. This should be done by the same medium through which your DEFENCE is to appear. It will be but candid towards the public. No extract from the papers, or general referrence to them can be satisfactory, and many thousands will undoubtedly see your publication, who may not have an opportunity of consulting *the history of the United States for 1796*, wherein they have been first published.

The [Philadelphia] *Merchants' Daily Advertiser,* July 12, 1797.
   1. For background to this letter, see the introductory note to Oliver Wolcott, Jr., to H, July 3, 1797; H to John Fenno, July 6, 1797.
   The letter printed above was preceded in the newspaper by the following letter from Callender, dated July 12, 1797, addressed to Thomas Bradford, publisher of *The Merchants' Daily Advertiser:* "In the 5th and 6th numbers,

of the history of the United States for 1796, &c. (see advertisement in this day's paper,) a number of documents are printed, relative to a mysterious connection between Mr. Alexander Hamilton, late secretary of the Treasury, and a certain James Reynolds. The papers are subscribed by Mr. F. A. Muhlenberg, Mr. Venable, and Mr. Monroe. In a letter in the Gazette of the United States of last Saturday, Mr. Hamilton makes an attack on the publication of these papers.

"The following answer was sent to Mr. Fenno who refused to insert it. From the superior independence & impartiality, of the Merchant's advertiser, I expect that you will permit its appearance. After the above explanation, I think the letter will be sufficiently intelligible to your readers."

2. Frederick A. C. Muhlenberg's statement, December 13, 1792, is document No. I (a) in the appendix to the printed version of the "Reynolds Pamphlet," August 25, 1797.

3. This is a reference to a letter which James Reynolds wrote to H on December 17, 1791. It reads in part: "If [you] think proper to Call at the sighn of the George tuesday morning at 8 oclock I will be there. for your house or office is no place to converse about these matters."

4. See H to James Monroe, July 5, 1797.

5. See H to Monroe, July 10, 1797.

To James Monroe [1]

[New York, July 10, 1797]

Mr. Hamilton requests an interview with Mr. Monroe at any hour tomorrow forenoon which may be convenient to him. Particular reasons will induce him to bring with him a friend to be present at what may pass. Mr. Monroe, if he pleases, may have another.

Monday July 10. 1797

AL, University of Rochester Library.

1. For background to this letter, see the introductory note to Oliver Wolcott, Jr., to H, July 3, 1797. See also Wolcott to H, July 7, 1797; H to Monroe, July 5, 8, 1797.

From James Monroe [1]

[New York, July 10, 1797]

Mr. Monroe readily consents to an interview with Colo. Hamilton tomorrow at ten in the morning at his lodgings with Mr. Knox [2] in Wall Street. He will bring whom he pleases.

July 10. 1797

AL, Hamilton Papers, Library of Congress.

1. For background to this letter, see the introductory note to Oliver Wolcott, Jr., to H, July 3, 1797; H to Monroe, July 10, 1797.

2. Thomas Knox, a New York City merchant, lived at 46 Wall Street.

From Frederick A. C. Muhlenberg [1]

Philada. July 10th. 1797

Sir

As I do not reside in the City at present, Your Letter of the 5th. inst [2] did not reach me time enough to answer by Saturdays post. Whilst I lament the publication of the papers respecting the Affair of Reynolds (of which I hope I need not assure you that I had neither Knowledge or Agency, for I never saw them since the Affair took place, nor was I ever furnished with a Copy) I do not hesitate to declare that I regretted the Trouble and Uneasiness this Business had occasioned, & that I was perfectly satisfied with the Explanation you gave at the same time permit me to remind You of Your Declaration also made in the presence of Mr. Wolcot that the Information & Letters in our possession justified the Suspicions we entertained before Your Explanation took place, and that our conduct towards You in this Business was satisfactory. Having no Share or Agency whatever in the publication or Comments You are pleased to cite I must beg to be excused from making any Remarks thereon. Were I to undertake to contradict the many Absurdities & falsehoods which I see published on a Variety of Subjects which heretofore came under my Notice, it would require more time than I am willing to sacrifice. I have the honor to be

Sir Your obdt. humble Servt. Fredk A C Muhlenberg

A. Hamilton Esqr.

ALS, Hamilton Papers, Library of Congress.

1. This letter is document No. XXIX in the appendix to the printed version of the "Reynolds Pamphlet," August 25, 1797. For background to this letter, see the introductory note to Oliver Wolcott, Jr., to H, July 3, 1797.

2. Letter not found. This letter was presumably the same as the letter that H wrote to James Monroe on July 5, 1797.

From Abraham B. Venable [1]

Philadelphia July 10th 97

Sir

I had written you yesterday in answer to your letter of the fifth, in which I informed you that I had no copy of the papers in question, the transaction took place at Mr Monroes, where I left the papers, since which I have not seen them. The paper alluded to as well as I can recollect was in the nature of a memorandum for our own use,[2] to refresh our memories in case we Should ever be called upon, and not intended for any other use, it related I believe chiefly to things which were said to [have] taken place pending the enquiry, and to the explanation. I cannot say whether it is an exact copy or not, tho' there was some such paper, the original I presume is in the possession of Mr Monroe, as I left them at his house Mr Mughlenberg being present; I do not know any means by which these papers could have got out, unless by the person who copyed them,[3] who had been present during the whole investigation, both before and after my being called on.

I am Sir   Your Hble Sert   Abm. B Venable

ALS, Hamilton Papers, Library of Congress.
    1. For background to this letter, see the introductory note to Oliver Wolcott, Jr., to H, July 3, 1797.
    2. This is a reference to a statement by Venable, James Monroe, and Frederick A. C. Muhlenberg on December 16, 1792, which was published in Callender, *History*, 216–18. For the text of this statement, see the introductory note to Wolcott to H, July 3, 1797.
    3. John Beckley.

David Gelston's Account of an Interview between Alexander Hamilton and James Monroe [1]

[New York] Tuesday Morning July 11th. 1797

Minutes of an Interview between Colo. Monroe and Colo. Hamilton at Colo. M's. lodgings in the presence of Mr Church [2] & myself.

Colo. Hamilton came about 10 oClk in the morning introduced Mr Church as his brother in law. Colo. H. appeared very much agitated upon his entrance into the room, and observed the cause or motives of this meeting being he presumed pretty well understood, he went into a detail of circumstances at considerable length upon a former meeting at Philada. between Mr Muhlenberg Mr. Venable and Colo. M.[3] after considerable time being spent in the detail Colo. M. asked what all that meant & said if you wish me to tell you any thing relating to the business all this history is unnecessary. Col. H said he should come to the point directly—some warmth appeared in both Gentln & some explanation took place Colo. M then began with declaring it was merely accidental his knowing any thing about the business at first he had been informed that one Reynolds from Virginia was in Gaol, he called merely to aid a man that might be in distress, but found it was a Reynolds from NYork and observed that after the meeting alluded to at Philada he sealed up his copy of the papers mentioned and sent or delivered them to his Friend in Virginia—he had no intention of publishing them & declared upon his honor that he knew nothing of their publication until he arrived in Philada from Europe [4] and was sorry to find they were published. Colo. H. observed that as he had written to Colo. M.[5] Mr Muhlenburgh & Mr. Venable [6] he expected an immediate answer to so important a subject in which his character the peace & reputation of his Family were so deeply interested. Colo. M replied that if he Colo. H would be temperate or quiet for a moment or some such word he would answer him candidly—that he recd his Colo. H.'s letter at 10 oClock at Night, that he had determined to leave Philada next Morng & actually did leave it for NYork, that immediately at a late hour that night after receiving the letter he went to Mr. Venables quarters that it was impossible to meet Mr. Muhlenberg & Mr. V. & that as at the meeting before alluded to they were all present (upon which Mr. C. took out of his pocket two pamphlets in which was a statement signed by Mr Muhlenburgh Mr Venable & Colo Monroe) [7] and all had signed it that he thought it most proper for them all to meet & return a joint answer to Colo. H.s letter which he meant to do on his return from Philada. Colo. M then observed if he Colo. H. wished him to give a relation of the facts & circumstances individually as they appeared to him, he would do

it then. Colo H. said he should like to hear it, Colo. M then proceeded upon a history of the business printed in the pamphlets and
said that the packet of papers before alluded to he yet believed
remained sealed with his friend in Virginia and after getting
through Colo. H. said this as your representation is totally false (as
nearly as I recollect the expression) upon which the Gentlemen
both instantly rose Colo. M. rising first and saying do you say I
represented falsely, you are a Scoundrel. Colo. H. said I will meet
you like a Gentleman Colo. M Said I am ready get your pistols,
both said we shall not or it will not be settled any other way. Mr C
& my self rising at the same moment put our selves between them
Mr. C. repeating Gentlemen Gentlemen be moderate or some such
word to appease them, we all sat down & the two Gentn, Colo. M.
& Colo. H. soon got moderate, I observed however very clearly to
my mind that Colo. H. appeared extremely agitated & Colo. M. appeared soon to get quite cool and repeated his intire ignorance of
the publication & his surprize to find it published, observing to Colo.
H. if he would not be so warm & intemperate he would explain
everything he Knew of the business & how it appeared to him. I
then addressed my self to Colo. H. and said if he pleased I would
make a proposition he said by all means. I then observed as Colo. M.
had satisfied him as to that part of the business which related to the
publication of the pamphlets, and as the other part was a transaction
of the three Gentlemen before alluded to whether it would not be
much the best way to let the whole affair rest until Colo. M returned
to Philada. and a meeting could be had with Mr. V & Mr. Muhlenburgh & a joint letter or answer given as Colo M. had proposed.
Colo. H. made some answer in a word or two which I understood
as not disapproving the mode I proposed, but what I cannot recollect with precision. I observed a silence & addressed my self to
Mr. C. with observing perhaps my proposition ought to have been
made or would have been made with more propriety to him than to
Colo. H & repeated the same thing over again to Mr. C. who after
asking Colo. M when he should return to Philada. he Colo. M.
answerd on friday [8] at farthest Mr C. then replied that as they
Mr. C. & Colo. H. would go on saturday [9] and as the business could
be finished on Sunday he thought it would be much the best way.
the Gentlemen all rose Mr. C observing that as there would be an

explanation by all three Gentlemen (vizt.) Mr V. Mr M. & Colo M that any warmth or unguarded expressions that had happened during the interview should be buried and considered as tho' it never had happened. Colo. M. said in that respect I shall be governed by Colo. H's conduct. Colo H said he thought that any intemperate expressions should be forgotten to which Colo. M. agreed.   David Gelston

the Interview continued about an hour or a little over myself being present through the whole.

N. York 11th July 1797

ADS, Historical Society of Pennsylvania, Philadelphia.
    1. Born in Bridgehampton, New York, Gelston was a New York City merchant and a Republican politician. He had been a member of the New York Provincial Congress, Continental Congress, New York Assembly, New York Senate, and Council of Appointment. When he wrote this document, he was surrogate of New York County.
    For background to this document, see the introductory note to Oliver Wolcott, Jr., to H, July 3, 1797. See also Wolcott to H, July 7, 1797; H to Monroe, July 8, 10, 1797; Monroe to H, July 10, 1797.
    2. John Barker Church.
    3. This is a reference to H's meeting with Monroe, Frederick A. C. Muhlenberg, and Abraham B. Venable on December 15, 1792.
    4. See Wolcott to H, July 3, 1797, note 52.
    5. See H to Monroe, July 5, 8, 10, 1797.
    6. H's letters to Muhlenberg and Venable have not been found.
    7. The two pamphlets were Nos. V and VI by James Thomson Callender.
    8. July 14, 1797.
    9. H changed his plans and went to Philadelphia on Wednesday, July 12. See Church to H, July 13, 1797.

From John B. Church

[*New York, July 12, 1797.* On July 13, 1797, Church wrote to Hamilton: "I wrote you a few Lines hastily Yesterday at the Post Office." *Letter not found.*]

From John B. Church [1]

New York July 13: 1797

My dear Sir

I wrote you a few Lines hastily Yesterday [2] at the Post Office just as the Post was setting out I am this Instant Return'd from your House, Eliza is well she Put into my Hand the Newspaper with James Thomsonn Callender's Letter to you,[3] but it makes not the least Impression on her, only that she considers the whole Knot of those opposed to you to be ⟨Scoundrels⟩, the Postman brought to your House whilst I was there a Letter which as I saw was from Mr Wolcott,[4] I took, the Liberty to open, it contained the inclos'd Certificate,[5] he mentions his Intention of setting out for New York this Day, but I suppose you saw him last Night, and that he will therefore postpone his Journey. Francis [6] has been with me this Morning he pretends that he has Papers in the Hands of his Brother [7] at Philadelphia which will be useful to you, and as he was very desirous to see you at Phila. I thought it was best to suffer him to set out, I imagine he will be with you before you Receive this Letter, he told me that Giles,[8] Maddison and Finlay [9] had frequent Meetings at his Brothers House and that they used a variety of Perswasions to prevail on him to accuse you of being concern'd with Reynolds in Speculation of Certificates altho he repeatedly assur'd them that it was not true, yet they were dispos'd to go every Length for the Purpose of injuring your Character. I suppose Munroe will be at Philadelphia tomorrow, and I think from what I observed Yesterday that he is inclin'd to be very generous and that he is much embarrass'd how to get out of the Scrape in which he has involv'd himself, I told him that Muhlenberg & Venable had both written to you [10] but I did not communicate any part of the Contents of their Letters. I Receiv'd a Letter Yesterday from Mr Cox [11] coverg a Copy of a Deed from Westcott [12] to him for 73 Patents of Land of which 17 & ½ Tracts are my Property to be drawn by Lot which he says cannot be done untill some Gentlemen to whom they have sold a Part of the Lands (who are now absent from Philadelphia)

Return there and offering to execute a Deed for my undivided Interest, but I wish if possible to have the Patents out of his Hands.[13] My Angelica is not very well—she complains that her Throat is a little sore, I hope it will not be of long Duration. I think from the present Appearances you will not be long detain'd at Philadelphia, but be able to Return on Sunday or Monday. Adieu I am ever sincerely

Yours   J B Church

ALS, Hamilton Papers, Library of Congress.

1. For background to this letter, see the introductory note to Oliver Wolcott, Jr., to H, July 3, 1797; "David Gelston's Account of an Interview between Alexander Hamilton and James Monroe," July 11, 1797.

On July 17, 1797, the following item appeared in the [Philadelphia] *Aurora. General Advertiser:* "Alexander Hamilton has favoured this city with a visit. He has certainly not come for the benefit of the *fresh air.* . . . Perhaps, however, he may have been called to town for the purpose of clearing up the mysterious business, which the 5th and 6th numbers of the History of the United States, just published, have brought to light."

2. Letter not found.

3. Callender to H, July 10, 1797.

4. Wolcott's letter has not been found.

5. This certificate, dated July 12, 1797, was Wolcott's recollection of the events in November and December, 1792, concerning the "Reynolds Affair." It is document No. XXIV in the appendix to the printed version of the "Reynolds Pamphlet," August 25, 1797.

6. Andrew G. Fraunces was a resident of New York City and a son of Samuel Fraunces, the erstwhile proprietor of Fraunces Tavern. He had been dismissed in March, 1793, from a clerkship in the Treasury Department and had returned to New York to open an office as a notary public. See Fraunces to H, May 16, 1793.

7. John Fraunces.

8. William B. Giles, a member of the House of Representatives from Virginia, had been one of H's most outspoken critics when H was Secretary of the Treasury.

9. William Findley was a Republican member of the House of Representatives from Pennsylvania.

10. Abraham B. Venable to H, July 9, 10, 1797; Frederick A. C. Muhlenberg to H, July 10, 1797.

11. Tench Coxe.

12. Robert Westcott. See the introductory note to Coxe to H, February 13, 1795.

13. This sentence concerns the Church partnership with Coxe for the purchase of lands in Pennsylvania. See the introductory note to Coxe to H, February 13, 1795.

From William Constable

[New York] July 13 [1797]. Requests Hamilton's opinion on whether he and his associates "are liable to the penalty of the Bond" signed as security for a deed of sale of Georgia lands.[1]

LC, MS Division, New York Public Library.

1. This letter deals with the controversy over the Georgia Yazoo lands. For information on these land grants and their revocations, see H to James Greenleaf, October 9, 1795, note 3; H to Oliver Wolcott, Jr., June 1–August 31, 1796. For information on the Yazoo land companies, which were organized in 1789, see H's "Defence of the Funding System," July, 1795, note 24.

On August 22, 1795, Senator James Gunn, a Federalist member of the Senate from Georgia, conveyed thirteen and one-half million acres of the Georgia Company's land to James Greenleaf. Greenleaf, in turn, on September 23, 1795, conveyed two million acres to Nathaniel Prime and Samuel Ward, New York City merchants. For H's role as attorney for Prime and Ward and for his opinion on the validity of Greenleaf's title, see H to Greenleaf, October 9, 1795. See also ASP, Public Lands, I, 218, 224; forthcoming Goebel, Law Practice, III. Greenleaf, a native of Massachusetts, who was appointed United States consul at Amsterdam in March, 1793 (Executive Journal, I, 136), speculated extensively in land and securities. He had been a partner with James Watson in the former New York City mercantile firm of Watson and Greenleaf. In 1793, Greenleaf, Robert Morris, and John Nicholson made vast purchases of land in the Federal City. See H to Morris, March 18, 1795, note 21; Morris to H, June 7, 1795, note 7.

By a deed dated February 1, 1796, Prime conveyed a tract of land in Georgia to Samuel Sewall, Samuel Dexter, and George Lane, all of Massachusets. On the same day, Prime, William Payne of Boston, and three New York City merchants, Comfort Sands, Constable, and Samuel Ward, signed a bond as security for the deed (copy, MS Division, New York Public Library). The bond required Prime to provide Sewall, Dexter, and Lane with specific documents to prove that the tract was free of any incumbrances. After the passage by the Georgia legislature in 1796 of the "Rescinding Act" (see H to Greenleaf, October 9, 1795, note 3), which provided for the destruction of all public records of the land sales of 1795, Prime and his associates were unable to fulfill this condition of the bond. Under these circumstances, Constable requested H's opinion on the liability of the vendors to the penalty of the bond.

In his undated opinion H agreed with Constable that the provisions of the "Rescinding Act" gave Prime and his associates a legitimate excuse for nonperformance of the bond. H further stated that the act violated Article I, Section 10, of the Constitution, which provided that no state should pass any law "impairing the Obligation of Contracts" (ADf, Hamilton Papers, Library of Congress; for H's opinion, see also forthcoming Goebel, Law Practice, III). An entry in H's Cash Book, 1795–1804, under the date of July 25, 1797, reads: "received Wm. Constable for opinion 50" (AD, Hamilton Papers, Library of Congress). For a discussion of the Georgia lands controversy along with relevant documents, see forthcoming Goebel, Law Pratice, III.

From James Monroe [1]

[Philadelphia, July 16, 1797]

Mr. Monroe has the honor to inform Colo Hamilton that he arrived in this city yesterday abt. 12.—that Mr. Muhlenburg & himself are to have a meeting this morning upon the subject which concerns him, & after wh. Colo. Hamilton shall immediately hear from them.

Sunday morning
July 16. 1797.

AL, Hamilton Papers, Library of Congress.
1. This letter is document No. XXXII in the appendix to the printed version of the "Reynolds Pamphlet," August 25, 1797. For background to this letter, see the introductory note to Oliver Wolcott, Jr., to H, July 3, 1797; "David Gelston's Account of an Interview between Alexander Hamilton and James Monroe," July 11, 1797.

From Samuel Dexter [1]

New York, July 17, 1797. Asks advice concerning notes he endorsed for James Greenleaf [2] for which Greenleaf provided encumbered lands in upstate New York as security. Encloses fifty dollars as a retainer.[3]

ALS, Hamilton Papers, Library of Congress.
1. Dexter was a Boston attorney who had been a Federalist member of the United States Senate from 1793 to 1795. He subsequently served as Secretary of War and Secretary of the Treasury during the last year of the presidency of John Adams.
2. Greenleaf, a native of Massachusetts, was a business associate of Robert Morris, and with Morris he speculated in land in various parts of the United States.
3. See the entry in H's Cash Book, 1795-1804, for August 26, 1797 (AD, Hamilton Papers, Library of Congress).

To John Fenno [1]

[Philadelphia, July 17–22, 1797]

Mr. Fenno

It has been a general maxim with me, to leave the evidence of my conduct and character to answer the calumnies which party spirit is so incessantly busied in heaping upon me; nor should I have deviated from this course in the present instance, had it not been, that the names of three citizens of political and personal importance in the community appeared to give sanction to the slander. But for this, indeed, I should have been intirely careless about it, relying on those internal characters of falsehood in the story, which could escape no discerning eye. It is necessary to suppose me, not only merely unprincipled but a fool, to imagine that I could not have found better means of gratifying a criminal avarice, and could have stooped to employ such *vile instruments* for such *insignificant ends.* When I determined to take notice of the slander, it was my intention, if the sanction of those names could not be taken away by the explicit declaration of the Gentlemen concerned—to place before the public an exact detail of the affair in all its circumstances, accompanied with the written documents which explain unequivocally its true nature.[2] But as such a disclosure would exhibit some features, which delicacy desires to suppress, and as I have obtained from the Gentlemen concerned a full testimony, that they were convinced by the evidence laid before them of the falsehood of the charge brought against me, and a disavoval of the implication contained in the ambiguous phraze of their Memorandum No. V in these words *"We left him under an impression our suspicions were removed"*— I have concluded to dispense with the proposed detail, and instead of it, to present to the public the documents at foot. No. 1 & 2 are answers to my letter to Messrs. Mughlenberg Monroe and Venable published in No. VI of the History of the U States for 1796.[3] The rest speak for themselves. But in addition to this, I have resolved to place in the hands of my friend   [4] a particular narrative of the affair and the original papers which support it, with permission to communicate them to respectable men of whatever political party on whose delicacy reliance may be placed.

A H

Philadelphia July   [5] 1797

ADfS, Hamilton Papers, Library of Congress.

1. For background to this letter, see the introductory note to Oliver Wolcott, Jr., to H, July 3, 1797. See also H to Fenno, July 6, 1797.

This letter, which has not been found in the *Gazette of the United States, and Philadelphia Daily Advertiser,* was written between July 17 and July 22, 1797. See James Monroe and Frederick A. C. Muhlenberg to H, July 17, 1797; H to Monroe, July 22, 1797.

2. See H to Fenno, July 6, 1797.

3. This is a reference to H to Muhlenberg, Monroe, and Abraham B. Venable, December 17, 1792, which James Thomson Callender printed (*History,* 224). "No. 1 & 2" are Muhlenberg to H, December 18, 1792, and Monroe to H, December 20, 1792.

4. Space left blank in MS.

5. Space left blank in MS.

From James Monroe and
Frederick A. C. Muhlenberg [1]

Phila. July 17. 1797.

Sir

It was our wish to have given a joint answer with Mr. Venable [2] to your favor of the 5th. instant concerning the publication of the proceedings in an enquiry in which we were jointly engaged with him in 1792, respecting an affair between yourself & Mr. Reynolds & into which, from the circumstances attending it, we deemed it our duty to enquire. His departure however for Virginia precludes the posibility of so doing at present. We nevertheless readily give such explanation upon that point as we are now able to give; the original papers having been deposited in the hands of a respectable character in Virga. soon after the transaction took place, & where they now are.

We think proper to observe that as we had no agency in or knowledge of the publication of these papers till they appeard, so of course we could have none in the comments that were made on them.

But you particularly wish to know what the impression was which yr. explanation of that affair made on our minds, in the interview we had with you upon that subject at your own house, as stated in the paper no. 5 of the publication referred to;[3] and to which we readily reply, that the impression which we left on your mind as stated in that number, was that which rested on our own, and which was that the explanation of the nature of yr. connection with Reynolds which you then gave, removed the suspicions we had before entertained of your being connected with him in speculation. Had not this been the case we shod. certainly not have left that impression on your mind, nor shod. we have desisted from the plan we had contemplated in the inquiry, of laying the papers before the President of the U States.

We presume that the papers to which our signatures are annexed are in all cases correct. Tis proper however to observe that as the notes contained in no. 5. were intended only as memoranda of the explanation which you gave us in that interview, as likewise of the information which was afterwards given us by Mr. Clingham on the same subject, and without a view to any particular use, they were entered concisely and without form. This is sufficiently obvious from the difference which appears in that respect, between the papers which preceded our interview & those contained in no. 5 of the publication.[4]

We cannot conclude this letter without expressing our surprise at the contents of a paper in the gazette of the U States of the 8th. instant,[5] which states that the proceedings in the inquiry in question, were the contrivance of two very profligate men who sought to obtain their liberation from prison by the favor of party spirit. You will readily recollect that one of these men Mr. Clingham was never imprisoned for any crime alledged against him by the department of the Treasury; & that the other Mr. Reynolds was upon the point of being released and was actually released & without our solicitation or even wish by virtue of an agreement made with him by that department before the enquiry began. We feel too very sensibly the injustice of the intimation that any of us were influenc'd by party spirit, because we well know that such was not the case: nor can we otherwise than be the more surprised that such an intimation shod. now be given, since we well remember that our conduct upon that

occasion excited yr. sensibility, and obtained from you an unequivocal acknowledgement of our candor.

with consideration we are Sir yr. most obt. & very humble servants   Fredk A C Muhlenberg
                                              Jas. Monroe

LS, in the handwriting of James Monroe, Hamilton Papers, Library of Congress; Df, in Monroe's handwriting, Columbia University Libraries.
    1. This letter is document No. XXXIII in the appendix to the printed ver-
sion of the "Reynolds Pamphlet," August 25, 1797. For background to this
letter, see the introductory note to Oliver Wolcott, Jr., to H, July 3, 1797.
See also "David Gelston's Account of an Interview between Alexander Hamilton and James Monroe," July 11, 1797; H to Monroe, July 5, 8, 10, 1797;
Monroe to H, July 10, 16, 1797.
    2. See Abraham B. Venable to H, July 9, 10, 1797.
    3. For document No. V, printed by James Thomson Callender, see Wolcott
to H, July 3, 1797, notes 1, 50, and 51.
    4. This is a reference to the depositions of Monroe, Muhlenberg, and Venable
on December 13, 1792, which are documents Nos. I (a)–III (a) in the appendix to the printed version of the "Reynolds Pamphlet," August 25, 1797.
Callender published these documents in his *History*, 209–18.
    5. H to John Fenno, July 6, 1797.

To James Monroe and
Frederick A. C. Muhlenberg [1]

[Philadelphia, July 17, 1797]

Gentlemen

I have your letter of this date. It gives me pleasure to receive your
explanation of the ambiguous phraze in the paper No V.,[2] published
with your signatures and that of Mr Venable, and your confirmation
of the fact, that my explanation had been satisfactory to you.

You express your surprise at the contents of a paper in the Gazette
of the U. States of the 8 instant.[3] If you will review that paper with
care, you will find, that what is said about *party spirit* refers to the
view with which the accusation was instituted by Reynolds and
Clingman, not to that with which the enquiry was entered into by
you. They sought, by the *favor of party Spirit*, to obtain liberation
from prison—but though they may have rested their hopes on this
ground it is not said nor in my opinion implied, that you in making
the Inquiry were actuated by that spirit. I cannot however alter my

opinion, that they were influenced by the motive ascribed to them. For though, as you observe, Clingman was not in prison (and so far my memory has erred) and though it may be true, that Reynolds was released [4] before the enquiry began by virtue of an agreement with the Treasury Department (that is the Comptroller of the Treasury) for a reason of public utility which has been explained to you. Yet it will be observed that Clingman, as well as Reynolds was actually under a prosecution for the same offence and that it appears by No. 1. of the papers [5] under your signatures, that for a period of more than three Weeks, while *Clingman* was in the act of soliciting the *"aid and friendship of Mr Mughlenburgh on behalf of himself and Reynolds to get them released or discharged from the prosecution"* he *Clingman* frequently dropped hints to *Mr Mughlenburgh,* that Reynolds had it in his power *very materially to injure the Secretary of the Treasury,* and that Reynolds *knew several very improper transactions of his;* and at last went so far as to state that Reynolds said he had it in his power to hang the Secretary of the Treasury who was deeply concerned in Speculation." From this it appears, that the suggestions to my prejudice were early made and were connected with the endeavour to obtain relief through Mr Mughlenburgh. I derive from all this a confirmation of my opinion, founded on the general nature of the proceeding, that *Reynolds* & *Clingman,* knowing the existence in Congress of a party hostile to my conduct in administration, and that the news papers devoted to it, frequently contained insinuations of my being concerned in improper speculations, formed upon that basis the plan of conciliating the favour and aid of that party towards getting rid of the prosecution by accusing me of Speculation. This is what I meant in the publication alluded to and what I must always believe.

With this explanation, you will be sensible that there is nothing in the publication inconsistent with my declaration to you at closing our interview. It is very true, that after the full and unqualified expressions which came from you together with Mr Venable, differing in terms but agreeing in substance, of your entire satisfaction with the explanation I had given, and that there was nothing in the affair of the nature suggested; accompanied with expressions of regret at the trouble and anxiety occasioned to me—and when (as I recollect it) some one of the Gentlemen expressed a hope that the manner of conducting the enquiry had appeared to me fair & liberal—I replied in substance, that though I had been displeased wtih the mode of introducing the subject to me (which you will remember I manifested at the time in very lively terms) yet that in other respects I was satisfied with and sensible to the candour with which I had been treated. And this was the sincere impression of my mind.

With Consideration   I am Gentlemen   Your Most Obed & humble Servant   Alex Hamilton

Philadelphia July 17. 1797

To Fred: A Mughlenberg ⎱ Esquires
& James Monroe   ⎰

LS, The Library, Lehigh University, Bethlehem, Pennsylvania; ADf, Hamilton Papers, Library of Congress.
    1. This letter is document No. XXXIV in the appendix to the printed version of the "Reynolds Pamphlet," August 25, 1797. For background to this letter, see the introductory note to Oliver Wolcott, Jr., to H, July 3, 1797. See also H to Monroe, July 5, 8, 10, 1797; Monroe to H, July 10, 16, 1797; Abraham B. Venable to H, July 9, 10, 1797; H to Monroe and Muhlenberg, July 17, 1797.
    2. For document No. V, printed by James Thomson Callender, see Wolcott to H, July 3, 1797, notes 1, 50, and 51.
    3. See H to John Fenno, July 6, 1797.
    4. For the suspension of the prosecution against Reynolds and Clingman, see the introductory note to Wolcott to H, July 3, 1797, and Wolcott's deposition of July 12, 1797, which is document No. XXIV in the appendix to the printed version of the "Reynolds Pamphlet," August 25, 1797.
    5. This is a reference to Muhlenberg's statement of December 13, 1792, which is document No. I (a) in the appendix to the printed version of the "Reynolds Pamphlet," August 25, 1797. Callender printed Muhlenberg's statement as document No. I in his *History*, 209–10.

To James Monroe [1]

[Philadelphia, July 17, 1797]

Sir

I send herewith an answer to the joint letter of Mr. Mughlenberg and yourself.[2] It appears to me on reflection requisite to have some explanation on the note of January 2. 1793 [3] with your signature and It may be inferred, from the attention to record the information of Clingman therein stated after what had passed between us, that you meant to give credit and sanction to the suggestion that the defence set up by me was an imposition. You will, I doubt not, be sensible of the propriety of my requesting you to explain yourself on this point also.

I remain with consideration   Sir Yr. obedient servant

ADf, Hamilton Papers, Library of Congress.
1. This letter is document No. XXV in the appendix to the printed version of the "Reynolds Pamphlet," August 25, 1797. For background to this letter, see the introductory note to Oliver Wolcott, Jr., to H, July 3, 1797. See also H to Monroe, July 5, 8, 10, 1797; Monroe to H, July 10, 16, 17, 1797; Abraham B. Venable to H, July 9, 10, 1797; H to Monroe and Frederick A. C. Muhlenberg, July 17, 1797; Monroe and Muhlenberg to H, July 17, 1797.
2. Monroe and Muhlenberg to H, July 17, 1797; H to Monroe and Muhlenberg, July 17, 1797.
3. Monroe's note of January 2, 1793, is printed in the introductory note to Wolcott to H, July 3, 1797.

From James Monroe [1]

Phila. July 17. 1797.

Sir

It is impossible for me to trace back at this moment, occupied as I am with other concerns, all the impressions of my mind at the different periods at which the memoranda [2] were made in the publication to which you refer in your favor of today, but I well remember that in entering the one which bears my single signature, altho' I was surprised at the communication given, yet I neither meant to give or imply any opinion of my own as to its contents. I simply entered the communication as I recd it, reserving to myself the liberty to form an opinion upon it at such future time as I found convenient, paying due regard to all the circumstances connected with it. I am Sir with consideratn. yr. very humble servant

Jas. Monroe

ALS, Hamilton Papers, Library of Congress.
1. This letter is document No. XXXVI in the appendix to the printed version of the "Reynolds Pamphlet," August 25, 1797. For background to this letter, see the introductory note to Oliver Wolcott, Jr., to H, July 3, 1797.
2. The "memoranda" were James Thomson Callender's document No. V and Frederick A. C. Muhlenberg's statement of December 13, 1792. Muhlenberg's statement is printed as document No. 1 (a) in the appendix to the printed version of the "Reynolds Pamphlet," August 25, 1797. For Callender's document No. V, see Wolcott to H, July 3, 1797, notes 1, 50, and 51.

To James Monroe [1]

[Philadelphia, July 18, 1797]

Sir

Your letter of yesterday in answer to mine of the same date was received last night. I am sorry to say, that as I understand it, it is unsatisfactory. It appears to me liable to this inference, that the information of *Clingman* had revived the suspicions which my explanation had removed. This would include the very derogatory suspicion, that I had concerted with Reynolds not only the fabrication of all the letters and documents under his hand, but also the forgery of the letters produced as those of Mrs. Reynolds—since these last unequivocally contradict the pretence communicated by Clingman. I therefore request you to say whether this inference be intended.

With consideration I am Sir   Yr. very Obed servant

A Hamilton
July 18. 1797

James Monroe Esqr

ALS, Lloyd W. Smith Collection, Morristown National Historical Park, Morristown, New Jersey; ALS (photostat), James Monroe Collection, Library of Congress; ADf, Hamilton Papers, Library of Congress.
    1. This letter is document No. XXXVII in the appendix to the printed version of the "Reynolds Pamphlet," August 25, 1797. For background to this letter, see the introductory note to Oliver Wolcott, Jr., to H, July 3, 1797. See also H to Monroe, July 5, 8, 10, 1797; Monroe to H, July 10, 16, 17, 1797; Abraham B. Venable to H, July 9, 10, 1797; H to Monroe and Frederick A. C. Muhlenberg, July 17, 1797; Monroe and Muhlenberg to H, July 17, 1797.

From James Monroe [1]

Phila. July 18. 1797.

Sir

I can only observe that in entering the note which bears my single signature [2] I did not convey or mean to convey any opinion of my own, as to the faith which was due to it, but left it to stand on its own merits reserving to myself the right to judge of it, as upon any fact afterwards communicated according to its import & authenticity.

    with due respect I am Sir yr. very humble servt   Jas. Monroe

ALS, Hamilton Papers, Library of Congress.
    1. This letter is document No. XXXVIII in the appendix to the printed version of the "Reynolds Pamphlet," August 25, 1797. For background to this letter, see the introductory note to Oliver Wolcott, Jr., to H, July 3, 1797. See also Monroe to H, July 10, 16, 17, 1797; H to Monroe, July 5, 8, 10, 17, 18, 1797; Abraham B. Venable to H, July 9, 10, 1797; H to Monroe and Frederick A. C. Muhlenberg, July 17, 1797; Monroe and Muhlenberg to H, July 17, 1797.
    2. Monroe's note of January 2, 1793, is printed in the introductory note to Wolcott to H, July 3, 1797.

To Elizabeth Hamilton

[Philadelphia, July 19, 1797]

    The affair, My Dearest Eliza, upon which I came here has come to a close.[1] But unavoidable delays in bringing it to this point & the necessity of communicating the result must very much against my will keep me here till the departure of the mail stage tomorrow, which will restore me to my Betsey on the day following. I need not tell her how very happy I shall be to return to her embrace and to the company of our beloved Angelica.[2] I am very anxious about you both, you for an obvious reason, and her because Mr. Church mentioned in a letter to me,[3] that she complained of *a sore throat*. Let me charge you and her to be well and happy, for you comprize all my felicity

    Adieu Angel   A H

                                              July 19. 1797

Give my Love to Mr. Church & tell him my moments have been too much employed to write to him. I have not been inattentive to his business.[4]

Mrs.

ALS, Hamilton Papers, Library of Congress.
    1. H had gone to Philadelphia to confer with James Monroe and Frederick

A. C. Muhlenberg about the revival of charges that H had speculated in public funds. See the introductory note to Oliver Wolcott, Jr., to H, July 3, 1797; "David Gelston's Account of an Interview between Alexander Hamilton and James Monroe," July 11, 1797.

An entry in H's Cash Book, 1795–1804, for July 25, 1797, reads: "Account of Expences—Dr. to Cash pd expences to & from Philadelphia 60." A second entry under the date of March, 1798, reads: "Expences Dr. to Cash paid for do. sometime since at Philadelphia 100" (AD, Hamilton Papers, Library of Congress).

2. Angelica Church, Elizabeth Hamilton's sister.
3. John B. Church to H, July 13, 1797.
4. H is referring to Church's land transactions with Tench Coxe. See the introductory note to Coxe to H, February 13, 1795.

To James Monroe [1]

[Philadelphia] July 20. 1797

Sir

In my last letter to you [2] I proposed a simple and direct question, to which I had hoped an answer equally simple and direct. That which I have received,[3] though amounting, if I understand it, to an answer in the negative, is conceived in such circuitous terms as may leave an obscurity upon the point which ought not to have remained. In this situation, I feel it proper to tell you frankly my impression of the matter.

The having any communication with Clingman, after that with me, receiving from him and recording information depending on the mere veracity of a man undeniably guilty of subornation of perjury, and one whom the very documents which he himself produced to you shewed sufficiently to be the accomplice of a vindictive attempt upon me,* leaving it in a situation where by possibility, it might rise up at a future and remote day to inculpate me, without the possibility perhaps from the lapse of time of establishing the refutation, and all this without my privity or knowlege, was in my opinion in a high degree indelicate and improper. To have given or intended to give the least sanction or credit after all that was known to you, to the mere assertion of either of the three persons *Clingman* Reynolds or his wife would have betrayed a disposition

---

* See the letter from Reynolds to Clingman [4] in which he declares that he will have satisfaction of me at all events & that he trusts only to Clingman.

towards me which if it appeared to exist would merit epithets the severest that I could apply.

With consideration I am   Sir   Your very humble serv

A Hamilton

James Monroe Esqr

ADfS, Hamilton Papers, Library of Congress.
    1. This letter is document No. XXXIX in the appendix to the printed version of the "Reynolds Pamphlet," August 25, 1797. For background to this letter, see the introductory note to Oliver Wolcott, Jr., to H, July 3, 1797. See also Monroe to H, July 17, 18, 1797; H to Monroe, July 17, 18, 1797.
    2. H to Monroe, July 18, 1797.
    3. Monroe to H, July 18, 1797.
    4. The letter reads: "I hope I have not forfeited your friendship, the last night's conversation, dont think any thing of it, for I was not myself. I know I have treated ******** friend ill, and too well I am convinced (Here about three lines are torn out.) to have satisfaction from HIM at all events, and you onely I trust too. I will SEE YOU THIS EVENING. HE HAS OFFERED TO FURNISH ME AND MRS. REYNOLDS WITH MONEY TO CARRY US OFF. If I will go, he will see that Mrs. Reynolds has money to follow me, and as for Mr. Francis, he sas he will make him swear back what he has said, and will turn him out of office. This is all I can say till I see you.
    "I am, dear Clingman, believe me, forever your sincere friend." (Callender, History, 221.)

To Elizabeth Hamilton

[Philadelphia, July 21, 1797]

My avocation here [1] my darling Eliza must detain me beyond the departure of the Mail stage but I expect certainly to leave town in the stage of tomorrow morning and still expect to reach New York tomorrow. Love to Angelica & Church. I shall return full freighted with it for My dear Brunettes

Adieu

A H

July 21. 1797

ALS, Columbia University Libraries.
    1. See H to Elizabeth Hamilton, July 19, 1797.

From James Monroe [1]

Phila. July 21. 1797.

Sir

Your favor of yesterday (to use your own language) gives an indelicate and improper coloring to the topic to which it refers. I will endeavor in a few words to place the points in discussion where they ought to stand.

It was never our intention other than to fulfill our duty to the publick, in our enquiry into your conduct, and with *delicacy* & *propriety* to yourself, nor have we done otherwise.

In this truth, in respect to the enquiry, & to our conduct upon that occasion, you have so often assented, that nothing need now be said on that point. In short I shod. have considered myself as highly criminal, advised as I was of your conduct, had I not united in the enquiry into it, for what offense can be more reprehensible in an officer charged with the finances of his country, than to be engaged in speculation? And what other officer who had reason to suspect this could justify himself for failing to examine into the truth of the charge? We did so. Apprized you of what we had done. Heared yr. explanation and were satisfied with it. It is proper to observe that in the expln. you gave, you admitted all the facts upon which our opinion was founded, but yet accounted for them, and for your connection with Reynolds, on another principle. Tis proper also to observe that we admitted your explanation upon the faith of your own statment, and upon the documents you presented, tho' I do not recollect they were proved or that proof was required of them.

You will remember that in this interview in wh. we acknowledged ourselves satisfied with the explanation you gave, we did not bind ourselves not to hear further information on the subject, or even not to proceed further in case we found it our duty so to do. This wod. have been improper, because subsequent facts might be disclosed which might change our opinion, and in which case it wod. be our duty to proceed further. And with respect to Mr. Clingman we thought it highly proper to hear what he had to say, because we had before heard him on the subject, and because you had acknowledged all his previous information to be true, and because he was a party and had a right to be heard on it. You will observe by the entry that we did not seek him, nor even apprize him of the expln. recd. from you. on the contrary that he sought us and in consequence of information recd. from Mr. Wolcott.[2]

The subject is now before the publick and I repeat to you what I have said before, that I do not wish any opinion of my own to be understood as conveyed in the entry which bears my single signature: because when I entered it I had no opinion upon it, as sufficiently appears by my subsequent conduct, having never acted upon it, and deposited the papers with a friend when I left my country,[3] in whose hands they still are. Whether the imputations against you as to speculation, are well or ill founded, depends upon the facts & circumstances which appear against you & upon yr. defense. If you shew that they are ill founded, I shall be contented, for I have never undertaken to accuse you since our interview, nor do I now give any opinion on it, reserving to myself the liberty to form one, after I see your defense: being resolved however so far as depends on me, not to bar the door to free enquiry as to the merits of the case in either view.

This contains a just state of this affr. so far as I remember it, which I presume will be satisfactory to you; and to which I shall only add that as on the one hand I shall always be ready to do justice to the claims of any one upon me, so I shall always be equally prepared to vindicate my conduct and character against the attacks of any one who may assail them. with due

respect I am Sir yr. obt. servt.   Jas. Monroe.

ALS, Hamilton Papers, Library of Congress; copy, in the handwriting of James Monroe, The Library, Lehigh University, Bethlehem, Pennsylvania.

1. This letter is document No. XL in the appendix to the printed version of the "Reynolds Pamphlet," August 25, 1797. For background to this letter, see the introductory note to Oliver Wolcott, Jr., to H, July 3, 1797. See also Monroe to H, July 17, 18, 1797; H to Monroe, July 17, 18, 20, 1797.

2. On January 2, 1793, Jacob Clingman mentioned to Monroe "that he had been apprized of Mr. Hamilton's vindication by Mr. Wolcott a day or two after our interview with him. . . ." See Monroe's statement, January 2, 1793, which is printed in the introductory note to Wolcott to H, July 3, 1797.

3. On March 28, 1794, the Senate confirmed Monroe's appointment as United States Minister Plenipotentiary to France (Executive Journal, I, 157). On June 18 he sailed from Baltimore on the Cincinnatus and arrived at Le Havre on July 31, 1794.

To James Monroe [1]

[Philadelphia, July 22, 1797]

Sir

I have maturely considered your letter of yesterday delivered to me at about Nine last and cannot find in it cause of satisfaction.

There appears to me in the first place an attempt to prop the veracity of Clingman by an assertion which is not correct, namely that I had acknowleged all his previous information to be true. This was not & could not be the fact. I acknowleged parts of it to be true but certainly not the whole—on the contrary, I am able to prove that a material part of it, according to its obvious intent, is false, and I know other parts of it to be so. Indeed in one sense I could not have made the acknowlegement alleged without acknowleging myself guilty.

In the second place, there appears a design at all events to drive me to the necessity of a formal defence—while you know that the extreme delicacy of its nature might be very disagreeable to me. It is my opinion that as you have been the cause, no matter how, of the business appearing in a shape which gives it an adventitious importance, and this against the intent of a confidence reposed in you by me, as contrary to what was delicate and proper, you recorded Clingman's testimony without my privity and thereby gave it countenance, as I had given you an explanation with which you was satisfied and which could leave no doubt upon a candid mind—it was incumbent upon you as a man of honor and sensibility to have come forward in a manner that would have shielded me completely from the unpleasant effects brought upon me by your agency. This you have not done.

On the contrary by the affected reference of the matter to a defence which I am to make, and by which you profess your opinion is to be decided—you imply that your suspicions are still alive. And as nothing appears to have shaken your original conviction but the wretched tale of Clingman, which you have thought fit to record, it follows that you are pleased to attach a degree of weight to that

communication which cannot be accounted for on any fair principle. The result in my mind is that you have been and are actuated
by motives towards me malignant and dishonorable; nor can I
doubt that this will be the universal opinion when the publication of
the whole affair which I am about to make shall be seen.

I am Sir   Your humble serv   A H

                                        Philadelphia July
                                        22. 1797

J M Esq

ADfS, Hamilton Papers, Library of Congress; copy, Hamilton Papers, Library
of Congress.
   1. This letter is document No. XLVI in the appendix to the printed version
of the "Reynolds Pamphlet," August 25, 1797. For background to this letter,
see the introductory note to Oliver Wolcott, Jr., to H, July 3, 1797. See also
Monroe to H, July 17, 18, 20, 21, 1797; H to Monroe, July 17, 18, 20, 1797.

From William Jackson [1]

Philadelphia July 24. 1797

Dear Hamilton,

In compliance with your request I waited upon Mr. Monroe, on
saturday morning, and delivered your letter to him [2]—telling him, at
the same time, that, in consequence of Mrs. Hamilton being in the
last stage of pregnancy,[3] you were under the necessity of going immediately to New York, but would return to Philadelphia in about
a fortnight.

Having read the letter, he said "it is very well, I shall attend to
Colonel Hamilton's movements—I mean to go to Virginia about
the last of next week, but expect to return shortly to Philadelphia."
A conversation ensued which was prefaced on my part by the observation "that, as I was not authorised by Colonel Hamilton to any
thing more than the delivery of the letter, and the verbal communication, which stated the necessity of your going immediately
to New York, on account of Mrs. H's situation, and your intention
to return to Philadelphia in about a fortnight, no conclusions affect-
ing Colonel Hamilton, shoud be drawn from what I might say in the

conversation." From this conversation I drew the following inferences.

That Mr. Monroe thought the correspondence which had passed
between you and him, since your visit to Philadelphia, should be
withdrawn—and destroyed—but that he wished not to be considered as making the proposal to withdraw it.

That if a letter was addressed by you to Mr. Muhlenberg, Mr.
Venable, and Mr. Monroe putting the question whether they meant
to offer any opinion upon, or to annex any sanction to, the last
paper given in by Clingman, he, Mr. Monroe, had no doubt they
would say that they neither meant to give any opinion, nor to annex
any sanction to that paper, as, he said, must naturally be inferred
from their not having acted upon it, which duty would have required of them had they annexed any sanction to the paper.

That he, Mr Monroe, had never intended to become your accuser, nor was he now so disposed.

That his letters to you, in your late correspondence, had been
respectful—and that yours to him he thought had been much otherwise.

These inferences, which I think correctly drawn, from the substance of such part of the conversation, as, considering the limitation which I had assigned to any of its conclusions compromitting
you, I think myself at liberty to repeat.

And, indeed, my dear Hamilton, unless there are very strong reasons to press you on the subject of publishing, I wish it could be
postponed until we meet, which meeting I will facilitate by any
means you may point out.

I am really of opinion that better effects may result from a
declaration on the part of Messrs. Monroe, Muhlenberg, and Venable that they annexed no sanction to Clingman's last paper, and
from the obvious inference that they did not believe it, since if
they had believed it, considering their original disposition towards
you, they would have acted upon it, than from entering into a detailed publication, which although it might fully satisfy all impartial
men, (who by the way are already satisfied) would only furnish
fresh *pabulum* for the virulent invective and abuse of faction to feed
on.

In any determination I think it will be best to suspend the publication until Mr. Monroe returns from Virginia, more especially as *your gauntlet is now before him.*

Let me repeat that your friends and every impartial Man are convinced of your purity as a public Officer—and no one among them can suppose that you are called on to furnish the Presbyterian pulpits with subject matter of declamation, however irrelevant, against the best political interests of our country.

Let me know that you have received this letter and believe me

With sincere affection and esteem   Your faithful friend and servant   W Jackson

Colonel Alexander Hamilton

ALS, Hamilton Papers, Library of Congress.
1. Jackson served as an aide to Major General Benjamin Lincoln during the American Revolution, and in 1781 he was named secretary to the French mission headed by John Laurens. H nominated Jackson to be secretary of the Constitutional Convention, and Jackson was elected on May 25, 1787. Jackson became one of George Washington's secretaries, serving until December, 1791, when he resigned. He subsequently formed a partnership with William Bingham, and in 1795 he married Elizabeth Willing, who was the daughter of Thomas Willing, president of the Bank of the United States. On January 13, 1796, Washington nominated Jackson as surveyor and inspector of the revenue for Philadelphia, and the Senate confirmed the nomination on the following day (*Executive Journal*, I, 197–98).
For background to this letter, see the introductory note to Oliver Wolcott, Jr., to H, July 3, 1797. See also James Monroe to H, July 17, 18, 20, 21, 1797; H to Monroe, July 17, 18, 20, 22, 1797.
2. H to Monroe, July 22, 1797.
3. William Stephen Hamilton was born on August 4, 1797.

From William Jackson [1]

Philadelphia July 25. 1797

Dear Hamilton,

In consequence of a conversation with Dr McHenry,[2] to whom I shewed my letter to you of yesterday, I believed it proper to see Mr. Monroe this morning. He says he shall write to you tomorrow. His letter will form a better rule for further proceeding than any thing I have said, or can say.

My letter of yesterday was too late for the mail, and will be received at the same time with this. But Mr. Monroes determination to write to you himself does away with the necessity of that letter, and, was it not already in the post office, I would not trouble you with it.

I am most sincerely   Your faithful & affectionate servant

W Jackson

ALS, Hamilton Papers, Library of Congress.

1. For background to this letter, see the introductory note to Oliver Wolcott, Jr., to H, July 3, 1797. See also James Monroe to H, July 17, 18, 20, 21, 1797; H to Monroe, July 17, 18, 20, 22, 1797; Jackson to H, July 24, 1797.
2. James McHenry.

From James Monroe [1]

Phila. July 25. 1797.

Sir

I received your Letter of the 22d. instant by Major Jackson [2] and have paid it the attention it merits.

Always anxious to do justice to every one it would afford me pleasure could I answer it in a manner satisfactory to your feelings: but while the respect which I owe to myself forbids my replying in that harsh stile which you have adopted, that same respect with an attention to truth, according to the impressions existing in my mind, will compell me upon all occasions to place this affr. on its true ground.

Why you have adopted this stile I know not. If your object is to render this affair a personal one between us you might have been more explicit, since you well know if that is yr disposition what my determination is, and to which I shall firmly adhere. But if it is to illustrate truth and place the question of its true merits, as I have always been disposed to do, it appears illy calculated to promote that end.

I have constantly said and I repeat again that in making an entry which appears after our interview with you,[3] and which ought to have been signed by the other gentln. as well as myself, I never intended to convey an opinion upon it, nor does it convey any opinion of my own, but merely notes what Clingman stated, leaving it upon his own credit only. But you wish me to state that this communication made no impression on my mind, and this I shall not state because in so doing I shod. be incorrect. On the other hand I do not wish to be understood as intimating that this communication had absolutely changed my opinion, for in that event I shod. have acted on it, whereas the contrary was the case as you well know. And with respect to the propriety of noting down that communication I have no doubt on that point, since I shod. have noted any other that might have been made on the same topic by that or any other party. Indeed if it was proper to note the communications first recd., it was equally so to note this, and *that* you did not disapprove. Had we proceeded in it you may be well assured we shod. have apprized of it, as in the other cases as well from motives of candor towards you, as propriety on our own parts.

It is not my wish to discuss the fact whether you admitted all or only part of Clingmans communication in our interview with you, because upon the principle in which I stand engaged in this affr., not as yr. accuser but called on to explain, it is one of no importance to me. Such was the impression upon my mind; if however the contrary were the case, & you shewed to be so, I shod. be equally contented as if it were otherwise, since it is my wish that truth appear in her genuine character, upon the present, as upon all other occasions. I am Sir with due respect

yr. obt. servant   Jas. Monroe [4]

ALS, Hamilton Papers, Library of Congress; ADf, Lloyd W. Smith Collection, Morristown National Historical Park, Morristown, New Jersey; copy, Hamilton Papers, Library of Congress.

1. This letter is document No. XLVII in the appendix to the printed version of the "Reynolds Pamphlet," August 25, 1797. For background to this letter, see the introductory note to Oliver Wolcott, Jr., to H, July 3, 1797. See also Monroe to H, July 17, 18, 20, 21, 1797; H to Monroe, July 17, 18, 20, 22, 1797; William Jackson to H, July 24, 25, 1797.

2. See Jackson to H, July 24, 1797.

3. For the text of Monroe's statement of January 2, 1793, see the introductory note to Wolcott to H, July 3, 1797.

4. On the back of this letter is an endorsement in Monroe's handwriting which reads: "If he chuses need not publish our correspondence—& may make the most of our certificate.

"No occasion for a reply, as it may lead on & irritate."

To James Monroe [1]

New York July 28. 1797

Sir

Your letter of the 25 instant reached me yesterday.

Without attempting to analize the precise import of your expressions, in that particular, and really at a loss for your meaning when you appeal to my knowlege of a determination to which you say you should firmly adhere, I shall observe, in relation of the idea of my desiring to make the affair personal between us, that it would be no less unworthy of me to seek than to shew such an issue. It was my earnest wish to have experienced a conduct on your part, such as was in my opinion due to me, to yourself and to justice. Thinking, as I did on the coolest reflection, that this had not been the case, I did not hesitate to convey to you the impressions which I entertained, prepared for any consequences to which it might lead.

Nevertheless, it would have been agreeable to me to have found in your last letter sufficient cause for relinquishing those impressions. But I cannot say that I do. The idea is every way inadmissible that *Clingman's* last miserable contrivance should have had weight to shake, though not *absolutely change* the opinion which my explanation had produced; and that having such an effect it should have been recorded and preserved in secret without the slightest intimation to me. There was a vast difference between what might have been proper before and after my explanation; though I am not disposed to admit that the attention which was paid to such characters, ever before, would have been justifiable had it not been for the notes in my handwriting.

But the subject is too disgusting to leave me any inclination to prolong this discussion of it. The public explanation to which I am driven must decide, as far as public opinion is concerned, between us. Painful as the appeal will be in one respect, I know that in the principal point, it must completely answer my purpose.

I am Sir   Your hum servant

ADf, Hamilton Papers, Library of Congress; copy, Hamilton Papers, Library of Congress.

1. This letter is document No. XLVIII in the appendix to the printed version

of the "Reynolds Pamphlet," August 25, 1797. For background to this letter, see the introductory note to Oliver Wolcott, Jr., to H, July 3, 1797. See also Monroe to H, July 17, 18, 20, 21, 25, 1797; H to Monroe, July 17, 18, 20, 22, 1797; William Jackson to H, July 24, 25, 1797.

To Jeremiah Wadsworth [1]

[New York, July 28, 1797]

My Dear Wadsworth

I regretted much, that I did not find you here.

I know you have seen the late publications, in which the affair of Reynold's is revived. I should have taken no notice of them had not the names of Mughlenberg Monroe & Venable given them an artificial importance. But I thought under this circumstance, I could not but attend to them. The affair has so turned that I am obliged to publish every thing.

But from the lapse of time I am somewhat embarrassed to prove Mrs. Reynold's hand writing. Thinking it probable, as she was a great scribbler you must have received some notes from her when she applied to you for assistance, I send you one of her notes to me and if your recollection serves would be much obliged to you to return it with your affidavit annexed—"That you received letters from Mrs. Reynolds, conceived yourself to be acquainted with her hand writing & that you verily believe this letter to be of her hand writing."

If your memory does not serve you then return the letter alone to me. If I remember right I never knew of your agency towards procuring Reynold's relief, till after he was discharged. If your memory stands in the same way, I will thank you to add a declaration to this effect.

Dont neglect me nor lose time.

Yrs. truly

A H

July 28. 1797

J Wadsworth Es

ALS, The Sol Feinstone Collection, Library of the American Philosophical Society, Philadelphia.

1. Wadsworth was a Hartford merchant and a member of the House of Representatives from 1789 to 1795.

For background to this letter, see the introductory note to Oliver Wolcott, Jr., to H, July 3, 1797.

From Edward Jones [1]

[*Philadelphia, July 29, 1797.* On July 30, 1797, Jones wrote to Hamilton and referred to "my letter of yesterday." *Letter not found.*]

1. Jones was a clerk in the Treasury Department.

From Edward Jones [1]

Philadelphia July 30th. 1797

Dear Sir,

In my letter of yesterday,[2] I mentioned an interview which I was to have with a person on the subject of the Conspirators. This interview has taken place. The person alluded to proves to be a Mr. Folwell by profession a printer,[3] and whose character I am told stands sufficiently fair to give weight to his testimony. The facts which he offers to substantiate are as follows—The improper conduct of Mrs. R—— whilst a lodger at his Mothers house—her Confession to him that her husband wished her to prostitute herself for money—her sending for him after she had assumed the Name of Clingman and telling among other things, that she had married Clingman before she had been divorced from Reynolds—in short if we were to pursue the clue which Folwell can furnish, we might obtain a very curious history of the means employed by those Caitiffs to levy contributions on the public—but as our time will not

ALS, Hamilton Papers, Library of Congress.
1. For background to this letter, see the introductory note to Oliver Wolcott, Jr., to H, July 3, 1797.
2. Letter not found.
3. In 1797 Richard Folwell wrote and published a *Short History of the Yellow Fever, that broke out in the city of Philadelphia, in July, 1797; with a list of the dead; of the donations for the relief of the poor, and a variety of other interesting particulars* (Philadelphia, 1797). He also published the *Journals of Congress: containing their proceedings from September 5, 1774, to January 1, 1788,* 13 Vols. (Philadelphia, 1800–1801). From 1805 to 1813 Folwell published *The* [Philadelphia] *Spirit of the Press.*

permit us to extend our enquiries, it will be best to content ourselves with such facts as come within his own knowledge.

Folwell does not wish it to appear as if he had volunteered this business—he therefore requests that you would address him a line, stating that you had been informed of his being acquainted with some circumstances relative to Reynolds & his Wife, and requesting that he would make oath to what he knew—this you can do without mentioning my name or that of Fenno.[4]

The moment I cast my eyes on the Copies of the original documents of the proceedings of the famous Committee of enquiry [5] I was enabled to account for their publication, admitting that the originals have not been resorted to—the fact is, they were transcribed by one of Beckley's [6] Clerks, who has very probably been directed to retain Copies of them.

Since writing the above, Mr. Folwell called on me and put into my possession the enclosed sheets,[7] which upon a careful perusal I

4. John Fenno.
5. From December, 1793, to May, 1794, a committee of the House of Representatives investigated H's conduct as Secretary of the Treasury. See the introductory note to H to Frederick A. C. Muhlenberg, December 16, 1793.
6. John Beckley.
7. The "enclosed sheets" have not been found, but on August 12, 1797, Folwell sent the following statement to Jones: "Having observed, by a Perusal of the History of the United States, that Odium was levelled at the Character of Col. Hamilton, and hearing that he intended to answer the Charges, I thought I possessed the Knowledge of some Traits in the Character of the Persons with whom he seems to be in Company with in that Work, that would in some Measure remove, if known, the Imputations levelled at the public Character of that Gentleman. Wishing, therefore, to see Right prevail, and Innocence protected, I suggested my Knowledge of the most material Incidents that would render improbable, in my Opinion, the Imputations contained in that work. By your Request, I roughly summoned them up; and am sorry, lest some material Point does not strike my Mind, that these Details have never come to the Hand of Col. Hamilton. To remove, however, this Disappointment, I will invoke my Recollection, and enter on the Particulars.
"A few days after Mrs. Reynolds' first appearance in Philadelphia, a Relation of hers requested my Mother to receive her for a few Days, into our House, as she was a Stranger in the City, and had come here to endeavour to reclaim a prodigal Husband, who had deserted her and his Creditors at New York. This was readily consented to when her innocent Countenance appeared to show an innocent Heart. Not more than two Days after she was at our House. She found her Husband was here—had been in Gaol, and was but just liberated. In a Day or two after she said, they had an Interview, but, could not come to Terms of Pacification. Her Mind, at this Time, was far from being tranquil or consistent, for, almost at the same Minute that she would declare her Respect for her Husband, cry, and feel distressed, they would vanish, and Levity would succeed, with bitter Execrations on her Husband. This Incon-

sistency and Folly was ascribed to a troubled, but innocent and harmless Mind. In one or other of these Paroxysms, she told me, so infamous was the Perfidy of Reynolds, that he had frequently enjoined and insisted that she should insinuate herself on certain high and influential Characters,—endeavour to make Assignations with them, and actually prostitute herself to gull Money from them. About five days after she first came at our House, Mr. Reynolds had an Interview; and we, while she commanded Commiseration, were induced to warn her to depart, that a Character so infamous as her Husband should not enter our House. She moved to a reputable Quaker Lady's at No. ——— North Grant Street; where they lived together; but, so the Family said, did not sleep together.

"Lately I have understood that Letters were frequently found in the Entry inviting her Abroad;—and that at Night she would fly off, as was supposed to *answer* their Contents. This House getting eventually too hot for them, they made their Exit. During the Period of their Residence there, she informed me she had proposed pecuniary Aid should be rendered by her to her Husband in his Speculations, by her placing Money in a certain Gentleman's Hands, to buy of him whatever public Paper he had to sell, and that she would have that which was purchased given to her,—and, if she could find Confidence in his future Prudence, she would eventually return him what he sold. From this House, if I recollect, they made their Exit for a short Time from Philadelphia; but soon returned; and gave me an Invitation to wait on them at No. ——— North Sixth Street. At this Time he wanted me to adventure with him in Turnpike Script,—to subscribe for which he was immediately to embark for Lancaster. The first Deposit for which was but trifling a Share—whether one or ten Dollars I do not recollect. Some considerable Time after (if necessary, Data can be procured) they removed and lived in stile in a large House in Vine Street, next to the Corner of Fifth. Here I had an Invitation, if I recollect, and being disposed to see if possible how People supported Grandeur, without apparently Friends, Money or Industry, I accordingly called. Mrs. Reynolds told me her Husband was in Gaol; and on asking her for what, she said he had got a Man to administer to the Estate of a supposed deceased Soldier and give him a Power of Attorney to recover what was due to him by the Public. That he had accordingly recovered it, but that *incautiously* and *imprudently* having given the Heir-Apparent an indemnifying Bond, that when the Soldier came to Life, the administration delivered the indemnifying Bond up to the real Heir, that then he was detected. That she said a Mr. Clingman, his Partner, was in the same Predicament. Before this Conversation was ended, in entered Mr. Clingman, to whom I was introduced. She referred to him for a more correct Narrative. But his Conversation seemed to me as if he wished to darken instead of throwing Light on this Information. He asked her what Luck she had in her Applications for Reynold's Liberation? She said she had called on the Governor, Mr. [Thomas] Mifflin, and that he felt for her: Referred her to Mr. [Alexander J.] Dallas and that he felt also. She said she called on Mr. Hamilton, and several other Gentlemen; and that they had all felt.

"In a few Days after Reynolds was liberated, possibly in consequence of the Coincidence of Sympathy these Gentlemen had in Feeling. Here the Curtain dropt from my View, their Career, till perhaps a Year or two after Mrs. Reynolds wrote me a Letter to call on her at a very reputable and genteel Lodging House in Arch Street, No.   . In this note she apprized me of her Marriage with Mr. Clingman, which is annexed. Her Business she gave me to understand, was with me, to clear up her Character in East Nottingham, Cecil County, Maryland. That she lived there happily with Mr. Clingman, at the House of a Distant Relation of mine, till she had mentioned the knowing of

find to contain the most important information. You will observe by his letter to you on the back of this last sheet,[8] that he wishes you to throw his communication into a better form, preserving however as much as possible the style, that the production may appear to be his own. This task I would have undertaken myself, but my health forbids the attempt. I have pledged myself to Mr. Folwell, that the rough draught shall be returned—you will therefore transmit it to me as soon as you have extracted everything useful to yourself. Preserve at all events, the anecdote of Mrs. R's application to Govr. Mifflin & Secretary Dallas. Now that I mention Mifflin's name, it is proper to inform you, he does not wish to recollect the fact referred to him in your publication—it has therefore been struck out.[9]

Just as I was going to close this long Epistle, Folwell called on me with a letter signed M. Clingman a copy whereof is enclosed. This letter proves two important facts—first—her hand writing—

---

our Family in Philadelphia; and that a Cousin of mine had given out that she must be the same Person who had left with her an infamous Character by the name of Mrs. Reynolds. She wished me to clear it up. I expostulated on the Inconsistency of this, that as it was bad before she had certainly increased it, as her Husband, Reynolds, I understood was alive in N. York. She said she had a Divorce; and that only one Fault she had incurred in her Change,—that she got married to Clingman one half Hour before she obtained the divorce. Since I have heard Nothing from her; only that she wrote me a very pathetic Letter—begging, as she was to return, that I would clear up her Character. This I have mislaid—but it would move any one almost to serve her, that was not perfectly acquainted with her Character, confirmed by actual Observation.

"I believe the Dates of these material Circumstances may be readily ascertained where necessary. I intended to digest the Confusion in which I throwed my former Observations that were mislaid. But you expressed Hurry. Had I a copy of that, this should be better arranged. The Same Reason of Hurry induces me to submit that this may be sent to Colonel Hamilton as it is. Relying that he will Retrench and improve—allowing me to alter what may not be agreeable to myself. My Brother told me, when he was in N. York, a young Man of good Character before,—Clerk to Henry Manly of this City once) was hung in N. York for Forgery. That he saw his Dying Speech—that it said, he was deluded by Clingman and Reynolds to the Fact for which he was to suffer. Mr. Hamilton can ascertain this.

"It is now two o'Clock on Sunday Morning. I am sleepy. I shall have Opportunity to do, with Mr. Jones's Approbation and my own, what Defect may be here, that Col. Hamilton with this may not entirely do." (Hamilton, *Intimate Life*, 473–76.)

Allan McLane Hamilton states incorrectly that Folwell's statement was addressed to C. W. Jones.

8. Letter not found.

9. In the draft of the "Reynolds Pamphlet," August 25, 1797, there is no reference to Mifflin.

Second, her connection with Clingman. Altho the motives which have governed Folwell in making these disclosures are highly disinterested—I should much approve of some means being adopted to convince him of your sense of the service he has rendered to you. The mode is submitted to yourself. He appears to possess a wish, that his communications might be cloathed in language favorable to his talents as a Writer—it is but reasonable therefore that he should be gratified—it is his desire also that his information may be published in the shape of a letter.

With esteem   I am   Dr Sir   Yours &c   E. Jones

Colo. Hamilton

From William Jackson [1]

Philadelphia July 31. 1797

Dear Hamilton,

Your letter to Mr. Monroe,[2] which I received under cover on saturday last, was delivered to him on that day—he said he should not leave Philadelphia until thursday, and gave me to understand that he would write to you.

It appears to me that your publication must go on, as Mr. M did not seem willing to grant the certificate, and I confess I should be unwilling to recommend any compromise short of that.

I am sincerely   Your faithful & affectionate servant   W Jackson

ALS, Hamilton Papers, Library of Congress.
    1. For background to this letter, see the introductory note to Oliver Wolcott, Jr., to H, July 3, 1797; Jackson to H, July 24, 25, 1797.
    2. H to James Monroe, July 28, 1797.

From James Monroe [1]

Phila. July 31. 1797.

Sir

Your letter of the 28th which I have recd. claims a short answer.

I have always stated to you that I had no wish to do you a personal injury. The several explanations wh. I have made accorded with truth & my ideas of propriety. Therefore I need not repeat them.

If these do not yield you satisfaction I can give no other, unless called on in a way which always for the illustration of truth, I wish to avoid, but which I am ever ready to meet. This is what I meant by that part of my letter [2] which you say you do not understand.[3] With due respect I am

Yr. humble servt   Jas. Monroe

ALS, Hamilon Papers, Library of Congress; two copies, in H's handwriting, Hamilton Papers, Library of Congress.

1. This letter is document No. XLIX in the appendix to the printed version of the "Reynolds Pamphlet," August 25, 1797. For background to this letter, see the introductory note to Oliver Wolcott, Jr., to H, July 3, 1797. See also Monroe to H, July 17, 18, 20, 21, 25, 1797; H to Monroe, July 17, 18, 20, 22, 28, 1797; William Jackson to H, July 24, 25, 31, 1797.

2. Monroe to H, July 25, 1797.

3. At the end of one of the copies of this letter H wrote: "The sequel of this correspondence is unnecessary to the present purpose."

From Jeremiah Wadsworth [1]

Hartford August 2d 1797

Dear Sir

your favor of the 28th July arrived late last evening. I have not the least knowledge of Mrs. Reynolds's hand writing nor do I remember ever to have recd a line from her if I did they were destroyed but a letter or two for you which by Your request I returned to her or destroyed. The first time I ever saw or heared of her She came to my lodgings one Morning [2]—and stated the Situation of her husband and desired me to apply to You Mr Woolcott & General Mifflin for his Liberation told me she was the Wife of Reynolds the Sister of Col DuBois. I told her I knew her husband. that his Character was bad and no interference of mind would be proper nor could it suceed: at this moment John Vaughn [3] came in on a Visit & supposeing me engaged offered to retire. I told him to stay the Lady was going she then said she wished to say something in private. Mr. V took leave. And she immediately fell into a flood of Tears and told me a long storey about her application to You for Money when in distress in her husbands Absence & that it ended in a amour & was discovered by her husband from a letter she had written to you which fell into his hands. I told her I would see Mr. Woolcott & G Mifflin The next Morning I told Mr. Woolcott what had passed he then related the transaction for which Clingn & Reys had been committed. I then went to Mifflin and told him I came at ye request of Mrs. Reynolds. he imediately told me that she had told him the Story of the amour. I imediately left him went to Mrs Reynolds and told her who I had seen that all interference on my part was at an end that in my Opinion her husband must undergo a trial. She then mention the transaction of Baron Glaubeck would be brot into View [4] and be injurious to You. I told her it was fortunate that I knew more about Glaubecks affair than any body and it could not injure you or Any body else. A Mr. Clingman whom I had never seen before and seemed to have been sent for was present part of the time. From this interview I was fully confirmed in my Opinion before formed that the whole business was a combination among them to Swindle you. Mrs Reynolds called on me again and urged me deliver letters to You. You refused to receive them & desired me to return letters for You or destroy them I do not know which.[5] I rec'd several Messages from her and again went to her house told her you would hold no correspondence with her and gave her my Opinion as at first that her husband must undergo a trial. I can not be particular as to time & date and I do not remember that I ever knew how he was liberated untill I lately saw Mr Woolcott. I certainly never considered myselfe as having any agency in procureing Reynolds's relief nor do I remember ever to have had any conversation with You on the subject untill after your meeting with the Mess Munroe Melenburg & Venables. and had supposed Reynolds to have been ⟨released⟩ by their influence he was ⟨ashamed⟩ to have been so ⟨–⟩ after an Explanation with you. I am sorry you have found it necessary to publish any thing for it will be easy to invent new Calumnies & you may be kept continualy employed in answring. be Assured it never will be in the power of your enemies to give the public an opinion that you have Speculated in ye funds, nor do they expect it: I should have replied by this days Post—but the Mail arrives here at nine at night & goes out at Two in the Morning.

I am D sir truly yours   J Wadsworth

ADfS, The Sol Feinstone Collection, Library of the American Philosophical Society, Philadelphia.
  1. For background to this letter, see the introductory note to Oliver Wolcott, Jr., to H, July 3, 1797.
  2. This meeting took place between November and December, 1792, while James Reynolds was in prison.
  3. Vaughan was a Philadelphia merchant.
  4. The claim of Baron de Glaubeck was at issue in the charges made against H by Andrew G. Fraunces in 1793. See Fraunces to H, May 16, 1793.
  5. At this point in the MS Wadsworth wrote and then crossed out: "She called on me again—to know if I had delivered You the Letters and wished you to furnish her with Means of geting out of Town. I then told her You would not receive the Letters she beged me to see You & urge you enable her to go out of Town. I called on You & you persisted in refusing her letters & said <-> any correspondance or giving any aid I waited on her imediately & told her your resolution."

From William North [1]

Duanesburg [New York] August 3, 1797. "I had the honour to write to you on the subject of an dispute with Voght some time since. . . .[2] You knew how much less calculated We are to combat our adversaries than Mr Duane was, & consequently how much more we must lean on you for support. If the thing could be arranged for the week after the Supreme Court in Octr, it would save us some expense . . . , & it would be conferring an Obligation on those who esteem You too much not to be pleased by receiving a mark of Your attention."

ALS, Hamilton Papers, Library of Congress.
  1. For an explanation of the contents of this letter, see Abraham Van Vechten to H, September 16, 1796.
  2. North to H, June 4, 1797.

From Egbert Benson [1]

[New York] August 4, 1797. "I take the first leisure moment to write to you on the Subject you mentioned to Me on Tuesday last, as to the Probability, whether after the Expiration of the seven Years granted by the first Law, the Legislature would prolong the Term for which the Dutch Gentlemen might hold the Lands they have purchased in our State? For four successive Sessions of the Legislature my Endeavours were unceasing, and yet nothing more could be effected than in the first Instance than a privilege for seven Years only, and that afterwards extended for thirteen Years more on Condition that the Purchasers would advance a Sum on Loan for the western Canal.[2] Both these Bills passed the Assembly with great Difficulty, and without meaning to make a Merit of it with these Gentlemen, I will venture to say and which I am perswaded You will readily beleive, that much is to be attributed to my personal Influence with many of the Members. . . ."

ALS, Gemeentearchief Amsterdam, Holland Land Company. These documents were transferred in 1964 from the Nederlandsch Economisch-Historisch Archief, Amsterdam.
    1. This letter was addressed to H in his capacity as an attorney for the Holland Land Company. For the full text of this letter and other relevant documents, see forthcoming Goebel, Law Practice, III.
    For an explanation of the contents of this letter, see H to Théophile Cazenove, January 22, 1796, notes 2 and 3; Cazenove to Benson and H, May 29, July 5, 1797. See also Robert Morris to H, June 7, 1795.
    2. This is a reference to the Western Inland Lock Navigation Company. See Cazenove to Benson and H, May 29, 1797, note 3.

From Alexander Hamilton [1]

Greenock [Scotland] 4th. August 1797

My Dear Sir.

I am about to introduce to your acquaintance a cousin & a name-sake, by the desire of my father, Mr. William Hamilton; who received the honor of your letter of the 2d. May, & being little in the habits of writing has given it to me to answer, by returning our United thanks for the information it conveyed relative to a person, whose conduct & character have acquired him a degree of reputation, in which our family is sensibly interested. As I hope to be

ALS, Hamilton Papers, Library of Congress.
    1. The author of this letter was the son of William Hamilton, who was the brother of H's father, James Hamilton. See H to William Hamilton, May 2, 1797.
    On the back of this letter the following note is written in an unidentified handwriting: "This gentleman was in 1802 imprisoned in France and released through the influence of Hamilton writing to Talyrand." For H's efforts to secure the release of his cousin Alexander Hamilton, see H to Charles Maurice de Talleyrand-Périgord, March 25, 1804.

favored with your future correspondence, it might be proper to give
you some idea of your correspondents, but alas! the trivial circumstances it would be my lot to record, must form a very unpleasant
contrast with the narrative you have sent my father. To tell you
that I went out at an early age to Bengal; that, in consequence of
some genuis for acquiring languages I Officiated as Persian & Bengal
Interpreter to the Governmt, during some years of my residence
there; & finally that bad health compelled me to relinquish my
propects in that country somewhat sooner than prudence would
have dictated, were a narrative little adapted to interest a man whose
life has been spent in rearing an infant state, in forming its constitution, & regulating its polity. Since my return to Scotland, about
two years ago my time has been chiefly devoted to literary pursuits,
particularly those connected with my early studies; the manners,
the genius & the history of oriental nations; subjects little attended
to in Europe, in consequence of being locked up in languages nearly
inaccessible, yet offering a rich feild of curious speculation to the
antiquarian, the historian & the philosopher. Permit me to ask, if
Mr. Thomas Law,[2] whom I had the pleasure of knowing in Bengal,
is still in New-york. If he is there, & of your acquaintance, I beg to
refer you to him for an account of the person who now solicits
the honor of your correspondence. My brother Robert, who intends himself the pleasure of waiting on you,[3] after his return to
America, is younger than me, & has from a very early age been
bred to the sea, (a line of life perfectly congenial to his disposition)
& has consequently acquired a very compleat knowledge of maritime affairs. His open, honest, & ingenuous mind is sufficiently
characteristic of the British Tar, & resembles in its best qualities the
real or Assumed character of which that body of men have so long
been in possession. The partiality of a brother may doubtless dis-
qualify me from appreciating exactly the worth of an object so
dear to me, but if I have the least knowledge of his disposition, you

2. Law, the son of the Bishop of Carlisle, went to India in 1773 in the service
of the East India Company. Because of poor health he returned to England in
1791. In 1794 he emigrated to the United States, and in 1796 he married Elizabeth Parke Custis, the granddaughter of Martha Washington. He settled in
Georgetown and invested heavily in real estate in the Federal City. Between
1794 and his death in 1834 he made two or three short visits to England.
3. See H to William Hamilton, May 2, 1797.

will have no reason to repent of the exertions you may bestow on the promotion of his views. My two younger brothers (Walter & William) are in India; the first in a mercantile line, & the latter who is a youth of sixteen on the Company's military establishment, as an Ensign, in Bengal. My oldest sister is married to Mr. Thos. Twemlaw, a merchant in Liverpool, & the youngest is at home with my father. I must intreat your forgiveness for this prolix account of a family of which you have hitherto heard so little, but the ties of consanguinity, which unite us so nearly must plead my excuse. My father has long resided at this place, where he formely carried on a pretty extensive commerce. At present he is entirely disengaged from business & as my habits were at all times averse to pecuniary pursuits, we propose next summer to remove from hence to Edinburgh, which affords a more varied society, & great facility for indulging my propensity to study. I hope, however, your other avocations will admit of your writing me oftener than once previous to our removal: I also beg you will have the goodness to write to my Brother Robert, who will reach St. Johns, New Brunswick, towards the close of the present autumn. He is master of a vessel belonging to that port, but will relinquish that situation & proceed to Newyork from St. Johns, if he should find on his arrival there that your letters encourage him to expect your assistance in procuring a better. Will you permit me to ask, if you destine any of your sons for the learned professions, & should that prove the case, might not the university of Edinburgh justly celebrated for the eminence of its professors, prove a proper place for their education? I need not say what pleasure it would afford us to see them in this country, & that you might rely on every attention being paid to them.

The eyes of all Europe are fixed on Lisle, the scene of the important negociations, which are (possibly) to decide the fate of England & France.[4] In the mean time, the former begins to revive from the constant alarms, which the dread of an invasion,[5] the revolt

4. See Rufus King to H, June 27, 1797, note 1.

5. On December 15, 1796, a French expedition of fourteen thousand men under the command of General Louis Lazare Hoche had set out from Brest for Bantry Bay in Ireland. Because of bad weather, the fleet was scattered and only part of it reached Bantry Bay, and those ships which did were ordered to turn back without landing. Another expedition, which left Brest on February 21, 1797, to attack Bristol, landed instead at Fishguard in South Wales and soon afterwards surrendered to British forces.

in the north of Ireland,[6] the mutiny of our seamen,[7] & the embarrassments of the Bank [8] have occasioned, during the whole of last
session of parliament. In the same proportion as our fears have subsided, our hopes (those fallacious hopes that have so often disappointed us) have returned, & I question if we should now accept
of the same terms, which a few months ago we would have wel-
comed as our only resource. The dissention between the Executive
Directory of France & the legislative Council assume daily a more
serious aspect, since the new third have taken their seats.[9] But I presume you receive more speedy & more accurate intelligence than is
in my power to furnish you with. My father & sister join me in best
wishes for you, Mrs. Hamilton & your whole family, to whom we
intreat you will offer our sincere regards

 I am My Dear Sir, Your faithful & Obedt. Servt. A. Hamilton

6. Acts of rebellion by the republican forces in northern Ireland led to the
proclamation of martial law on March 13, 1797. A stricter version of martial
law was proclaimed on May 17, 1797. Following acts of terrorism by Orange-
men and British forces, a temporary peace was established by the middle of
the summer.

7. In mid-April, 1797, the crews of the Channel Fleet under Lord Bridport
at Spithead, having unsuccessfully petitioned Lord Howe for an increase in
wages, mutinied and refused to put to sea. Other causes for grievance were
the poor and insufficient food and the bad treatment of the sick and wounded.
The mutiny was ended by the cabinet's agreement to the demands within a
week and a royal pardon. The following month, however, the sailors of the
North Sea fleet at the Nore mutinied. In July, 1767, their leader, Richard
Parker, and twenty-two others were hanged.

8. On February 26, 1797, the Bank of England temporarily suspended payments. See Rufus King to H, March 8, 1797, note 1.

9. The elections of April, 1797, for replacing one-third of the French deputies to the French legislative councils resulted in a majority for the right-
wing Constitutionalists. During the following months the new councils re-
pealed legislation against priests and émigrés and sought to gain administrative
power and control of the war from the Directory. Meanwhile, in July, 1797,
prompted by the leaders of the Constitutional party, François Barthélemy and
Lazare Nicolas Marguerite Carnot, the two more moderate members of the
Directory, proposed the dismissal of the government's four Revolutionary
ministers. On July 16, however, the "triumvirs" in the Directory (Paul François
Jean Nicolas Barras, Jean François Reubell, and Louis Marie de La Révellière-
Lépeaux) overrode this decision and dismissed the three Constitutionalist min-
isters.

To James Monroe [1]

New York Aug 4. 1797

Sir

In my opinion the idea of a personal affair between us ought not to have found a place in your letters [2] or it ought to have assumed a more positive shape. In the state to which our correspondence had brought the question, it lay with you to make the option whether such an issue should take place. If what you have said be intended as an advance towards it, it is incumbent upon me not to decline it. On the supposition that it is so intended I have authorised Major Jackson to communicate with you and to settle time and place.

I am Sir   Your Humble servant

James Monroe Esq

ADf, Hamilton Papers, Library of Congress; copy, in Monroe's handwriting, The Library, Lehigh University, Bethlehem, Pennsylvania.
    1. This letter is document No. L in the appendix to the printed version of the "Reynolds Pamphlet," August 25, 1797. For background to this letter, see the introductory note to Oliver Wolcott, Jr., to H, July 3, 1797.
    2. For the correspondence between H and Monroe, see Monroe to H, July, 17, 18, 20, 21, 25, 31, 1797; H to Monroe, July 17, 18, 20, 22, 28, 1797. See also William Jackson to H, July 24, 25, 31, 1797.

From William Jackson [1]

Philadelphia August 5. 1797

My dear Sir,

Immediately on the receipt of your Letter this morning,[2] I waited on Colonel Monroe and observing that "Colonel Hamilton considering your letter [3] as an overture to a personal meeting, has directed me to deliver this letter from him to you [4]—and I have further to inform you that I am prepared to give effect to the purpose of his letter."

Mr. Monroe received the letter, and then asked me if it was a challenge. I told him that propriety, in every relation, forbad me to say that I was the Bearer of a challenge—the letter would explain its purport. He then returned the letter to me, and said he would consult a friend.[5]

I desired him to attend the message, which I would repeat, as stated within the inverted commas, On which he requested me to lay down the letter, and as soon as he had consulted with his friend, he would give an answer either to you or myself. Here we parted. By to-morrow's post I may be able to give you the result of his determination.

I have delivered the other paper to Mr. Jones.[6]

Accept my congratulations on the birth of your Son [7]—and always believe me

Affectionately yours   W Jackson

ALS, Hamilton Papers, Library of Congress.

1. For background to this letter, see the introductory note to Oliver Wolcott, Jr., to H, July 3, 1797; Jackson to H, July 24, 25, 31, 1797.

2. Letter not found.

3. Monroe to H, July 31, 1797.

4. H to Monroe, August 4, 1797.

5. On August 6, 1797, Monroe wrote to Aaron Burr: "I enclose you a copy of my correspondence with Colo. Hamilton since my return to this city which I hope you will immediately peruse. I send likewise a letter to him in reply to his last which after reading & sealing I wish you to present him. I have written this last letter as you will perceive to demd. whether he meant his as a direct challenge on his part or as the acceptance of one on mine (the latter being the idea of Major Jackson), or of an invitation on my part. If the former be the case, then you will accept it of course. If the latter then the expln. which I give ends the affr., as I never meant to give him a challenge, on acct. of what has passed between us, seeing no cause so to do; having conceded nothing wh. as a man of honor and truth I ought not: and in this stile following his example, especially when our interview at New York is also notic'd: an example however which ought not to have been given.

"If the affr. takes the first course, then time must be given me on acct. of my publication, the adjustment of my family affrs. &c having been long absent and they requiring much attention, especially when it is considered that in case of accident I shod. leave Mrs. M. almost friendless in Virga., she being of New York. For the whole of this abt. three months wod. be necessary—two wod. be for the publication only. The place I shod. wish to be abt. or near the Susquehannah, but on this head I shod. not be vigorous. As you have a child & a familly I wod. not trouble you unless in yr. neighbourhood, but shall calculate on the aid of Mr. Dawson. However tis probable I shod. be forced to ask yr. aid, <– –> much confidence in you.

"You will explain to him, if he asks expln., why I referr'd him to you and did not adjust it with Major Jackson, that I supposed it wod. be more agreable to him to have you authorized to represent me fully in the affr. for the purpose of closing it at once with him on the spot: and that to me it was an object of importance, since being much occupied in other concerns and meaning soon to leave town, I wished to have my time & mind free from interruption.

"I hope you will settle this disagreeable affr. finally so that we write no more either to the other on it. Nor need I observe that as I have entire confidence in your judgment, honor and friendship for me, so I equally confide that you will close it in such a manner, as duly observing that a certain result, ought always to be avoided, whilst it can with propriety, especially by a person with a family, yet it is not to be avoided by the slightest sacrifice or condescention.

"If the affr. takes an amicable issue, and he enters into conversation on the publication &c afterwards then you may hint to him that if he chuses, you think all the letters between him & me had better be suppress'd or not published in his publication: since they certainly weaken the ground of Muhlenburg's & my letter to him, wh. was written in a spirit of conciliation, as well as of truth. In that case too he may make his inferences from *that* as he pleases for we never mean to say a word on the subject, if he does not attack us. Indeed I was never averse to the simple question 'did you mean to give any opinion of yr. own as to the credibility due to the entry bearing your single signature'? to answer 'that I did not but meant it to stand on the credibility of the man.' This wod. have been perhaps of some service to him, <‑‑> never asked it, always endeavouring to get more from me than in conscience, I cod. give. Nor shod. I now hesitate (provided you approved it) after the affr. is settled (if settled amicably) to give such an answer to such a question; observing that the affr. be first settled, before any other <‑>.

"I am satisfied he is pushed on by his party friends here, who to get rid of me, wod. be very willing to hazard him. Of this I have many reasons to be well assured of.

"In truth I have no desire to persecute this man, tho' he justly merits it, and except giving a certificate to what in truth I cod. not, did not from the first moment of my arrival care, how favorable the affr. appeard for him. I had no hand in the publication, was sorry for it—and think he has acted, by drawing the publick attention to it, & makeing it an affr. of more consequence than it was in itself, very indiscreetly. And in case he manages his defense so as to make Muhlenburg Venable & myself, become his accusers in our own defense he loses the benefit of our certificate &c. However this is between ourselves. . . ." (ALS, Lloyd W. Smith Collection, Morristown National Historical Park, Morristown, New Jersey.)

See also Monroe to H, July 25, 1797, note 4.
6. See Edward Jones to H, July 30, 1797.
7. William Stephen Hamilton was born on August 4, 1797.

From Rufus King

London Aug. 6 [–10] 1797

Dear sir

No satisfactory Opinion can yet be formed concerning the termination of the negotiations for Peace. Even those who are supposed to have the best information are without confidence—on the one

Hand peace may be concluded sooner than any one thinks probable, on the other the negotiations at Lisle [1] and montebello [2] may be suddenly broken off, and France again engaged with austria as well as England. A great Struggle in which all Europe think themselves interested, exists between the two Councils and a majority of the Directory, for it is well understood that almost every question is decided in this latter Body by three against two.[3] If the councils prevail, peace is believed to be more probable—if the war continues Denmark, and the neighbouring free Cities, Portugal, perhaps Switzerland, and even Greece [4] as well as the whole of Italy will be revolutionized. I wish I could write to you with the same freedom as we could converse: how far the new order of things is to extend, which are still to be overturned, and who are to be spared, is a subject concerning which we may amuse ourselves with Conjectures; it would be a consolation, could we any where discover a mind of adequate foresight and authority, to influence, combine, and apply to their proper and legitimate uses, the dispositions, and the means, which unquestionably exist, to resist and baffle the monstrous Force, which overturns, and will continue to lay waste every Country against which it bends its energies—paradoxical as it may appear, the People are less wrong than their Governments, which every where seem to be destitute of both wisdom and courage. I cannot except even the Government of this Country, which possessing the command of the Resources of the Richest nation in Europe, with a clear and distinct view of the total insecurity of any compromise with their Enemy, still dismount and lower the national Spirit and Courage by fruitless and repeated Efforts to restore Peace. Men are mortal, and by a Law to which they are subject, can exist but for a limited time. Societies are exempt from this Law, and there is nothing in their nature that limits their improvement, or Duration; still the Analogy is but too strict, and we seem to be doomed to witness, if not to suffer in, the Dissolution of the present social organization.

Farewell, when I am able to give you a gayer prospect, I will write to you again.

Yours very sincerely

PS. 10 Aug. a very short time will ascertain who are to rule in Fr—the armies are loud and publish their sentiments with great

Boldness [5]—it wd. not be surprizing shd. they try their hands and give another Constitution to the imperishable Republic. The negotiations at Lisle are suspended in Effect (tho in form they continue) and will continue so till the Parties decide which shall govern.[6]

AL[S], Hamilton Papers, Library of Congress.

1. See King to H, November 30, 1796, note 3; June 27, 1797, note 1.

2. After the conclusion of preliminaries for a peace between France and Austria at Leoben on April 18, 1797 (see King to H, April 29, 1797, note 4), Napoleon established himself at Mombello (Montebello), near Milan, and began negotiations for a treaty. Early in July the negotiators moved to Udine. Determined to extend the French possessions beyond the limits established at Leoben, Napoleon demanded that France be granted the left bank of the Rhine as its eastern frontier and that Austria, in exchange for Salzburg, Passau, and the city of Venice, move its southwestern boundary from the Oglio to the Adige so that Mantua would be included in the new Cisalpine Republic. The Austrians procrastinated throughout the summer and finally accepted Napoleon's terms on October 17, 1797, at the Treaty of Campo Formio.

3. See Alexander Hamilton to H, August 4, 1797, note 9.

4. After the fall of Venice in May, 1797, Napoleon sent forces to occupy the Venetian islands of Corfu, Zante, and Cephalonia.

5. On July 14, 1797, Napoleon read a proclamation to the army of Italy warning it of a possible royalist plot and urging it to swear loyalty to the enemies of the Republic. In response to an appeal from the Directors, he sent one of his generals, Pierre François Charles Augereau, to Paris. Augereau, who arrived on August 5, 1797, made a public show of belligerence toward the royalists and was immediately created head of the Paris military division.

6. On August 6, 1797, James Harris, first earl of Malmesbury, wrote to Lord Grenville: "Had I no other grounds at this moment to form an opinion but the conduct of the Directory, I should look upon the negotiation as in a very precarious state, and apprehend its breaking up to be a very near event. But, if what I hear . . . can be relied on, I must hold a contrary belief; I must suppose the French will contend only for terms and give way in substance, and that they will affect to perform their engagements (real or supposed) in appearance, but break them in fact. . . .

"From every thing you read and hear to-day you will, I am sure, be confirmed in your opinion that on the upshot of the present contest at Paris depends the fate of the treaty. . . ." (Dropmore Papers, III, 345.) See also Malmesbury's dispatch of the same date giving an account of the negotiations at Lille from July 31 to August 6, 1797 (Dropmore Papers, III, 347–52).

From James Monroe [1]

Phila. augt. 6th. 1797.

Sir

I do not clearly understand the import of your letter of the 4th. instant and therefore desire an explanation of it. With this view I will give an explanation of mine which preceded it.[2]

Seeing no adequate cause by any thing in our late correspondence, why I shod. give a challenge to you, I own, it was not my intention to give or even provoke one by any thing contained in those letters. I meant only to observe that I shod. stand on the defensive & receive one in case you thought fit to give it. If therefore you were under a contrary impression I frankly own you are mistaken. If on the other hand you meant this last letter as a challenge to me, I have then to request that you will say so, and in which case have to inform you, that my friend Colo Burr who will present you this, and who will communicate with you on the subject, is authorized to give you my answer to it, and to make such other arrangements, as may be suitable in such an event.[3] with due respect

I am yr. very humble servt   Jas. Monroe

ALS, Hamilton Papers, Library of Congress; ADfS, Lloyd W. Smith Collection, Morristown National Historical Park, Morristown, New Jersey.
   1. This letter is document No. LI in the appendix to the printed version of the "Reynolds Pamphlet," August 25, 1797. For background to this letter, see the introductory note to Oliver Wolcott, Jr., to H, July 3, 1797.
   2. Monroe to H, July 31, 1797.
   3. See William Jackson to H, August 5, 1797, note 5.

From William Jackson [1]

Philadelphia, August 7. 1797

Dear Hamilton,

I have informed Mr. Dawson,[2] who called on me yesterday, on the part of Mr. Monroe, that, as you had expressly told Mr. M in one of your letters, that you thought the motives of his conduct towards you had been "malignant and dishonorable," [3] I had advised you against throwing the affair into a more formal challenge, it resting, in my opinion, with Mr. Monroe either to submit to, or to resent these expressions.[4]

I am always   Your faithful affectionate friend   W Jackson

This letter has been shewn to Mr. Dawson.   W. J.

ALS, Hamilton Papers, Library of Congress.
   1. For background to this letter, see the introductory note to Oliver Wolcott, Jr., to H, July 3, 1797; Jackson to H, July 24, 25, 31, August 5, 1797.
   2. John Dawson. See Jackson to H, August 5, 1797, note 5.

3. H to Monroe, July 22, 1797.

4. Dawson's account of this interview with Jackson is dated August 17, 1797, and reads: "On the morning of sunday the   th Int I called on Majr. Jackson, at the request of Colo Monroe, & shewd to him a letter which Colo Monroe had written to Hamilton, in answer to one which he had received on the day before by Mjr. Jackson.

"I then askd him, whether he considerd the letter from Colo Hamilton as a challenge—he said he did not, but as a declaration of his readiness to accept one—I then informd him that it was not Colo Monroe's intention to c[h]allenge, but to accept one, whenever Colo Hamilton shoud think proper to give one, as he coud give no certificate different from those he had already of which Colo Hamilton complained.

"On the next evening Majr. Jackson called on me, & said he had calld in the forenoon when I was out—he then shewd me a short letter which he had written to Colo Hamilton, stating as his opinion, that it was not incumbent on him to give a challenge to Colo Monroe, on what had passd between them.

"These are the material points in the interviews between Majr. Jackson & my self, as far as I recollect. Colo Ms letter to Colo H. alluded to above went by mondays mail." (ADS, Lloyd W. Smith Collection, Morristown National Historical Park, Morristown, New Jersey.)

On the back of Dawson's statement Monroe wrote: "in a case in wh. you compld. of an injury, however unjustly, I of none, it wod. have been improper for me to do so. Tis possible."

From William Jackson [1]

Philadelphia, August 7. 1797

Dear Hamilton

Mr. Dawson (of Virginia) called upon me yesterday morning to shew to me a letter from Mr. Monroe to you,[2] wherein he says "that if you considered his last letter as a challenge, he will frankly acknowledge that you were mistaken—that he meant not to give but to be prepared to receive one—that he admits, if any one has been injured in the correspondence between you, it has been you—and, if your letter was intended as a direct challenge,[3] Colonel Burr is charged with his answer." [4]

I hold it to be a duty to say something on the subject of this letter, and to offer my opinion on the manner of treating it.

It is certainly a question of feeling which of you is to consider yourself as the Party injured by the correspondence—and Mr. Monroe may possibly think you the injured party—or, by saying so, he may endeavor to extort a *direct challenge:* But it by no means appears to me that you are the Person injured by the correspondence —injured you may be by his conduct—but there is not a word in *his correspondence,* since I became acquainted with it, which will bear that construction, or that calls for a direct challenge from you. On the other hand I declare it to be an opinion, growing out of my sense of propriety, that the man, whose sense of injury is not to be awakened by being told (as you have expressly told Mr Monroe) that the motives to his conduct have been "malignant and dishonorable" [5] and whose resentment, after such indignity, is not to be excited by a proposal to settle the time and place of a personal meeting, is not a Person to whom I would offer a direct defiance, which might be accepted or which might be used to other purposes.

Under this impression of your situation, I am free to advise you to decline giving a direct challenge to Mr. Monroe—and to wait the effect of your publication, which will, I doubt not, be the removal of any opinion, if any such has been formed, against your official conduct.

I am, most sincerely My dear Hamilton Your faithful and affectionate friend   W Jackson

ALS, Hamilton Papers, Library of Congress.
   1. For background to this letter, see the introductory note to Oliver Wolcott, Jr., to H, July 3, 1797. See also Jackson to H, July 24, 25, 31, August 5, 7 (first letter), 1797.
   2. James Monroe to H, August 6, 1797.
   3. H to Monroe, August 4, 1797.
   4. See Jackson to H, August 5, 1797, note 5; Monroe to H, August 6, 1797
   5. H to Monroe, July 22, 1797.

From James McHenry [1]

[Philadelphia, August 7, 1797]

I have recd and read the enclosed. I think the advice contained in the last paragraph ought to be adopted.[2]

Mr J—— will say to *Dawson* [3] "that inasmuch as you have expressly told Mr M—— that in your opinion his motives were malignant and conduct dishonorable,[4] that he would advise you against throwing it into a more formal challenge, it resting with Mr Munroe to submit it to the expressions or resent them."

Yours most affectionately   James McHenry

Webster has been sent to Jones.[5]

ALS, Lloyd W. Smith Collection, Morristown National Historical Park, Morristown, New Jersey.

1. For background to this letter, see the introductory note to Oliver Wolcott, Jr., to H, July 3, 1797; William Jackson to H, July 24, 25, 31, August 5, 7 (two letters), 1797.

2. McHenry is referring to the second letter which Jackson wrote to H on August 7, 1797.

3. John Dawson. See Jackson to H, Jackson to H, August 5, 1797, note 5, and August 7 (two letters), 1797.

4. See H to James Monroe, July 22, 1797.

5. McHenry is referring to a statement by Noah Webster, Jr., dated July 13, 1797, which is document No. XLIII in the appendix to the printed version of the "Reynolds Pamphlet," August 25, 1797. See H to John Fenno, July 6, 1797. The statement was sent to Edward Jones, who was assisting H in the collection of documents for the "Reynolds Pamphlet." See Jones to H, July 30, 1797.

To James Monroe [1]

New York August 9. 1797

Sir

The intention of my letter of the 4th instant, as itself imports, was to meet and close with an advance towards a personal interview, which it appeared to me had been made by you.

From the tenor of your reply of the 6th, which disavows the inference I had drawn, any further step on my part, as being inconsistent with the ground I have heretofore taken, would be improper.

I am Sir   Your humble servt   A Hamilton

James Monroe Esq

ALS, Lloyd W. Smith Collection, Morristown National Historical Park, Morristown, New Jersey; ALS (photostat), Hamilton Papers, Library of Congress; copy, in H's handwriting, Hamilton Papers, Library of Congress; ADf, Hamilton Papers, Library of Congress; ADf, Hamilton Papers, Library of Congress; ADfS, Hamilton Papers, Library of Congress; copy, in Monroe's handwriting, The Library, Lehigh University, Bethlehem, Pennsylvania.

1. This letter is document No. LII in the appendix to the printed version of the "Reynolds Pamphlet," August 25, 1797. For background to this letter, see the introductory note to Oliver Wolcott, Jr., to H, July 3, 1797.

The first two drafts are on the same sheet of paper. The first draft reads: "My letter of the fourth instant was meerly to meet and close with an overture which it appeared to me was intimated in your preceding one.

"The complexion altogether of Yours of the 6th., received this day appears to me to be such as with consistency or propriety will admit of no further step on my part."

The second draft, all of which is crossed out, reads: "My letter of the fourth instant was meerly to meet and close with an advance towards a personal interview which it appeared to me had been made by you.

"Your letter of the 6th received this day puts this affair upon a ground which would render any further step on my part inconsistent and improper."

On the back of the sheet containing the first two drafts H wrote: "A letter of which the inclosed is a copy was written & dld to Col Burr, who advised a revision & alteration as best adapted to some eventual course which might obviate the necessity of publication. Aug. 9 1797."

The third draft, which H signed, reads: "My letter of the 4th instant was manifestly to meet and close with an overture which it appeared to me was intimated in your preceding one—

"The complexion altogether of yours of the 6th received this day appears to me to be such as, with consistency or propriety, will admit of no further step on my part"

The copy in the Hamilton Papers, Library of Congress, of the letter which was finally sent to Monroe is in H's handwriting and is endorsed by H: "copy of second letter dld August 9, 1797." The "second letter dld" to Monroe on this date is the letter printed above.

Aaron Burr believed that "a personal interview" had been averted, for on August 9, 1797, he wrote to Monroe: "The Thing *will* take an amicable course and terminate, I believe to your Satisfaction" (ALS, deposited in the Library of The Phillips Exeter Academy, Exeter, New Hampshire).

From William Jackson [1]

Philadelphia August 11. 1797

Dear Sir,

I have received your letter, without date,[2] enclosing the copies of Mr. Monroes two last letters [3] to you, which I have delivered to Mr. Jones [4]—to whom I have shewn your letter.

He is surprised that you should not have received a packet containing some interesting documents, among others Folwell's testimony,[5] which he forwarded to you [6] under the Comptroller's [7] frank. I am no less surprised that you should not have acknowledged the receipt of my two last letters,[8] one of which, expressing my advice to you on Mr. Monroes last letter, I had shewn to his friend Mr. Dawson [9]—a copy of this letter, which is a short one, I must request you to transmit to me, as I mean to annex it to the certificate which I shall give to Mr. Jones.

I applaud your decision on Monroe's last letter, and congratulate you on the recent evidence received through Folwell, a duplicate of which Mr. Jones will forward tomorrow.

I am always   Your faithful affectionate friend   W Jackson

ALS, Hamilton Papers, Library of Congress.

1. For background to this letter, see the introductory note to Oliver Wolcott, Jr., to H, July 3, 1797. See also Jackson to H, July 24, 25, 31, August 5, 7 (two letters), 1797.
2. Letter not found.
3. Monroe to H, July 31, August 6, 1797.
4. Edward Jones.
5. See Jones to H, July 30, 1797, note 7.
6. Letter not found.
7. John Steele.
8. Both letters were written on August 7, 1797.
9. John Dawson. See Jackson to H, August 5, 1797, note 5, and two letters of August 7, 1797. The letter shown to Dawson was the first letter which Jackson wrote to H on August 7, 1797.

From George Clarke [1]

Catskill [New York] August 15. 1797. ". . . I waited on Mr. Scott [2] Attorney at Law at Cattskill, to know if he had obtained your Answer & Opinion respecting my Title to the Land at Cattskill Point. . . . I have made every enquiry in my Power in order to discover the deed of Trust from John Lindesay [3] . . . (which Deed is not recorded but only noted as a memorandum on the Margin of the Patent to Lindesay) but have not as yet been fortunate enough to discover in whose Hands it is. . . . I should wish to know your sentiments as to the loss of the Deed, & what effect the memorandum may produce in a Court of Law. . . . I request the favor of your forwarding your advice generally & Particularly on the Subject, to Mr. Scott at Kattskill. . . . [4] "

ALS, Hamilton Papers, Library of Congress.

1. Clarke was the owner of extensive lands in New York State.
2. John Vander Speigle Scott was a lawyer and politician of Catskill.
3. John Lindesay was the sheriff of Albany County. The Lindesay patent, located in what is now Catskill, New York, contained four hundred and sixty acres. On July 26, 1684, Gysbert Uytden Bogaert purchased the land from the Indians, but a patent was not obtained until August 22, 1783, when the land was owned by John Lindesay (from information supplied by Mr. Raymond Beecher, Curator, Greene County Historical Society, Coxsackie, New York). In July, 1738, Lindesay had received a draft of a certificate "for a tract of land, in the county of Albany, lying on the west side of Hudson's river, near Katts kill, of which Helmer Janse died seized, leaving no heirs" (*N.Y. Colonial Manuscripts*, 235).
4. An entry in H's Cash Book, 1795–1804, under the date of June 16, 1797, reads: "received of George Clarke Retainer v. Patentee of Salisbury 75" (AD, Hamilton Papers, Library of Congress). In his Law Register, 1795–1804, H re-

corded: "George Clark ex patent Lindsay v Patentees of Salisbury" (D, partially in H's handwriting, New York Law Institute, New York City). For the Salisbury patent near Catskill, New York, see the map at the end of Alexander C. Flick, ed., *Conquering the Wilderness*, Vol. 5 of *History of the State of New York* (New York, 1934). A later entry in H's Law Register, 1795–1804, reads: "Clark

v   } Ejectments
Divers } Ulster

Scot for Plaintif of Counsel" (D, partially in H's handwriting, New York Law Institute, New York City). Catskill is currently the county seat of Greene County, which was formed on March 25, 1800, out of Albany and Ulster counties. Until that date Catskill was in Ulster County.

Certificate by James Monroe [1]

[Philadelphia, August 16, 1797]

I hereby certify that it was not my intention to give any sanction to, or opinion of my own, as to the entry which bears my single signature, in the papers containing an enquiry into Colo. Hamiltons conduct, by messrs. Muhlenburg Venable & myself in 1792, but that I meant it to stand on the credit of Mr. Clingman only upon whose application the entry was made. Phila. Augt. 16. 1797.   Jas. Monroe

ADS, Lloyd W. Smith Collection, Morristown National Historical Park, Morristown, New Jersey.

1. For background to this document, see the introductory note to Oliver Wolcott, Jr., to H, July 3, 1797. See also Monroe to H, July 10, 16, 17, 18, 21, 25, 31, August 6, 1797; H to Monroe, July 10, 17, 18, 20, 22, 28, August 4, 9, 1797; William Jackson to H, July 24, 25 31, August 5, 7 (two letters), 11, 1797; James McHenry to H, August 7, 1797; "David Gelston's Account of an Interview between Alexander Hamilton and James Monroe," July 11, 1797.

Although H had already indicated to Monroe (H to Monroe, August 9, 1797) that he had withdrawn his challenge for a duel, Monroe nevertheless prepared the certificate printed above. On August 6, 1797, Monroe had written to Aaron Burr that he had no objection to making a statement. See Jackson to H, August 5, 1797, note 5. On August 13, 1797, Burr wrote to Monroe: "The enclosed from Col. H. was left with me I believe on friday— it requires no comment." If Burr received any document written by H on Friday, August 11, 1797, it has not been found. Burr continued: "I have again read over the correspondence [between H and Monroe] & wish it all burnt; which I hope and believe will be the result. If you and Muhlenburgh really believe, as I do, and think you must, that H is innocent of the charge of any concern in speculation with Reynolds, It is my opinion that it will be an act of magnanimity & Justice to say so in a joint certificate. You expressed to me the same idea when we were together here. This is, and should be treated as a distinct thing from any personal impropriety of Conduct to you. Resentment is more dignified when Justice is rendered to its' object—but this remark is now ill-timed. I take your personal differences to be settled & they had best remain so. I enclose you a Sketch of what would appear to me to suffice as a Certificate in Case you shall choose to give one—should such be your determination, send it to me by return of Mail" (ALS, The Huntington Library, San Marino, California). The sketch of a certificate which Burr enclosed was probably the following, dated August, 1797: "we certify that, in consequence of Information which we received in December 1792 of a concern in speculation between A H. then Sec. of the T. and one J. Reynolds, we had an explanation on the subject with said A. H. who by that explanation supported by written documents satisfied us that the above charge was ill founded as we declared to him at the time: That the impression under which we left him of our being so satisfied was reciprocal and is still the same" (quoted in Samuel H. Wandell and Meade Minnigerode, *Aaron Burr* [New York, 1927], I, 283).

Monroe, however, did not take Burr's advice and prepared instead the certificate printed above. No evidence has been found that Monroe ever sent it to H.

To James McHenry

[New York, August 17, 1797]

My Dr Sir

Inclosed are some papers,[1] which were sent me shortly after my return to this City from Philadelphia[2] but which from Mrs. Hamilton's situation[3] hurry of business &c have been forgotten. If there is any thing to be said to my correspondent you will enable me as speedily as possible to say it. I send you the 100 Dollars you sent me and a further sum to reimburse some money paid for me by *Lewis*.[4]

 Yrs affectly   A Hamilton

                  Aug. 17. 1797

Js. Mc. Henry Esq

ALS, Maryland Historical Society, Baltimore.

1. The enclosed papers, sent to H by James Tillary, a New York City physician and politician, concerned the trading house of William Panton, Robert Leslie, and Company. The enclosures have not been found. For Panton's earlier correspondence with Tillary, see Panton to Tillary, May 5, 1794 (ALS, Hamilton Papers, Library of Congress).

2. H had been in Philadelphia collecting documents for the appendix to the "Reynolds Pamphlet," August 25, 1797.

3. William Stephen Hamilton was born on August 4, 1797.

4. Samuel Lewis was a clerk in the War Department.

From James McHenry

Philad. 19 Augt. 1797.

My dear Sir

I have received this morning your letter of the 17th inst.

Mr Jones [1] is without your letter of the 4th to Mr Monroe, and the want of it delays the publication.

With respect to the papers inclosed to you by Mr. Tillery.[2] I wrote to McKee [3] on the 25th of July ulto.[4]

"I will state to you briefly the difficulty which prevents any final determination at present on the two propositions which respect the house of Panton Leslie & Co. and what I think that house may reasonably look forward to."

"As the assumption of their Indian debts or compensation for them in land would require the consent of Congress, it would be to hazard a great deal too much to make any promise to them founded on its being obtainable. In a case so circumstanced it is proper that they should understand the difficulty and be convinced that the President has no authority to conclude such an engagement or make it binding on the U.S. In giving them this information you will mention how very sensible I am of the good offices which they have it in their power to render, and that whatever favour they can ask that can be granted by the President will not be refused. It would be easy I should conceive to afford them such indulgences as would greatly facilitate the effectual and prompt collection of their debts within our Indian nations and this is what I think they may ask and reasonably look forward to."

"Considering how infinitely precious the friendship of the U.S. is to Spain I can only ascribe the late conduct of some of her officers to an influence which controuls their better judgment. War is not desired by the U.S. They will shun it if possible, and sure I am Spain ought carefully to avoid forcing them into it. My last accounts from Natches is up to the 19 May. Then every thing was seemingly quiet."

Yours affectionately   James McHenry

P.S. There was no money in your letter.

ALS, Hamilton Papers, Library of Congress; ADf, James McHenry Papers, Library of Congress.

1. Edward Jones. See the introductory note to Oilver Wolcott, Jr., to H, July 3, 1797; Jones to H, July 30, 1797; McHenry to H, August 7, 1797.

2. James Tillary's enclosures have not been found. See H to McHenry, August 17, 1797.

3. John McKee was an agent of the Southern Indian Department. McKee's activities in 1797 are described as follows by A. P. Whitaker: "In view of the meagerness of transportation facilities and the remoteness of the centers of population on the Atlantic seaboard from the Mississippi, the war party needed all the support it could get from the Western frontiersmen and the Southern Indians. One of the most important efforts made in this direction, and certainly the most singular, was the sending of John McKee to the head-quarters of the Anglo-Spanish trading firm of Panton, Leslie and Company at Pensacola in 1797. Though the mission was regarded by some observers as a move in the Blount conspiracy, there is good reason to believe that it was in fact engineered by the Federalist war party in order to pave the way for the conquest of Florida by enlisting the services of Panton, Leslie and Company, whose influence was paramount among the Indian tribes on the Florida border. It is certainly not without significance that McKee . . . was under the orders of Secretary of War McHenry, and that Secretary of State Pickering was privy to the purpose of his mission. . . . The American government had known for nearly a decade that Panton, Leslie and Company was the chief agent of Spanish resistance to American influence among the Southern tribes within the limits which the United States claimed, and that, by stirring up the Indians to ravage the frontiers of Georgia and Tennessee, the company had stained its hands with the blood of American citizens. Yet high officials of the government were now offering the company facilities for collecting from these very Indian tribes the debts which were the most eloquent reminder of that long and cruel warfare" (*The Mississippi Question, 1795–1803: A Study in Trade, Politics, and Diplomacy* [New York and London, 1934], 125–26).

4. AL, letterpress copy, James McHenry Papers, Library of Congress; ADf, James McHenry Papers, Library of Congress.

From George Washington

Mount Vernon 21st Aug 1797

My dear Sir,

Not for any intrinsic value the thing possesses, but as a token of my sincere regard and friendship for you, and as a remembrancer of me; I pray you to accept a Wine cooler for four bottles, which Coll. Biddle [1] is directed to forward from Philadelphia (where with other articles it was left) together with this letter, to your address.

It is one of four, which I imported in the early part of my late Administration of the Government; two only of which were ever used.

I pray you to present my best wishes, in which Mrs. Washington joins me, to Mrs. Hamilton & the family; and that you would be persuaded, that with every sentiment of the highest regard, I remain your sincere friend, and affectionate Hble Servant

Go: Washington

Alexr Hamilton Esqr.

ALS, Hamilton Papers, Library of Congress.
1. Clement Biddle, a Philadelphia merchant, had served with the rank of colonel in the Continental Army. During the war he was both aide-de-camp to Nathanael Greene and commissary general of forage. From 1789 to 1793 he was United States marshal of Pennsylvania.
On August 21, 1797, Washington wrote to Biddle: "The large Plated wine cooler . . . I pray you to have carefully packed up and sent with the letter enclosed by a safe conveyance to Colo. Hamilton of New York" (LC, George Washington Papers, Library of Congress).

Draft of the "Reynolds Pamphlet" [1]

[August 25, 1797]

The spirit of Jacobism, <– – –> if not intirely a new spirit in the world, has at least acquired an organisation which it had not before —has been reduced to a more regular system, and ~~bears~~ armed with more powerful weapons than it ~~has~~ formerly possessed: And it is

                                        complicated
not too much to say of it, that it threatens ~~gre~~ more numerous and

ADf, Hamilton Papers, Library of Congress.
1. For background to this document, see the introductory note to Oliver Wolcott, Jr., to H, July 3, 1797.
Although H had completed the untitled draft of the document printed above before the end of July, 1797, he had to delay publication until he had collected the supporting documents which he included in the appendix. On August 27, 1797, John Fenno's Gazette of the United States, and Philadelphia Daily Advertiser contained an advertisement announcing the publication on August 25, 1797, of H's pamphlet which was entitled Observations on Certain Documents Contained in No. V & VI of "The History of the United States for the Year 1796," In Which the Charge of Speculation Against Alexander Hamilton, Late Secretary of the Treasury, is Fully Refuted. Written by Himself (Philadelphia: Printed for John Fenno, by John Bioren, 1797).
Because of numerous differences between the draft and the published version of the pamphlet, both are printed above. The published version, but not the draft, has been annotated.

extensive evils to mankind than have been experienced from the united operation of its three great scourges *War Pestilence* and *Famine*. Where it will ultimately land society, it is impossible for any human comprehension to foresee—but there is just ground to apprehend that its progress may be marked with horrors and miseries of which the dreadful incidents of the French Revolution afford

perspective only a faint ^presage^ image. Incessantly busied in undermining all the props of ~~social and~~ public security and private happiness it seems to threaten the political and moral word with a complete chaos.^1^

A principal engine by which it aims at effecting its purposes is that of Calumny. It is essential to its success, that the weight and influence of men of upright principles,^disposed and able to^ ~~shall be at all events destroyed~~ disposed and ^able^ ~~qualified~~ to resist its enterprises, shall be at all events destroyed. Not contented with traducing their best endeavours for the public good, with misrepresenting their purest motives, with inferring criminality from actions innocent or laudable, the most direct falshoods are invented and and propagated with undaunted effrontery and unwearied perseverance. Lies often detected and re-futed are ^still^ revived and ~~repeated retailed afresh~~ repeated, in the hope that the refutation may have been forgotten, or that the frequency

hardihood and ^defect^ boldness of accusation may supply the want of truth and proof. The most profligate men are encouraged, probably bribed, certainly with patronage, if not with money, to become informers and accus-ers. And when ~~their falsehoods~~ tales, which their characters alone were sufficient to discredit, are disproved by facts and evidence ^that^ ~~which do not permit an~~ compel their patrons to shrink from the ^open^ support of them, they still continue in ^corroding^ whispers to ~~pollute steal away steal away~~ wear away the reputations which they could not over-throw. If luckily ~~any private foible~~ for the conspirators ~~against~~ some little ~~personal~~ foible folly or indiscretion can be dis[c]overed in any of those whom they desire to persecute it becomes at once in their hands a two edged ^poignard^ sword by which to wound the public fame and to stab the private felicity of the person. With ~~these~~ ^such^ cannibals of character, nothing is sacred. The peace even of an innocent and amiable ^virtuous~~ wife is a ~~good victim~~ welcome victim to their ^greedy^ insatiate fury against the husband. And the secret irregularities of a father are without scruple to be recorded and handed down for the imitation of his children.

~~To this~~ ^poisonous and^ ~~detestable spirit we are to ascribe /// not only the continual calumnies which resound in the Jacobin Prints of this Country but the p~~

In the indulgence of this ~~poisonous~~ baleful ~~and detestable~~ spirit, we not only hear the Jacobin news papers of this country continually ~~with~~ ^with^ ring ~~the most~~ odious insinuations and charges against many of our most ~~distinguished and~~ virtuous citizens. But not satisfied with this a measure new in this country appears to have been lately adopted to give greater system and efficacy to the plan of defamation. Periodical pamphlets issue from the same presses full freighted with ~~artful~~ misrepresentation and frequently barefaced falshood ~~calculated~~ artfully calculated to hold up the chief ~~of the Anti-Jacobin f~~ opponents of the Jacobin faction to the jealously and distrust of the present generation and to transmit their names with dishonor to posterity. Even the great and multiplied services the tried and rarely equalled virtuous of a Washington can secure no exemption, can form no rampart round his his fame which these daring marauders will not attempt to invade.

How then can I, with pretensions ^every way^ ~~so~~ inferior, expect to be exempt; and if truly this be, as every appearance indicates, a conspiracy of vice against virtue, ought I not rather to be flattered that I have been so long and so peculiarly an object of ~~bitter~~ persecution? Ought I to regret, if there be any thing about me so formi ^d^ able to the Faction as to have made me worthy of ~~its most venomous~~ being distinguished by ~~its~~ the plentitude of its rancour and venom? If indeed a zeal to withstand the pernicious tenets of the ~~Section~~ which ^ready to encounter^ can only be ^every difficulty to run every hazard^ extinguished with my breadth, ~~intitles~~ intitles me to so honorable ^a^

distinction, I may lay claim to it as not unmerited; and shielded as I
_Λfeel myself to be   can
~~can~~_Λby conscious rectitude, I ~~shall~~ never cease to defy the utmost
efforts of the malignity.

                               had
    It is certain that I have already_Λa pretty copious experience of
them. For the honor of human nature it is to be hoped that the
examples are not numerous of men so greatly calumniated and per-
secuted as I have been with so little cause.

    I dare appeal to all my immediate fellow citizens of whatever
                      truth of the
political party for the fact that no man ever~~y~~ ~~undertook~~ carried into
          life
public ~~office~~ a more unblemished character as to pecuniary affairs
than that with which I undertook the Office of Secretary of the
Treasury—~~distinguished by~~ a character disinterested and ~~wh~~ careless
about property rather than marked by an avidity for wealth. I had
even ~~scrupulously~~ refrained from motives of delicacy from speculations not culpable in themselves which I saw making the fortunes of
many around me.

    With such a character, however natural it was to expect opposi-
             censure
tion and even ~~censure~~ as to the policy of the plans which issued from
my department as to the ~~skilfulness and propr~~ diligence care and
skilfulness with which the measures connected with it were executed
& as to modes of political ~~opinion~~ thinking—it was not natural to
expect nor was it expected that imputations ~~on~~ would be made on
the fidelity and integrity, in a pecuniary sense, of the conduct which
was pursued.

    But on this head a painful and mortifying disappointment has been
experienced. Without the sligh[t]est foundation in any respect I
have been repeatedly and cruelly held up to the suspicions of ~~my~~
~~fellow~~ ~~citizens~~ the community as one who was directed in his ad-
                                     the
ministration by the most sordid views who has sacrificed ~~his~~ public
to his private interest his duty and honor to the sinister accumulation
                                        poorer
of fortune; while the truth is that I withdrew from office ~~worse~~ than
                                       1
I went into it and certainly not worth 2000 £ in the word.

an
Merely because I persevered in ~~the~~ opinion ~~that~~ once common to
me—
me and the most influential of those who opposed—that the public
debt ought to be provided for on the basis of the contract upon
which it was created ~~and~~ without discrimination between original
or
holders and purchasers without deduction on account of the depreci-
ation which it had incurred—I ~~am ac~~ have been accused with wantonly increasing the public burthen to promote a stock-jobbing interest of myself and friends; while the truth is that from the time I
went into office to the present moment I have never been directly or
indirectly
interested in the public funds beyond the sum of   ² dollars and
~~I did not know while in office~~ when I framed or proposed my plan
was wholly ignorant of the situation of any particular friend or
connection of mine in this respect and did believe whether righ[t]ly
or wrongly to this money I cannot say that the only connection
whose situation could be supposed to influence my mind would
not be materially ~~or~~ if at all affected by ~~the~~ discrimination—between
original holders and purchasers.

chiefly
At another time, ~~merely~~ because a member of the house of representatives did not understand accounts and ~~construed certain the~~
the
entertained a different idea from me as to∧legal effect of appropria-
accused in that body
tion$ ~~by~~ laws, I was ~~openly arraigned~~ of ~~undem~~ deliberate and
criminal violations of ~~the~~ law ~~and~~ was by implication if not expressly
stigmatised as a defaulter for millions—and was driven to the unpleasant necessity of calling for a solemn Inquiry.

This inquiry took place. It was conducted by a Committee of
³ members of the House of Representatives most of them my
political adversaries some of them of the most active part and one of
them (Mr. Giles from Virginia) the very person who had commenced the attack.

officers
The∧Books and records of the Treasury were strictly scrutinized.

2. Space left blank in MS.
3. Space left blank in MS.

The transactions between the several banks and the Treasury were
~~carefully~~ also examined. Even ~~the~~ my private accounts with those
institutions were placed before the Committee and every possible
facility given to the Inquiry. The result was a complete demonstration that the suspicions which had been entertained were without
foundation. ~~The~~

After ~~stating in considerable detail~~ presenting in considerable
detail the regulations and state of the Department ~~with evidence~~ The
Committee conclude thus—"It appears from the affidavits of the
Cashier and several officers of the Bank of the UStates and several
of the Directors, the Cashier & other officers of the Bank of New
York that the *Secretary of the Treasury*, never has either directly or
indirectly ₍for himself or any other person₎ procured any discount or credit from either of the said
Banks upon the basis of any public monies which at any time have
been deposited therein under his direction: And The Committte are
satisfied that no monies of the United States whether before or after
they have passed to the Credit of the Treasurer have ever been
directly or indirectly used for or applied to any purposes but those
of the Government, except so far as all monies deposited in a Bank
are concerned in the *general operations* thereof."

* ~~Not only every pretence of~~

Here was a direct contradiction of the principal insinuations,
which had been thrown out, namely that the public monies had been
~~made leg turned to the ace~~ converted through the medium of the
Bank to the accommodation of myself and friends for purposes of
Speculation either by way of direct loan or as a fund of credit with
the Banks. Every idea of dilapidation vanished like an idle dream.
And my enemies finding no handle for their malice abandonned the
pursuit.

~~To leave no ambiguity upon the subject I gave earl~~ When I had
concluded to resign my office, to leave no ambiguity upon the subject, I gave early previous notice to the House of Representative for
the declared purpose of affording an opportunity before I left the
office of legislative inculpation if any ground for it had been discovered. Not the least step towards it was taken. I have a right
therefore to infer the universal conviction that no cause existed and
consider the result as a complete triumph over the malice of my
enemies.

In another instance, a profligate man found encouragement to bring before the House of Representatives a formal accusation of criminal conduct in Office. A Committee of the House was appointed to inquire. In this case some of my most intelligent and active enemies were the inquisitors. The ~~unanimous~~ Report of the Committee ~~confirmed~~ accepted by the House in decisive terms declared my innocence and

Was it not to have been expected, that these repeated demonstrations of the injustice of the accusations hazarded against me would not only have effectually vindicated my reputation, in the minds of the community, ~~woul~~ but would also have abashed the enterprize of my culumniators? However natural such a conclusion may have ~~been~~ B Yet seemed it would have betrayed an ignorance of ~~the Jacobin Spirit~~ Jacob Policy. It is a maxim too well ~~understood by it~~ ingrafted in that dark system that no character, however upright ~~and pure~~, is a match for incessantly repeated attacks however false. Every calumny makes some proselites, ~~The justificaton~~ and it keeps some, because justification ~~is~~ seldom circulates as rapidly and as ~~far~~ widely as slander. The number of those who first doubt, next suspect, and at last believe guilty, is continually increasing. And the public at large is ~~very~~ apt at length to sit down with the opinion that a character very often accused cannot be intirely free from guilt substituting the repitition and accumulation of charges for proof of culpability.

Relying upon this weakness of human nature the Jacobin phalanx though often defeated constantly returns to the charge. Old calumnies against me are served up with scarcely any variety of ~~sacrifice~~ sauce and every pretext is embraced to add to the catalogue.

Of all the base attempts to injure my character that which has been lately revived in number V & 6 of the History of the United States for 1796 is the most base. This it will be impossible for any intelligent man to doubt, when I have finished the examination.

~~The charge is a connection with one Reynolds in some plan~~

~~of~~   I ought perhaps to apologize to my friends for condescending to make it. A just pride with reluctance stoops to a vindication against so vile and despicable a contrivance and admonishes me that I ought silently to oppose the evidence of an upright character to so wretched a tale. Did it not derive a sanction from three names of some consequence in Society contrary to every rule of fair proceeding, names the aid of which I had a right to challenge towards the discredit—I should probably pursue that course. And even In other times—in times when the ~~human~~ ^{public} mind free from the delirium of the Jacobin influenza ~~could dispassionately analize and judge for itself that course would be preferable~~ ^{was} I should with much hesitation attempt to exculpate myself from such a charge with all the weight it can derise from such names. But in times like the present public Opinion must be regarded as a ~~sickly~~ ^{capricious} patient demanding some indulgence to its humours and caprices.

The charge against me is a connection with one James Reynolds ~~in speculation~~ for ∧purposes of∧ speculations ~~in the funds or in some other very improper object of profit~~ ^{some} ^{improper pecuniary}. My real crime is a loose connection with his wife which there is every reason to believe I was drawn into by a combination between husband and wife with design to extort money from me.

I do not make this confession without a blush. I shall not be the apologist of any Vice because the ardour of passion has made it mine. I ~~shall never~~ can never cease to censure myself for the pang which the publication of it may inflict upon a bosom ~~which~~ ^{that} has every title to be the depository of my utmost∧gratitude∧and love. ^{∧fidelity ~~fidelity~~} ~~And I can only throw myself upon its gener But there are occasions when a man ought to~~ But she herself will approve that even at so great an expence I wipe away a more serious stain from a ~~name~~ fame so interesting and so dear to her.

Before I proceed to a statement of the positive circumstances which serve to exculpate me∧I shall offer some preliminary remarks ^{beyond a doubt} which will tend to ~~prove that there are intrinsic characters which~~

~~serve to shew that the accusation is intitled to no credit~~—corroborate
the conclusion.

1   ~~It appears on all hands that~~

It appears from the documents themselves and is otherwise a
matter of notoriety that Reynolds was an obscure insignificant and
profligate man. ~~If~~ Taking it even for granted that I ~~was~~ unprincipled
^{a Secretary of the Treasury was}
enough to be willing to speculate for gain in ways inconsistent with
^{his}   ^{he}
~~my~~ office and character is it probable that I should have been dis-
^{to give my}   ^{to}
posed ~~my~~ confidence ~~in~~ a man of such a description and make use
of him as an instrument? ~~A Secretary of the Treasury must have
been very stupid who could not~~ He must have been a very stupid
one indeed if he could not have contrived objects large enough to
have interested men of much greater importance and with whom he
could have been perfectly safe. The supposition, besides ascribing
to him a wickedness ~~whie~~ with which his enemies have liberally
charged him, ascribes to him also a degree of folly with which he has
not before been charged.

2   ~~All the suggest The supplies of money which are suggested
All~~

~~The su~~ All the evidence which appears of supplies of monies to
Reynolds exhibits a very narrow scheme for a speculating secretary
of the Treasury. Clingman alleges that Mrs. Reynolds ~~sometime be-
fore~~ informed him that at a certain time her husband received upwards of Eleven hundred Dollars from Col Hamilton. By a note
which is among the documents, it appears that at one time Fifty
Dollars were sent. And there is an application for another sum of
300 Dollars which was refused—and with the declaration that it was
utterly out of my power to comply with it. What a scale of speculation is this not only for a Secretary of the Treasury but for one who
in the very publication which brings forward this charge is represented as having funded at forty Millions a debt which ought to have
been discharged at ten or fifteen Millions for the corrupt purpose
of benefitting myself and my friends. Surely I must have been a very

clumsy knave not to have secured enough of this excess of 25 or 30 Millions to either to have taken away ⫽ every inducement to be concerned to have risked my character in such bad hands and in so huckstering a traffic—It or as would have enabled me to employ the person with more means and to better purpose. Is it not extraordinary that at one time the Secretary should have furnished the speculating Agent with the paltry sum of 50 Dollars, at another time that he should have refused him the inconsiderable sum of 300 Dollars declaring upon his honor that it was not in his power to furnish

it? This declaration was true or not —if true it ill co if not true ⌃it
            ⌃the refusal
ill comports with the idea of a speculating connection—if true, it is very extraordinary that the head of a department engaged in such vast schemes of profit as are ascribed to him should have been
            But
destitute of so small a sum. If the Secretary lived upon an inadequate salary without any concern in speculation then there is no difficulty in the case.

3   It appears on all hands that Reynolds and Clingman were de-
                    contemptible
tected by the Comptroller of the Treasury in the crime of suborning a witness to swear to the death of

It certainly must be deemed very extraordinary that a confidential Agent of the head of the Treasury Department should have been driven to so miserable and despicable an expedient.

4   The documents relied upon as evidence against me shew that there was great intimacy between Clingman and Reynolds and his wife which continued down to a period subsequent to Reynolds liberation from prison—that both Reynolds and his wife as Clingman pretends informed him of my connection with Reynolds in specula-
            one
tion; yet no mention was made by any of them of any ⌃object of this speculation. The pretext that letters from Mr. H were destroyed which might contain the evidence is no answer. For the objects of speculation might no doubt have been recollected and cou[l]d have been marked specified. This never was done and for the obvious reason that any detail might have exposed the parties to detection. The destruction of letters which might explain is a fiction which is

refuted by the laconic and mysterious form of the notes which were found. This proves that there was great caution not to put much

upon paper—and ~~it is~~ without this_∧it ~~were~~ utterly ~~absurd to imagine~~

that I would have run the risk of ~~committing~~ to paper unnecessarily

~~the~~ transactions which would involve me in infamy, seeing that I

could have made my communications personally or_∧through some other Agent. In ~~every~~ whatever light it is viewed the supposed scheme charges me with as much folly as weakness and with both in an extremes for no adequate object.

5 The accusation against me is never heared of till Clingman and Reynolds are under prosecution by the Treasury for an infamous crime. It appears by the document No. 1 that during the endeavours of Clingman to procure the aid of Mr. Muglenbergh for his relief from the prosecution the disclosure of my prended criminality was made by him. It further appears by Document No. 2 that Reynolds supposed he was kept in prison by a design on my part to *oppress* him—and by the letter from him to Clingham of the 13 December that he felt a vindictive spirit towards me threatening to have satisfaction from me at all Events, and adding as addressed to Clingman "And you *only I trust too*"—which with the comment

Three inferences ~~were~~ to be drawn from these circumstances—one

that the accusation_∧was made an auxiliary to the efforts of the parties ~~to extricate~~ to obtain aid in getting relieved from the prosecution under which they laboured—another that there was a spirit of revenge against me on the part of Reynolds at least and the third, that he trusted in Clingham as a coadjutor in the plan of obtaining satisfaction from me *at all events*. Such circumstances are alone sufficient to destroy the Credit of the accusers; but when we add to it their ~~adm~~ very bad characters and the admitted fact that they were at the time of the transaction under a just prosecution for a heinous offence, it will follow that their mere allegations ~~unsp~~ unsupported by other testimony ought to have no weight whatever against an important officer of the Government or even against any ~~respectable~~

Citizen. As to Mrs. Reynolds testimony ~~when it shall appear that she was in a combination with her husband to prostitute herself, the inference will be a natural one that she was in the other plot to criminate & it will be presently seen~~ it will be equally undeserving of credit either from the supposition that she acted under the duress of her husband or was a party to the plot as will fuly appear in the sequel.

If therefore the supposed profits of criminality, which are independent of the assertions of such unworthy accusures can be satisfactorily answered and explained ~~and an easy clue be furnished out a key can~~ be furnished ~~as to those frauds particulars which are ambiguous or mysterious to unlock the mystery where appearances~~ may seem ~~unfavourable~~ no doubt can ~~rest~~ remain with any honest or candid mind as to the innocence of the accused.

I proceed to furnish the Key which is to unlock the mighty mystery in the following narrative and proofs.

Some time in the Summer of the year 1791 a woman called at my house in the City of Philadelphia and asked to speak with me ~~apart~~. ^in private. She was shewn into the parlour ~~and I where I quickly after went~~ where I went to her. ~~She introduced herself by telling~~ With ap^~~ap~~ ^seeming parent air of distress, ^she informed me that she was a daughter of a Mr. Lewis ~~of the State of New York and a~~ sister to a Mrs. G—— Livingston of the State of New York and wife to a Mr. Reynolds whose father was in the Commissary or Quarter Master department during the war with Great Britain—~~that he had lately lef~~ that her husband ^who ^had for a long time treated her very cruelly ~~y~~ had lately left her to live with another woman and so destitute that though desirous of returning to her friends she had not the means—that knowing I was a citizen of the same State of New York she had take the liberty to address herself to my humanity for relief. There was something odd in the application and the story yet there was a ~~genuineness~~ ^simplicity and modesty in the manner of relating it which gave an impression of its truth. I replied that her situation was an interesting one & that I was disposed to afford her as much aid as might be ~~necessary~~ ^sufficient to convey her to her

but   (which was truly the case)
friends—that at the instant it was not convenient to me, that if she
would inform me where she was to be found I would send or bring
                                    me
it to her in the course of the day. She gave the Street and the number
                                    lodged.
of the house where she ~~would be found~~. In the Evening I put a
thirty dollar bill in my Pocket and went to the house ~~where~~ I inquired for Mrs. Reynolds and was shewn up Stairs ~~into~~ at the head of
which she met me and conducted me into a bed room. I took the
bill out of my pocket and delivered it to ~~him~~ her. Some conversation
ensued which made it quickly apparent that other than pecuniary
consolation would not be unacceptable. It required a harder heart
                        Beauty
than mine to refuse it to ~~a pretty woman~~ in distress.

After this, I had frequent meetings with her—most of them at
my own house. Mrs. Hamilton being absent on a visit to her father
with her Children. In the course of a short time she mentioned to me
that ~~her husband she had reason to think~~ her husband had solicited ~~an~~
a reconciliation
~~accommodation~~ with her and pretended to ask my advice. I advised
her to the accommodation; which she shortly afterwards told me had
                                                had
taken place and informed me that her husband∧been engaged in some
speculations ~~upo~~ in *claims* upon the Treasury and she believed could
give me information respecting the conduct of ~~some~~ persons in the
department which would be useful to me. I desired an interview with
him and he came to me accordingly.

In the course of it, ~~he informed~~ after having engaged a promise
that I would endeavour to serve him as the consideration for the dis-
∧of an important secret
covery∧he told me ~~he~~ that he was possessed of a list of certain
claims upon the Treasury which he had obtained ~~from the Treasury~~
from ~~a person in the department at New York a list of certain
claims~~ Mr. Duer while in the department at New York ~~a list of certain
claims on the Treasury~~ for the purpose of ~~speculating upon them~~
speculation.

This discovery, if true, was not very important, as Mr. Duer had
a considerable time before resigned his office—yet I ~~appeared to ae~~
did not tell Reynolds ~~so~~ what I thought of the matter but contented

                                     ~~befriending him~~
              with
myself ~~my~~ a general assurance of ~~rendering him any service which~~
    ∧serving him
~~might~~∧if a proper opportunity should occur accompanied with some
gracious expressions which in a similar situation would naturally occur.

    He told me he was shortly going to Virginia and when he re-
turned he should point out something in which I might be of service
to him. On his return he asked employment as a Clerk in the Treasury Department. The knowlege he had given me of himself was
decisive against such a request. I parried it by telling him there was
no vacancy in my immediate Office and that the ~~Cl~~ appointment of
Clerks in the other branches of the department was left to the chiefs
of the respective branches. Reynolds ~~states as~~ alleged (as Clingman
relates No. IV (a) that I promised him employment and had disappointed him. It is possible (though I do not recollect it) that to
conciliate him I may have given him some expectation of this sort
in case of future opportunity—but the knowlege I acquired of the
man rendered this more and more inadmissible.[4]

                                         ∧meantime
    The intercourse with Mrs Reynolds in the∧continued ~~for some~~
~~time~~ and though various reflections (among these the knowlege I
                     speculating
had acquired of Reynolds∧character and pursuits and certain symptoms of contrivance ~~& plot~~ between her husband & her) induced
me to wish to drop it—yet her conduct made it very difficult to disentangle myself. The appearances of a violent attachment ~~were~~
        a genuine
~~played of~~ and of ~~extreme~~ distress at the idea of an interruption of
the connection were played off with such infinite art, aided by the
~~most~~ more genuine effects of an ardent temperament and a quick
                                     the
sensibility, that though I was not completely the dupe of∧illusion
—yet I was made to doubt as to the real state of things; and my
                                       real
vanity perhaps admitting too ~~express~~ easily the _possibility_ of a ~~sincere~~
fondness on the part of Mrs. Reynolds, ~~my hum~~ I adopted the plan
of a gradual discontinuance rather than a sudden cessation of the
            _as_
intercourse ~~so~~ likely to occasion least pain.

    4. At this point, H left half a page blank.

                      while

Perceiving after a ~~little time~~ that this was not attended with the desired effect that a more frequent intercourse continued to be pressed upon me on the pretext of its being essential to the peace of the party and my suspicions of some ~~foul p~~ sinister contrivance at the same time increasing I resolved to put an end to the affair and to see Mrs. Reynolds no more.

              persisted in   ing

She ~~nevertheless~~ persecut~~ed~~ me with letters filled with the strong-
                                       grief
est professions of tenderness and ~~distress~~—to which I made no re-ply.

One day I received a letter from her which is in the appendiz (numbere~~d~~ I) from which I concluded either that her husband had accidently discovered the connection or that ~~my resolution to end it having now become unequivacal~~ the time was arrived for ~~a denou~~ the catastrophe of the plot.

             (December 15, 1791)
The same day, I received from Mr. Reynolds the letter No. 2 by
                           me
which it will be seen that he informs∧of his having detected his wife ~~of~~ writing a letter to me and had obtained from her a full discovery of her connection with me, with the pretence that it was the con-
        ∧an undue
sequence of∧advantage taken of her distress. ~~and declaring that concludes with announcing his resolution to have satisfaction of me.~~

In answer to this I sent him a message to call at my office which he did the same day.

He in substance repeated the topics contained in his ~~and~~ letter and concluded as he had done there that he was resolved to have satis-faction.

I replied that he knew best what evidence he had of the alleged connection between his wife and myself—that I should neither ac-knowlege nor deny—that if he knew of any injury I had done him which intitled him to satisfaction he ought to name it.

Had there been & improper con-nections other-wise there would have been no need of this shift

He then went over the same ground he had trodden before and concluded again with the same vague claim of satisfaction which he had already thrown but without specifying any thing. I could be no longer at a loss to understand that he wanted money and I resolved to gratify him. I ~~told~~ observed to him that I had upon a former oc-
ı   do   service
casion told him I should be glad to ~~render~~ him∧and desired him to

I

think in what manner ~~he~~ could do it & to write to me. I thought it well by this mode if he had any delicacy to manage it. He withdrew with a promise to do as I desired.

Two days after (the 17 of December) he wrote me the letter No. III. This letter is evidently calcul[at]ed to exaggerate the importance of the injury I had done, to exhibit an affected sensibility in strong colours, and to magnify the attonement ~~wa~~ which was to be made. It however comes to no conclusion but proposes a meeting at
the
~~at~~ George Tavern or at some other place more agreeable to me which I should name.

~~Having received this letter I went~~

In consequence of this letter I called upon Reynolds and assuming a pretty decisive tone with him, I insisted upon his telling me explicitly what it was he desired. He again promised to do it by letter.

On the 19th, I received the promised letter No. IV, the essence of which is that he was willing to take a thousand Dollars as the plaister for his wounded honor.

I resolved to give it to him and accordingly ~~paid the amount~~ did so in two different payments the 22 of December and 3 of January ~~for~~ of 600 & 400 Dollars as ℀ receipts No. V & 6. It will ~~sti~~ strike ob-
not
servant men as∧a little extraordinary that a rapacious speculating
had so little money at command as to have
Secretary of the Treasury should have∧been ~~been~~ under the necessity of satisfying a trifling engagement of this sort by two distinct payments.

On the 17 of January I received the letter No. V which is an invitation to me from Reynolds to *renew my visits to his wife*. He had before requested that I would not see her again. The real motive
∧concluding
to this step appears in the∧~~following~~ passage of the letter. "I rely on your befriending me if there should any thing offer that should be to my advantage as you express a wish to befriend me."

If I recollect rightly I did not immediately accept the invitation nor till after I had received several very ~~importu~~ importunate & pathetic letters from Mrs. Reynolds. See No ~~VI & VII~~—VIII—IX & X.

On the 24 of March I received a letter from Reynolds No. XI and on the same day one from his wife No. XII. This will further illustrate the amiable concert between the husband and wife to ~~con~~
keep alive my
~~tinue me in~~ connection with her.

              are
The letters from Reynolds No. XIII to XVI inclusively ~~are~~ additional comments upon the motives to this concert. ~~No pains~~ It was a persevering plan to spare no pains to levy money upon my passions on the one hand and my apprehensions of discovery on the other.

The letter No. XVII is a Master piece. The husband there forbids my future visits to his wife chiefly because I was careful to avoid publicity in seeing her. It was ~~perhaps ne~~ probably necessary to the plan of some deeper treason against me that I should be seen at the house.

The interdiction was every way welcome and I complied with it strictly. On the second of June following I received the letter No. XVIII from Mrs. Reynolds—which shews that it was not her plan
               the
yet to let me off. It was probably the prelude to∧letter from Reynolds No XIX in which he requests a ~~letter No~~ loan of 300 Dollars to enable him to subscribe to the Lancaster Turnpike. This letter ~~to~~ is that to which ~~my note~~ the following note was an answer *"It is utterly out of my power, I assure you, 'pon my honor, to comply with your request. Your note is returned."* ~~Clingman states this in the narrative No. IV~~ Clingmans statement in No IV shews this. It makes Reynolds inform him "that I had supplied him with money to speculate, that about June 1792 Reynolds had informed him that he had applied to me for money to subscribe to the Turnpike road at Lancaster and had received a note from me in the above words." The letter itself, to which the note is an answer, proves clearly that ~~the application to me on that occasion~~ there was no view to any speculation in which I was to participate, that the money asked of
    ∧as a matter of *favour*
me was merely∧as a *loan* to be *simply* reimbursed without any profit ~~in the fort~~ in less than a fortnight.

                     ∧my
The letter No. XX from Reynolds explains fully the object of∧ note in these words "Inclosed are 50 dollars, they could not be sent

sooner"—It proves that this sum ~~y~~ also was asked merely as a *loan* and in a very apologetic stile.

           24th.

The letters of the ~~XXIV~~ and 30th. of August No. XXI & XXII explain the affair of the 200 Dollars mentioned by Clingman in No. IV, shewing that this sum was asked of me by way of loan to aid

him   small   & his wife were

in furnishing a_∧Boarding house which Reynolds ~~pretended was~~ or pretended to be about to set up.

The foregoing letters furnish a complete elucidation of the nature of the connection between Reynolds and myself. They prove ~~an~~

                                       me

indubitably an amorous connection between the wife and ~~myself~~,

                                  it

the detection or pretended dectection of by the husband, the necessity I was under of making a pecuniary compromise with him, the duress upon me in consequence of this ~~and the for~~ for fear of a disclosure and the forced loans which were levied upon me from time

                                      fully

to time. They meet directly and explain_∧the mysterious notes which

                                    excited

Reynolds so carefully preserved. and which had ~~occasionned~~ suspicion~~s~~ shewing ~~that the monie~~ not by implication or reference but in express terms, that the monies advanced by me to Reynolds, except the sum of 1000 Dollars, which was the ~~mo~~ composition for

                                 as

his wifes ~~fav~~ chastity, were solicited as favours and_∧loans to be repaid simply without any participation in the profits of employment —and ~~manifestly show~~ particularly that in the single where a purpose of speculation appears, ~~in the~~ it was intended to be for the sole benefit of Reynolds and the money was asked as a loan, but in this case was refused.

                                      with

Three of the five notes which are produced and those ~~which~~ the most point are explained not only by the general ~~comp~~ nature of the affair but by a specification in the letters of their objects. I shall notice the three which remain.

1 "Tomorrow what is requested will be done. Twill hardly be possible to day." ~~It has been stated that the 1000 Dollars which was the composition with Reynolds was advanced in two sums.~~ This

was an answer to Reynolds letter of the 7 of April No. XIV. The plundering Secretary was often not a little straitened for Cash.

II "My Dear Sir—I expected to have heared the day after I had the pleasure of seeing you." This if part of a letter to Reynolds denotes nothing more than a disposition to be civil to a man whom
pleasures
it was the interest of my passions to manage. But I ~~verily~~ ~~believe~~ ~~it~~ ~~was~~ am well satisfied it was no part of a letter to him because I do not believe that I ever addressed him in the stile of "*My Dear Sir*." It may have been a part of a letter to some one else procured by means of which I am ignorant or what is most probable it may have been the commencement of a letter which was not continued but torn off and thrown into the Chinney at my office which was a common practice, swept out and picked up by Reynolds or by Fraunces (who appears to have been implicated with Reynolds & Clingman) and given to him.

The endeavour shewn by the letter No.   5 to ~~vi~~ induce me to visit Mrs. Reynolds more openly and the care with which my little notes were preserved authorise a belief that at a period before it was attempted the idea of implicating me in some accusation with a view to the advantage of the parties was conceived. Hence the motive to pick up any fragment which might favour the idea of a confidential correspondence.

III "The person Mr. Reynolds inquired for on friday waited for him all the Evening at his house from a little after *seven*. Mr. R may see him at any time to day or tomorrow between the hours of two and three."

Mrs. Reynolds had informed me with that art of which she was so much mistress that Reynolds had again become very discontented and violent that he had treated her ill and thrown out ~~various~~ threats of ⟨>×<⟩ ~~the~~ disclosure. After this he called to inquire for me and left word he would call again in the Evening. I waited for him accordingly and being uneasy at his not coming and apprehensive of an eruption I wrote him the above note. I had an interview with him and he parted in better humour.

                    ^it
Thus ~~it~~ will_∧be seen that these different notes admit of a very easy

5. Space left blank in MS.

solution. I return to the verbal declarations of the three ~~complotters~~ confederates, as they have been recorded, for further confirmation of the falsehood of the charge.

Reynolds (No. II) ~~is made to state~~ alleges "that a Merchant came to him and offered as a volunteer to be his bail who he suspected had been instigated by me, and after being decoyed to the place the Merchant wished to carry him to, he refused being his bail unless he would deposit a sum of money to some considerable amount which he could not do, and was in consequence committed to prison." Clingman No. IV tells the same story in substance, though in̸ a
it
different form, and applies to Henry Seckel Merchant. The affidavit of the respectable Citizen No.   ⁶ gives the lie to both and shews that he was in fact the Agent of Clingman from motives of good will to him, that he never had any communication with me concerning either of them till they were both in custody and that ̸
when applied to,
⟨~~could~~-⟩ not only ̸ declined interposing in their behalf but advised Mr. *Sekel* to have nothing to do with them. This ⟨-⟩ alone is sufficient to discredit the whole story—shewing the disregard of truth and malice against me by which the parties were actuated. ~~It appears also~~ It is evident also from this transaction that I manifested the reverse of a disposition to skreen them from prosecution. Instead of encouraging Mr. *Seckel* to become their bail I advised him to have nothing to do with them as being bad and dangerous men. It appears likewise from Clingman's narrative No. V that I would not permit *Francis* a Clerk in my departt. to become their bail & gave him to understand that if he did it, he must quit the department.

                                    makes   say
~~Reynolds~~ *Chingman* No 4 ~~asserts~~ that Reynolds ᴧ~~had~~ told ~~him~~ that I had informed him that I was connected in speculation with
                                                    likely
Duer. Let any man of sense judge whether it is ~~probable~~ I should be so prodigal of confidence in such a character.

Clingman states in the same number that my Note in answer ~~in answer~~ to the application ~~for money to~~ for a loan of money towards a subscription to the Lancaster Turnpike was in his possession from about the time it was written (June 1792). This slight circumstance

6. Space left blank in MS.

is very illustrative of the general plan. For what purpose had *Clingman the* custody of this note all that time?

~~No. V.~~ In No. V Clingman speaks of something that *Francis* had said and ~~my~~ of ˄an observation of mine upon it. The particulars of this part of the business have escaped me, but it deserves notice that this same *Francis* afterwards became my ~~public~~ accuser to the house of Representatives and was ~~disa~~ disgraced by it—which is a sample of the materials that were employed by this ~~base~~ ˄vile confederacy to inculpate me.

I shall conclude with taking notice of some comments that have been made upon this transaction.

~~It has been remarked that the languge of one of~~

The soft language of one of my notes is criticised as being addressed to a man who was in the habit of threatening me with disgrace. How does it appear that he was in such a *habit?* No otherwise than by the declaration of Reynolds & Clingman. If the mere assertions of these ~~persons were to be~~ wretches ~~were~~ ˄are to be admitted as proofs there ~~would be~~ ˄is an end of the question. I am then certainly guilty of atrocious misconduct. ~~But no man not worthless as themselves would give credit to their assertions And~~ There ~~is~~ ˄can be no need of elaborate argument from *parts* of their *assertions* to prove what their assertions collectively ~~allege~~ ˄affirm. But no man not as worthless as themselves would believe them, independent of the positive disproof of them in the documents which are now produced.

As to the affair of threats, ~~of~~ except as to the disclosure of the connection with the wife, not the least idea of the sort ever reached me till after the imprisonment of Reynolds. Mr. Wolcotts certificate shews my conduct on that occasion. Nothwithstanding the powerful motives ~~I had~~ I may be presumed to have had to ~~desire that the man by being set at liberty might be under no temptation to give eclat to the affair~~ desire the liberation of the man on account of my situation with the ~~wif~~ wife, ~~I caution~~ it will be seen by Mr. Wolcotts certificate that I cautionned him against facilitating that liberation till the affair of the threat was satisfactorily cleared. Reynolds by his

Burning of the letters—

Cautious conduct of Mrs Reynolds when examined—

Duers *failure*

After inquiry into my Conduct

Transaction
with Monroe &c

What motives
Chastity

Omission in the
inquisition agency

letter No.   ⁷ having denied it_∧Mr. Wolcot thought my in-

^{∧in the most solemn manner}

junction satisfied. All the argument consequently from this source
falls to the ground.

Strong inferences are drawn from the release of Reynolds and
Clingman from imprisonment, from the_∧disappearance of Reynolds

^{subsequent}

and his wife, and from their not having_∧produced by me in order

^{been}

to be confronted at the time of the explanation to the three members
of Congress.

As to the first, as far as I now recollect, it was transacted by Mr.
Wolcot solely; but there was a very adequate motive for what he
did. It certainly was of more consequence to the ~~Government~~ Public, that a perfidious Clerk should be detected and expelled from the
Treasury Department, to prevent extensive future mischief, than
that the two ~~culprits~~ should have ~~suffered~~ ~~such~~ ~~punishment~~ been

^{individuals}

punished. Besides that a~~n~~ _∧influence foreign to me was exerted to

^{∧powerful}

procure indulgence to them—that of Mr. Mughlenberg and Col
Burr—that of Col Wadsworth which though insiduously placed to
my account was certainly put in motion by the entreaty of Mrs.
Reynolds. I do not believe that I had the least knowlege of Col
Wadsworths interference till after the affair was over. Candid men
will perceive strong evidence of innocence on my part when they consider, that under circumstances so peculiar, ~~my~~ these men were
driven to the necessity of giving a real and substantial equivalent,
for the relief they obtained, to a department over which I presided.

As to the disappearance of the parties how am I responsible for it?
Is it probable that the instance discovered was the only offence of the
kind of which these persons were guilty? Is it not on the contrary
very probable that Reynolds fled to avoid detection and punishment
in other cases? But exclusive of this, it is matter of notoriety, and
Mr. Mughlenberg ~~may~~ himself may be appealed to for the fact that
Reynolds was very much ~~in debt~~ involved in debt? What more
natural for him after having been exposed by confinement for a
crime, to get out of the way of his creditors as fast as possible?

7. Space left blank in MS.

Besides ~~inf~~ atrocious as his conduct had been towards me was he not to fear when discovered the effects of the resentment which it might excite. ~~Might he~~ Was it not natural for him to fear that his business ~~would be deemed in sufficon~~ sufficient ~~to dispense the department~~ might induce the department to renew against him the prosecution from which he escaped?

~~As to Mrs. Reynolds after her having~~

This disappearance of Reynolds rendered it impracticable to bring him forward to be confronted. As to Mrs. Reynolds, after her having become my accuser, is it presumable ∧that she was easily accessible by me? Does it not even appear that she was through Clingman more in the power of those who undertook the inquiry? If they supposed it necessary to the elucidation of the affair why did not they ∧attempt to bring her forward? But to what purpose this confronting? What light would it have afforded, if Mr. and Mrs. Reynolds had asserted things which I had denied. Character & the written documents must still ~~decide~~ determine. These could decide without it, and these were ~~produced~~ relied upon. Moreover was it to be imagined that I could so debase myself as to consent or seek to be confronted with a fellow who was confessedly guilty of so vile a crime as that of ~~subornation~~ of ~~perjury?~~ Could I for a moment suffer my veracity to be exposed to so humiliating a competition? The man who could expect it must be himself mean and ~~despicable beyond~~ groveling beyond measure.

Full satisfaction of the Inquiry

My desire to repel this slander completely has ∧I am aware led me into a ~~more~~ more copious and particular examination of it than was necessary. The bare perusal of the letters from Reynolds and his wife must be sufficient to convince the bitterest enemy that there is nothing in the affair worse than ~~a~~ an ~~culpable and~~ indelicate ∧amour—. For this I bow to the just censure which it merits. Taken in all its circumstances I feel myself humbled by it. Tis needless to say more.

To evince still more clearly the ~~very culpable~~ odious temper with which the publication has been made I ~~subjoin~~ shall annex the affidavits of Mr. Webster and myself to disprove the ∧strange story fabricated in the advertisement of it.

Last Story of
Clingman connec-
tion *with him*

> And to let the public fairly judge between Messrs. Mughlenberg Monroe Venable & myself I shall also annex th~~ th~~ the communications between us ~~from No.~~ ———— ~~to~~ ————in the pieces Numbered from to   .[8]

Printed Version of the "Reynolds Pamphlet" [9]

THE spirit of jacobinism, if not entirely a new spirit, has at least been cloathed with a more gigantic body and armed with more powerful weapons than it ever before possessed. It is perhaps not too much to say, that it threatens more extensive and complicated mischiefs to the world than have hitherto flowed from the three great scourges of mankind, WAR, PESTILENCE and FAMINE. To what point it will ultimately lead society, it is impossible for human foresight to pronounce; but there is just ground to apprehend that its progress may be marked with calamities of which the dreadful incidents of the French revolution afford a very faint image. Incessantly busied in undermining all the props of public security and private happiness, it seems to threaten the political and moral world with a complete overthrow.

A principal engine, by which this spirit endeavours to accomplish its purposes is that of calumny. It is essential to its success that the influence of men of upright principles, disposed and able to resist its enterprises, shall be at all events destroyed. Not content with traducing their best efforts for the public good, with misrepresenting their purest motives, with inferring criminality from actions innocent or laudable, the most direct falshoods are invented and propagated, with undaunted effrontery and unrelenting perseverance. Lies often detected and refuted are still revived and repeated, in the hope that the refutation may have been forgotten or that the frequency and boldness of accusation may supply the place of truth and proof. The most profligate men are encouraged, probably

8. Spaces in this paragraph were left blank in the MS.
9. *Observations on Certain Documents Contained in No. V & VI of "The History of the United States for the Year 1796," In Which the Charge of Speculation Against Alexander Hamilton, Late Secretary of the Treasury, is Fully Refuted. Written by Himself* (Philadelphia: Printed for John Fenno, by John Bioren, 1797).

bribed, certainly with patronage if not with money, to become informers and accusers. And when tales, which their characters alone
ought to discredit, are refuted by evidence and facts which oblige
the patrons of them to abandon their support, they still continue in
corroding whispers to wear away the reputations which they could
not directly subvert. If, luckily for the conspirators against honest
fame, any little foible or folly can be traced out in one, whom they
desire to persecute, it becomes at once in their hands a two-edged
sword, by which to wound the public character and stab the private
felicity of the person. With such men, nothing is sacred. Even the
peace of an unoffending and amiable wife is a welcome repast to their
insatiate fury against the husband.

In the gratification of this baleful spirit, we not only hear the
jacobin news-papers continually ring with odious insinuations and
charges against many of our most virtuous citizens; but, not satisfied
with this, a measure new in this country has been lately adopted to
give greater efficacy to the system of defamation—periodical pamphlets issue from the same presses, full freighted with misrepresentation and falshood, artfully calculated to hold up the opponents of
the FACTION to the jealousy and distrust of the present generation and
if possible, to transmit their names with dishonor to posterity. Even
the great and multiplied services, the tried and rarely equalled virtues
of a WASHINGTON, can secure no exemption.

How then can I, with pretensions every way inferior expect to
escape? And if truly this be, as every appearance indicates, a conspiracy of vice against virtue, ought I not rather to be flattered, that
I have been so long and so peculiarly an object of persecution? Ought
I to regret, if there be any thing about me, so formidable to the
Faction as to have made me worthy to be distinguished by the plentitude of its rancour and venom?

It is certain that I have had a pretty copious experience of its
malignity. For the honor of human nature, it is to be hoped that the
examples are not numerous of men so greatly calumniated and per-
secuted, as I have been, with so little cause.

I dare appeal to my immediate fellow citizens of whatever political
party for the truth of the assertion, that no man ever carried into
public life a more unblemished pecuniary reputation, than that with
which I undertook the office of Secretary of the Treasury; a charac-

ter marked by an indifference to the acquisition of property rather than an avidity for it.

With such a character, however natural it was to expect criticism and opposition, as to the political principles which I might manifest or be supposed to entertain, as to the wisdom or expediency of the plans, which I might propose, or as to the skill, care or diligence with which the business of my department might be executed, it was not natural to expect nor did I expect that my fidelity or integrity in a pecuniary sense would ever be called in question.

But on his head a mortifying disappointment has been experienced. Without the slightest foundation, I have been repeatedly held up to the suspicions of the world as a man directed in his administration by the most sordid views; who did not scruple to sacrifice the public to his private interest, his duty and honor to the sinister accumulation of wealth.

Merely because I *retained* an opinion once common to me and the most influencial of those who opposed me, *That the public debt ought to be provided for on the basis of the contract upon which it was created*, I have been wickedly accused with wantonly increasing the public burthen many millions, in order to promote a stock-jobbing interest of myself and friends.

Merely because a member of the House of Representatives entertained a different idea from me, as to the legal effect of appropriation laws, and did not understand accounts, I was exposed to the imputation of having committed a deliberate and criminal violation of the laws and to the suspicion of being a defaulter for millions; so as to have been driven to the painful necessity of calling for a formal and solemn inquiry.

The inquiry took place. It was conducted by a committee of fifteen members of the House of Representatives—a majority of them either my decided political enemies or inclined against me, some of them the most active and intelligent of my opponents, without a single man, who being known to be friendly to me, possessed also such knowledge and experience of public affairs as would enable him to counteract injurious intrigues. Mr. Giles of Virginia who had commenced the attack was of the committee.[10]

10. This investigation into H's conduct as Secretary of the Treasury took place from December, 1793, to May, 1794. For this investigation and William B.

The officers and books of the treasury were examined. The transactions between the several banks and the treasury were scrutinized. Even my *private accounts* with those institutions were laid open to the committee; and every possible facility given to the inquiry. The result was a complete demonstration that the suspicions which had been entertained were groundless.

Those which had taken the fastest hold were, that the public monies had been made subservient to loans, discounts and accommodations to myself and friends. The committee in reference to this point reported thus: "It appears from the affidavits of the Cashier and several officers of the bank of the United States and several of the directors, the Cashier, and other officers of the bank of New-York, that the Secretary of the Treasury never has either *directly* or *indirectly*, for himself or any other person, procured any discount or credit from either of the said banks upon the basis of any public monies which at any time have been deposited therein under his direction: And the committee are *satisfied*, that *no monies* of the United States, whether *before* or *after* they have passed to the credit of the Treasurer have ever been *directly* or *indirectly* used for or applied to *any purposes* but those of the government, except so far as all monies deposited in a bank are concerned in the *general operations* thereof." [11]

The report, which I have always understood was unanimous, contains in other respects, with considerable detail the materials of a complete exculpation. My enemies, finding no handle for their malice, abandoned the pursuit.

Yet unwilling to leave any ambiguity upon the point, when I determined to resign my office, I gave early previous notice of it to the House of Representatives, for the declared purpose of affording an opportunity for legislative crimination, if any ground for it had been discovered.[12] Not the least step towards it was taken. From which I have a right to infer the universal conviction of the House,

---

Giles's role in it, see the introductory note to H to Frederick A. C. Muhlenberg, December 16, 1793.

11. H is quoting from the report of the select committee appointed to investigate H's conduct as Secretary of the Treasury, May 22, 1794 (D, RG 233, Papers of the Select Committee Appointed to Examine the Treasury Department, Third Congress, National Archives).

12. See H to Frederick A. C. Muhlenberg, December 1, 1794.

that no cause existed, and to consider the result as a complete vindication.

On another occasion, a worthless man of the name of Fraunces found encouragement to bring forward to the House of Representatives a formal charge against me of unfaithful conduct in office.[13] A Committee of the House was appointed to inquire, consisting in this case also, partly of some of my most intelligent and active enemies. The issue was an unanimous exculpation of me as will appear by the following extract from the Journals of the House of Representatives of the 19th of February 1794.

"The House resumed the consideration of the report of the Committee, to whom was referred the memorial of Andrew G. Fraunces: whereupon,

"*Resolved*, That the reasons assigned by the secretary of the treasury, for refusing payment of the warrants referred to in the memorial, are fully sufficient to justify his conduct; and that in the whole course of this transaction, the secretary and other officers of the treasury, have acted a meritorious part towards the public."

"*Resolved*, That the charge exhibited in the memorial, against the secretary of the treasury, relative to the purchase of the pension of Baron de Glaubeck is wholly illiberal and groundless *." [14]

Was it not to have been expected that these repeated demonstrations of the injustice of the accusations hazarded against me would have abashed the enterprise of my calumniators? However natural such an expectation may seem, it would betray an ignorance of the true character of the Jacobin system. It is a maxim deeply ingrafted in that dark system, that no character, however upright, is a match for constantly reiterated attacks, however false. It is well understood by its disciples, that every calumny makes some proselites and even retains some; since justification seldom circulates as rapidly and as widely as slander. The number of those who from doubt proceed to suspicion and thence to belief of imputed guilt is continually augmenting; and the public mind fatigued at length with resistance to the calumnies which eternally assail it, is apt in the end

* Would it be believed after all this, that Mr. Jefferson Vice President of the United States would write to this Fraunces friendly letters? Yet such is the fact as will be seen in the Appendix, Nos. XLIV & XLV.

13. See the introductory note to Andrew G. Fraunces to H, May 16, 1793.
14. *Journal of the House*, II, 67.

to sit down with the opinion that a person so often accused cannot be entirely innocent.

Relying upon this weakness of human nature, the Jacobin Scandal-Club though often defeated constantly return to the charge. Old calumnies are served up a-fresh and every pretext is seized to add to the catalogue. The person whom they seek to blacken, by dint of repeated strokes of their brush, becomes a demon in their own eyes, though he might be pure and bright as an angel but for the daubing of those wizard painters.

Of all the vile attempts which have been made to injure my character that which has been lately revived in No. V and VI, of the history of the United States for 1796 is the most vile.[15] This it will be impossible for any *intelligent*, I will not say *candid*, man to doubt, when he shall have accompanied me through the examination.

I owe perhaps to my friends an apology for condescending to give a public explanation. A just pride with reluctance stoops to a formal vindication against so despicable a contrivance and is inclined rather to oppose to it the uniform evidence of an upright character. This would be my conduct on the present occasion, did not the tale seem to derive a sanction from the names of three men [16] of some weight and consequence in the society: a circumstance, which I trust will excuse me for paying attention to a slander that without this prop, would defeat itself by intrinsic circumstances of absurdity and malice.

The charge against me is a connection with one James Reynolds for purposes of improper pecuniary speculation. My real crime is an amorous connection with his wife, for a considerable time with his privity and connivance, if not originally brought on by a combination between the husband and wife with the design to extort money from me.

This confession is not made without a blush. I cannot be the apologist of any vice because the ardour of passion may have made it mine. I can never cease to condemn myself for the pang, which it

15. James Thomson Callender, *The History of the United States for 1796; Including a Variety of Interesting Particulars Relative to the Federal Government Previous to that Period* (Philadelphia: Snowden & McCorkle, 1797). For information on the publication of this pamphlet, see Wolcott to H, July 3, 1797, note 1.

16. James Monroe, Frederick A. C. Muhlenberg, and Abraham B. Venable.

may inflict in a bosom eminently intitled to all my gratitude, fidelity and love. But that bosom will approve, that even at so great an expence, I should effectually wipe away a more serious stain from a name, which it cherishes with no less elevation than tenderness. The public too will I trust excuse the confession. The necessity of it to my defence against a more heinous charge could alone have extorted from me so painful an indecorum.

Before I proceed to an exhibition of the positive proof which repels the charge, I shall analize the documents from which it is deduced, and I am mistaken if with discerning and candid minds more would be necessary. But I desire to obviate the suspicions of the most suspicious.

The first reflection which occurs on a perusal of the documents is that it is morally impossible I should have been foolish as well as depraved enough to employ so vile an instrument as *Reynolds* for such *insignificant ends*, as are indicated by different parts of the story itself. My enemies to be sure have kindly pourtrayed me as another *Chartres* [17] on the score of moral principle. But they have been ever bountiful in ascribing to me talents. It has suited their purpose to exaggerate such as I may possess, and to attribute to them an influence to which they are not intitled. But the present accusation imputes to me as much folly as wickedness. All the documents shew, and it is otherwise matter of notoriety, that Reynolds was an obscure, unimportant and profligate man. Nothing could be more weak, because nothing could be more unsafe than to make use of such an instrument; to use him too without any intermediate agent more worthy of confidence who might keep me out of sight, to write him numerous letters recording the objects of the improper connection (for this is pretended and that the letters were afterwards burnt at my request) to unbosom myself to him with a prodigality of confidence, by very unnecessarily telling him, as he alleges, of a connection in speculation between myself and Mr. Duer.[18] It is very

17. In 1793 Louis Philippe d'Orleans, duc de Chartres, the son of Louis Philippe Joseph, duc d'Orleans, deserted to the Austrians with his commander, General Charles François Dumouriez. Louis Philippe spent three years in exile in northern Europe. In 1796 the Directory agreed to release from prison his two brothers, the Duc de Montpensier and the Duc de Beaujolais, if Louis Philippe would go to America. The Duc de Chartres arrived in Philadelphia in October, 1796, and his brothers joined him there in February, 1797. Louis Philippe was King of France from 1830 to 1848.
18. William Duer.

extraordinary, if the head of the money department of a country, being unprincipled enough to sacrifice his trust and his integrity, could not have contrived objects of profit sufficiently large to have engaged the co-operation of men of far greater importance than Reynolds, and with whom there could have been due safety, and should have been driven to the necessity of unkennelling such a reptile to be the instrument of his cupidity.

But, moreover, the scale of the concern with Reynolds, such as it is presented, is contemptibly narrow for a rapacious speculating secretary of the treasury. *Clingman, Reynolds* and his wife were manifestly in very close confidence with each other. It seems there was a free communication of secrets. Yet in clubbing their different items of information as to the supplies of money which Reynolds received from me, what do they amount to? *Clingman* states, that Mrs. Reynolds told him, that at a certain time her husband had received from me upwards of eleven hundred dollars.[19] A note is produced which shews that at one time fifty dollars were sent to him,[20] and another note is produced, by which and the information of Reynolds himself through Clingman, it appears that at another time 300 dollars were asked [21] and refused. Another sum of 200 dollars is spoken of by *Clingman* as having been furnished to Reynolds at some other time.[22] What a scale of speculation is this for the head of a public treasury, for one who in the very publication that brings forward the charge is represented as having procured to be funded at forty millions a debt which ought to have been discharged at ten or fifteen millions for the criminal purpose of enriching himself and his friends? He must have been a clumsy knave, if he did not secure enough of this excess of twenty five or thirty millions, to have taken away all inducement to risk his character in such bad hands and in so huckstering a way—or to have enabled him, if he did employ such an agent, to do it with more means and to better purpose. It is curious, that this rapacious secretary should at one time have furnished his speculating agent with the paltry sum of fifty dollars, at

19. Clingman's deposition, dated December 13, 1792, is document No. IV (a) in the appendix to this pamphlet.
20. James Reynolds to H, June 23, 1792, which is document No. XX in the appendix to this pamphlet.
21. James Reynolds to H, June 3–22, 1792, which is document No. XIX in the appendix to this pamphlet.
22. Clingman's deposition, dated December 13, 1792, is document No. IV (a) in the appendix to this pamphlet.

another, have refused him the inconsiderable sum of 300 dollars, declaring upon his honor that it was not in his power to furnish it. This declaration was true or not; if the last the refusal ill comports with the idea of a speculating connection—if the first, it is very singular that the head of the treasury engaged without scruple in schemes of profit should have been destitute of so small a sum. But if we suppose this officer to be living upon an inadequate salary, without any collateral pursuits of gain, the appearances then are simple and intelligible enough, applying to them the true key.

It appears that *Reynolds* and *Clingman* were detected by the then comptroller of the treasury,[23] in the odious crime of suborning a witness to commit perjury, for the purpose of obtaining letters of administration on the estate of a person who was living in order to receive a small sum of money due to him from the treasury.[24] It is certainly extraordinary that the confidential agent of the head of that department should have been in circumstances to induce a resort to so miserable an expedient. It is odd, if there was a speculating connection, that it was not more profitable both to the secretary and to his agent than are indicated by the circumstances disclosed.

It is also a remarkable and very instructive fact, that notwithstanding the great confidence and intimacy, which subsisted between *Clingman*, *Reynolds* and his wife, and which continued till after the period of the liberation of the two former from the prosecution against them, neither of them has ever specified the objects of the pretended connection in speculation between Reynolds and me. The pretext that the letters which contained the evidence were destroyed is no answer. They could not have been forgotten and might have been disclosed from memory. The total omission of this could only have proceeded from the consideration that detail might have led to detection. The destruction of letters besides is a fiction, which is refuted not only by the general improbability, that I should put myself upon paper with so despicable a person on a subject which might expose me to infamy, but by the evidence of extreme caution on my part in this particular, resulting from the laconic and disguised form of the notes which are produced. They prove incontestibly that there was an unwillingness to trust Reynolds with my

23. Oliver Wolcott, Jr.
24. The perjurer was John Delabar. The claimant was Ephraim Goodenough. See Wolcott to H, July 3, 1797, note 14.

hand writing. The true reason was, that I apprehended he might make use of it to impress upon others the belief of some pecuniary connection with me, and besides implicating my character might render it the engine of a false credit, or turn it to some other sinister use. Hence the disguise; for my conduct in admitting at once and without hesitation that the notes were from me proves that it was never my intention by the expedient of disguising my hand to shelter myself from any serious inquiry.

The accusation against me was never heard of 'till Clingman and Reynolds were under prosecution by the treasury for an infamous crime. It will be seen by the document No. 1 (a) that during the endeavours of *Clingman* to obtain relief, through the interposition of Mr. Mughlenberg, he made to the latter the communication of my pretended criminality. It will be further seen by document No. 2 [(a)] that Reynolds had while in prison conveyed to the ears of Messrs. Monroe and Venable that he could give intelligence of my being concerned in speculation, and that he also supposed that he was kept in prison by a design on my part to oppress him and drive him away. And by his letter to *Clingman* of the 13 of December, after he was released from prison, it also appears that he was actuated by a spirit of revenge against me; for he declares that he will have *satisfaction* from me *at all events;* adding, as addressed to *Clingman,* "And *you only I trust.*" [25]

Three important inferences flow from these circumstances—one that the accusation against me was an auxiliary to the efforts of *Clingman* and *Reynolds* to get released from a disgraceful prosecution—another that there was a vindicative spirit against me at least on the part of Reynolds—the third, that he confided in *Clingman* as a coadjutor in the plan of vengeance. These circumstances, according to every estimate of the credit due to accusers, ought to destroy their testimony. To what credit are persons intitled, who in telling a story are governed by the double motive of escaping from disgrace and punishment and of gratifying revenge? As to Mrs. Reynolds, if she was not an accomplice, as it is too probable she was, her situation would naturally subject her to the will of her husband. But enough besides will appear in the sequel to shew that her testimony merits no attention.

The letter which has been just cited deserves a more particular

25. See H to James Monroe, July 20, 1797, note 4.

attention. As it was produced by Clingman, there is a chasm of three lines, which lines are manifestly essential to explain the sense. It may be inferred from the context, that these deficient lines would unfold the cause of the resentment which is expressed. 'Twas from them that might have been learnt the true nature of the transaction. The expunging of them is a violent presumption that they would have contradicted the purpose for which the letter was produced. A witness offering such a mutilated piece descredits himself. The mutilation is alone satisfactory proof of contrivance and imposition. The manner of accounting for it is frivolous.

The words of the letter are strong—satisfaction is to be had *at all events, per fas et nefas,* and *Clingman* is the chosen confidential agent of the laudable plan of vengeance. It must be confessed he was not wanting in his part.

Reynolds, as will be seen by No. II (a) alleges that a merchant came to him and offered as a volunteer to be his bail, who he suspected had been instigated to it by me, and after being decoyed to the place the merchant wished to carry him to, he refused being his bail, unless he would deposit a sum of money to some considerable amount which he could not do and was in consequence committed to prison. Clingman (No. IV a) tells the same story in substance though with some difference in form leaving to be implied what Reynolds expresses and naming *Henry Seckel* as the merchant. The deposition of this respectable citizen (No. XXIII) gives the lie to both, and shews that he was in fact the agent of *Clingman,* from motives of good will to him, as his former book-keeper, that he never had any communication with me concerning either of them till after they were both in custody, that when he came as a messenger to me from one of them, I not only declined interposing in their behalf, but informed Mr. Seckel that they had been guilty of a crime and advised him to have nothing to do with them.

This single fact goes far to invalidate the whole story. It shews p[l]ainly the disregard of truth and the malice by which the parties were actuated. Other important inferences are to be drawn from the transaction. Had I been conscious that I had any thing to fear from *Reynolds* of the nature which has been pretended, should I have warned Mr. *Seckel* against having any thing to do with them? Should I not rather have encouraged him to have come to their assistance? Should I not have been eager to promote their liberation? But this is not the only instance, in which I acted a contrary part. *Clingman* testifies in No. V. that I would not permit *Fraunces* a clerk in my office to become their bail, but signified to him that if he did it, he must quit the department.[26]

Clingman states in No. IV. (a) that my note in answer to Reynolds' application for a loan towards a subscription to the *Lancaster Turnpike* was in his possession from about the time it was written (June 1792.) This circumstance, apparently trivial, is very explanatory. To what end had *Clingman* the custody of this note all that time if it was not part of a project to lay the foundation for some false accusation?

It appears from No. V.[27] that *Fraunces* had said, or was stated to have said, something to my prejudice. If my memory serves me aright, it was that he had been my agent in some speculations. When *Fraunces* was interrogated concerning it, he absolutely denied that he had said any thing of the kind. The charge which this same *Fraunces* afterwards preferred against me to the House of Representatives, and the fate of it, have been already mentioned. It is illustrative of the nature of the combination which was formed against me.

There are other features in the documents which are relied upon to constitute the charge against me, that are of a nature to corroborate the inference to be drawn from the particulars which have been noticed. But there is no need to be over minute. I am much mistaken if the view which has been taken of the subject is not sufficient, without any thing further, to establish my innocence with every discerning and fair mind.

I proceed in the next place to offer a frank and plain solution of the enigma, by giving a history of the origin and progress of my connection with Mrs. Reynolds, of its discovery, real and pretended by the husband, and of the disagreeable embarrassments to which it exposed me. This history will be supported by the letters of Mr. and Mrs. Reynolds, which leave no room for doubt of the principal

26. H mistakenly referred to document "No. V." He is actually referring to document No. IV (a) in the appendix to this pamphlet.

27. H is referring to document No. V in James Thomson Callender's *History*. See Wolcott to H, July 3, 1797, notes 1, 50, and 51.

facts, and at the same time explain with precision the objects of the little notes from me which have been published, shewing clearly that such of them as have related to money had no reference to any concern in speculation. As the situation which will be disclosed, will fully explain every ambiguous appearance, and meet satisfactorily the written documents, nothing more can be requisite to my justification. For frail indeed will be the tenure by which the most blameless man will hold his reputation, if the assertions of three of the most abandoned characters in the community, two of them stigmatized by the discrediting crime which has been mentioned, are sufficient to blast it. The business of accusation would soon become in such a case, a regular trade, and men's reputations would be bought and sold like any marketable commodity.

Some time in the summer of the year 1791 a woman called at my house in the city of Philadelphia [28] and asked to speak with me in private. I attended her into a room apart from the family. With a seeming air of affliction she informed that she was a daughter of a Mr. Lewis, sister to a Mr. G. Livingston of the State of New-York, and wife to a Mr. Reynolds whose father was in the Commissary Department during the war with Great Britain, that her husband, who for a long time had treated her very cruelly, had lately left her, to live with another woman, and in so destitute a condition, that though desirous of returning to her friends she had not the means—that knowing I was a citizen of New-York, she had taken the liberty to apply to my humanity for assistance.

I replied, that her situation was a very interesting one—that I was disposed to afford her assistance to convey her to her friends, but this at the moment not being convenient to me (which was the fact) I must request the place of her residence, to which I should bring or send a small supply of money. She told me the street and the number of the house where she lodged. In the evening I put a bank-bill in my pocket and went to the house.[29] I inquired for Mrs. Reynolds and was shewn up stairs, at the head of which she met me and conducted me into a bed room. I took the bill out of my pocket

28. 79 South Third Street.
29. A Philadelphia directory for 1791 states that a "Mrs. Reynolds" lived at 154 South Fourth Street (Clement Biddle, *The Philadelphia Directory* [Philadelphia: Printed by James & Johnson, No. 147, High-Street, 1791], 107).

and gave it to her. Some conversation ensued from which it was quickly apparent that other than pecuniary consolation would be acceptable.

After this, I had frequent meetings with her, most of them at my own house; Mrs. Hamilton with her children being absent on a visit to her father.[30] In the course of a short time, she mentioned to me that her husband had solicited a reconciliation, and affected to consult me about it. I advised to it, and was soon after informed by her that it had taken place. She told me besides that her husband had been engaged in speculation, and she believed could give information respecting the conduct of some persons in the department which would be useful. I sent for Reynolds who came to me accordingly.

In the course of our interview, he confessed that he had obtained a list of claims from a person in my department which he had made use of in his speculations. I invited him, by the expectation of my friendship and good offices, to disclose the person. After some affectation of scruple, he pretended to yield, and ascribed the infidelity to Mr. Duer from whom he said he had obtained the list in New-York, while he (Duer) was in the department.

As Mr. Duer had resigned his office some time before the seat of government was removed to Philadelphia; this discovery, if it had been true, was not very important—yet it was the interest of my passions to appear to set value upon it, and to continue the expectation of friendship and good offices. Mr. Reynolds told me he was going to Virginia, and on his return would point out something in which I could serve him. I do not know but he said something about employment in a public office.

On his return he asked employment as a clerk in the treasury department. The knowledge I had acquired of him was decisive against such a request. I parried it by telling him, what was true, that there was no vacancy in my immediate office, and that the appointment of clerks in the other branches of the department was left to the chiefs of the respective branches. Reynolds alleged, as *Clingman* relates No. IV (a) as a topic of complaint against me that I had promised him *employment* and had *disappointed* him. The situ-

30. Elizabeth Hamilton left Philadelphia for a visit with her parents in Albany in the middle of July, 1791. See H to Rufus King, July 8, 1791; H to Elizabeth Hamilton, July 27, 1791.

ation with the wife would naturally incline me to conciliate this man. It is possible I may have used vague expressions which raised expectation; but the more I learned of the person, the more inadmissible his employment in a public office became. Some material reflections will occur here to a discerning mind. Could I have preferred my private gratification to the public interest, should I not have found the employment he desired for a man, whom it was so convenient to me, on my own statement, to lay under obligations. Had I had any such connection with him, as he has since pretended, is it likely that he would have wanted other employment? Or is it likely that wanting it, I should have hazarded his resentment by a persevering refusal? This little circumstance shews at once the delicacy of my conduct, in its public relations, and the impossibility of my having had the connection pretended with Reynolds.

The intercourse with Mrs. Reynolds, in the mean time, continued; and, though various reflections, (in which a further knowledge of Reynolds' character and the suspicion of some concert between the husband and wife bore a part) induced me to wish a cessation of it; yet her conduct, made it extremely difficult to disentangle myself. All the appearances of violent attachment, and of agonizing distress at the idea of a relinquishment, were played off with a most imposing art. This, though it did not make me entirely the dupe of the plot, yet kept me in a state of irresolution. My sensibility, perhaps my vanity, admitted the possibility of a real fondness; and led me to adopt the plan of a gradual discontinuance rather than of a sudden interruption, as least calculated to give pain, if a real partiality existed.

Mrs. Reynolds, on the other hand, employed every effort to keep up my attention and visits. Her pen was freely employed, and her letters were filled with those tender and pathetic effusions which would have been natural to a woman truly fond and neglected.

One day, I received a letter from her, which is in the appendix (No. I. b) intimating a discovery by her husband. It was matter of doubt with me whether there had been really a discovery by accident, or whether the time for the catastrophe of the plot was arrived.

The same day, being the 15th of December 1791, I received from Mr. Reynolds the letter (No. II. b) by which he informs me of the detection of his wife in the act of writing a letter to me, and that he had obtained from her a discovery of her connection with me, suggesting that it was the consequence of an undue advantage taken of her distress.

In answer to this I sent him a note, or message desiring him to call upon me at my office, which I think he did the same day.[31]

He in substance repeated the topics contained in his letter, and concluded as he had done there, that he was resolved to have satisfaction.

I replied that he knew best what evidence he had of the alleged connection between me and his wife, that I neither admitted nor denied it—that if he knew of any injury I had done him, intitling him to satisfaction, it lay with him to name it.

He travelled over the same ground as before, and again concluded with the same vague claim of satisfaction, but without specifying the kind, which would content him. It was easy to understand that he wanted money, and to prevent an explosion, I resolved to gratify him. But willing to manage his delicacy, if he had any, I reminded him that I had at our first interview made him a promise of service, that I was disposed to do it as far as might be proper, and in my power, and requested him to consider in what manner I could do it, and to write to me. He withdrew with a promise of compliance.

Two days after, the 17th of December, he wrote me the letter (No. III. b). The evident drift of this letter is to exaggerate the injury done by me, to make a display of sensibility and to magnify the atonement, which was to be required. It however comes to no conclusion, but proposes a meeting at the *George Tavern*, or at some other place more agreeable to me, which I should name.

On receipt of this letter, I called upon Reynolds, and assuming a decisive tone, told him, that I was tired of his indecision, and insisted upon his declaring to me explicitly what it was he aimed at. He again promised to explain by letter.

On the 19th, I received the promised letter (No. IV. b) the essence of which is that he was willing to take a thousand dollars as the plaister of his wounded honor.

I determined to give it to him, and did so in two payments, as per receipts (No. V and VI) dated the 22d of December and 3d of January. It is a little remarkable, that an avaricious speculating

31. Letter not found.

secretary of the treasury should have been so straitened for money as to be obliged to satisfy an engagement of this sort by two different payments!

On the 17th of January, I received the letter No. V.[32] by which Reynolds invites me to *renew my visits to his wife*. He had before requested that I would see her no more. The motive to this step appears in the conclusion of the letter, "*I rely* upon your befriending me, *if there should any thing offer that should be to my advantage*, as you *express a wish to befriend me*." Is the pre-existence of a speculating connection reconcileable with this mode of expression?

If I recollect rightly, I did not immediately accept the invitation, nor 'till after I had received several very importunate letters from Mrs. Reynolds—See her letters No. VIII, (b) IX, X.

On the 24th of March following, I received a letter from *Reynolds*, No. XI, and on the same day one from his wife, No. XII. These letters will further illustrate the obliging co-operation of the husband with his wife to aliment and keep alive my connection with her.

The letters from Reynolds, No. XIII to XVI, are an additional comment upon the same plan. It was a persevering scheme to spare no pains to levy contributions upon my passions on the one hand, and upon my apprehensions of discovery on the other. It is probably to No. XIV that my note, in these words, was an answer; "To-morrow what is requested will be done. 'Twill hardly be possible *to-day*." [33] The letter presses for the loan which is asked for *to-day*. A scarcity of cash, which was not very uncommon, is believed to have modelled the reply.

The letter No. XVII is a master-piece. The husband there forbids my future visits to his wife, chiefly because I was careful to avoid publicity. It was probably necessary to the project of some deeper treason against me that I should be seen at the house. Hence was it contrived, with all the caution on my part to avoid it, that *Clingman* should occasionally see me.

The interdiction was every way welcome, and was I believe,

32. H is mistaken, for he intended to refer to document No. VII in the appendix to this pamphlet.
33. H to James Reynolds, April 7, 1792.

strictly observed. On the second of June following, I received the letter No. XVIII, from Mrs. Reynolds, which proves that it was not her plan yet to let me off. It was probably the prelude to the letter from Reynolds, No. XIX, soliciting a *loan* of 300 dollars towards a subscription to the Lancaster Turnpike. *Clingman's* statement, No. IV [(a)], admits, on the information of Reynolds, that to this letter the following note from me was an answer—"*It is utterly out of my power I assure you 'pon my honour to comply with your request. Your note is returned.*" The letter itself demonstrates, that here was no concern in speculation on my part—that the money is asked as a *favour* and as a *loan*, to be reimbursed simply and without profit *in less than a fortnight.* My answer shews that even the loan was refused.

The letter No. XX, from *Reynolds*, explains the object of my note in these words, "*Inclosed are 50 dollars, they could not be sent sooner,*" [34] proving that this sum also was begged for in a very apologetic stile as a mere loan.

The letters of the 24th and 30th of August, No. XXI and XXII, furnish the key to the affair of the 200 dollars mentioned by *Clingman* in No. IV, shewing that this sum likewise was asked by way of loan, towards furnishing a small boarding-house which *Reynolds* and his wife were or pretended to be about to set up.

These letters collectively, furnish a complete elucidation of the nature of my transactions with *Reynolds.* They resolve them into an amorous connection with his wife, detected, or pretended to be detected by the husband, imposing on me the necessity of a pecuniary composition with him, and leaving me afterwards under a duress for fear of disclosure, which was the instrument of levying upon me from time to time *forced loans.* They apply directly to this state of things, the notes which *Reynolds* was so careful to preserve, and which had been employed to excite suspicion.

Four, and the principal of these notes have been not only generally, but particularly explained—I shall briefly notice the remaining two.

"My dear Sir, I expected to have heard the day after I had the pleasure of seeing you." This fragment, if truly part of a letter to *Reynolds*, denotes nothing more than a disposition to be civil to a man, whom, as I said before, it was the interest of my passions to

34. H to James Reynolds, June 24, 1792.

conciliate. But I verily believe it was not part of a letter to him, because I do not believe that I ever addressed him in such a stile. It may very well have been part of a letter to some other person, procured by means of which I am ignorant, or it may have been the beginning of an intended letter, torn off, thrown into the chimney in my office, which was a common practice, and there or after it had been swept out picked up by Reynolds or some coadjutor of his. There appears to have been more than one clerk in the department some how connected with him.

The endeavour shewn by the letter No. XVII, to induce me to render my visits to Mrs. Reynolds more public, and the great care with which my little notes were preserved, justify the belief that at a period, before it was attempted, the idea of implicating me in some accusation, with a view to the advantage of the accusers, was entertained. Hence the motive to pick up and preserve any fragment which might favour the idea of friendly or confidential correspondence.

2dly. "The person Mr. Reynolds inquired for on Friday waited for him all the evening at his house from a little after seven. Mr. R. may see him at any time to-day or to-morrow between the hours of two and three."

Mrs. Reynolds more than once communicated to me, that Reynolds would occasionally relapse into discontent to his situation—would treat her very ill—hint at the assassination of me—and more openly threaten, by way of revenge, to inform Mrs. Hamilton—all this naturally gave some uneasiness. I could not be absolutely certain whether it was artifice or reality. In the workings of human inconsistency, it was very possible, that the same man might be corrupt enough to compound for his wife's chastity and yet have sensibility enough to be restless in the situation and to hate the cause of it.

Reflections like these induced me for some time to use palliatives with the ill humours which were announced to me. Reynolds had called upon me in one of these discontented moods real or pretended. I was unwilling to provoke him by the appearance of neglect— and having failed to be at home at the hour he had been permitted to call, I wrote her the above note to obviate an ill impression.

The foregoing narrative and the remarks accompanying it have prepared the way for a perusal of the letters themselves. The more attention is used in this, the more entire will be the satisfaction which they will afford.

It has been seen that an explanation on the subject was had cotemporarily that is in December 1792, with three members of Congress—F. A. Muhlenberg, J. Monroe, and A. Venable. It is proper that the circumstances of this transaction should be accurately understood.

The manner in which Mr. Muhlenberg became engaged in the affair is fully set forth in the document (No. I. a). It is not equally clear how the two other gentlemen came to embark in it. The phraseology, in reference to this point in the close of (No. I. [(a)]) and beginning of (No. II. [(a)]) is rather equivocal. The gentlemen, if they please, can explain it.

But on the morning of the 15th of December 1792, the above mentioned gentlemen presented themselves at my office. Mr. Muhlenberg was then speaker. He introduced the subject by observing to me, that they *had discovered a very improper connection* between me and a Mr. Reynolds: extremely hurt by this mode of introduction, I arrested the progress of the discourse by giving way to very strong expressions of indignation. The gentlemen explained, telling me in substance that I had misapprehended them—that they did not intend to take the fact for established—that their meaning was to apprise me that unsought by them, information had been given them of an improper pecuniary connection between Mr. Reynolds and myself; that they had thought it their duty to pursue it and had become possessed of some documents of a suspicious complexion—that they had contemplated the laying the matter before the President, but before they did this, they thought it right to apprise me of the affair and to afford an opportunity of explanation; declaring at the same time that their agency in the matter was influenced solely by a sense of public duty and by no motive of personal ill will. If my memory be correct, the notes from me in a disguised hand were now shewn to me which without a moment's hesitation I acknowledged to be mine.

I replied, that the affair was now put upon a different footing— that I always stood ready to meet fair inquiry with frank communication—that it happened, in the present instance, to be in my power by written documents to remove all doubt as to the real nature of the business, and fully to convince, that nothing of the kind imputed to me did in fact exist. The same evening at my house was by mutual consent appointed for an explanation.

I immediately after saw Mr. Wolcott, and for the first time informed him of the affair and of the interview just had; and delivering into his hands for perusal the documents of which I was possessed, I engaged him to be present at the intended explanation in the evening.

In the evening the proposed meeting took place, and Mr. Wolcott according to my request attended. The information, which had been received to that time, from *Clingman, Reynolds* and his wife was communicated to me and the notes were I think again exhibited.

I stated in explanation, the circumstances of my affair with Mrs. Reynolds and the consequences of it and in confirmation produced the documents (No. I. b, to XXII.) One or more of the gentlemen (Mr. Wolcott's certificate No. XXIV, mentions one, Mr. Venable, but I think the same may be said of Mr. Muhlenberg) was struck with so much conviction, before I had gotten through the communication that they delicately urged me to discontinue it as unnecessary. I insisted upon going through the whole and did so. The result was a full and unequivocal acknowlegement on the part of the three gentlemen of perfect satisfaction with the explanation and expressions of regret at the trouble and embarrassment which had been occasioned to me. Mr. Muhlenberg and Mr. Venable, in particular manifested a degree of sensibility on the occasion. Mr. Monroe was more cold but intirely explicit.

One of the gentlemen, I think, expressed a hope that I also was satisfied with their conduct in conducting the inquiry. I answered, that they knew I had been hurt at the opening of the affair—that this excepted, I was satisfied with their conduct and considered myself as having been treated with candor or with fairness and liberality, I do not now pretend to recollect the exact terms. I took the next morning a memorandum of the substance of what was said to me, which will be seen by a copy of it transmitted in a letter to each of the gentlemen No. XXV.

I deny absolutely, as alleged by the editor of the publication in question, that I intreated a suspension of the communication to the President, or that from the beginning to the end of the inquiry, I asked any favour or indulgence whatever, and that I discovered any symptom different from that of a proud consciousness of innocence.[35]

Some days after the explanation I wrote to the three gentlemen the letter No. XXVI already published. That letter evinces the light in which I considered myself as standing in their view.

I received from Mr. Muhlenberg and Mr. Monroe in answer the letters No. XXVII and XXVIII.

Thus the affair remained 'till the pamphlets No. V and VI of the history of the U. States for 1796 appeared; with the exception of some dark whispers which were communicated to me by a friend in Virginia, and to which I replied by a statement of what had passed.[36]

When I saw No. V though it was evidence of a base infidelity somewhere, yet firmly believing that nothing more than a want of due care was chargeable upon either of the three gentlemen who had made the inquiry, I immediately wrote to each of them a letter of which No. XXV is a copy [37] in full confidence that their answer would put the whole business at rest. I ventured to believe, from the appearances on their part at closing our former interview on the subject, that their answers would have been both cordial and explicit.

I acknowledge that I was astonished when I came to read in the pamphlet No. VI the conclusion of the document No. V, containing

35. This is a reference to the following statement by Callender: ". . . When some of the papers which are now to be laid before the world, were submitted to the secretary; when he was informed that they were to be communicated to President Washington, he entreated, in the most anxious tone of deprecation, that this measure might be suspended. Mr. Monroe was one of the three gentlemen who agreed to a delay. They gave their consent to it, on his express promise of a guarded behaviour in future, and because he attached to the suppression of these papers, a mysterious degree of solicitude . . ." (Callender, *History*, 205).

36. On May 6, 1793, Henry Lee wrote to H from Richmond, Virginia: "Was I with you I would talk an hour with doors bolted & windows shut, as my heart is much afflicted by some whispers which I have heard." H's letter to Lee, which was dated June 15, 1793, has not been found.

37. H to Monroe, July 5, 1797. H's letters on the same date to Muhlenberg and Venable have not been found.

the equivocal phrase "*We left him under an impression our suspicions were removed,*" [38] which seemed to imply that this had been a mere piece of management, and that the impression given me had not been reciprocal. The appearance of duplicity incensed me; but resolving to proceed with caution and moderation, I thought the first proper step was to inquire of the gentlemen whether the paper was genuine. A letter was written for this purpose the copy of which I have mislaid.[39]

I afterwards received from Messrs. Muhlenberg and Venable the letters No. XXIX, XXX, and XXXI.[40]

Receiving no answer from Mr. Monroe, and hearing of his arrival at New-York I called upon him.[41] The issue of the interview was that an answer was to be given by him, in conjunction with Mr. Muhlenberg and Mr. Venable on his return to Philadelphia, he thinking that as the agency had been joint it was most proper the answer should be joint, and informing me that Mr. Venable had told him he would wait his return.

I came to Philadelphia accordingly to bring the affair to a close; but on my arrival I found Mr. Venable had left the city for Virginia.

Mr. Monroe reached Philadelphia according to his appointment. And the morning following wrote me the note No. XXXII. While this note was on its way to my lodgings I was on my way to his. I had a conversation with him from which we separated with a repetition of the assurance in the note. In the course of the interviews with Mr. Monroe, the *equivoque* in document No. V, (a) and the paper of January 2d, 1793, under his signature were noticed.[42]

I received the day following the letter No. XXXIII, to which I

38. This is a reference to a memorandum by Monroe, Muhlenberg, and Venable, dated December 16, 1792. For the text of the memorandum, see Wolcott to H, July 3, 1797, note 50.

39. H to Monroe, July 8, 1797.

40. H was mistaken, for he skipped the number XXXI in numbering the letters in the appendix to this pamphlet. For this letter, see Venable to H, July 10, 1797.

41. See H to Monroe, July 10, 1797; Monroe to H, July 10, 1797; "David Gelston's Account of an Interview between Alexander Hamilton and James Monroe," July 11, 1797.

42. H did not include any document numbered "V (a)" in the appendix to the pamphlet printed above. Callender, however, printed it as document No. V in his *History.* See Wolcott to H, July 3, 1797, notes 1, 50, and 51.

returned the answer No. XXXIV,—accompanied with the letter No. XXXV. which was succeeded by the letters No. XXXVI—XXXVII —XXXVIII—XXXIX—XL. In due time the sequel of the correspondence will appear.

Though extremely disagreeable to me, for very obvious reasons, I at length determined in order that no cloud whatever might be left on the affair, to publish the documents which had been communicated to Messrs. Monroe, Muhlenberg and Venable,[43] all which will be seen in the appendix from No. I, (b) to No. XXII, inclusively.

The information from *Clingman* of the 2d January 1793, to which the signature of Mr. Monroe is annexed, seems to require an observation or two in addition to what is contained in my letter to him No. XXXIX.

Clingman first suggests that he had been apprized of my vindication through Mr. Wolcott a day or two after it had been communicated. It did not occur to me to inquire of Mr. Wolcott on this point, and he being now absent from Philadelphia,[44] I cannot do it at this moment. Though I can have no doubt of the friendly intention of Mr. Wolcott, if the suggestion of Clingman in this particular be taken as true; yet from the condition of secrecy which was annexed to my communication, there is the strongest reason to conclude it is not true. If not true, there is besides but one of two solutions, either that he obtained the information from one of the three gentlemen who made the inquiry, which would have been a very dishonourable act in the party, or that he conjectured what my defence was from what he before knew it truly could be. For there is the highest probability, that through Reynolds and his wife, and as an accomplice, he was privy to the whole affair. This last method of accounting for his knowledge would be conclusive on the sincerity and genuineness of the defence.

But the turn which *Clingman* gives to the matter must necessarily fall to the ground. It is, that Mrs. Reynolds denied her amorous connection with me, and represented the suggestion of it as a mere contrivance between *her husband* and *myself* to cover me, alleging that there had been a fabrication of letters and receipts to countenance it.

43. See H to John Fenno, July 6, 17–22, 1797.
44. Wolcott was in Connecticut visiting his father, who was ill.

The plain answer is, that Mrs. Reynolds' own letters contradict absolutely this artful explanation of hers; if indeed she ever made it, of which *Clingman's* assertion is no evidence whatever. These letters are proved by the affidavit No. XLI, though it will easily be conceived that the proof of them was rendered no easy matter by a lapse of near five years. They shew explicitly the connection with her, the discovery of it by her husband and the pains she took to prolong it when I evidently wished to get rid of it. This cuts up, by the root, the pretence of a contrivance between the husband and myself to fabricate the evidences of it.

The variety of shapes which this woman could assume was endless. In a conversation between her and a gentleman whom I am not at liberty publicly to name,[45] she made a voluntary confession of her belief and even knowledge, that I was innocent of all that had been laid to my charge by *Reynolds* or any other person of her acquaintance, spoke of me in exalted terms of esteem and respect, declared in the most solemn manner her extreme unhappiness lest I should suppose her accessary to the trouble which had been given me on that account, and expressed her fear that the resentment of Mr. Reynolds on *a particular score*, might have urged him to improper lengths of revenge—appearing at the same time extremely agitated and unhappy. With the gentleman who gives this information, I have never been in any relation personal or political that could be supposed to bias him. His name would evince that he is an impartial witness. And though I am not permitted to make a public use of it, I am permitted to refer any gentleman to the perusal of his letter in the hands of William Bingham, Esquire; who is also so obliging as to permit me to deposit with him for similar inspection all the original papers which are contained in the appendix to this narrative. The letter from the gentleman above alluded to has been already shewn to *Mr. Monroe.*

Let me now, in the last place, recur to some comments, in which the hireling editors of the pamphlets No. V and VI has thought fit to indulge himself.

The first of them is that the *soft* language of one of my notes addressed to a man in the habit of threatening me with disgrace, is in-

45. Probably Richard Folwell. See Edward Jones to H, July 30, 1797.

compatible with the idea of innocence.[46] The threats alluded to must be those of being able to hang the Secretary of the Treasury. How does it appear that Reynolds was in such a *habit?* No otherwise than by the declaration of *Reynolds* and *Clingman.* If the assertions of these men are to condemn me, there is an end of the question. There is no need, by elaborate deductions from *parts* of their assertions, to endeavour to establish what their assertions collectively affirm in express terms. If they are worthy of credit I am guilty; if they are not, all wire-drawn inferences from parts of their story are mere artifice and nonsense. But no man, not as debauched as themselves, will believe them, independent of the positive disproof of their story in the written documents.

As to the affair of threats (except those in Reynolds letters respecting the connection with his wife, which it will be perceived were very gentle for the occasion) not the least idea of the sort ever reached me 'till after the imprisonment of Reynolds. Mr. Wolcott's certificate [47] shews my conduct in that case—notwithstanding the powerful motives I may be presumed to have had to desire the liberation of Reynolds, on account of my situation with his wife, I cautioned Mr. Wolcott not to facilitate his liberation, till the affair of the threat was satisfactorily cleared up. The solemn denial of it in Reynold's letter No. XLII was considered by Mr. Wolcott as sufficient. This is a further proof, that though in respect to my situation with his wife, I was somewhat in Reynolds's power. I was not disposed to make any improper concession to the apprehension of his resentment.

As the threats intimated in his letters, the nature of the cause will shew that the soft tone of my note was not only compatible with them, but a natural consequence of them.

But it is observed that the dread of the disclosure of an amorous connection was not a sufficient cause for my humility, and that I had nothing to lose as to my reputation for chastity concerning which the world had fixed a previous opinion.

46. In discussing a note which H wrote to Reynolds, Callender wrote: ". . . The gentle tone of the refusal, also, deserves notice. It expressly implies a high degree of previous intimacy" (Callender, *History,* 219).
47. See document No. XXIV in the appendix to this pamphlet.

I shall not enter into the question what was the previous opinion entertained of me in this particular—nor how well founded, if it was indeed such as it is represented to have been. It is sufficient to say that there is a wide difference between vague rumours and suspicions and the evidence of a positive fact—no man not indelicately unprincipled, with the state of manners in this country, would be willing to have a conjugal infidelity fixed upon him with positive certainty. He would know that it would justly injure him with a considerable and respectable portion of the society—and especially no man, tender of the happiness of an excellent wife could without extreme pain look forward to the affliction which she might endure from the disclosure, especially a *public disclosure*, of the fact. Those best acquainted with the interior of my domestic life will best appreciate the force of such a consideration upon me.

The truth was, that in both relations and especially the last, I dreaded extremely a disclosure—and was willing to make large sacrifices to avoid it. It is true, that from the acquiescence of Reynolds, I had strong ties upon his secrecy, but how could I rely upon any tie upon so base a character. How could I know, but that from moment to moment he might, at the expence of his own disgrace, become the *mercenary* of a party, with whom to blast my character in *any way* is a favorite object!

Strong inferences are attempted to be drawn from the release of *Clingman* and *Reynolds* with the consent of the Treasury, from the want of communicativeness of Reynolds while in prison—from the subsequent disappearance of Reynolds and his wife, and from their not having been produced by me in order to be confronted at the time of the explanation.

As to the first, it was emphatically the transaction of Mr. Wolcott the then Comptroller of the Treasury, and was bottomed upon a very adequate motive—and one as appears from the document No. I, (a) early contemplated in this light by that officer. It was certainly of more consequence to the public to detect and expel from the bosom of the Treasury Department an unfaithful Clerk to prevent future and extensive mischief, than to disgrace and punish two worthless individuals. Besides that a powerful influence foreign to me was exerted to procure indulgence to them—that of Mr. Muhlenberg and Col. Burr [48]—that of Col. Wadsworth,[49] which though insidiously placed to my account was to the best of my recollection utterly unknown to me at the time, and according to the confession of Mrs. Reynolds herself, was put in motion by her entreaty. Candid men will derive strong evidence of my innocence and delicacy, from the reflection, that under circumstances so peculiar, the culprits were compelled to give a real and substantial equivalent for the relief which they obtained from a department, *over which I presided.*

The backwardness of Reynolds to enter into detail, while in jail, was an argument of nothing but that conscious of his inability to communicate any particulars which could be supported, he found it more convenient to deal in generals, and to keep up appearances by giving promises for the future.

As to the disappearance of the parties after the liberation, how am I answerable for it? Is it not presumable, that the instance discovered at the Treasury was not the only offence of the kind of which they were guilty? After one detection, is it not very probable that Reynolds fled to avoid detection in other cases? But exclusive of this, it is known and might easily be proved, that Reynolds was considerably in debt! What more natural for him than to fly from his creditors after having been once exposed by confinement for such a crime? Moreover, atrocious as his conduct had been towards me, was it not natural for him to fear that my resentment might be excited at the discovery of it, and that it might have been deemed a sufficient reason for retracting the indulgence, which was shewn by withdrawing the prosecution and for recommending it?

One or all of these considerations will explain the disappearance of Reynolds without imputing it to me as a method of getting rid of a dangerous witness.

That disappearance rendered it impracticable, if it had been desired to bring him forward to be confronted. As to *Clingman* it was not pretended that he knew any thing of what was charged upon me, otherwise than by the notes which he produced, and the information of Reynolds and his wife. As to Mrs. Reynolds, she in fact ap-

48. Aaron Burr. See document No. I (a) in the appendix to this pamphlet.
49. Jeremiah Wadsworth. See document No. III (a) in the appendix to this pamphlet.

pears by *Clingman's* last story to have remained, and to have been accessible through him, by the gentlemen who had undertaken the inquiry. If they supposed it necessary to the elucidation of the affair, why did not they bring her forward? There can be no doubt of the sufficiency of Clingman's influence, for this purpose, when it is understood that Mrs. Reynolds and he afterwards lived together as man and wife.[50] But to what purpose the confronting? What would it have availed the elucidation of truth, if Reynolds and his wife had impudently made allegations which I denied. Relative character and the written documents must still determine These could decide without it, and they were relied upon. But could it be expected, that I should so debase myself as to think it necessary to my vindication to be confronted with a person such as Reynolds? Could I have borne to suffer my veracity to be exposed to the humiliating competition?

For what?—why, it is said, to tear up the last twig of jealousy—but when I knew that I possessed written documents which were decisive, how could I foresee that any twig of jealousy would remain? When the proofs I did produce to the gentlemen were admitted by them to be completely satisfactory, and by some of them to be more than sufficient, how could I dream of the expediency of producing more—how could I imagine that every twig of jealousy was not plucked up?

If after the recent confessions of the gentlemen themselves, it could be useful to fortify the proof of the full conviction, my explanation had wrought, I might appeal to the total silence concerning this charge, when at a subsequent period, in the year 1793, there was such an active legislative persecution of me.[51] It might not even perhaps be difficult to establish, that it came under the eye of Mr. Giles,[52] and that he discarded it as the plain case of a private amour unconnected with any thing that was the proper subject of a public attack.

Thus has my desire to destroy this slander, completely, led me to

50. See Jones to H, July 30, 1797, note 7.

51. This is a reference to the investigation into H's conduct as Secretary of the Treasury in January–March, 1793. See H's "Report on the Balance of All Unapplied Revenues at the End of the Year 1792 and on All Unapplied Monies Which May Have Been Obtained by the Several Loans Authorized by Law," February 4, 1793.

52. William Branch Giles. See John B. Church to H, July 13, 1797.

a more copious and particular examination of it, than I am sure was necessary. The bare perusal of the letters from Reynolds and his wife is sufficient to convince my greatest enemy that there is nothing worse in the affair than an irregular and indelicate amour. For this, I bow to the just censure which it merits. I have paid pretty severely for the folly and can never recollect it without disgust and self condemnation. It might seem affectation to say more.

To unfold more clearly the malicious intent, by which the present revival of the affair must have been influenced—I shall annex an affidavit of Mr. Webster [53] tending to confirm my declaration of the utter falsehood of the assertion, that a menace of publishing the papers which have been published had arrested the progress of an attempt to hold me up as a candidate for the office of President. Does this editor imagine that he will escape the just odium which awaits him by the miserable subterfuge of saying that he had the information from a respectable citizen of New-York? Till he names the author the inevitable inference must be that he has fabricated the tale.

ALEXANDER HAMILTON.

Philadelphia, July, 1797.

APPENDIX.[54]

No. I. (a)[55]

Philadelphia, 13th of December, 1792.

Jacob Clingman being a clerk in my employment, and becoming involved in a prosecution commenced against James Reynolds, by the comptroller of the treasury, on a charge or information exhibited before Hillary Baker, Esq. one of the aldermen of this city, for subornation of perjury, whereby they had obtained money from the treasury of the United States, he (Clingman) applied to me for my aid, and friendship on behalf of himself and Reynolds, to get them

53. See H to John Fenno, July 6, 1797.
54. The texts of the documents in this appendix which are printed below have been taken from the published version of the "Reynolds Pamphlet." When manuscripts of these documents are known to exist, the location of each is noted.
55. Copy, Hamilton Papers, Library of Congress; copy, The Sol Feinstone Collection, Library of the American Philosophical Society, Philadelphia.

released or discharged from the prosecution. I promised, so far as respected Clingman, but not being particularly acquainted with Reynolds, in a great measure declined, so far as respected him. In company with Col. Burr, I waited on Col. Hamilton, for the purpose, and particularly recommended Clingman, who had hitherto sustained a good character. Col. Hamilton signified a wish to do all that was consistent. Shortly after, I waited on the comptroller, for the same purpose, who seemed to have some difficulties on the subject; and from some information I had, in the mean time, received, I could not undertake to recommend Reynolds; as I verily believed him to be a rascal; which words I made use of, to the comptroller. On a second interview with the comptroller, on the same subject, the latter urged the propriety of Clingman's delivering up a certain list of money due to individuals, which, Reynolds and Clingman were said to have in their possession, and of his informing him, of whom, or thro' whom, the same was obtained from the public offices: on doing which, Clingman's request might, perhaps, be granted with greater propriety. This, Clingman, I am informed, complied with, and also refunded the money or certificates, which they had improperly obtained from the treasury. After which, I understand the action against both was withdrawn, and Reynolds discharged from imprisonment, without any further interference of mine whatsoever. During the time, this business was thus depending, and which lasted upwards of three weeks, Clingman, unasked, frequently dropped hints to me, that Reynolds had it in his power, very materially to injure the secretary of the treasury, and that Reynolds knew several very improper transactions of his. I paid little or no attention to those hints, but when they were frequently repeated, and it was even added, that Reynolds said, he had it in his power to hang the secretary of the Treasury, that he was deeply concerned in speculation, that he had frequently advanced money to him (Reynolds) and other insinuations of an improper nature, it created considerable uneasiness on my mind, and I conceived it my duty to consult with some friends on the subject. Mr. Monroe and Mr. Venable were informed of it yesterday morning.

Signed by Mr. Muhlenberg.

No. II. (a)[56]

Philadelphia, 13th December, 1792.

Being informed yesterday in the morning, that a person, of the name of Reynolds, from Virginia, Richmond, was confined in the jail, upon some criminal prosecution, relative to certificates, and that he had intimated, he could give some intelligence of speculations by Mr. Hamilton, which should be known, we immediately called on him, as well to be informed of the situation of the man, as of those other matters, in which the public might be interested. We found, it was not the person, we had been taught to believe, but a man of that name from New-York, and who had, for some time past resided in this city. Being there, however, we questioned him, respecting the other particular: he informed us, that he could give information of the misconduct, in that respect, of a person high in office, but must decline it for the present, and until relieved, which was promised him, that evening: that at ten to-day, he would give us a detail of whatever he knew on the subject. He affirmed, he had a person in high office, in his power, and has had, a long time past: That he had written to him in terms so abusive, that no person should have submitted to it, but that he dared not to resent it. That Mr. Wolcott was in the same department, and, he supposed, under his influence or controul. And, in fact, expressed himself in such a manner, as to leave no doubt, he meant Mr. Hamilton. That he expected to be released by Mr. Wolcott, at the instance of that person, altho' he believed that Mr. Wolcott, in instituting the prosecution, had no improper design. That he was satisfied the prosecution was set on foot, only to keep him low, and oppress him, and ultimately drive him away, in order to prevent his using the power he had over him; that he had had, since his residence here, for eighteen months, many private meetings with that person, who had often promised to put him into employment, but had disappointed: That, on hearing the prosecution was commenced against him, he applied to this person for counsel, who advised him to keep out of the way, for a few days:

56. DS, The Library, Lehigh University, Bethlehem, Pennsylvania; copy, Hamilton Papers, Library of Congress; copy, The Sol Feinstone Collection, Library of the American Philosophical Society, Philadelphia.

That a merchant came to him, and offered, as a volunteer, to be his bail, who, he suspects, had been instigated by this person, and after being decoyed to the place, the merchant wished to carry him, he refused being his bail, unless he would deposit a sum of money to some considerable amount, which he could not do, and was, in consequence, committed to prison: As well as we remember, he gave, as a reason why he could not communicate to us, what he knew of the facts alluded to, that he was apprehensive, it might prevent his discharge, but that he would certainly communicate the whole to us, at ten this morning; at which time, we were informed, he had absconded, or concealed himself.

Signed by James Monroe and Abraham Venable.

No. III. (a)[57]

Philadelphia, 13*th December,* 1792.

Being desirous, on account of their equivocal complection, to examine into the suggestions which had been made us respecting the motive for the confinement and proposed enlargement of James Reynolds, from the jail of this city, and inclined to suspect, for the same reason, that, unless it were immediately done, the opportunity would be lost, as we were taught to suspect he would leave the place, immediately after his discharge, we called at his house last night for that purpose; we found Mrs. Reynolds alone. It was with difficulty, we obtained from her, any information on the subject, but at length she communicated to us the following particulars:

That since Col. Hamilton was secretary of the treasury, and at his request, she had burned a considerable number of letters from him to her husband, and in the absence of the latter, touching business between them, to prevent their being made public; she also mentioned, that Mr. Clingman had several anonymous notes addressed to her husband, which, she believed, were from Mr. Hamilton (which we have) with an endorsement "from secretary Hamilton,

57. DS, Lloyd W. Smith Collection, Morristown National Historical Park, Morristown, New Jersey; copy, Hamilton Papers, Library of Congress; copy, The Sol Feinstone Collection, Library of the American Philosophical Society, Philadelphia.

Esq." in Mr. Reynolds's hand writing: That Mr. Hamilton offered her his assistance to go to her friends, which he advised: That he also advised that her husband should leave the parts, not to be seen here again, and in which case, he would give something clever. That she was satisfied, this wish for his departure did not proceed from friendship to him, but upon account of his threat, that he could tell something, that would make some of the heads of departments tremble. That Mr. Wadsworth had been active in her behalf, first at her request; [58] but, in her opinion, with the knowledge and communication of Mr. Hamilton, whose friend he professed to be; that he had been at her house yesterday and mentioned to her, that two gentlemen of Congress had been at the jail to confer with her husband; enquired if she knew what they went for; observed, he knew, Mr. Hamilton had enemies, who would try to prove some speculations on him, but, when enquired into, he would be found immaculate: to which, she replied, she rather doubted it. We saw in her possession two notes; one in the name of Alexander Hamilton, of the sixth of December,[59] and the other signed "S.W." [60] purporting to have been written yesterday, both expressing a desire to relieve her.

She denied any recent communication with Mr. Hamilton, or that she had received any money from him lately.

Signed by James Monroe and F. A. Muhlenberg.

No. IV. (a)[61]

Philadelphia, 13th December, 1792.

Jacob Clingman has been engaged in some negociations with Mr. Reynolds, the person, who has lately been discharged from a prosecution instituted against him, by the comptroller of the treasury: That his acquaintance commenced in September, 1791: That a mu-

58. See H to Wadsworth, July 28, 1797; Wadsworth to H, August 2, 1797.
59. Note not found.
60. This is presumably a typographical error. "S.W." should read "J.W." to indicate Jeremiah Wadsworth.
61. DS, The Library, Lehigh University, Bethlehem, Pennsylvania; copy, Hamilton Papers, Library of Congress; copy, The Sol Feinstone Collection, Library of the American Philosophical Society, Philadelphia.

tual confidence and intimacy existed between them; That in January or February last, he saw Col. Hamilton, at the house of Reynolds; immediately on his going into the house Col. Hamilton left it: That in a few days after, he (Clingman) was at Mr. Reynold's house, with Mrs. Reynolds, her husband being then out, some person knocked at the door; he arose and opened it, and saw that it was Col. Hamilton: Mrs. Reynolds went to the door; he delivered a paper to her, and said, he was ordered to give Mr. Reynolds that: He asked Mrs. Reynolds, who could order the secretary of the treasury of the United States to give that; she replied, that she supposed, he did not want to be known: This happened in the night. He asked her how long Mr. Reynolds had been acquainted with Col. Hamilton; she replied, some months; That Col. Hamilton had assisted her husband; that some few days before that time, he had received upwards of eleven hundred dollars of Col. Hamilton. Some time after this, Clingman was at the house of Reynolds, and saw Col. Hamilton come in; he retired and left him there. A little after Duer's failure,[62] Reynolds told Clingman in confidence, that if Duer had held up three days longer, he should have made fifteen hundred pounds, by the assistance of Col. Hamilton: that Col. Hamilton had informed him that he was connected with Duer. Mr. Reynolds also said, that Col. Hamilton had made thirty thousand dollars by speculation; that Col. Hamilton had supplied him with money to speculate. That, about June last, Reynolds told Clingman, that he had applied to Col. Hamilton, for money to subscribe to the turnpike road at Lancaster, and had received a note from him, in these words, "It is utterly out of my power, I assure you upon my honor, to comply with your request. Your note is returned." Which original note, accompanying this, has been in Clingman's possession ever since. Mr. Reynolds has once or twice mentioned to Clingman, that he had it in his power to hang Col. Hamilton; that if he wanted money, he was obliged to let him have it: That he (Clingman) has occasionally lent money to Reynolds, who always told him, that he could always get it from Col. Hamilton, to repay it. That on one occasion Clingman lent him two hundred dollars, that Reynolds promised to pay him thro' the means of Col. Hamilton, that he went with him, saw him go into Col. Hamilton's; that after he came out, he paid him one hundred

62. Duer's financial collapse occurred in March, 1792.

dollars, which, he said, was part of the sum he had got; and paid the balance in a few days; the latter sum paid, was said to have been received from Col. Hamilton, after his return from Jersey, having made a visit to the manufacturing society there.[63] After a warrant was issued against Reynolds, upon a late prosecution, which was instituted against him, Clingman seeing Reynolds, asked him, why he did not apply to his friend Col. Hamilton, he said, he would go immediately, and went accordingly; he said afterwards, that Col. Hamilton advised him to keep out of the way, a few days, and the matter would be settled. That after this time, Henry Seckel [64] went to Reynolds, and offered to be his bail, if he would go with him to Mr. Baker's [65] office, where he had left the officer, who had the warrant in writing; that he prevailed on Reynolds to go with him; that after Reynolds was taken into custody, Seckel refused to become his bail, unless he would deposit, in his possession, property to the value of four hundred pounds; upon which, Reynolds wrote to Col. Hamilton, and Mr. Seckel carried the note; after two or three times going, he saw Col. Hamilton; Col. Hamilton said, he knew Reynolds and his father; that his father was a good whig in the late war; that was all he could say: That it was not in his power to assist him; in consequence of which, Seckel refused to be his bail, and Reynolds was imprisoned. Mr. Reynolds also applied to a Mr. Francis,[66] who is one of the clerks in the treasury department: he said, he could not do any thing, without the consent of Mr. Hamilton; that he would apply to him. He applied to Mr. Hamilton; who told him, that it would not be prudent; if he did, he must leave the department.

After Reynolds was confined, Clingman asked Mrs. Reynolds, why she did not apply to Col. Hamilton, to dismiss him, as the money was ready to be refunded, that had been received; she replied, that she had applied to him, and he had sent her to Mr. Wolcott, but directed her, not to let Mr. Wolcott know, that he had sent her

63. H attended meetings of the directors of the Society for Establishing Useful Manufactures on May 16, 17, 18 and July 4, 5, 6, 7, 1792 ("Minutes of the S.U.M.," 35–55).
64. See Seckel's deposition, which is document No. XXIII in the appendix to this pamphlet.
65. Hilary Baker, a Philadelphia alderman in 1792, was mayor of Philadelphia in 1797.
66. Andrew G. Fraunces.

there; notwithstanding this injunction, she did let Mr. Wolcott know, by whom she had been sent; who appeared to be surprized at the information, but said, he would do what he could for her, and would consult Col. Hamilton on the occasion. Col. Hamilton advised her to get some person of respectability to intercede for her husband, and mentioned Mr. Muhlenberg.

Reynolds continued to be kept in custody, for some time; during which time, Clingman had conversation with Mr. Wolcott, who said, if he would give up a list of claims which he had, he should be released: After this, Mrs. Reynolds informed Clingman, that Col. Hamilton had told her, that Clingman should write a letter to Mr. Wolcott, and a duplicate of the same to himself, promising to give up the list, and refund the money, which had been obtained on a certificate, which had been said to have been improperly obtained.

Clingman asked Mrs. Reynolds, for the letters, that her husband had received from Col. Hamilton, from time to time, as he might probably use them to obtain her husband's liberty; she replied, that Col. Hamilton had requested her to burn all the letters, that were in his hand writing, or that had his name to them; which she had done; he pressed her to examine again, as she might not have destroyed the whole, and they would be useful; She examined and found   [67] notes, which are herewith submitted, and which, she said, were notes from Col. Hamilton.

Mrs. Reynolds told Clingman, that having heard, that her husband's father was, in the late war, a commissary under the direction of Col. Wadsworth, waited on him, to get him to intercede for her husband's discharge; [68] he told her, he would give her his assistance, and said, now you have made me your friend, you must apply to no person else. That on Sunday evening Clingman went to the house of Reynolds, and found Col. Wadsworth there: he was introduced to Col. Wadsworth by Mrs. Reynolds: Col. Wadsworth told him, he had seen Mr. Wolcott; that Mr. Wolcott would do any thing for him (Clingman) and Reynold's family, that he could; that he had called on Col. Hamilton but had not seen him; that he might tell Mr. Muhlenburg, that a friend of his (Clingman's) had told him, that Col. Wadsworth was a countryman and schoolmate of Mr. Inger-

67. Space left blank in document.
68. See Wadsworth to H, August 2, 1797.

soll,[69] and that Col. Wadsworth was also intimate with the governor,[70] and that the governor would do almost any thing to oblige him; that his name must not be mentioned to Mr. Muhlenburg, as telling him this; but that if Mr. Muhlenburg could be brought to speak to him first, on the subject, he would then do any thing in his power for them; and told him not to speak to him, if he should meet him in the street, and said, if his name was mentioned, that he would do nothing: That on Wednesday, Clingman saw Col. Wadsworth at Reynold's house; he did not find her at home, but left a note; but on going out, he met her, and said he had seen every body, and done every thing,

Mrs. Reynolds told Clingman, that she had received money of Col. Hamilton, since her husband's confinement, enclosed in a note, which note she had burned,

After Reynolds was discharged, which was eight or nine o'clock on Wednesday evening: [71] about twelve o'clock at night, Mr Reynolds sent a letter to Col. Hamilton by a girl; [72] which letter Clingman saw delivered to the girl; Reynolds followed the girl, and Clingman followed him; he saw the girl go into Col. Hamilton's house: Clingman then joined Reynolds, and they walked back and forward in the street, until the girl returned, and informed Reynolds, that he need not go out of town that night, but call on him, early in the morning. In the morning, between seven and eight o'clock, he saw Reynolds go to Col. Hamilton's house and go in: he has not seen him since, and supposes he has gone out of the state.

Mr. Clingman further adds, that some time ago, he was informed by Mr. and Mrs. Reynolds, that he had books containing the amount of the cash due to the Virginia line, at his own house at New-York, with liberty to copy, and was obtained thro' Mr. Duer.

The above contains the truth to the best of my knowledge and recollection, and to which I am ready to make oath.

> Given under my hand, this 13th
> of December, 1792.
> Signed by Jacob Clingman.

---

69. Jared Ingersoll, attorney general of Pennsylvania.
70. Thomas Mifflin.
71. December 12, 1792.
72. Letter not found.

Nos. I–XXII [73]

I	From Maria Reynolds	December 15, 1791
II	From James Reynolds	December 15, 1791
III	From James Reynolds	December 17, 1791
IV	From James Reynolds	December 19, 1791
V	From James Reynolds	December 22, 1791
VI	From James Reynolds	January 3, 1792
VII	From James Reynolds	January 17, 1792
VIII	From Maria Reynolds	January 23–March 18, 1792
IX	From Maria Reynolds	January 23–March 18, 1792
X	From Maria Reynolds	January 23–March 18, 1792
XI	From James Reynolds	March 24, 1792
XII	From Maria Reynolds	March 24, 1792
XIII	From James Reynolds	April 3, 1792
XIV	From James Reynolds	April 7, 1792
XV	From James Reynolds	April 17, 1792
XVI	From James Reynolds	April 23, 1792
XVII	From James Reynolds	May 2, 1792
XVIII	From Maria Reynolds	June 2, 1792
XIX	From James Reynolds	June 3–22, 1792
XX	From James Reynolds	June 23, 1792
	From James Reynolds	June 24, 1792
XXI	From James Reynolds	August 24, 1792
XXII	From James Reynolds	August 30, 1792

No. XXIII.

City of Philadelphia, ss.

Henry Seckel of the City aforesaid Merchant maketh oath that on or about the thirteenth day of November in the year one thousand seven hundred and ninety two Jacob Clingman sent for this Deponent to the house of Hilary Baker, Esquire then Alderman, that this Deponent went accordingly to the house of the said Alderman and was there requested by the said Jacob Clingman to become his bail which he did upon the promise of the said Clingman to deposit

73. Any letters to or from H which appear in the appendix to the "Reynolds Pamphlet" are printed in *The Papers of Alexander Hamilton* under the date on which they were written and therefore are not reprinted above.

with him a sum in certificates sufficient to cover and secure him for so becoming bail. That the said Clingman having failed to make the said deposit according to his promise this Deponent applied to the said Hilary Baker and obtained from him a warrant upon which the said Clingman was arrested and carried again to the said Hilary Baker. That the said Clingman again urged this Deponent to become his bail but he declining said Clingman requested this Deponent to go and bring to him one James Reynolds from whom as this Deponent understood the said Clingman expected to obtain assistance towards his release from Custody. That this Deponent went accordingly to the said James Reynolds and in the name of Clingman engaged him to accompany the Depondent to the House of the said Alderman where the said James Reynolds was also apprehended and detained That thereupon the said James Reynolds requested this Deponent to carry a letter for him to Alexander Hamilton then Secretary of the Treasury—that this Deponent carried the said letter as requested and after two or three calls found the said Alexander Hamilton and delivered the letter to him—that the said Hamilton after reading it mentioned to this Deponent that he had known the father of the said Reynolds during the war with Great-Britain, and would be willing to serve the said James, if he could with propriety, but that it was not consistent with the duty of his office to do what Reynolds now requested; and also mentioned to this Deponent that Reynolds and Clingman had been doing something very bad and advised this Deponent to have nothing to do with them lest he might bring himself into trouble. And this Deponent further saith that he never had any conversation or communication whatever with the said Alexander Hamilton respecting the said Reynolds or Clingman till the time of carrying the said letter. And this Deponent further saith that the said Clingman formerly lived with this Deponent and kept his books which as he supposes was the reason of his sending for this Deponent to become his bail thinking that this Deponent might be willing to befriend him.   HENRY SECKEL.

Sworn this 19th day of July
MDCCXCVII before me
HILARY BAKER, Mayor.

———————————

No. XXIV.

Having perused the fifth and sixth numbers of a late publication in this City entitled "The History of the United States for the year 1796" and having reviewed certain letters and documents which have remained in my possession since the year 1792, I do hereby at the request of Alexander Hamilton Esquire of New York Certify and declare,

That in the Month of December 1792, I was desired by Mr. Hamilton to be present at his house as the witness of an interview which had been agreed upon between himself and James Monroe, Frederick Augustus Muhlenberg and Abraham Venable, Esquires, with which I accordingly complied.

The object of the interview was to remove from the minds of those Gentlemen, certain suspicions which had been excited by suggestions of James Reynolds then in Prison and Jacob Clingman a Clerk to Mr. Muhlenberg, (against both of whom prosecutions had been instituted for frauds against the United States,) that Mr. Hamilton had been concerned in promoting or assisting speculations in the public funds, contrary to Law and his duty as Secretary of the Treasury.

The conference was commenced on the part of Mr. Monroe by reading certain Notes from Mr. Hamilton and a Narrative of conversations which had been held with the said Reynolds and Clingman. After the grounds upon which the suspicions rested, had been fully stated, Mr. Hamilton entered into an explanation and by a variety of written documents, which were read fully evinced, that there was nothing in the transactions to which Reynolds and Clingman had referred, which had any connection with, or relation to speculations in the Funds, claims upon the United States, or any public or Official transactions or duties whatever. This was rendered so completely evident, that Mr. Venable requested Mr. Hamilton to desist from exhibiting further proofs. As however an explanation had been desired by the Gentlemen before named, Mr. Hamilton insisted upon being allowed to read such documents as he possessed, for the purpose of obviating every shadow of doubt respecting the propriety of his Official conduct.

After Mr. Hamilton's explanation terminated Messrs. Monroe, Muhlenberg and Venable, severally acknowledged their entire satisfaction, that the affair had no relation to Official duties, and that it ought not to affect or impair the public confidence in Mr. Hamilton's character; at the same time, they expressed their regrets at the trouble which the explanation had occasioned. During a conversation in the streets of Philadelphia immediately after retiring from Mr. Hamilton's house, Mr. Venable repeated to me, that the explanation was entirely satisfactory, and expressed his concern, that he had been a party to whom it had been made. Though in the course of the conversation Mr. Venable expressed his discontent with public measures which had been recommended by Mr. Hamilton, yet he manifested a high respect for his Talents, and confidence in the integrity of his character.

When Mr. Reynolds was in Prison, it was reported to me, that he had threatened to make disclosures injurious to the character of some head of a Department. This report I communicated to Mr. Hamilton, who advised me to take no step towards a liberation of Reynolds, while such a report existed and remained unexplained. This was antecedent to the interview between Mr. Hamilton and Messrs. Monroe, Muhlenberg and Venable, or to any knowledge on my part of the circumstances by which it was occasioned.

The Offence for which Reynolds and Clingman were prosecuted by my direction, was for suborning a person to commit perjury for the purpose of obtaining Letters of Administration on the estate of a person who was living. After the prosecution was commenced, Clingman confessed to me, that he and Reynolds were possessed of lists of names and sums due to certain Creditors of the United States, which lists had been obtained from the Treasury. Both Clingman and Reynolds obstinately refused for some time to deliver up the lists or to disclose the name of the person, through whose infidelity they had been obtained. At length on receiving a promise from me, that I would endeavour to effect their liberation from the consequences of the prosecution, they consented to surrender the lists, to restore the balance which had been fraudulently obtained, and to reveal the name of the person, by whom the lists had been furnished.

This was done conformably to the proposition contained in a letter from Clingman dated December 4, 1792, of which a copy is hereunto annexed. The original letter and the lists which were surrendered now remain in my possession. Agreeably to my engagement I informed Jared Ingersol Esqr. Attorney General of Pennsylvania, that an important discovery had been made, and the condition by which it could be rendered useful to the public in preventing future frauds; in consequence of which, the prosecutions against Clingman and Reynolds were dismissed.

In the publication referred to, it is suggested that the lists were furnished by Mr. Duer; this is an injurious mistake—nothing occurred at any time to my knowledge, which could give colour to a suspicion, that Mr. Duer, was in any manner directly or indirectly concerned with or privy to the transaction. The infidelity was committed by a clerk in the office of the Register. Mr. Duer resigned his office in March, 1790, while the Treasury was at New-York—the Clerk who furnished the lists was first employed in Philadelphia in January 1791. The Accounts from which the lists were taken, were all settled at the Treasury subsequent to the time last mentioned; on the discovery above stated the Clerk was dismissed, and has not since been employed in the public offices.

The name of the Clerk who was dismissed has not been publicly mentioned, for a reason which appears in Clingman's letter; but if the disclosure is found necessary to the vindication of an innocent character, it shall be made.

Certified in Philadelphia, this twelfth day of July, 1797.

OLIV. WOLCOTT.

Copy of a letter from Jacob Clingman, to the Comptroller of the Treasury.

Phila. 4 December, 1792.

Sir,

Having unfortunately for myself, been brought into a very disagreeable situation, on account of Letters of Administration taken out by a certain John Delabar on the effects of a certain Ephraim Goodanough, who, it since appears, is still living. I beg leave to mention that I am ready to refund the money to the Treasury or to the proper owner or his order, and if it can be of any service to the Treasury Department or to the United States, in giving up the lists of the names of the persons to whom pay is due, and to disclose the name of the persons to whom pay is due, and to disclose the name of the person in the utmost confidence from whom the list was obtained, earnestly hoping that may be some inducement to withdraw the action against me, which if prosecuted can only end in injuring my character without any further advantage to the United States.

I have the honour to be   your most humble Servant

Signed Jacob Clingman.

Hon. Oliver Wolcott, Esq.

Nos. XXV–XL [74]

XXV	To James Monroe	July 5, 1797
XXVI	To Frederick A. C. Muhlenberg, James Monroe, and Abraham Venable	December 17, 1792
XXVII	From Frederick A. C. Muhlenberg	December 18, 1792
XXVIII	From James Monroe	December 20, 1792
XXIX	From Frederick A. C. Muhlenberg	July 10, 1797
XXX	From Abraham Venable	July 9, 1797
XXXII	From James Monroe	July 16, 1797
XXXIII	From James Monroe and Frederick A. C. Muhlenberg	July 17, 1797
XXXIV	To James Monroe and Frederick A. C. Muhlenberg	July 17, 1797
XXXV	To James Monroe	July 17, 1797
XXXVI	From James Monroe	July 17, 1797
XXXVII	To James Monroe	July 18, 1797
XXXVIII	From James Monroe	July 18, 1797
XXXIX	To James Monroe	July 20, 1797
XL	From James Monroe	July 21, 1797

---

74. See note 73.

No. XLI.

City of Philadelphia, ss.

Mary Williams of the City aforesaid Boarding House Keeper maketh Oath that She is acquainted with Mrs. M. Reynolds formerly reputed to be the Wife of Mr. James Reynolds that her acquaintance commenced by the said Mrs. Reynolds calling upon her to obtain admission as a lodger which the Deponent declined that afterwards the Deponent frequently saw the said Mrs. Reynolds and also frequently saw her write that from this she the Deponent conceives herself to be well acquainted with the hand writing of the said Mrs. Reynolds and is well satisfied that the hand writing of the letters hereunto annexed numbered I—VIII—IX—X—XII—XIII is of the proper hand writing of the said Mrs. Reynolds to identify which letters the more particularly this Deponent hath upon each of them endorsed her name.

Sworn this XXIst day of
July MDCCXCVII. be-   Mary Williams
fore me
   Robert Wharton
     One of the Aldermen of the
     City of Philadelphia.

No. XLII.

Wednesday 5th, December, 1792.

Honnoured Sir,

too well you are acquainted with my unfortenate setuvation, to give you an explanation thereof, I am informed by a Note from Mrs. Reynolds this Evening, wherein She informed Me that you have bin informed that I Should have Said, if I were not discharged in two days. that I would make Some of the heads of the Departments tremble. now Sir I declare to god, that I never have said any Such thing. nor never have I said any thing, against any Head of a departmet whatever. all I have Said, Sir. is that I am under the Necessaty of letting you Know. which of the Clarks in the publick Office has givein out the List, of the ballance due. from the United States. to the individual States. and when it Comes to your knowledge, that the would tremble, Now Can I have an Enemy So base as to lodge such False alligations to my Charge, which is tottely Groundless. and without the least foundation Immaginable. now Sir, if you will give me the pleashure of waiting uppon your honnor tomorrow I will give you every information that lies in my power Respecting the Matter. which I hope it will give you final Satisfaction. what I have done never Was with a wish to Rong the United States or any Other person whatever, the person that Administer On this mans pay. which he Received from the United States. had my monies in his hands and would not transfer the Certificate to Mrs. Clingman and myself untill wee signed the bond of indamnification. to him now dear Sir. that was our Situvation. to Secure our own Intrest. wee executed the Bond, which was an Oversight of ours. now Sir Can you Suppose In my present Setuvation, that I would say any thing against you Sir or any Other head of department whatever, where it even was in my power which was not. Espicially where all my hopes and Dependance where. now dear Sir think of my poor innocent family. not of me, for them I Onely wish to live.

I am, honnored Sir   Your most Obedient and Humble Servt.

James W, Reynolds

Oliver Woolcot Esqr.

No. XLIII.

Having seen in a pamphlet published in Philadelphia entitled "The History of the United States No. 5." a paragraph to the following Effect:

"During the late Canvass for the Election of a President, Webster in his Minerva, gave a Hint that Mr. Hamilton would be an adviseable Candidate. A person in this City who chanced to see this News-Paper, wrote immediately to a Correspondent in New-York. The letter desired him to put himself in the way of Mr. Hamilton and inform him that, if Webster should in future print a single paragraph on the Head, the papers referred to were instantly to be laid before the World. The Message was delivered to Mr. Hamilton and the Minerva became silent."

I declare that the Contents of the foregoing paragraph, as far as they relate to myself, are totally *false*. I never entertained an idea that Mr. Hamilton was a Candidate for the Presidency or Vice-Presidency at the late Election. I never uttered, wrote or published a Hint or Suggestion of the kind; nor did I ever receive from Mr. Hamilton or any other person either directly or indirectly, any Hint or Communication to discontinue any notice or Suggestions on that subject. I have examined the Minerva for several Months previous to the late Election, and I cannot find a Suggestion published in that paper, of Mr. Hamilton's being a Candidate as aforesaid, either from any Correspondent or republished from any other paper; nor have I the least knowledge what the suggestions in the foregoing paragraph allude to.

My own idea uniformly was, that Mr. Adams and Mr. Pinckney were the only Candidates supported by Mr. Hamilton and the friends of our Government in general.

Sworn the 13th, July 1797.

before me Abm. Skinner N. P. }   Noah Webster Jun.

No. XLIV.

Philadelphia, June 27, 1797.

Sir,

It would have highly gratified me had it been in my power to furnish the relief you ask: but I am preparing for my departure and find, on winding up my affairs, that I shall not have one dollar to spare. It is therefore with sincere regret I have nothing better to tender than the sentiments of good will of

Sir,   Your most obedient servant,   Th. Jefferson.

No. XLV.

Philadelphia, June 28, 1797.

Sir,

I know well that you were a clerk in the Treasury Department while I was in the office of Secretary of State; but as I had no relation with the interior affairs of that office, I had no opportunity of being acquainted with you personally, except the single occasion on which you called me. The length of time you were in the office affords the best presumption in your favour, and the particular misunderstanding which happened to you with your principals may account for your not having obtained from them those certificates of character which I am not able to supply. I doubt not however that a knowledge of your conduct wherever you establish yourself will soon render all certificates unnecessary, and I sincerely wish you may obtain employment which may evince and reward good conduct.

I am, Sir,   Your very humble servant,   Th. Jefferson.

Nos. XLVI–LII [75]

XLVI	To James Monroe	July 22, 1797
XLVII	From James Monroe	July 25, 1797
XLVIII	To James Monroe	July 28, 1797
XLIX	From James Monroe	July 31, 1797
L	To James Monroe	August 4, 1797
LI	From James Monroe	August 6, 1797
LII	To James Monroe	August 9, 1797

N. B. It may be proper to observe that in addition to the original letters from Mrs. Reynolds, there are in the hands of the gentleman with whom the papers are deposited, two original letters from her, one addressed to Mr. R. Folwell—the other to a Mrs. Miller, and both of them signed MARIA CLINGMAN, in the former of which she mentions the circumstance of her being married to Clingman.

75. See note 73.

To Timothy Pickering [1]

[New York, August 27, 1797]

Dr Sir

Sometime since I received the inclosed being directions concerning measures requisite to be pursued to obtain indemnification in cases of Captures by British Cruisers. I laid it by in haste & have since overlooked it. I do not recollect to have seen it in the news papers & yet it appeared to me necessary that it should be so. As it came to me from some one of our public characters in London, I presume you must have received the Equivalent. I am curious to know if this has been the case & if any thing has been done upon it. After perusal & making such use as you may think proper you will oblige me by returning it.[2]

Yrs. truly   A H

Aug 27. 1797

Col Pickering

ALS, Massachusetts Historical Society, Boston.
1. For an explanation of the contents of this letter, see Rufus King to H, April 29, 1797.
2. Pickering endorsed this letter: "returned the papers inclosed Oct. 21. 1797. being rules in prosecuting appeals from the British Vice-Admiralty courts." Pickering's letter of October 21, 1797, has not been found.

To George Washington

New York Aug 28. 1797

My Dear Sir

The receipt two days since of your letter of the 21 instant gave me sincere pleasure. The token of your regard, which it announces, is very precious to me, and will always be rememberd as it ought to be.

Mrs. Hamilton has lately added another boy to our Stock.[1] She and the Child are both well. She desires to be affectionately remembered to Mrs. Washington & yourself.

We have nothing new here more than our papers contain; but are anxiously looking forward to a further developement of the negotiations in Europe with an ardent desire for general accommodation. It is at the same time agreeable to observe that the public mind is adopting more and more sentiments truly American and free from foreign tincture.

I beg my best respects to Mrs. Washington, and that you will always be assured of the most respectful & affectionate attachment of Dr. Sir

Yr obliged & very Obed serv   A Hamilton

                                               Aug 28. 1797

George Washington Esq

ALS, William Cabel Rives Papers, Library of Congress; copy, Hamilton Papers, Library of Congress.
   1. William Stephen Hamilton was born on August 4, 1797.

To Robert Morris

[*New York, August 29, 1797.* On September 9, 1797, Morris wrote to Hamilton: "I have received your favour of the 29th." *Letter not found.*]

From Thomas Spencer [1]

Albany, August 30, 1797. Asks Hamilton to examine the validity of the title to various tracts of land owned by Spencer lying between Lake Superior and Lake Huron.[2]

ALS, Hamilton Papers, Library of Congress.
   1. Spencer was an Albany merchant.
   2. The following receipt, written by H and signed by Spencer, appears at the bottom of this letter: "Received of Alexander Hamilton the papers above-mentione[d]
NYork Jany 1 1799   Thos Spencer."

From Isaac Parker [1]

[Castine, District of Maine, August 31, 1797]

Honble Alexander Hamilton Esqr.

Please to deliver Doctor Oliver Mann or his order two notes of Hand lodged with you by John Lowell Jr. Esq for collection, signed by Edward & Elias Parker for $750 each—in which notes my name is mentioned.[2]   Isaac Parker

Castine 31. August 1797.

ALS, Hamilton Papers, Library of Congress.
   1. For background to this letter, see John Lowell, Jr., to H, December 19, 1795; Oliver Mann and Parker to H, June 28, 1797.
   2. The following receipt in Mann's handwriting is at the bottom of this letter: "Recd the abovementioned notes of Col Hamilton.
September 27th 1797   Oliver Mann."

["Reynolds Pamphlet"] [1]

[Philadelphia, August 31, 1797] [2]

   1. Observations on Certain Documents Contained in No. V & VI of "The History of the United States for the Year 1796," In Which the Charge of Speculation against Alexander Hamilton, Late Secretary of the Treasury, is Fully Refuted. Written by Himself (Philadelphia: Printed for John Fenno, by John Bioren, 1797).
   2. In Volumes X–XIV of The Papers of Alexander Hamilton the "Reynolds Pamphlet" is incorrectly dated August 31, 1797. See the "Reynolds Pamphlet," August 25, 1797.

From David Meade Randolph [1]

Newport [Virginia] September 3, 1797. "I have witnessed the decease of Majr. Lindsay,[2] the collector of Norfolk in Virginia; and feel myself greatly interested in the appointment of his successor. Mr. Francis S. Taylor, the bearer, I have had a personal acquaintance with several years, and in addition to the high character whh. I know him to support, he has acted as deputy in the office for some time—until his qualifications for other business, and the small pittance afforded him in *that office*, induced him to resign—since which period, possessing the confidence of the Collector, and understanding the business better, he has had the superintendance of the same—and that too from no other consideration, than friendship for the deceased. . . . This application to you for an exertion of your influence, I hope will be pardoned. . . ." [3]

ALS, RG 59, General Records of the State Department, Applications and Recommendations, 1792–1801, National Archives.
   1. Randolph was appointed marshal of the Virginia District on November 3, 1791, and was reappointed to that position in 1795 and 1799 (*Executive Journal,* I, 88, 194, 326).
   2. William Lindsay.
   3. Taylor did not receive the appointment. On November 24, 1797, President John Adams nominated Otway Bird, and the Senate approved the appointment the following day (*Executive Journal,* I, 251).

From Jonathan Williams [1]

Mount Pleasant [2] *[near Philadelphia] September 3, 1797.* "I took the Liberty when I saw you last in New York to intimate a wish to be employed in the treasury department, and you were so kind as to offer your aid in this respect whenever a specific object should be pointed out. The Death of D Way [3] having left a vacancy in the mint, I have been induced to make application to be appointed Treasurer in that Department. I hope I do not presume too far on your friendship to flatter myself that you will take occasion to serve me in such way as to you may seem best. . . ." [4]

ALS, Hamilton Papers, Library of Congress.
   1. Williams, a native of Boston and a great-nephew of Benjamin Franklin, served as prize and commercial agent at Nantes during the American Revolution. After the Revolution, he settled in Philadelphia and invested in stock and land speculations. In 1796 he became associate judge of the Court of Common Pleas.
   2. This was the name of Williams's estate, which was located on the east bank of the Schuylkill River and had formerly belonged to Benedict Arnold.
   3. Dr. Nicholas Way, a physician in Philadelphia, had been appointed Treasurer of the Mint in 1794. On September 4, 1797, Elias Boudinot, Director of the Mint, wrote to Timothy Pickering: "It is with inexpressible Grief, that I

announce to you the unexpected Death of our excellent friend Dr. Nicholas
Way, Treasurer of the Mint—He dyed last Saturday Evening of a most malignant fever—He was ill but seven days." On September 15, 1797, Boudinot wrote
to Pickering that Williams had applied for the position of Treasurer of the
Mint (Jane J. Boudinot, ed., *The Life, Public Services, Addresses and Letters
of Elias Boudinot, LL.D* [Boston and New York, 1896], II, 129, 131).

4. Williams did not receive the appointment. On November 24, 1797, John
Adams nominated Benjamin Rush, and the Senate agreed to this appointment
on November 27 (*Executive Journal*, I, 251). For a discussion of Rush's appointment as Treasurer of the Mint, including relevant letters, see L. H. Butter-
field, ed., *Letters of Benjamin Rush* (Princeton, 1951), II, 1209–12.

To Oliver Wolcott, Junior

[New York, September 8, 1797]

My Dr. Sir

I have received the inclosed letter [1] which I send to you with only
this remark that I have a good opinion of the *writer*. I know that
the pretensions of the person recommended will be weighed in an
equal scale & will have all the attention to which they are intitled.

Yrs. truly   AH

Sep. 8. 1797

O Wolcott Jun Esq

ALS, RG 59, General Records of the State Department, Applications and Recommendations, 1792–1801, National Archives.
1. David Meade Randolph to H, September 3, 1797.

From Rufus King [1]

London. Sat. Sep. 9. 1797

Dear Sir

We have this day accounts from Paris, which tho~ very important and interesting, are not unexpected. The Breach between
the Councils and the directory has for some time destroyed all
Prospect of a reconciliation between them; and either an organized

civil war, in consequence of the different sides adopted by the several armies, or a Measure like that which has happened, had become inevitable—the march of the unreducable divisions of the army into the interior, the removal of Generals in whom they did not confide, the various messages in the stile of manifestoes addressed to the councils, and the sending for General Jourdan, who commanded the army of the Rhine, to Paris, and putting his army in the interim of his absence under Hoche, are now explained.[2]

Augereau who had been called from Italy for the purpose, upon the alarm Cannon being fired on the morning of the 4th. instant, marched his Troops and surrounded without opposition the Place of sitting of the Council of 500; he then proceeded to arrest Pichegru, and a considerable number of the other most influential Members of that Council, on the charge of a royalist conspiracy; having for its object the Massacre of three of the Directory, to make way for successors who would place Louis XVIII on the Throne of France. Carnot say the same accts. has fled, and Barthelemy say others is also arrested.[3] I do not give you this account as authentic, tho I have little doubt that it is so, as far at least as it states an attack of the Directory upon the Council of 500. If the consequence of this proceeding was confined to France, it would be less the Subject of regret tho' all must deplore the sanguinary scenes so frequently there exhibited; but in reference to the pending Negotiations,[4] and the Return of Peace, this Transaction is very important. The two Councils who in this respect are supposed to have faithfully represented their Constituents desired Peace with sincerity: the Directory most certainly differed from them in their inclinations on this Subject—if the Directory overwhelm the Councils, the war must and will continue. But how will the armies, how will the nation conduct on this Occasion. I fear there is little consolation to the friends of humanity from ⟨the dou⟩bt wh. for a moment exists on these points. The nation are nothing—the Armies are most probably deceived—and the Directory will triumph.

   Adieu   yrs &c   R King

P. S. If I do not forget names a majority of the Comee. to whom Pastorets Speech on our affairs was referred, are among the members

now arrested.⁵ You will readily see how mischievous to us this success of the Directory may and probably will be.

ALS, Hamilton Papers, Library of Congress.
    1. This letter describes the *coup d'état* of 18 Fructidor an V (September 4,
1797).
    2. After the failure of his German campaign in the late summer of 1796 (see
King to H, November 30, 1796, note 1), General Jean Baptiste Jourdan resigned
from the command of the army of the Sambre and Meuse and was temporarily
replaced by Pierre de Riel, marquis de Beurnonville. In February, 1797, General
Louis Lazare Hoche took command of the army after returning from an
unsuccessful expedition to Ireland. In July, 1797, the Directors diverted Hoche
from his second Irish expedition and ordered him to prepare a force to march
on Paris. After returning with the greater part of his army to eastern France,
Hoche sent to Paris a detachment of troops under General Louis Chérin which
assisted in the *coup d'état* of September 4, 1797.
    3. Pierre François Charles Augereau, formerly a general in Napoleon's army
of Italy (see King to H, August 6–10, 1797, note 5), commanded the Paris mili-
tary division which effected the *coup d'état* of September 4, 1797. Entering the
Tuileries at dawn on September 4, Augereau's men arrested General Jean-
Charles Pichegru, president of the Council of Five Hundred and a monarchist,
General Jean-Pierre Ramel, commandant of the guard of the legislature, the
Director François Barthélemy, and a number of deputies. The Director Lazare
Nicolas Marguerite Carnot escaped from Paris on the night of September 3.
On September 4, 1797, Barthélemy, Pichegru, and Ramel, with sixty-two others,
were banished (Duvergier, *Lois*, X, 44). Pichegru was the only one of those
arrested who was actually guilty of treason, for, as general of the army of the
Rhine and Moselle, he had accepted money from both the English and their
ally, the Prince de Condé, who was at the head of a monarchist army which
fought to place Louis XVIII, the brother of Louis XVI, on the throne. The
full story of Pichegru's relations with England did not reach the Directory,
however, until several months after the *coup d'état*. Instead, on September 4,
the Directory published the proposals made by the Prince de Condé in June,
1795, that Pichegru should hand over the city of Huningue to the monarchists
and join his army with the army of the Prince de Condé to promote a monarchist rising in Alsace. Pichegru had agreed "in principle" with these proposals,
but he did not carry them out.
    4. See King to H, June 27, 1797, note 1; King to H, August 6–10, 1797, note
2.
    5. Claude-Emanuel-Joseph Pierre, marquis de Pastoret, a monarchist, was one
of the new members elected to the Council of Five Hundred in April, 1797. On
June 20, 1797, at a meeting of the Council, he spoke against the injustice of
French policy toward the United States and ordered the *arrêts* of the Directory
concerning the United States to be sent to a special commission appointed by
the legislature to examine the constitutionality of the Directory's actions (*Réimpression de L'Ancien Moniteur*, XXVIII, 731). Pastoret left Paris in time to
escape the effects of the *coup d'état*.

From Robert Morris [1]

Hills [2] near Philada. Septr. 9th. 1797

Dear Sir

I have received your favour of the 29th.[3] with the Papers enclosed therewith and should have acknowledged the receipt of them immediately but that I observed you had inserted a larger Sum as the bala. of my Note than I thought could be due thereon & lest you may not have kept a regular acct of the payments I have made on that account I wrote Mr Cottringer [4] to make an extract from My Books & you will find it herein. I wish I could remit you the balance, but that is not yet in my power, I hope it may [be] soon.

I was much disappointed at not seeing you when in Philada.[5] I went thither on purpose one Sunday Morning & sent my Son Charles to every place I could think of to bring you to dine with us, but he was unsuccessful and I regretted it much & more so afterwards when I found you had departed without giving me a call at this place.

I am most truly your obedt. Servant   Robt Morris

Colo. Hamilton

ALS, Hamilton Papers, Library of Congress; LC, Robert Morris Papers, Library of Congress.

1. This letter concerns Morris's efforts to pay the balance of a debt which he owed to H. For an account of this debt and Morris's efforts to pay it, see the introductory note to H to Morris, March 18, 1795. See also Morris to H, March 31, June 2, 23, 30, July 18, 20, 1795; July 17, 27–30, November 19, December 8, 1796; June 2, 10, 1797.

2. "The Hills" was the name of Morris's estate on the eastern bank of the Schuylkill River. It was about three miles from what was then Philadelphia.

3. Letter not found.

4. For Garrett Cottringer, Morris's bookkeeper, see H to Morris, March 18, 1795, note 17.

5. H had been in Philadelphia from July 19 to July 22–24, 1797, in connection with the "Reynolds Affair." See H to Elizabeth Hamilton, July 19, 1797; H to James Monroe, July 22, 1797.

To Elizabeth Hamilton

Rye 30 Miles from
New York
Tuesday Even [September 12, 1797]

I am arrived here [1] My Dear Eliza in good health but very anxious about my Dear Philip.[2] I pray heaven to restore him and in every event to support you. If his fever should appear likely to prove obstinate, urge the Physician to consider well the propriety of trying the cold bath—I expect it will, if it continues assume a nervous type and in this case I believe the cold bath will be the most efficacious remedy—but still do not attempt it without the approbation of the Physician. Also my Betsey how much do I regret to be separated from you at such a juncture. When will the time come that I shall be exempt from the necessity of leaving my dear family? God bless my beloved and all My Dear Children   AH

Mrs. Hamilton

ALS, Hamilton Papers, Library of Congress.
    1. H was on his way to Hartford, Connecticut, to represent New York in the Connecticut Gore controversy before the United States Circuit Court, District of Connecticut, at Hartford. For information on the Connecticut Gore controversy, and H's role in it, see Goebel, *Law Practice*, I, 657–84.
    On April 9, 1798, Samuel Jones, comptroller of New York State, signed a warrant for eight hundred dollars to be paid to H for his services in the Connecticut Gore controversy (DS, Onandaga Historical Association, Syracuse, New York). See also John Jay to Jones, March 31, 1798 (L[S], Onandaga Historical Association, Syracuse, New York); Josiah Ogden Hoffman, attorney general of New York, to Aaron Burr and Abraham Van Vechten, an Albany attorney, March 13, 1798 (D[S], Onandaga Historical Association, Syracuse, New York). On a separate sheet of paper in the Onandaga Historical Association is the following receipt: "Received Albany 14th April 1798 from Robert McClallen Treasurer of the State of New York Eight Hundred Dollars in full of the Within Warrant $800   to be transmitted to Colo Hamilton   Daniel Hale." Hale was an Albany merchant and politician.
    Under the date of January 4, 1797, H recorded in his Cash Book, 1795–1804: "Cash for this sum received of Atty General for State Adsm Connecticut Gore 250" (AD, Hamilton Papers, Library of Congress).
    H also attended the April, 1798, session of the United States Circuit Court, District of Connecticut, at New Haven. Three entries in H's Cash Book, 1795–1804, under the date of April 1, 1798, read:
"paid on journey to N: Haven 100
"Cash received State Ads Connecti 103

"State of New York second journey to N Haven 8 days at 50Ds ℞ Da 400" (AD, Hamilton Papers, Library of Congress).

For H's earlier involvement in the Connecticut Gore controversy, see H to Jeremiah Wadsworth, September 29, 1796.

2. Philip Hamilton, H's eldest son. Dr. David Hosack, whose recollections are not entirely accurate, described Philip's illness in a letter to John C. Hamilton on January 1, 1833: "I was first introduced into Your Father's family as a physician, during the dangerous illness of your oldest brother Philip. . . . He was attacked with a severe, bilious fever which soon assumed a typhus character, attendant with symptoms which gave great alarm to his family and anxiety to his physician the late Dr. [John] Charlton. . . . The son's complaints increasing in violence and danger, at the suggestion of Dr. Charlton and some of your family connexions I was called in consultation.

"Great distress then existing in your family added to the anxiety pervading their numerous friends, indeed I may say the community. I resolved at the request of Mrs. Hamilton and of Dr. Charlton, to remain with your brother while his situation continued thus perilous. His disease continuing to increase in violence, and scarcely a ray of hope remaining, your Father was sent for by an express, informing him that his son's recovery was entirely despaired of. In the meantime more malignant symptoms appeared attended with delirium, insensibility to external objects, loss of pulse, and general prostration, insomuch that his Mother, overwhelmed with distress, by my advice, was removed to another room that she might not witness the last struggles of her son.

"At this moment it occurred to me that a stimulant bath prepared with a strong decoction of *Peruvian bark* with the addition of some bottles of *rum*, and that made use of at a *high temperature*, might possibly prove beneficial at least in prolonging his existence. The bath was immediately prepared. He was carefully immersed in it, and occasionally it was rendered still more stimulant, by the frequent addition of small quantities of the *spirits of hartshorne*. After a few minutes he was aroused from his delirium, his senses for the time were restored, his pulse acquired strength, and he was enabled to swallow some draughts of strong wine whey, which I had directed to be prepared. After remaining in the bath about 15 minutes, he was removed to his bed, and covered with warm dry blankets. He immediately fell into a sleep by which he was sensibly improved, but in a few hours he relapsed into delirium, with a return of the former alarming symptoms. The warm bath was renewed and the same salutary effects were produced as before. The third application of the bath upon the recurrence of a similar train of symptoms in the course of the day, placed him in a relatively safe situation, from which he gradually acquired strength and ultimately recovered." (Typescript, furnished by Columbia University Libraries.) An entry in H's Cash Book, 1795–1804, under the date of September 8, 1797, reads: "paid Doct Charleton 60" (AD, Hamilton Papers, Library of Congress).

From Samuel Dexter

Charlestown, Massachusetts, September 16, 1797. "More than two Months ago I handed to a young gentleman in your Office (a student I presume) a letter directed to you [1] containing a lengthy detail of my concern in Onondago Land & requesting your opinion as soon as possible. I also enclosed fifty Dollars, not as a stimulus to your friendship, but to quiet my own feelings. Having heard nothing from you I have been apprehensive that the letter with its enclosures had been mislaid. . . . If you are eno' at leisure, will you now answer my former letter, & also acquaint me with . . . what my prospects are? It is a business that interests me as deeply as any concern meerly pecuniary can do."

ALS, Hamilton Papers, Library of Congress.
  1. Dexter to H, July 17, 1797.

To Elizabeth Hamilton

[Hartford, September 18–19, 1797] [1]

I have received only one letter from my beloved Eliza since I left the city. I am very anxious to hear further and especially to know that my beloved Philip [2] is recovered.

My health continues pretty good—but I am excessively engaged with our cause. I impatiently wish it at an end that I may return to the fond bosom of my Eliza.

If our Dear Angelica [3] is returned remember me affectionately to her.

Adieu my beloved and assure yourself always of my tenderest affection.

In great haste   **AH**
                                            Tuesday 18th Sepr.

ALS, MS Division, New York Public Library.
  1. There is some difficulty concerning the date of this letter, for H dated it "Tuesday 18th Sepr" and the envelope is postmarked "Hartford." In 1798, September 18 was a Tuesday. There is, however, no evidence that H was in Hartford in September, 1798. On the other hand, he was in Hartford in September, 1797. See H to Elizabeth Hamilton, September 12, 1797, note 1. On September 18, 1797, a Monday, H attended the United States Circuit Court, District of Connecticut, at Hartford. See Goebel, *Law Practice*, I, 673.
  2. For Philip Hamilton's illness, see H to Elizabeth Hamilton, September 12, 1797, note 2.
  3. Angelica Church was Elizabeth Hamilton's sister.

From Robert Morris [1]

Hills near Philada. Octr. 2d. 1797

Dear Sir

I cannot help feeling some chagrin when I find you constantly treating the debt I owe you as if you were in danger of loosing it, because I wish to stand higher in your confidence than it seems is the case. I have assured you that you should not loose and I am happy to see my way clear to effect the payment pretty soon, perhaps some influen⟨ce o⟩n your part over those who are to pay may ⟨b⟩e necessary, and as soon as I receive a Copy of the Treaty made with the Indians [2] I will write again and explain myself on this point in the mean while I am as ever   Dr Sir

Your Obedt hble servt.   Robt Morris

Alexr Hamilton Esqr
New York

ALS, Hamilton Papers, Library of Congress; LC, Robert Morris Papers, Library of Congress.

1. This letter concerns the balance of a debt which Morris owed to H. For an account of this debt and Morris's efforts to pay it, see the introductory note to H to Morris, March 18, 1795. See also Morris to H, March 31, June 2, 23, 30, July 18, 20, 1795; June 17, 27–30, November 19, December 8, 1796; June 2, 10, September 9, 1797.

2. See H to Herman LeRoy, William Bayard, and James McEvers, December 16, 1796; March 4–July 19, 1797.

From Ezekiel Gilbert [1]

Hudson [*New York*] *October 4, 1797.* "My friend Doctor Benton,[2] holds a Note for 5000 Dols. against Peirpoint Edwards [3] of New Haven—he desires me to enclose to you a copy of it, in order that you may, if any Occasion admits of his being found within the Jurisdiction of our Supreme Court, have him taken and prosecuted to recovery. Should you be disposed to accept this business, or to place it where it will receive due attention, so that Benton may secure & collect the payment, he will be happy to make a most generous reward. . . ."

ALS, Hamilton Papers, Library of Congress.
    1. Gilbert, a Hudson, New York, lawyer, was a member of the New York Assembly in 1789 and 1790 and a member of the House of Representatives from 1793 to 1797.
    2. Dr. Caleb Benton of Hillsdale, New York, engaged in land speculation. He was a member of the New York Assembly from 1796 to 1798.
    3. Pierpont Edwards, a New Haven lawyer, had been a member of the Connecticut legislature, the Continental Congress, and the Connecticut Ratifying Convention. He had been appointed United States attorney for the District of Connecticut in September, 1789.

To Robert Morris

[*New York, October 5, 1797.* On October 27, 1797, Morris wrote to Hamilton and referred to "your last letter dated the 5th inst." *Letter not found.*]

From George Washington

Mount Vernon 8th. Octr. 1797.

My dear Sir,
    The ardent desire which Mr. La Fayette [1] feels to embrace his Parents and Sisters in the first moment of their liberation,[2] induces him to set out for New York, or further Eastward, in search of a Passage to France.
    It was my opinion that he had better have awaited authentic accounts of this event; but his eagerness to see his friends—the fear of a Winter passage—and a conviction that he is under no predicament that would render his reception in France at all embarrassing to him, even if he should be disappointed in meeting his friends there, has prevailed.
    I am sure it is unnecessary that I should recommend him and Mr. Frestal to your civilities while they may be detained in New York; or to your aid in procuring them a passage to France: but I will request, if circumstances should call for greater pecuniary means

than they possess, that you would be so good as to furnish them, and draw upon me for the amount, & it shall be paid at sight.

Present Mrs Washington and myself in the most affectionate manner to Mrs. Hamilton—and be assured always of the very high esteem and regard with which

I am Yours Go: Washington

Colo. Hamilton

ALS, Hamilton Papers, Library of Congress.
    1. This is a reference to George Washington Motier Lafayette, son of the Marquis de Lafayette, who had arrived in the United States in the late summer of 1795. For information on young Lafayette and his tutor, Felix Frestel, see H to Washington, October 16, 26, November 19, 26, December 24, 27–30, 1795, March 7, April 2, 9, 1796; Washington to H, October 29, November 18, 23, 28, December 22, 1795, February 13, 1796.
    2. In 1792 the Austrians arrested Lafayette and handed him over to the Prussians. In 1794 the Prussians returned Lafayette to the Austrians, who imprisoned him in the fortress of Olmütz in Moravia. See "Cabinet Meeting. Opinion on Writing to the King of Prussia Concerning the Marquis de Lafayette," January 14, 1794. For the several unsuccessful efforts to arrange Lafayette's escape, see H to William Bradford, June 13, 1795; Bradford to H, July 2, 1795; H to Washington, January 19, 1796; Washington to H, April 13, May 8, 1796; Justus Erich Bollman to H, April 13, 1796. In October, 1795, Madame de Lafayette and her daughters arrived at Olmütz. On September 19, 1797, at the intercession of the French, Lafayette and his family were released from Olmütz and settled temporarily in Holstein. In February, 1798, George Washington Motier Lafayette and Frestel arrived in Holstein from the United States.

To Théophile Cazenove [1]

New York, October 14, 1797. States: "The question of interest on the contract with Mr Morris of the 24th of December 1792 [2] is not free from difficulty and doubt. I however think it the better opinion that interest is payable *until* the 24th of December 1795 and *no longer*." Gives reasons for this opinion.[3]

ALS, Gemeentearchief Amsterdam, Holland Land Company. These documents were transferred in 1964 from the Nederlandsch Economisch-Historisch Archief, Amsterdam.
    1. H wrote this letter in his capacity as an attorney for the Holland Land Company. For the full text of this letter and other relevant documents, see forthcoming Goebel, *Law Practice*, III.
    2. On December 24, 1792, Robert Morris deeded to Herman LeRoy and John Lincklaen as trustees of the Holland Land Company two tracts of land in the

Genesee country totaling one and one-half million acres. The Dutch bankers paid £75,000 for the western tract of one million acres, but the agreement stipulated that within three years they could declare the sum to be a loan to Morris secured upon the land. It was also agreed that the eastern tract of five hundred thousand acres could also be mortgaged or purchased for £37,000 and that the Holland Land Company would pay Morris after he had secured titles for the tracts from the Indians and had made the requisite surveys. See Orsamus Turner, *History of the Pioneer Settlement of Phelps and Gorham's Purchase, and Morris's Reserve* . . . (Rochester, 1870), 646. The Dutch bankers decided to purchase the land.

Morris described this contract as follows: "1,000,000 ⎫
500,000 ⎬ Acres were sold to
Mr. Cazenove and conveyed to Herman Le Roy and John Lincklaen. This sale was made conditional by certain articles of agreement, and held at the option of the purchasers to make it a sale or a mortgage at a time fixed, and at that time they elected to make it a purchase, whereby it was supposed the deeds of conveyance became absolute; and this was my opinion, as I always after that election did consider the sale as absolute; but after the Indian Right was purchased, Mr. Cazenove thought proper to get deeds of confirmation drawn, which he presented and left for my examination, and to be executed. Instead of examining and comparing them myself, I put them under the inspection of two Gentlemen bred to the Law, who very soon informed me that from the nature of the writings and circumstances of relating to this 1,500,000 Acres, I had an equal Right with the purchasers to elect that it should be a sale absolute or a Mortgage; in the latter case to be redeemed by re-payment of the consideration money, (£112,500 sterling,) and interest agreeably to the articles of agreement. And it was urged, that as my affairs were then so deranged, that I was obliged to keep close house; it became my duty to reserve this Right to my Creditors, and not to sign the deeds of confirmation. To this reasoning, I submitted reluctantly, because I thought the sale a fair one, intended at the time by me to be positive; and which, if my affairs had been in such a situation as that no creditors could have been affected, I certainly would have signed the new deeds without hesitation; that I did not do it, was to me a matter of regret, under which I have never felt perfectly satisfied" (*In the Account of Property*, 5-6).

For the purchase of the Indian right, see H to Herman LeRoy, William Bayard, and James McEvers, December 16, 1796; March 4-July 19, 1797.

For additional information on Morris's sale to the Holland Land Company, see Paul Demund Evans, *The Holland Land Company* (Buffalo, 1924), 25-36, 177-78.

3. On October 13, 1797, H made the following entry in his Cash Book, 1795–1804: "Le Roy & Bayard Dr . . . opinion concerning interest on the 37.500 £ Sterling payable to R Morris if retained 15" (AD, Hamilton Papers, Library of Congress).

To Théophile Cazenove [1]

[*New York, October 14, 1797.*] Answers Cazenove's letters of May 29 and July 5, 1797, concerning ownership of lands in New York State by aliens.[2]

ADf, Hamilton Papers, Library of Congress; two copies, Gemeentearchief Amsterdam, Holland Land Company. The Holland Land Company documents were transferred in 1964 from the Nederlandsch Economisch-Historisch Archief, Amsterdam.

1. H wrote this letter in his capacity as attorney for the Holland Land Company. For the full text of this letter and other relevant documents, see forthcoming Goebel, *Law Practice*, III.

2. The following entry appears in H's Cash Book, 1795–1804, for October 13, 1797: "Le Roy & Bayard Dr for opinion given to Mr Cazenove as to the validity of mortgages on the lands of the Dutch Company if sold on Credit 15" (AD, Hamilton Papers, Library of Congress).

From David Ross [1]

Bladensburgh [Maryland] Octr. 16th. 1797

Dear Sir

The subject of the letter I alluded to in my last,[2] did not relate to Colo. Mercer but to a public assertion of a letter of yours, being seen in one of the West India Islands in favour of a change of our Government to Monarchy.[3] I had concluded you had agreed with me in sentiment that nothing Co. Mercer could say was worth your notice after I had furnished you with Capt. Campbells [4] & my answer to a piece of his, filed in the Printing Office at Annapolis & which he suffered to pass unnoticed: [5] & I had put it in that point of view the only time I heard the subject mentioned, that is, the close of your corrispondence with him.[6] I still think the same. If you can make up your mind to determine in favor of my opinion it would be right to put it in my power to ascertain it, if the subject should ever again be introduced, as he has yet some political friends in this Neighbourhood & you of course some political enemies.

Mr. Monroes application for the reasons of his recall,[7] was a surprize, it being so directly in opposition to the principles of our Government; but this surprize has vanished when it is found by your Publication [8] that he thinks nothing of sacrificing the happiness of a private family, to his Party-views: for if he should be able to show he was not a voluntary means of the Publication yet his conduct in obliging you to answer it or admit yourself a dishonest man will ever be sufficient to condemn him & prevent his being considered as a man of honour even if he had not evaded as he has done your charges of Malignancy & dishonour. This is the general sentiment here & I may with truth say universal with the friends of Government so far as has come to my knowledge.

Your Publication has also confirmed impressions made here by a private letter of Mr. Jefferson, since his being Vice President, which does not approve of the change in our Representation it being in favor of Government & addressed to one, in a district that elected a federal member & who was opposed to his election; [9] and this has done away the hopes some had from his Speech as V-President, that he meant to support the measures of the Executive—or at least would have restrained any observations on that representation that has been its support.[10]

Little is to be expected from Partizans, but with those who are yet open to conviction, your Publication is thought will have a happy influence & prevent their rallying round any other Standard than that of their own Government.

I am Dr Sir   Your friend & obedt. Servt.   David Ross

Alexander Hamilton

ALS, Hamilton Papers, Library of Congress.

1. After service in the American Revolution, Ross practiced law and managed his family's estate in Frederick County, Maryland. He corresponded with H about H's protracted dispute with John Francis Mercer, a member of the House of Representatives from Maryland from 1791 to 1794. See the introductory note to H to Mercer, September 26, 1792.

2. Presumably Ross to H, November 16, 1796.

3. See Ross to H, November 16, 1796.

4. Captain William Campbell. See Ross to H, November 23, 1792.

5. See Ross to H, November 16, 1796.

6. See the introductory note to H to Mercer, September 26, 1792.

7. On July 6, 1797, soon after his return from France, James Monroe wrote to Timothy Pickering and asked for a "statement as a matter of right" on why he had been recalled, (Stanislaus Murray Hamilton, ed., The Writings of James Monroe Including a Collection of His Public and Private Papers and Correspondence Now for the First Time Printed, 7 Vols. [New York, 1898–1903; reprinted: New York, 1969], III, 66–68).

8. Ross is referring to H's "Reynolds Pamphlet," August 25, 1797.

9. This is a reference to a letter which Thomas Jefferson wrote to Peregrine Fitzhugh of Washington County, Maryland, on June 4, 1797. After discussing the role of the Republicans in blocking preparedness measures, Jefferson wrote: ". . . In fact I consider the calling of Congress so out of season an experiment of the new administration to see how far & on what line they could count on it's [the Republican majority in Congress] support. Nothing new had intervened between the late separation & the summons, for Pinckney's non-reception was then known. It is possible from the complexion of the President's speech that he was disposed or perhaps advised to proceed on a line which would endanger the peace of our country: & though the address is nearly responsive

yet it would be too bold to proceed on so small a majority. . . . The nomination of the envoys for France does not prove a thorough conversion to the pacific system . . ." (Ford, *Writings of Jefferson*, VII, 298–300).

Fitzhugh described the contents of this letter to some Republican friends, one of whom mentioned the letter to a Federalist, who in turn sent its substance to correspondents in Frederick and Georgetown (Fitzhugh to Jefferson, October 15, 1797 [ALS, Thomas Jefferson Papers, Library of Congress]).

The district to which Ross is referring was Maryland's fourth congressional district, which included Washington County, Fitzhugh's home. In the first session of the fifth Congress which assembled on May 15, 1797, George Baer, Jr., a Federalist, replaced Thomas Sprigg, a Republican, as the Representative of that district.

10. Ross is referring to the speech which Thomas Jefferson delivered in the Senate chamber following his inauguration as Vice President. In this speech Jefferson said: ". . . The rules which are to govern the proceedings of this House, so far as they shall depend on me for their application, shall be applied with the most rigorous and inflexible impartiality, regarding neither persons, their views, nor principles, and seeing only the abstract proposition subject to my decision. If, in forming that decision, I concur with some and differ from others, as must of necessity happen, I shall rely on the liberality and candor of those from whom I differ, to believe, that I do it on pure motives" (*Annals of Congress*, VI, 1581).

From Timothy Pickering

[*Philadelphia, October 21, 1797.* On the back of a letter which Hamilton wrote to him on August 27, 1797, Pickering wrote: "returned the paper inclosed Oct. 21. 1797." *Letter not found.*]

From Robert Morris [1]

Alexander Hamilton Esqr
New York   Hills [near Philadelphia] October 27th 1797

Dear Sir

In my last letter to you [2] I said I saw the means of discharging my debt to you in consequence of the purchase made of the Indians and that your influence might be usefull in the recovery of the money, it is thus; Doctor Craigie in Co with Watson & Greenleaf purchased of Mr Saml. Ogden with my consent 100000 acres of Genesee land for which they paid, except $12500 Watson and Greenleaf were half and Doctr Craigie half, unfortunately at the solicitation of Greenleaf when he was settling accounts with Mr Watson I released the latter of his responsibility and took Greenleaf's Bond for their half.[3] Doctor Craigie is to pay me the other half in specie or in certain Bonds which he then held of mine those Bonds I have satisfied by a sale of lands to him since; therefore he is to pay me $6250 in specie in 60 days after the Indian title is acquired to the 100000 Acres of land, that title was acquired on the 15th day of September last being the date of the Indian Deed of conveyance [4] for the whole Country of which that 100000 Acres is a part and none of the Indian reservations are near it. I wrote to Mr Craigie last Week [5] and enclosed a Copy of the instructions I gave for the survey and sent that letter open under cover to his relation and Agent Mr Seth Johnston of New York but have not heard from either of them. I do not Know of or suspect any demur to this payment unless they or either of them should have possessed themselves of some of the notes in circulation on which unfortunately my Name is. I think you have influence with both these Gentln and in your last letter dated the 5th inst.[6] you promise the exertion of it. I request that you will apply to them upon this subject as if the debt was assigned to you and prevail on them to pay without any attempt at defalcation. If they agree I will send you an order or assignment as you may think best, you had best in your first application only to mention that you are to receive this Money & hear what they have to say, if they agree to pay all is well, if they make any objections I will send you the papers on which the debt rests. There are two orders in the hands of Mr Hazlehurst [7] amount to about £ 500 to £ 600 which I am to get up or they will stop the Amot. these I expect to obtain in time. I shall await your Answer and remain   Dr Sir yrs

RM

LC, Robert Morris Papers, Library of Congress.
   1. This letter concerns Morris's efforts to pay the balance of a debt which he owed to H. For an account of this debt and Morris's plans for paying it, see the introductory note to H to Morris, March 18, 1795. See also Morris to H, March 31, June 2, 23, 30, July 18, 20, 1795; June 17, 27–30, November 19, December 8, 1796; June 2, 10, September 9, October 2, 1797.
   2. Morris to H, October 2, 1797.
   3. For an explanation of the transactions described in this sentence and in the remainder of this letter, see the introductory note to H to Morris, March 18, 1795.
   4. See Morris to H, March 3, 1797, note 6.
   5. Morris to Andrew Craigie, October 19, 1797 (LC, Robert Morris Papers, Library of Congress).
   6. Letter not found.
   7. In summarizing his accounts with Robert and Isaac Hazlehurst, Morris

wrote: "*Robert Hazlehurst & Co., Robert Hazlehurst* of Charleston, South Carolina. These are old long standing accounts; and as Isaac Hazlehurst conceived that upon a settlement of his accounts with me I should prove the debtor, I assigned to him my claims on his Brother, altho. I differ from his opinion as to the result of the settlement.

"*Isaac Hazlehurst* of Philadelphia, Old and lengthy accounts are depending; and in a settlement with him must be included my dependencies with his brother. And as I owe a debt to John Thompson of Philadelphia, Merchant, attended with peculiar circumstances, I have assigned all my claims upon Mr. Hazlehurst to Mr. Thompson, with Reservation of any surplus to me, my heirs or assigns." (Morris, *In the Account of Property*, 28–29.)

From James T. Callender [1]

[Philadelphia, October 29, 1797]

Sir

I have perused your observations on the history of 1796.[2] As the facts which you there bring forward, and the conclusions which you attempt to draw from them, do not appear Satisfactory to me, I intend introducing a reply to them in a volume upon your administration,[3] that I am now engaged in writing. My object in this letter is, to request that you will give an order to a friend of mine and myself to inspect the papers lodged with Mr. Bingham,[4] that I may judge what credit is due to them. Such an order, I conceive from your own words in *the Observations*, to be necessary to obtain a perusal of them; and if they appear to be genuine, I Shall be as ready to confess my conviction to the public, as I was to declare my former opinion, I hope that there is nothing improper in this application. I am Sure that I have no personal enmity at you, nor any pleasure in giving you uneasiness. The freedom which I take with all parties ought to have convinced you that I am the "hireling" of none.[5]

With sincere admiration of your Superior talents, I am Sir Your most obedt servt. Jas Thomson Callender
Corner of Walnut and
eleventh Street

Philadelphia
Octr. 29. 1797

P.S. The treatment which I have got from Some of your friends, while I was writing defences of your right to attend the western army,[6] and in Such a guarded and candid Stile that I have no reason at this time to disavow them, was of a nature so monstrous that they left me no terms to keep with them, and when I began to search I did find what I had not expected. If an answer is to come to this letter, I would think it a favour to Send it soon, as I mean in a few days to print a prospectus of my new Volume. I have always Spoke of your talents as of the highest class. This was a tribute that I Could not help paying.

Permit me to State one palpable mistake, as I Judge it to be. In No. 5 of the documents you tell of *visiting her at Inskeep's*. The George never was a house of that sort.[7] Inquiry was made at the time, and it was affirmed that neither Mrs. R. nor you ever had been there. Besides, in the letters there is no trace of Such a thing. I tell You honestly and as a friend, that this has an air of inconsistency; and I would gladly, if you can give me a reconcilement of it, save you the trouble of inserting one in your Second pamphlet; for that you must come out again I firmly believe. I might mention other things, but perhaps have already Stretched my letter to a disagreeable length.[8]

ALS, Hamilton Papers, Library of Congress.
    1. For background to this letter, see the introductory note to Oliver Wolcott, Jr., to H, July 3, 1797; the "Reynolds Pamphlet," August 25, 1797. See also Callender to H, July 10, 1797.
    2. See the "Reynolds Pamphlet," August 25, 1797.
    3. *Sketches of the History of America* (Philadelphia: Snowden and McCorkle, 1798).
    4. William Bingham.
    5. In the "Reynolds Pamphlet," August 25, 1797, H wrote: "Let me now, in the last place, recur to some comments, in which the hireling editors of pamphlets No. V and VI has thought fit to indulge himself."
    6. This is a reference to H's participation in 1794 in the expedition against the Whiskey Insurrection in western Pennsylvania.
    7. This is a reference to the memorandum, dated December 16, 1792, in which James Monroe, Frederick A. C. Muhlenberg, and Abraham B. Venable described their meeting with H on the evening of December 15. Callender published this memorandum as part of document No. V in his *History*. For the text of this memorandum, see Wolcott to H, July 3, 1797, note 50.
    8. H endorsed this letter: "Impudent Experiment NO *Notice*."

From Ambrose Spencer [1]

Hudson [New York] October 30, 1797. Discusses a case involving a land dispute between William Proctor, for whom Hamilton was counsel, and "Avery & others," who were represented by Spencer.[2]

ALS, Hamilton Papers, Library of Congress.

1. Spencer was a Hudson, New York, attorney. In 1794 he represented Columbia County in the New York Assembly, and from 1796 to 1802 he was a member of the state Senate. In 1796 he was appointed state district attorney for the third district, and in 1797 he was a member of the Council of Appointment of New York.

2. In 1774 surveys were made for Samuel Avery "and others" for twenty-four thousand acres of land in Charlotte County and for Humphrey Avery "and others" for twenty-eight thousand acres of land in the same county (Mix, *Catalogue: Maps and Surveys,* 204). Charlotte County was located in what is now Vermont.

H made the following entry in his Law Register, 1795–1804:

"In Chancery
Proctor
  adsm
William Avery   Recd Retr. $25
Ebenezer Brackill   Mr Proctor
Samuel Olmstead   39 Fair Street
Eliphalet Ackley
Ichabod Olmstead
and Ansyl Willey"

(D, partially in H's handwriting, New York Law Institute, New York City). An entry in H's Cash Book, 1795–1804, for February 24, 1797, reads: "Dr. to Costs & Fees Cash received retainer of *Proctor* v *Avery* 25" (AD, Hamilton Papers, Library of Congress). On May 8, 1799, the New York Court of Chancery "ordered that the injunction issued in this Cause be dissolved so far as to permit the defendant to proceed to trial at law in the ejectment suits mentioned on the pleadings in this cause . . ." (MS Minutes of the New York Court of Chancery, 1798–1801 [Hall of Records, New York City]).

Conversation with Robert Liston [1]

[New York, October, 1797]

"It remains to be considered whether His Majesty's Service might not reap considerable advantage from a general stipulation for the restitution of deserters [2] in nearly the same terms with those employed in the French Treaty.[3] Our friends in this Country think it would, and they strongly advise that an article of that tenour should be concluded. Among the number of these is Colonel Hamilton of New York, who expressed to me his opinion that we ought carefully to avoid urging the American Ministry to any stipulations which might add strength to that imputation of partiality to Great Britain which has of late been cast upon them by the Democratic Party."

PRO: F.O. (Great Britain), 5/18.
1. This conversation has been taken from Liston to Lord Grenville, October 28, 1797 (ALS, PRO: F.O. [Great Britain], 5/18). Liston was the British Minister to the United States. George Grenville was the British Foreign Secretary.
2. On May 12, 1797, Liston wrote to Grenville and proposed that a new article be added to the Jay Treaty which would provide for the reciprocal restitution of deserters (Mayo, *Instructions to British Ministers*, 135, note 27). On July 5, 1797, Grenville sent Liston "the Draft of an Article stipulating the reciprocal Restitution of all Deserters from the Naval or Land Service of Great Britain or the United States who may take refuge in the Territories of either Country" (Mayo, *Instructions to British Ministers*, 135).
3. This is a reference to Article 23 (originally 25) of the 1778 Treaty of Amity and Commerce between the United States and France (Miller, *Treaties*, II, 20–21).

From Robert Morris [1]

Hills [near Philadelphia] Novr. 1st. 1797

Dear Sir

I wrote to you some days ago,[2] but have not yet heard in reply. I take the liberty to enclose herein a letter for Mr. Church and to ask your interference. If it is only his Money that he is Seeking I will get it for him, and I would fain hope that he does not wish to take advantage of my Necessities and obtain my property at less than its worth.

I am willing to Sell it at a fair price to him if he chooses, but if he really does not wish to have the Land, procure for me a little time and I will do him ample justice.

If he were pressed by Necessity I could not think hard of his pressure, but as that is not the case and I am willing to pay for indulgence I hope he will grant it, and you will oblige me by letting Mr Rd. Harison [3] and myself know what to expect. I hope I am not imposing a disagreable task on you, but that you will do the needfull for a real Friend.

Your hble servt.   Robt Morris

Alexr. Hamilton Esqr

[ENCLOSURE]

Robert Morris to John B. Church [4]

John B. Church Esqre   Hills near Philada Novr 1st 1797
New York

Sir

I informed you some time since that I was in Treaty for money to pay the interest due to you, it so happened that I could not bring the agreement to a close before the Citizens of Philadelphia began to disperse on account of the Yellow fever, and since they did so, it has been next to impossible to get any business done. They are now returning to their homes and I shall renew my negotiations and doubt not but in a short time I shall be able to secure the money to pay the interest due as well as that which is coming due. Under this expectation I request your patience for a little longer time and you shall hear from me again I hope with the remittance. I shall not object to pay interest for the delay of the payment which ought to have been made on the 1st Jany last.

Yrs.   RM

ALS, Hamilton Papers, Library of Congress; LC, Robert Morris Papers, Library of Congress.

1. This letter and its enclosure concern a debt which Morris owed to John B. Church, Morris's efforts to pay this debt, and Church's suit in Chancery to secure the payment of interest on this debt. For information on these matters, see the introductory note to Morris to H, June 7, 1795. See also Morris to H, July 20, November 16, December 18, 1795, January 15, March 6, 12, 14, 30, April 27, May 3, 10, 17, 18, 31, 1796, March 3, 27, May 20, 23, June 2, 10, July 2, 1797; William Lewis to H, May 4, 1796; H to Charles Williamson, May 17–30, 1796.

2. Morris to H, October 27, 1797.

3. Morris had retained Richard Harison of New York as his attorney in the suit brought by Church. On November 1, 1797, Morris wrote to Harison: ". . . I have this day written to Mr Church asking his forbearance a little while, as I am going to renew a negotiation for raising his money which was broken of[f] in consequence of the Yellow fever dispersing our Citizens. If

he means only to get his money I shall expect his compliance but if he means to acquire plunder out of my distress it will be in vain to look for money. I will enclose the letter for him to Colo Hamilton and ask his interference and to let you know the effect. In the mean time I will thank you to inform me how soon he can bring the matter to a close. If he will not grant my request and what delay will be obtained by filing an answer; If that is done I cannot go to N York and of course a commission will be necessary & say how much money for I have but little at present" (LC, Robert Morris Papers, Library of Congress).

4. LC, Robert Morris Papers, Library of Congress.

From Stephen Van Rensselaer

Water Vliet [New York] November 6. 1797

Dear Sir

I received your letter [1] on the subject of Mr. Hoffmans embarrassments [2] altho I always feel disposed to aid those who are in distress & particularly those for whom I have a friendship yet when I reflect on the extent of the operation proposed & the sacrifices I should be obliged to make to fulfill my engagements if I became responsible a sense of duty to my family forbids me acceding to the proposition. I congratulate you on the birth of your son.[3] I hope he may inherit your talents & virtues. My wife as well as myself are much flattered with the name & joins me in love to Mrs H & Children.

Your Aff   S. V Rensselear

The Genl.[4] has had an attack in the stomach. He is better again & out.

ALS, Hamilton Papers, Library of Congress.
     1. Letter not found.
     2. Josiah Ogden Hoffman, attorney general of New York, had speculated heavily in land and securities. Hoffman's speculations were unsuccessful and led to his arrest for non-payment of debts in 1798. On October 22, 1798, Governor John Jay wrote to Hoffman: ". . . your pecuniary Embarrassments are considered as being incompatible with the Attention and Independence with which the Duties of your office should be executed" (ADf, Columbia University Libraries). Hoffman explained his financial difficulties in a letter to Jay on October 31, 1798: ". . . I observe, that I was arrested for near $11000, when the sum actually due, by the united opinions of General Hamilton, Mr [Richard] Harrison and Mr. [Robert] Troup, was only $1090. . . . It may be remarked, that the Cause of this Arrest was not for any debt of my own. As to the Unsettled state of my Accounts with the Publick, you will suffer me to remark, and I am sure, the force of the remark cannot escape your attention, *that the unsettled state of a Public Officer's Accounts, unaccompanied,* by any Refusal to *state* and *settle the same,* can never in itself, be a just cause of Crimination. . . .
     "There is one other source of Incompatibility, mentioned by your Excel-

lency, '*My pecuniary Embarassments*' . . . . they have been occasioned by unforeseen Events, and principally from my being *Security* for others. . . . I have long determined, that if ever they should render me incapable of attending to the duties of my Office, that Moment it should be resigned. . . . It is flattering to me, to believe, from your professions of personal friendship and Regard, that you will be gratified in being informed, that *these Embarassments* have greatly subsided, that several of the most important demands against me, have been conveniently arranged, and that the few remaining ones, will, in all probability, be accomodated in a few Weeks. . . ." (ALS, Columbia University Libraries.) Hoffman settled his financial affairs and remained in office until February, 1802.

3. William Stephen Hamilton was born on August 4, 1797.

4. Philip Schuyler, father-in-law of H and Van Rensselaer.

From Stephen Van Rensselaer [1]

Albany, November 8, 1797. "I take the liberty of sending for your examination & opinion a Deed which was given to me by Mr. Hoffman as an indemnification against any losses I might sustain by reason of my endorsement for him. The security is ample if the instrument is valid. I wish it not to be made public unless it may be necessary for my security. I however submit this to your discretion. I shall be happy to hear from you on this subject."

ALS, Independence National Historical Park, Philadelphia.

1. For background to this letter, see Van Rensselaer to H, November 6, 1797.

From Rufus King [1]

[*London, November 13, 1797. Letter not found.*]

1. Letter listed in Rufus King's "Memorandum of Private Letters, &c. dates & persons from 1796 to Augt. 1802," owned by Mr. James G. King, New York City.

From Alexander Baring [1]

Philadelphia, November 16, 1797. "I have not till now been able to meet Mr. Field [2] to make the necessary inquiries about the land Coll. Burr proposed transferring as a security for his debt to Mr Angerstien [3] and I am sorry to say the result of a conversation I have had with him leaves little reason to hope that this property can be applied to the object in question or that it will afford any tolerable security for it. . . ."

ALS, Hamilton Papers, Library of Congress.

1. Baring, the son of Sir Francis Baring, who was head of the House of Baring, arrived in the United States in December, 1795. As an agent for his father's firm, he invested in Maine lands, speculated in foreign exchange, and made alliances with several leading mercantile firms and banking houses in the United States. Although he traveled extensively, his headquarters were in Philadelphia. In 1798 he married a daughter of William Bingham.

2. John Field was a Philadelphia merchant.

3. John J. Angerstein was a London merchant, a philanthropist, and one of the outstanding art collectors of his time. His extensive economic interests included holdings in western lands in the United States.

In a statement which H enclosed in a letter to John Rutledge, dated January 4, 1801, H wrote: "He [Aaron Burr] is without doubt insolvent for a large *deficit*. All his visible property is deeply mortgaged, and he is known to owe other large debts, for which there is no specific security. Of the number of these is a Judgment in favour of Mr. Angerstien for a sum which with interest amounts to about 80,000 Dollars." The same enclosure was sent to James McHenry on January 4, 1801.

The case of *Aaron Burr* v *John Julius Angerstein,* in which H represented Angerstein, was finally dismissed "On motion of the Complainant and with the consent of Mr Hamilton of Counsel for the defendant" on February 8, 1803 (MS Minutes of the New York Court of Chancery, 1801–1804 [Hall of Records, New York City]). On December 16, 1802, H made the following entry in his Cash Book, 1795–1804: "Receipts Dr. Costs (Angerstien) 300" (AD, Hamilton Papers, Library of Congress).

For a history of the case and its political implications for Burr, see James Cheetham, *A View of the Political Conduct of Aaron Burr, Esq. Vice-President of the United States* (New York: Denniston & Cheetham, 1802), 70–75.

To Robert Morris

[*New York, November 20, 1797.* On November 23, 1797, Morris wrote to Hamilton: "I have this minute received your favour of the 20th inst." *Letter not found.*]

To Oliver Wolcott, Junior

[New York, November 20, 1797]

Dr Sir

Give me leave to remind you of your promise to send me the documents and information which authenticate the situation of Mr. Beaumarchais as to the unaccounted for *Million.*[1]

Allow me also to mention to you another point. I hear there is a plan among the Directors of the Bank to transfer the management of their concerns from the House of *Cazenove* [2] to that of Baring.[3] When the arrangement was originally upon the Tapis, I felt some preference to the House of *Baring* as of more known solidity. But after its having taken a different course I should regret a change unless upon grounds which I am persuaded do not exist—circumstances of insecurity in the conduct or affairs of the existing Agents. I verily believe they unite prudence & solidity. The change might, without cause, injure their *credit* and do them *positive* harm. It was one thing to have entrusted them in the first instance. It is another to recall that trust; which neither Justice nor the Reputation of the Bank will countenance but for valid reasons of change of Opinion. My friendship for Mr. Cazenove the Father [4] corresponds with my sense of Propriety, to induce the wish that you may see fit to exert your influence in every proper way to prevent a change.[5]

   Yrs Affectly   A H

                                           Nov 20. 1797

O Wolcott Junr Esq

ALS, Connecticut Historical Society, Hartford.
  1. For information on Pierre Augustin Caron de Beaumarchais and the "lost million," see the introductory note to Oliver Wolcott, Jr., to H, March 29, 1792; H to Thomas Jefferson, June 10, 1793; Beaumarchais to H, October 29, 1796.
  2. The London banking house of J. H. Cazenove, Nephew, and Company.
  3. This is a reference to the fact that among the many duties of the Bank of the United States as fiscal agent of the Treasury Department was the obligation to facilitate the Treasury's various foreign exchange operations. The bank, in turn, paid a designated foreign bank to perform these duties.
  4. The father of J. Henry Cazenove was Théophile Cazenove, a member of a French Protestant family that had lived for many years in Switzerland. H was well acquainted with J. Henry Cazenove's brother, Théophile, who was American agent of the Holland Land Company.
  5. Wolcott endorsed this letter: "Ansd. Decr. 10." Letter not found.

From Jeremiah Condy [1]

Philadelphia, November 21, 1797. "I feel very much embarassed to discover the cause of my being without any reply to the several Letters I did myself the Honor to address you,[2] and am really sorry Sir, that I should have given you the trouble of attending to a Correspondence which has yet been of no advantage to you or Utility to me, for I can make no other Conclusion than that you have declined the Business proposed and mean to return the papers in your hands and the Fee. If so . . . I will be glad *to receive them by the first mail* and you will please to deduct from the fee you return the Expences you have paid. . . ." [3]

ALS, Hamilton Papers, Library of Congress.
    1. Condy was a Charleston, South Carolina, merchant.
    2. Letters not found.
    3. H endorsed this letter: "J Condy Ans 22 Nov." Letter not found.

To Jeremiah Condy

[*New York, November 22, 1797.* Hamilton endorsed the letter Condy wrote to him on November 21, 1797: "Ans 22 Nov." *Letter not found.*]

From Robert Morris [1]

Hills [near Philadelphia] Novr. 23d. 1797

Dear Sir

I have this minute received your favour of the 20th inst. [2] and sit down immediately to acknowledge my fear that the mistake respecting Doctr Cragies Bond is with me, I am seperated from the Bulk of my Papers and when I wrote you respecting it [3] I had only his letter agreeing for the purchase of the Land and terms of payment, not hearing from you I sent to Town a few days ago for the Bond intending to Send it to you, but it could not be found amongst my Papers and then it occurred for the first time, that Colo. Ogden must have it, as he made the Sale of that Land to Greenleaf Watson & Cragie, and I have Greenleafs Bond for their half, which I have just put in Suit against him, for I had at his request in the days of my Confidence in him released Mr Watson and taken him alone of which I now repent as I do of every transaction between him & me. I beg your pardon for having given you this trouble, and I will immediately turn my attention to another source of reimbursement for you. My promise to you on this point is sacred and shall be full-filled, you will speedily hear again from me in regard to it. I hope Mr Church has too much Spirit and too high a Sense of honor to entertain a desire of possessing himself of my property at less than its Value, and at its Value I am willing to Sell it to him.[4] I trust to your assurance of serving me in this business and remain as ever Dr Sir

Your Sincere Friend & Servant   Robt Morris

Alexr Hamilton Esqr
New York

ALS, Montague Collection, MS Division, New York Public Library; LC, Robert Morris Papers, Library of Congress.

1. This letter, except for the last two sentences, concerns Morris's efforts to pay the balance of a debt which he owed to H. For an account of this debt and Morris's plans to pay it, see the introductory note to H to Morris, March 18, 1795. See also Morris to H, March 31, June 2, 23, 30, July 18, 20, 1795; June 17, 27–30, November 19, December 8, 1796; June 2, 10, September 9, October 2, 27, 1797.

For the individuals and specific transactions mentioned in this letter, see the introductory note to Morris to H, June 7, 1795, and Morris to H, October 27, 1797. See also Morris to Andrew Craigie, October 19, 1797 (LC, Robert Morris Papers, Library of Congress).

2. Letter not found.

3. Morris to H, October 27, 1797.

4. This sentence refers to a debt which Morris owed to John B. Church, Morris's efforts to pay this debt, and Church's proceedings in Chancery to secure the payment of the interest on this debt. For information on these matters, see the introductory note to Morris to H, June 7, 1795. See also Morris to H, July 20, November 16, December 18, 1795, January 15, March 6, 12, 14, 30, April 27, May 3, 10, 17, 18, 31, 1796, March 3, 27, May 20, 23, June 2, 10, July 2, November 1, 23, 1797; William Lewis to H, May 4, 1796; H to Charles Williamson, May 17–30, 1796.

On November 23, 1797, Morris wrote to Richard Harison, his attorney in the suit brought by Church, as follows: ". . . I hope Mr. Church is not seeking to obtain my property for less than its value. I have that confidence in your exertions which makes me to look to you for protection in this business; in the meantime I have removed the negotiation I mentioned to you but my own situation renders such things more dilatory than otherwise they would be" (LC, Robert Morris Papers, Library of Congress).

From Ezekiel Gilbert

Hudson [New York] November 30, 1797. "I took Occasion Some weeks ago, at the Desire of Doctor Benton, to enclose a Copy of a

Note for 5000 Dols given him by Pierpoint Edwards Esqr of New Haven, with an Intimation that in case Mr Edwards could be taken within New York, Dr Benton's wish was that you would issue process and pursue the suit for him.[1] Not having heard from you, the Doctor requests me to gain some Information from you, and your Advise respecting the business."

ALS, Hamilton Papers, Library of Congress.
  1. See Gilbert to H, October 4, 1797.

From James Monroe [1]

Albemarle [Virginia] decr. 2. 1797.

Sir

I requested Colo. Burr to inform you immediately after the recit of yours of augt. 9th that I was not satisfied with the explanation given by it of yr. preceding one of the 4th, since wh. my mind & time have been devoted to other objects claiming with me a priority of attention.[2]

It was not my intention to make the subject into the discussion whereof I was drawn by you upon my arrival, a personal affr., because in a case in which you complained of an injury, however unjustly, I of none, it would have been highly improper for me so to do; nor was there any thing in my letters which countenanc'd that idea. It was suggested by certain passages in yours having that tendency, to which I replied if you invited it, I shod. accept it. But by this I did not mean to become an aggressor nor was it justly inferable. It was however not my intention to decline that issue if sought by you in any mode whatever, either by challenge invitation or advance (for with me these terms are synonimous), in which light it seems to me as if yr. letter of the 4th. thus explained may be conceived. I have therefore requested Mr. Dawson to communicate with you further upon the subject of that letter and impowered him in case you meant it as such to give you my answer to it and otherwise arrange the affr. for the interview thus invited on yr. part.

  I am Sir Yr. Obt. servt   Jas. Monroe

ALS, Lloyd W. Smith Collection, Morristown National Historical Park, Morristown, New Jersey.

1. For background to this letter, see the introductory note to Oliver Wolcott, Jr., to H, July 3, 1797; the "Reynolds Pamphlet," August 25, 1797.

In August, 1797, the threatened duel between H and Monroe was averted (see Monroe to H, July 10, 16, 17, 18, 21, 25, 31, August 6, 1797; H to Monroe, July 10, 17, 18, 20, 22, 28, August 4, 9, 1797; William Jackson to H, July 24, 25, 31, August 5, 7 [two letters], 11, 1797; James McHenry to H, August 7, 1797; "David Gelston's Account of an Interview between Alexander Hamilton and James Monroe," July 11, 1797; "Certificate by James Monroe," August 16, 1797). On October 19, 1797, however, James Madison wrote to Monroe: "I have recd yours of the 15th. and according to its request enclose back the pamphlet to Mr. Jefferson. I have looked over attentively the part of it which regard you. It does not seem to me to present any ground on which you could resumed the controversy with Col. H. with an appearance either of obligation or propriety. All the points deserving attention which grew out of the course of the correspondence, as well as incident to the original state of the case between you seem to have been brought to a final close . . ." (ALS, James Madison Papers, Library of Congress).

On December 2, Monroe wrote to Thomas Jefferson enclosing a letter to Aaron Burr, dated December 1, and a letter to John Dawson, dated November 27, 1797 (ALS, Thomas Jefferson Papers, Library of Congress). Monroe's letter to Burr, to whom during the previous August he had entrusted the negotiations for the abortive duel (see William Jackson to H, August 5, 1797, note 5), reads: "Now that I have in some measure adjusted an affr to wh. that of Mr. H. formed an unreasonable intrusion, I am able to pay some attention to that of Mr. H.

"When I recd. Mr. H's. last letter I was not satisfied with it & desired you to tell him so, giving you a full power over the case in my behalf. To this letter I have no answer from you, which I impute either to an opinion on your part, that I ought to leave the affair where it is, or that it was then proper that I shod. not be interrupted by it, nor till I had finished the other which was a more important one. Permit me however to call your attention to it again.

"My opinion was and is that this gentn. ought to have been satisfied with the explanations I gave him, or to have called me to the field. Such wod. have been my conduct in his case. The contrary however was his.

"Whether I shod. have taken other notice of the stile of his letters at another time & under other circumstances I will not pretend to say. I shall only observe that as the publication of the papers to wh. he referred, did not injure me, and might him (especially if inocent), altho' I was much provoked when I received those letters, yet I did not then find in them a sufficient cause why I shod. take other ground than the defensive, wh. was strictly the proper ground for me in such a controversy.

"Tis possible however the letter in question as expld. may be considered as a species of invitation, & if so intended it becomes me to accept it. To ascertain this I have written him the enclosed letter, & have to request if you approve my acting further in it & the manner, that you will perform the office designated in it for you to perform.

"I give you full power over this affr. either by proceeding or otherwise as you deem it most honorable for me to do. I wish you to take precisely that course you would take in a like case of yr.self. You will decide in the first instance how far an explan., in the sentimt. proposed, alters the case as it now stands, so as to make it a suitable thing to desire such an expln.

"If you present the letter and he gives a satisfactory answer I want no publication of letters. Perhaps it may be proper to insert a pargh. in the gazette to the effect stated below. But if he does not make a suitable expln. you will of course close the affr. & arrange the time & place of meeting, & the sooner the better, & I care little where. If he gives no expln. but leaves it to me to expln., then you will consider his letter as an *advance &c.* and close it as above." (ALS, Historical Society of Pennsylvania, Philadelphia; ADf, Lloyd W. Smith Collection, Morristown National Historical Park, Morristown, New Jersey.)

The "paragraph . . . stated below" reads: "We have the pleasure to inform the publick that the affr. between Messrs. H. & M. so far as of a personal nature has been adjusted without the necessity of a personal interview. Mr. H. having upon the application of Mr. M. thro Mr. B. declared that he did not mean by his letter of augt. the 4th. to make any advance or give any invitation on his part to a personal interview, but only to meet and accept an advance which he supposed was made on the part of Mr. M." (D, in Monroe's handwriting, Historical Society of Pennsylvania, Philadelphia).

The letter which Monroe enclosed for Burr to deliver to H is dated November 27, 1797, and reads: "I requested Colo. Burr to inform you immediately after the receit of yours of Augt. the 9th. that I was not satisfied with the explanation given by it of yr. preceding one of the 4th; since which my mind and time have been devoted to other objects claiming with me a priority of attention.

"In my judgment you ought either to have been satisfied with the explanations I gave you, or to have invited me to the field. There seemed to be no intermediate ground for a man of honor to take; yet you found one.

"The explanations I gave you upon the subject to wh. those letters referred were liberal. They withdrew my own opinion from the scale against you, upon the possibility you might be inocent, leaving you to combat the testimony alone. To ask more if a proof of any thing was a proof of guilt.

"Still however it was not my intention to invite or even provoke a personal interview in that discussion, because I have many reasons of great weight to avoid it at the time & none to make it at any time. The idea was suggested by certain passages in yours having that tendency, to wh. I replied if you invited I shoud. accept it. But by this I did not mean to become an aggressor nor was it justly inferable. It was however not my intention to decline that issue if sought by you in any mode whatever, either by challenge invitation or advance, (for with me these terms are synonimous) in which light it seems to me as if that letter thus explained might be conceived. I have therefore requested Colo. Burr to communicate with you further upon the subject of that letter & impowered him." (ADf [incomplete], James Monroe Law Office Museum, Fredericksburg, Virginia.)

In the letter which Monroe wrote to Dawson on November 27, 1797, he enclosed the letter to H of December 2 printed above. On December 10 Monroe wrote again to Dawson: "I am much surprised I have heard nothing from you since yr. arrival in Phila. I committed to a late private conveyance a letter for you which will arive before this, on a subject of some delicacy & importance to me, the content of wh. subject I submitted to yours & his judgement. But if taken up, tis possible the mode suggested was not with sufficient dignity & tone. I therefore send another letter—wh. in that case will be examined, & the most suitable one preferred. I am sure you will weigh this subject with due attention, & take that step it becomes me to take. I think Mr Livingston ought to be consulted as a man of judgment and candour & very friendly to me. Consult however whom you please. You will fill up the blank with yours or Burrs name in case it be and as likewise the date . . ." (ALS, Lloyd W. Smith Collection, Morristown National Historical Park, Morristown, New Jersey). The letter to H which contains the "blank with yours or Burrs name . . . and as likewise the date" is similar, with minor variations in wording, to the letter Monroe wrote to H and sent to Burr on December 1, 1797.

In compliance with Monroe's request, Dawson conferred with Edward Livingston, Congressman from New York, Aaron Burr, and others. On December 24, 1797, Dawson wrote Monroe the following "candid history of what has passed": "I have been favour with your letters . . . with the several enclosures—and I have delayd an answer in order to weigh well a matter of delicacy & importance, & to give you one which might point out a course satisfactory & honourable to you.

"On the day after the receipt of your letters by a private conveyance, and after reading them with attention & reflecting on what passed last summer, I called on that character & had a consultation with him—the result of which was that we united in opinion, that it wd. be unwise, impolitic & unnecessary for you to take any farther step in the business.

"I will here observe that I had had conversation with several gentlemen previous to the receipt of any letter from you, & the foregoing was the opinion of all, except Mr. Livingston, who declared explicitly, that you ought to have challengd him for the terms 'malignant & dishonourable'—this I communicated in this consultation, & it produced no change in either of us, except that Mr. L—— ought not to be advisd with, as the gentlemen from that state might have an improper bias on their minds. About this time Colo: Burr came to Phia—this I communicated to the gentleman who brought your letters of the 27th Ulo. (& whom I will hereafter call Mr. A——) & we agreed, that it would be proper to speak to him in general terms, without saying any thing particular—accordingly I went into his room & after some loose conversation, I observed that I had seen you when in Virginia, & had since recievd letters from you, & that you were astonishd at geting none from him in answer to yours of last summer, as it was on a subject interesting to you. He declared that the reason was that he did not know what to write—for had the whole business been left to him he shoud have brought you & Mr. H—— together immediately, not liking that childish mode of writing—observing that he was convinced H—— woud not fight, as he had insinuated to you. I expressed some astonishment at this conversation, & told him that he certainly had an entire controul over the business committed by you; and urgd him to write to you, which he said he woud do immediately, & I presume did, as I went out, & in a short time communicated to Mr. A—— what had passed. He made the same observation that he had respecting Mr. L—— and as we agreed that there might be the same bias, it was deemed unwise to say any thing to him.

"After that I had several conversations with gentlemen, and they all agreed that you ought not to move in this affair any farther. On the reciept of yours of the 10 Int I communicated it to Mr A—— whose opinion remains unchanged—on yesterday I dined . . . with Mr. Livingston & five or six others, mostly foriegners—the dispute between you & Mr. H—— became the subject of conversation, & Mr. L—— expressed the same opinion he had to me before; I a different one, as I saw no just cause on your part—the book, which was upstairs was sent for, from which I endeavour to prove my position—& his, declaring that it was the general sentiment where he had been, altho he himself was convincd that the truth was different from the impression which the correspondence made, that is, that you were willing to fight, & Colo H—— not. I then declard that if you ought to have gone farther than you did the fault was with Colo [James] Innes & myself by whom you had been prevented—that even now coud I be persuaded that you ought to challenge Colo: H—— I was authorisd to do it—but this I did not think you ought to do.

"Thus have I given you a candid history of what has passd, with my real opinion—and altho it differs from that of some gentlemen's whom I respect, it is not changd—with you it rests to determine, as I shall not take any step before I hear from you—shoud your opinion differ from mine on a review of all circumstances, I will repeat here an observation which I made before 'that the correspondence has been already too long' & that the object of H—has been to attract the public mind to it, & thereby to withdraw it from his guilt in another business, which has sunk him as low as possible—and farther to suggest to you, in that case, the propriety of coming on, if convenient—think not that this arises from a unwillingness to do any & every thing in my power, & according to the best of my judgement—I assure you the contrary, & that it proceeds from an opinion that the business might be better conducted, & even that step make some impression on the public mind, & on the nerves of Mr. H.

"I must again repeat that *my* opinion is that you have nothing farther to do. . . ." (ALS, Lloyd W. Smith Collection, Morristown National Historical Park, Morristown, New Jersey.)

On December 27, 1797, Jefferson wrote to Monroe: "I communicated to Mr M. the evening I was with him the papers you sent by me for Mr. D. he was clearly of opinion nothing farther ought to be done. D. was decisively of the same opinion. this being the case then there was no ground for consulting L. or B. and accordingly nothing has been said to them" (ALS, letterpress copy, Thomas Jefferson Papers, Library of Congress).

No evidence has been found that Burr or Dawson ever sent a letter to H from Monroe. Although Monroe wrote to H on January 1, 1798, that letter has not been found.

2. Monroe had been engaged in the preparation of a pamphlet to explain his conduct as United States Minister Plenipotentiary to France from 1794 to 1796. Monroe's pamphlet, which was published in Philadelphia on December 21, 1797, is entitled: *A View of the Conduct of the Executive, in the Foreign Affairs of the United States, Connected with the Mission to the French Republic, During the Years 1794, 5, & 6.* See the [Philadelphia] *Aurora. General Advertiser*, December 29, 1797.

From Elisha Boudinot [1]

New Ark [New Jersey] December 4, 1797. "I am anxious to consult you relative to a particular friend & connection of mine—Mr. Griffith [2] a gentleman of the bar in this State. . . . He has had several severe fits of sickness. . . . This has induced him to think of moving into a City, if practicable. . . . As I know of no Gentleman in the City whose candor on this subject I would put so much confidence in as yours and none who I would choose to lay under obligations to, but yourself—I have therefore taken the liberty of asking your friendly advice on the occasion—whether under your rules, he could get admittance at your bar and whether you know of any Gentleman who would like to connect himself with him. . . . I only mention that he was not only in full practice as a lawyer —was surrogate of the County but within a year has published a book on the office of a Justice of the peace [3]—Exrs &c which has gone thro' two editions already. . . . I will, if the weather permits call on you to morrow with him. . . . Independant of the particular business which interests him—I should like to introduce (as if by accident) the conversation he has lately had with Tench Coxe, who dined with him—Justifying himself for his conduct. This *Janus* (enter nos) will not be in office many days. . . ."

ALS, Hamilton Papers, Library of Congress.

1. Boudinot was a Newark lawyer and businessman.
2. William Griffith had married Abigail Hetfield, Boudinot's niece (George Adams Boyd, *Elias Boudinot; Patriot and Statesman, 1740-1821* [Princeton, 1952], 287).
3. *A Treatise on the Jurisdiction and Proceedings of Justices of the Peace in Civil Suits. With an Appendix, containing Advice to Executors, Administrators and Guardians. Also an Epitome of the Law of Landlord and Tenant; the whole interspersed with Proper Forms, and calculated for General Instruction* (Burlington: Elderkin and Miller, 1796).

From John Jay

Albany 5 Decr. 1797

Dr. Sir

Yours of the 4th Ult: [1] relative to Mr. Richardson,[2] was delivered to me Yesterday.

On Mr. Dunscombs [3] Resignation, Col. Troup [4] recommended Mr. Keese [5] to succeed him, and in Terms very explicit. If I recollect right, he had conversed with Mr. Keese on the Subject. Considering the Population of New York, and the Delays which might be caused by the Death Sickness Resignation or absence of the Examiner, and the Inconveniences which Mr. Dunscombs Resignation had actually occasioned, I have been inclined to think that it might be expedient to appoint two Examiners; [6] and in that Case, I had thought of nominating Mr Keese & Mr. Ab. Walton.[7] Whether the latter would accept it I do not know. If he would I think he should be preferred to any junior Counsellor—supposing their Competency to be adequate. Besides, that Family has, on account of their attachmt. to our present Constitution & Governmt., claims to attention; and the fact is, that as yet they have recd. very little. It would give me pleasure to have your Sentiments on these heads, provided

no circumstances or considerations should render it inconvenient.
Yours   John Jay

Col. Hamilton

ALS, Hamilton Papers, Library of Congress.
  1. Letter not found.
  2. Presumably Charles I. Richardson, a New York City lawyer.
  3. Edward Dunscomb, a New York City lawyer and notary public, had resigned as an examiner in Chancery. In 1797 he became clerk of the United
States Court for the District of New York.
  4. Robert Troup, a close friend of H since the time when they had been
students at King's College, was a New York City and Albany attorney. A
veteran of the American Revolution, he served as secretary of the Board
of War in 1778 and 1779 and secretary of the Board of Treasury in 1779 and
1780. In 1786 he was a member of the New York Assembly. Troup was involved
in land speculation in western New York and was associated with Charles
Williamson in the development of the Pulteney purchase in the Genesee
country.
  5. John Keese, a New York City lawyer.
  6. Three examiners in Chancery were appointed. They were Abraham G.
Lansing, Gabriel V. Ludlow, and Edward W. Laight (David Longworth,
*Longworth's American Almanack, New-York Register, and City Directory
for the Twenty-third Year of American Independence* . . . [New York, 1798],
55).
  7. Abraham Walton had played a prominent part in the movement for independence in New York, serving as a member of the Committee of One Hundred and of the First Provincial Congress which met in New York City on
May 23, 1775.

From Mathieu Dumas [1]

LehmKuhl [Holstein] 8 Xbre. 1797

Monsieur

Un intervalle de 17 années écoulées depuis l'époque ou J'eus
l'avantage de faire votre Connoissance, et des occasions plus fré-
quentes de la cultiver pendant la Campagne de 1781, n'en a point
affaibli le souvenir. Les orages de la révolution française, nos efforts
pour Conquérir et fixer notre liberté, nos malheurs même m'ont
souvent ramené vers ces temps heureux ou nous concourions a
achever la révolution américaine, ou nous appercevions l'aurore des
prosperités auxquelles vous aves eû depuis tant de part, et comme
Citoyen, et comme homme public.

je n'ose me flatter que Vous m'ayés distingué dans cette foule de personnes que la Confiance de leurs concitoyens a mis dans une fûneste ou périlleuse évidence; mais j'ai cette Confiance que si dans les débats auxquels j'ai dû prendre part, mes opinions m'ont retracé quelquefois à Votre pensée, Vous y aurés retrouvé les principes que dans ma jeunesse, j'allai puiser près de Vous à leur Veritable Source. la place que Vous m'aurés vû occuper sur les nouvelles tables de proscription Confirmera sans doute ce jugement favorable.

Depuis long temps je me proposais d'avoir l'honneur de Vous écrire, je dois Vous solliciter pour une affaire qui m'interesse personellement, et du succés de laquelle dependent le sort futur de mes enfants, la réparation de ma fortune deux fois renversée. Je ne pouvais commencer cette Correspondance sous un auspice plus favorable que celui de ma réunion avec notre ami commun Le Gal. Lafayette que je suis venû joindre ici aprés sa résurrection du tombeau d'olmuttz.[2]

Vous Conoissés monsieur, Les réclamations constantes et jusqu'à présent infructueuses de Mr. de beaumarchais, tant auprés du gouvernement qu'auprés de l'état de Virginie en particulier:[3] Je vois par les dernières correspondances que l'acte de justice que Vous avés exercé comme ministre[4] ne vous permet pas d'en poursuivre Vous même la Consequence naturelle, et trop differee, mais vous avés fait espérer à beaumarchais par Le canal de ses amis MMrs *Chevalier & Rainetaux de Newyork*[5] que Vous emploiriés Vos bons offices auprés de Mr. Le ministre des finances: L'opposition qu'a mis Mr. Walcot, et son délai à faire rechercher et produire la preuve que beau marchais a reçu un fort *a-compte*,[6] arrête la Conclusion de son procés avec l'état de Virginie. Ce procés déjà jugé favorablement pour nous a la cour de la Chancellerie ne peut être terminé à la Cour d'appel ou la Cause a été évoquée, que lorsque cette opposition, qui n'a accun fondement, aura été levée.[7]

Mon beau-frêre Edouard delarûe (l'un des aides-de camp du général Lafayette) a épousé la fille unique de Mr. de beaumarchais L'un de mes plus anciens amis;[8] sa fortune en europe a été avec La mienne presque détruite par les sequestres les confiscations: telle est la communauté d'intéret qui éxiste entre nous, que Le payement des créances d'amerique, créances si bien prouvées, si sacrées par leur origine, est aujourdhuy la seule espérance des deux familles.

J'ajoutterai que dans l'etat présent des affaires si ce payement s'effectûait; de quelque nature que fussent les valeurs et Les termes, nous ne songerions pas à deplacer notre fortune, mais bien plutot à en aller jouir en bons et vieux américains d'adoption, sur la terre natale de la liberté, ou je serais trés heureux de Vous revoir.

Veuillés bien offrir mon hommage respectueux à Madame hamilton & à Madame Church,[9] et recevoir celui de L'estime la plus constante, et du plus sincére dévouement.   Mathieu Dumas

P. S. Si Vous avés la bonté de me répondre veuillés bien addresser Votre lettre à *Mr. Elias funck,*[10] *chés MMs Bellamy, Riccé & Co. a hambourg.*[11]

J'ai preferé de Vous écrire en français n'ayant point oublié la perfection et L'aimable préférence avec lesquelles Vous parliés notre langue, mais je n'ai pas entièrement perdu l'usage de la langue américaine.

ALS, Hamilton Papers, Library of Congress.

1. General Mathieu Dumas had served in the French army as aide-de-camp to the Count de Rochambeau during the American Revolution and in Europe after 1784. He was elected to the Legislative Assembly in 1791, joining the Constitutionalist Party of the Feuillants. In August, 1792, as president of the Assembly, he defended the Marquis de Lafayette against an indictment for royalism. Condemned to death under the Terror, he fled to Switzerland, returned under the Directory, and 1795 was elected to the Council of Ancients as a member of the Constitutionalist Party. Proscribed once again in the Directorial purge which accompanied the *coup d'état* of September 4, 1797, he escaped with the false passport of a Danish citizen and established himself at Tremsbüttel in Holstein.

This letter was enclosed in Marquis de Lafayette to H, December 8, 1797. See H to Lafayette, April 28, 1798.

2. See Lafayette to H, December 8, 1797.

3. For information on the claims of Pierre Augustin Caron de Beaumarchais against the United States, see the introductory note to Oliver Wolcott, Jr., to H, March 29, 1792; H to Thomas Jefferson, June 10, 1793; Beaumarchais to H, October 29, 1796.

4. See Beaumarchais to H, October 29, 1796, note 7.

5. See Beaumarchais to H, October 29, 1796, note 5.

6. See Beaumarchais to H, October 29, 1796, note 5; H to Wolcott, November 20, 1796.

7. Beaumarchais's case was not decided by the Virginia Court of Appeals until November 2, 1801 (Daniel Call, *Reports of Cases Argued and Adjudged in the Court of Appeals of Virginia* [Richmond: Thomas Nicolson, 1805], III, 122–80).

8. André-Toussaint (not Edouard) Delarue, brother of Dumas's wife Julie, married Eugénie Beaumarchais on July 11, 1796.

9. Angelica Church, Elizabeth Hamilton's sister.

10. Elias Funck was Dumas's alias as a Danish citizen.

11. The banking house of Bellamy, Riccé, and Company had been established by two French Constitutionalist refugees.

From Marquis de Lafayette [1]

LehmKuhl. holstein. Xber the 8th. 1797

my dear hamilton

As my former letters have already given, and you shall in posterior ones find a regular account of every thing relating to me, give me leave to-day to confine myself to one very interesting object, which being highly momentous to the future welfare of gal. dumas,[2] & his brother, cannot be considered as foreign to me, & has of course a right to your attention.

Dumas himself has during the war deservedly obtained your personal friendship and regard. He continued, on his return to france to be confidentially & honourably employed down to the time when on the ruins of the bastille, we founded a popular government. There also dumas entered into a course of important services to our cause, among which I Shall only mention the first & the last viz that to him I am under great obligations from the organisation of the national guards, & that on the overthrow of the national constitution in 1792, being at that time one of the ablest members of the legislative body, he Conducted himself with a firmness So Conspicuous & persevering, that it not only exposed him to the greatest dangers, but forced a tribute of praises from the very enemies whom it had been his duty to resist.

When liberty began to revive in france, the nomination of dumas to the council of elders, was one of the first effects of the restored freedom of elections, as in that *third* & the ensuing one you may (among Some Choices which from a Spirit of indignation against the jacobins were in the other extreme very bad) you may, say I, find the names of several strenuous friends to liberty & legal order who had miraculously escaped the Snare & the axe of tyrannical anarchy.

To these honest Senators in both houses, fully impressed with the rights of national Sovereignity, & the religion of a civic oath, it had become a Sacred obligation to Support the republican Constitution of the *third year*. Some did it from duty—others from inclination &

I would have been among the latter—all who were my personal friends, whatever be the motive, did it in earnest whether others have, or have not acted otherwise, it has nothing to do with the object of this letter. Nor is it necessary with you who have read the arguments pro & con the revolution of the 18th fructidor [3] to expatiate on the nature of those measures. Suffice it to say that one of its consequences whas to throw dumas into the same country where you know that we have found it convenient & even necessary on account of our, & particularly my wife's health, to fix our winter quarters.

His brother delarûe, my aide de camp in the national guards one of the cleverest & best young men I ever knew, has married beaumarchais's daughter [4]—both he & his brother in law are to divide between themselves the payement of the Sums which in the united States are düe to the young lady's father.[5] I have for twenty years often heard, yet I know very little of that affair—this I am told that on the one part of it, the States of Virginia have favourably decided, & that on the other article the two brothers are willing to abide by the decision which you as a minister have given.[6] I do not presume to discuss, much less to decide in this business—but I am bound by friendship to interest myself in the welfare of dumas, & his brother, the more So as the faithfull good Will of both, & the exertions of the former in my behalf during my captivity entitle them to my gratitude.

My most affectionate respects wait on Mrs. hamilton & Mrs. Church—remember me most friendly to their father her husband, & all your families—adieu, my dear hamilton.

your affectionate friend   Lafayette

ALS, Hamilton Papers, Library of Congress.
    1. For background to this letter, see George Washington to H, October 8, 1797, note 2.
    2. See Mathieu Dumas to H, December 8, 1797.
    3. See Rufus King to H, September 10, 1797.
    4. See Dumas to H, December 8, 1797, note 8.
    5. See Pierre Augustin Caron de Beaumarchais to H, October 29, 1796.
    6. See Beaumarchais to H, October 29, 1796, note 7.

From John Laurance [1]

Philadelphia Dec 10 1797

My dear sir

I have sent our Friend R Lennox [2] 2000 Dollars on account of the obligation given by us to J Mark payable this Month. I have remitted the Sum on Condition it is Credited on the Mortgage of J Mark to R Gilchrist and indorsed on the Note as being so. My intention was, to have paid also, 2000 Dollars more, without any determination on the Interest I shall eventually hold in the purchase, but because I could have done it: but in addition to the Sums I have paid for T Cooper [3] I had a Note from Ogden Hoffman [4] Indorsed by his Father, [5] for that amount. This Note I supposed would be paid but it was protested the 14th of November and now lies unpaid at the Branch Bank.

I have paid, on the purchase from J Mark, before the remittance to R Lennox upwards of 10.100 Dollars, exclusive of Interest on the same from 9 Jany 1796 and the present remittance will make my payment in full, or very near it: provided your Interest and mine are equal, but not so, if I am to take the quantity you suppose: however if that Note had been paid I should have applied the Money that way, which would have exceeded my Share. You offered me a Loan of 1500 Dollars [6] in case I took the quantity you supposed I ought to take. I hope therefore you will not be embarrassed, in making such payment as will satisfy Mr Lennox. I am confident he will be very well disposed to grant any indulgence that may not be unreasonable. I am satisfied the question of Interest, between us, should remain open; for I am not indisposed to hold the Interest you think I ought to take, but the heavy payments I have made for T Cooper added to the disappointment of payment of the Note from Messrs Hoffmans have drained me of nearly all my active Funds, and money from the Country, although I have much due to me, is very tardy in its progress. Pry how are the affairs of Ogden Hoffman and his Father circumstanced? I have proposed Ogden an arrangement but have not heard from him. If he can't make it, and can make any with you, so that the produce of the Note can come into your hands to be applied to the payment of R Lennox to be credited on the Mortgage and indorsed on the Note aforesaid as being so, I shall be well satisfied, leaving the question of Interest, in the purchase from J Mark still open between us. It may be in your power to do it, as I have understood some Friends meant to come forward with a Loan to extricate Ogden & his Father. The Note lies under protest in the Branch Bank is for 2000 Dollars with Interest from 14 Novr last and charge of protest.

I am   My dear sir   very sincerely yours   John Laurance

Col A Hamilton

ALS, Hamilton Papers, Library of Congress.
    1. For background to this letter, see Jacob Mark and Company to John B. Church, H, and Laurance, May 30, 1797; Laurance to H, June 3, 1797.
    2. Robert Lenox, a native of Scotland, emigrated to New York City, where he became a prominent merchant and an investor in city real estate. He remained in New York City during part of the American Revolution and served the British as a clerk in the office of commissary of naval prisoners. In 1797 he was also a New York City alderman and a director of the New York branch of the Bank of the United States. See "Certificate on Robert Lenox," January 11, 1796.
    3. Thomas Cooper was a New York City attorney.
    4. Josiah Ogden Hoffman, a New York City attorney and attorney general of New York, had speculated heavily in land and securities. For Hoffman's financial difficulties in 1797 and 1798, see Stephen Van Rensselaer to H, November 6, 8, 1797.
    5. Nicholas Hoffman.
    6. An entry in H's Cash Book, 1795–1804, for December 29, 1797, reads: "John Laurance   Dr to Cash paid R Lenox at his request by way of loan   1500" (AD, Hamilton Papers, Library of Congress).

From Oliver Wolcott, Junior

[*Philadelphia, December 10, 1797.* Wolcott endorsed the letter Hamilton wrote to him on November 20, 1797: "ansd. Decr. 10." *Letter not found.*]

From William Duer

[New York, December 11, 1797]

Dear Sir,

I was in hopes not to have troubled you again on any Subject of a Pecuniary, but my Necessities constrain me to sollicit the Loan of Fifteen Dollars. In the Course of three or four Months I shall have it in my Power to reimburse this, and the former Advances you was so obliging to make me. I know you have use for all your Profession brings in, but Necessity constrains me to borrow out of your small Stock.[1]

I am Dear Sir, Your Affectionate Humble servt.   W Duer.

New York Dec. 11th. 1797

ALS, Hamilton Papers, Library of Congress.
    1. An entry in H's Cash Book, 1795–1804, for December 26, 1797, reads: "Wm. Duer Dr. to Cash lent him some days since   15" (AD, Hamilton Papers, Library of Congress).

From John Ferrers [1]

New York, December 12, 1797. "The Friendly attention with which you have at all times received any application from me, has encouraged me to assure myself, that you will not think me troublesome, in requesting from you a piece of information. . . . Having been inform'd that Mr. Bayard the Agent from the United States in England,[2] intends to return in the Spring, I am desirous of knowing if any other Appointment will be made on the Business of British Captures in his Stead. . . . The purport of the application I now trouble you, with is to request you will procure for me, through the Secretary of State, the information I have mention'd, and to favour me also with your Friendly opinion, as it respects the propriety of such an application on my part, which will be received and attended to, with the utmost respect."

ALS, Hamilton Papers, Library of Congress.

1. Ferrers was a New York City merchant.

2. Samuel Bayard, a former law partner with William Bradford in Philadelphia and a former clerk of the Supreme Court of the United States, had been selected by George Washington in October, 1794, to prosecute before the British Admiralty courts United States claims for losses sustained by United States citizens from captures of their ships on the high seas by British cruisers. With the organization of the mixed commission authorized by Article 7 of the Jay Treaty to settle these claims, Bayard served as United States agent for presenting them to the commission. See Rufus King to H, April 29, 1797. Bayard resigned as agent in August, 1797.

From Robert Morris [1]

Hills [near Philadelphia] Decemr 21st. 1797

Dear Sir

I have this day been informed that an attachment has been laid by your order in the Name of Mr Church, in the hands of Messrs Le Roy Bayard & McEvers,[2] what this is for or why it is done I cannot conceive; your agency in its astonishes me, if it is for the balance of the Money *you lent me*,[3] I shall deem my self more unfortunate than ever (altho sufficiently so before) to have such measures taken at the time I was making arragements to satisfy you perfectly.

Will you be so good as to explain to me Candidly What this attachment is for and why it is done and you will so far oblige

Your Obedt hble servt   Robt Morris

Alexr Hamilton Esqr
New York

ALS, Hamilton Papers, Library of Congress, LC, Robert Morris Papers, Library of Congress.

1. This letter concerns an order by Chancellor Robert Livingston to secure the payment of interest on a debt which Morris owed to John B. Church. For this debt and the Chancellor's order, see the introductory note to Morris to H, June 7, 1795. See also Morris to H, July 20, November 16, December 18, 1795, January 15, March 6, 12, 14, April 27, May 3, 10, 17, 18, 31, 1796, March 3, 27, May 20, 23, June 2, 10, July 2, November 1, 1797; William Lewis to H, May 4, 1796; H to Charles Williamson, May 17–30, 1796.

2. See the introductory note to Morris to H, June 7, 1795.

3. Morris's assumption was incorrect, for, as indicated in note 1 above, the debt in question was one which Morris owed to Church. For the debt which Morris owed to H, see the introductory note to H to Morris, March 18, 1795. See also Morris to H, March 31, June 2, 23, 30, July 18, 20, 1795; June 17, 27–

30, November 19, December 8, 1796; June 2, 10, September 9, October 2, 27, November 23, 1797.

To Robert Morris

[*New York, December 26, 1797.* On January 17, 1798, Morris wrote to Hamilton: "I have been a long time possessed of your letter of the 26 Decemr." *Letter not found.*]

To Theodore Sedgwick

[*New York, December 26, 1797.* "I beg your pardon for not having written to you sooner. Blame my excessive avocations & particularly my engagements with the Court of Chancery. . . . The declaration sent us by Van Shack [1] has been examined and returned. We do not find, that our statute contains any provision." [2] *Letter not found.*]

ALS, sold by American Art Association–Anderson Galleries, March 3, 1925, Lot 275.
    1. Peter Van Schaack, a former Tory, was a lawyer in Kinderhook, New York.
    2. Text taken from dealer's catalogue.

1798

From Cornelius I. Bogert [1]

[*New York*] *January 1, 1798*. "Permit me to request your attention to the case of Bull agt Armstrong & Barnewall. . . ." [2]

ALS, Hamilton Papers, Library of Congress.
1. Bogert was a New York City attorney.
2. This is a reference to the case of *Henry Bull* v *William Armstrong and George Barnwall*. For a discussion of this case, along with the relevant documents, see Goebel, *Law Practice*, II, 183–88.

From James Monroe

[*Albemarle, Virginia, January 1, 1798*. In January, 1798, Hamilton wrote to Monroe and referred to "your letter of the first instant." *Letter not found.*]

To Timothy Pickering [1]

[New York, January 1, 1798]

Dr. Sir

By some unaccountable delay the inclosed [2] which came in a letter to me [3] has been extremely postponed. I hope not injuriously for the interest of the party concerned. Do me the favour to acknowlege its receipt. [4]

Yrs. with esteem & regard   A H

Jany. 1. 1798

ALS, Massachusetts Historical Society, Boston.
1. For background to this letter, see the Marquis de Fleury to H, May 28, 1796; Oliver Wolcott, Jr., to H, September 1, 1796; H to Charles Cotesworth Pinckney, September 12, 1796.
2. The "inclosed" is a letter from Fleury to Pickering, February 21, 1797 (ALS, Massachusetts Historical Society, Boston), which contains copies of

documents supporting Fleury's claim for compensation for his services during the American Revolution. The enclosures, in Fleury's handwriting, are in the Massachusetts Historical Society, Boston.

During the American Revolution, Fleury, who had served in the French army, was made a brigade major on the staff of Casimir Pulaski in 1777 after the Battle of Brandywine, and later that year he became a lieutenant colonel of engineers. He fought with Rochambeau at Yorktown in 1781. At the end of the war Fleury went to South America, and in 1784 he returned to France. See Fleury to H, October 15–19, 1777; August 4, 1784.

3. Letter not found.

4. Pickering endorsed this letter: "Inclosing Colo. Fleurys packet dated Feby. 21. 1797."

From Timothy Pickering

Philadelphia Jany. 3. 1798.

Dr Sir

I have to-day received your letter of the 1st inclosing a letter from Colo. Fleury, dated the 21st. of February last, with powers to receive & remit to Europe the amount of his dues from the U.S. which he hoped to receive in six months. He will be uneasy at not hearing from me in near eleven months,[1] and will lose the benefits which the possession of the money might have yielded. These circumstances arising from the accidental detention of his letter you will regret as much as I do.

I am very respectfully yours   Timothy Pickering.

Alexander Hamilton Esq

ALS, Hamilton Papers, Library of Congress; copy, Massachusetts Historical Society, Boston.

1. Pickering had written to Fleury on September 24, 1796 (ALS, Massachusetts Historical Society, Boston).

From Isaac Gouverneur [1]

New York, January 7, 1798. "The cause which has been so long depending between Louis le Guen and my commercial house in this city, has excited so much attention . . . I can only address you on the subject through the medium of a public newspaper. . . . To

satisfy me more fully on the subject . . . I resorted to Philadelphia
to take further advice from three more gentlemen that were thought
most eminent in the law in that place, whose opinions will herewith
accompany this letter. . . ." [2]

The [New York] *Commercial Advertiser,* January 10, 1798.
    1. This letter concerns the case of *Louis Le Guen* v *Isaac Gouverneur and
Peter Kemble,* which was one of a series of cases in which H served as the
attorney for Le Guen. For a discussion of these cases, see Goebel, *Law Practice,*
II, 48–164. See also H to Gouverneur and Kemble, January 19, 1797; H to
Elizabeth Hamilton, April 16, 1797; Le Guen to H, April 24, 1797.
    2. The opinions, which were furnished by William Lewis, Jared Ingersoll,
and William Tilghman, are printed in *The* [New York] *Commercial Advertiser,* January 10, 11, 1798.

From Moses Lopez [1]

New York, January 7, 1798. ". . . I am informed you intend going to Albany in a day or two with Mr. Le Guen. My long confinement of 2 years the 19th Instant [2] will I trust . . . induce you to
see Mr. Le Guen, and come to some conclusion in his consenting
to my discharge on Common Bail, which Mr. Livingston [3] is Ready
to do in behalf of Mr. Governeur. . . ."

ALS, Hamilton Papers, Library of Congress.
    1. This letter, like the preceding one, concerns H's role as attorney for
Louis Le Guen.
    2. Lopez had been imprisoned in January, 1796, because of an action of
debt which Isaac Gomez, Jr., had brought against him (MS Minutes of the
New York Supreme Court under the date of January 30, 1796 [Hall of Rec-
ords, New York City]). See also Goebel, *Law Practice,* II, 54, note 22. In his
deposition, dated June 11, 1798, on cross-interrogatories in the case of *Isaac
Gomez, Jr., and Abraham R. Rivera* v *Louis Le Guen, Isaac Gouverneur, Peter
Kemble, and Moses Lopez,* Lopez stated "that altho' he was then [November,
1796] discharged from the suit of the said Isaac Gomez still he remained in
Confinement on other suits" (copy, Hamilton Papers, Library of Congress).
    3. Brockholst Livingston was attorney for the defendants in *Louis Le Guen*
v *Isaac Gouverneur and Peter Kemble.*

From Isaac Gouverneur [1]

New York, January 9, 1798. "I had the honor to pay my respects
to you on the 7th inst. to give the opinions of the able counsellors
at the bar in Philadelphia, on the case of Le Guen's. . . . I think

you, as a professional man of the law, should act with more caution in committing yourself with a mistaken opinion; for it frequently acts as a spur to make individuals unreasonably obstinate afterwards. It would also be more becoming in the practice, to be less abusive. I remember at the pleadings of the last tryal in this cause of Le Guen's, in order to move the feelings of the jury, that you spoke of his sufferings in a very sympathetic manner . . . and that you finally compared me to the odious character of 'Shylock in the Play.' I felt extremely hurt upon this observation, my dear Colonel, because I thot you was wounding yourself, as I am not without a regard for you. . . ."

The [New York] *Commercial Advertiser*, January 11, 1798.
  1. This letter, like the preceding two, concerns H's role as attorney for Louis Le Guen.

To Elizabeth Hamilton

Rhinebeck [New York]
½ past twelve. [January 14, 1798]

This moment my Dear Eliza, we descended from the carriage— after a journey,[1] so far, much more comfortable than we could possibly have anticipated. It makes me repent that we had not pursued our original plan. But we must console ourselves with the hope of a speedy reunion which you may be assured I do every thing in my power to accelerate—For I give up too much of my happiness by my absence not to be anxious to abridge it. I rely on your promise to compose your dear heart; and to be as happy as you can be. Give my love to Angelica [2] & kiss my dear Children for me.

Adieu my excellent & beloved Betsy   A H.

Jany 14th.

To Mrs. Elisabeth Hamilton
No 26 BroadWay
New York.

Copy, Columbia University Libraries.
  1. H was on his way to Albany to attend the session of the New York Supreme Court.
  2. Angelica Church.

From Robert Morris [1]

Hills [near Philadelphia] Jany 17th. 1798

Dear Sir

I have been a long time possessed of your letter of the 26 Decemr [2] without replying, which has been Occasioned by my waiting to hear from my Son Thomas whether he had made any arrangement for paying the debt I owe you. It seems he wrote to me at New York on the 4th. inst but his Servant instead of putting the letter in the Post Office, put it with some others into his Trunk and took it to Albany from whence I have received it this day and thereby learn that an agreement has taken place between you which I find to be indulgent to him, for which I am thankfull. Mr Rees [3] is possessed of the Deed of Conveyance of the Lands for which my Son is to pay [4] & the Sum he assumes to pay you on my Account is in part thereof, Mr Rees will be the bearer of the Deed and on his arrival you & my son can finish the business. The explanation contained in your letter of Mr Church's proceedings [5] is the only one I have received and it was very satisfactory So far as it conveys the Idea that you were not the *Willing* instrument of his Severity, for I was much shocked at the first contrary Idea that was held out.

This ought to be considered as a proof of my respect for you, since the experience I have acquired leads me to disregard very much the Conduct of those whom I have not found cause to esteem.

The Complaint you make of delay in providing for the payment of the balance [6] is but too well founded, I often thought of it and made many efforts that you're not acquainted with because they did not succeed. The horrid usury of the times, threw difficulties in my way in every attempt to raise Money and I have frequently been without what was necessary for the Market. Property would not sell or serve, as formerly, as the basis for Loans, and I may truely Say, that I am a Martyr to the times, had the State of things remained as formerly I would not have trespassed on you, nor have had my property Advertized, Sold, Sacrificed & plundered in the manner it has. As to your Ultimate safety, that was never in danger for I had included you in an Arrangement for Securing all who had lent me Money or Names disinterestedly I would sooner perish than let one such Creditor suffer. You surprize me by the manner in which you mention Mr Cragies debt & the Occurrence respecting it.[7] I do not know what kind of suspicion you can have taken up on that subject. When I first wrote to you [8] I certainly expected that the Money was to be received by me, otherwise why should I have written at all about it, my only fear was that he might have bought Paper and would oppose that to the payment, but being Seperated from my Papers and it being a transaction of many years standing I had really forgot that upon agreement the Bond had been assigned to Mr Ogden. My design Certainly was to have put that Money into your hands which I think should rather carry conviction of my desire to pay, than have given rise to any sentiment that should Weaken Confidence. I will send on by Mr Rees the Account exactly Stated and you will find the balance of the principal to be as I formerly made it in an Acct sent you,[9] the Interest will increase it I mean the Legal interest for I dare not propose any other for fear of Offending a disinterested Mind, altho I should be very ready to make additional Compensation for the delay. I am Sensible that I have lost the Confidence of the World as to my pecuniary ability, but I believe not as to my honor or integrity and I shall certainly deem myself unhappy if yours is diminished in any respect; for I remain with sincere attachment Dr Sir

   Your faithful Friend & humble Servant   Robt Morris

Alexr Hamilton Esqr
at New York
or Albany

ALS, Hamilton Papers, Library of Congress; LC, Robert Morris Papers, Library of Congress.

  1. This letter, unless otherwise noted, concerns Morris's efforts to pay the balance of a debt which he owed to H. For this debt and Morris's attempts to pay it, see the introductory note to H to Morris, March 18, 1795. See also Morris to H, March 31, June 2, 23, 30, July 18, 20, 1795; June 17, 27–30, November 19, December 8, 1796; June 2, 10, September 9, October 2, 27, November 23, December 21, 1797.

  2. Letter not found.

  3. During the American Revolution, James Rees had been a clerk for the firm of Willing and Morris in Philadelphia. He was later the clerk for the commissioners of the "Morris Treaty" with the Indians. In 1798 he moved to Geneva where he became a private agent for Charles Williamson.

  4. The remainder of Morris's debt to H had been assigned to Morris's son

Thomas, who had secured its payment with lands in the Genesee country.

5. "Mr Church's proceedings" were instituted in Chancery to obtain the payment of the interest on a debt which Morris owed to Church. Morris had asked H about this matter in a letter to him dated December 21, 1797.

For Morris's debt to Church, see the introductory note to Morris to H, June 7, 1795. See also Morris to H, July 20, November 16, December 18, 1795; January 15, March 6, 12, 14, 30, April 27, May 3, 10, 17, 18, 31, 1796; March 3, 27, May 20, 23, June 2, 10, July 2, November 1, 23, December 21, 1797.

6. This is a reference to the payment of the balance of the debt which Morris owed to H. See note 1.

7. Although H's letter to Morris on this point has not been found, H had complained that Morris's claim against Andrew Craigie for $6,250, which Morris planned to use to pay H, had been assigned to Samuel Ogden and therefore could not be used for the payment to H. See Morris to H, October 27, November 23, 1797.

8. Morris to H, October 27, 1797.

9. This account, which has not been found, was sent to H on June 30, 1795 (see Morris to H, June 30, 1795). For H's account with Morris, see the introductory note to H to Morris, March 18, 1795.

From Jacob Read [1]

Philadelphia, January 18, 1798. ". . . The President having thought proper to dismiss Mr Tench Coxe [2] from the office of Commissr of the Revenue a Successor is Wanted. The Gentlemen of the So Carolina delegation in both Houses are anxious to have Wm. Ward Burrows [3] appointed & have Warmly recommended him to the President. . . . Mr Wolcott . . . Objects to him on the score Of a probable want of Industry. . . . For my own part I conceive him fully Equal to the office. . . . He thinks you can serve him and that a line from you to Mr Wolcott woud remove Mr W's objections. . . ."

ALS, Hamilton Papers, Library of Congress.

1. Read was a South Carolina Federalist who had fought in the American Revolution and served in the Continental Congress from 1783 to 1786. From 1795 to 1801 he was a member of the United States Senate.

2. For H's break with Coxe, see H to George Washington, February 2, 1795. For a Republican defense of Coxe, see the [Philadelphia] *Aurora. General Advertiser*, April 6, 1798.

3. Burrows, a resident of Kinderton, Pennsylvania, who had been involved in William S. Smith's speculative ventures (see Oliver Wolcott, Jr., to H, April 22, 1797, note 10), did not get the job. Instead, on January 18, 1798, Adams nominated William Miller of Philadelphia as commissioner of the revenue, and the Senate confirmed the nomination on January 23 (*Executive Journal*, I, 259–60).

From James McHenry

Philad. 26 Jany. 1798

My dear Hamilton.

Will you assist me or rather your country with such suggestions and opinions as may occur to you on the subject of the within paper. Some of the questions it contains are very important, and an immature step or a wrong policy pursued or recommended respecting them may become extremely injurious or beget disagreeable consequences. I am sure I cannot do such justice to the subject as you can. Let me therefore intreat you to favour me as soon as possible with your ideas. Take care of the paper. I reced. it only this morning.

Yours most affectionately   James McHenry

Col Hamilton.

[E N C L O S U R E]

*John Adams to James McHenry, Timothy Pickering,
Oliver Wolcott, Junior, and Charles Lee* [1]

Philad. Jany 24 1798

The President of the U S. requests the Secy of State, the Secy of the treasury, the Secy of War and the Atty. general to take into consideration the state of the nation and its foreign relations especially with France. These indeed may be so connected with these, with England Spain Holland and others that perhaps the former cannot be well weighed without the other.

If our Envoys extraordinary [2] should be refused an audience, or after an audience be ordered to depart without accomplishing the object of their mission [3]

1. They may all repair to Holland, or 2d. two of them may return home, leaving one abroad 3. all of them may return to America.

In the first case will it be prudent to call them all home and in the second to recall the one?

In any of the three cases what will be necessary or expedient for the Executive authority of the government to do here?

In what manner should the first intelligence be announced to Congress by message or speech?

What measures should be recommended to Congress?

Shall an immediate declaration of war be recommended or suggested? If not what other system shall be recommended more than a repetition of the recommendations heretofore repeatedly made to both houses?

Will it in any case and in what cases be adviseable to recommend an embargo?

What measures will be proper to take with Spain? What with Holland? What with Portugal? but above all what will policy dictate to be said to England? And how shall it be said? By Mr King? [4] or to Mr Liston? [5] And how shall it be conveyed to Mr. King? By packet? By an ordinary conveyance? or by some special trusty and confidential messenger?

Will it not be the soundest policy even in case of a declaration of war on both sides between France and the U. S. for us to be totally silent to England and wait for her overtures? Will it not be imprudent in us to connect ourselves with Britain in any manner, that may impede us in embracing the first favourable moment or opportunity to make a seperate peace? What aids or benefits can we expect from England, by any stipulations with her, which her interest will not impel her to extend to us without any? On the brink of the dangerous precipice on which she stands will not shaking hands with her, necessitate us, to fall with her, if she falls? On the other hand, what aid could we stipulate to afford her, which our own interest would not oblige us to give without any other obligation? In case of a revolution in England, a wild democracy, will probably prevail, for as long a time as it did in France; in such case will not the danger of reviving and extending that delerium in America, be increased in proportion to the intimacy of our connection with that nation?

ALS, Hamilton Papers, Library of Congress; ADf, James McHenry Papers, Library of Congress.

1. Copy, in the handwriting of McHenry, Hamilton Papers, Library of Congress.

2. On May 31, 1797, Adams had sent the following message to the Senate: "I nominate General Charles Cotesworth Pinckney, of South Carolina, Francis Dana, Chief Justice of the State of Massachusetts, and General John Marshall,

of Virginia, to be jointly and severally Envoys Extraordinary and Ministers Plenipotentiary to the French Republic.

"After mature deliberation on the critical situation of our relations with France, which have long engaged my most serious attention, I have determined on these nominations of persons to negotiate with the French Republic, to dissipate umbrages, to remove prejudices, to rectify errors, and adjust all differences, by a treaty between the two powers.

"It is, in the present critical and singular circumstances, of great importance to engage the confidence of the great portions of the Union, in the characters employed, and the measures which may be adopted: I have therefore thought it expedient to nominate persons of talents and integrity, long known and intrusted in the three great divisions of the Union; and, at the same time, to provide against the cases of death, absence, indisposition, or other impediment, to invest any one or more of them with full powers." (*Executive Journal*, I, 241–42.) On June 5, 1797, the Senate consented to the President's nominations (*Executive Journal*, I, 243–44).

On June 20, 1797, Adams sent the following message to the Senate: "I nominate the honorable Elbridge Gerry, Esq., of Massachusetts, to be Envoy Extraordinary and Minister Plenipotentiary to the French Republic, jointly and severally with Charles Cotesworth Pinckney and John Marshall, in the place of Francis Dana, who has declined his appointment on account of the precarious state of his health" (*Executive Journal*, I, 244). The Senate confirmed Gerry's nomination on June 22, 1797 (*Executive Journal*, I, 245).

For the instructions to Pinckney, Marshall, and Gerry, see *ASP, Foreign Relations*, II, 153–57.

3. Although in this and the following sentences Adams appears to know what had actually happened in the so-called XYZ affair, this was not the case. The first dispatches from the three commissioners describing their experiences in France did not reach Philadelphia until March 4, 1798. See Adams's message to Congress, March 5, 1798, in *ASP, Foreign Relations*, II, 150.

4. Rufus King was the United States Minister Plenipotentiary to Great Britain.

5. Robert Liston was the British Envoy Extraordinary and Minister Plenipotentiary to the United States.

To James McHenry

[New York, January 27–February 11] 1798 [1]

It may serve to prepare the way for a direct answer to the questions stated by the President [2] to make some preliminary observations.

AD, in the United States Naval Academy Museum; AD (photostat), James McHenry Papers, Library of Congress.

1. This undated document was written after January 26, 1798, when McHenry wrote to H, and before February 12, the date of McHenry's acknowledgment to H of the receipt of the document. In the letter he wrote to the President, McHenry incorporated almost verbatim H's answers to the questions which Adams had submitted to his cabinet (McHenry to Adams, February 15, 1798 [ALS, Adams Family Papers, deposited in the Massachusetts Historical Society, Boston; ADf, James McHenry Papers, Library of Congress]).

2. For these questions, see the enclosure to McHenry to H, January 26, 1798.

1   It is an undoubted fact that there is a very general and strong aversion to War in the minds of the people of this Country—and a considerable part of the community (though even this part has been greatly alienated from France by her late violent conduct towards this country) is still peculiarly averse to a War with that Republic.

2   A formal rupture between the two countries *ipso facto* carries matters to the greatest extremity, and takes all the chances of evil which can accrue from the Vengeance of France stimulated by success.

3   A mitigated hostility leaves still a door open to negotiation and takes some chances, to avoid some of the extremities of a formal war.

4   By a formal war with France there is nothing to be gained. Trade she has none—and as to territory, if we could make acquisitions they are not desireable.

These premisses if just lead to this conclusion, that in the event of a failure of the present attempt to negotiate, a truly vigorous defensive plan, with the countenance of a readiness still to negotiate, is the course adviseable to be pursued.

Then if one or more of our Commissioners remain in Europe it may be expedient to leave them there (say in Holland) to have the air of still being disposed to meet any opening to accommodation.

If they all Return, there is an end of that question, for they certainly are not to be sent back.

The further measures presumed to be expedient for the Government in the event supposed are— [3]

1   To give permission to Merchant Vessels under proper guards to arm for defence.

2   To prepare as fast as possible a number of *Sloops* of *War*, say Twenty of from 10 to 20 guns each. Vessels already built may be procured fit for the purpose and perhaps in sufficient number.

3   To complete as fast as possible the three remaining Frigates.[4]

3. The recommendations which follow are substantially the same as those which H sent to Timothy Pickering on March 17, 1798, and to Theodore Sedgwick on March 1–15, 1798.

4. On March 27, 1794, Congress had passed "An Act to provide a Naval Armament" (1 *Stat.* 350–51), which reads in part: "Whereas the depredations committed by the Algerine corsairs on the commerce of the United States

4 To give authority to the President in case of open rupture to provide equip &c by such means as he shall judge best a number of ships of the line not exceeding ten in number. Tis not impossible these may be procured from G B—to be manned & commanded by us. A provisional negotiation for this purpose may be opened. The authority ought to be broad enough, though covert in the terms, to permit the contracting with a foreign power to take such a number of its navy into the pay of our Government.

In the first instance our Merchant & other armed vessels should be authorised to capture and bring or send in all vessels which may attack them and all French privateers which they may find hovering within   [5] leagues of our Coast. The Vessels to be condemned & the crews liberated.

5 To this end and for more important reasons the Treaties of Alliance & Commerce between the UStates & France to be declared suspended.[6]

6 A substantial regular Force of 20,000 men to be at once set on foot and raised as soon as may be. Of these not less than 2000 to be cavalry. An auxiliary *provisional* army to be likewise constituted of 30000. Infantry on the plan heretofore suggested.[7]

---

render it necessary that a naval force should be provided for its protection: . . . *Be it therefore enacted* . . . That the President of the United States be authorized to provide by purchase or otherwise, equip and employ four ships to carry forty-four guns each, and two ships to carry thirty-six guns each." Following the Treaty of Peace and Amity with Algiers in 1795 (Miller, *Treaties*, II, 275–317), construction on three of the six frigates was stopped. The *Constitution*, the *United States*, and the *Constellation* were the three frigates to be completed, and under the provisions of "An Act supplementary to an act entitled 'An act to provide a Naval Armament'" (1 *Stat.* 453–54 [April 20, 1796]) funds were appropriated for their completion. By Section 1 of "An Act providing a Naval Armament" the President was empowered "to cause the frigates United States, Constitution and Constellation to be manned and employed" (1 *Stat.* 523–25 [July 1, 1797]). On March 27, 1798, Congress enacted "An Act for an additional appropriation to provide and support a Naval Armament," which appropriated funds "to complete and equip for sea . . . the United States, the Constitution and the Constellation . . ." (1 *Stat.* 547).
5. Space left blank in MS.
6. On February 6, 1778, the United States signed a Treaty of Amity and Commerce and a Treaty of Alliance with France. For the texts of these treaties, see Miller, *Treaties*, II, 3–47.
7. In the margin opposite this paragraph H wrote: "A Regiment to form two batalions commanded by a Colonel—Each batalion to be commanded by a Major & to consist of 5 Companies each Company to have a Captain two Lieutenants 4 sergeants & 100 rank & file."

7 To furnish the means all the sources of revenue to be immediately seized and put in action with boldness & a loan to the requisite extent on computation to be authorised.

The more Revenue we have the more vigour evidently we can act with & by taking a *rank* hold from the commencement we shall the better avoid an accumulation of debt. This object is all important nor do I fear any serious obstacles from popular opposition.

The measures to be taken by the Executive will therefore be—

To communicate to Congress with *manly* but *calm* and *sedate* firmness & without strut, the ill success of the attempt to negotiate & the circumstances attending it—

To deplore the failure of the measure—

To inculcate that the crisis is a very serious one & looking forward to possible events in Europe may involve the safety liberty & prosperity of this Country—[8]

That the situation points out two objects 1 measures of immediate defence to our Commerce and 2 of ulterior security in the event of open Rupture. Towards these the abovementioned measures to be recommended but without detail as to *numbers* of *Ships troops* &c.

The idea to be thrown in that the hope of an accommodation without proceeding to open Rupture ought not to be abandoned or precluded while measures of self preservation ought not to be omitted or delayed & ought to be prosecuted with a vigour commensurate with the present urgency & eventual greatness of the danger.

The further idea ought to be thrown out that France by formally violating has in fact suspended the Treaties—that they ought consequently *ad interim* to be suspended by us—since the observance on one side & not on the other can only produce inconvenience & embarrassment.

The necessity of ample provision of revenue & force ought to be dwelt upon with emphasis accompanied by strong allusions to great future possible dangers. In all this a stile *cautious, solemn, grave*, but free from asperity or insult is all important.[9]

8. In the margin opposite this paragraph H wrote: "I think the overthrow of England & the Invasion of this Country very possible so possible that any other calculation for our Government will be a bad one."

9. In the margin opposite this paragraph H wrote: "There has been latterly too much *Epigram* in our Official Stile."

An Embargo seems now to be out of place & ineligible.

With regard to Spain nothing more seems adviseable at present than to instruct our Minister at that Court [10] to make respectful but energetic representations pressing the fulfilment of the Treaty. The less is done with her Officers [11] here the better.

With regard to Holland or Portugal it is not perceived that any thing is requisite except to endeavour to continue & cultivate good understanding.

As to England it is believed to be best in any event to avoid *alliance*. Mutual interest will command as much from her as Treaty. If she can maintain her own ground she will not see us fall a prey —if she cannot, Treaty will be a feeble bond. Should we make a Treaty with her & observe it we take all the chances of her fall. Should France endeavour to detach us from a Treaty if made, by offering advantageous terms of Peace it would be a difficult & dangerous Task to our Government to resist the popular cry for acceptance of her terms. Twill be best not to be entangled.

Nothing more therefore seems proper to be done than through Mr. King [12] to communicate the measures in Train—to sound as to cooperation in case of open Rupture, the furnishing us with naval force—pointing the cooperation to the Floridas Louisiana & South American possessions of Spain,[13] if rupture as is probable shall extend to her. To prevail on Britain to lodge in her Minister here [14] ample authority for all these purposes; but all this without engagement or commitment in the first instance. All on this side the Mississippi must be *ours* including both Floridas. Twill be best to charge with the instructions a confidential Messenger.

In addition to these measures Let the President recommend a day to be observed as a day of fasting humiliation & prayer. On religious ground this is very proper—On political, it is very expedient. The Government will be very unwise, if it does not make the most of the religious prepossessions of our people—opposing the honest

10. David Humphreys was United States Minister Plenipotentiary to Spain.

11. Carlos Martinez, Marquis de Casa Yrujo, was the Spanish Minister to the United States and Josef de Viar was the Spanish commissioner and consul general in the United States.

12. Rufus King.

13. For information on Francisco de Miranda's plans to liberate Spain's American colonies, see Miranda to H, April 1, 1797; February 7, 1798.

14. Robert Liston.

enthusiasm of Religious Opinion to the phrenzy of Political fanaticism. The last step appears to me of the most precious importance & I earnestly hope, it will by no means be neglected.

To James Monroe [1]

[New York, January, 1798] [2]

Sir

A resolution long formed to act with deliberation in any case which should involve the extremity, to which I am now driven, has occasionned me to defer my reply to your letter of the first instant.[3]

Though I have it in my power completely to satisfy any candid mind, that I never give a shadow of cause for the resentment you avow; yet the indelicate doubt of the veracity of my representation to you, and the deliberate spirit of animosity, which are manifested in your letter, forbid any further attempts on my part to pursue the road of explanation.

I therefore acquiesce in the necessity you impose on me.

And have accordingly authorised   [4] who will deliver you this, and who will act as my friend in the affair, to adjust with you a time and place of meeting for such a decision of the matter as you appear to desire.[5]

I am Sir   Your humble servant

ADf, Hamilton Papers, Library of Congress.
    1. For background to this letter, which H presumably decided not to send, see Monroe to H, December 2, 1797. See also the introductory note to Oliver Wolcott, Jr., to H, July 3, 1797; the "Reynolds Pamphlet," August 25, 1797.
    2. H did not date this letter. The letter "of the first instant," however, had to be dated January 1, 1798, because as of December 24, 1797, Monroe was still receiving advice on whether or not to send any letter to H (see Monroe to H, December 2, 1797, note 1).
    3. Letter not found.
    4. Space left blank in MS.
    5. On February 8, 1797, Thomas Jefferson wrote to Monroe: "I had expected Hamilton would have taken the field . . ." (AL [incomplete], Thomas Jefferson Papers, Library of Congress; copy, James Monroe Papers, Library of Congress).

Certificate of Admission to Practice Law in the United States Circuit Court for the New York District in the Eastern Circuit

[New York, February 4, 1798]

United States of America, ⎱
New York District.   ⎰ ss.   I Edward Dunscomb, Clerk of the

Circuit Court of the United States for the New York District in the Eastern Circuit Pursuant to the Statute of the United States, entitled, "An Act laying Duties on stamped Vellum, Parchment and Paper." [1] Do hereby Certify, that on the Sixth Day of April, in the year of our Lord, one thousand seven hundred and Ninety six Alexander Hamilton was duly admitted a Counsellor of the said Court,[2] in the same to appear, and therein to practice as such according to the Rules and Orders of the same Court, and the Constitution and Laws of the said United States.

In Testimony whereof, and pursuant to the Statute aforesaid, I have hereunto subscribed my name as Clerk as aforesaid, this Fourth Day of February in the twenty-third year of the Independence of the United States.

Edward Dunscomb
Clerk

DS, Hamilton Papers, Library of Congress.
 1. Section 7 of this act reads: "That every counsellor, solicitor, attorney, proctor or advocate, who hath been or shall be admitted, enrolled or registered, in any court of the United States, before he shall at any time after the said thirty-first day of December next, prosecute, carry on, or defend any action, suit or proceeding in any court of the United States, shall take out a certificate of such admission, enrolment or registry from the clerk or prothonotary of the court granting such admission . . ." (1 *Stat.* 529 [July 6, 1797]).
 2. See "Admission to Practice Law in the United States Circuit Court for the New York District in the Eastern Circuit," April 6, 1796.

From Theodore Sedgwick

Philadelphia, February 4, 1798. "I hope you will be able to procure a dismissal of the injunction in the case of Morris and Bacon,[1] and I am the more anxious, as I have lately heard there is some doubt of the solidity of the circumstances of Mr. Morris. . . ."

ALS, Hamilton Papers, Library of Congress.

1. Sedgwick is referring to the case of *Thomas Morris and James Wadsworth* v *William Bacon,* in which H was counsel for the defendant. In H's Law Register, 1795–1804, the following entry appears:

"Bacon ⎤
adsm ⎬   In Chancery
Morris ⎦

March 1799 hearing for dissolution of injunction" (D, partially in H's handwriting, New York Law Institute, New York City). The injunction was dissolved on March 2, 1799 (MS Minutes of the New York Court of Chancery, 1798–1801 [Hall of Records, New York City]). On May 18, 1799, the Court ruled further: "Upon a petition for Rehearing this Cause . . . the Chancellor doth order and direct, that the complainants confess a Judgment to the defendant's for the sum due upon the Bond . . ." (MS Minutes of the New York Court of Chancery, 1798–1801 [Hall of Records, New York City]).

From Francisco de Miranda

a Londres ce 7. Fevrier 1798.

il-y-a quelque tems mon respectable et cher ami que j'eûs le plaisir de vous ecrir de Paris,[1] et de vous envoier en même tems une Certaine Correspondence du ministre Diplomatique Munrroe [2]—ainsi que une histe. de la Revolution française par Desodoard.[3] je n'ai reçü aucune repponse encore; ce qui ne me surprends pas, atendü la suitte des evenements: et sur tout ma nouvelle proscription du 18. frutidor,[4] que je crois être le Coup-de-grace pour toutte ⟨es⟩pece de Liberté en france—à moins d'un miracle!!! mais c'est le conti⟨ne⟩nt Americain tout entier qui semble se preparer à secour le joug d'une maniere sage et raisonable—et de former un corps d'allience avec les Etats-Unis, et l'Angleterre. C'est sur cet objet que je suis venü ici. je ne peus pas vous dire davantage pour le moment; mais J'espere que bientôt vous en sçaurez plus.[5] Le Pamphlet de Harper [6] est une chose excelente, et qui s'accorde parfaitement avec nos dispositions, et celles de ce pais-ici. Conduisez vous en consequence—et je crois que nous aurons gain de Cause à la fin, tant pour le bonheur du nouveaux monde, que pour la tranquilité de celui-ci. Mr. King votre ministre-ici, me parait un homme excelent, et fort instruit. Je le frequente avec plaisir, et je commence à lui faire quelques confidences sachant qu'il vous est ataché—ecrivez lui à ce sujet, et envoiez moi vos Lettres sous son addresse.

je n'ai pas le tems aujour'hui d'ecrir à notre Ami le Genl. Knox,[7] ni au Col: Smith—[8] faisez moi le plaisir de leurs dire mille choses de ma part, et de leurs communiquer la partie que vous jugerez à propos de celle-ci. mes compliments respectueux a mad. Hamilton.[9]

à Dieu.   yours sincerely   F. de Miranda.

Alexander Hamilton, Esq.

ALS, Hamilton Papers, Library of Congress.
  1. Miranda to H, April 1, 1797.
  2. James Monroe.
  3. See Miranda to H, April 1, 1797, note 3.
  4. This is a reference to the *coup d'état* of 18 Fructidor (September 4, 1797). See Rufus King to H, September 9, 1797. Miranda was banished by a resolution of September 4, 1797 (Duvergier, *Lois*, X, 44). See also *Réimpression de L'Ancien Moniteur*, September 6, 1797.
  5. On February 7, 1798, Rufus King wrote in cipher to Timothy Pickering: "I have had some reason to believe that the prospect of our being engaged in the war has revived the project that on more than one occasion has been meditated against South America. . . . Miranda who was certainly engaged in this scheme at the time of the affair of Nootka . . . came to this Country a few weeks since. He has been with the Ministry here by their desire or with their permission. The object is the compleat independence of South America; to be effected by the cooperation of England and the United States" (LS [deciphered], RG 59, Despatches from United States Ministers to Great Britain, 1791–1906, Vol. 7, January 9–December 22, 1798, National Archives). On February 26, 1798, King wrote to Pickering: "Two points have within a fortnight been settled in the English cabinet respecting South America. If Spain is able to prevent the overthrow of her present government and to escape being brought under the entire controul of France, England, between whom and Spain, notwithstanding the war, a certain understanding appears to exist, will at present engage in no scheme to deprive Spain of the possessions of South America. But if, as appears probable, the army destined against Portugal, and which will march thro' Spain, or any other means which may be employed by France, shall overthrow the Spanish government, and thereby place the resources of Spain and of her colonies at the disposal of France, England will immediately commence the execution of a plan long since digested and prepared for the compleat independence of Sh. America. If England engages in this plan, she will propose to the United States to cooperate in its execution. Miranda will be detained here, under one pretence or another, until events

shall decide the conduct of England" (copy [deciphered], RG 59, Despatches from United States Ministers to Great Britain, 1791–1906, Vol. 7, January 9–December 22, 1798, National Archives).

6. *Observations on the Dispute between the United States and France: Addressed by Robert G. Harper, Esq. of South Carolina to His Constituents, in May, 1797* (Philadelphia: Thomas Bradford, 1797).

7. Henry Knox.

8. William S. Smith, John Adams's son-in-law, who had been secretary of the American legation in London in 1785, toured Europe with Miranda before returning to the United States in 1788.

9. H endorsed this letter: "Several Years ago this man was in America much heated with the project of liberating S Amer from the Spanish Domination. I had frequent conversation with him on the subject & I presume expressed ideas favourable to the object and perhaps gave an opinion that it was one to which the UStates would look with interest. He went then to England upon it. Hence his present letter. I shall not answer because I consider him as an intriguing adventurer."

From Robert Morris [1]

Alexander Hamilton Esqr
at New York or Albany

Hills [near Philadelphia]
Feby 7th 1798

Dear Sir

You will find annexed the exact statement of your Acct with me for the ten thousand dollars which you lent me with the Interest computed to the 27th Novr last Balance in your favour on that day being $6002.25.[2] This Balance my Son Tom is to assume with interest from that date accordingly I have closed the Acct in my Books by charging you and crediting him for the same which I hope will meet with your & his approbation. I shall ever be gratefull for your Kindness in this transaction and lament that it should have been attended with inconvenience as to loss it was ever my determination to secure you against, Mr Rees [3] is still here settling his own affair, he has the Deed the execution of which he will prove (being one of the Witnesses) before a Master in Chancery or Judge of your State so as to entitle it to be recorded [4]

Yrs   RM

LC, Robert Morris Papers, Library of Congress.

1. This letter concerns the payment of the balance of a debt which Morris owed to H. For an explanation of the contents of this letter, see the introductory note to H to Morris, March 18, 1795. See also Morris to H, March 31, June 2, 23, 30, July 18, 20, 1795; June 17, 27–30, November 19, December 8, 1796; June 2, 10, September 9, October 2, 27, November 23, December 21, 1797; January 17, 1798.

2. Copy, Hamilton Papers, Library of Congress. See also the enclosure to Morris to H, February 17, 1798.
3. James Rees.
4. For the transactions in this sentence, see Morris to H, January 17, 1798.

From Henry Sheaff [1]

Philadelphia, February 10, 1798. "Mr Robert Morris by Art and address has nearly Ruined me. . . .[2] I have paid Ten Thousand Dollars have yet to pay Seven Thousands. . . .[3] It was suggested to me by applying to you, as Mr. Morris holds large quantity of Lands in your State,[4] you have it in your power to put me on Some plan to Secure my Debt. . . . Any mode you can devise for me will be thankfully Received. . . ."

ALS, Hamilton Papers, Library of Congress.
1. Sheaff was a Philadelphia wine merchant.
2. Sheaff had endorsed notes for Morris, which were protested. For Morris's unsuccessful efforts to settle this debt, see Morris to Sheaff, June 5, 19, July 11, 24, August 8, 15, 21, September 4. October 31, December 11, 28, 1797; January 25, 1798 (LC, Robert Morris Papers, Library of Congress).
3. In the summary of his various debts Robert Morris wrote: "*Henry Sheaff.* The balance at his credit is $7,684.30.
"Ledger C. Folio 118. It is but lately that I enter'd up his accounts, and struck the balance. I have not given him the statement, and he thinks the balance is much larger; and so I thought before entering up his accounts against me. Under that impression, he is included in the Genesee security to T[homas]. F[itzSimons]., J[oseph]. H[igbee]. & R[obert]. M[orris]. jun'r. I also assigned to him my claim on Henry Philips. Mr. Sheaff lent me his name; and the balance arising from the use of it forms his claim, which is therefore considered of the first class." (Morris, *In the Account of Property*, 54.) The "Ledger C," to which Morris refers above, is located in the Historical Society of Pennsylvania, Philadelphia.
4. For Morris's original purchases in the Genesee country, see H to Morris, March 18, 1795, note 29. For Morris's explanation of the disposition of these lands, see Morris, *In the Account of Property*, 1–7.

From James McHenry

Philad. 12 Feby 179[8] [1]

My dear Sir

I have recd. the result of my request to you [2] and cannot be otherwise than pleased with it and thankful to you for it.

The inclosed is my first conceptions on certain past transactions [3] in which you were a participator and perhaps adviser.[4] I believe every thing was then conducted as it has been since, after due deliberation and for the best. It is however no easy matter to account for the great expenditures that have taken place beyond what had been expected, and not involve predecessors in some censure, and at the same time insinuate a belief or expectation that similar expences may in future be avoided, thereby to encourage to the prosecution of the same object. Will you run over the pages and make such notes or alterations as may appear to you proper. I have no copy of what I send. It is the first draught. I pray you therefore not to lose any of the sheets and to return it as soon as may be with your commentary.

Will it not be proper to subjoin to my letter certain propositions for consideration. Such as

The expediency of using the timber that has been procured for the purposes for which it was obtained or

2. The propriety of making a provision for a permanent navy yard and gradual or prompt purchase of timber &c proper for building and equipping ships of different rates &c.

Give me some reflexions on this point.

Yours affectionately   J McHenry

ALS, Hamilton Papers, Library of Congress.
    1. McHenry mistakenly dated this letter "1797."
    2. See McHenry to H, January 20, 1798; H to McHenry, January 27–February 11, 1798.
    3. The enclosure was a draft of McHenry's report on "Naval Expenditures, and the Disposition of Materials." This report is dated March 22, 1798, and it was communicated to the House of Representatives on May 1, 1798 (*ASP, Naval Affairs*, I, 37–56).
    4. On March 27, 1794, Congress passed "An Act to provide a Naval Armament" (1 *Stat.* 350–51) authorizing the President to provide four ships of forty-four guns each and two ships of thirty-six guns each. Although the War Department was responsible for the construction of the ships, the Treasury Department had been charged with responsibility for procuring the supplies for them. See Henry Knox to H, April 21, 1794.

To James McHenry

[New York, February 13, 1798]

My Dear Sir
    Yours of yesterday with its inclosure are come to hand & will be attended to as speedily as possible.

I take the liberty to trouble you with the inclosed to receive the amount (which though the accumulated interest on all my Stock from the beginning of the funding system will be short of 200 Dollars). When received, pay yourself one hundred, our friend *Lewis* [1] seven, & deliver the rest to Wolcott who has lately been paying for some books for me.

This idea, drawing my attention to this little object, as the sum is not worth retaining, has induced me to make sale of the principal to Le Roy Bayard & McEvers.[2] While at the Notary's & not having previously consulted them, I put your name in the power to transfer the Stock.[3] This power they will send you. Pray comply with it & excuse this almost *indecorum* on my part.[4]

Yrs. truly A H

Feby 13. 1798

James Mc.Henry Esq

ALS, Montague Collection, MS Division, New York Public Library; copy, Hamilton Papers, Library of Congress.

1. William Lewis was an attorney in Philadelphia who had been a judge of the Federal District Court for the Eastern District of Pennsylvania in 1791 and 1792. See H to James McHenry, August 17, 1797.

2. Herman LeRoy, William Bayard, and James McEvers. An entry in H's Cash Book, 1795–1804, for February 14, 1798, reads: "Cash Dr to Stock received of Le Roy &c for the amount of my three ℔ Cents 411.55" (AD, Hamilton Papers, Library of Congress).

3. DS, Charles Roberts Autograph Collection of the Haverford College Library, Haverford, Pennsylvania.

4. In the margin opposite this paragraph McHenry wrote:

"recd at the Bank of U.S. 144 48
N. A. B. 24 8
168 56
Paid Mr Woolcot 40 20
Lewis 7
Self 100
147 20
Balance sent 21 36
168 56."

The following entries appear in H's Cash Book, 1795–1804:
"Mar 24. 1798
Cash Dr. to Stock received of J Mc.Henry for interest on my 3 ℔ C Stock from the commencement of the funding system to this day 168.65
"Expences Dr. to Cash
paid for drs. sometime since at Philadelphia 100
paid Lewis 7
107.
"April 1
Library Acct. for paid toward Enciclopedia 40.20"
(AD, Hamilton Papers, Library of Congress).

From Elihu H. Smith [1]

[New York, February 14, 1798]

Sir,

The New York Society for promoting the Manumission of Slaves &c.[2] at their Stated meeting in January last,[3] directed the referrence, of the two following articles, (of a report then made to them by their Committee on the Circular Address of the last Convention,[4]) to the Counsellors [5] of the Society: "Art. 1st. To transmit Copies to the ensuing Convention, of any Laws, relative to Slaves, which may be enacted, by the Legislature of this State, previous to the Session of the said Convention, and since the Convention of 1797."

"Art. 5th (of the Report) To give information to the Convention of the exertions, and of their issue, which have been made by this Society, to obtain a repeal, or amelioration, of the Laws relative to Slaves."

The Report represents these as duties to be fulfilled by the Society; which they have, accordingly, determined to execute, & for this purpose have ordered this referrence to their Counsellors—who are further directed "to prepare their report therein, with all convenient dispatch; and, when prepared, to deliver it over to such persons as may, hereafter, be chosen to represent the Society, in the Convention to be held in June 1798."

The other members of the Counsel of the Society, of which you are first-named, are: Peter Jay Munro, William Johnson, & Martin S. Wilkins, Esquires.[6]

I am respectfully Yours,   E. H. Smith Secy.

Feb: 14. 1798.
Alexr. Hamilton Esqr.

ALS, Hamilton Papers, Library of Congress.
    1. Smith was a physician, poet, and author who served as secretary of the New York Society for Promoting the Manumission of Slaves. On September 19, 1798, he died of yellow fever.
    2. The first meeting of the society was held on January 25, 1785 ("Minutes

of the Society for Promoting the Manumission of Slaves," New-York Historical Society, New York City). For H's participation in the establishment of
the society, see "Attendance at a Meeting of the Society for Promoting the
Manumission of Slaves," February 4, 1785.

3. This meeting was held on January 16, 1798 ("Minutes of the Society for
Promoting the Manumission of Slaves," New-York Historical Society, New
York City).

4. The convention met in Philadelphia, May 3–9, 1797. See *Minutes of the
Proceedings of the Fourth Convention of Delegates from the Abolition Societies Established in Different Parts of the United States. Assembled at Philadelphia, on the third day of May one thousand seven hundred and ninety-
seven, and continued by adjournments until the ninth day of the same month,
inclusive* (Philadelphia: Zachariah Paulson, Jr., 1797).

5. H was elected a counsellor on January 16, 1798 ("Minutes of the Society
for Promoting the Manumission of Slaves," New-York Historical Society,
New York City).

6. Munro, Johnson, and Wilkins were New York City attorneys. In addition,
Johnson was one of the vice presidents of the Society for Promoting the
Manumission of Slaves and president of Columbia College from 1787 to 1800.

From Robert Morris [1]

Alexr Hamilton Esqr   Philada Feby 17th 1798

Dear Sir

The bearer hereof Mr James Rees [2] takes with him the deed for
the genesee land which is to be lodged with you for my son Thomas
and it may either be lodged with you as an Escrow to secure in the
first instance the payment of the bala due to you which is $6002 as
℔ the accot which is forwarded to Thomas so that you and he may
settle and the remainder of the purchase money is to be paid to me
but if Tom wants the deed not to be lodged as an escrow, for my
part I shall be content with such arrangements as you & he may
agree for

Your Obedt hble servt   RM

LC, Robert Morris Papers, Library of Congress.

1. This letter concerns the balance of a debt which Morris had owed to H
and which had been assumed by his son Thomas. For this debt and for an explanation of the contents of this letter, see the introductory note to H to
Morris, March 18, 1795. See also Morris to H, March 31, June 2, 23, 30, July
18, 20, 1795; June 17, 27–30, November 19, December 8, 1796; June 2, 10, September 9, October 2, 27, November 23, December 21, 1797; January 17, February 7, 1798.

2. See Morris to H, January 17, 1798.

[ENCLOSURE] [3]

Dr.   Alexander Hamilton Esqre in Accot. Currt. with Robert Morris   Cr.

1794		Dollars		1794		Dolls.
Augt 2	To Cash paid this day	500.		June 4	By Cash received this day	10,000.
1795				1797		
July 18	To my Remittance this day in Harrison & Stererts Bills on J. H. Cazenove nephew & Co favr Josiah Bacon at 60 days			Novr 27	By Int on $10,000 from 4 June 1794 to this day is 3 years 5 Mos 23 days	2 088.33
	no 13. £250 } £500 Stg @ 5 pct	2333.33			[Received the Balance of this account from Thomas Morris by his Bond and Mortgage dated the first of February last to John B. Church Albany March 8th. 1798 A Hamilton]	
	14. 250					
	To my Remitte. 30 June last in Jos. Higbees order at 30 ds. on Hartshorne & Linsey	1500				
Decr. 8	To my Remitte this day in sd. Higbees order at 30 ds. on Hartshorne & Linsey	1000				

		yr	mos	ds	Dollars
1797					
Novr. 27	To Int on $500 from 2d. Augt. 1794.	3	3	25	99 58
	2333.33 from 18 July 1795	2	4	9	330 17
	1500 from 30 July "	2	4	—	210
	1000 from 8 Jany 1796	1	10	18	113
	To Thomas Morris who assumes to pay the Balance of this Account.				6002.25
	Dollars				12,088.33

Cr. side totals:

	Dollars
	12,088.33
Ballance brought down	6002 25
[Interest to last of Jany on 4666.67	46 66
	6048 91]

3. D, partially in H's handwriting, Mr. Walter N. Eastburn, East Orange, New Jersey.

With the exception of the bracketed material, which is in H's handwriting, this account is a copy of the one which Morris enclosed in Morris to H, February 7, 1798. On February 7, 1798, Morris wrote to his son Thomas: "You will receive inclosed with this my letter of today to Colo Alexr Hamilton with a State of his Acct with me balle in his favour due on the 27th. Novr last being $6002.25 say six thousand & two dollars twenty five Cents, which you are to assume with interest from that day being the date. . . . I have left open the letter to Colo Hamilton for your inspection and you may if you think proper Keep a copy of the Acct. When you have done with it Seal and deliver or send the letter and Acct as directed" (LC, Robert Morris Papers, Library of Congress). The account printed above is apparently the copy which Thomas Morris made.

To James McHenry

[New York, February 20, 1798]

My Dear Friend

I regret that my occupations have not permitted me to give your report [1] more than a cursory reading, before my being obliged to leave the city for Albany.[2] I have put it under a cover addressed to you. If it cannot conveniently wait my return, which will be in a fortnight, it will be sent you upon a line directed to Mr. "James Inglis [3] at Col Hamilton's No. 26 Broad Way N York." desiring him to forward you the Packet left in his care for you which will be done.

Interpret favourably & forgive

Yr. Affect

A Hamilton
N York 20 Feby
1798

ALS, James McHenry Papers, Library of Congress.
1. See McHenry to H, February 12, 1798.
2. H was going to Albany to attend the Court of Errors for an argument on behalf of his client Louis Le Guen. See Goebel, *Law Practice*, II, 48–164. See also H to Isaac Gouverneur and Peter Kemble, January 19, 1797; H to Elizabeth Hamilton, April 16, 1797; Le Guen to H, January 7, 1798; Gouverneur to H, January 7, 9, 1798; Moses Lopez to H, January 7, 1798.
3. James Inglis, Jr., was a clerk in H's law office.
On August 6, 1798, the New York Supreme Court read and filed "A Certificate of Alexander Hamilton bearing date the 4th of August 1798 . . . whereby it appears that James Inglis junior has served a Clerkship in his Office

from the eighth day of June 1795 to the fourth day of July & that he is of good moral Character." Inglis was admitted to practice before the New York Supreme Court on August 9, 1798 (MS Minutes of the New York Supreme Court, July 31–August 11, 1798 [Hall of Records, New York City]).

From Marquis de La Tour du Pin [1]

London, February 21, 1798. ". . . J'ai bien plus de pardons a vous demander pour un objet particulier. Je desire vendre ma ferme d'albany. . . .[2] Les bontés a jamais pretieuses, qu'ont eues pour nous, la famille de Madame hamilton, me font esperer qu'à votre Sollicitation elle voudra bien encore nous rendre le Service de faire vendre ce petit objet. . . ."

ALS, Hamilton Papers, Library of Congress.
    1. Frédéric-Séraphin, marquis de La Tour du Pin, was an aide-de-camp to Lafayette during the American Revolution. After the war he was named colonel of the Royal-Vaisseaux and served as an aide to his father, Jean-Frédéric de Paulin, comte de La Tour du Pin, the Minister of War. La Tour du Pin served as minister to Holland until his recall in 1792. In 1794 he emigrated to the United States, where he bought and operated a farm near Albany. Three or four years later he went to England.
    2. On March 1, 1796, La Tour du Pin's property was described as follows in an advertisement in the [Philadelphia] *Courrier de la France et des Colonies:* "A farm newly occupied by the undersigned, situated in Watervleit, five miles north of Albany, and two miles north of Troy; it contains 206 acres. There is a pleasant house with dependencies, all in very good order; a large orchard full of choice trees, and a good sized vegetable garden where there are also fruit trees and bushes. The farm utensils are also for sale, a complete assortment, with several milk cows and mares that will bear . . ." (quoted in Francis S. Childs, *French Refugee Life in the United States, 1790–1800* [Baltimore, 1940], 94).

From Oliver Wolcott, Junior

[Philadelphia] Feby 24. 1798

Dr. Sir

I have recd. a Letter from Mr. Josiah Meigs [1] one of the Professors of Yale College, informing me that he has been offered one half of the establishment of the Daily Advertizer published in your City, which it is proposed should be edited & conducted jointly by Mr. Meigs & Mr. Morten [2] the present Proprietor. To enable Mr. Meigs to accept the proposal it will however be necessary for him to advance by the first of May next, the Sum of Eight Thousand Dollars, which he wishes to obtain on Loan to be repaid in four annual Installments with Interest at seven per Centum per Annum—On condition that the property purchased together with the monies & debts to be recd. shall be pledged to the lenders as security.

As the success of the publication & of course the security of the Lenders will in a great measure depend on the talents & discretion of the Editor, it is important that the character & qualifications of Mr. Meigs should be known, and with this view I address you.

Mr. Meigs & myself were Classmates at Yale College; he is unquestionably a man of talents & was early distinguished as a literary & scientific proficient; as a man of honour he has ever [been] highly esteemed by his acquaintance.

I believe Mr. Meigs to be well qualified to be the Editor of a paper; he has had some experience in this line; a paper conducted by him at New Haven about ten years since was deservedly esteemed one of the best printed at that time; & it certainly contributed considerably to establish in the scene where it circulated the principles & opinions upon which the present Government rests for support.

But candour requires me [to] say that Mr. Meigs has been latterly considered as opposed to the leading measures of the Government; In what degree the report is well founded I cannot say: It is probable that his feelings were irritated during a residence in Bermuda in the years 1793 & 1794, when he was a witness to the violent & unjust conduct of the British Cruizers & may have thought that different measures ought to have been adopted by the Govt.[3] It is my opinion notwithstanding any contrary suggestions that entire reliance may be placed in the good sense & candour of Mr. Meigs that he will not suffer a paper edited under his direction to assume a complexion justly displeasing to the friends of the Government, whose opinion may be different from his own.

I make this communication that you may so far as may be convenient as you shall judge proper obviate any obstacle to the success of his plan, on the score of erroneous political sentiments.

I am Dear Sir with perfect respect, y   O W.

A Hamilton Esq

ADfS, Connecticut Historical Society, Hartford.

1. Meigs, a lawyer, had been graduated from Yale in 1778. He had been the founder and publisher of *The New Haven Gazette* from 1784 to 1786 and the *New Haven Gazette, and Connecticut Magazine* from 1786 to 1789, city clerk of New Haven, and professor of mathematics and natural philosophy at Yale College. He did not get the money or job for which Wolcott recommended him in this letter.

2. *The* [New York] *Daily Advertiser*, which had been founded by Francis Childs in 1785 and published by Childs and John Swaine from 1788 to 1794, was published by John Morton from 1796 to July 10, 1798.

3. From 1789 to 1794, Meigs was in Bermuda looking after the interests of Connecticut clients. Toward the end of his stay there, he was arrested for treason and acquitted only after the intercession of Governor Henry Hamilton. While in Bermuda he argued the causes of American claimants of captured property in the Court of Vice Admiralty.

Wolcott's suspicions about Meigs's oppositon to the Federalists were well founded; he was an enthusiastic Republican as early as 1795.

To Elizabeth Hamilton

[Albany, March 1, 1798]

This, My beloved Eliza, is the third letter I have written to you [1] since I left—but I am still without a line from you. I hope the Post of today will bring me one, or I shall be uneasy.

We are getting on in our cause [2] so that I expect to leave this place on Sunday or Monday.

Your father is better again. All the rest of your family are well. They speak of you with tenderness and this you know gives me much pleasure.

We cannot yet judge how our cause will end; but the appearances hitherto are not against us. Poor Le Guen is much buyoyed up. It is to be hoped he may not have cause to be proportionally depressed. Kiss My Dear Children for me & accept a thousand kisses for yourself.

Yrs. ever Affect   A H
                                                                   March 1. 1798

ALS, Hamilton Papers, Library of Congress.
1. Letters not found.
2. See H to James McHenry, February 20, 1798, note 2.

From Effingham Lawrence [1]

Flushing, New York, March 1, 1798. Seeks to retain Hamilton as his attorney in a case involving patent rights for a brickmaking machine.

ALS, Hamilton Papers, Library of Congress.
  1. Lawrence, a veteran of the American Revolution, "commenced buisness in 1781 at No. 199 Pearl street, one door below Maiden lane, and retired from business in 1794 with an ample competency, purchasing . . . [an] elegant country residence . . . fronting the water, in the town of Flushing, to which place he removed the same year, and died in 1800" (Walter Barrett [pseud. for Joseph A. Scoville], *The Old Merchants of New York City* [New York, 1885], V, 98).

To Theodore Sedgwick [1]

[Albany, March 1–15, 1798]

My Dear Sir
  In my opinion these things—
  The President ought to make a solemn and manly communication to Congress the language grave and firm but without invective—in which after briefly recapitulating the progress of our controversy with France the measures taken toward accommodation & stating their degrading result—he ought to advert to the extremely critical posture of Europe the excessive pretensions of France externally her treatment to the neutral powers generally dwelling emphatically on the late violent invasion of their Commerce as an act destructive of the Independence of Nations [2]—to state that eventual dangers of the most serious kind hang over us and that we ought to consider ourselves as bound to provide with the utmost energy for the immediate security of our invaded rights & for the ultimate defence of our liberty and Independence—and conclude with a recommendation on general terms to adopt efficient measures for increasing our revenue for protecting our commerce, for guarding our sea ports and ultimately for repelling Invasion—intimating also that the rela-

tions of Treaty which have subsisted between us and France & which have been so intirely disregarded by her, ought not to remain by our Constitution & laws binding upon us but ought to be suspended in their Operation till an adjustment of differences shall re-establish a basis of connection and intercourse between the Two Countries—taking especial care however that merely defensive views be indicated.

The measures which I should contemplate would be these— [3]

To authorise our Merchantmen to arm and to defend themselves against any attempt to capture them by French Cruisers—and to capture & bring in any vessels by which they should be attacked.

To complete our Frigates already begun and to enable our president to provide equip & arm immediately a number of vessels of from 16 to 20 guns to serve as Convoys. These vessels also to be authorised to capture all those that may attack them and all French *privateers* found within Twenty leagues of our Coast.

The President to be likewise authorised in case a War should break out to provide Ten ships of the line. The terms to be broad enough to enable him to purchase them or take them in pay of a foreign power, but this idea to be covered under general expressions.

Our regular army to be increased to 20000 Men horse foot & infantry & a provisional army of 30000 more to be added.

The fortification of our ports to be seriously prosecuted & not less than a million of Dollars appropriated to this purpose.

All the sources of Revenue Land Tax house tax &c. &c. to be immediately resorted to—that we may be equal to this expenditure & early providing the most essential sinew of War may be able to carry it on with Vigour & avoid Running in Debt. A loan commensurate with the objects to be authorized.

The Treaties between the two Countries to be declared suspended.

These measures to a feeble mind may appear gigantic. To yours they can only appear excessive as far as it may seem impracticable to get them adopted. For my part I contemplate the possible overthrow of England—the certainty of invasion in that case, without unqualified submission and the *duty* and *practicability* even in that event of defending our honor and rights.

Let the President also call to his aid the force of religious Ideas by a day of fasting humiliation & prayer. This will be in my opinion no less proper in a political than in a Religious View. We must oppose to political fanaticism religious zeal.

I do not enter into a detail of reasons for the respective measures. They will all occur to you. I consider the Independence of Nations as threatened and I am willing to encounter every extremity in the preservation of ours.

In all our measures however, let it be seen that final rupture is desired to be avoided as far as may consist with security & the UStates still stand ready to accommodate. I write in extreme haste.

Yrs.   A H

P.S. I beseech you Exert yourself to induce the New England Representatives if not already done to forward the Bill for providing an indifferent mode of Trial in Cases in which *States are* concerned. Without it a civil war may ensue between us & Connecticut & the Foederal Interest will at any rate be much injured.[4]

ALS, Massachusetts Historical Society, Boston; copy, Massachusetts Historical Society, Boston.
  1. The first paragraph has been inked out. The paragraph reads: "An extreme pressure of professional engagements has prevented 'til now a reply to the political ‹–› of your last letter. The late European Advices have brought matters to a ‹crisis›, and the ‹–› must speedily be decided. What is to be done?" H wrote in the margin opposite this paragraph: "Temperate language but bold measures suit the situation."
  2. See H to McHenry, January 27–February 11, 1798.
  3. The recommendations which follow are substantially the same as those which H sent to McHenry on January 27–February 11, 1798, and to Timothy Pickering on March 17, 1798.
  4. This is a reference to a land dispute between Connecticut and New York which was known as the Connecticut Gore controversy. For this controversy, H's part in it, and the relevant documents, see Goebel, *Law Practice*, I, 657–84.
  On March 1, 1798, Representative James A. Bayard of Delaware "reported a bill supplementary to the act for establishing the Judicial Courts of the United States" (*Annals of Congress*, VII, 1116). In the House of Representatives on March 15, 1798, "The bill supplementary to the act establishing the Judicial Courts of the United States, was read the third time, and the yeas and nays were called on the question of passing. (This bill originated upon a resolution brought forward by a member from New York, . . . [Edward Livingston] in order to provide for the trial of causes in which two States are concerned, in the next adjoining State, in order to obtain an impartial trial. What gave immediate cause to the bill was a case which is now pending between the States of New York and Connecticut.) After considerable debate, the yeas and nays were taken, and stood 29 to 58 . . ." (*Annals of Congress*, VIII, 1266–67).

From James McHenry

[Philadelphia, March 8, 1798]

My dear Hamilton.

I have transferred your certificates and received your interest. I have also paid to Mr. Wolcott 40 20/100. I will pay to Mr. Lewis 7 dolls who says he does not recollect that you owed him any thing. I have retained 100, and herewith inclose the balance or 21 36/100.[1]

If this should find you at New-York I intreat you to spare an hour or two to the essay, and to send it to me as soon as possible. If you should not have returned to New York I have desired Mr. Inglis to transmit it.[2]

Apathy prevails as yet within and out of Congress.

Yours affectionately   James McHenry
                                                        8 March 1798

Interest reced at the Bank of the U.S.   144 48
        4 quarters at the B. N. Am.   24 8
                                    Total   168 56

Alexr Hamilton Esq

ALS, Hamilton Papers, Library of Congress.
    1. For an explanation of the contents of this paragraph, see H to McHenry, February 13, 1798.
    2. For an explanation of the contents of this paragraph, see McHenry to H, February 12, 1798; H to McHenry, February 20, 1798.

To Timothy Pickering

New York March 17. 1798

Dr. Sir

I make no apology for offering you my opinion on the present state of our affairs.

I look upon the Question before the Public as nothing less than whether we shall maintain our Independence and I am prepared to do it in every event and at every hazard. I am therefore of opinion that our Executive should come forth on this basis.

I wish to see a *temperate*, but *grave solemn* and *firm* communication from the President to the two houses on the result of the advices from our Commissioners.[1] This communication to review summarily the course of our affairs with France from the beginning to the present moment—to advert to her conduct towards the neutral powers generally, dwelling emphatically on the last decree respecting vessels carrying B Manufacture⟨s⟩ [2] as an unequivocal act of hostility against all of them [3]—to allude to the dangerous and vast projects of the French Government—to consider her refusal to receive our Ministers as a virtual denial of our Independence and as evidence that if circumstances favour the plan we shall be called to defend that Independence our political institutions & our liberty against her enterprizes—to conclude that leaving still the door to accommodation open & not proceeding to final rupture. Our duty our honor & safety require that we shall take vigorous and comprehensive measures of defence adequate to the immediate protection of our Commerce to the security of our Ports and to our eventual defence in case of Invas⟨ion⟩ with a view to these great objects calling forth and organising all the resources of the Country. I would at the same time have the President to recommend a day of fasting humiliation and prayer. The occasion renders it proper & religious ideas will be useful. I have this last measure at heart.

The measures to be advocated, by our friends in Congress to be these— [4]

I   Permission to our Merchant Vessels ⟨to⟩ arm and to capture those which may ⟨attack⟩ them.

II   The completion of our frigates & the provision of a considerable number of sloops of war not exceeding 20 Guns. Authority to capture all attacking & *privateers* found within 20 leagues of our Coast.

III   Power to the President in genera⟨l⟩ terms to *provide* and *equip* 10 Ships of the line in case of open rupture with any foreign power.

IV   The increase of our military establishment to 20000 & a provisional army of *3000⟨0⟩* besides the Militia.

V   The efficacious fortification of our principal ports say Portsmouth Boston New Port, New London, N York, Philade⟨lphia⟩ Norfolk Baltimore Wilmington NC Charlest⟨on⟩ Savannah. Tis waste of money to be more diffusive.

VI   The extension of our Revenue to all the principal objects of Taxation & a loan commensurate with the contemplated expenditure.

VII   The *suspension* of our Treaties with France till a basis of Connection shall ⟨be⟩ reestablished by Treaty.

In my Opinion bold language & bold measures are indispensable. The attitude of *calm defiance* suits us. Tis vain to talk of Peace with a Power with which we are actually in hostility. The election is between a tame surrender of our rights or a state of mitigated hostility. Neither do I think that this state will lead to general rupture, if France is unsuccessful ⟨and⟩ if successful there is no doubt in my mind tha⟨t⟩ she will endeavour to impose her Yoke upon us.

Yrs. with true esteem   A Hamilton

Dr Sir   If Robert Troupe [5] resigns his office of District Judge The President cannot make a better choice than of Samuel Jones Esqr. the present comptroller of the State.[6] I understand he will accept.

Timothy Pickering Esq

ALS, Masachusetts Historical Society, Boston.
    1. This is a reference to the dispatches which President John Adams had received from Charles Cotesworth Pinckney, Elbridge Gerry and John Marshall, Envoys Extraordinary to France. On March 5, 1798, Adams sent a message to Congress stating that the dispatches had been received but had not been deciphered (*ASP, Foreign Relations*, II, 150).
    2. The material within broken brackets in this letter has been taken from *JCHW*, VI, 269–71.
    3. The French decree, dated January 11, 1798, reads: "1st. The character of a vessel, relative to the quality of neuter or enemy, is determined by her cargo. In consequence, every vessel loaded in whole or in part, with English merchandise, is declared lawful prize, whoever the owner of the said merchandise may be.
    "2. Every foreign vessel which in the course of her voyage, shall have entered an English port, shall not enter France, except in case of distress: she shall depart thence as soon as the causes of her entry shall have ceased." (*ASP Foreign Relations*, II, 151.)
    4. The recommendations which follow are substantially the same as those which H sent to James McHenry on January 27–February 11, 1798, and to Theodore Sedgwick, March 1–15, 1798.
    5. Troup had been appointed on December 10, 1796 (*Executive Journal*, I,

215). Following his resignation he was replaced by John Sloss Hobart on April 12, 1798 (*Executive Journal*, I, 269).

6. Jones, a New York lawyer with whom H had been associated in several cases during the seventeen-eighties, was the state's first comptroller, serving from 1797 to 1800. He had been a member of the Continental Congress, the New York Ratifying Convention, and the New York Assembly from 1786 to 1790; he was a member of the New York Senate from the Southern District from 1791 to 1799.

To Pierre Charles L'Enfant [1]

[New York, March 20, 1798]

Dr. Sir

On my return from Albany,[2] I received a letter[3] referring to one[4] I sometime since received from you. I am ashamed to tell you that the extreme pressure of my engagements has hindered my attending hitherto to your wish. I shall in the course of this week pay such attention to it as my relative situation permits, guided by a real desire to be useful to you.

Yrs. with regard

A Hamilton
March 20 1798

Major L'Enfant.

ALS, Digges-L'Enfant Morgan Collection, Library of Congress.

1. L'Enfant was a French volunteer in the Corps of Engineers during the American Revolution. In order to provide adequate accommodation for the new Federal Government in New York City, its temporary seat, L'Enfant was commissioned to convert City Hall on Wall Street into Federal Hall. He was hired to plan the new Federal City, but because of a dispute with the commissioners of the Federal District, he stopped working on this project in February, 1792. In July, 1792, the directors of the Society for Establishing Useful Manufactures hired L'Enfant to lay out the society's manufacturing center in Paterson, New Jersey. In April, 1794, he was appointed temporary engineer at Fort Mifflin on Mud Island in the Delaware River.

2. An entry in H's Cash Book, 1795–1804, under the date of March, 1798, reads: "Expences Dr. for journey to Albany & back 40" (AD, Hamilton Papers, Library of Congress). H had been in Albany, among other reasons, for the case of *Louis Le Guen* v *Isaac Gouverneur and Peter Kemble*. For this case and H's part in it, see Goebel, *Law Practice*, II, 48–164.

3. Letter not found.

4. Letter not found.

To Timothy Pickering

[New York, March 23, 1798]

My Dear Sir

I understand that the *Senate* have called upon the President for papers.[1] Nothing certainly can be more proper; and such is the universal opinion here. And it appears to me essential that so much, as possibly can, be communicated. Confidence will otherwise be wanting—and criticism will ensue which it will be difficult to repel. The observation is that Congress are called upon to discharge the most important of all their functions & that it is too much to expect that they will rely on the influence of the Executive from materials which may be put before them. The recent examples of the British King are cited.[2] Pray let all that is possible be done.

Yrs. truly   A Hamilton
                                                         March 23. 1798

T Pickering Es

ALS, Mr. Hugh Fosburgh, New York City; copy, Massachusetts Historical Society, Boston.

1. On March 5, 1798, President John Adams sent the following message to Congress: "The first despatches from our envoys extraordinary, since their arrival at Paris, were received at the Secretary of State's office at a late hour last evening. They are all in a character which will require some days to be deciphered, except the last, which is dated the 8th of January, 1798. The contents of this letter are of so much importance to be immediately made known to Congress, and to the public, especially to the mercantile part of our fellow citizens, that I have thought it my duty to communicate them to both Houses, without loss of time" (*ASP, Foreign Relations*, II, 150).

The dispatch from Charles Cotesworth Pinckney, John Marshall, and Elbridge Gerry, to which Adams refers, reads: "We embrace an unexpected opportunity to send you the 'Redacteur' of the 5th instant, containing the message of the Directory to the council of five hundred, urging the necessity of a law to declare, as good prizes, all neutral ships having on board merchandises and commodities, the production of England, or of the English possessions, that the flag, as they term it, may no longer cover the property. And declaring, further, that the ports of France, except in case of distress, shall be shut against all neutral ships, which, in the course of their voyage, shall have touched at an English port. A commission has been appointed to report on the message, and it is expected that a decree will be passed in conformity to it.

"Nothing new has occurred since our last, in date of the 24th ultimo. We can only repeat that there exists no hope of our being officially received by the Government, or that the objects of our mission will be in any way accomplished." (*ASP, Foreign Relations*, II, 150–51.)

For the French decree of January 11, 1798, see H to Pickering, March 17, 1798, note 3.

On March 19, 1798, Adams sent the following message to Congress: "The despatches from the envoys extraordinary of the United States to the French Republic, which were mentioned in my message to both Houses of Congress, of the 5th instant, have been examined and maturely considered.

"While I feel a satisfaction in informing you that their exertions for the adjustment of the differences between the two nations have been sincere and unremitted, it is incumbent on me to declare that I perceive no ground of expectation that the objects of their mission can be accomplished on terms compatible with the safety, the honor, or the essential interests of the nation.

"This result cannot, with justice, be attributed to any want of moderation on the part of this Government, or to any indisposition to forego secondary interests for the preservation of peace. Knowing it to be my duty, and believing it to be your wish, as well as that of the great body of the people, to avoid, by all reasonable concessions, any participation in the contentions of Europe, the powers vested in our envoys were commensurate with a liberal and pacific policy, and that high confidence which might justly be reposed in the abilities, patriotism, and integrity of the characters to whom the negotiation was committed. After a careful review of the whole subject, with the aid of all the information I have received, I can discern nothing which could have insured or contributed to success, that has been omitted on my part, and nothing further which can be attempted, consistently with maxims for which our country has contended, at every hazard, and which constitute the basis of our national sovereignty.

"Under these circumstances I cannot forbear to reiterate the recommendations which have been formerly made, and to exhort you to adopt, with promptitude, decision, and unanimity, such measures as the ample resources of the country can afford, for the protection of our seafaring and commercial citizens; for the defence of any exposed portions of our territory; for replenishing our arsenals, establishing foundries, and military manufactures; and to provide such efficient revenue as will be necessary to defray extraordinary expenses, and supply the deficiencies which may be occasioned by depredations on our commerce.

"The present state of things is so essentially different from that in which instructions were given to the collectors to restrain vessels of the United States from sailing in an armed condition, that the principle on which those orders were issued has ceased to exist. I therefore deem it proper to inform Congress that I no longer conceive myself justifiable in continuing them, unless in particular cases, where there may be reasonable ground of suspicion, that such vessels are intended to be employed contrary to law.

"In all your proceedings it will be important to manifest a zeal, vigor, and concert, in defence of the national rights, proportioned to the danger with which they are threatened." (*ASP, Foreign Relations*, II, 152.)

On March 20, 1798, "A motion was made [in the Senate], by Mr. [Joseph] Anderson [of Tennessee], as follows: *Resolved*, That the President of the United States be requested to lay before the Senate the instructions given to the American Commissioners at Paris; and, also, all communications he hath received from them relative to the object of their mission" (*Annals of Congress*, VII, 525). On April 3 the Senate agreed that "further consideration" of Anderson's motion "be postponed" (*Annals of Congress*, VII, 535). In the meantime, the House had acted, for on April 2 it approved the following resolution: "*Resolved*, that the President of the United States be requested to communicate to this House, the instructions to and despatches from, the Envoys Extraordinary of the United States to the French Republic, mentioned in the Message of the 19th instant" (*Annals of Congress*, VIII, 1370–71). On April 3 Adams sent copies of the instructions to and dispatches from the commissioners to both the House and the Senate (*Annals of Congress*, VII, 535–36; VIII, 1374–75). The dispatches, which are a documentary history of the XYZ affair, are printed along with the instructions and Adams's message in *ASP, Foreign Relations*, II, 153–68. Adams sent further material from Pinckney, Marshall, and Gerry to Congress on May 4 (*ASP, Foreign Relations*, II, 169–82).

2. On November 3, 1797, for example, the King presented to both Houses of Parliament the "Papers respecting the Negotiation for Peace with France" (*The Parliamentary History of England*, XXXIII [London, 1818], 909–63).

From Timothy Pickering

Philadelphia March 25. 1798.

Dear Sir,

I duly received your letter of the 17th. No apology will be necessary for a communication of your opinion at any time; and at the present crisis your opinion is peculiarly acceptable.

Prior to the receipt of your letter, the President had determined to recommend the observance of a general fast; and had desired one or both the chaplains of Congress to prepare the draught of a proclamation. This has since been issued.[1]

The idea of a solemn and firm communication from the President to the two Houses of Congress, on the state of our affairs with France, had occurred to me; with this addition, that it might be more impressive if delivered personally by the President himself from the Speaker's chair, as at the opening of a session. That this speech should comprehend as brief a statement of our relations to France as would consist with an adequate representation of *our good faith* and of *her perfidy and hostile acts,* from the commencement of the French

ALS, Hamilton Papers, Library of Congress; ALS, letterpress copy, Massachusetts Historical Society, Boston.

1. John Adams's proclamation, which was issued on March 23, 1798, reads in part: ". . . And as the United States of America are, at present, placed in a hazardous and afflictive situation, by the unfriendly disposition, conduct and demands of a foreign power, evinced by repeated refusals to receive our Messengers of Reconciliation and Peace, by depredations on our commerce, and the infliction of injuries on very many of our Fellow-Citizens, while engaged in their lawful business on the seas: Under these considerations it has appeared to me that the DUTY of imploring the mercy and benedictions of Heaven on our Country demands, at this time, a special attention from its inhabitants.

"I have therefore thought fit to recommend, and I do hereby recommend

Revolution to the present moment.[2] This paper should be prepared by me: [3] I wish I were able to do full justice, to the subject. A proper time to deliver this communication would be when the letters from our envoys should be laid before Congress: for a motion has been made in the Senate for that purpose; & it is expected a like motion will be made in the House: [4] but independently of these motions, it is really desirable that not Congress only but the people at large should know the conduct of the French Government towards our Envoys, and the abominable corruption of that Government; together with their enormous demands for *money*. These are so monstrous as to shock every reasonable man, when he shall know them. It pretended that the Directory was vastly exasperated against the American Government for some expressions in the President's speech to Congress on the 16th of May last; [5] that those

---

that *Wednesday the ninth day of May* next be observed throughout the United States, as a day of solemn humiliation, fasting and prayer. . . ." ([Philadelphia] *Aurora. General Advertiser*, March 28, 1798.)

2. For Adams's messages to Congress on United States relations with France, see H to Pickering, March 23, 1798, note 1.

3. No such "paper" was sent to Congress by Adams. Instead, on April 3, 1798, he sent to Congress a brief note enclosing the XYZ papers. See H to Pickering, March 23, 1798, note 1.

4. For the Senate and House resolutions, see H to Pickering, March 23, 1798, note 1.

5. The paragraphs of the President's message of May 16, 1797, to which the Directory objected read: "I With this conduct of the French government it will be proper to take into view the public audience, given to the late minister of the United States, on his taking leave of the Executive Directory. The speech of the President discloses sentiments more alarming than the refusal of a minister, because more dangerous to our independence and union, and at the same time studiously marked with indignities towards the Government of the United States. It evinces a disposition to separate the people of the United States from the Government; to persuade them, that they have different affections, principles and interests from those of their fellow-citizens, whom they themselves have chosen to manage their common concerns; and thus to produce divisions fatal to our peace. Such attempts ought to be repelled with a decision, which shall convince France and the world, that we are not a degraded people, humiliated under a colonial spirit of fear, and sense of inferiority, fitted to be the miserable instruments of foreign influence, and regardless of national honour, character and interest.

"II The diplomatic intercourse between the United States and France being at present suspended; the Government has no means of obtaining official information from that country; nevertheless there is reason to believe that the Executive Directory passed a decree on the 2d of March last, contravening, in part, the treaty of amity and commerce of 1778, injurious to our lawful commerce and endangering the lives of our citizens. A copy of this decree will be laid before you.

"III While we are endeavouring to adjust all our differences with France,

expressions, or their application to the Government of France, must be *disavowed*. This however was a bold pretence only, as the means of extorting moneys; for after it had been said that the *Directory for its own honor and the honor of the Republic* would insist on this reparation, our Envoys were plainly told that there was a practicable substitute, *more valuable than both*. They asked what? Money! Money! was the answer. This reparation when it should be made, was only paving the way for new and I may say unlimited demands of more money—a sum equal to all the spoliations of the French on our commerce! to enable the Republic to pay our merchants? No! for the present use of the Republic. Then a mode might be agreed on for the *liquidation* of the merchants claims, to be compensated at some future period—and in the mean time, until the treaty should be concluded, (which that government might procrastinate indefinitely) their depredations were not to be restrained! Besides this, we must purchase promptly 32 millions of Dutch inscriptions (12,800,000 dollars) at par, and rely on the existence and ability of the Batavian Republic to redeem them. The sum of all was, in the words of the agent "Il faut de l'argent—il faut beaucoup d'argent;" and without this our envoys were explicitly told, *by the secret but unofficial agents*, that if they remained in Paris six months longer, they would not advance one step.[6]

You will be aware that I communicate these important facts to you *in perfect confidence;* for as you interest yourself so deeply in public affairs and are so obliging as to communicate your opinions,

---

by amicable negotiation, the progress of the war in Europe, the depredations on our commerce, the personal injuries to our citizens, and the general complexion of affairs, render it my indispensable duty to recommend to your consideration effectual measures of defence.

"IV It is impossible to conceal from ourselves, or the world, what has been before observed, that endeavours have been employed to foster and establish a division between the Government and the people of the United States. To investigate the causes which have encouraged this attempt is not necessary. But to repel, by decided and united councils, insinuations so derogatory to the honour, and aggressions so dangerous to the constitution, union and even independence of the nation, is an indispensable duty." (*ASP, Foreign Relations,* II, 160–61.)

For the speech in its entirety, see *Annals of Congress,* VII, 54–59.

6. Pickering's information on the XYZ affair was taken from the dispatches which were sent by the three United States commissioners and submitted to Congress by President Adams on April 3, 1798 (*ASP, Foreign Relations,* II, 150–68).

I thought you should be possessed of facts. I communicate them of myself, without the privity of any one.

Yet after all these inadmissible demands, and the peremptory declaration with which I closed the above detail, the envoys meant to make one more formal application by letter to Talleyrand, on the 10th of January; [7] 2 days after their last letter to me [8] which you have seen was communicated to Congress, and in which they say "there existed no hope of their being officially recd. or in any way accomplishing the object of their mission." These objects they meant to state and *discuss*, as if they had been formally received. There is but one solution of this measure of the envoys, & of their long suffering patience in their mortifying situation—To convince all their countrymen that it was not *possible* to adjust our differences with the present government of France. We do not know the result of this intended application; nor whether the envoys have left France: and it is these uncertainties which prevented the President's displaying this scene of insults, extortion, ambition & iniquity, by communicating the envoys letters before Congress and the country.

I must assure you further that Portugal *purchased* her peace [9]—

7. This letter was not sent. Instead the American commissioners wrote to Charles Maurice de Talleyrand-Périgord, Minister of Foreign Affairs, on January 27, 1798 (*ASP, Foreign Relations*, II, 169–82).

8. See Elbridge Gerry, John Marshall, and Charles Cotesworth Pinckney to Pickering, January 8, 1798 (*ASP, Foreign Relations*, II, 150–51).

9. On August 10, 1797, a treaty of peace and amity between France and Portugal was signed at Paris guaranteeing the neutrality of Portugal on condition that France should be treated in Portuguese ports as the most favored nation. See Rufus King to H, June 27, 1797, note 5. For the text of the treaty, incorrectly dated August 20, see Martens, *Recûeil*, VI, 413–19. The Council of Ancients ratified the treaty on September 12, 1797. On October 26, 1797, however, the Directory declared the treaty to be void on the ground that the Queen of Portugal had not ratified it within the stipulated two months (Duvergier, *Lois*, X, 102). Although the Portuguese ambassador, Antonio D'Araujo D'Azevedo, produced the Portuguese ratification on December 1, 1797, he was imprisoned from January through March, 1798 (*The* [London] *Times*, January 6, 11, April 9, 1798).

In describing these events, *The* [London] *Times*, March 10, 1798, stated: "In the course of July last, the Portuguese Minister at Paris, Chevalier d'Araujo, *purchased a Peace* at the rate of 6 millions of Livres Tournois, which were paid down in hard cash. When afterwards, by the revolution of the 18th Fructidor (4th September) the Directory had got rid of the majority of the two Councils, which was in favour of Peace, it refused to ratify the treaty, on pretence that the Court of Portugal had industriously protracted the consumation of the treaty. On the Chevalier d'Araujo's desiring the business to be definitely set-

that the very money paid by her in hand, enabled the triumvirs in the Directory to march troops and effect the revolution of September 4th: [10] and yet the day after they received the intelligence of the peace finally concluded with the Emperor,[11] these same villains declared the Portuguese treaty void. Doubtless they now demand more money to renew it than Portugal can conveniently muster; and probably nothing would satisfy the monsters, short of the riches of Lisbon, and the pillage of the Churches, and the subversion of the kingdom. Then will come the turn of Spain, of whom they have demanded the cession of Louisiana—and *pressed* their demand until the Prince of Peace knows not how any longer to resist it. And in order to plunder Spain and subvert the monarchy, unprincipled men will not want pretences—perhaps this will be sufficient—that Spain has not contributed as she ought to the common warfare, as an ally bound by a league offensive as well as defensive.[12]

What ought we to do, in respect to *Louisiana?* A Letter this day recd. from Colo. Humphreys dated at Madrid the 4th of January renders it probable that the information we have had from New Orleans is true—that Gayoso has recd. orders to evacuate the posts.[13] His information (Colo. Humphreys') was from a man em-

---

tled, a new ransom was demanded by the French Government. Surprised at this demand, the Portuguese Minister strongly reprobated this scandalous imposition, but instead of an answer, he was sent to the *Temple prison. . . .*"

10. This is a reference to the *coup d'état* of 18 Fructidor, Year V (September 4, 1797).

11. The Treaty of Campo Formio, October 17, 1797.

12. By the Treaty of San Ildefonso, August 19, 1796, Spain joined France in the war against England. For the text of the treaty, see *Réimpression de L'Ancien Moniteur,* XXVIII, 426–28.

13. David Humphreys was United States Minister Plenipotentiary to Spain. Manuel Gayoso de Lemos was the Spanish governor of Louisiana from 1797 until his death in 1799. In the Treaty of Friendship, Limits, and Navigation between the United States and Spain, October 27, 1795 (Pinckney's Treaty), Article II provided for a boundary line between the United States and Spanish territories and that "if there should be any troops, Garrisons or settlements of either Party in the territory of the other according to the above mentioned boundaries, they shall be withdrawn from the said territory . . ." (Miller, *Treaties,* II, 319–20).

Humphreys's letter, which is dated January 5 (not January 4), reads in part: ". . . I hasten to advise you that a Spanish Gentleman, in public Office, who has been conversant with the Proceedings of this Government in relation to the U. S., has just informed me, that there is almost a certainty (after several contradictory proceedings) positive orders have been dispatched some months since, for the delivery of the Posts on the Mississipi to the U. S." (ALS, RG 59,

ployed in a public office conversant in American affairs; and Colo.
H. considered it *almost certain*. Perhaps these orders may have resulted from Spain's seeing or fearing the necessity of ceding Louisiana to France—and hence concluding that she might as well do a
grateful thing to us before the surrender.[14] Louisiana is easy to be
defended by a force commanding the Mississipi at its mouth, another at the *English Turn* (half way between New Orleans and the
mouth of the river) and at the entrance from the sea into the lake
Pontchartrain. The Spanish force in all Louisiana is small—probably
not rising to a thousand men, from the Bellize to the Missouri. The
deepest channel of the three mouths of the Mississipi does not exceed fifteen feet of water; and it requires a pretty strong breeze to
advance against the current.

I have one more important fact to mention—That since Lord
Malmsbury's negociation was broken off by the French,[15] that Gov-

---

Despatches from United States Ministers to Spain, 1792–1906, Vol. 4, October
27, 1797–October 29, 1799, National Archives).

14. On August 27, 1796, James Monroe wrote to Pickering: "I am told the
treaty with Spain is probably concluded; and by which France is to have
Louisiana and the Floridas" (Monroe, *A View of the Conduct of the Executive*,
363). In a subsequent letter, however, Monroe wrote: "I send you a copy of the
treaty of alliance, offensive and defensive, between France and Spain; and
which, as you will observe, contains no stipulation respecting Louisiana, and
the Floridas. Nor have I any reason to conclude that there is any secret article
on that subject. I rather think, from what I can collect, that it is a point still
in negociation between those powers; and protracted by the indecision of
France, whether to accept or reject it; and whose decision upon it may be essentially influenced by the relation which is to subsist, for the future between
this country and ours. If this relation is established upon the close footing they
wish it, then I think it probable (should the question be so long protracted)
this government will decline accepting it; from the fear it might prove a cause
of jealousy between us and weaken that connection. But should the contrary be
the result, then I think, they will act otherwise, and endeavor not only in this
respect, but by every other practicable means, to strengthen their own resources; and to make themselves as independent of us as possible . . ." (Monroe
to Pickering, September 21, 1796 [Monroe, *A View of the Conduct of the
Executive*, 378]).
On June 5, 1797, Charles Cotesworth Pinckney, Monroe's successor, informed
Pickering that "the negotiations respecting the exchange of Louisiana and
Florida are at present suspended but will probably be resumed" (LC, RG 59,
Despatches from United States Ministers to France, 1789–1869, Vol. 5, Novem-
ber 17, 1796–September 24, 1797, National Archives).
15. In the autumn of 1796, James Harris, first earl of Malmesbury, unsuccess-
fully sought to negotiate a peace treaty with France at Lille. In July, 1797, he
tried once more, but negotiations broke down completely after the events of
September 4, 1797, and by September 19, 1797, Malmesbury had returned to
England.

ernment has offered more advantageous terms to the British administration than Lord Malmsbury demanded—on the single condition of a *douceur* of *one million sterling*—to be divided among the Directory and the ministers: Talleyrands share was to be one hundred thousand pounds sterling, for his department! I might have mentioned, that these miscreants had the modesty to ask of our envoys a douceur of but fifty thousand pounds sterling. Merlin [16] was to have no part of the 50,000. because the privateersmen had paid him liberally for his opinions against our vessels and those of other neutrals. This reminds me of another very important omission in my preceeding details—In regard to the adjustment of our claims for spoliations, all the vessels condemned for want of the rôle d'equipage were not to be brought into view: their condemnations were to be admitted as irrevocable—because Merlin had written a treatize [17] to justify their condemnation!! Were there ever such devils out of pandemonium? There was afterwards some relaxation on this point—Claims might be made for such vessels—and if Citizen *Merlin* could be *convinced* they were just—why they might be considered.

Of the measures you recommend [18]

1. Permission to arm merchant vessels is given by the President's withdrawing his restriction: [19] but there should be a law to regulate them. The opposition are very angry with the president's act on this point.

2. The frigates are to be completed: [20] but the providing of a number of sloops of war will be vehemently opposed.

16. Philippe Antoine Merlin of Douai was appointed Minister of Justice in 1795 and was made a member of the Directory following the *coup d'état* of September 4, 1797.

17. See the "Report of the French Minister of Justice [Merlin], made to the Executive Directory the 12th Brumaire, an 5me. (3d November, 1797) of the French Republic" (*Message from the President of the United States, Transmitting Copies of the Several Instructions to the Ministers of the U. States to the Government of France, and of the Correspondence with Said Government, Having Reference to The Spoliations by that Power, on the Commerce of the United States, Anterior to September 30, 1800, &c. . . . .* [Washington, 1826], 178–79).

18. See H to Pickering, March 17, 1798.

19. For Adams's message to Congress of March 19, 1798, see H to Pickering, March 23, 1798, note 1.

20. See "An Act for additional appropriation to provide and support a Naval Armament" (1 *Stat.* 547 [March 27, 1798]).

3. To authorize the President to provide ten ships of the line would be still more opposed. I have supposed they might easily be obtained of Great Britain: and that even for the bare act of *victualling* such a fleet by us, the British would keep one on our coast—and perhaps subject them to our orders, the British Minister concurring: but to command them fully, they must be our own.

4. There would be equal opposition to an increase of our military establishment.

5. There would perhaps be little opposition to a better, perhaps to a formidable fortifying of our principal ports. Where are the Engineers? The Frenchmen in general employed in 1794 [21] only wasted our money: almost any artillery officer of our revolution army would probably do better. Colo. Vincent's plans at New-York are probably a fortunate exception.[22]

6. The revenue will not be extended but on the adoption of the defensive measures that will make additional revenues indispensible.

7. Instead of a *suspension,* I have for some time thought we should declare the *annihilation* of all our treaties with France. The repeated infractions of them on her part would justify us in making void the whole.

A disclosure of our actual situation with France, by communicating the Envoys letters, would, I presume, detach so many of the adherents to opposition leaders as to enable the real friends to their country to take promptly all the requisite measures. On these details, favour me with your opinions.

Truly & respectfully yours,   T. Pickering.[23]

Alexander Hamilton Esqr.

21. On March 20, 1794, Congress passed "An Act to provide for the Defence of certain Ports and Harbors in the United States" (1 *Stat.* 345–46). Consistent with the provisions of this act, Henry Knox in the spring of 1794 appointed the following men as engineers to provide plans for the fortification of the stipulated ports and harbors: Etienne Nicholas Marie Bechet, chevalier de Rochefontaine; Charles Vincent; Pierre Charles L'Enfant; John Jacob Ulrich Rivardi; John Vermonnet; Nicholas Francis Martinon; and Paul Hyacinte Perrault (*ASP, Military Affairs,* I, 72–102).

22. Vincent's "General observations on the defence of the Harbor and City of New York," dated "New York, 1794," is printed in *ASP, Military Affairs,* I, 78–80.

23. In the margin Pickering wrote and crossed out the following incomplete postscript: "P S A vessel is in two or three days to be dispatched with letters to recall our envoys, if they should still be in France; unless the."

From Timothy Pickering

Philaa. March 25. 1798.

Dr. Sir

The inclosed [1] I wrote last evening for your information. This morning I received your *open* letter of the 23d. As soon as a vessel shall be dispatched for France with letters of recall to our envoys, I presume the President will communicate their letters to Congress —whether demanded or not. If the envoys or any of them should be found in France (of which there is a bare possibility) they are to demand their passports and return—unless they shall have concluded a treaty, or are *actually* in treaty with persons vested with equal powers, and that the treaty proceeds with candour on the part of the French Government.[2] This vessel will probably sail the ensuing Thursday.

What shall we say to the British Government? You hint at nothing. The opposition party have often insinuated that a treaty offensive & defensive has doubtless been already concluded with Great Britain—a friend of mine yesterday told me that he was asked if such a treaty had not arrived. The truth is, that not one syllable has been written to Mr. King or any one else upon the subject. I confess it to have been for some time my opinion that provisional orders should be sent to Mr. King. Mr. King in one of his latest letters desires to be particularly instructed.[3] The dispatch boat [4] may be diverted to go from France to England with such instructions (which will be in cypher) or may go directly to Falmouth, and there may ascertain whether our Envoys are or are not in France.

Your ideas communicated on this subject, and on the facts stated in the inclosed, will be highly acceptable to me: I wish to receive them on Wednesday.

Very truly & respectfully yours   T. Pickering

Alexander Hamilton Esq

ALS, Hamilton Papers, Library of Congress; ALS, letterpress copy, Massachusetts Historical Society, Boston.
    1. This enclosure was the first of two letters which Pickering wrote to H on March 25, 1798.

2. On March 23, 1798, Pickering wrote to Pinckney, Marshall, and Gerry: ". . . the President presumes that you have long since quitted paris and the French dominions: yet actuated as you were with an ardent desire to preserve peace, which you knew would be so grateful to your country; and having for this object manifested unexampled patience, and submitted to a series of mortifications; as you also proposed to make one more direct attempt, subsequent to the date of your last letter, to draw the French Government to an open negotiation; there is a bare possibility that this last effort may have succeeded: The President, therefore, thinks it proper to direct

"1. That if you are in treaty with persons duly authorized by the Directory, on the subjects of your mission, then you are to remain and expedite the completion of the treaty, if it should not have been concluded. Before this letter gets to hand, you will have ascertained whether the negotiation is or is not conducted with candour on the part of the French Government: and if you shall have discovered a clear design to procrastinate, you are to break off the negotiation, demand your passports and return. For you will consider that *suspense* is ruinous to the essential interests of your country.

"2. That if on the receipt of this letter, you shall not have been received, or, whether received or not, if you shall not be in treaty with persons duly authorized by the Directory, with full and equal powers, you are to demand your passports and return.

"3. In no event is a treaty to be purchased with money, by loan or otherwise. There can be no safety in a treaty so obtained. A loan to the Republic would violate our neutrality: and a douceur to the men now in power might by their successors be urged as a reason, or as a precedent for further and repeated demands." (LC, RG 59, Diplomatic and Consular Instructions of the Department of State, 1791–1801, Vol. 4, February 1, 1797–November 30, 1798, National Archives.)

3. On January 9, 1798, Rufus King wrote to Pickering: "If, as now I believe, our Mission to France shall totally fail, it will be very important in guiding my opinions and conduct, that I should be early and fully possessed of the views of our Government . . ." (King, *The Life and Correspondence of Rufus King,* II, 270).

4. On December 14, 1800, Pickering sent to H a copy of the second paragraph of the letter printed above. On the copy Pickering placed an asterisk after "dispatch boat" and wrote: "The 'dispatch boat' was the U. S. brig. Sophia, then going to France with orders to the envoys relative to their return."

To Timothy Pickering

[New York] March 27. 1798
10 oClock Tuesday

My Dear Sir

I have this moment received your two favours of the 25th. I am delighted with their contents; but it is impossible for me to reply particularly to them so as to reach you *tomorrow* as you desire.

I will therefore confine myself to one point. I am against going immediately into alliance with Great Britain. It is my opinion that her interest will ensure us her cooperation, to the extent of her power, and that a Treaty will not secure her further. On the other hand a Treaty might entangle us; public opinion is not prepared for it—it would not fail to be represented as to the *point to which our previous conduct was directed* and in case of offers from France satisfactory to us the public faith might be embarrassed by the calls of the people for accommodation & peace.

The *desideratum* is that Britain could be engaged to lodge with her *Minister here* powers commensurate with such arrangements as exigencies may require & the progress of Opinion permit. I see no good objection on her part to this plan. It would be good policy in her to send to this Country a dozen frigates to pursue the directions of this Government.

If *Spain* would cede *Louisiana* to the UStates I would accept it, absolutely if obtainable absolutely, or with an engagement to *restore* if it cannot be obtained absolutely.

I shall write again tomorrow.[1]

Yrs. truly   A Hamilton

T Pickering Esq

ALS, Hamilton Papers, Library of Congress; copy, Massachusetts Historical Society, Boston.

1. The copy is endorsed: "original sent to Col. Hamilton Decr. 14, 1800 as requested in his letter of November 13, 1800."

From George Washington

[*Mount Vernon, March 27, 1798.*[1] *Letter not found.*]

1. "List of Letters from G—— Washington to General Hamilton," Columbia University Libraries.

Account with Robert H. Dunkin [1]

[New York, March 30, 1798]

Upon an Order of R H Dunkin & Wife dated the 14 of March for £384.10 NYC—I have paid Mrs. Watkins 936 Dollars & 25 Cents this being the sum actually received by me on her account.[2]

NY March 30. 1798
A Hamilton [3]

ADS, Hamilton Papers, Library of Congress.

1. Dunkin (or Duncan) was a Philadelphia attorney and notary public.
2. This is a reference to the case of *Elisha Lamoreux* v *Robert Henry Duncan and Elizabeth his wife*. On August 31, 1786, Lamoreux, a resident of Rensselaerville in Albany County, New York, borrowed £384.10 New York Currency from Elizabeth Watkins, who later married Dunkin. As security for this debt, Lamoreux gave Elizabeth Watkins a mortgage on a tract of land in Philipse Manor in Westchester County, New York. In 1795 Lamoreux filed a bill in the New York Court of Chancery to prevent Dunkin from selling the mortgaged land (Bill, filed January 22, 1795 [Chancery Decrees Before 1800, L-244, Historical Documents Collection, Queens College, New York City]). On December 13, 1797, with H as counsel for the defendants and Peter J. Munro for the complainant, the Court of Chancery ordered Dunkin to reconvey the land to Lamoreux upon receipt of $961.25 (or £384.10, which was the original debt), plus $31.81 for "Costs at Law" (MS Minutes of the New York Court of Chancery, 1793–1797 [Hall of Records, New York City]).
An entry in H's Cash Book, 1795–1804, under the date of January 4, 1798, reads: "Cash Dr. to Robert H. Dunkin received of A Brown on his Account 936.25" (AD, Hamilton Papers, Library of Congress). Andrew Brown was a New York City merchant. A second entry in H's Cash Book, 1795–1804, under the date of March 24, 1798, reads: "Robert H Dunkin Dr to Cash paid C. Watkins ⅌ his order 936.25" (AD, Hamilton Papers, Library of Congress). Charles Watkins was a New York City merchant.
3. An endorsement on the back of this document reads: "Recd. New York July 12 1799 of A Hamilton Esqr Twenty five Dollars Being in full of the within A/c for Mrs E. Dunkin $25."

The Stand No. 1 [1]

[New York, March 30, 1798]

The enlightened friend of America never saw greater occasion of disquietude than at the present juncture. Our nation, thro its official

The [New York] *Commercial Advertiser*, March 30, 1798.
1. The other numbers of "The Stand" are dated April 4, 7, 12, 16, 19, 21, 1798.

organs, has been treated with studied contempt and systematic insult; essential rights of the country are perseveringly violated, and its independence and liberty eventually threatened, by the most flagitious, despotic and vindictive government that ever disgraced the annals of mankind; by a government marching with hasty and colossal strides to universal empire, and, in the execution of this hideous project, wielding with absolute authority the whole physical force of the most enthralled, but most powerful nation on earth. In a situation like this, how great is the cause to lament, how afflicting to every heart, alive to the honor and interest of its country, to observe, that distracted and inefficient councils, that a palsied and unconscious state of the public mind, afford too little assurance of measures adequate either to the urgency of the evils which are felt, or to the magnitude of the dangers which are in prospect.

When Great Britain attempted to wrest from us those rights, without which we must have descended from the rank of freedom, a keen and strong sense of injury and danger ran with electric swiftness thro the breasts of our citizens. The mass and weight of talents, property and character, hastened to confederate in the public cause. The great body of our community every where burnt with a holy zeal to defend it, and were eager to make sacrifices on the altar of their country.

If the nation, with which we were called to contend was then the preponderating power of Europe; if by her great wealth and the success of her arms she was in a condition to biass or to awe the cabinets of princes; if her fleets covered and domineered over the ocean, facilitating depredation and invasion; if the penalities of rebellion hung over an unsuccessful contest; if America was yet in the cradle of her political existence; if her population little exceeded two millions; if she was without government, without fleets or armies, arsenals or magazines, without military knowlege;—still her citizens had a just and elevated sense of her rights, were thoroughly awake to the violence and injustice of the attack upon them, saw the conduct of her adversary without apology or extenuation; and, under the impulse of these impressions and views, determined with little short of unanimity to brave every hazard in her defence. This magnanimous spirit was the sure pledge, that all the energies of the country would be exerted to bring all its resources into action, that whatever was possible would be done towards effectual opposition; and this, combined with the immense advantage of distance, warranted the expectation of ultimate success. The event justified the expectation and rewarded the glorious spirit from which it was derived.

Far different is the picture of our present situation! The FIVE TYRANTS of France,[2] after binding in chains their own countrymen, after prostrating surrounding nations, and vanquishing all external resistance to their revolutionary despotism at home, without the shadow of necessity, with no discernible motive, other than to confirm their usurpation and extend the sphere of their domination abroad—These implacable TYRANTS obstinately and remorselessly persist in prolonging the calamities of mankind, and seem resolved as far as they can to multiply and perpetuate them. Acting upon the pretension to universal empire, they have at length, in fact tho not in name, decreed war against all nations not in league with themselves; and towards this country, in particular, they add to a long train of unprovoked aggressions and affronts the insupportable outrage of refusing to receive the extraordinary ambassadors whom we sent to endeavor to appease and conciliate.[3] Thus have they, in regard to us, filled up the measure of national insult and humiliation. 'Tis not in their power, unless we are accomplices in the design, to sink us lower. 'Tis only in our own power to do this by an abject submission to their will.

2. This is a reference to the Directory, whose members at this time were Paul François Jean Nicholas Barras, Louis Marie de La Révellière-Lépeaux, Nicolas Louis François de Neufchâteau, Philippe Antoine Merlin of Douai, and Jean François Reubell.

In the Hamilton Papers, Library of Congress, is an undated document, in an unknown handwriting, addressed to H, which consists of brief biographies of these five members of the Directory. The document is endorsed: "Sketches of the Characters of certain Frenchmen." On the cover of the document John Church Hamilton wrote: "Author unknown; but a Frenchman from the style of calligraphy & some of the turns of phrase. It is well executed. The characters are the same as those of Canning's group in the 'New Morality;' but they are set in a friendlier & falser light."

The "New Morality" referred to above is a poem written by the English statesman George Canning. See Alfred Howard, ed., *The Works of George Canning, Consisting of His Poems, Essays, and Select Speeches* (New York, 1829), 5–21.

3. For a documentary account of the experiences of the United States envoys in France, see *ASP, Foreign Relations*, II, 153–82. See also H to Timothy Pickering, March 23, 1798, note 1; Pickering to H, two letters of March 25, 1798.

But tho a knowlege of the true character of the citizens of this country will not permit it to be suspected that a majority either in our public councils or in the community can be so degraded or infatuated; yet to the firm and independent lover of his country, there are appearances at once mortifying and alarming.

Among those who divide our legislative councils, we perceive hitherto, on the one side unremitting efforts to justify or excuse the despots of France, to vilify and discredit our own government, of course to destroy its necessary vigor, and to distract the opinions and to damp the zeal of our citizens, what is worse, to divert their affections from their own to a foreign country: on the other side, we have as yet seen neither expanded views of our situation, nor measures at all proportioned to the seriousness and extent of the danger. While our independence is menaced, little more is heard than of guarding our trade, and this too in very feeble and tremulous accents.

In the community, though in a sounder state than its representatives, we discover the vestiges of the same divisions which enervate our councils. A few, happily a contemptible few, prostituted to a foreign enemy, seem willing that their country should become a province to France. Some of these dare even to insinuate the treasonable and parricidal sentiment, that in case of invasion, they would join the standard of France. Another and a more considerable part are weak enough to appear disposed to sacrifice our commerce, to endure every indignity and even to become tributary, rather than to encounter war or increase the chances of it; as if a nation could preserve any rights, could even retain its freedom, which should conduct itself on the principle of passive obedience to injury and outrages; as if the debasement of the public mind did not include the debasement of the individual mind and the direlection of whatever adorns or exalts human nature; as if there could be any security in compounding with tyranny and injustice by degrading compliances; as if submission to the existing violations of our sovereignty would not invite still greater, and whet the appetite to devour us by the allurement of an unresisting prey; as if war was ever to be averted by betraying unequivocally a pusillanimous dread of it as the greatest of all evils.

This country has doubtless powerful motives to cultivate peace.

It was its policy, for the sake of this object, to go a great way in yielding secondary interests, and to meet injury with patience as long as it could be done without the manifest abandonment of essential rights; without absolute dishonor. But to do more than this is suicide in any people who have the least chance of contending with effect. The conduct of our government has corresponded with the cogent inducements to a pacific system. Towards Great-Britain it displayed forbearance—towards France it has shewn humility. In the case of Great Britain, its moderation was attended with success. But the inexorable arrogance and rapacity of the oppressors of unhappy France barr all the avenues to reconciliation as well as to redress, accumulating upon us injury and insult till there is no choice left between resistance and infamy.

My countrymen! can ye hesitate which to prefer? can ye consent to taste the brutalizing cup of disgrace, to wear the livery of foreign masters, to put on the hateful fetters of foreign bondage? Will it make any difference to you that the badge of your servitude is a *cap* rather than an *epaulet?* Will tyranny be less odious because FIVE instead of ONE inflict the rod? What is there to deter from the manful vindication of your rights and your honor?

With an immense ocean rolling between the United States and France—with ample materials for ship building, and a body of hardy seamen more numerous and more expert than France can boast, with a population exceeding five millions, spread over a wide extent of country, offering no one point, the seizure of which, as of the great capitals of Europe, might deside the issue, with a soil liberal of all the productions that give strength and resource, with the rudiments of the most essential manufactures capable of being developed in proportion to our want, with a numerous and in many quarters well appointed militia, with respectable revenues and a flourishing credit, with many of the principle sources of taxation yet untouched, with considerable arsenals and the means of extending them, with experienced officers ready to form an army under the command of the same illustrious chief who before led them to victory and glory, and who, if the occasion should require it, could not hesitate again to obey the summons of his country—what a striking and encouraging contrast does this situation in many respects form, to that in which we defied the thunder of Britain? what is there in it to excuse or palliate the cowardice and baseness of a tame surrender of our rights to France?

The question is unnecessary. The people of America are neither idiots nor dastards. They did not break one yoke to put on another. Tho a portion of them have been hitherto misled; yet not even these, still less the great body of the nation, can be long unaware of the true situation, or blind to the treacherous arts by which they are attempted to be hood winked. The unfaithful and guilty leaders of a foreign faction, unmasked in all their intrinsic deformity, must quickly shrink from the scene, appalled and confounded. The virtuous whom they have led astray will renounce their exotic standard. Honest men of all parties will unite to maintain and defend the honor and the sovereignty of their country.

The crisis demands it. 'Tis folly to dissemble. The despots of France are waging war against us. Intoxicated with success and the inordinate love of power, they actually threaten our independence. All amicable means have in vain been tried towards accommodation. The Problem now to be solved is whether we will maintain or surrender our sovereignty. To maintain it with firmness is the most sacred of duties, the most glorious of tasks. The happiness of our country, the honor of the American name demands it. The genius of Independence exhorts to it. The secret mourning voice of oppressed millions in the very country whose despots menace us, admonish to it by their suffering example. The offended dignity of man commands us not to be accessary to its further degradation. Reverence to the SUPREME GOVERNOR of the universe enjoins us not to bow the knee to the modern TITANS who erect their impious crests against him and vainly imagine they can subvert his eternal throne.

But 'tis not enough to resist. 'Tis requisite to resist with energy. That will be a narrow view of our situation which does not contemplate, that we may be called, at our very doors, to defend our independence and liberty, and which does not provide against it, by bringing into activity and completely organizing all the resources of our country. A respectable naval force, ought to protect our commerce, and a respectable army ought both to diminish the temptation to invasion, by lessening the apparent chance of success, and to guarantee us, not only against the final success of such an attempt, but against the serious tho partial calamities, which in that case would certainly await us, if we have to rely on militia alone against the enterprises of veteran troops, drenched in blood and slaughter and led by a skillful and daring Chief!   TITUS MANLIUS.

[*Marcellus No. I and No. II*] [1]

[New York, March 31, 1798]

Gazette of the United States, and Philadelphia Daily Advertiser, March 31, 1798.

1. On April 5, 1798, Thomas Jefferson wrote to James Madison: "You will see in Fenno two numbers of a paper signed Marcellus. They promise much mischief, and are ascribed, without any difference of opinion, to Hamilton" (Ford, *Writings of Jefferson*, VII, 231). No conclusive evidence that H was the author of these essays has been found.

From Philip Schuyler

[Albany] Saturday 31st March 1798

My Dear Sir

I learned with great Satisfaction that altho you had experienced much fatigue in your Journey,[1] you arrived in perfect health and found my Dear Eliza and the Children so.

After a fortnights confinement to my bed room I am so well recovered as to return to the hall,—the wounds in my leg are on the point of being healed. The inner bark of the London or Bass wood was applied on Sunday last and in twenty four hours I was relieved from the most excruciating torments and have since had less pain, then in any equal number of days for Six months past. Indeed I have hardly any pain at all and my Appetite is gradually restoring —please to communicate this to my Children.

The Chancellor is here and he and his friends are Assiduous in blackening Mr Jays Character.[2] The Chancellor called on me Yesterday Morning and began a Conversation on the State of our Affairs in relation to france, he imputed the impending rupture to the Intemperance of our Government, which wished to connect Itself with britain to the prejudice of France, I asked for the proof, he replied that Mr Jay was instructed to yield every thing, and had done So. Chagrined I replied that altho I was already an Old and Infirm man I was not yet so much of a Child as to have an Assertion so notoriously false made to me—that he must reserve Such assertions to be made to Idiots That If a rupture with france should Ensue It was Undoubtedly to be imputed to the *Antifoederalists*, and to such foederalists as had apostatized, and Joined them in all their nefarious Scheme to reduce America to a disgraceful dependance on france,—he attempted to Justify the directory for banishing Pitchgrou & the other Members of their Legislature,[3] and supposed the directory apprehended If their deputies had been brought to Trial their friends would [have] caused an Insurrection. I exposed the weakness of Such a reason, and observed that If It was a really good and Justifiable measure, and that he believed It, I must conclude he would applaud ⟨the Executive of the⟩ U. States If he should Send thirty or forty members of Congress to some inhospitable shore, there to perish by famine and disease. The Man my dear Sir has worked himself up to such a pitch of Enmity against our Government as approaches to Madness.

A   I hope every exertion will be made In Your quarter to ensure Mr Jays Election. I fear the result in Dutchess County as I [do] not recollect Since Mr Radcliffs [4] departure thence that we have any Active Influencial friend there. I wish Mr Radif could go into that County—or at least that he would write to his friends.   B

Mrs. Schuyler and all here are well and Join in love to you My Eliza & Mr & Mrs Church [5] and the Children of both families. God bless you

Yours ever most Affectionately

Alexr Hamilton Esqr

If Colo Hamilton is from Home Mrs. Hamilton will please to Extract the paragraph marked A to B. and give It to Colo. Troup [6] as from me.   P S.

AL[S], Columbia University Libraries.

1. H had returned to New York City from Albany. See H to James McHenry, February 20, 1798, note 2.

2. John Jay, the governor of New York, was running for re-election against Chancellor Robert R. Livingston.

3. This is a reference to the *coup d'état* of September 4, 1797. See Rufus King to H, September 9, 1797, note 3.

4. From February, 1796, to January, 1798, Jacob Radcliff was an assistant attorney general for the Second District of New York, which included Dutchess, Orange, and Ulster counties. In 1798 he became a New York City attorney.

5. John B. and Angelica Church.

6. Robert Troup.

From Henry A. Williams [1]

New York, March 31, 1798. "I am again necessitated to write you from this gloomy place (Viz. the Goal) where a trifling sum . . . holds me. You will therefore I hope excuse me for Troubling you and as Imediately as possible take the Necessary Steps to Recover that Money. . . ."

ALS, Hamilton Papers, Library of Congress.

1. When he was not in jail, Williams was a grocer at 102 Broad Street in New York City (David Longworth, *Longworth's American Almanack, New-York Register, and City Directory for the Twenty-Third Year of American Independence* . . . [New York, 1798]).

H was Williams's attorney in the suit of *John Schenck, Hendrick Schenck, Abraham Schenck, Letty Schenck, and Margaret Schenck by Frederick Froelinghuysen her next Friend* v *Paul Schenck and Henry A. Williams* (MS Minutes of the New York Court of Chancery, under the date of December 14, 1797 [Hall of Records, New York City]).

For H's earlier service as Williams's attorney in matters involving the Schencks, see H's "Cash Book," March 1, 1782–1791.

To Rufus King

[New York, March, 1798] [1]

It is a great while, My Dr. friend, since I have written to you a line. You will not I am sure impute my silence to any cause impeaching my friendship, for that must be always cordial and intire. The truth is that my professional avocations occupy me to the extent of the exertions my health permits, and I have been unwilling to sit down to write you without leisure to say something interesting. But I now depart from this rule that my persevering silence may not make me sin beyond Redemption. I have however only time to tell you that your friends are generally well & as much attached to you as ever; & that I hear of no cabals against you.

Being just returned from Albany,[2] I could say nothing about the political juncture as it is affected by the unpleasant advices from our Commissioners in France.[3] I will only say that the public mind is much sounder than that of our Representatives in the national Councils & that there is no danger of our actively disgracing ourselves, that is by any unworthy compliances with the exorbitant pretensions of "The Great *Monster*." *

Yrs. affecly   A Hamilton

Rufus King Esqr

* soit disant "The Great Nation"

ALS, New-York Historical Society, New York City.
   1. At the top of this letter King wrote: "Probably Mar say 12. 98."
   2. See H to Pierre Charles L'Enfant, March 20, 1798, note 2.
   3. The dispatches from the United States envoys in France are printed in *ASP, Foreign Relations*, II, 153–82. See also H to Timothy Pickering, March 23, 1798, note 1; Pickering to H, two letters of March 25, 1798.

The Stand No. II [1]

[New York, April 4, 1798]

The description of VICE, by a celebrated poet, may aptly be applied to the REVOLUTIONARY GOVERNMENT of France. It is,

"A MONSTER of such horrid mien,
     As to be *hated*, needs but to be *seen*." [2]

Unfortunately, however, for mankind, a species of moral pestilence has so far disordered the mental eye of a considerable portion of it, as to prevent a distinct view of the deformities of this PRODIGY of human wickedness and folly. It is the misfortune of this country in particular, that too many among its citizens have seen the Monster in all its dreadful transformations with complacency or toleration.

The [New York] *Commercial Advertiser*, April 4, 1798.
   1. The other issues of "The Stand" are dated March 30, April 7, 12, 16, 19, 21, 1798.
   2. Alexander Pope, *Essay on Man*, Epistle II, lines 217–18.

Nor is it among the least of the contradictions of the human mind, that a religious, moral and sober people should have regarded with indulgence so frightful a volcano of atheism, depravity and absurdity; that a gentle and humane people should have viewed without detestation, so hateful an instrument of cruelty and bloodshed; that a people having an enlightened and ardent attachment to genuine liberty, should have contemplated without horror so tremendous an engine of despotism and slavery. The film indeed begins to be removed, but the vision of many of those who have been under its influence is not yet restored to the necessary energy or clearness.

It is of the last importance to our national safety and welfare, that the remaining obscurity should be speedily dispelled. Till this shall be the case, we shall stand on the brink of a precipice.

To exhibit the hydra in all its horrible preeminence of guilt and mischief, would require volumes. Slight sketches chiefly to pourtray its character in reference to other nations, are all that will comport with the plan of these papers.

In retracing the progress of a war which has immersed Europe in blood and calamity, it is an error as common as it is strange, to acquit France of responsibility, and to throw the whole blame upon her adversaries. This is a principal source of the indulgence which is shewn to the extravagances and enormities of her revolution. And yet the plainest facts demonstrate, that the reverse of this supposition is far more agreeable to truth. It required all the bold imposing pretences of the demagogues of France, all the docile partiality of a warm admiration for her revolution, to have secured a moment's success to so glaring a deception.

The origin of the war is usually charged to the treaty of *Pilnitz*,[3] and to the counter-revolutionary projects of the parties to it.

To this day we are without authentic and accurate evidence of the nature of that treaty. Taking its existence for granted, there is not

3. The Treaty of Pillnitz, drawn up secretly by Emperor Leopold II of Austria and King Frederick William II of Prussia, on August 27, 1791, provided among other things for safeguarding the existing treaties with France. On the same day, the two rulers issued a declaration calling on the other European powers to assist them in restoring full authority to the king of France. They also stated that they would intervene in France only with the unanimous consent of the other powers (Martens, *Recûeil*, V, 260–62).

the least proof that it comprehended any other powers than *Austria*, *Prussia*, and *Sardinia*.* Beyond these, therefore, unless suspicion be substituted for fact, it could not afford even a pretext for hostility. It is likewise certain,† that after the date assigned to the treaty of *Pilnitz*, the Emperor, who was the reputed head of the confederacy, gave strong proof of the renunciation of its object, if hostile to the revolution; by signifying, thro his ministers, to all the foreign courts, his determination to acquiesce in the constitution of 1792, accepted by Louis the XVI.

The diplomatic correspondence between *France* and *Austria*, which preceded the rupture, evinces that the treaty of *Pilnitz* was not the cause of the war, for it is not even mentioned. The immediate ostensible cause, as it there appears, was the refusal of Austria to disarm in compliance with the peremptory demand of France; a demand to which this, apparently, very reasonable reply was given, that France had previously armed to a greater extent; and that Austria could not safely reduce her force while France remained in so disturbed and inflamed a state as to leave her neighbors every moment exposed to the enterprises of her revolutionary fervor.[5] There is no absolute criterion by which it can be pronounced whether this reply was merely a pretext, or the dictate of a serious apprehension. But it is certain that the correspondence discovers great appearance of candor and moderation on the part of the Imperial cabinet; and it is not to be denied, that the state of effervescence of the French nation at this juncture furnished real cause of alarm to the neighboring governments.

It is then, at best, problematical, whether France in declaring war, as she did at the same time against *Austria* and *Prussia*, was actuated by the conviction that it was necessary to anticipate and disconcert

---

* *I am not certain that ever Sardinia was a party. Writing from memory some minute circumstances may be mistated.*
† *See State paper by* Debret.[4]

4. "Copy of a circular Dispatch of the Aulic and State Chancellor, Prince de Kaunitz, to the Ambassadors and Ministers of his Imperial and Royal Majesty at the several foreign Courts," November 1, 1791 (Debrett, *A Collection of State Papers*, I, 150–51).

5. See "Decree of War against the King of Hungary and Bohemia," April 20, 1792 (Debrett, *A Collection of State Papers*, I, 18–19), and "Counter Declaration of the Court of Vienna against France," July 5, 1792 (Debrett, *A Collection of State Papers*, I, 24–28).

the unfriendly views of those powers; or whether the war, as has been suggested with great probability, was fought by the republican party as a mean of embarrassing the executive government, and paving the way for the overthrow of the royalty. Two things, well established, are instructive on this point. The one, that the king was driven against his wish, by a ministry forced upon him by the popular party, to propose the declaration of war, which he considered as the tomb of his family—the other, that BRISSOT, the head of the then prevailing faction, some time afterwards exultingly boasted, that *"but for this war the revolution of the tenth of August would never have taken place; that but for this war, France would never have been a republic."* [6]

Admitting, nevertheless, that the true source of the war with Austria and Prussia is inveloped in some obscurity, there is none as to the wars in which France became subsequently engaged. It is clear as to them that she was the original aggressor.

It appeared from cotemporary testimony, that one of the first acts of that assembly which dethroned the king, was in a paroxism of revolutionary frenzy, to declare itself "A COMMITTEE OF INSURRECTION of the whole human race, for the purpose of overturning all existing governments." This extravagant declaration surpasses any thing to be found in the ample records of human madness. It amounted to an act of hostility against mankind. The republic of America, no less than the despotism of Turkey, was included in the anathema. It breathed that wild and excessive spirit of fanaticism, which would scruple no means of establishing its favorite tenets; and which, in its avowed object, threatening the disorganization of all governments, warranted a universal combination to destroy the monstrous system of which it was the soul.

6. Jacques Pierre Brissot de Warville, leader of the Girondins and one of the principal organizers of the massacre of August 10, 1792.

Although it cannot be stated with certainty, it seems likely that H first saw this quotation in *Observations on the Dispute between the United States and France: Addressed by Robert G. Harper, Esq. of South Carolina to His Constituents, in May, 1797* (Philadelphia: Thos. Bradford, [June,] 1797). On page 84 of that pamphlet, Harper wrote: "After the king was dethroned, Brissot justified the war, and took the credit of it to himself and to his friends. 'Without the war,' says he in his gazette of September 22, 1792, 'the revolution of the 10th of August would never have taken place; without the war, France never would have been a republic.'" The reference is to *La Patriote français*, which Brissot edited.

The decrees of the 19th of November [7] and 15th of December 1792,[8] were modifications of the same spirit. The first offered fraternity and assistance to every people who should wish to recover their liberty, and charged the executive power to send orders to their generals to give that assistance and to defend *those citizens,* who had been or might be vexed for the cause of liberty. The last declared that the French nation would *treat as* enemies *any people* who, refusing or *renouncing liberty* and *equality,* were desirous of *preserving,* recalling, or entering into accommodation with their *prince* and *privileged casts.*

The first was a general signal to insurrection and revolt. It was an invitation to the seditious of every country, in pursuit of chimerical schemes of more perfect liberty, to conspire under the patronage of France against the established government, however free. To assist a people in a reasonable and virtuous struggle for liberty, already begun, is both justifiable and laudable; but to incite to revolution every where, by indiscriminate offers of assistance before hand, is to invade and endanger the foundations of social tranquility. There is no term of reproach or execration too strong for so flagitious an attempt.

The last of the two decrees is not merely in spirit—it is in terms equivalent to a manifesto of war against every nation having a prince or nobility. It declares explicitly and formally, that the French nation will *treat as enemies every people,* who may desire to preserve or restore a government of that character.

It is impossible not to feel the utmost indignation against so presumptuous and so odious a measure. It was not only to scatter the embers of a general conflagration in Europe—it was to interfere coercively in the interior arrangements of other nations—it was to dictate to them, under the penalty of the vengeance of France, what form of government they should live under—it was to forbid

7. The decree of November 19, 1792, reads: "La convention national déclare, au nom de la nation françoise, qu'elle accordera fraternité et secours à tous les peuples qui voudront recouvrer leur liberté, et charge le pouvoir exécutif de donner aux généraux les ordres nécessaires pour porter secours à ces peuples, et défendre les citoyens qui auroient été vexés, ou qui pourroient l'être, pour la cause de la liberté" (Martens, *Recûeil,* V, 365).

8. "Décret par lequel La France proclame la liberté et la souveraineté de tous les peuples chez lesquels elle a porté et portera ses armes," December 15–17, 1792 (Duvergier, *Lois,* V, 105–07).

them to pursue their political happiness in their own way—it was to set up the worst of all despotisms, a despotism over opinion, not against one nation, but against almost all nations. With what propriety is the interference of the powers, *ultimately* coalesced against France, in her interior arrangements, imputed to them as an unpardonable crime, when her leaders had given so terrible an example, and had provoked retaliation as a mean of self-preservation? *

These decrees preceded the transactions which immediately led to rupture between France and the other powers, Austria and Prussia excepted.

It is idle to pretend, that they did not furnish to those powers just cause of war. There is no rule of public law better established or on better grounds, than that whenever one nation unequivocally avows maxims of conduct dangerous to the security and tranquility of others, they have a right to attack her, and to endeavor to disable her from carrying her schemes into effect. They are not bound to wait till inimical designs are matured for action, when it may be too late to defeat them.

How far it may have been wise in a particular government to have taken up the gauntlet, or if in its option, to have left France to the fermentations of the pernicious principles by which its leaders were actuated, is a question of mere expediency, distinct from the right. It is also a complicated and difficult question—one which able and upright men might decide different ways. But the right is still indisputable. The moment the convention vomited forth those venomous decrees, all the governments threatened were justifiable in making war upon France.

Neither were they bound to be satisfied with after explanations or qualifications of the principles which had been declared. They had a right to judge conscientiously whether reliance could be placed on any pretended change of system, and to act accordingly. And while the power of France remained in the same men, who had dis-

---

* *If it be true, as pretended, that Austria and Prussia first interfered in this way with France, it was no plea for her to retaliate on all the rest of Europe. Great-Britain in particular, as far as appears, had observed a fair neutrality. Yet the principle of the French decree was emphatically pointed against her, by the open reception of deputations, of malcontents and public declarations to them, on behalf of the French government, avowing the desire of seeing all thrones overturned, of a National Convention and a Republican revolution in England.*

covered such hostile views, and while the effervescence of the public mind continued at its height, there could not have been, in the nature of things, any security in assurances of greater moderation. Fanaticism is a spirit equally fraudulent and intractable. Fanatics may dissemble the better to effect their aims, but they seldom suddenly reform. No faith is due to the reformation which they may affect, unless it has been the work of time and experience.

But whether a wrong or a right election in point of expediency, may have been made by all or any of the powers, which after the passing of those decrees became engaged in hostility with France, it is not the less true, that her government was the first aggressor, and is primarily chargeable with the evils which have followed. This conclusion is greatly aided by the striking fact, that it was France which declared war, not only against Austria and Prussia, but against England, Spain, Sardinia and Holland.

Two very important inferences result from the facts which have been presented—one, that in blowing up the dreadful flame which has overwhelmed Europe in misfortune, France is the party principally culpable—the other, that the prominent original feature of her revolution is the spirit of proselytism, or the desire of new modelling the political institution of the rest of the world according to her standard. The course of the revolutions also demonstrates that whatever change of system may have been at any time pretended, or however the system may in particular instances have yielded to a temporary policy; it has continued in the main to govern the conduct of the parties who have successively triumphed and tyrannized.   TITUS MANLIUS.

From Oliver Wolcott, Junior [1]

Private   Phila. Apl. 5. 1798

Dear Sir

I recd your note [2] and delivered the enclosure to Fenno [3] who will publish it with its Successors. I hope it will do good, for if the Country cannot be roused from the Lethargy into which it fell in consequence of the miserable conduct of Congress last Summer,[4] the Government will not in one year be worth defending.

The papers relative to the Negotiation which has been attempted with France have been laid before Congress.[5] Many in both Houses I believe find that the gratification of their curiosity has made them responsible, for the management of a pretty difficult subject. The disclosure was I suppose *necessary, though I regret the necessity*. The dose will kill or cure, and I wish I was not somewhat uncertain which; not that I doubt the expediency of what the Government had done, or attempted, but I believe Faction & Jacobinism to be natural & immortal Enemies of our system. It is some satisfaction however to know, that the instructions & the conduct of the President generally in this affair, have enlisted the reluctant approbation of our most inveterate opposers.

A few days will determine whether the Legislature can act with that decision & energy which the Crisis demands. Nothing further by way of impression can be done except recourse is had to the *desperate* & *doubtful* remedy of a popular appeal.

The Revenue does not decline so much as I expected, but the management of the Treasury becomes more & more difficult. The Legislature will not pass laws in gross. Their appropriations are minute. Gallatin to whom they all yield, is evidently intending to break down this Department by charging it with an impracticable detail.[6] The duties are high, the merchants are embarrassed. There is some considerable smuggling in places where correction is difficult. In common with the rest of the Country, the public Officers have grown lazy or dishonest. The sum which has been lost by delinquencies of the Revenue Officers would alarm you—see below.# I have done all in my power, the delinquents are dismissed promptly & without mercy—and yet new discoveries are making. I pray God, that we may not find that most of the old fashioned honesty has left the Country. But I will complain no more at present.

I am assuredly yours   Oliv Wolcott.

see above # Randolph embezled 50.000 Dolls while Secy of State [7] besides which, there ought to be 200.000 Dollars in the Treasy which rests in the Accounts of Revenue Officers—most of this money will be lost. You will at first suspect that I have been careless in suffering the money to remain too long in their hands. The fact however is that in most instances I have been imposed on by fictitious accounts or by other frauds equally alarming.   O. W.

ALS, Connecticut Historical Society, Hartford; LC, Connecticut Historical Society, Hartford.

1. At the bottom of the last page of this letter Wolcott wrote: "July 23d. 1811. This Letter to Genl Hamilton was recd. from Mrs Hamilton on this day. O. W."

2. Letter not found.

3. John Fenno was the editor of the *Gazette of the United States, and Philadelphia Daily Advertiser*. The enclosure, which has not been found, was a copy of the "The Stand No. I," which first appeared in *The* [New York] *Commercial Advertiser*, March 30, 1798, and which was reprinted in the *Gazette of the United States* on April 5, 1798.

4. Although Congress had passed "An Act to provide for the further Defence of the Ports and Harbors of the United States" (1 *Stat.* 523–25 [July 1, 1797]) and "An Act providing a Naval Armament" (1 *Stat.* 350–51 [March 27, 1794]), it had defeated a bill "to raise a provisional army" (*Annals of Congress*, VII, 25) and had refused to give the President authority to establish an embargo similar to that of 1794 (*Annals of Congress*, VII, 386, 531).

5. This is a reference to the papers concerning the XYZ affair, which President John Adams submitted to Congress on April 3, 1798 (*ASP, Foreign Relations*, II, 150–68).

6. On January 31, 1797, Albert Gallatin, a leading opponent of Federalist fiscal policies in the House of Representatives, proposed an amendment to a resolution for an appropriation for the civil list. The original resolution stated that "there be appropriated a sum not exceeding ———, viz." Gallatin's amendment proposed striking out those words and substituting: "The following sums be respectively appropriated, viz." In defending his proposed amendment, Gallatin "said his object in this amendment was, that each appropriation should be specific; that it might not be supposed to be in the power of the Treasury Department to appropriate to one object money which had been specifically appropriated for any other object. He did not know, he had never investigated the subject, whether, as to the Civil List, appropriations had ever been mixed, or whether it was understood they might be so mixed; but they knew it had been officially declared that so far as related to the Military Department, the items had been totally mixed: for instance, if the estimate for clothing or any other item fell short, the officers of the Treasury did not think themselves bound by that particular appropriation, but had recourse to other items, for which larger sums were granted than there was occasion for. Such construction of the law, Mr. G. said, totally defeated the object of appropriation, and it was necessary, therefore, so to express the law that no color for such a construction should be given. The amendment he proposed would have this effect" (*Annals of Congress*, VI, 2040). See also *Annals of Congress*, VI, 2341–42.

7. The Secretary of State, when Edmund Randolph was in office, was held accountable for all money advanced to the diplomatic representatives of the United States if he could not produce receipts from the agents to whom the money had been allocated. Under this arrangement the Secretary of State could be held personally responsible for funds lost through the sinking of a ship, the failure of a bank, and a variety of other natural or man-made disasters. After Randolph resigned in 1795, the Government charged that there were

no receipts in his accounts for $49,154.89. Part of this money had been lost because of a failure of a bank in Amsterdam, and another shortage had occurred because of the failure of an American firm whose bills had been purchased by the Government. Randolph's biographer has argued convincingly that Randolph was at most guilty of carelessness (Moncure Daniel Conway, *Omitted Chapters of History Disclosed in the Life and Papers of Edmund Randolph* [New York, 1889], 370–77).

From Francisco de Miranda [1]

à Londres ce 6. Avril [–June 7] 1798

Celle-ci vous sera remise, mon Cher et respectable Ami, par mon Compatriote D. Pedro Josef de Caro,[2] chargé des Depéches de la

ALS, Hamilton Papers, Library of Congress; LS, marked "Dup:," Hamilton Papers, Library of Congress; LS, marked "3d," Hamilton Papers, Library of Congress; copy, Academia Nacional de la Historia, Caracas, Venezuela.

1. For background to this letter, see Miranda to H, April 1, 1797; February 7, 1798. When Miranda wrote this letter, he did not realize how unlikely it was that England would cooperate in carrying out his plans for the liberation of Spanish America. On April 6, 1798, for example, Rufus King wrote to Timothy Pickering: ". . . England since the arrival of Miranda here but without his knowledge has informed Spain not only that she will not countenance or assist the Spanish colonies in becoming independent—but that she will join her in resisting the endeavours of others to accomplish it provided that Spain will oppose the views of France against her own dominions and those of Portugal. At the same time that this communication has been made to Spain, an expedition has been prepared and the correspondent arrangements at Trinidad have been ordered, for the purpose of beginning the revolution of South America. In this event as I have before intimated to you England will at Philadelphia open herself to and ask the co-operation of the UStates. Miranda who is impatient with the delays that he experiences, as well as ignorant of the provisional decisions of this cabinet has concluded to send his friend and associate Mr. [Pedro José] Carro to Philadelphia" (LS [deciphered], RG 59, Despatches from United States Ministers to Great Britain, 1791–1906, Vol. 7, January 9–December 22, 1798, National Archives).

2. Caro, a native of Cuba, was conspiring to secure the independence of the Spanish American colonies by taking advantage of the conflict between England and Spain.

In his instructions to Caro, dated April 6, 1798, Miranda wrote: "A su arrivo de Vm. á New Yorck entregará la Carta que lleva para Mr Hamilton, á quien solamente podrá hablar con confianza en el asunto; y luego sin perdida de tiempo se pondrá en marcha para Philadelfia. . . . y sin perdida de tiempo entregar tambien la Carta de Mr King al Ministro de Negocios extrangeros de quien solicitará immediatamente una audiencia, afin de entregar al Presidente en propia mano los despachos de que está encargado; ó si algun motivo lo impideise en el momento, hará pasar estos Despachos por mano del Ministro al Presidente, solicitando el ser presentado á este privadamente, lo mas pronto que fuese posible" (*Archivo, Miranda*, XV, 231). In these instructions Miranda is referring to his letter to H printed above; his letter to John Adams, March 24,

plus haute importance pour le President des Etats Unis: [3] il vous dirà Confidentiellement ce que vous voudrez apprendre sur ce Sujet. Il paroit que le moment de nottre emancipation aproche, et que

1798 (ALS, Adams Family Papers, deposited in the Massachusetts Historical Society, Boston; copy, Adams Family Papers, deposited in the Massachusetts Historical Society, Boston); King to Pickering, April 6, 1798 (LS, RG 59, Despatches from United States Ministers to Great Britain, 1791–1906, Vol. 7, January 9–December 22, 1798, National Archives). Miranda also asked Caro to deliver a letter to Henry Knox (Pickering to Adams, August 21, 1798 [ALS, Adams Family Papers, deposited in the Massachusetts Historical Society, Boston]). Miranda's letter to Knox has not been found.

Caro, however, never came to the United States. On April 25, 1798, Miranda instructed him to go directly to Barbados and to send the letters entrusted to him to Pickering for transmittal (*Archivo, Miranda*, XV, 248–49). On May 10, 1798, Caro wrote to Pickering, enclosed the letters in question, and explained the change in his plans (ALS, Massachusetts Historical Society, Boston). Caro's letter to Pickering is printed in *Archivo, Miranda*, XV, 256. A translation of Caro's letter is in the Adams Family Papers, deposited in the Massachusetts Historical Society, Boston, and is printed in King, *The Life and Correspondence of Rufus King*, II, 658. Pickering received Caro's letter on August 20, 1798, and on August 21 he wrote to Adams: "I enclose a letter which I received last evening under cover from Mr. Pedro Josef Caro, accompanied by a letter from Mr. King intended as an introduction to Mr. Caro; but the latter having missed a passage to the U. States, in the British Cutter which sailed from Falmouth for New-York on the 20th of April, & circumstances requiring his arrival in So. America with as little delay as possible, he forwarded the packet to me. A copy of the translation of his letter to me I have the honor to enclose.

"Under the same cover were enclosed two letters, one for Colo. Hamilton, the other for General Knox, which I forward by this post to those gentlemen." (ALS, Adams Family Papers, deposited in the Massachusetts Historical Society, Boston.)

3. In his letter to Adams, dated March 24, 1798, Miranda enclosed a copy of his "instructions," December 22, 1797, and an estimate of the population and products of Spanish America (ALS, Adams Family Papers, deposited in the Massachusetts Historical Society, Boston; copy, Adams Family Papers, deposited in the Massachusetts Historical Society, Boston). Miranda's "instructions" were, in fact, a plan for the liberation of Spain's American colonies and were signed at Paris by Miranda and two other revolutionists, José del Pozo y Sucre and Manuel José de Salas (two copies, Adams Family Papers, deposited in the Massachusetts Historical Society, Boston). The estimate was probably a copy of "Vista Politica de la América Española," which is printed in *Archivo, Miranda*, XV, 216–25. On March 20, 1798, Miranda sent a copy of this estimate to William Pitt, first lord of the treasury and chancellor of the exchequer (*Archivo, Miranda*, XV, 212–14). The copy of Miranda's letter to Adams, March 24, 1798, has a postscript dated April 28, which explains the change in Caro's plans. Miranda wrote to Adams again on August 17, 1798 (ALS, Adams Family Papers, deposited in the Massachusetts Historical Society, Boston). On October 3, 1798, Adams wrote to Pickering: "Inclosed is a duplicate of a letter from Miranda, with some estimates. Read it and think of it. A number of questions and considerations occur. We are friends with Spain. If we were enemies, would the project be useful to us? It will not be in character for me to answer the letter . . ." (Adams, *Works of John Adams*, VIII, 600).

l'etablissement de la Libertè sur tout le Continent du Nouveau-monde nous est confiè par la Providence! Le seul danger que je prevois c'est l'introduction des principes-français, qui empoisonnerai la Libertè dans son berçèau, et finirai pour en detruir bien-tôt la votre; mais si nous prenons des Sages precautions à tems, tout pourrà fort bien-y reussir. Qu'il vous fasse voir mes instructions à cet egard, et vous pourriez-y ajouter ce qui me serait echapè.

On est convenü d'avance d'une forme de gouvernement mixte, qui me parai pourrà fort bien convenir au Pays: J'aurois l'honneur de vous le Soumetre à tems; mais je vous previens, que nous voudrions vous avoir *avec nous* pour cet important object, et que c'est le Veux de ceux de mes Compatriotes à qui j'ai parlè sur cette affaire; ainsi J'espere que Vous ne nous refuserez pas quand le moment Arriverà —vottre Greque predecesseur Solon, ne l'aurai pas fait au moins J'en suis sur! et il serà possible que J'aille bien tôt vous prendre moi-même—il-y-a une autre Persone chez vous, qui m'est connüe de reputation, et que je crois, pourroit fort bien nous rendre des services tres important dans la partie militaire; c'est le general *H. Lee* de la Virginie.[4] Come je reçüs au Commencement de la Revolution en france (par mon ami le Co: W. Smith) une Letter de lui [5] Souhaitant d'entrer au Service de la Repl. alors; je me flatte qu'il ne nous refuserà non plus, quand il s'agit de la vrai-Libertè, que nous aimons tous et du bonheur de ses Compatriotes du Perou et du Mêxique—fairez-moi le plaisir de le presentir d'avance pour qu'il se prepare à nous

4. Henry Lee, a veteran of the American Revolution, was a member of the Continental Congress from 1785 to 1788, a member of the Virginia Ratifying Convention, and governor of Virginia from 1791 to 1794.

5. On November 24, 1792, William S. Smith wrote to Miranda: "I have received a letter from my friend Colonel henry Lee at present Governor of Virginia, dated Richmond 21st of September, he writes thus: 'will you be so good, my dear friend, as to inform me of the real state of affairs in france, whether the Disunion prevalent there will endanger the Revolution—I am solicitous to know *your sentiments* on this subject, as I very much wish to cross the atlantic & offer to that illustrated Nation my humble services as a soldier. . . .'

"Permit me to congratulate you, my friend, on the offer of service of this soldier for one of more military address never enter'd the field:—he is a great acquisition for *our great project* & I will nourish him accordingly—send an extract of this letter to the Minister & ask a Commission for henry Lee as Brigadier general, Commandant of a legionary Corps. . . ." (*Archivo, Miranda,* XV, 147.) On December 26, 1792, Miranda sent an extract of Smith's letter to Jean Pierre Brissot de Warville, a member of the National Convention (*Archivo, Miranda,* XV, 156).

acompagner, lui recomandant toujours toute la reserve qu'est indispensable—Nottre ami Knox [6] voudra-t-il venir? J'en serois bien charmè, mais je crains que non.

Enfin Portez-vous bien mon Cher Ami—donnez-moi des vous nouvelles, sous l'adresse de Mr. King votre ministre Plenipe. ici—presentez mes compliments respectueux à Made. Hamilton—et croyez moi toujours avec un atachement inviolable votre sincere Ami.   F. de Miranda.

Alexr. Hamilton, Esqe. New-York.

P.S. ce 7. Juin 1798.[7]
Mr. Caro est parti en droiture au Continent Americain, par des circonstances pressantes qui nous ont force à cette demarche. Les evenements pressent, et tout se prepare pour notre grande enterprise. J'ai vü vos Lettres à Mr. King, inclusivement jusques au 5. may dernier—je vous prie de repondre le plus-tôt possible, et de me communiquer vottre avis sur tout de qui regarde *toutte l'Amerique*. à Dieu

yours,   M——a.

6. Henry Knox.
7. This postscript, in Miranda's handwriting, appears only on the letter marked "Dup:" in the Hamilton Papers, Library of Congress.

The Stand No. III [1]

[New York, April 7, 1798]

In reviewing the disgusting spectacle of the French revolution, it is difficult to avert the eye entirely from those features of it which betray a plan to disorganize the human mind itself, as well as to undermine the venerable pillars that support the edifice of civilized society. The attempt by the rulers of a nation to destroy all religious opinion, and to pervert a whole people to Atheism, is a phenomenon of profligacy reserved to consummate the infamy of the

The [New York] *Commercial Advertiser*, April 7, 1798.
1. The other issues of "The Stand" are dated March 30, April 4, 12, 16, 19, 21, 1798.

unprincipled reformers of France. The proofs of this terrible design are numerous and convincing.

The animosity to the Christian system is demonstrated by the single fact of the ridiculous and impolitic establishment of the decades, with the evident object of supplanting the Christian Sabbath. The inscription by public authority on the tombs of the deceased, affirming death to be an eternal sleep, witness the desire to discredit the belief of the immortality of the soul. The open profession of Atheism in the Convention,* received with acclamations; the honorable mention on its journals of a book professing to prove the *nothingness* of all religion; † the institution of a festival to offer public worship to a courtezan decorated with the pompous [title] [5] of "GODDESS OF REASON;" [6] the congratulatory reception of impious children appearing in the hall of the Convention to lisp blasphemy against the King of Kings; are among the dreadful proofs of a conspiracy to establish Atheism on the ruins of Christianity—to deprive mankind of its best consolations and most animating hopes —and to make a gloomy desert of the universe.

Latterly the indications of this plan are not so frequent as they were, but from time to time something still escapes which discovers that it is not renounced. The late address of *Buonaparte* to the Di-

* By Dupont,[2] Danton &c.[3]

† Written and presented by Anacharsis Clootz,[4] calling himself orator of the human race.

2. This is a reference to Pierre Samuel Du Pont de Nemours, a French physiocrat. On November 13, 1790, as a member of the National Assembly, he proposed the suppression of religious orders (*Révolution Française, ou Analyse Complette et Impartiale du Moniteur: Suivie d'une Table Alphabétique des Personnes et des Choses* [Paris, 1801], I, 114).

3. For Georges-Jacques Danton's views on religion, see his speech to the Convention on November 26, 1793 (*Réimpression de L'Ancien Moniteur*, XVIII, 535).

4. John Baptiste du Val de Grace, Baron von Cloots, who was better known as Anacharsis Cloots, was a member of the Prussian nobility who went to France in 1789 and on June 19, 1790, delivered to the Assembly an address in favor of the Declaration of the Rights of Man which earned him the title "the orator of the human race." In August, 1792, he announced that he was a personal enemy of Jesus and that he rejected all revealed religions. He was elected to the Convention a month later. On March 24, 1794, he was guillotined as a Hébertist. For Cloots's speech against religion, see *Réimpression de L'Ancien Moniteur*, XXVIII, 454.

5. This word was taken from *JCHW*, VII, 651.

6. On November 10, 1793, the National Convention passed a decree converting the Metropolitan Church in Paris into the Temple of Reason (Duvergier, *Lois*, VI, 347).

rectory is an example. That unequalled conqueror, from whom it is painful to detract; in whom one would wish to find virtues worthy of his shining talents, prophanely unites RELIGION (not superstition) with royalty, and the feudal system as the scourges of Europe for centuries past.[7] The decades likewise remain the CATAPULTA which is to batter down Christianity.

Equal pains have been taken to deprave the morals as to extinguish the religion of the country, if indeed morality in a community can be separated from religion. It is among the singular and fantastic vagaries of the French revolution, that while the Duke of Brunswick was marching to Paris,[8] a new law of divorce was passed; which makes it as easy for a husband to get rid of his wife, and a wife of her husband, as to discard a worn out habit.* [9] To complete the dissolution of those ties, which are the chief links of domestic and ultimately of social attachment, the Journals of the Convention record with guilty applause accusations preferred by children against the lives of their parents.

It is not necessary to heighten the picture by sketching the horrid groupe of proscriptions and murders which have made of France a den of pillage and slaughter; blackening with eternal opprobrium the very name of man.

---

* This law it is understood has been lately modified, in consequence of its manifestly pernicious tendency; but upon a plan which, according to the opinion of the best men in the two Councils, lately banished, would leave the evil in full force.[10]

7. On December 10, 1797, Napoleon presented the Directory with the Treaty of Campo Formio of October 17, 1797, and the ratification of it by the Austrians. In his speech he said: "La religion, la féodalité et le royalisme, ont successivement, depuis vingt siècles, gouverné l'Europe; mais de la paix que vous venez de conclure, date l'ère des gouvernements représentatifs" (*Réimpression de L'Ancien Moniteur*, XXIX, 90).

8. Karl Wilhelm Ferdinand, duke of Brunswick, commanded a Prussian detachment of the coalition army which entered eastern France on August 19, 1792. After a month's campaign, Brunswick was defeated by the French at Valmy on September 20, 1792, and withdrew into Flanders.

9. "Décret qui détermine les causes, le mode et les effets du divorce," September 20, 1792 (Duvergier, *Lois*, IV, 556–62). Two other decrees dealing with divorce were issued on December 28, 1793, and April 23, 1794: "Décret qui attribue aux tribunaux de famille la connaissance des contestations relatives aux droits des époux divorcés" (Duvergier, *Lois*, VI, 442–43) and "Décret contenant des dispositions additionelles à celui du 20 septembre 1792 sur la divorce" (Duvergier, *Lois*, VII, 183–84).

10. This may be a reference to a law passed on February 17, 1798, entitled "Arrêté du Conseil des Cinq-Cents, relatif à la reconnaissance des enfans naturels" (Duvergier, *Lois*, X, 235).

The pious and the moral weep over these scenes as a sepulchre destined to entomb all they revere and esteem. The politician, who loves liberty, sees them with regret as a gulph that may swallow up the liberty to which he is devoted. He knows that morality overthrown (and morality *must* fall with religion) the terrors of despotism can alone curb the impetuous passions of man, and confine him within the bounds of social duty.

But let us return to the conduct of revolutionary France towards other nations, as more immediately within our purpose.

It has been seen that she commenced her career as the champion of universal liberty; and, proclaiming destruction to the governments which she was pleased to denominate despotic, made a tender of fraternity and assistance to the nation whom they oppressed.[11] She, at the same time, disclaimed conquest and aggrandizement.

But it has since clearly appeared, that at the very moment she was making these professions, and while her diplomatic agents were hypocritically amusing foreign courts * with conciliatory explanations and promises of moderation, she was exerting every faculty, by force and fraud, to accomplish the very conquest and aggrandizement which she insidiously disavowed.

The people of Belgium, ensnared by fair pretences, believed that in abandoning the defence of their country and the cause of their ancient sovereign, they acquired a title to enjoy liberty under a government of their own choice, protected by France. Contrary to the hopes which were inspired—contrary to the known will of a large majority of that people, contrary to all their religious and national prejudices—they have been compelled to become departments of France. And their violated temples have afforded a rich plunder to aliment further conquest and oppression.[12]

The Dutch, seduced by the same arts to facilitate rather than obstruct the entrance of a French army into their country, thot they

* England among the rest.

11. See "The Stand No. II," April 4, 1798, notes 7 and 8.

12. The first phase of French control over Belgium, which had lasted from the defeat of the Austrians at Jemappes on November 6, 1792, until the Austrian victory at Neerwinden on March 18, 1793, had been largely unsuccessful despite the enforcement of the French decree of December 15–17, 1792, promoting revolution ("The Stand No. II," April 4, 1798, note 9). In July, 1794, France regained control of Belgium and incorporated that country into the republic by a decree of October 1, 1795 (Duvergier, *Lois*, VIII, 367–69).

were only getting rid of their stadtholder and nobles, and were to retain their territory, and their wealth secured by such a civil establishment as they should freely choose. Their reward is the dismemberment of their country and the loss of their wealth by exhausting contributions; and they are obliged to take a government, dictated by a faction openly countenanced, and supported by France. Completely a province of France in imitation of their frantic masters, they are advancing with rapid strides to a lawless tyranny at home.* [13]

France professing eternal hatred to kings was to be the tutelary Genius of Republics—HOLLAND, GENOA, VENICE, the SWISS CANTONS and the UNITED STATES, are agonizing witnesses of her sincerity.

Of undone *Holland* no more need be said; nothing remains for us but to exercise tender sympathy in the unfortunate fate of a country which generosity lent its aid to establish our independence, and to deduce from her melancholy example an instructive lesson to repel with determined vigor, the mortal embrace of her seducer and destroyer.

Genoa, a speck on the Globe, for having at every hazard resisted the efforts of the enemies of France to force her from a neutral station, is recompensed with the subversion of her government, and the pillage of her wealth by compulsory and burthensome contributions.[14]

VENICE, is no more! In vain had she preserved a faithful neutrality, when perhaps her interposition might have inclined the scale of victory in Italy against France. A few of her citizens kill † some French soldiers. Instant retaliation takes place. Every attonement is offered. Nothing will suffice but the overthrow of her government. 'Tis effected. Her own citizens attracted by the lure of democracy become accessary to it, and receive a popular government at the hand

* By the last accounts some of their most independent citizens have been siezed and imprisoned merely for the constitutional exercise of their opinion.
† Were they not French agents employed to create the pretext?

13. In January, 1795, the French armies, supported by the Dutch Patriot party, overran the Netherlands, and the Stadtholder William V fled to England. On May 16, 1795, the States General accepted the terms of a treaty proposed by France, according to which the Netherlands became autonomous under the name of the Batavian Republic, accepted an army of occupation, ceded Flanders, Maestricht, and Venlo to France, and paid France an indemnity of one hundred million florins (Martens, *Recûeil*, VI, 88–98).

14. See Rufus King to H, June 27, 1797, note 4.

of France.[15] What is the sequel—what the faith kept with them? It suits France to bribe the Emperor to a surrender of the Netherlands and to peace, that she may pursue her projects elsewhere with less obstacle. It suits France to extend her power and commerce by the acquisition of portions of the *Venetian* territories. The bribe is offered and accepted. VENICE is divided. She disappears from the mass of nations. The tragedy of Poland is reacted with circumstances of aggravated atrocity.[16] France is perfidious enough to sacrifice a people, who at her desire had consented to abrogate their *privileged casts*, to the chief of those Despots, against whom she had vowed eternal hatred.

The Swiss cantons—the boast of Republicans—the model to which they have been glad to appeal in proof, that a republican government may consist with the order and happiness of society—the old and faithful allies of France, who are not even pretended to have deviated from a sincere neutrality—what are they at this moment? Perhaps like Venice, *a story told!* The despots of France had found pretences to quarrel with them—commotions were excited—the legions of France were in march to second the insurgents.[17] Little other hope remains than that the *death* of this respectable people will be as glorious as their *life;* that they will sell their independence as dearly as they bought it. But why despair of a brave and virtuous

15. See King to H, June 27, 1797, note 3. On April 21, 1797, a French gunboat had entered the Lido at Venice in defiance of the local law excluding foreign warships, and four Frenchmen had been killed. Although the Venetian Senate offered reparation to Napoleon, he refused to receive the Venetian envoys. Within a month after the incident, Venice, fearing a French invasion, adopted a democratic form of government subordinate to France.

16. Late in 1794 Russian troops had defeated the Polish uprising led by Tadeusz Kosciusko against the second partition of Poland by Russia and Prussia. Russia and Austria then arranged for a third partition which on January 3, 1795, awarded the greatest share to Russia; a smaller one, including Cracow and part of Galicia, to Austria; and the smallest, including Warsaw, to Prussia (Martens, *Recûeil*, VI, 168–71). The Convention of St. Petersburg, signed by the three powers on October 24, 1795, slightly modified this arrangement and gave to Prussia part of the territory to the north of Warsaw previously claimed by Austria (Martens, *Recûeil*, VI, 171–75). On November 25, 1795, the King of Poland, Stanislas Poniatowski, formally abdicated.

17. In 1797 a number of Swiss democrats, notably Peter Ochs of Basel, had appealed first to the Directory and later to Napoleon for support in unifying the cantons and overthrowing the oligarchs. Early in 1798, after an attack by Bernese troops, the French invaded the canton of Vaud. In February, 1798, French troops occupied Berne. Subsequently civil war broke out between the Catholic and Protestant cantons and continued through the spring of 1798.

people who appear determined to meet the impending danger with a countenance emulous of their ancient renown?

The United States—what is their situation? Their sovereignty trampled in the dust and their commerce bleeding at every pore, speak in loud accents the spirit of oppression and rapine, which characterises the usurpers of France. But of this a distinct view is requisite and will be taken.

In these transactions we discover ambition and fanaticism marching hand in hand—bearing the ensigns of hypocrisy, treachery and rapine. The dogmas of a false and fatal creed second the weapons of ambition. Like the prophet of Mecca, the tyrants of France press forward with the alcoran of their faith in one hand, and the sword in the other—They proselyte, subjugate and debase—no distinction is made between republic and Monarchy—all must alike yield to the aggrandizement of the "GREAT NATION;" the distinctive, the arrogant appellation lately asumed by France to assert in the face of nations her superiority and ascendency. Nor is it a mere title with which vanity decorates itself. It is the substantial claim of dominion. France, swelled to a gigantic size and aping ancient Rome, except in her virtues, plainly meditates the controul of mankind, and is actually giving the law to nations. Unless they quickly rouse and compel her to abdicate her insolent claim, they will verify the truth of that philosophy, which makes man in his natural state a quadruped, and it will only remain for the miserable animal, converting his hands into paws, in the attitude of prone submission to offer his patient and servile back to whatever burthens the LORDLY TYRANTS of France may think fit to impose.   TITUS MANLIUS.

From Timothy Pickering

Philadelphia April 9. 1798.

Dear Sir,

This morning the dispatches from our envoys are published, and I inclose a copy.[1]

In your letter of March 27th in answer to mine of the 25th just then received, you say, "I shall write again to-morrow." I have received no letter from you since that of the 27th. which I mention on the presumption that you may have written, and because if you have, it is important on every account that it should be known.

You will readily imagine what apologies our internal enemies make for the French Government. Jefferson says that the Directory are not implicated in the villainy and corruption displayed in these dispatches—or at least that these offer no proof against them.[2] Bache's paper of last saturday says "That M. Talleyrand is notoriously anti republican; that he was the intimate friend of Mr. Hamilton, Mr. King and other great federalists,[3] and that it is probably owing to the determined hostility which he discovered in them towards France, that the Government of that country consider us only as objects of plunder." [4]

I am very truly yours   T Pickering

Alexander Hamilton Esqr.

ALS, Hamilton Papers, Library of Congress; ALS, letterpress copy, Massachusetts Historical Society, Boston.

    1. This is a reference to the first dispatches concerning the XYZ affair from the United States Envoys to France, Elbridge Gerry, John Marshall, and Charles Cotesworth Pinckney (*ASP, Foreign Relations*, II, 153–68). For the decision of Congress to have these dispatches printed, see *Annals of Congress*, VII, 536–37; VIII, 1377–80.

    The pamphlet in which the dispatches were published on April 9, 1798, is entitled *Message of the President of the United States, to both Houses of Congress, April 3, '98, With the Despatches from the Envoys of the United States at Paris, which accompanied the Same* (Philadelphia: John Fenno, 1798).

    2. It has not been possible to discover how Pickering knew that Thomas Jefferson was attempting to make a distinction between Talleyrand and the Directory in the XYZ affair, for no record has been found that Jefferson stated these views publicly. Malone states: "Jefferson entered into no public discussion of the XYZ dispatches . . ." (Dumas Malone, *Jefferson and the Ordeal of Liberty* [Boston, 1962], 373). On the other hand, on April 12, 1798, Jefferson wrote to Peter Carr: "As the instructions to our envoys & their communications have excited a great deal of curiosity, I enclose you a copy. You will perceive that they have been assailed by swindlers whether with or without the participation of Taleyrand is not very apparent. The known corruption of his character renders it very possible he may have intended to share largely in the 50.000 £ demanded. But that the Directory knew anything of it is neither proved nor probable. On the contrary, when the Portuguese ambassador yielded to like attempts of swindlers, the conduct of the Directory in imprisoning him for an attempt at corruption, as well as their general conduct, really magnanimous places them above suspicion. It is pretty evident that mr A's speech [to Congress on May 16, 1797] is in truth the only obstacle to negociation. That humiliating disavowals of that are demanded as a preliminary, or, as a commutation for that a heavy sum of money, about a million sterling. This obstacle removed, they seem not to object to an arrangement of all differences and even

to settle & acknolege themselves debtors for spoliations" (ALS, letterpress copy, Thomas Jefferson Papers, Library of Congress). See also Jefferson to James Madison, April 6, 1798 (ALS, letterpress copy, Jefferson Papers, Library of Congress); Jefferson to Madison, April 15, 1798 (ALS, James Madison Papers, Library of Congress).

3. After the overthrow of the French monarchy in 1792, Charles Maurice de Talleyrand-Périgord left France for England. Expelled from that country early in 1794, he sailed for the United States, where he remained until June, 1796. He returned to Paris in September of the same year.

4. This quotation is from an editorial entitled "The Dispatches of the Envoys" in Benjamin Franklin Bache's [Philadelphia] *Aurora. General Advertiser,* April 7, 1798.

From David Ford [1]

Morris Town [New Jersey]
April 11th. 1798

Dear Sir

The endeavours & industry of the Enemies of America, The French Faction, is becoming every day greater. Nothing bounds their Ambition, but a total over throw of the Government, to this end evry possible scheem of villany is used. Now under the Spacious pretence of Peace, they are in evry part of this state, endeavouring to raise distrust towards the Gouvernment. Our Town Meetings in this part of New Jesey are held by law the 2d. Monday in April. On that day by a concerted plan the demons came forward at allmost evry pole and surprized the People with a Remonstrance as they called it against War.[2] These in general were drawn so as to Criminate our own Chief Magistrate & those who support him—and in Most places the Idea of its being a Petition for Peace, obtained it support. All this is a prelude to the succeeding Election in Octr., for Members of Congress.

But the greatest evil that prevades our Country is the Country Presses, these have been many of them set up & supported by the Democratic party in different places, and those not Actually raised by their Private Collections of Money Have been as it were siezed, or hired, by the party to retail scandal against the Gouvernment, so that 9 tenths of the Presses out of the great towns in America to the South of the Hudson are Democratic & most of them in direct pay, or by influences. While the opposes of the Gouvernment are doing all this & ten times as much by misrepresentation—The Wealth Information & Abilities of our Country, are not Exalted at all, or very little indeed. But not at all to my knowledge by establishing & supporting with Money good Presses throughout the Country, whereby the People would be truely informed for I am bold to say if they knew the Truth the French faction may sink. But there is an Attatchment for Paper printed among ourselves, and it is easily got & Cheap, by this means there is a Constant stream of misrepresentation overwhelming the people. And those rightly disposed at last are corrupted. I know of no other way to remedy this evil than for the Gentlemen of the Federal Interest to become subscribers in the different out Towns to these Papers, and then Write for them, so as that evry paper should contain a good piece or two in favor of Gouvernment. It is very singular yet True, that the People of Elizabeth Town are Federal, & Yet there Issue from that Town, as infamous & inflamatory a Paper [3] as any in the Country. Your Wisdom & advice will best decide what is to do. If something is not speedily & spiritedly done, I fear we shall have some Jacobins elected.

My Present Ideas are that now is a very favorable Opportunity for the Federal Interest to rally & by Public County or Town Meetings, give that tone & current which the late dispatches so fully furnish, now the Spirit is up, Keep it up by addresses ⟨in⟩ the Public Papers & Mee⟨ting⟩s, the Rascally French are down, but they will make out a set of lies to at least palsey the Proceedings of Gouvernment.

I hope You will excuse this Liberty of addressing You, but I know of no man whose Abilities & Interest is sufficient to Stem the torrent—unless You exert yourself.

With Great Respect & Esteem I am Dear Sir Your Very Hle.
Sert   David Ford

Alexr. Hambleton Esqr

ALS, Hamilton Papers, Library of Congress.

1. Ford, a native of Morristown, New Jersey, and a member of the New Jersey militia, commanded a troop of New Jersey soldiers during the Whiskey Insurrection. For further information on Ford, see Samuel Ogden to H, October 5, 1795.

2. At a town meeting at Newark, New Jersey, on April 9, 1798, "an address to both houses of Congress was brought forward, and adopted by almost the

unanimous voice of the meeting, earnestly desiring the government to restrain the arming of our merchant ships, and to refrain from instituting or augmenting a naval armament—but at the same time expressed their firm determination to support the constitution of the United States with their lives and fortunes . . ." ([Philadelphia] *Aurora. General Advertiser*, April 14, 1798).

3. This is a reference to *The New-Jersey Journal*, which was published by Shepard Kollock.

The Stand No. IV [1]

[New York, April 12, 1798]

In the pursuit of her plan of universal empire, the two objects which now seem chiefly to occupy the attention of France, are a new organization of Germany favorable to her influence, and the demolition of Great Britain. The subversion and plunder, first of Portugal, next of Spain, will be merely collateral incidents in the great drama of iniquity.

In the new distribution of the territories, population and political power of the Germanic body, which has been announced as in contemplation of the Directory, three characters are conspicuous—a disposition to build up rivals to the Imperial chief, strong enough to feel the sentiment of competition, but too weak to hazard it alone, who will therefore stand in need of the patronage of France, and as a consequence will facilitate her influence in the affairs of the Empire—a generosity in making compensation, at the expense of others, for the spoils with which she has aggrandized herself—a facility in transferring communities, like herds of cattle, from one master to another, without the privilege of an option. In a project like this, it is impossible to overlook the plain indications of a restless, overbearing ambition, combined with a total disregard of the rights and wishes of nations. The People are counted for nothing, their Masters for everything.

The conduct of France towards Great Britain is the copy of that of Rome towards Carthage. Its manifest aim is to destroy the principal obstacle to a domination over Europe. History proves, that

The [New York] *Commercial Advertiser*, April 12, 1798.

1. The other issues of "The Stand" are dated March 30, April 4, 7, 16, 19, 21, 1798.

Great Britain has repeatedly upheld the balance of power there, in opposition to the grasping ambition of France. She has no doubt occasionally employed the pretence of danger as the instrument of her own ambition; but it is not the less true, that she has been more than once an essential and an effectual shield against real danger. This was remarkably the case in the reign of Louis the XIVth, when the security of Europe was seriously threatened by the successful enterprizes of that very ambitious monarch.

The course of the last negociation between France and Britain leaves no doubt, that the former was resolved against peace on any practicable terms.[2] This of itself indicates, that the destruction of the latter is the direct object in view. But this object is not left to inference. It has been fastidiously proclaimed to the world—and the necessity of crushing the TYRANT of the SEA has been trumpeted as a motive to other powers to acquiesce in the execution of a plan, by which France endeavors to become the Tyrant both of SEA and LAND. The understanding of mankind has, at the same time, been mocked, with the proposition that the Peace of Europe would be secured by the aggrandizement of France on the ruins of her rivals; because then, it is said, having nothing to fear, she would have no motive to attack; as if moderation was to be expected from a government or people having the power to impose its own will without control. The peace of Europe would in such case be the peace of vassalage.

Towards the execution of the plan of destroying Great Britain, the rights of other nations are openly and daringly invaded. The confiscation is decreed of all vessels with their cargoes, if composed in any part of articles of British fabric; and all nations are to be compelled to shut their ports against the meditated victim[3] Hamburgh is stated to have already reluctantly yielded to this humiliating compulsion.[4]

2. See Timothy Pickering to H, first letter of March 25, 1798, note 15.
3. See H to Pickering, March 17, 1798, note 3.
4. According to The [London] Times, February 22, 1798, "the Directory had obtained sufficient influence with the Senate of Hamburgh to cause that port to be shut against the English." French efforts to halt trade between Hamburg and Britain failed, however, and on September 11, 1798, the [Paris] Gazette Nationale ou Le Moniteur Universel reported: "Hambourg—Commerce florissant entre l'Angleterre et cette ville" (Réimpression de L'Ancien Moniteur, XXIX, 384).

While the demolition of Great Britain is eagerly pursued as a primary object, that of Portugal seems designed to form an Episode in the Tragedy. Her fears had induced her to buy a peace.[5] The money which she had paid was the immediate instrument of the revolution of September last [6]—Yet no sooner had the news of pacification with the Emperor [7] reached Paris, than pretences were sought to elude the ratification of the purchased treaty. A larger tribute was demanded, more, probably, than it was expected Portugal would be able to pay, to serve as an excuse for marching an army to revolutionize and plunder.* The blow may perhaps be suspended by further sacrifices, but it is not likely to be finally averted.

Spain, too, was in a fair way of enjoying the fruits of her weakness in putting on the yoke of France, and of furnishing another proof of the general scheme of aggrandizement and oppression. The demand of the cession of *Louisiana*, long pressed upon her, had at length become categoric. The alternative was to comply or offend. The probability is that before this time the cession has been made; and *Spain* has learnt, to her cost, that the chief privilege of an ally of France is to be plundered at discretion. With the acquisition of Louisiana, the foundation will be laid for stripping her of South America and her mines; and perhaps for dismembering the United States. The magnitude of this mighty mischief is not easy to be calculated.[8]

Such vast projects and pretensions pursued by such unexampled means are full evidence of a plan to acquire an absolute ascendant among nations. The difficulties in the final execution of a plan of this kind are, with many, decisive reasons against its existence. But in the case of ancient Rome, did it not in fact exist, and was it not substantially realized? Does the experience of the present day warrant the opinion that men are not as capable of mad and wicked projects as they were at any former period? Does not the conduct of the French government display a vastness and sublimation of

* Such is the account of this transaction received thro authentic channels.
    5. See Pickering to H, first letter of March 25, 1798, note 9.
    6. This is a reference to the *coup d'état* of September 4, 1797 (18th Fructidor).
    7. H is referring to the Treaty of Campo Formio, October 17, 1797.
    8. See Pickering to H, first letter of March 25, 1798, notes 12, 13, and 14.

views, and enormity of ambition, and a destitution of principle, which render the supposition of such a design probable? Has not a more rapid progress been made towards its execution, than was ever made by Rome in an equal period? In their intercourse with foreign nations, do not the directory affect an ostentatious imitation of Roman pride and superiority? Is it not natural to conclude that the same spirit points to the same ends?

The project is possible. The evidence of its existence is strong, and it will be the wisdom of every other state to act upon the supposition of its reality.

Let it be understood, that the supposition does not imply the intention to reduce all other nations formally to the condition of provinces. This was not done by Rome in the zenith of her greatness. She had her provinces and she had her allies. But her allies were in fact her vassals. They obeyed her nod. Their Princes were deposed and created at her pleasure.

Such is the proud pre-eminence to which the ambition of France aspires! After securing as much territory as she thinks it expedient immediately to govern, after wresting from Great-Britain and attaching to herself the command of the sea, after despoiling Spain of the riches of Mexico and Peru, after attaining by all these means to a degree of strength sufficient to defy and awe competition, she may be content, under the modest denomination of allies, to rule the rest of the world by her frown or her smile.

The character of the actual Directory of France justifies the imputation to them of any project the most extravagant and criminal. Viewed internally, as well as externally, their conduct is alike detestable. They have overturned the constitution, which they were appointed to administer with circumstances of barefaced guilt that disgrace a revolution, before so tarnished as seemed scarcely to admit of greater degradation; and have erected in its stead a military despotism, cloathed, but not disguised with the mere garb of the constitution which they have abolished. In the accomplishment of this usurpation, they have assassinated one of their colleagues,* and

* Carnot—as was reported at the time, and as is confirmed by nothing having been since heard of him.[9] He had been too deeply in the horid secrets of the violent party. It was necessary to silence him.

9. Lazare Nicholas Marguerite Carnot was a French revolutionist who as a member of the Committee of Public Safety organized and determined the

seized and banished another,[10] together with all those members of the two councils, who were disposed and able to combat their pernicious aims. They have done more; not content with rendering themselves masters of the two councils, and converting them into the mere pageants of national representation, they have thot it proper to secure their own power by exiling or imprisoning such private citizens as they feared might promote the future election of men hostile to their views, on the futile pretence of a counter-revolutionary plot to be effected by *royalizing* the elections. Thus have they not only monopolized all the power for the present, but they have made provisions for its perpetuation; so long at least as the PRÆTORIAN BANDS will permit.

No impartial man can doubt that the Plot charged upon the exiled members is a forgery. The characters of several of the accused bely it. *Barthelemy* and *Pichegru*[11] are virtuous men. The former has long merited and possessed this character. The latter has given numerous proofs of a good title to it—his only fault seems to have been that of enthusiasm in the worst of causes. Neither of them, like DUMOURIER,[12] had been from his entrance on Public life marked out as the votary of an irregular ambition. The alledged object of the plot, as to such men, from the circumstances of the conjuncture, was wholly improbable; nothing like satisfactory proof has come to light. But the decisive argument of their innocence is, that the usurpers did not dare to confront them with a fair legal accusation and trial. It was so clearly their interest and policy to have justified themselves by establishing the guilt of the accused, if in their power, that the omission to attempt it is the demonstration of its

---

strategy of the French army. He became a member of the Directory, but in 1797 was sentenced to deportation. After the *coup d'état* of September 4, 1797 (18th Fructidor), Carnot fled the country. He returned to France in 1799 and lived until 1823.

10. François Barthélemy, who had been ambassador to Switzerland for five years, was elected to the Directory in May, 1797. He was arrested as a result of the *coup d'état* of September 4, 1797, was deported to Cayenne, but escaped and returned to France in 1799.

11. See Rufus King to H, September 9, 1797, note 3.

12. Following his defeat by the Austrians at Neerwinden on March 18, 1793, Charles François Dumouriez, a French general, tried unsuccessfully to persuade his troops to march on Paris and destroy the revolutionary government. He then went over to the enemy and spent the last years of his life in England intriguing against France.

impossibility. Having all authority in their own hands, and the army at their devotion, they had nothing to fear from the pursuit; and they must have foreseen that the banishment, without trial, would finally marshal public opinion against them. There can be little doubt that the people of France at this moment regard, with compassion and regret, the banished Directors and Deputies, and with horror and detestation the authors of their disgrace. But the people of France internally are annihilated. To their liberty and happiness this last usurpation gave a more fatal blow than any or all of the former. It has more of system in it; and being less sanguinary is less likely to provoke resistence from despair.

The inference from the transaction is evident. The real crime of the banished was the desire of arresting the mad career of the directory and of restoring peace to France, in the hope that peace might tend to settle the government on the foundations of order, security and tranquility. The majority of the directory foresaw that Peace would not prove an element congenial with the duration of their power; or perhaps under the guidance of SIEYES, the conjuror of the scene, they judged it expedient to continue in motion the revolutionary wheel, till matters were better prepared for creating a new DYNASTY and a new ARISTOCRACY,* to regenerate the exploded monarchy of France with due regard to their own interest.

Thus we perceive, that the interior conduct of the directory has the same characters with their exterior—the same irregular ambition, the same contempt of principle, the same boldness of design, the same temerity of execution. From such men, what is not to be expected? The development of their recent conduct towards the United States will no doubt confirm all the inferences to be drawn from other parts of the portrait; and will contribute to prove that

---

* There is good evidence that this is at bottom the real plan of the Abbe Sieyes; [13] and some of the most influential in the Executive Department are his creatures.

13. During the *coup d'état* of September 4, 1797, Abbé Emmanuel Joseph Sieyès was appointed by the Council of Five Hundred to a committee of five to help "ensure the public safety and the preservation of the Constitution of the Year Three" (J. H. Clapham, *The Abbé Sieyès* [London, 1912], 197). In May, 1799, Sieyès was chosen a Director of France, and in June he began actively to plot against the Directory. He allied with Napoleon, and through this alliance the Directory was overthrown by the *coup d'état* of Brumaire (November 9–10, 1799).

there is nothing too abandoned or too monstrous for them to medi-
tate or attempt.

Who that loves his country or respects the dignity of his nature,
would not rather perish than subscribe to the prostration of both
before such men and such a system? What sacrifice, what danger is
too great to be incurred in opposition to both? What security in
any compromise with such unprincipled tyranny? What safety but
in union, in vigor, in preparation for every extremity, in a decisive
and corageous stand for the rights and honor of our injured and
insulted Country?   TITUS MANLIUS.

The Stand No. V [1]

[New York, April 16, 1798]

To estimate properly the conduct of revolutionary France
towards the United States the circumstances which have reciprocally
taken place must be viewed together. It is a WHOLE not a PART which
is to be contemplated. A rapid Summary, nevertheless, of the most
material is all that can be presented.

Not only the unanimous good wishes of the citizens of this country spontaneously attached themselves to the Revolution of France
in its first stages But no sooner was the change from monarchy to
a Republic officially announced than our Government, consulting
the principles of our own revolution and the wishes of our citizens,
hastened to acknowlege the new order of things. This was done to
the last Minister [2] sent by Louis the XVI, before the arrival of the

ADf, Hamilton Papers, Library of Congress; *The* [New York] *Commercial
Advertiser,* April 16, 1798.

   1. The other issues of "The Stand" are dated March 30, April 4, 7, 12, 19,
21, 1798. H mistakenly numbered this issue of "The Stand" "No. IV."

   2. Jean Baptiste de Ternant. On March 5, 1792, George Washington sent to
Congress a translation of a letter from Louis XVI, dated September 19, 1791,
announcing his acceptance of the new French constitution (*ASP, Foreign
Relations,* I, 133). On March 10, 1792, the House of Representatives resolved:
"That this House had received, with sentiments of high satisfaction, the notification of the King of the French, of his acceptance of the Constitution presented to him in the name of the Nation: And that the President of the United
States be requested, in his answer to the said notification, to express the sincere
participation of the House in the interests of the French Nation, on this great
and important event, and their wish that the wisdom and magnanimity dis-

first envoy from the republic. Genet afterwards came—his reception by the Government was cordial, by the people enthusiastic.

The Government did not merely receive the Minister of the Republic, in fact, and defer the obligation of Treaties till the contest concerning its establishment had been terminated by success: But giving the utmost latitude to the maxim that real treaties bind nations notwithstanding revolutions of Government, ours did not hesitate to admit the immediate operations of the antecedent treaties between the two countries; though the revolution could not be regarded as yet fully accomplished; though a warrant for a contrary policy might have been found in the example of France herself and though the treaties contained several stipulations which gave to her important preferences relative to war & which were likely to give umbrage to the powers coalesced against her.[3]

In acknowleging the republic, the U States preceded every other nation. It was not till a long time after that any of the neutral powers followed the example. Had prudence been exclusively consulted, our Government might not have done all that it did at this juncture, when the case was very nearly EUROPE in arms against FRANCE.

But good faith and a regard to consistency of principle prevailed over the sense of danger. It was resolved to encounter it; qualify-

_____

played in the formation and acceptance of the Constitution, may be rewarded by the most perfect attainment of its object, the permanent happiness of so great a people" (*Annals of Congress,* III, 456–57). On March 13, 1792, the Senate resolved: "That the President of the United States be informed that the Senate have received with satisfaction the official intelligence that the King of the French has accepted the Constitution presented to him by the National Assembly, and are highly gratified by every event that promotes the freedom and prosperity of the French nation and the happiness and glory of their King" (*Annals of Congress,* III, 107). On March 13, 1792, Ternant wrote to Claude Antoine de Valdec de Lessart, French Minister for Foreign Affairs, describing the actions of Congress and his reception by Washington and Thomas Jefferson (Frederick J. Turner, ed., "Correspondence of French Ministers to the United States, 1791–1797," *Annual Report of the American Historical Association for the Year 1903* [Washington, 1904], II, 94–97).

3. For a description of the provisions of the 1778 treaties of Alliance and of Amity and Commerce with France and their effect on the diplomatic position of the United States in 1793, see H to John Jay, first letter of April 9, 1793; Washington to H, Jefferson, Henry Knox, and Edmund Randolph, April 18, 1793; "Cabinet Meeting. Opinion on a Proclamation of Neutrality and on Receiving the French Minister," April 19, 1793; H and Knox to Washington, May 2, 1793; H to Washington, May 20, 1796, note 4.

ing the step by the manifestation of a disposition to observe a sincere neutrality as far as should consist with the stipulations of Treaty. Hence the proclamation of neutrality.

It ought to have no small merit in the eyes of France that at so critical a period of her affairs we were willing to run risks so imminent. The fact is, that it had nearly implicated us in the war on her side at a juncture when all calculations were against her, and when it was certain she could have afforded us no protection or assistance.

What was the return? *Genet* came with neutrality on his lips but war in his heart. The instructions published by himself [4] and his practice upon them demonstrate that it was the premeditated plan to involve us in the contest not by a candid appeal to the judgment friendship or interest of our country but by alluring the avarice of bad citizens into acts of predatory hostility by instituting within our territory military expeditions against nations with whom we were at peace.[5] And when it was found that our Executive would not connive at this insidious plan, bold attempts were made to create a scism between the people and the government and consequently to sow the seeds of civil discord insurrection and revolution. Thus began the Republic.

It is true that the *Girondist* Faction having been subverted by that of Robespierre,[6] our complaint of the Agent of the former was attended with success. The spirit of vengeance came in aid of the justice of our demand. The offending Minister was recalled with disgrace.[7] But Robespierre did not fail in a public speech to give a

4. *The Correspondence between Citizen Genet, Minister of the French Republic, to the United States of North America, and the officers of the Federal government, to which are prefixed the Instructions from the constituted authorities of France to the said minister. All from authentic documents* (Philadelphia: Benjamin Franklin Bache, 1793).

5. For the activities of Edmond Charles Genet, see "Cabinet Meetings. Proposals Concerning the Conduct of the French Minister," August 1–23, 1793; Proposed Presidential Message to Congress Concerning Revocation of Edmond Charles Genet's Diplomatic Status," January 6–13, 1794.

6. The "revolution" of May 31–June 2, 1793, resulted in the expulsion and arrest of the Girondin leaders. On July 27, 1793, Maximilien François Marie Isidore de Robespierre became a member of the Committee of Public Safety. For a discussion of these events and Robespierre's continued rise in power, see Georges Lefebvre, *The French Revolution From 1793 to 1799*, trans. John Hall Stewart and James Friguglietti (London and New York, 1964), 39–136.

7. On September 15, 1793, Jefferson informed Genet that the United States

gentle hint of delinquency in the United States, sufficiently indicating that the *authors* and the *manner* were more in fault in his opinion than the thing.[8] It was not then expedient to quarrel with us. There was still a hope that a course of things, or more dextrous management might embark us in the war as an auxiliary to France.

The Treaties were made by us the criterion of our duty; but as they did not require us to go to war, as France did never even pretend this to be the case, listening to the suggestions not only of interest but of safety, we resolved to endeavour to preserve peace. But we were equally resolved to fulfil our real obligations in every respect. We saw without murmur our property seized in belligerent vessels;[9] we allowed to French Ships of War and privateers all the peculiar exclusive privileges in our ports to which, they were entitled by our treaties upon fair construction, *upon a construction fully concurred in by the political leader* * *of the adherents to France*[10]—we went further, and gratuitously suffered her to sell her prizes in our country, in contravention perhaps of the true principles of neutrality[11]—we paid to her new government the debt contracted by us with the old not only as fast as it became due but

* Mr. Jefferson.

Government had requested his recall (ADf, Thomas Jefferson Papers, Library of Congress). For the decision to ask for Genet's recall, see "Cabinet Meetings. Proposals Concerning the Conduct of the French Minister," August 1–23, 1793; "Conversation with George Hammond," August 2–10, 1793; "Notes for a Letter to Gouverneur Morris," August 2–16, 1793; H to Washington, August 5, 1793; "Proposed Presidential Message to Congress Concerning Revocation of Edmond Charles Genet's Diplomatic Status," January 6–13, 1794; "Cabinet Meeting. Opinion on a Presidential Message to Congress on the Recall of Edmond Charles Genet," January 19, 1794. See also Jefferson to Morris, August 16, 1793 (*ASP, Foreign Relations*, I, 167–72). In his message to Congress on January 20, 1794, Washington wrote that Genet's "conduct has been unequivocally disapproved; and that the strongest assurances have been given, that his recall should be expedited without delay" (LC, George Washington Papers, Library of Congress). Washington received Jean Antoine Joseph Fauchet, the new French Minister, on February 22, 1794 (JPP, 274). In November, 1793, the French Ministry had ordered Fauchet to arrest Genet and return him to France (Turner, "Correspondence of French Ministers," 288–94).

8. This is a reference to Robespierre's speech of November 17, 1793 (*Réimpression de L'Ancien Moniteur*, XVIII, 459).

9. For British depredations on United States commerce, see, for example, the introductory note to H to Washington, March 8, 1794.

10. See Jefferson to Washington, April 28, 1793 (ADS, George Washington Papers, Library of Congress). See also H and Knox to Washington, May 2, 1793.

11. See H to John Jay, first letter of April 9, 1793, note 2; "Treasury Department Circular to the Collectors of the Customs," May 30, 1793.

by an anticipation which did not give pleasure to her enemies.[12] While our government was faithful; our citizens were zealous. Not content with good wishes they adventured their property and credit in the furnishing of supplies to an extent that showed in many cases the cooperation of zeal with interest. Our country, our Merchants and our ships in the gloomy periods of her Revolution have been the organs of succours to France to a degree which give us an undoubted title to the character of very useful friends.

Reverse the medal. France from the beginning has violated essential points in the Treaties between the two countries. The first formal *unequivocal* act by either of the belligerent parties interfering with the rule that "free ships make free goods" was a decree of the French Convention.[13] This violation has been persisted in and successive violations added till they amount to a general war on our commerce.

First the plea of necessity repelled our feeble and modest complaints of infractions. Next the plea of delinquencies on our part was called in aid of the depredations which it was found convenient to practice upon our trade. Our refusal to record privileges not granted by our Treaties but claimed by [14] misconstructions destitute even of plausibility, privileges which would have put us at once in a state of war with the enemies of France the reciprocal application to them of principles originally established against their remonstrances in favour of France * occasioned embarrassments to her

---

* *Note.* This was the case as to the horses procured by the British in Virginia. France had before freely procured military supplies in our Country. The British Minister had remonstrated. The reply, adhered to, was that belligerent powers had a right to procure supplies in a neutral country.[15]

12. See the introductory note to H to George Latimer, January 2, 1793; H to Fauchet, May 5, 1794; "Report on Loans Negotiated in Europe Not Already Laid Before the Legislature," May 27, 1794, notes 2 and 8; Randolph to H, first letter of June 23, 1794, note 1.

13. This is a reference to the decree of May 9, 1793, which authorized French vessels to seize and carry into French ports vessels laden with provisions for an enemy port (Duvergier, *Lois*, V, 343–44).

14. In MS, "my."

15. On February 16, 1796, Timothy Pickering wrote to Phineas Bond, the British chargé d'affaires at Philadelphia at that time: "On the receipt of your note of the 8th. instant, relative to the proceedings at Norfolk in Virginia, to prevent the shipments of Horses or the departure of vessels hired at the instance of [John Hamilton] his Britannic Majesty's Consul, and having Horses on board, to be conveyed to the west Indies, I had the honor personally to inform you, that the President of the united States deemed such Shipments

privateers, arising from the established forms of our courts and the necessity of vigilance to frustrate her efforts to entangle us against our will in the war—delays in giving relief in a few instances rendered unavoidable by the nature of our government and the great extent of our territory—these were so many topics of bitter accusation against our government and of insult as rude as was unmerited. Our citizens in judging whether the accusation was captious or well founded ought to bear in mind that most of the transactions on which it was predicated happened under the administrations of *Jefferson* and *Randolph;* and, as is well ascertained with their full assent & cooperation. They will not readily suppose that these *very cunning* men were the dupes of colleagues actuated by ill will towards France; but they will discover in this union opinon among men of very opposite principles, a strong probability that our government acted with propriety and that the dissatisfaction of France, if more than a colour, was unreasonable.

Hitherto the progress, no less than the origin of our controversy with France, exhibits plain marks of a disposition on her part to disregard those provisions in the treaties which it was our interest should be observed by her, to exact from us a scrupulous performance of our engagements and even the extension of them beyond their true import—to embroil us with her enemies contrary to our inclination and interest and without even the allegation of a claim upon our faith—to make unreasonable demands upon us the grounds of complaints against us and excuses to violate our property and rights, to divide our nation and to disturb our government.

---

not repugnant either to the laws of nations, to the laws of the united States or to our treaty with France: That this opinion had been first communicated to the minister of the French Republic in answer to his complaints, and afterwards to the Executive of Virginia, whose interposition had been directly requested by [Martin Oster] the French vice-Consul at Norfolk" (LC, Domestic Letters of the Department of State, Vol. 9, October 12, 1795–February 28, 1797, National Archives; copy, Massachusetts Historical Society, Boston). Pickering's letter to Pierre Auguste Adet is dated January 20, 1796 (LC, Domestic Letters of the Department of State, Vol. 9, October 12, 1795–February 28, 1797, National Archives), and his letter to Robert Brooke, governor of Virginia, is dated January 29, 1796 (LC, Domestic Letters of the Department of State, Vol. 9, October 12, 1795–February 28, 1797, National Archives). See also Pickering to Brooke, February 6, 1796 (LC, Domestic Letters of the Department of State, Vol. 9, October 12, 1795–February 28, 1797, National Archives; copy, Massachusetts Historical Society, Boston); Adet to Pickering, January 12, March 11, 1796 (*ASP, Foreign Relations,* I, 645–49).

Many of the most determined advocates of France among us appear latterly to admit that previous to the Treaty with Great Britain, the complaints of France against the U States were frivolous, those of the United States against France real and serious. But the Treaty with G Britain,[16] it is affirmed, has changed the ground. This, it is said, has given just cause of discontent to France—this has brought us to the verge of war with our first ally and best friend —to this fatal instrument are we indebted for the evils we feel and the still greater which impend over our heads.

These suggestions are without the shadow of foundation; They prove the infatuated devotion to a foreign power of those who invented them and the easy credulity of those with whom they have obtained currency. The evidence of a previous disposition in France to complain without cause and to injure without provocation is a sufficient comment upon the resentment she professes against the Treaty. The partiality or indulgence with which the ill treatment received from her prior to that event was viewed by her decided partisans is a proof of the facility with which they credit her pretences and palliate her aggressions.

The most significant of the charges against the Treaty, as it respects France, is that it abandonned the rule of free ships making free goods [17]—that it extended unduly the list of contraband articles and gave colour to the claim of a right to subject provisions to seizure [18]—that a Treaty of amity with the enemy of France in the midst of a war was a mark of preference to that enemy and of ill will to her. The replies which have been given to these charges are conclusive.[19]

16. The Jay Treaty was signed on November 19, 1794, and proclaimed on February 29, 1796. For the text of the treaty, see Miller, *Treaties*, II, 245–67.
17. Article 17 of the Jay Treaty provided that "in all cases where Vessels shall be captured or detained on just suspicion of having on board Enemy's property or of carrying to the Enemy, any of the articles which are Contraband of war; The said Vessels shall be brought to the nearest or most convenient Port, and if any property of an Enemy, should be found on board such Vessel, that part only which belongs to the Enemy shall be made prize, and the Vessel shall be at liberty to proceed with the remainder without any Impediment . . ." (Miller, *Treaties*, II, 258).
18. This is a reference to the provisions of Article 18 of the Jay Treaty. For the text of this article, see "Remarks on the Treaty . . . between the United States and Great Britain," July 9–11, 1795, note 63.
19. For H's "replies," see "Remarks on the Treaty . . . between the United States and Great Britain," July 9–11, 1795; "The Defence Nos. XXXI, XXXII, XXXIII," December 12, 16, 19, 1795.

As to the first point—The stipulation of two powers to observe between themselves a particular rule in their respective wars a rule too innovating upon the general law of nations can on no known or reasonable principle of interpretation be construed to intend that they will insist upon that rule with all other nations, and will make no treaty with any however beneficial in other respects which does not comprehend it. To tie up the will of a nation and its power of providing for its own interests to so immense an extent required a stipulation in positive terms. In vain shall we seek in the Treaty for such a stipulation or its equivalent. There is not even a single expression to imply it. The idea is consequently no less ridiculous than it is novel. The cotemporary proceedings legislative and judiciary of our government shew that it was not so understood in this country. Congress even declined to become a formal party to the armed neutrality,[20] of which it was the basis; unwilling to be pledged for the coercive maintenance of a principle which they were only disposed to promote by particular pacts. It is equally futile to seek to derive the obligation of the U States to adhere to this rule from the supposition of a change in the law of nations by the force of that league. Neither theory nor practice warrants the attributing so important an effect to a military association springing up in the war and ending with it; not having had the universal consent of nations nor a course of long practice to give it a sanction.

Were it necessary to resort to an auxiliary argument, it might be said with conclusive force, that France having before our Treaty with Great Britain violated in practice the rule in question absolved us from all obligation to observe it, if any did previously exist.

As to the second point—it has been repeatedly demonstrated that the enumeration of contraband in the treaty with Great Britain is agreeable to the *general* law of nations. But this is a matter from its nature liable to vary according to relative situation, and to be variously modified not only between different nations but between one nation and different nations. Thus in our Treaty with Great Britain some articles are enumerated which are omitted in that with France; in that with France some articles are inserted which are

20. For information on the armed neutrality and United States reaction to it, see Randolph to William Bradford, H, and Knox, March 13, 1794; H to Washington, April 23, 1794, note 13; "Conversation with George Hammond," July 1–10, 1794; H to Randolph, July 8, 1794.

omitted in that with Britain. But it is perhaps the first time that a diversity of this sort has been deemed a ground of umbrage to a third party.

With regard to provisions, the treaty only decides that where *by the law of nations* they are subject to seizure they are to be paid for. It does not define or admit any new case. As to its giving colour to abuse in this respect, thus if true would amount to nothing. For till some abuse has actually happened and been tolerated to the prejudice of France there was no cause of complaint. The possibility of abuse from a doubtful construction of a Treaty between two powers is no subject of offence to a third. It is the fact which must govern. According to this indisputable criterion, France has had no cause to complain on this account; for since the ratification of the Treaty no instance of the seizure of provisions has occurred & it is known that our government protested against such a construction.[21]

Further, the Treaty has made no change whatever in the actual antecedent state of things to the disadvantage of France.

Great Britain had before the Treaty with the sanction of our Government acted upon the principles, as to free ships making free goods and generally as to the affair of contraband which the treaty recognizes. Nor was That sanction merely tacit but explicit and direct. It was even diplomatically communicated to the Agents of France.[22] If there was any thing wrong therefore in this matter, it was chargeable, not upon the Treaty, but upon the prior measures of the Government, which had left these points mere points of form in the Treaty.

The remaining charge against that instrument involves a species of political metaphysics. Neither the theory of Writers nor the history of nations will bear out the position, that a treaty of amity, between a neutral state and one belligerent party not granting either succours or new privileges relative to war not derogating from any obligation of the neutral state to the other belligerent party is a cause of umbrage to the latter. There can be no reason why a

21. See Adet to Pickering, October 27, 1796; Pickering to Adet, November 1, 1796 (*ASP, Foreign Relations,* I, 576–78).

22. See Jefferson to Jean Baptiste de Ternant, May 15, 1793 (*ASP, Foreign Relations,* I, 147); Jefferson to Genet, July 24, 1793 (LC, RG 59, Domestic Letters of the Department of State, Vol. 5, February 4, 1792–December 31, 1793, National Archives).

neutral power should not settle differences or adjust a plan of intercourse beneficial to itself with another power because this last happens to be at war with a third. All this must be a mere question of curtesy; and might be uncurtious or otherwise according to circumstances, but never a ground of quarrel. If there even might have been want of curtesy in the U States to have entered into a Treaty of this sort with the enemy of France, had they volunteered it without cogent motives—there could be none in the particular situation. They were led to the Treaty by preexisting differences which had nearly ripened to a rupture, and the amicable settlement of which affected very important interests. No favourable conjunction for this settlement was to be lost. The settlement, by the usual formulas in such cases, would amount to a Treaty of Amity.

Thus is it evident, that the Treaty, like all the rest, has been a mere pretence for ill treatment. But admitting that this was not the case, that it really afforded some cause of displeasure, was this of a nature to admit of no atonement, or of none short of the humiliation of our country?

If the contrary must be conceded, it is certain that our Government has done all that was possible towards reconciliation, and enough to have satisfied any reasonable or just government.

France after the treaty proceeded to inflict still deeper wounds upon our commerce. She has endeavoured to intercept [23] and destroy it with all the ports of her enemies. Nor was this the worst. The spoliation has frequently extended to our trade with her own dominions attended with unparall[el]ed circumstances of rapacity and violence.

The diplomatic representative of the French Government to the U States was ordered to deliver to our government a most insulting manifesto and then to withdraw.[24]

Yet our government, notwithstanding this accumulation of

23. In MS, "incercept."
24. H is referring to Adet's letter to Pickering, dated November 15, 1796. The letter with its appended documents is printed in *ASP, Foreign Relations*, I, 579–667. See Oliver Wolcott, Jr., to H, November 17, 1796; H to Washington, November 19, 1796; Washington to H, November 21, 1796. For Adet's earlier attack on United States foreign policy, see Adet to Pickering, October 27, 1796 (*ASP, Foreign Relations*, I, 576–77). See also H to Wolcott, November 1, 1796; H to Washington, November 5, 11, 1796; Washington to H, November 2, 3, 1796.

wrongs, after knowing that it had been repeatedly outraged in the person of one Minister, condescended to send another specially charged to endeavour to conciliate. This Minister was known to unite fidelity to his country with principles friendly to France and her revolution. It was hoped that the latter would make him acceptable and that he would be able by amicable explanations and overtures to obviate misunderstanding and restore harmony. He was not received.[25]

Though it was very problematical whether the honor of the U States after this permitted a further advance; yet, the Government anxious if possible to preserve peace concluded to make another and more solemn experiment. A new mission, confided to three extraordinary ministers took place.[26] They were all three in different degrees men well affected to France and her revolution. They were all men of high respectability and among the purest characters of our country. Their powers and instructions were so ample as to have extorted from the most determined opposers of the government, in the two houses of Congress, a reluctant approbation in this instance of the Presidents conduct.

In contempt of established usage and of the respect due to us as an independent people, with the deliberate design of humbling and mortifying our government, these special and extraordinary ministers have been refused to be received.[27] Admitting all the charges brought against us by France to be well founded, still ministers of that description ought on every principle to have been accredited and conferred with, 'till it was ascertained that they were not ready to do as much as was expected. Not to pursue this course was to deny us the rank of an independent nation; it was to treat us as Great Britain did, while we were yet contending with her for this character.

Instead of this, informal Agents probably panders and mistresses, are appointed to intrigue with our envoys.[28] These attending only

25. For the French refusal to receive Charles Cotesworth Pinckney as United States Minister Plenipotentiary to France, see Pickering to H, March 30, 1797.

26. For the appointment of Pinckney, John Marshall, and Elbridge Gerry as Envoys Extraordinary and Ministers Plenipotentiary to France, see James McHenry to H, January 26, 1798, note 2.

27. For the French refusal to receive Pinckney, Marshall, and Gerry, see Pickering to H, first letter of March 25, 1798.

28. There has been some confusion as to the identities of the French agents "W," "X," "Y," and "Z," and the women to whom H is referring. "W" was

to the earnest wish of their constituents for peace, stoop to the conference. What is the mishapen result?

Nicholas Hubbard of the Dutch banking house of Nicholaas and Jacob Van Staphorst and Nicholas Hubbard, which served as bankers for the United States; "X" was Jean Conrad Hottinguer, a financier, who had been a banker in Paris and had connections in Holland; "Y" was Bellamy, who owned property in America and was a partner in the Hamburg banking firm of Bellamy and Riccé (Pinckney, Marshall, and Gerry to Pickering, October 22–27, 1797 [LS (duplicate and deciphered), RG 59, Despatches from United States Ministers to France, 1798–1869, Vol. 6, October 22, 1797–April 3, 1798, National Archives]). In 1795 Hottinguer was in the United States. As the agent of three commercial houses, Jean Samuel Couderc, Jan Brants, and Daniel Changuion of Amsterdam, James Curry and Company of Amsterdam, and Philip Lom of Seville, he signed articles of agreement on October 1, 1795, with Robert Morris, John Nicholson, and Walter Stewart for three hundred thousand acres of land in Northumberland and Huntingdon counties in Pennsylvania (DS, Historical Society of Pennsylvania, Philadelphia). On July 10, 1798, the following item appeared in *The* [London] *Times:* "A long narrative of the share which M. Y. had in the negociation carried on between the American Plenipotentiaries at Paris, and TALLEYRAND, the Minister for Foreign Affairs, has been addressed to the Editor of *L'Ami des Loix*, dated Hamburgh, the 25th of June. The writer of it, Mr. BELLAMY, avows himself to be the person designed by M. Y. and he enters into a very laboured justification of his conduct. It is the most uninteresting narrative we ever read.

"Mr. BELLAMY admits that he proposed to the Plenipotentiaries to buy up some Batavian Inscriptions, merely with a view *of shewing their attachment to the French Republic;* but he pleads in his vindication for doing so, that the proposition was made from 'his private individual opinion.' Yet in the beginning of his apology, he expressly says, speaking of and referring to Citizen Talleyrand—'*Without whose orders I have done nothing, said nothing, written nothing.*' Was then the proposition made to the American Commissioners to take 32 millions of Dutch Inscriptions at 20s. in the pound, which were only worth 10s. the act of TALLEYRAND or of BELLAMY? If we are to give credit to B's solemn declaration in the very outset of his justification, we must consider it only as the act of Talleyrand.

"If the charge brought against Citizen TALLEYRAND by the American Ministers stood in need of any additional proof, Mr. BELLAMY's letter would be strong corroboration of what is already before the Public, to convict the Ex-BISHOP and his Colleagues of the most gross fraud and corruption; for a more wretched attempt to vindicate was never before submitted to the tribunal of public opinion."

For the activities of Hottinguer and Bellamy, see Raymond Guyot, *Le Directoire Et La Paix De L'Europe Des Traités De Bâle A La Deuxième Coalition, 1795–1799* (Paris, 1911), 560–63.

"Z" was Lucien Hauteval, a Frenchman, who served as messenger and interpreter in the XYZ affair (diary, enclosed in Pinckney, Marshall, and Gerry to Pickering, November 8, 1797 [LS (deciphered), RG 59, Despatches from United States Ministers to France, 1789–1869, Vol. 6, October 22, 1797–April 3, 1798, National Archives]; Talleyrand to Gerry, June 1, 1798 [*ASP, Foreign Relations*, II, 210]). Gerry stated that he had known Hauteval "in the United States when driven from St. Domingo" (Gerry to John Adams, October 20, 1798 [ALS, Adams Family Papers, deposited in the Massachusetts Historical Society, Boston]). On June 1, 1798, Hauteval explained his role in the XYZ affair in a letter to Talleyrand: "In the beginning of last Brumaire, (October 22,

MONEY, MONEY is the burthen of the discordant song of these
foul birds of prey. Great indignation is at first professed against

---

1797,) having been to pay my respects to the citizen Minister of Exterior Relations [Talleyrand], and, the conversation turning upon the United States of
America, he expressed to me his surprize that none of the Americans, and
especially the new envoys, ever came to his house; that this was not the way
to open a negotiation, the success of which they had more reason than we to
wish; that he would receive them individually with great pleasure, and particularly Mr. Gerry, whom he had known at Boston. Knowing my friendly connexions with Mr. Gerry, he charged me to impart to them what he had
said. I accordingly waited on Mr. Gerry, who, having sent for his colleagues,
I communicated to them the conversation I had had with the citizen minister.
    "Messrs. Pinckney and Marshall declined waiting on the minister upon
the ground of ceremony; but as the same reason did not apply to Mr. Gerry,
it was agreed that he should the next day, and that I should accompany him,
Mr. Gerry at that time not being able to express himself in French. The next
day we went; but not finding the minister at home, Mr. Gerry requested him
to appoint a time for an interview, which was fixed for a few days after. We
attended accordingly, and, after the usual compliments, Mr. Gerry having expressed to the minister his desire to see harmony and a good understanding
re-established between the two republics, the minister anwered him that the
Directory had made a determination not to treat with them, unless they previously made reparation for some parts of the President's speech at the opening
of Congress, and gave an explanation of some others; that he could not delay,
but for a few days, communicating this determination officially to them; that,
until then, if they had any propositions to make, which could be agreeable to
the Directory, he would communicate them with alacrity; that considering the
circumstance, and the services of the same kind which France had formerly
rendered to the United States, the best way would be for them to offer to
make a loan to France, either by taking Batavian inscriptions for the sum
of fifteen or sixteen millions of florins, or in any other manner. Mr. Gerry,
after having replied in a polite, but evasive manner to the first article, added,
on the subject of the loan, that their powers did not extend so far, but that
he would confer with his colleagues upon the subject. It is to be observed that,
as the minister spoke nothing but French, I repeated in English to Mr. Gerry
what he had said to him, and that, although certain that he very well understood the answers of Mr. Gerry, I repeated them to him in French. We took
our leave of the minister who had just received a courier, and he charged me,
on parting, to repeat to Mr. Gerry and his colleagues what he had said to us.
Accordingly I repeated to Messrs. Pinckney and Marshall, in the presence of
Mr. Gerry, the conversation which we had had with the minister.
    "A few days afterwards Mr. Gerry requested me to accompany him again
on a visit to the minister, and having repeated to him the extreme desire he
felt to see the most perfect union re-established between the two nations, he
resorted to the insufficiency of their powers, and proposed, in the name of
his colleagues and himself, that one of them should immediately depart for
America with the propositions which the French Government might make.
The minister answered that it would require six months to have an answer,
and that it was of importance to have a speedy determination; that he was
extremely desirous to have frequent communications with them individually
and amicably. This course appearing to him to be the best adapted to come at
the issue of a speedy negotiation, he therefore lamented that he had yet had
no communication with them.

expressions in the Presidents speech of May last.[29] The reparation of a disavowal is absolutely due to the honor of the Directory and of the republic; but it turns out that there is a practicable substitute more valuable. The honor of both being a marketable commodity— is ready to be committed for gold.

A douceur of 50000 pounds Sterling for the special benefit of the Directory was to pave the way. Instead of reparation for the spoliations of our commerce exceeding twenty Millions of Dollars, a loan equal to the amount of them is to be made by us to the French Government. Then perhaps a mode might be settled for the liquidation of the claims of our Merchants to be compensated at some future period. The depredations nevertheless were to continue till the Treaty should be concluded, which from the distance between the two countries must at all events take a great length of time, and might be procrastinated [30] indefinitely at the pleasure of the Directory.

In addition to all this we must purchase of the Directory at par Dutch Inscriptions to the amount of thirty two millions of florins and look to the ability of the Batavian Republic [31] to redeem them.

"Such, citizen minister, as far as my memory serves me, are the particulars of the only two conferences at which I was present. . . ." (*ASP, Foreign Relations,* II, 226–27.) See also Hauteval to Gerry, June 10, 1798 (*ASP, Foreign Relations,* II, 223).

Two of the women "appointed to intrigue with our envoys" were Madame Catherine-Noël Worlée Grand, Talleyrand's mistress (Guyot, *Le Directoire Et La Paix De L'Europe,* 562), and Reine-Philiberte Rouph de Varicourt, marquise de Villette, at whose house Gerry and Marshall lived during their stay in Paris. For information on the Marquise de Villette, see Gerry to his wife, Ann Thompson Gerry, November 25, 1797, in Russell W. Knight, ed., *Elbridge Gerry's Letterbook: Paris 1797–1798* (Salem, Massachusetts, 1966), 22–25. For a review of the XYZ affair, see Pickering's report to Adams, January 18, 1799, which is printed in *ASP, Foreign Relations,* II, 229–38.

29. This is a reference to Adams's speech of May 16, 1797, which is printed in its entirety in *Annals of Congress,* VII, 54–59. For the passage in this speech to which the Directory objected, see Pickering to H, first letter of March 25, 1798, note 5.

30. In MS, "procrastinately."

31. In their dispatch to Pickering, dated October 22–27, 1797, the United States envoys wrote that "Y" said "that there were thirty two millions of florins of Dutch inscriptions, worth ten shillings in the pound, which might be assigned to us at twenty shillings to the pound; and he proceeded to state to us the certainty that, after a peace the Dutch government would repay us the money; so that we should ultimately lose nothing; and the only operation of the measure would be, an advance from us to France of thirty two millions, on the credit of the government of Holland" (LS [duplicate and de-

Already are these Assignats depreciated to half their nominal value and in all probability will come to nothing; serving merely as a flimsy viel to the extortion of a further & immense contribution.

"Money a great deal of money" * is the cry from the first to last; and our commissioners are assured that without this they may stay in Paris six months without advancing a step. To enforce the argument they are reminded of the fate of VENICE.[33]

At so hideous a compound of corruption and extortion, at demands so exorbitant and degrading, there is not a spark of virtuous indignation in an American breast which will not kindle into a flame. And yet there are men—could it have been believed? There are men to whom this country gave birth—vile and degenerate enough to run about the Streets to contradict to palliate to justify to preach the expediency of Compliance. Such men merit all the detestation of all their fellow citizens; and there is no doubt that with time and opportunity they will merit much more from the offended justice of the laws.   T M

* Il faut de'largent—il faut beaucoup d'argent" [32]

---

ciphered], RG 59, Despatches from United States Ministers to France, 1789–1869, Vol. 6, October 22, 1797–April 3, 1798, National Archives).

32. On October 22–27, 1797, Pinckney, Marshall, and Gerry wrote to Pickering: "On reading the speech M. Bellami dilated very much upon the keenness of the resentment it had produced, & expatiated largely on the satisfaction he said was indispensably necessary as a preliminary to negotiation. But, said he, gentlemen, I will not disguise from you, that this satisfaction, being made, the essential part of the treaty remains to be adjusted; 'il faut de l'argent—il faut beaucoup d'argent.' *you must pay money—you must pay a great deal of money* . . ." (LS [duplicate and deciphered], RG 59, Despatches from United States Ministers to France, 1789–1869, Vol. 6, October 22, 1797–April 3, 1798, National Archives).

33. In the diary which they sent to Pickering on November 8, 1797, the United States envoys wrote that on October 30 "Y" told them that "the fate of Venice was one which might befall the U. States" if money was not forthcoming (LS [deciphered], RG 59, Despatches from United States Ministers to France, 1789–1869, Vol. 6, October 22, 1797–April 3, 1798, National Archives). For "the fate of Venice," see Rufus King to H, June 27, 1797, note 3.

From John Jay

Albany 19 April 1798

Dear Sir

I have this Instant recd. a Letter dated the 14th. Instant from Judge Hobart,[1] resigning his Seat in the Senate of the united States, and as our Legislature is not now in Session, it hath become my Duty to appoint a Senator to succeed him and take his place, untill the next Meeting of the Legislature.[2]

The present delicate State of our public affairs, and the evident Expediency of filling this Vacancy without Delay, induce me without requesting your Permission and waiting for your answer, to determine to send you a Commission to fill that place, by the next Post. I can say nothing that will not occur to You.

adieu   yours sincerely   John Jay

Alexander Hamilton Esqr.

ALS, Hamilton Papers, Library of Congress; copy, from the original in the New York State Library, Albany.

1. John Sloss Hobart was a justice of the New York Supreme Court from 1777 to 1798. On January 11, 1798, he was appointed to the United States Senate to fill the vacancy caused by Philip Schuyler's resignation (*Journal of the Senate of the State of New-York; At their Twenty-First Session, Began and Held At the City of Albany, the second day of January, 1798* [Albany: Loring Andrews & Co., n.d.], 15). On April 11, 1798, John Adams nominated Hobart to be judge of the United States District Court for New York, and the Senate agreed to his appointment on the following day (*Executive Journal*, I, 269).

In May, 1798, William North of Duanesburg, New York, was appointed to the Senate in place of Hobart (*Annals of Congress*, VII, 559–60).

2. The New York legislature met on August 9, 1798 (*Journal of the Senate of the State of New York; At their Twenty-Second Session, Began and Held At the City of Albany, the Ninth day of August, 1798* [Albany: Loring Andrews & Co., n.d.]).

From John Jay

Albany 19 Ap. 1798

Dr. Sir

I wrote you a few Lines this Morning informing you that Judge Hobart had resigned his Seat in the Senate, and that by the next post I should send you a Commission to fill his place.

On further Reflection I doubt the propriety of appointing you without your previous permission, and therefore shall postpone it untill I receive your answer. If after well considering the Subject you should decline an appointmt. be so good as to consult with some of our most judicious Friends and advise me as to the Persons most proper to appoint and at the same time likely to accept.

yours sincerly   John Jay

Col. A. Hamilton

ALS, Hamilton Papers, Library of Congress; copy, from the original in the New York State Library, Albany.

The Stand No. VI [1]

[New York, April 19, 1798]

The inevitable conclusion from the facts which have been presented is, that Revolutionary France has been and continues to be governed by a spirit of proselytism, conquest, domination and rapine. The detail well justifies the position, that we may have to contend at our very doors for our independence and liberty.

When the wonders atchieved by the arms of France are duely considered the possibility of the overthrow of Great Britain seems

ADf, Hamilton Papers, Library of Congress; *The* [New York] *Commercial Advertiser*, April 19, 1798.
    1. The other issues of "The Stand" are dated March 30, April 4, 7, 12, 16, 21, 1798.
    H mistakenly numbered this issue of "The Stand" "No. V."

not to be chimerical. If by any of those extraordinary coincidences of circumstances, which occasionally decide the fate of empires, the meditated expedition against England shall succeed, or if by the immense expence to which that Country is driven and the derangement of her commerce by the powerful means employed to that end her affairs shall be thrown into such disorder as may enable France to dictate to her the terms of peace; in either of these unfortunate events the probability is, that the UStates will have to choose between the surrender of their sovereignty, the new modelling of their government according to the fancy of the Directory, the emptying of their wealth by contributions into the coffers of the greedy and insatiable monster—and resistance to invasion in order to compel submission to those ruinous conditions.

In opposition to this, it is suggested that the interest of France concurring with the difficulty of execution is a safeguard against the enterprize. It is asked what incentives sufficiently potent can stimulate to so unpromising an attempt?

The answer is—the strongest passions of bad hearts—inordinate ambition, the love of domination, that prime characteristick of the despots of France—the spirit of vengeance for the presumption of having thought and acted for ourselves, a spirit which has marked every step of the revolutionary leaders—the fanatical egotism of obliging the rest of the world to adapt their political system to the French standard of perfection—the desire of securing the future controul of our affairs by humbling and ruining the independent supporters of their country and of elevating the partisans and tools of France—the desire of entangling our commerce with preferences and restrictions which would give to her the monopoly—these passions the most imperious, these motives the most enticing to a crooked policy, are sufficient persuasives to undertake the subjugation of this country.

Added to these primary inducements, the desire of finding an outlet for a part of the vast armies which on the termination of the European war are likely to perplex and endanger the men in power would be an auxiliary motive of Great Force. The total loss of the troops sent would be no loss to France. Their cupidity would be readily excited to the undertaking by the prospect of dividing among themselves the fertile lands of this Country. Great Britain once silenced, there would be no insuperable obstacle to the transportation. The divisions among us, which have been urged to our commission[er]s as one motive to a compliance with the unreasonable demands of the Directory [2] would be equally an encouragement to invasion. It would be believed that a sufficient number would flock to the standard of France to render it easy to quell the resistance of the rest. Drunk with success nothing would be thought too arduous to be accomplished.

It is too much a part of our temper to indulge an overweening security. At the close of our revolution war the phantom of perpetual peace danced before the eyes of every body. We see at this early period with how much difficulty war has been parried and that with all our efforts to preserve peace we are now in a state of partial hostility. Untaught by this experience, we now seem inclined to regard the idea of invasion as incredible and to regulate our conduct by the belief of its improbability. Who would have thought eighteen months ago that Great Britain would have been at this time in serious danger of invasion from France? Is it not now more probable that such a danger may overtake us than it was then that it would so soon assail G B?

There are currents in human affairs, when events at other times less than miraculous are to be considered as natural and simple. Such were the æras of Macedonian, of Roman of Gothic of Saracen inundation. Such is the present æra of French fanaticism. Wise men, when they discover the symptoms of a similar æra, look for prodigies and prepare for them with foresight and energy.

Admit, that in our case invasion is upon the whole improbable; yet

2. On October 30, 1797, "Y" stated to Elbridge Gerry, John Marshall, and Charles Cotesworth Pinckney: "Perhaps . . . you believe that, in returning and exposing to your countrymen the unreasonableness of the demands of this government, you will unite them in their resistance to those demands: you are mistaken; you ought to know that the Diplomatic skill of France and the means she possesses in your country, are sufficient to enable her, with the French party in America, to throw the blame which will attend the rupture of the negotiations on the Federalists, as you term yourselves, but on the British party, as France terms you; and you may assure yourselves this will be done" (diary, enclosed in Pinckney, Marshall, and Gerry to Pickering, November 8, 1797 [LS (deciphered), RG 59, Despatches from United States Ministers to France, 1789–1869, Vol. 6, October 22, 1797–April 3, 1798, National Archives]).

if there are any circumstances which pronounce that the apprehension of it is not absolutely chimerical, it is the part of wisdom to act as if [it] was likely to happen. What are the inconveniences of preparation compared with the infinite magnitude of the evil if it shall surprise us unprepared? They are lighter than air weighed against the smallest probability of so disastrous a result.

But what is to be done? It is not wiser to compound on any terms than to provoke the consequences of resistance?

To do this is dishonor—it is ruin—it is death. Waving other considerations there can be no reliance on its efficacy. The example of Portugal [3] teaches us that it is to purchase disgrace, not safety. The cravings of despotic rapacity may be appeased but they [are] not to be satisfied. They will quickly renew their fires and call for new sacrifices in proportion to the facility with which the first were made. The situation of France is likely to make plunder for a considerable time to come an indispensable expedient of government. Excluding the great considerations of public right and public policy, and bringing the matter to the simple test of pecuniary calculation, resistance is to be preferred to submission. The surrender of our whole wealth would only procure respite, not safety. The disbursements for war will chiefly be at home. They will not necessarily carry away our riches, and they will preserve our honor and give us security.

But in the event supposed can we oppose with success? There is no event in which we may not look with confidence to a successful resistance. Though G Britain should be impolitic or wicked enough (which is hoped to be impossible) to compromise her differences with France by an agreement to divide the U States, according to the insulting threat of the Agents of France, still it is in our power to maintain our independence and baffle every enemy. The people of the UStates from their number situation and resources are invincible if they are provident and faithful to themselves.

The Question returns—what is to be done? Shall we declare war? No—there are still chances for avoiding a general rupture which ought to be taken. Want of future success may bring the present despots to reason. Every day may produce a revolution which may

3. See Pickering to H, first letter of March 25, 1798, note 9.

substitute better men in their place and lead to honorable accommodation.

Our true policy is, in the attitude of calm defiance, to meet the aggressions upon us by proportionate resistance, and to prepare vigorously for further resistance. To this end, the chief measures requisite are to invigorate our treasury by calling into activity the principal untouched resources of revenue—to fortify in earnest our chief sea ports—to establish founderies and increase our arsenals—to create a respectable naval force and to raise with the utmost diligence a considerable army. Our Merchant vessels ought to be permitted not only to arm themselves but to sink or capture their assailants. Our vessels of war ought to cruise on our coast and serve as convoys to our trade. In doing this, they also ought to be authorised not only to sink or capture assailants, but likewise to capture & bring in privateers found hovering within twenty leagues of our coast. For this last measure, precedent if requisite is to be found in the conduct of neutral powers on other occasions.

This course, it will be objected implies a state of war. Let it be so. But it will be a limited and mitigated state of war, to grow into general war or not at the election of France. What may be that election will probably depend on future and incalculable events. The continuation of success on the part of France would insure war. The want of it might facilitate accommodation. There are examples in which states have been for a long time in a state of partial hostility without proceeding to general rupture. The duration of this course of conduct on our part may be restricted to the continuance of the two last decrees of France, that by which the trade of neutrals with the ports of her enemies has been intercepted, and that by which vessels and their cargoes, if composed in whole or in part of British fabrics are liable to seizure and condemnation.[4]

The declared suspension of our treaties with France[5] is a measure of evident justice and necessity. It is the natural consequence of a total violation on one side. It would be preposterous to be fettered by treaties which are wholly disregarded by the other party. It is

4. This is a reference to the decree of January 11, 1798. See H to Pickering, March 17, 1798.

5. For the texts of the treaties of Alliance and of Amity and Commerce, signed at Paris on February 6, 1778, see Miller, *Treaties*, II, 3–29, 35–46.

essentially our interest to get rid of the guarantee in the treaty of alliance,[6] which on the part of France is likely to be henceforth nugatory, on the part of the U States it is a substantial and dangerous stipulation; obliging them in good faith to take part with France in any future defensive war, in which her West India colonies may be attacked. The consular convention [7] is likewise a mischievous instrument devised by France in the spirit of extending her influence into other countries, and producing to a certain extent *imperium in imperio.*

It may be happy for the U States that an occasion has been furnished by France, in which with good faith they may break through these trammels; readjusting when reconciliation shall take place a basis of connection or intercourse more convenient and more eligible.

The resolution to raise an army,[8] it is to be feared, is that one of the measures suggested, which will meet with greatest obstacle; and yet it is the one which ought most to unite opinion. Being merely a precaution for internal security, it can in no sense tend to provoke war, and looking to eventual security, in a case, which if it should happen would threaten our very existence as a nation, it is the most important.

The history of our revolution-war is a serious admonition to it.

---

6. H is referring to Article 11 of the 1778 Treaty of Alliance with France, which reads: "The two Parties guarantee mutually from the present time and forever, against all other powers, to wit, the united states to his most Christian Majesty the present Possessions of the Crown of france in America as well as those which it may acquire by the future Treaty of peace: and his most Christian Majesty guarantees on his part to the united states, their liberty, Sovereignty, and Independence absolute, and unlimited, as well in Matters of Government as commerce and also their Possessions, and the additions or conquests that their Confédération may obtain during the war, from any of the Dominions now or heretofore possessed by Great Britain in North America, conformable to the 5th. & 6th articles above written, the whole as their Possessions shall be fixed and assured to the said States at the moment of the cessation of their present War with England" (Miller, *Treaties,* II, 39–40).

7. For the text of the "Convention Defining and Establishing the Functions and Privileges of Consuls and Vice Consuls," signed by the United States and France on November 14, 1788, see Miller, *Treaties,* II, 228–41.

8. On March 26, 1798, Humphrey Marshall of Kentucky moved in the Senate that a provisional army be raised (*Annals of Congress,* VII, 531). On April 13 Senator Benjamin Goodhue of Massachusetts reported a bill "authorizing the President of the United States to raise a provisional army" (*Annals of Congress,* VII, 540). The Senate passed the bill on April 23 and the House on May 18, 1798 (*Annals of Congress,* VII, 546; VIII, 1771–72). For the text of this act, see 1 *Stat.* 558–61 (May 28, 1798).

The American cause had nearly been lost for want of creating in the first instance a solid force commensurate in duration with the war. Immense additional expence and waste and a variety of other evils were incurred which might have been avoided.

Suppose an invasion, & that we are left to depend on Militia alone. Can it be doubted that a rapid and formidable progress would in the first instance be made by the invader? Who can answer what dismay this might inspire—how far it might go to create general panic—to rally under the banners of the enemy the false and the timid? The imagination cannot without alarm anticipate the consequences. Prudence commands that they shall be guarded against. To have a good army on foot will be best of all precautions to prevent as well as to repel invasion.

The propriety of the measure is so palpable, that it will argue treachery or incapacity in our councils, if it be not adopted. The friends of the government owe it to their own characters to press it; its opposers can give no better proof that they are not abandonned to a foreign power than to concur in it. The public safety will be more indebted to its advocates than to the advocates of any other measure, in proportion as our Independence & liberty are of more consequence than our Trade.

It is the fervent wish of patriotism that our councils and nation may be united and resolute. The dearest interests call for it. A great public danger commands it. Every good man will rejoice to embrace the adversary of his former opinions if he will now by candour and energy evince his attachment to his country. Whoever does not do this consigns himself to irrevocable dishonor. But tis not the triumph over a political rival, which the true lover of his country desires— 'tis the safety, 'tis the welfare of that Country—and he will gladly share with his bitterest opponent the glory of defending and preserving her. Americans! rouse! be unanimous be virtuous be firm, exert your courage, trust in heaven and nobly defy the enemies both of god and man!   T M

To Abraham Van Vechten

New York, April 20, 1798. "I wrote to you from N Haven [1] on the subject of two suits *Low* Adsm *Graham* [2] & *Gracie* Adsm *Brot*.[3] I continue in the wish that the argument for a new trial may be postponed till *July.* . . ."

ALS, MS Division, New York Public Library.
  1. Letter not found. H had been in New Haven for the Connecticut Gore controversy. See H to Elizabeth Hamilton, September 12, 1797, note 1.
  2. This is a reference to the case of *Charles M. Graham* v *Nicholas Low* in the New York Supreme Court and the New York Court of Chancery. For an account of this case with relevant documents, see Goebel, *Law Practice*, II, 488–510.
  3. This is a reference to the case of *Andrew Brott* v *Archibald Gracie* in the New York Supreme Court and the New York Court of Chancery. For an account of this case, see Goebel, *Law Practice*, II, 510–11.

The Stand No. VII [1]

[New York, April 21, 1798]

The dispatches from our envoys have at length made their appearance.[2] They present a picture of the French government exceeding in turpitude whatever was anticipated from the previous intimations of their contents. It was natural to expect, that the perusal of them would have inspired a universal sentiment of indignation and disgust; and that no man, calling himself an American, would have had the hardihood to defend, or even to palliate a conduct so atrocious. But it is already apparent, that an expectation of this kind would not have been well founded.

There are strong symptoms that the men in power in France understand better than ourselves the true character of their faction in this country, at least of its leaders; and that as to these, the agents

The [New York] *Commercial Advertiser*, April 21, 1798.
  1. The other issues of "The Stand" are dated March 30, April 4, 7, 12, 16, 19, 1798.
  2. For the publication of these dispatches, see Timothy Pickering to H, April 9, 1798, note 1.

who conferred with our envoys, were not mistaken in predicting that the unreasonableness of the demands upon us would not serve to detach the party from France, or to re-unite them to their own country.[3] The high-priest of this sect, with a tender regard for the honor of the immaculate Directory, has already imagined several ingenious distinctions to rescue them from the odium and corruption unfolded by the dispatches. Among these is the suggestion that there is no proof of the privity of the Directory—all may have been the mere contrivance of the minister for foreign relations.[4]

The presumption from so miserable a subterfuge is, that had the propositions proceeded immediately from the Directory, the cry from the same quarter would have been—there is no evidence that the councils or nation approved of them; they at least are not implicated; the friendship of the two republics ought not to be disturbed on account of the villainy of the transitory and fugitive organs of one of them. The inventor of the subterfuge, however, well knew, that the Executive organ of a nation never comes forward in person to negociate with foreign ministers; and that unless it be presumed to direct and adopt what is done by its agents, it may always be sheltered from responsibility or blame. The recourse to so pitiful an evasion, betrays in its author a systematic design to excuse France at all events—to soften a spirit of submission to every violence she may commit—and to prepare the way for implicit subjection to her will. To be the pro-consul of a despotic Directory over the United States, degraded to the condition of a province, can alone be the criminal, the ignoble aim of so seditious, so prostitute a character.

The subaltern mercenaries go still farther. Publications have appeared, endeavoring to justify or extenuate the demands upon our envoys, and to inculcate the slavish doctrine of compliance.[5] The United States, it is said, are the aggressors, and ought to make atonement; France assisted them in their revolution with loans, and they ought to reciprocate the benefit; peace is a boon worth the price required for it, and it ought to be paid. In this motley form, our country is urged to sink voluntarily, and without a struggle, to a state

3. See "The Stand No. VI," April 19, 1798, note 2.
4. See Pickering to H, April 9, 1798, note 2.
5. See the five articles entitled "The Catastrophe" and signed "Nestor," and three articles signed "Sidney" in the [Philadelphia] Aurora. General Advertiser, April 14, 16, 17, 19, 20, 1798.

of tributary vassalage. Americans are found audacious and mean enough to join in the chorus of a foreign nation, which calls upon us to barter our independence for a respite from the lash.

The charge of aggression upon the United States is false; and if true, the reparation, from the nature of the case, ought not to be pecuniary. This species of indemnification between nations, is only proper where there has been pecuniary injury.

The loans received by us from France were asked as a favor, on the condition of reimbursement by the United States; and were freely granted for a purpose of mutual advantage. The advances to be made by us were exacted as the price of peace. Tho, in name loans, they would be in fact contributions, by the coertion of a power which has already wrested from our citizens an immense property, for which it owes to them compensation.

To pay such a price for peace, is to prefer peace to independence. The nation which becomes tributary takes a master.* Peace is doubtless precious, but it is a bauble compared with national independence, which includes national liberty. The evils of war to resist such a precedent, are insignificant, compared with the evil of the precedent. Besides that there could be no possible security for the enjoyment of the object for which the disgraceful sacrifice was made.

To disguise the poison, misrepresentation is combined with sophistry. It is alledged, that finally no more was asked than that the United States should purchase sixteen millions of Dutch inscriptions,

---

* The argument of what has been done in the cases of *Algerines* and *Indians*,[6] has nothing pertinent but in the comparison of relative ferocity. In this view, the claim of the Directory is indisputable—but in every other it is preposterous. It is the general practice of civilized nations to pay barbarians— there is no point of honor to the contrary. But as between civilized nations, the payment of tribute by one to another, is by the common opinion of mankind, a badge of servitude.

6. In their diary, which the United States envoys to France sent to Pickering on November 8, 1797, they wrote that "X" on October 27 stated: ". . . that we paid money to obtain peace with the Algerines, and with the Indians; and that it was doing no more to pay France for peace. To this it was answered, that when our government commenced a treaty with either Algiers or the Indian tribes, it was understood that the money was to form the basis of the treaty and was it's essential article; that the whole nation knew it, and was prepared to expect it as a thing of course; but that in treating with France, our government had supposed that a proposition, such as he spoke of, would, if made by us, give mortal offence" (LS [deciphered], RG 59, Despatches from United States Ministers to France, 1789–1869, Vol. 6, October 22, 1797– April 3, 1798, National Archives).

and that by doing this, they would have secured compensation to their citizens for depredations on their trade to four times the amount, with an intermission of the depredations; that no hazard of ultimate loss could have attended the operation, because the United States owed the Dutch a much larger sum which would be a pledge for payment or discount.

This is a palpable attempt to deceive. The first propositions were such as to have been represented in a former paper; [7] but it appears in the sequel, that the French agents seeing the inflexible opposition of our envoys to their plan, and hoping to extort finally a considerable sum, tho less than at first comtemplated, relaxed so far in their demands as to narrow them down to the payment of a douceur of twelve hundred thousand livres with a positive engagement to advance to the French government a sum equal to the amount of the spoliations of our trade, and a further engagement to send to our government for power to purchase of France thirty two millions of the inscriptions (12,800,000 dollars) in return for all which, our envoys were to be permitted to remain six months in Paris, depredations on our trade during that time, were to be suspended, and a commission of five persons was to be appointed to liquidate the claims for past depredations which were to be satisfied "in a *time* and *manner* to be agreed upon." The substance of these demands is to pay immediately twelve hundred thousand livres and to bind ourselves to pay absolutely twenty millions of dollars more (the estimated amount of the spoliations) for what?—barely for the acknowlegement of a debt to our citizens, which without it, is not the less due, and for a suspension of *hostilities* * for six months.

Afterwards, in a conversation between the French Minister himself and one of our envoys, the propositions assumed still another form.[8] The United States were required to purchase of France at par sixteen millions of inscriptions, and to promise *further aid when in their power.* This *arrangement being first made* and not before,

---

* It is observable that the French give themselves the denomination of *hostilities* to their depredations upon us. Our Jacobins would have us consider them as gentle caresses.

7. See "The Stand No. V," April 16, 1798, note 28.

8. The envoy was Elbridge Gerry. For the conversation, see Exhibit C enclosed in Pinckney, Marshall, and Gerry to Pickering, December 24, 1797 (LS [deciphered], RG 59, Despatches from the United States Ministers to France, 1789–1869, Vol. 6, October 22, 1797–April 3, 1798, National Archives).

France was to take measures for reimbursing the equitable demands of our citizens on account of captures.

The purchase of the inscriptions was to be preliminary. The arrangement for reimbursing our merchants was to follow. The nature of it was not explained; but it is to be inferred from all that preceeded, that the expedient of the advance of an equal sum by the United States would have been pressed as the basis of the promised arrangement.

This last proposal was in its principle as bad as either of the former; its tendency worse. The promise of future assistance would have carried with it the privilege to repeat at pleasure the demand of money, and to dispute with us about our ability to supply; and it would have immediately embarked us as an *associate* with France in the war. It was to promise her the most effectual aid in our power, and that of which she stood most in need.

The scheme of concealment was a trick. The interest of France to engage us in the war against Great Britain, as a mean of wounding her commerce, is too strong to have permitted the secret to be kept by her. By the ratification of the treaty, in which the Senate must have concurred, too many would have obtained possession of the secret to allow it to remain one. While it did, the apprehension of discovery would have enabled France to use it as an engine of unlimited extortion. But a still greater objection is, that it would have been infamous in the United States, thus covertly to relinquish their neutrality, and with equal cowardice and hypocrisy to wear the mask of it, when they had renounced the reality.

The idea of securing our advances, by means of the debt which we owe to the Dutch is without foundation.[9] The creditors of the United States are the *private citizens* of the Batavian republic. Their demands could not be opposed by a claim of our government upon their government. The only shape in which it could be attempted must be in that of reprisals for the delinquency of the government. But this would not only be a gross violation of principle—it would be contrary to *express* stipulations in the contracts for the loans.*

In the same spirit of deception, it has also been alleged that our envoys by giving the douceur of twelve hundred thousand livres and

* They all provide against seizure or sequestration by way of reprisals, &c.
9. See note 6.

agreeing to send for powers to make a loan, might have obtained a suspension of depredations for six months. There is not a syllable in the dispatches to countenance this assertion. A large advance in addition, either on the basis of the spoliations, or by way of purchase of the inscriptions, is uniformly made the condition of suspending hostilities.

Glosses so false and insidious as these, in a crisis of such imminent public danger, to mislead the opinion of our nation concerning the conduct and views of a foreign enemy, are shoots from a very pernicious trunk. Opportunity alone is wanting to unveil the treason which lurks at the core.

What signifies the quantum of the contribution, had it been really as unimportant as is represented? 'Tis the principle which is to be resisted at every hazard. 'Tis the pretension to make us tributary, in opposition to which every American ought to resign the last drop of his blood.

The pratings of the Gallic faction at this time remind us of those of the British faction at the commencement of our revolution. The insignificance of a duty of three pence per pound on tea was echoed and re-echoed as the bait to an admission of the right to bind us in all cases whatsoever.

The tools of France incessantly clamor against the treaty with Britain as the just cause of the resentment of France. It is curious to remark, that in the conferences with our envoys this treaty was never once mentioned by the French agents. Particular passages in the speech of the President [10] are alone specified as a ground of dissatisfaction. This is at once a specimen of the fruitful versatility, with which causes of complaint are contrived, and of the very slight foundations on which they are adopted. A temperate expression of sensibility at an outrageous indignity, offered to our government by a member of the directory, is converted into a mortal offence. The tyrants will not endure a murmur at the blows they inflict.

But the dispatches of our envoys, while they do not sanction the charge preferred by the Gallic faction against the treaty, confirm a very serious charge which the friends of the government bring

10. For the passages in John Adams's speech to Congress, dated May 16, 1797, which the French thought objectionable, see Pickering to H, first letter of March 25, 1798, note 5.

against that faction. They prove, by the unreserved confession of her agents, that France places absolute dependence on this party in every event, and counts upon their devotion to her as an encouragement to the hard conditions which they attempt to impose. The people of this country must be infatuated indeed, if after this plain confession they are at a loss for the true source of the evils they have suffered or may hereafter suffer from the despots of France. 'Tis the unnatural league of a portion of our citizens with the oppressors of their country.   TITUS MANLIUS.

To John Jay

New York April 24. 1798

Dr. Sir

I have received your two favours of the 19th instant. I feel as I ought the mark of confidence they announce. But I am obliged by my situation to decline the appointment. This situation you are too well acquainted with to render it necessary for me to enter into explanation. There may arrive a crisis when I may conceive myself bound once more to sacrifice the interest of my family to public call. But [1] I must defer the change as long as possible.

I do not at present think of a person to recommend as adapted to the emergency. I shall reflect & consult and write you by the next post. This, the first day, is not decisive of our election here; [2] but there is as yet nothing to discourage. With respect & attachment,

I remain Dr. Sir   Yr. Obed serv   A Hamilton

Governor Jay

ADfS, Hamilton Papers, Library of Congress.
   1. At this point, H wrote and then crossed out: "the period is not yet."
   2. H is referring to the elections for representatives to the Sixth Congress, which by the provisions of "An Act for electing representatives for this state in the house of representatives of the Congress of the United States of America" were scheduled to begin on the last Tuesday in April (*New York Laws*, 20th Sess., Ch. LXII [March 28, 1797]). The canvassing of votes for congressional representatives began on June 13, 1798 (*Gazette of the United States, and Philadelphia Daily Advertiser*, June 14, 1798). The canvassing of votes for the state offices of governor, lieutenant governor, and senators began on May 29, 1798 (*Gazette of the United States, and Philadelphia Daily Advertiser*, May 30, 1798).

From Asher Robbins [1]

Newport [Rhode Island] 26th Apl. 1798

Sir

Mr Gibbs [2] of this Town, who is doubtless known to you, will deliver you this. I have mentioned to him & to others that you were kind enough to engage to reflect on the situation of this Island, & to give an opinion, upon the most elegible mode of putting it into a State of defence. To enable you to do this Mr Gibbs, will put into your hands, a map, which is esteemed a very correct one, & some observations of Colo Crary and Colo Sherburne; [3] two of our most experienced military characters. Colo Olney [4] living at Providence I have not been able to consult with him, but Mr Gibbs will be able to make or procure you any further explanations you many want.

With the most perfect esteem   I am Sir   Your hble servt

Asher Robbins

Alexander Hamilton Esqr.

ALS, Hamilton Papers, Library of Congress.
1. Robbins, a former tutor at Rhode Island College (now Brown University), had studied law and practiced in Providence, Rhode Island. In 1795 he moved to Newport. He became a United States Senator in 1825.
2. George W. Gibbs was a Newport merchant and shipowner.
3. "Observations upon the points of defence of Rhode Island by Colo Archibald Crary & Colo Henry Sherburne," April 28, 1798 (DS, Hamilton Papers, Library of Congress). Crary, a Revolutionary War veteran, was a colonel in the Second Rhode Island Regiment and was agent for the War Department in Rhode Island. Sherburne, a Revolutionary War veteran, was treasurer of Rhode Island from 1792 to 1818.
4. Jeremiah Olney was collector of customs at Providence.

From Henry A. Williams [1]

New York, April 26, 1798. "I am much supprized by being informed by my Wife that you cannot find either my papers or any way of Coming at the property so long withheld from me. . . . Exert yourself & not lett me Linger Longer in this Bastile while my family are Sufferring at home. . . ."

ALS, Hamilton Papers, Library of Congress.
1. For background to this letter, see Williams to H, March 31, 1798.
An entry in H's Law Register, 1795–1804, reads:
"Henry A. Williams ⎱
      v   ⎰
Schencks
I have accepted conditionally an order in favour of Thomas Payne for 221
Dollars" (AD, partially in H's handwriting, New York Law Institute, New
York City). A similar entry appears in H's Cash Book, 1795–1804, under the
date of April, 1798, in a section entitled "Memoranda" (AD, Hamilton Papers,
Library of Congress).
Payne, a New York City cabinetmaker, was Williams's creditor.

From Robert G. Harper [1]

Philadelphia April 27th. [1798]

My dear sir

Could any thing prevail on you to undertake the war-department?
Reflect on the importance of the station at this moment. Consider
how much more important a war minister is than a general, & how
much more difficult to be found.

We shall have an army of 20,000 men, with the power to revive
voluntary inlistments ad libitum in addition to it the volunteers to
be armed & cloathed at their own expence.[2] This, under proper direction, will give us the flower of the country; and put arms into the
hands of all our friends. But every thing will depend on the *name* of
the general, & the *talents* of the minister.

I write this without any authority: but I have good reason to
believe, from late conversations with the President, that if he were to
understand your willingness to come forward, the arrangement
would immediately take place. In that case Mr. Mc.Henry would
give way: and there is no difference in opinion among the federal
party on the absolute necessity of his doing so.

Genl. Pinckney & Carrington of Virginia have been thought of
among our friends, if you cannot be got: but the first is absent,[3] &
the 2d.[4] however able, wants the weight of Character requisite at this
time. Besides he may be more fit for the marine, where also will be
wanted a man of athorty & detail.

Yours truly   Rob: G. Harper.

Col. Hamilton

ALS, Hamilton Papers, Library of Congress.

1. Harper was a Federalist member of the House of Representatives from South Carolina.

2. "An Act authorizing the President of the United States to raise a Provisional Army" (1 *Stat.* 558–61) did not become law until May 28, 1798.

3. Charles Cotesworth Pinckney, who had been appointed on June 5, 1797, as one of the three Envoys Extraordinary to France from the United States, had not yet returned to America.

4. Edward Carrington was supervisor of the revenue in Virginia.

To Marquis de Lafayette [1]

[New York] April the 28th. 1798.

I was very happy, My dear Marquis to receive lately a letter [2] from you. It inclosed one from Général Dumas,[3] which also gave me pleasure. I fear, shall hardly have time to write to him by this opportunity; but I beg you to assure him of the interest I take in what ever concerns him. As to the affair of Mr. de Beaumarchais,[4] while I was in the office of secretary of the Treasury, I procured his account to be settled provisionally and asked an appropriation for the ballance to depend for its application on the event of an inquiry then making concernin[g] a certain million of livres of which you have no doubt heard. The result of this inquiry was not had, when I left the department; [5] but I presume before this, Mr. Beaumarchais has information more precise through the agency of Mr. Casenove [6] whose application for that purpose to the actual Secy of the Treasury was supported by all my influence and who wrote me [7] that it had been effectual.

Your letter implied, as I had before understood, that though your engagements did not permit you to follow the fortunes of the republic yet your attachments had never been separated from them. In this, I frankly confess, I have differed from you. The suspension of the King and the massacre of September [8] (of which events a temporary intelligence was received in this Country) cured me of my good will for the French Revolution.

I have never been able to believe that France can make a republic and I have believed that the attempt while it continues can only produce misfortunes.

Among the events of this revolution I regret extremely the misunderstanding which has taken place between your country and ours and which seems to threaten an open rupture. It would be useless to discuss the causes of this state of things. I shall only assure you that a disposition to form an intimate connection with Great Britain, which is charged upon us forms no part of the real Cause, though it has served the purpose of a party to impose the belief of it on france. I give you this assurance on the faith of our former friendship. And the effect will prove to you that I am not wrong. The basis of the policy of the party, of which I am, is to avoid intimate and exclusive connection with any foreign powers.

But away with politics the rest of my letter Shall be dedicated to assure you that my friendship for you will survive all revolutions & all vicissitudes.

No one feels more than I do the motives which this country has to love you, to desire and to promote your happiness. And I Shall not love it, if it does not manifest the sensibility by unequivocal acts. In the present state of our affairs with france, I cannot urge you to us—but until some radical change in france I Shall be sorry to learn you have gone elsewhere. Should the continuation of an evil course of things in your own country lead you to think of a permanent asylum elsewhere you will be sure to find in America a most cordial and welcome reception. The only thing in which our parties agree is to love you.

May I presume to beg you to make my respectful compliments & those of Mrs. Hamilton acceptable to Madame Lafayette.

Yours ever   A Hamilton.

April 28. 1798.

Sparks Transcripts, Harvard College Library.

1. For information on Lafayette's release from Olmütz, see George Washington to H, October 8, 1797, note 2.

2. Lafayette to H, December 8, 1797.

3. Mathieu Dumas to H, December 8, 1797.

4. This is a reference to Pierre Augustin Caron de Beaumarchais and the problem of the "lost million." For information on the "lost million," see the introductory note to Oliver Wolcott, Jr., to H, March 29, 1792. See also H to Thomas Jefferson, June 10, 1793; Beaumarchais to H, October 29, 1796; Charles Maurice de Talleyrand-Périgord to H, November 12, 1796; H to Wolcott, November 20, 1797; Dumas to H, December 8, 1797; Lafayette to H, December 8, 1797.

5. At this point H wrote and then crossed out: "but it has since been obtained and I am informed that it traces to Mr de Beaumarchais the missing

million which I believe extinguishes his ballance. This is the state of the business according to my information."

H resigned his office as Secretary of the Treasury on January 31, 1795. See H to Washington, December 1, 1794; January 20, 31, 1795.

6. Théophile Cazenove was the agent of the Holland Land Company.

7. Wolcott's letter to H has not been found.

8. H is referring to the massacres of September 2–7, 1792. See Gouverneur Morris to H, December 24, 1792, note 8.

A French Faction

[April, 1798] [1]

There is a set of men, whose mouths are always full of the phrazes *British Faction, British Agents British Influence*. Feeling that they themselves are enlisted in a foreign faction, they imagine, that it must be so with every one else—and that whoever will not join with them in sacrificing the interests of their country to another Country must be engaged in an opposite foreign faction. *Frenchmen* in all their feelings and wishes they can see in their opponents nothing but *Engglishmen*. Every true *American*, every really independent man becomes in their eyes a British Agent a British Emissary.

The truth is, that there is in this Country a decided *French Faction* but no other foreign faction. I speak as to those who have a share in the public councils or in the political influence of the country. Those who adhered to Great Britain during the Revolution may be presumed generally to have still a partiality for her. But the number of those who have at this time any agency in public affairs is very insignificant. They are neither numerous nor weighty enough to form in the public councils a distinct faction. Nor is it to this description of men that the phraze is applied.

The satellites of France have the audacity to bestow it upon men who have risked more in opposition to Great Britain than but few of them ever did—to men who have given every possible proof of their exclusive Devotion to the interests of their own country.

Let facts speak. The leaders of the French Faction during the War managed to place the Ministers of this Country abroad in a servile dependence on the Ministry of France—and but for the virtuous independence of those men, which led them to break their instructions,[2] it is very problematical whether we should have had as early or as good a peace as that we obtained. The same men, during the same period, effected the revocation of a Commission which had been given for making a commercial Treaty with Great Britain, and again, on the approach of peace, defeated an attempt to produce a renewal of that Commission; and thus lost an opportunity known to have been favourable for establishing a beneficial Treaty of Commerce with that Country [3]—though they have since made the obtaining of such a Treaty the pretext for reiterated attempts to renew hostilities with her. The same men have been constantly labouring from the first institution of the present Government to render it subservient, not to the advancement of our own manufactures, but to the advancement of the Navigation & Manufactures of France.

Is a plan proposed which aims at fostering our own Navigation and elevating our own manufactures by giving them advantages over those of *all foreign Nations?* A thousand obstacles occur. A thousand alarms are sounded. Usurpation of ungranted powers—Designs to promote the interests of particular parts of the Union at the expence of other parts of it—and innumerable other spectres are conjured up to terrify us from the pursuit. Is the project to confer particular favours upon the navigation and manufactures of France even at the expence of the UStates? Then all difficulties vanish. This is the true and *only* object of the constitution. For this it was framed—by this alone it can live and have a being. To this precious end, we are assured, the states who may particularly suffer, will be willing to sacrifice. In this holy cause, we are to risk every thing. Our Trade our Navigation our manufactures our agriculture, our revenues our peace. Not to consent is to want spirit to want honor to want patriotism.

Thus does *Gallicism* assume the honorable garb of Patriotism!

ADf, Hamilton Papers, Library of Congress.
   1. In *JCHW*, VII, 682, this document is dated "1798."
   2. The instructions of the Continental Congress of June 6, 1781, to John Adams, John Jay, Benjamin Franklin, Henry Laurens, and Thomas Jefferson, the commissioners appointed to negotiate a treaty of peace with Great Britain, read in part: "You are to make the most candid and confidential communications, upon all subjects, to the ministers of our generous ally the king of France; to undertake nothing in the negotiations for peace without their knowledge and concurrence; and to make them sensible how much we rely upon his Majesty's influence for effectual support, in every thing that may be necessary to the present security or future prosperity of the United States of America" (*JCC*, XX, 606–07). The commissioners, however, signed the preliminary

articles of peace without consulting the French, and they explained their decision in a letter to Robert R. Livingston, the Secretary of Foreign Affairs, on December 14, 1782: "As we had reason to imagine that the articles respecting the boundaries, the refugees, and fisheries did not correspond with the policy of this court [France], we did not communicate the preliminaries to the minister until after they were signed. . . . We hope that these considerations will excuse our having so far deviated from the spirit of our instructions . . ." (Wharton, *Revolutionary Diplomatic Correspondence*, VI, 131–33).

3. On September 28, 1779, the Continental Congress approved instructions to the Minister Plenipotentiary for the negotiation of a treaty of commerce with Great Britain (*JCC*, XV, 1116–17). On July 12, 1781, these instructions were revoked (*JCC*, XX, 746).

To Oliver Wolcott, Junior

[April, 1798] [1]

Dr Sir

I thank you for your last letter. The opinion with regard to the conduct of the President is very important.

As to our finances all will be well, if our councils are wise & vigorous; if not, all will go to ruin. I fear there is not among the friends sufficient capaciousness of views for the greatness of the occasion.

I send the inclosed because it required correction.

AL, Connecticut Historical Society, Hartford.
1. This letter is undated. It was written in reply to Wolcott to H, April 5, 1798. In *HCLW*, X, 274, this letter is dated "1797."

To Rufus King

[New York, May 1, 1798] [1]

My Dear Sir

It is a great while since I received a line from you—nor indeed have I deserved one. The vortex of business, in which I have been, having kept me from writing to you. At this moment I presume you will not be sorry to know my opinion as to the course of our public affairs.

In Congress, a good spirit is gaining ground; and though measures march slowly, there is reason to expect that almost every thing which the exigency requires will be done. The plan is, present defence against depredations by sea and preparations for eventual danger by land. In the community, indignation against the French Government and a firm resolution to support our own discover themselves dayly by unequivocal symptoms. The appearances are thus far highly consoling.

But in this posture of things, how unfortunate is it, that the new instructions issued by Great Britain, which appear, according to the reports of the day, to be giving rise to many abusive captures of our vessels,[2] are likely to produce a counter current—and to distract the public dissatisfaction between two powers, who it will be said are equally disposed to plunder and oppress. In vain will it be urged that the British Government cannot be so absurd as at such a juncture to intend us injury. The effects will be alone considered and they will make the worst possible impression. By what fatality has the British Cabinet been led to spring any new mine, by new regulations, at such a crisis of affairs? What can be gained to counterballance the mischievous tendency of abuses? Why are weapons to be furnished to our Jacobins?

It seems the captured vessels are carried to the *Mole* * where there is a virtuous Judge of the name of *Comboult* disposed to give sanction to plunder in every shape.[3] Events are not yet sufficiently unfolded to enable us to judge of the extent of the mischief—but nothing can be more unlucky than that the door has been opened. The recency of the thing may prevent your hearing any thing about it from the Government by this opportunity.

Yrs. Affecty   A Hamilton

PS

* It is said Privateers are fitting out at Antigua & St Kitts.[4]

R King Esq.

ALS, New-York Historical Society, New York City.

1. Although this letter is undated, it is endorsed: "May Packet. 1798 recd June 8th." In *JCHW*, VI, 287, and *HCLW*, X, 283, this letter is dated "May, 1798."

2. On January 25, 1798, Great Britain revoked its order of January 8, 1794, and substituted the following order: ". . . And whereas in consideration of the present state of the Commerce of this Country, as well as that of neutral Countries, it is expedient to revoke the said Instructions, we are pleased hereby

to revoke the same, and in lieu thereof, we have thought fit to issue these
our Instructions to be observed from henceforth, by the Commanders of all our
Ships of war and Privateers that have or may have Letters of marque against
France Spain and the *united Provinces.*

"1. That they shall bring in, for lawful adjudication, all vessels, with their
Cargoes, that are laden with Goods the Produce of any Island, or Settlement
belonging to *France, Spain,* or the *united Provinces,* and coming directly from
any Port of the said Islands, or Settlements to any Port in Europe not being
a Port of this Kingdom, nor a port of that Country to which such Ships,
being neutral Ships shall belong.

"2. That they shall bring in, for lawful adjudication all Ships with their
Cargoes, that are laden with Goods the Produce of the said Islands or Set-
tlements, the property of which Goods shall belong to subjects of *France
Spain* or the *united Provinces,* to whatsoever Ports the same may be bound.

"3. That they shall seize all Ships that shall be found attempting to enter
any Port of the said Islands or Settlements, that is or shall be, blockaded by
the arms of His Majesty, and shall send them in with their Cargoes, for
adjudication, according to the Terms of the second article of the former
Instructions, bearing date the 8th. day of June 1793.

"4. That they shall seize all vessels laden wholly, or in part with Naval or
Military Stores, bound to any Port of the said Islands or Settlements, and shall
send them into some convenient Port belonging to His Majesty, in order that
they, together with their Cargoes, may be proceeded against according to
the Rules of the Law of Nations." (Copy, RG 59, Despatches from United
States Ministers to Great Britain, 1792–1870, Vol. 7, January 9–December 22,
1798, National Archives; copy, Hamilton Papers, Library of Congress.)

3. On December 5, 1797, Timothy Pickering wrote to King: "Another
grievance, which has for some time past excited much complaint, is the proceeding of the Judge of the Court of vice-admiralty in St. Domingo. This
Court was erected by governor [John Graves] Simcoe, who appointed a Mr.
Richard Cambauld the judge. . . .

"It is not only the frequence of captures that are made, that complaints
have been preferred; but the judge . . . has an extraordinary facility in condemning. . . ." (LC, RG 59, Diplomatic and Consular Instructions of the
Department of State, 1791–1801, Vol. 4, February 1, 1797–November 30, 1798,
National Archives.)

Again, in a letter to Samuel Sewall, dated December 27, 1797, Pickering
wrote: "Few complaints have been made of American vessels being captured
by the British; except such as have been conducted within the jurisdiction of
a Court of Vice Admiralty lately organized at the Mole of St. Nickolas"
(*Naval Documents, Quasi-War, February, 1797–October, 1798,* 21).

On February 26, 1798, King wrote to Pickering: "Annexed you have
Copies of three Notes which I have lately received from Lord Grenville—the
first is an answer to my Note respecting the Proceedings of the vice admiralty
Court at St. Domingo. As this Court was not legally constituted, its proceedings are void, and those who have suffered from its acts are referred . . . to
the High Court of Admiralty for redress . . ." (LS, RG 59, Despatches from
United States Ministers to Great Britain, 1792–1870, Vol. 7, January 9–December 22, 1798, National Archives).

On February 20, 1798, Grenville had written to King: "Lord Grenville
presents his compliments to Mr. King and has the honor to inform him, in
answer to his Note of the 3d. instant, that he does not find on Enquiry that
any regular authority has been given for the Institution of the vice-Admiralty
Court at St. Domingo mentioned in that note: It does not belong to Lord
Grenville to anticipate the Decisions of the regular Courts here in any Indi-

vidual cases. The proper resort of such Parties as may conceive themselves to be aggrieved by the proceedings had in St. Domingo, is to the high Court of admiralty in this Kingdom, where claims must be given, and the consequent legal steps taken thereupon; and there is no doubt that the Judgement of the Court will be guided by the same principles as have already been acted upon in cases of a similar nature" (copy, RG 59, Despatches from United States Ministers to Great Britain, 1792–1870, Vol. 7, January 9–December 22, 1798, National Archives).

In May, 1798, Robert Liston reported to Grenville that the Adams Administration was complaining of the unusually severe sentences handed out by the British Admiralty Court which recently had been established at Môle-Saint-Nicolas, Santo Domingo (Mayo, *Instructions to British Ministers*, 160, note 43).

Grenville, on June 8, 1798, replied: "Immediate Enquiry shall be made respecting the Court of Vice Admiralty at Cape Nicola Mole. I have no knowledge that any such Court exists there, under any competent Authority. If, as I apprehend will be found the Case, it has been irregularly established, Directions will without Delay be given for it's being discontinued, and in that Case the Government of the United States will be aware that all it's Proceedings will be considered here as Nullities" (Mayo, *Instructions to British Ministers*, 160).

For newspaper reports on the activities of the British Vice Admiralty Court at Môle-Saint Nicolas, see the [Philadelphia] *Aurora. General Advertiser*, June 7, 9, 11, 1798.

4. On April 30, 1798, the following item appeared in the *Gazette of the United States, and Philadelphia Daily Advertiser:* "Captain [William] H[ampton, of the brig *Sally*] further informs, that in consequence of the late instructions of the Court of London, respecting neutrals, several privateers were fitting out at St. Kitt's, and 9 at Antigua. . . ."

To Richard Varick [1]

[New York, May 4, 1798]

Dr Sir

A friend of mine has a sudden and unexpected call for 5000 Dollars which I am anxious to assist him with. Can you assist me with *1000* under the certainty that it will be replaced on Wednesday next? If you can you will do me a pleasure.[2]

Yrs.   A Hamilton
                                                                             May 4. 1798

ALS, from a typescript supplied by an anonymous donor.

1. Varick was mayor of New York City.

2. At the bottom of this letter the following receipt is written: "Received from Richard Varick Esqr a check for 1000 Dollars above Mentioned. J. W. Patterson for Coll. Hamilton. May 4th, 1798."

John W. Patterson was a clerk in H's law office. See John Patterson to H, January 12, 1796.

From Rufus King

London May 12. 1798

Dear Sir

It will not surprise you to hear that an open Scism, accompanied by mutual reproaches took place between our Envoys before they separated. Mr. Gerry remains at Paris; and there is a strong opinion that great pains will be taken to persuade him to consent to a public reception, in order to deceive and mock his Country with overtures of an insidious negociation. Marshall & Pinckney left Paris about the middle of April; the former I hope is on his passage to Philadelphia; the latter will embark early in June.[1]

You will be at no loss to understand this state of things. Nothing but vigour and energy will save our Country. Unanimity cannot be expected. Moderation and forbearance with all the virtues that meekly follow in their train, have been faithfully employed, and without success. It is now time, and the wretched Picture exhibited by the Countries where France has introduced her detestable Principles should admonish us, to give up halfway measures with halfway men: they do not belong to the Times in which we live. The people of America will support their Government, if that Government acts with decision, if it appeals to the Pride, the Patriotism, and the Honor of the Nation! But if it temporises, if it wastes itself in words, if it stops short of the only course that remains for its adoption, consistently with the public safety; the next Election will convulse the Country and may, as the Directory intend and expect it shall, give the Government to those who will deliver us up to the same ruin that continues to dessolate Europe.

There is a slight appearance that things are mending upon the Continent; but little interests, little jealousies and little men, whose united influence is opposed to the only effectual Remedy for the mischief, forbid us to expect it until the Evil has spread still wider: for so wretched are the Governments on the Continent, not yet subverted, that the best hope is from the People who are cured when the Fire has passed over them.

I received a short Letter from you a few days since without date,[2] which gave me great satisfaction, as it authorized the hope that the public opinion was sounder than that of its Representatives. War will encrease the public Taxes; these are unpleasant subjects for meditation; the Passions must be attended to; they must have an object; there is a great one. I can't explain myself. I have had no occasion for reserve with the Secretary of State, because I write to him in Cipher.[3]

Yours &c   R.K.

Col. Hamilton

LS, Hamilton Papers, Library of Congress; LC, New-York Historical Society, New York City.

1. In April, 1798, following the breakdown of the XYZ negotiations, John Marshall and Charles Cotesworth Pinckney asked for and received their passports. Marshall sailed for the United States on April 24, 1798. Pinckney, who could not embark immediately because of the illness of his daughter, moved to the south of France. Elbridge Gerry remained in Paris, where he continued to negotiate with the French until July 26, 1798 (*ASP, Foreign Relations,* II, 199–201, 204–27).

2. H to King, March, 1798.

3. King is referring to Francisco de Miranda's plans to liberate South America through the cooperation of England and the United States. See Miranda to H, April 1, 1797; February 7, April 6–June 7, 1798. King described Miranda's proposals in cipher to Timothy Pickering on February 7, 26, April 6, 1798. See Miranda to H, February 7, 1798, note 5; April 6–June 7, 1798, note 1.

From James McHenry

Philad. 12 May 1798.

My dear Hamilton.

I shall in a short time be able to get to sea, one or two of our frigates,[1] and perhaps, in less than six or seven days, Cap Dale, in the Ganges, a lately purchased vessel.[2] Can you spare an hour or two to help me to the instructions that it will be proper to give to their captains. Our ships of war, it is probable, will meet with French privateers, who may be in possession of our merchantmen, or with our merchant vessels having French prize masters on board; or with French privateers cruising upon our coast to capture american vessels. They may also when acting as convoys be obliged to employ force to protect their convoy, and may even be obliged to board a French ship of war to terminate a contest and insure its safety. What instructions ought to be given to meet such cases, or enable them to afford competent protection to our merchantmen and preserve the Executive from any future accusation, of having by its orders involved the country in war. I foresee these instructions will fall to my lot, there being no chance that we shall have a Secretary of the Navy [3] in time to frame them or relieve me from the responsibility. Neither the President has mentioned the subject yet to me nor any other gentleman. You will easily conceive how necessary it is I should be assisted with your ideas and a sketch of such instructions as in your opinion will comport with the existing state of things, and the profound reserve of Congress.

Yours sincerely & Affectionately James McHenry

ALS, Hamilton Papers, Library of Congress; ADfS, James McHenry Papers, Library of Congress.

1. For the construction of the frigates, see H to McHenry, January 27–February 11, 1798, note 4.

2. Richard Dale, a Loyalist in the early years of the American Revolution, joined the Navy as a midshipman and by the end of the war had attained the rank of captain. He then entered the merchant service. In 1794 George Washington appointed him one of the six captains of the newly organized navy (*Executive Journal*, I, 160, 161; Henry Knox to Dale, June 5, 1794 [LC, RG 45, Bound Volumes, Letters Sent Concerning Naval Matters, National Archives]). In 1795 Dale obtained a furlough (Timothy Pickering to Dale, March 14, 1795 [LC, RG 45, Bound Volumes, Letters Sent Concerning Naval Matters, National Archives]). Dale re-entered the merchant service and sailed to China in command of the *Ganges*. On April 27, 1798, Congress enacted "An Act to provide an additional Armament for the further protection of the trade of the United States; and for other purposes" (1 *Stat.* 552). Section 1 of this act reads: "That the President of the United States shall be, and he is hereby authorized and empowered, to cause to be built, purchased or hired, a number of vessels, not exceeding twelve, nor carrying more than twenty-two guns each, to be armed, fitted out and manned under his direction." In pursuance of this act, the United States purchased the *Ganges* from the firm of Thomas Willing, Thomas Mayne Willing, and Thomas Willing Francis for fifty-eight thousand dollars (Bill of Sale, May 3, 1798 [DS, RG 217, Miscellaneous Treasury Accounts, 1790–1894, Account No. 9749, National Archives]). On May 10, 1798, John Adams nominated Dale to be a captain in the Navy, and the Senate confirmed his appointment on the following day (*Executive Journal*, I, 274–75). Dale accepted the command of the *Ganges* (McHenry to Willing and Francis, May 4, 1798 [LC, RG 45, Bound Volumes, Letters Sent Concerning Naval Matters, National Archives]), and on May 24, 1798, the *Ganges* sailed from Philadelphia (*Gazette of the United States, and Philadelphia Daily Advertiser*, May 24, 1798) and patrolled the coastal waters of the United States from Long Island to the Virginia Capes (Benjamin Stoddert to Dale, June 27, 1798 [*Naval Documents, Quasi-War, February, 1797–October, 1798*, 145]).

3. On April 30, 1798, Congress enacted "An Act to establish an Executive department, to be denominated the Department of the Navy" (1 *Stat.* 553–54). On May 2, 1798, Adams nominated George Cabot, who had been United States Senator from Massachusetts from 1791 to 1796, as the first Secretary of the Navy (*Executive Journal,* I, 272). Cabot refused the appointment (*Executive Journal,* I, 275). Adams then nominated Benjamin Stoddert of Maryland to the position, and the Senate agreed to the appointment on May 21, 1798 (*Executive Journal,* I, 275–76). Stoddert did not assume office until June 18, 1798.

To Jonathan Burrall

[New York, May 17, 1798]

Dr Sir

Of the sum deposited in the Office of the B of the U States in my name in trust for Louis LeGuen [1] you will please to cause to be paid upon his orders or Checks as they may be presented The *excess beyond* thirty thousand Dollars, which 30000 Dollars are to remain in *deposit* until a further communication from me.

With esteem   Yr Obd Svt.   A Hamilton
                                    New York May 17. 1798

Jonathan Burrall Esqr
Cashier

ALS, from a typescript supplied by the Lincoln Library, Shippensburg, Pennsylvania.
    1. See Isaac Gouverneur to H, January 7, 1798.

To James McHenry

[New York, May 17, 1798]

My Dear Sir

I have received your letter of the   instant.[1] Not having seen the law which provides the *Naval Armament,*[2] I cannot tell whether it gives any new power to the President that is any power whatever with regard to the employment of the Ships. If not, and he is left on the foot of the Constitution, as I understand to be the case, I am not ready to say that he has any other power than merely to employ the Ships as Convoys with authority to *repel* force by *force*, (but not to capture), and to repress hostilities within our waters including a marine league from our coasts.

Any thing beyond this must fall under the idea of *reprisals* & requires the sanction of that Department which is to declare or make war.

In so delicate a case, in one which involves so important a consequence as that of War—my opinion is that no doubtful authority ought to be exercised by the President—but that as different opinions about his power have been expressed in the house of Representatives,[3] and no special power has been given by the law, it will be expedient for him, and his duty, and the true policy of the Conjuncture to come forward by a Message to the two houses of Congress declaring that "so *far* and no *farther*" he feels himself *confident* of his authority to go in the employment of the naval force; that as in his opinion the depredations on our trade demand a more extensive protection he has thought it his duty to bring the subject under the review of Congress by a communication of his opinion of his own powers— having no desire to exceed the constitutional limits.

This course will remove all clouds as to what The President will do—will gain him credit for frankness and an unwillingness to chicane the Constitution—and will return upon Congress the Question in a shape which cannot be eluded.

I presume you will have heared before this reaches you that a French Privateer has made captures at the mouth of our harbour.[4] This is too much humiliation after all that has passed. Our Merchants are very indignant. Our Government very prostrate in the view of every man of energy.

Yrs. truly   A Hamilton
                                                     May 17. 1798
James McHenry Esq.

ALS, Montague Collection, MS Division, New York Public Library; ALS (photostat), James McHenry Papers, Library of Congress; copy, Hamilton Papers, Library of Congress.

1. McHenry to H, May 12, 1798.
2. "An Act to provide an additional Armament for the further protection of the trade of the United States; and for other purposes" (1 *Stat.* 552 [April 27, 1798]). See McHenry to H, May 12, 1798, note 2.
3. On April 18, 19, 1799, in the debates preceding the enactment of "An Act to provide an additional Armament for the further protection of the trade of the United States; and for other purposes," there was considerable discussion

of one section of the bill. The section in question reads: "That, to secure and maintain the independent rights of commerce and navigation which the laws of nations and the stipulations of treaties acknowledge and sanction, the President of the United States is hereby authorized and empowered to employ the armed vessels of the United States, as convoys, whenever he may think proper to afford such protection, or in any other manner which, in his judgement, will best contribute to the general interests of the United States" (*Annals of Congress*, VIII, 1440). Jonathan Dayton of New Jersey, Robert G. Harper of South Carolina, Harrison Gray Otis and Samuel Sewall of Massachusetts argued that even if this section were rejected, the President had been granted the right to employ the vessels as he saw fit by the Constitution. John Nicholas of Virginia and Albert Gallatin of Pennsylvania, on the other hand, maintained that the President had no such right. The House voted to eliminate the section in question (*Annals of Congress*, VIII, 1440–59).

4. "The ship Merchant, Rosseter, of and from this port, bound to Bristol, and the ship Thomas, Holland, from Liverpool, bound to Philadelphia, are taken in lat 35, 45, by the French privateer Jean Bart, of 14 guns, and sent for Curracoa. The privateer was in chace of another ship" (*Greenleafs* [New York] *New Daily Advertiser*, May 16, 1798). See also the *Gazette of the United States, and Philadelphia Daily Advertiser*, May 16, 1798.

From Uriah Tracy [1]

Philada. 17th. May 1798.

Sir

Our Envoys continuing so long in Paris, is not only a mortifying circumstance, but will probably prevent any energy of Govt. even in the Senate.[2] A Committee of Senate to take into consideration the Subject, was together this morning consisting of 5 members.[3] I laid before them, the followg Bill (viz)—

"A bill declaring the Treaties between the U. S. and the Republic of France, to be void, and more effectually to protect the Commerce & Coasts of the U. States."

Whereas the Govt of the French Republic has repeatedly violated the Treaties subsisting between the U S and the French Nation, and whereas under authority of the sd Govt. armed Vessels, belonging to the French Republic and Citizens thereof, have repeatedly captured the Ships and property of the Citizens of the U.S. on the coasts thereof, while engaged in commerce authorized by sd Treaties, and the law of Nations. Therefore Be it enacted &c.

That the Treaties of "*Alliance*" and of "*Amity and Commerce*" now subsisting between the U.S. and the French Nation, which were agreed upon and signed at Paris on the 6th day of Feby 1778, by the authority of the U. S. & the then King of France, and the stipulations contained therein, be and they are hereby declared to be void, and of no effect. And the U. S. and every Citizen thereof, are hereby declared to be released & discharged from all and singular the Obligations & stipulations contained in sd. Treaties or either of them."

"And be it further enacted. That the President of the U. S. be and he hereby is authorized to instruct the Commanders of all armed Vessels of the U. States, to take and bring into Port all armed Vessels belonging to the Republic of France, or any citizen thereof, which may be found within 40 leagues of any part of the Coast of the U. States—and further to instruct sd. Commanders, who are employed to convoy any Merchant Vessel or Vessels of the U. States, not to permit search to be made on board of such Vessel or Vessels, by Officers or Crew of a French cruizer or armed Vessel on any pretence whatever."

This bill you will see is a rought draught, but the ideas were too strong for our Committee. We may possibly, with immense, labor, drive thro' the Senate a bill authorizing, instructions to capture a cruizer that has unjustifiably taken one of our Vessels on our Coast—but the Treaty must remain intangible until our Envoys are out of Paris.[4] I never permit myself to despair of the Common Wealth, but I am sometimes exhausted & discouraged & think the U. S. must succumb under the intrigues of the *"great Nation."* Our best men are so timid, and our worst so active and profligate—that nothing is done, but with excessive fatigue & industry—confidence in one another is lost—and among ourselves, I mean federalists, there is a look out, to secure against possible events, and protections from the French who may invade us, are now thought of, and qualifications, for friendship from French clemency, are now in calculation.

Pardon me, Sir, for troubling you so long. I wish for your assistance, and that of all good men to excite our friends, our Enemies I fear not, if our friends will be faithful to themselves.

Yours respectfully   Uriah Tracy

Mr. Hamilton

ALS, Hamilton Papers, Library of Congress.

1. Tracy was a Federalist member of the United States Senate from Connecticut.

2. Although news of the fact had not reached the United States, John Marshall and Charles Cotesworth Pinckney had ended their negotiations with the French Directory, while Elbridge Gerry remained in Paris and continued negotiations. See Rufus King to H, May 12, 1798, note 1.

3. This is a reference to a Senate committee which was appointed on November 29, 1797, to consider "that part of the President's Speech, which recommends some measures being adopted for the security and protection of the commerce of the United States . . ." (Annals of Congress, VII, 475). Its members were Benjamin Goodhue of Massachusetts, William Bingham of Pennsylvania, James Gunn of Georgia, John Laurance of New York, and Tracy.

4. On June 21, 1798, the committee "reported a bill, declaring void the treaties between the United States and the French Republic . . ." (Annals of Congress, VII, 586). On July 7, 1798, "An Act to declare the treaties heretofore concluded with France, no longer obligatory on the United States" (1 Stat. 578) became law.

From Oliver Wolcott, Junior

Phila. May 18. 1798

Dr. Sir   (Private)

You may render great service by corresponding occasionally with your acquaintances in Congress, prompting them to vigorous measures, & dispelling whims & hysterics. Mr. Lawrence & Mr. Bingham have frequently created much embarrassment—The former is now firm—the latter troublesome [1]—both want stimulants occasionally. No person here can say anything to them with advantage.

Congress appears to be but little better than before the publication of the dispatches.[2] All their measures are feeble and qualified with some *proviso*, or *limitation*, which shows that they are not in earnest.

Mr. Cabot will not accept the naval Department [3] & I almost despair of obtaining a tolerably fit character. The purchase, building & providing of the Ships [4] falls upon me, & you know that my other duties are enough to employ a mind more active & vigorous than I possess. To diminish the care as much as possible I must employ efficient agents to whom much must be confided. John Blagge [5] does not appear to answer this description. Colo. Stevens [6] wishes to be employed—but he certainly has not all the requisite qualifications. Will you be so good as to turn the thing in your mind, & mention a number of the most suitable characters.

We hear nothing from the Envoys, I fear that their delay will

ruin our Affairs. Their continuance in France[7] furnishes the only
plausible argument for inaction.

I am Dr. Sir yours   Oliv Wolcott.

Alexander Hamilton Esq.

ADfS, Connecticut Historical Society, Hartford; LC, Connecticut Historical
Society, Hartford.
  1. John Laurance and William Bingham.
  On April 9, 1798, in a letter describing the views of various members of Congress, Theodore Sedgwick wrote to Rufus King: "Lawrence is as you knew him
so-so" (King, The Life and Correspondence of Rufus King, II, 311). Bingham
was "troublesome" on at least two occasions. On April 9, 1798, he deserted the
Federalists to vote in the Senate against the printing of the papers relating to
the negotiations in the XYZ affair (Annals of Congress, VII, 538), and on April
24, 1798, he joined the opposition in the voting on amendments to "An act to
provide an additional armament for the further protection of the trade of the
United States; and for other purposes" (Annals of Congress, VII, 547).
  2. For the decision of Congress to print the dispatches from the United States
envoys to France concerning the XYZ affair, see Annals of Congress, VII, 536–
37; VIII, 1377–80. See also Timothy Pickering to H, April 9, 1798, note 1.
  3. For the appointment of Benjamin Stoddert to be Secretary of the Navy,
see James McHenry to H, May 12, 1798, note 3.
  4. Wolcott is referring to "An Act to provide an additional Armament for
the further protection of the trade of the United States; and for other purposes" (1 Stat. 552 [April 27, 1798]) and "An Act to authorize the President
of the United States to cause to be purchased, or built, a number of small vessels to be equipped as gallies, or otherwise" (1 Stat. 556 [May 4, 1798]).
  5. Blagge, a New York City businessman, was a director of the New-York
Insurance Company. In 1794 Henry Knox had appointed him United States
naval agent at New York City. See Knox to H, June 25, 1794.
  6. Ebenezer Stevens, New York merchant and director of the New-York Insurance Company, served throughout the American Revolution and at the end
of the war held the rank of lieutenant colonel. In 1794 the New York legislature had named him to a seven-man committee in charge of "repairing or erecting fortifications at or near the city and port of New-York" ("An Act authorizing the erecting of Fortifications within this State" [New York Laws,
17th Sess., Ch. XLI (March 26, 1794)]). In 1794 Stevens was also the Federal
agent in charge of construction of the fortifications for New York City. See
Henry Knox to H, March 29, 1794, note 5; Stevens to H, December 1, 1794.
  7. See Rufus King to H, May 12, 1798, note 1.

To George Washington

New York May 19. 1798

My Dear Sir

At the present dangerous crisis of public affairs, I make no apology
for troubling you with a political letter. Your impressions of our

situation, I am persuaded, are not different from mine. There is certainly great probability that we may have to enter into a very serious struggle with France; and it is more and more evident that the powerful faction which has for years opposed the Government is determined to go every length with France. I am sincere in declaring my full conviction, as the result of a long course of observation, that they are ready to *new model* our constitution under the *influence* or *coertion* of France—to form with her a perpetual alliance *offensive* and *defensive*—and to give her a monopoly of our Trade by *peculiar* and *exclusive* privileges. This would be in substance, whatever it might be in name to make this Country a province of France. Neither do I doubt, that her standard displayed in this country would be directly or indirectly seconded by them in pursuance of the project I have mentioned.

It is painful and alarming to remark that the Opposition-Faction assumes so much a Geographical complexion. As yet from the South of Maryland nothing has been heared but accents of disapprobation of our Government and approbation of or apology for France.[1] This is a most portentous symptom & demands every human effort to change it.

In such a state of public affairs it is impossible not to look up to you; and to wish that your influence could in some proper mode be brought into direct action. Among the ideas which have passed through my mind for this purpose—I have asked myself whether it might not be expedient for you to make a circuit through Virginia and North Carolina under some pretence of health &c. This would call forth addresses public dinners &c. which would give you an opportunity of expressing sentiments in Answers Toasts &c. which would throw the weight of your character into the scale of the Government and revive an enthusiasm for your person that may be turned into the right channel.

I am aware that the step is delicate & ought to be well considered before it is taken. I have even not settled my own opinion as to its propriety—but I have concluded to bring the general idea under your view, confident that your judgment will make a right choice and that you will take no step which is not well calculated. The conjuncture however is extraordinary & now or very soon will demand extraordinary measures.

You ought also to be aware, My Dear Sir, that in the event of an open rupture with France, the public voice will again call you to command the armies of your Country; and though all who are attached to you will from attachment, as well as public considerations, deplore an occasion which should once more tear you from that repose to which you have so good a right—yet it is the opinion of all those with whom I converse that you will be compelled to make the sacrifice. All your past labour may demand to give it efficacy this further, this very great sacrifice.

Adieu My Dear Sir   Respectfully & Affecly Yr very obed servt

A Hamilton

General Washington

ALS, George Washington Papers, Library of Congress.
   1. See Washington to H, May 27, 1798.

For The Time Piece

[New York, May 22, 1798]

A most unprovoked & wanton attack upon me appeared in the Time pi[e]ce of yesterday under the signature of *William Keteltas*.[1] Were this man as well known elsewhere as in his own state his attack would [be] treated with silent contempt. As it is, a very slight notice only can be taken of it. It is barely necessary to state that where he is known, the doubt is whether he is most *madman* or *knave*, that he is so contemptible as to have been the missionary of a party to go three hundred miles into the Western parts of this state, with saddle bags full of addresses to be distributed for an electioneering purpose,[2] and that his present publication is replete with gross falshoods. By the allusion to *Caesar* and *Brutus* [3] he plainly hints at assassination. Though his fears may be the only, it is not doubted that they will be a full security that he will not attempt to be the *assassin*. But while he is conscious that the worthlessness of his character renders it impossible to descend to his level he may be assured he will not find me unprepared to repel attack and that he is *despised* and *defied*.[4]

AH

ADfS, Hamilton Papers, Library of Congress; *The* [New York] *Time Piece,* May 25, 1798.

1. Keteltas was a New York lawyer and a Republican. For H's earlier relations with Keteltas, see "Certificate on Robert Lenox," January 11, 1796, note 1. The "unprovoked & wanton attack" to which H refers was written and signed by Keteltas and was printed in *The Time Piece,* May 21, 1798. Keteltas placed his principal emphasis on H's alleged admiration of monarchy and his alleged hostility toward popular government.

2. In his attack on H in *The Time Piece,* May 21, 1798, Keteltas wrote: ". . . In conversation with you, at your house, a few days since on the subject of the late ass[ass]inating treatment I received in the dark, from four villains in the county of Herkimer, for exposing Mr Jay's unrepublican conduct as respected the union, and in our own state in particular as the executive thereof, you was pleased to remark that you did not approve of personal violence; which in my mind was the result of fear, and not sincerity, from what followed. You attempted to palliate that conduct, by observing, I ought not to have opposed the administration as I did in the year 1796, or spoke my sentiments and circulated hand bills through the country descriptive of its conduct."

3. After stating in his attack on H in *The Time Piece* that H had attempted to introduce a monarchical form of government at the Constitutional Convention in 1787, Keteltas wrote: ". . . What renders these vile attempts in you peculiarly criminal and ungrateful is, that your infant years was the paternal and maternal care of the sons and daughters of America, who may say as did Cesar et too Brute, the first to plunge the dagger in their bosom and enslave them; but like Caesar you are ambitious, and for that ambition to enslave his country Brutus slew him; and are ambitious men less dangerous to American than Roman Liberty?"

4. On May 28, 1798, Keteltas wrote an open letter in reply to H's letter. Keteltas's letter, which is printed in *The Time Piece,* May 28, 1798, in large part reiterates the charges he made in *The Time Piece* on May 21, 1798. In addition, in *The Time Piece,* June 11, 1798, Keteltas wrote: "A Mr. [John W.] Patterson, clerk to Alexander Hamilton, having declared in public company, that I, the undersigned, would be murdered, I offer 500 dollars for the apprehension of the assassin, or his abettors, that may be given up to the justice of their country, to be treated as the law directs."

Conveyance from Alexander Hamilton, Elizabeth Hamilton, Isaac Bronson, and Ann Bronson to John B. Church [1]

New York, May 24, 1798. Convey two and one-half lots of land in New York City to Church.[2]

Copy, Conveyances in the Office of the Register, City of New York, Liber 60, 176–79, Hall of Records, New York City.

1. Bronson, a prominent New York City moneylender and land speculator, had been a surgeon's mate in the American Revolution.

2. For information on this conveyance, see "Receipt from Morgan Lewis," March 18, 1796, note 3.

From Rufus King [1]

[*London, May 26, 1798.* King's notation for this letter reads: "Hamilton. Politicks." *Letter not found.*]

1. Letter listed in Rufus King's "Memorandum of Private Letters, &c., dates & persons, from 1796 to Augt 1802," owned by Mr. James G. King, New York City.

From George Washington

Mount Vernon 27th of May 1798.

My dear Sir,

Yesterday, brought me your Letter of the 19th. instant.

You may be assured, that my Mind is deeply impressed with the present situation of our public affairs, and not a little agitated by the outrageous conduct of France towards the United States; and at the enemical conduct of its partisans among ourselves, who aid & abet their measures: You may believe further from assurances equally sincere, that if there was any thing in my power, which could be done with consistency to avert, or lessen the danger of the Crisis, it should be rendered with hand and heart.

The expedient however, which has been suggested by you, would not, in my opinion, answer the end which is proposed. The object of such a tour could not be veiled by the ostensible cover to be given to it; because it would not apply to the state of my health, which never was better; and as the measure would be susceptible of two interpretations, the enemies to it—always more active & industrious than friends—would endeavour, as much as in them lay, to turn it to their own advantage, by malicious insinuations; unless they should discover that the current against themselves was setting too strong, & of too serious a nature for them to stem; in which case the journey

ALS, Hamilton Papers, Library of Congress; ALS, letterpress copy, George Washington Papers, Library of Congress.

would be unnecessary, and in either case, the reception might not be such as you have supposed.

But, my dear Sir, dark as matters appear at present, and expedient as it is to be prepared at *all* points, for the worst that can happen; (and no one is more disposed to this measure than I am)—I cannot make up my mind, *yet*, for the expectation of *open War;* or, in other words, for a formidable Invasion, by France. I cannot believe, although I think them capable of *any thing bad*, that they will attempt to do more than they have done; that when they perceive the spirit, & policy of this country rising into resistance; and that they have falsely calculated upon support from *a large* part of the *People* thereof, to promote their views & influence in it, that they will desist, *even from those practices;* unless unexpected events in Europe, or their possession of Louisiana & the Floridas, should induce them to continue the measure. And I believe further, that although the *leaders* of their party, in this country, will not change their sentiments, that they will be obliged nevertheless to change their plan, or the mode of carrying it on; from the effervescence which is appearing in all quarters, and the desertion of their followers, which must frown them into silence—at least for a while.

If I did not view things in this light, my mind would be infinitely more disquieted than it is; for if a crisis should arrive when a sense of duty, or a call from my Country, should become so imperious as to leave me no choice, I should prepare for the relinquishment, and go with as much reluctance from my present peaceful abode, as I should do to the tombs of my Ancesters.

To say at this time, determinately, what I should do under such circumstances, might be improper, having once before departed from a similar resolution; [1] but I may declare *to you*, that as there is no conviction in my breast that I could serve my country with more efficiency in the command of the Armies, it might Levy, than many others, an expression of its wish that I should do so, must, some how or other, be unequivocally known, to satisfy my mind that, notwithstanding the respect in which I may be held on account of former services, that a preference might not be given to a man more in his

1. Washington is referring either to his reversal of his decision not to be a candidate for a second term as President (see the introductory note to H to Washington, May 10, 1796) or to his decision to come out of retirement and accept the Presidency in 1789 (*JCC*, XXV, 837–38; Washington to John Landon, April 14, 1789 [*GW*, XXX, 284–85]).

prime. And it may well be supposed too, that I should like, previously, to know who would be my coadjutors, and whether you would be disposed to take an active part, if Arms are to be resorted to.

Before this letter can get to your hands, you will have seen the Resolutions & proposed Address from the Citizens of Charleston, in South Carolina.[2] Their proceedings will, I am persuaded, give the ton to other parts of *that* State. Two or three very good Addresses have already appeared from No. Carolina; one with the Signature of a late Governor thereof, Spaight.[3] All the upper, most populous, and hardy yeomanry of this State, have come, & are coming forward, with strong Addresses to the Executive, and assurances of Support. The Address from Norfolk [4] (I do not mean the impertinent one from Magnien's Grenadier Company) [5] is a good one. The middle counties

2. The resolutions of the "Citizens of Charleston" are dated May 5, 1798 (D, Adams Family Papers, deposited in the Massachusetts Historical Society, Boston; *Gazette of the United States, and Philadelphia Daily Advertiser*, May 24, 1798). The "address" from the citizens of Charleston has been dated in a later handwriting "[May? 1798]." This address reads in part: ". . . your memorialists feel themselves irresistibly impelled to make a full, Solemn and explicit declaration of the sincere attachment to the Constitution and Government of the United States; and of their fixed resolution to maintain and support them against All foreign encroachment & domination at the hazard of their Lives & fortunes . . . and they submit, to the discretion of the Government, the measures essential to the attainment and Security of these great objects" (DS, Adams Family Papers, deposited in the Massachusetts Historical Society, Boston; *Gazette of the United States, and Philadelphia Daily Advertiser*, June 15, 1798).

3. This "address," which is dated May 3, 1798, was from the citizens of New Bern, North Carolina. It is printed in the *Gazette of the United States, and Philadelphia Daily Advertiser*, May 22, 1798. Richard Dobbs Spaight was governor of North Carolina from 1792 to 1795.

4. The "address" from the citizens of Norfolk, Virginia, is dated May 10, 1798, and is printed in the *Gazette of the United States, and Philadelphia Daily Advertiser*, May 19, 1798.

5. This address, which was prepared at a "meeting of Capt. Bernard Magnien's Company of Grenadiers, at . . . Portsmouth [Virginia] the 5th of May, '98," reads in part: "That we view with extreme concern, the attempts that are evidently making by men high in authority, to widen the breach between the United States and the French Republic, by holding up to the good people of these states, the late unworthy propositions of certain unauthorized persons at Paris, as the act of the French government, when, in reality, the face of the dispatches cannot warrant any such conclusions.

"That we cannot but view the man, or set of men, as inimical to the RIGHTS of the PEOPLE and the sound principle of their self-government, who shall endeavour, by any false colouring, to give the stamp of authenticity to that which is in itself extremely doubtful and problematical: and who shall, by such means, strive to involve us in all the calamities of war with the most powerful Republic on earth.

"That without reference to our well founded complaints, or to occurances

of this State, with two or three exceptions, have hitherto been silent; they want leaders; but I shall be much mistaken if a large majority of them do not forsake, if they have heretofore been with, those who have pretended to speak their Sentiments. As to the Resolutions which were entered into at Fredericksburgh, it is only necessary to point to the Manager of them; [6] & add, that the meeting was partial. From Georgia, no developement of the public sentiment has yet made its appearance; but I have learnt from a very intelligent Gentleman just returned from thence, where he has been sometime for the benefit of his health; travelling, going & returning, slowly, and

---

fresh in the memory of us all, nothing can be more abhorrent to our feelings, than the idea of being by such a war driven into an alliance with a nation which is at present unhappily under the guidance of the most foul and corrupt government upon earth." (*Gazette of the United States, and Philadelphia Daily Advertiser,* May 16, 1798.)

For the debate in the House of Representatives on this address, see *Annals of Congress,* VIII, 1707–24.

6. The "manager" was John F. Mercer, a former Republican member of the House of Representatives from Maryland, who had played a prominent role in opposing H's fiscal policies in 1792. See the introductory note to H to Mercer, September 26, 1792. See also David Ross to H, October 16, 1797. On April 10, 1798, "At a numerous Meeting of the Freeholders and other inhabitants of Spotsylvania County" in Fredericksburg, Virginia, it was resolved: ". . . We heartily deprecate *any measure* which may be so offensive, as to close the door of reconciliation, and mar all future prospects of accomodation; in this view, whilst we doubt the constitutionality of that part of the President's message, which permits armed vessels to be cleared, we trust that as the constitution has given the Power of Declaring War to Congress alone, the Representatives of the People will not be influenced in their deliberations by a personal consideration, but by those only, which involve the Happiness and Dearest Interests of their Country.

". . . That Peace with France, upon any terms, less than an abandonment of our Rights as a Free People, is preferable to a Connection with England upon terms, that would embark our Interests and Happiness in the same bottom with her's, and eventually subject us to the same Despotism, Corruption and Bankruptcy, under which she is now labouring.

". . . That viewing the calamities which will ensue from a War with France, we are led to apprehend the aid that such an event would afford to the unremitted exertions of the Enemies of Republicanism, in the United States, before our government is matured, and its principles permanently established, by a liberal and correct construction of its Constitution, and fearfully to anticipate, that it would give additional and unconstitutional weight to Executive Influence, always most prompt and active to acquire Power in the time of War.

". . . That to an enlightened People, every information ought to be afforded by those in Power, which can ameliorate the unhappy difference, that subsists between America and her Sister Republic; that if there be just cause for War they may be convinced of it and not pressed into measures, which can never be effectual, without unanimity; but must expose our Country to all the misfortunes that usually befal a divided People, and finally end in all the horrors of a Civil War and consequent Despotism." ([Fredericksburg] *Virginia Herald,* April 14, 1798.)

making considerable halts, that the people of that State, as also those of South & North Carolina, seem to be actuated by one spirit, *and that*, a very friendly one to the General Government. I have likewise heard, that the present Governor of the first (Georgia) [7] professes to be strongly attached to it. These disclosures, with what may yet be expected, will, I conceive, give a different impression of the sentiments of our people to the Directory of France, than what they have been taught to believe; while it must serve to abash the partizans of it for their wicked, & presumptive information.

Your free communication on these political topics, is so far from needing an apology, that I shall be much gratified, & thankful to you, for the continuation of them; & I would wish you to believe that with great truth and sincerity, I am always

Your Affectionate friend, & Obedt Sert.   Go: Washington

Alexr. Hamilton Esqr.

7. James Jackson was governor of Georgia from January 12, 1798, to March 3, 1801.

To James McHenry

[New York, June 1, 1798]

Introductory Note

This letter contains the first of many references to the plans for the fortification of New York City during the Quasi-War with France. What on the surface should have been a relatively simple operation became extraordinarily complex because of the division of responsibility among the United States Government, the Military Committee of New York City, the state government, and the city government.

The fortification of ports and harbors in the United States was first undertaken in 1794 when war with Great Britain seemed imminent. On March 20, 1794, Congress enacted "An Act to provide for the Defence of certain Ports and Harbors in the United States." [1] This statute was implemented by "An Act making appropriations for the support of the Military establishment of the United States, for the year one thousand seven hundred and ninety-four," which appropriated "For fortifying certain ports and harbors of the United States, and purchasing the lands necessary for the erection of the same, seventy-six thousand dollars.

ALS (photostat), James McHenry Papers, Library of Congress; ALS, from a typescript furnished by Mr. Joseph M. Roebling, Trenton, New Jersey.
1. 1 *Stat.* 345–46.

. . ." [2] As a result of this legislation, the fortification of New York City was begun in 1794, but the work was not completed.

In his eighth annual message to Congress on December 7, 1796, George Washington inquired ". . . whether our Harbours are yet sufficiently secured," [3] and on December 16, 1796, the House of Representatives "*Resolved,* That inquiry ought to be made into the actual state of the fortifications of the ports and harbors of the United States, and whether any, and what, further provision is necessary on that subject." [4] On June 23, 1797, "An Act to provide for the further Defence of the Ports and Harbors of the United States" appropriated not more than one hundred and fifteen thousand dollars "for fortifying certain ports and harbors of the United States." [5] More money was appropriated for fortifications on May 3, 1798, by "An Act supplementary to the act providing for the further defence of the ports and harbors of the United States." This act provided "That a sum not exceeding two hundred and fifty thousand dollars, in addition to the sums heretofore appropriated, remaining unexpended, shall be, and is hereby appropriated, and shall and may be paid out of any monies not before appropriated, to make and complete, at the discretion of the President of the United States, the fortifications heretofore directed for certain ports and harbors, and to erect fortifications in any other place or places as the public safety shall require, in the opinion of the President of the United States; and which other fortifications he is hereby authorized to cause to be erected, under his direction from time to time as he shall judge necessary." [6]

Following the enactment of the 1794 statutes, Henry Knox, Secretary of War, appointed Ebenezer Stevens agent of the War Department for the fortification of New York City.[7] In this capacity, Stevens was responsible for the funds allocated for the defense of New York. In the late spring of 1798, Secretary of War James McHenry reappointed Stevens as War Department agent.[8]

The city government first became interested in measures for the defense of New York Harbor on April 30, 1798, when, in response to a petition from the Chamber of Commerce, the Common Council requested that "sixteen long eighteen Pounders of those now at West Point mounted upon travelling Carriages or as many of them as can be spared" be transferred to New York City and "Ordered that Mr Mayor [Richard Varick] issue his Warrant on the Treasr to pay Colo Ebenr Stevens $1000, on Acct towards providing Timber for Carriages & other Apparatus. . . ." [9] On May 28, 1798, the Common Council ordered that

2. 1 *Stat.* 346–47 (March 21, 1794).
3. LC, George Washington Papers, Library of Congress.
4. *Annals of Congress,* VI, 1672.
5. 1 *Stat.* 521–22.
6. 1 *Stat.* 554–55.
7. See Knox to H, March 29, 1794; "Treasury Department Circular to the Collectors of the Customs," April 3–June 4, 1794; Stevens to H, December 1, 1794.
8. See Stevens to H, February 28, 1799. See also Stevens to H, April 4, 1799, note 2.
9. *Minutes of the Common Council,* II, 435–36.

Aldermen John B. Coles, Gabriel Furman, and John Bogert "be a Committee in conjunction with Colo Stevens to attend to the Measures . . . for the Defence of the City & Harbor of New York. . . ." [10] Subsequently the Council "Resolved that this Board will provide a Sum not exceeding fifty thousand Dollars to be applied towards the Defence of this Port & City And that an Application shall be made to Congress and, if necessary, to our State Legislature for the Reimbursement thereof." [11] Instead of appropriating the money in question, the Council authorized Furman to borrow it from the Bank of New York, which he did.[12] On October 14, 1799, the state reimbursed the city with "the Sum of Sixty thousand Dollars . . . borrowed last Year . . . and also a further Sum . . . for Interest thereof. . . ." [13]

The Military Committee of New York City originated as a citizens' organization with neither official standing nor authority. At a meeting at City Hall on June 11, 1798, representatives of the "Officers of the late army and navy of the United States," various city wards, and the Chamber of Commerce discussed measures for the defense of the city and appointed a Military Committee consisting of Aaron Burr, Hamilton, and Stevens.[14] Although the power and responsibilities of the Military Committee were never clearly defined, its members—particularly Hamilton and Stevens—took an active part in formulating the plans for the city's defenses, and more often than not they were responsible for the supervision of the projects initiated by the Federal, state, and city governments.

The New York legislature first acted on the city's defenses on March 26, 1794, when it passed "An Act authorising the erecting of Fortifications, within this State." [15] This act stated: "Whereas the monies that may be appropriated by the Congress, for the purpose of repairing or erecting fortifications at or near the city and port of New-York, may not be sufficient to put the said city and port in a proper state of defence,

". . . That a sum or sums of money not exceeding in the whole the sum of thirty thousand pounds, shall be appropriated. . . ."

Ebenezer Stevens was one of seven commissioners appointed by this act.

On August 27, 1798, the legislature passed "An Act for the further defence of this State and for other purposes." [16] In a letter to President

10. *Minutes of the Common Council*, II, 444.
11. *Minutes of the Common Council*, II, 447.
12. *Minutes of the Common Council*, II, 452, 458, 462, 467, 473.
13. *Minutes of the Common Council*, II, 577.
14. [New York] *Argus. Greenleaf's New Daily Advertiser*, June 11, 1798. For this meeting and the events leading up to it, see "Call for a Meeting," June 4, 1798, note 2.
15. *New York Laws*, 17th Sess., Ch. XLI.
16. *New York Laws*, 22nd Sess., Ch. V. This act reads in part: "*Be it enacted* . . . , That a sum not exceeding one hundred and fifty thousand dollars be, and the same is hereby appropriated, for the purposes of repairing and compleating such fortifications, as have already been erected and constructed in the said city and its vicinity, and for constructing and erecting such other fortifications at such place or places, upon the Island of New-York, Governor's

Adams on September 26, 1798, Governor John Jay described the contents of this act and wrote: "I . . . take the liberty of submitting to your Consideration whether as Majr. Genl. Hamilton is a national Officer in whom great confidence may be reposed, it would not be expedient to authorize him to concert with me the plan of laying out this money to the best advantage and to appoint him to superintend the execution of it. . . ." [17] Adams accepted this proposal. [18] The upshot of this arrangement was that Hamilton was the principal officer of both the state and Federal governments for the fortification of the city and

---

Island, Bedlow's Island, Ellice's or Oyster Island and Long Island, and for providing such other means of defence, for the security of the said city and port of New-York, as the person administering the government of this State for the time being, shall or may deem best adapted to the security and defence of the same, and provided that the said sum shall be expended under the direction of the President of the United States.

"*And be it further enacted,* That there be appropriated a sum not exceeding one hundred and sixty-five thousand dollars for the purchase of a further quantity of arms, and to provide ammunition for the use of the militia of this State; to mount and equip the cannon belonging to this State; to purchase military stores, and for building an arsenal or arsenals in such parts of this State as the person administering the government of this State for the time being shall order and direct. That the person administering the government of this State for the time being do cause the said arsenal or arsenals to be built and the said purchases to be made, in such manner and on such terms as to him shall seem most conducive to the interest of this State.

"*And be it further enacted,* That the arms, ammunition, cannon and military stores now belonging to the people of the State, and such as may be purchased by virtue of this act, shall be distributed or deposited in such place or places, as the person administering the government of this State shall from time to time direct.

"*And be it further enacted,* That it shall and may be lawful to and for the person administering the government of this State for the time being, to employ such agent or agents, as he may deem proper to superintend the works intended to be repaired, erected and constructed in conformity to this act, and to purchase the requisite materials and military stores herein provided for.

"*And be it further enacted,* That the Comptroller of this State shall on the order of the person administering the government of this State for the time being draw his warrant on the Treasurer of this State, for the payment of the aforesaid several sums of money hereby appropriated, or for such parts thereof, as may from time be requested or directed for the purposes aforesaid by the person administering the government of this State; and the said Comptroller shall audit the accounts of the expences and disbursements which may accrue by reason of the premises, and shall annually lay the same before the Legislature at their stated meetings. . . ."

A copy of this act is in the Hamilton Papers, Library of Congress. Also in the Hamilton Papers, Library of Congress, is an unsigned and undated draft written by Philip Schuyler of a statute for fortifying New York City. This draft differs in several significant features from the statute adopted by the New York legislature.

17. LC, Governor's Letter Books, from the original in the New York State Library, Albany; copy, Dr. Frank Monaghan, Washington, D.C.

18. Adams to H, October 17, 1798.

port of New York and that Ebenezer Stevens was his immediate subordinate in this undertaking.

That this system—or lack of system—of overlapping authority worked as well as it did can be attributed to the fact that Hamilton and Stevens were the leading figures in each of the participating agencies. The Military Committee (or Hamilton and Stevens, for Burr took little part in the committee's activities) worked closely with—and were often the designated agents of—the Federal, state, and city governments. More important, Stevens was agent for the War Department in New York City, and both men were the principal state and Federal officials responsible for the city's fortification. In any given instance, Hamilton and Stevens may not have known under what authority they were acting, but they seldom, if ever, had to doubt that such authority existed.

My Dear Sir

Our citizens are extremely anxious that some further measures for their defence should take place. Do me the favour to inform me confidentially what means are *actually* in the disposition of your department for this purpose when & how they will be applied.

Yrs truly   A Hamilton

June 1. 1798

A Capt *Hacker* [19] formerly of our Navy is desirous of being employed. One or two good men have recommended him to me. It seems however that he has been heretofore rather Democratic. I barely wish that his pretensions may be fairly but carefully considered & that he may have such chance as he merits.

The sooner I hear from you the *better*.

J McHenry Esq

19. Hoystead Hacker, who was among the first group of commissioned officers in the Continental navy in 1775, entered the navy as a lieutenant and was promoted to captain. In 1779 he was in command of the *Providence* when it defeated the *Diligent*. When this letter was written, he was a resident of New York City, a pilot for Long Island Sound, and a member of the standing committee of the Marine Society of New York City.

To George Washington

New York June 2d
1798

My Dear Sir

I have before me your favour of the 27. of May.

The suggestion in my last was an indigested thought begotten by my anxiety. I have no doubt that your view of it is accurate & well founded.

It is a great satisfaction to me to ascertain what I had anticipated in hope, that you are not determined in an *adequate emergency* against affording once more your Military services. There is no one but yourself that could unite the public confidence in such an emergency, independent of other considerations—and it is of the last importance that this confidence should be *full* and *complete*. As to the wish of the Country it is certain that it will be *ardent* and *universal*. You intimate a desire to be informed what would be my part in such an event as to entering into military service. I have no scruple about opening myself to you on this point. If I am invited *to a station in which the service I may render may be proportioned to the sacrifice I am to make*—I shall be willing to go into the army. If you command, the place in which I should hope to be most useful is that of Inspector General with a command in the line. This I would accept. The public must judge for itself as to whom it will employ; but every individual must judge for himself as to the terms on which he will serve and consequently must estimate himself his own pretensions. I have no knowlege of any arrangement contemplated but I take it for granted the services of all the former officers worth having may be commanded & that your choice would regulate the Executive. With decision & care in selection an excellent army may be formed.

The view you give of the prospects in the South is very consoling. The public temper seems every where to be travelling fast to a right point. This promises security to the Country in every Event.

I have the honor to remain very truly My Dr. Sir   Yr. faithful & Affectionate servant   A Hamilton

General Washington

ALS, George Washington Papers, Library of Congress; copy, Hamilton Papers, Library of Congress.

To Oliver Wolcott, Junior

[New York, June 2, 1798]

My Dear Sir

I received from you not long since a letter [1] on the subject of a fit person for naval Agent which in the hurry of my business I forgot. I think you mentioned in it for consideration Col Stevens & Mr. Blagg.

Col Stevens is an active man not wanting in intelligence [2] who has latterly been employed in navigation & probably has some relative ideas. He is however pretty largely in other business & perhaps would make this too secondary an object. Besides this he has till lately been connected in French Trade & generally unfriendly to our politics; though he come forward now explicitly on the right side & I believe is in earnest. But the employment of a man of this description in preference to staunch friends is apt to occasion criticism & one is not always certain of such a person.

Blagge is a very good but I fear not a very active [3] man.

Some other characters have occured to me—

James Watson [4] whom you know is a man of understanding & leisure. He has taken pretty good care of his own affairs and I should think competent. I must however say that he has latterly had the air [5] to me of being rather disposed to inactivity.

There is a Mr. George Barnewall whom I should prefer to either of these if it were not for his situation in some respects. He has been bred a sailor is well acquainted with all that appertains to vessels—has done considerable business as a Merchant & is of very good reputation for integrity. But he was an officer in the British Navy last War & his appointment to a *money getting* place would be dissatisfactory to many & be represented as an evidence of British inclination in The Governt. This however would not prevent me from appointing him to the command of one of our sloops of War where I think he would be an acquisition & which being considered more as an employt. of danger than profit would attract less criticism.[6]

Anthony Rutgers.[7] This man is well acquainted with Shipping business—is indefatigable in his pursuits—honest well principled & a man of property. But he is 54 years old & garrulous. He would do the business well upon a small scale but would I imagine be incompetent to an extensive Scene.

Mr. Charles Smith. A Merchant Sailor—very competent industrious attentive honest—a man of property & respectability. He is advanced in life but of considerable activity & vigor of body.

John B Church, my brother in law, a man of fortune & integrity —of strong mind, very exact very active & very much a man of business. He is about fifty but of uncommon strength of constitution. I have no reason to believe the employment would be acceptable to him but that he has little to do his time hangs heavy on his hands—& he has a son [8] grown up whom he wants to employ. You know he was *Wadsworth's* [9] associate in the supply of the French & our Army—in which he gave full proofs of ability and efficiency. If he should be thought of it should come by way of inquiry of me from you & put upon the footing that he is understood to be unengaged in business and to have a son grown up whom he might wish to employ. You must also state the objects & the compensation.

Of the men I have mentioned except Mr Church I should upon the whole prefer Mr. Smith if he would accept. Say nothing to any body of this hint about Mr Church. I am not sure that he would be pleased with my doing what I have done.

Yrs. truly   A Hamilton
                                                   June 2. 1798

O Wolcot Esq

ALS, Connecticut Historical Society, Hartford.
    1. Wolcott to H, May 18, 1798.
    2. H placed an asterisk at this point and in the margin wrote: "Mr. W Constable who is a good Judge says there has appeared to him some confusion in his business arrangements." William Constable was a New York City merchant.

3. At this point H placed an asterisk and in the margin of the last page of this letter wrote: "NB This Gentleman has some propensity to Gaming, but it is in perfect command & now confined to a party at Bragg once a week with *Low Clarkeson Le Roy Harrison* & one or two others of similar description." Brag was a card game resembling poker. Nicholas Low, Matthew Clarkson, and Herman LeRoy were New York City merchants. Richard Harison was United States attorney for the District of New York.

4. Watson was a New York City attorney and merchant. A veteran of the American Revolution, he had been a member of the New York Assembly in 1791 and from 1794 to 1796. He had been speaker of the Assembly in 1794. He was a member of the state Senate from 1796 to 1798, and he entered the United States Senate on August 17, 1798, having been elected to replace William North. For North's appointment to the Senate to fill the vacancy created by the resignation of John Sloss Hobart, see the first letter from John Jay to H, April 19, 1798, note 1.

5. In MS, "aid."

6. At this point H wrote and then crossed out: "Isaac Bronson deserves attention. He is a sensible active man—is not I believe much occupied & as far as I know has a fair character."

7. Rutgers was a New York City merchant and brewer. He was the son of Elizabeth Rutgers, plaintiff in the case of *Rutgers* v *Waddington*. See H to Thomas Jefferson, April 19, 1792. See also Goebel, *Law Practice*, I, 282–419.

8. Philip Church, who later became H's aide-de-camp.

9. Jeremiah Wadsworth.

To Elizabeth Hamilton [1]

[New York] June 3d. 1798

I have been extremely uneasy, My beloved Eliza, at the state of health and state of mind in which you left me. I earnestly hope that there has been a change of both for the better. Let me entreat you as you value my happiness to tranquillize yourself and to take care of yourself. You are infinitely dear to me. You are of the utmost consequence to our precious Children. You have every motive to study your own health and repose.

I will not hurry you to return because you must do as duty and affection to your father demand and because I know you will be glad to come back to my arms as soon as possible. These when you arrive will welcome you with increased affection. I always feel how necessary you are to me. But when you are absent I become still more sensible of it, and look around in vain for that satisfaction which you alone can bestow.

I dined with Angelica [2] today—Margaret [3] was with her. My spirits were not very good—though every body tried to make my time pass pleasantly. Give my love to your father & mother. Kiss the dear Children with you for me and receive the assurance of my fond & unalterable tenderness.   A H

ALS, Hamilton Papers, Library of Congress.
  1. Elizabeth Hamilton was visiting her parents, Philip and Catharine Schuyler, in Albany.
  2. Elizabeth's sister, Angelica Schuyler Church.
  3. Elizabeth's sister, Margaret Schuyler Van Rensselaer.

Call for a Meeting [1]

[New York, June 4, 1798]

CARD.

The officers of the late army and navy of the United States are requested to meet at Gautier's,[2] on Tuesday evening, 7 o'clock, to consult on the subject of measures for the immediate security of our port and city.[3]   A. HAMILTON,

M. CLARKSON,[4]

E. STEVENS.

June 4.

[New York] *Argus. Greenleaf's New Daily Advertiser*, June 4, 1798.
  1. For background to this document, see the introductory note to H to James McHenry, June 1, 1798.
  2. The report of this meeting states that it was held on June 5, that sixty officers were present, and that a seven-man committee, including H, was appointed "to devise and pursue in concert with our fellow-citizens at large, such measures as may be judged expedient for the security of the port and city of New York, being in conformity and in aid of the views of the government . . ." ([New York] *Argus. Greenleaf's New Daily Advertiser*, June 6, 1798). On the following day, the officers' committee met with a committee from the Chamber of Commerce and "recommend[ed], that the citizens of each ward assemble therein on Friday next . . . and appoint three persons in each Ward, as a Committee to meet the Committees above-mentioned, in order to devise and adopt such measures as they may judge expedient and necessary in aid of those adopted by the Government, for the immediate defence of the . . . Port and City . . . and that the said several Committees convene together on Friday Evening next, at 7 o'clock, at the City-Hall . . ." ([New York] *Argus. Greenleaf's New Daily Advertiser*, June 7, 1798). On June 8, following the elections in the wards ([New York] *Argus. Greenleaf's New Daily Advertiser*, June 9, 11, 1798), the "Committees from the different Wards, met the Committee from the Chamber of Commerce and the Officers of the late army and navy of the

United States at the City-Hall. . . . The utmost harmony prevailed in the meeting. The necessity of some measures of immediate and effectual defence of the port and city was the universal sentiment, and for this purpose, they appointed a MILITARY COMMITTEE, consisting of Cols. Hamilton, [Aaron] Burr and [Ebenezer] Stevens, to provide cannon, ammunition, etc . . ." ([New York] *Argus. Greenleaf's New Daily Advertiser,* June 11, 1798).

3. Louis Gautier was the proprietor of an assembly room at 68 William Street (David Longworth, *Longworth's American Almanack, New-York Register, and City Directory, for the Twenty-second Year of American Independence* . . . [New York, 1797], 186).

4. Matthew Clarkson, a resident of New York City, served as chairman of each of the three meetings mentioned in note 2. At the conclusion of the American Revolution he held the rank of major, and in 1798 he was a major general of the New York State militia. Clarkson had served as United States marshal of the District of New York in 1791 and 1792, and in February, 1795, he had been appointed commissioner of loans for New York. See H to George Washington, January 14, 1795. Clarkson had been a member of the New York Assembly in 1789 and 1790 and of the state Senate in 1794 and 1795. Like Ebenezer Stevens, in 1794 he had been named by the New York legislature to the committee in charge of New York City's fortifications. On May 21, 1796, Washington nominated Clarkson as the United States commissioner under Article 21 of the treaty between Spain and the United States signed at San Lorenzo el Real on October 27, 1795, and the Senate agreed to the appointment in May 24, 1796 (*Executive Journal,* I, 210–11).

From James McHenry

Philada. 4 June 1798

My dear Hamilton

I have just recd. yours of the 1st.

I have calculated to be able to leave this on Wednesday, to examine the harbour of New York, and to with the aid of the best advice I can procure, determine what further works can be constructed out of the means that can be spared.

Be kind enough to Tell Col. Stevens[1] to have a pilot boat engaged and the proper apparatus ready to take depths and ascertain the quality of the ground on bottom.

Yours

Col. Hamilton

ADf, James McHenry Papers, Library of Congress.
1. Ebenezer Stevens.

To Elizabeth Hamilton

[New York, June 5, 1798]

I wrote to you, My beloved Eliza, by the Monday's Post.[1] You will be glad to hear that your dear boys & myself continue in good health & that they thus far behave well. I hope they will continue to do so—for in our mutual love & in them consist all our happiness.

I trust you are by this time arrived & shall impatiently look out for a letter from you. Our public affairs continue to march in a good train; & when you shall return to me my private affairs cannot fail to be in as good a train as I desire them.

Yrs. most faithfully & affec   A H

June 5th 1798

Mrs. Hamilton

ALS, Hamilton Papers, Library of Congress.
1. H to Elizabeth Hamilton, June 3, 1798.

To Oliver Wolcott, Junior

[New York, June 5, 1798]

My Dear Sir

The answer from The President to the Commander in Chief &c of New Jersey contains in the close a very indiscreet passage.[1] The sentiment is intemperate & revolutionary. It is not for us, particularly for the Government, to breathe an irregular or violent spirit. Hitherto I have much liked the Presidents answers, as in the main within proper bounds & calculated to animate and raise the public mind. But there are limits which must not be passed. And from my knowlege of the ardour of the Presidents mind & this specimen of the effect of that ardour, I begin to be apprehensive that he may run into indiscretion. This will do harm to the Government, to the cause & to himself. Some hint must be given for we must make no mistakes.

Inclosed is a sketch of some ideas which have run through my mind. They are perhaps none of them new but they are offered as the evidence of my Opinion on the points. As yet we are far short of the point of vigour.

Yrs. truly   A H
                                                                          June 5

[ENCLOSURE]

Further measures adviseable to be taken *without delay* [2]

I   To authorise the President to proceed forthwith to raise the 10000 men already ordered.[3]

II To establish an academy for naval & military instruction. This is a very important measure and ought to be permanent.

III To provide for the immediate raising of a corps of Non Commissioned officers (viz) *serjeants & Corporals* sufficient with the present establishment for an army of 50000 men. The having these men prepared & *disciplined* will accelerate extremely the disciplining of an additional force.

IV To provide before Congress rise, that in case it shall appear that an invasion of this country by a large army is actually on foot—there shall be a draft from the Militia, to be classed, of a number sufficient to complete the army to 50000 men. Provision for volunteers in lieu of drafts. A bounty to be given.

V   To authorise the President to *provide* a further naval force of six ships of the line & 12 frigates with 20 small vessels not exceeding sixteen Guns. It is possible the Ships of the line & frigates may be purchased from G Britain to be paid for in *Stock*. We ought to be ready to cut up all the small privateers & gun boats in the West Indies so as at the same time to distress the French Islands as much as possible & protect our own Trade.

VI Is not the Independence of the French Colonies under the Guarantee of the UStates to be aimed at? If it is there cannot be too much promptness in opening negotiations for the purpose. Victor Hughes [4] is probably an excellent subject. This idea however deserves mature consideration.

VII It is essential the Executive should have half a million of secret service money. If the measure cannot be carried without it, The expediture may be with the approbation of three members of each house of Congress. But Twere better without this incumbrance.

obable

VIII Revenue in addition to the 2000000 of land tax   say

oduce
o.ooo

a Stamp duty on hats as well manufactured at home as imported distributed into three Classes 10. 15. 25 Cents

Saddle horses 1 Dollar each excluding those engaged in agriculture &

o.ooo

Salt add so as to raise the present Duty to 25 Cents ℔ Bushel.

Male Servants of those capacities by whatever name *Maitre D'hotel house steward valet de chambre Butler Underbutler Confectioner Cook house Porter Waiter footman Coachman Groom Postilion Stable boy*

In lieu of tax on slaves which is liable to much objection

o.ooo

For one such servant   1 Dollar

for 2 such servants & not more   2 Dollars each

For three & not more   3 Dollars each

Above three   4 Dollars each

One Dollar additional by Batchelors

o.ooo

New Modification with greater diversity of licenses for sale of Wines &

o.ooo

1 ℔ Cent on all succession by descent or devise

IX A loan of 10,000 000 of Dollars. The interest to be such as will insure the loan at par. Tis better to give high interest redeemable at pleasure than low interest with accumulation of Capital as in England.

ALS, Connecticut Historical Society, Hartford; copy, Hamilton Papers, Library of Congress.

1. On May 31, 1798, the New Jersey militia presented John Adams with an "address" supporting his foreign policy. This address was signed by Governor Richard Howell in his capacity as commander in chief of the militia and by several other officers. On the same day, Adams replied to this address. Both documents are printed in the *Gazette of the United States, and Philadelphia Daily Advertiser*, June 1, 1798.

The paragraph of Adams's reply to which H objected reads: "Your voice of confidence and satisfaction, of firmness and determination to support the laws and Constitution of the United States, has a charm in it irresistible to the feelings of every American bosom; but when, in the presence of the God of armies and in firm reliance on his protection, you solemnly pledge your lives and fortunes, and your sacred honor, you have recorded words which ought to be indelibly imprinted on the memory of every American youth. With these sentiments in the hearts and this language in the mouths of Americans in general, the greatest nation may menace at its pleasure, and the degraded and the deluded characters may tremble, lest they should be condemned to the severest punishment an American can suffer—that of being conveyed in safety within the lines of an invading enemy."

2. AD, Connecticut Historical Society, Hartford; copy, Hamilton Papers, Library of Congress.

In *JCHW*, VII, 686, and *HCLW*, VII, 48, this enclosure is entitled "Measures for Defence" and is dated "1799".

3. See "An Act authorizing the President of the United States to raise a Provisional Army" (1 *Stat.* 558–61 [May 28, 1798]).

4. Victor Hugues was the French Directory's special agent in the French West Indies. See John Williams to H, June 7, 1797.

From Rufus King

London June 6. 1798

My Dear Sir

We have certain intelligence that the Toulon expedition has sailed.[1] The number of Troops, of Transports, and of men of war are variously stated, but it is known that Buona parte commands and that the fleet is a very great one—its Destination is the subject of inquietude and of conjecture. A few Days will bring us more perfect accounts, and from the Force and Position of the Br. fleet under Ld. St. Vincents the public are in daily, not to say hourly expectation of hearing that he has discovered and destroyed this boasted Armada.[2]

If Ireland is the object, the Insurrection has been ill judged and premature—in almost every instance the insurgents have been dispersed and killed, and the quarter round Dublin is now nearly restored to the Kings Peace.[3] Still however if a moderate french force with a supply of Arms could now be thrown into Ireland, the issue wd. be dubious, so deep and general is the Defection. Great Britain is unquestionably in a better and more secure, as well as more united state than she has been since the commencement of the war. With her the question with france is at issue; and so far as regards Europe upon her alone must it essentially depend, for upon the continent french principles & french Influence seem still to extend themselves in every Direction. Tho it is more than a fortnight since the Publication of the Instructions & Dispatches of our Envoys must have been received at Paris [4] neither their Papers, nor Letters from France take any notice of them. Gerry is still there, but about to return home, and if I mistake not will be the bearer of a soothing and treacherous Message from the Directory.[5] Be upon your Guard; france will not declare war agt us; no her policy will be to pursue with us the same course she already has done, and which has served her purpose in Italy and among the honest but devoted and ruined Swiss.[6]

I will say if after all that ⟨has occured⟩ [7] among ourselves, and in other Countries, we are content ⟨to⟩ be duped, and cajoled, and betrayed, we shall deserve the fate which they are preparing for us.

Yours affectionately. R K

ALS, Hamilton Papers, Library of Congress; copy, New-York Historical Society, New York City.

1. Napoleon sailed from Toulon with thirty-five thousand men on May 19, 1798. He took Malta on June 12, landed in Egypt on July 1, and occupied Alexandria the following day.

2. The English at first thought that Ireland was the objective of the French expedition. On May 2, 1798, Admiral Sir John Jervis, earl of St. Vincent, who was commanding the English fleet blockading Cadiz, sent Rear Admiral Sir Horatio Nelson with a few ships to ascertain the nature of the French plans. After the French had sailed from Toulon, St. Vincent dispatched Nelson with a large squadron with orders to follow and destroy the Toulon fleet.

3. In 1791 Wolfe Tone had founded the society of "United Irishmen," which enlisted the support of both Protestants and Catholics in Ireland and which became the principal organization in Ireland opposed to British rule. The outbreak of war between France and England in 1793 increased Irish hopes of independence, and the French on more than one occasion sent expeditions—all of them unsuccessful—to Ireland. In the spring of 1798 the Irish, like the English, thought Ireland was the objective of the Toulon expedition. Anticipating the arrival of the French fleet, the Irish rebels took up arms in May, 1798. Their efforts, however, were unsuccessful, and on June 21, 1798, they were defeated at Vinegar Hill.

4. For Congress's decision to print the dispatches concerning the XYZ affair from the United States envoys to France, see Annals of Congress, VII, 536–37; VIII, 1377–80. See also Timothy Pickering to H, April 9, 1798, note 1.

5. At the request of Charles Maurice de Talleyrand-Périgord, French Minister of Foreign Affairs, Elbridge Gerry remained in France after his fellow envoys, John Marshall and Charles Cotesworth Pinckney, had left the French capital (Gerry to Pickering, October 1, 1798 [ASP, Foreign Relations, II, 204–08]). Marshall sailed for the United States on April 24, 1798. Pinckney, who remained in France because of his daughter's illness, moved to the south of France. See King to H, May 12, 1798, note 1. On June 25, 1798, Secretary of State Pickering ordered Gerry to return to the United States (ASP, Foreign

Relations, II, 204); Gerry arrived in the United States on October 1, 1798 (Gerry to Pickering, October 1, 1798 [*ASP, Foreign Relations,* II, 204–08]).

6. See "The Stand No. III," April 7, 1798.

7. The words within broken brackets in this paragraph have been taken from King, *The Life and Correspondence of Rufus King,* II, 338.

To Rufus King

[New York, June 6, 1798]

My Dear Sir

Official information & the public papers will give you all the information I could give of the measures going on in this Country. You will have observed with pleasure a spirit of patriotism kindling every where. And you will not be sorry to know that it is my opinion that there will shortly be *national unanimity* as far as that idea can ever exist. Many of the leaders of Faction will persist and take ultimately a station in the public estimation like that of the *Tories* of our Revolution.

Our Chief embarrassment now is the want of energy among some of our friends, and our Councils containing too strong an infusion of these characters who cannot reform, and who though a minority are numerous enough and artful enough to *perplex* and *relax.* We do far less than we ought towards organising & maturing for the worst the resources of the Country. But I count that there is a progess of opinion which will shortly overcome this obstacle.

How vexatious that at such a juncture there should be officers of Great Britain who actuated by a spirit of plunder are doing the most violent things—calculated to check the proper current of popular feeling & to furnish weapons to the enemies of the Government. *Comboult* at the Mole is acting a part quite as bad as the Directory & their Instruments.[1] I have seen several of his condemnations. They are wanton beyond measure. It is not enough that his acts are disavowed & a late and defective redress given through the Channels of the Regular Courts. Justice & the policy of the crisis demand and advise that he be decisively punished and disgraced. I think it probable you will be instructed to require this. It would be happy if the Government where you are would anticipate.

It is unlucky too that Cochran of the *Thetis* appears to be doing some ill things.² The Southern papers announce a number of captures lately made by him & in some instances, if they say true, on very frivolous pretexts. The character of that Gentleman would lead me to hope that there is in this some misrepresentation; but the present appearances against him are strong.

There seems a fatality in all this. It cannot be doubted that the British Cabinet must at this time desire to conciliate this Country. It is to be hoped they will not want vigour to do it with effect by punishing those who contravene the object.

Yrs. Affecty   *A Hamilton*
                                                                June 6. 1798

R King Esq

ALS, New-York Historical Society, New York City.

1. See H to King, May 1, 1798, note 3.

2. As early as 1794, United States officials had complained of alleged infringements on American rights by Captain Alexander F. Cochrane of the frigate *Thetis*. See Edmund Randolph to George Hammond, July 24, September 3, October 23, 1794 (LS, RG 59, Domestic Letters of the Department of State, Vol. 7, June 27–November 3, 1794, National Archives). See also H to Phineas Bond, September 15, 1796; Robert Liston to H, September 30, 1796.

In 1798 Republicans repeatedly complained that because of its pro-British bias the Adams Administration had refused to protest the capture of American ships by Cochrane. For example, on June 9, 1798, the [Philadelphia] *Aurora. General Advertiser*, an anti-administration paper, wrote: "Altho' the Thetis has besieged Charleston harbour and captured our vessels by wholesale, Mr. Adams himself, who is all sensibility on the subject of French spoliations, has been dumb about soft Cochron." H was not the only Federalist worried over the effects on American opinion of Cochrane's captures, for on June 11, 1798, Robert Troup wrote to Rufus King: ". . . Capt Cochran of the Thetis has . . . recently captured several vessels. . . . This business has created very unpleasant sensations in the public mind" (King, *The Life and Correspondence of Rufus King*, II, 346).

From James McHenry ¹

Philadelphia 6 June 1798

My Dear Hamilton.

I had reckoned upon the immediate arrival of the Secry. of Marine ² when I wrote you ³ that I should leave this City for New York to-day. He will not be here before Friday. I cannot of course set out sooner than monday. I have requested Lt. Col. Doughty [4] to join me at Brunswick, and will bring with me one Hill [5] who possesses information which may be useful.

Yours sincerely   James McHenry

Alexander Hamilton.

ADfS, James McHenry Papers, Library of Congress.

1. For background to this letter, see the introductory note to H to McHenry, June 1, 1798.

2. Although Benjamin Stoddert was appointed the first Secretary of the Navy on May 18, 1798, and confirmed three days later (*Executive Journal*, I, 275, 276), he did not take office until June 18, 1798.

3. McHenry to H, June 4, 1798.

4. A veteran of the American Revolution, John Doughty of Morris County, New Jersey, had been appointed a lieutenant colonel commandant in the Corps of Artillerists and Engineers on June 1, 1798 (*Executive Journal*, I, 277–78).

5. John Hills wrote to John Jay on April 14, 1798: "Having been Educated in . . . London and at the Royal Academy at Woolwich in the Theory of Engineering for near Eight years, in the practical part during the Revolutionary War, particularly at New York and its environs . . . I have plans by me of the different works that were erected by the British forces for the protection of the Harbour and City of New York, and . . . if you wish, I can have recommendations from most of the Old Inhabitants of the City of New York, and from Genl. [Henry] Knox, late secretary of War whose service I was in for four years" (ALS, Hamilton Papers, Library of Congress, enclosed in Jay to Matthew Clarkson, April 20, 1798 [ALS, Hamilton Papers, Library of Congress]).

In his capacity as agent for the War Department, Ebenezer Stevens hired Hills and George Flemming to draw up plans for the defense of New York City (McHenry to Stevens, June 16, 1798 [copy, George Washington Papers, Library of Congress]; McHenry to Hills and Flemming, June 16, 1798 [copy, George Washington Papers, Library of Congress]). See also McHenry to Stevens, January 12, 1799 (extract, Hamilton Papers, Library of Congress).

From Robert Morris [1]

Philadelphia, June 6, 1798. "In a letter which I wrote to you on the 27th of October last you will find it Stated that Doctor Craigie stood indebted to me in the Sum of $6,250 which it was my wish that you should receive in discharge of the debt I owed you. Sometime after you wrote [2] that Mr. Johnson [3] Agent of Doctr Craigie informed you that this Claim was Assigned by me to Colo Ogden, and as I had not with me at that time my Books and Papers I yielded to that information supposing that it must be so.

I have however just discovered that my Claim was founded, that it
Still exists, and my intention still continues that you shall have
this Money. . . ." [4]

ALS, Hamilton Papers, Library of Congress.
    1. This letter concerns Morris's efforts to pay the balance of a debt which
he owed to H and which had been assumed by Morris's son Thomas. For
information concerning this debt and the transactions discussed in this letter,
see the introductory note to H to Morris, March 18, 1795. See also Morris to
H, March 31, June 2, 23, 30, July 18, 20, 1795; June 17, 27, 27–30, November
19, December 8, 1796; June 2, 10, September 9, October 2, 27, November 23,
December 21, 1797; January 17, February 7, 17, 1798.
    2. H's letter has not been found, but see Morris to H, November 23, 1797.
    3. Seth Johnson was a New York merchant and speculator.
    4. In the remainder of this letter Morris explains in detail why he thinks
both that Andrew Craigie did in fact owe him $6,250 and that Craigie's bond
could be used to pay Morris's debt to H. See Morris to H, October 27, November 23, 1797.

From William North [1]

Philadelphia, June 7, 1798. "I offer the enclosed. . . ,[2] leaving
out what was not necessary to be published, with an intention of
sending it to One of your printers, in the idea, that the Citizens
perhaps might, from knowing the Barons opinion on the subject,
the more readily come into the measure. The paper, as it is, I would
not give to any body but yourself. . . . Mr McHenry is to Visit
New York,[3] to see the state of the fortifications, & to form further
plans of defence—but the man is a small man."

ALS, Hamilton Papers, Library of Congress.
    1. North, who served throughout the American Revolution and was an aide-
de-camp to Baron von Steuben, held the rank of major and was inspector of
the army from 1784 to 1788. He served in the New York Assembly in 1792,
1794, 1795, and 1796, and was speaker in 1795 and 1796. From May 5, 1798, to
August 17, 1798, he was United States Senator, filling the vacancy which had
been created by the resignation of John Sloss Hobart. See John Jay to H, two
letters of April 19, 1798. On July 19, 1798, North was appointed adjutant general of the army with the rank of brigadier general (*Executive Journal*, I, 293).
    This letter was addressed to H in his capacity as a member of the Military
Committee of New York City. See the introductory note to H to James
McHenry, June 1, 1798; "Call for a Meeting," June 4, 1798, note 2.
    2. Copy, Hamilton Papers, Library of Congress. This undated document, en-
titled "Observations on the proposed defence of New York," is a plan which
Steuben had drawn up in 1794 for the defense of New York City. See Steuben
to H, March 27, 1794.

North and Steuben remained close associates until Steuben's death on November 28, 1794. On March 26, 1794, the New York legislature had appointed both men to a commission in charge of fortifying the western and northern frontiers of New York State ("An Act authorizing the erecting of Fortifications, within this state" [*New York Laws,* 17th Sess., Ch. XLI]). When he died, Steuben left his property in the United States to North and Benjamin Walker, who had also been Steuben's aide-de-camp (Friedrich Kapp, *The Life of Frederick William von Steuben* [New York, 1859], 702).

3. See McHenry to H, June 4, 6, 1798.

To Timothy Pickering

[New York, June 7, 1798]

My Dear Sir

As Mc.Henry will probably have left Philadelphia,[1] before this reaches that place, I take the liberty to address the subject of it to you.

I have received a letter from Capt Van Rensselaer,[2] in which he informs me that he is a candidate for a Commission on board of our navy, and requests my recommendation of it. As a connexion of our family [3]—I cannot refuse it as far as truth & propriety will warrant. When he first began his carreer the young man did things which were not pretty; but he has since that retrieved his character by a conduct which has rapidly raised him to the command of a Ship which he has had of several.[4] I have particularly inquired concerning him; & my inquiries have been satisfactorily answered—so that I really conclude he is a deserving man. But of this you can be better ascertained from persons in Philadelphia in whose employ I believe he has sailed.

My only intention is to request *attention* to his *pretensions* as far as they may appear to be good & in the proportion which they bear to those of other candidates. I owe this to him as a family connection and I may add that he is of a *brave* blood.

What do the British mean? What are these stories of the *Thetis* [5] &c.? In my opinion our Country is now to act in every direction with spirit. Will it not be well to order one of our frigates to Charlestown to protect effectually our Commerce in that quarter & if necessary controul the *Thetis?* This Conduct will unite & animate.

Yrs. truly

A Hamilton

June 7. 1798

PS If an alien Bill passes I should like to know what policy in execution is likely to govern the *Executive*.[6] My opinion is that while the mass ought to be obliged to leave the Country—the provisions in our Treaties in favour of Merchants ought to be observed & there ought to be *guarded* exceptions of characters whose situations would expose them too much if sent away & whose demeanour among us has been unexceptionable. There are a few such. Let us not be cruel or violent.

A H

T Pickering Esq

ALS, Massachusetts Historical Society, Boston.

1. See James McHenry to H, June 6, 1798.

2. Letter not found. Killian Henry Van Rensselaer was commissioned a lieutenant in the Navy on January 7, 1799 (*Executive Journal*, I, 302–03, where his first name is misspelled "Killeair").

3. Killian Henry Van Rensselaer was the son of Henry K. Van Rensselaer, who was the cousin of Hamilton's mother-in-law, Catharine Schuyler.

4. In 1794 Killian Henry Van Rensselaer sailed to Holland, where he visited the Dutch branch of the Van Rensselaer family. He returned to New York in 1795 aboard the ship *Minerva*. He then purchased part of the brig *Peggy* and sailed as master for France and Amsterdam. On February 15, 1797, he sailed from Wilmington, North Carolina, on the schooner *Two Friends,* which was owned by Thomas White, a merchant in Lexington, Kentucky. On March 6 the French privateer *La Voitisseur* captured the schooner *Two Friends*. Van Rensselaer returned to the United States on April 23 in the schooner *Betsey* (James Cuyler to Captain Solomon Van Rensselaer, Killian's brother, March 9, 1795, and Solomon Van Rensselaer to Harriot (or Arriett), his wife, May 18, 1797, in Catharina V. R. Bonney, *A Legacy of Historical Gleanings* [Albany: J. Munsell, 1875] I, 116–17, 138–39; Killian K. Van Rensselaer, Killian Henry's uncle, to J. C. and S. Van Rensselaer of Amsterdam, November 14, 1794, J. C. and S. Van Rensselaar to K. K. Van Rensselaer, April 17, 1795, K. K. Van Rensselaer to Jan Jacob Van Rensselaar, March 15, 1795, in Maunsell Van Rensselaer, *Annals of the Van Rensselaers in the United States, especially as they relate to the family of Killian K. Van Rensselaer, Representative from Albany in the Seventh, Eighth, Ninth and Tenth Congresses* [Albany, 1888], 61–64).

5. See H to Rufus King, June 6, 1798, note 2.

6. This is a reference to the debate in the Senate on the bill that eventually became "An Act concerning Aliens" (1 *Stat.* 570–72 [June 25, 1798]). The bill originated in the Senate as a result of a motion introduced by James Hillhouse of Connecticut on April 25, 1798 (*Annals of Congress*, VII, 548). On the following day, Hillhouse's resolution was referred to a committee which reported a bill on May 4 (*Annals of Congress*, VII, 549, 554–55). It was not until June 8 that the Senate passed the bill (*Annals of Congress*, VII, 575). The House passed the bill with amendments on June 21 (*Annals of Congress*, VIII, 2028), and the Senate concurred in the House amendments on June 22 (*Annals of Congress*, VII, 586). "An Act concerning Aliens" should not be confused with "An Act supplementary to and to amend the act, intituled 'An act to establish an uniform rule of naturalization; and to repeal the act heretofore passed on that subject'" (1 *Stat.* 566–69 [June 18, 1798]) and "An Act respecting Alien Enemies" (1 *Stat.* 577–78 [July 6, 1798]).

As early as July 1, 1797, David Brooks of New York, a member of the House of Representatives, unsuccessfully proposed a revision of the naturalization law (*Annals of Congress*, VII, 421). The law in question was "An Act to establish an uniform rule of Naturalization; and to repeal the act heretofore passed on that subject" (1 *Stat.* 414–15 [January 29, 1795]). On April 17, 1798, Joshua Coit of Connecticut again proposed to the House the need to amend the current naturalization law (*Annals of Congress*, VIII, 1427). On May 15 Samuel Sewall of Massachusetts "reported a bill supplementary to, and to amend the act establishing an uniform rule of naturalization, and to repeal the act heretofore passed . . ." (*Annals of Congress*, VIII, 1707). The House passed the bill on May 22 and agreed to the Senate amendments on June 13 (*Annals of Congress*, VIII, 1783, 1925).

On May 8, 1798, the House ordered the select committee on commerce and defence to report a bill on alien enemies, and on May 18 Sewall reported a bill (*Annals of Congress*, VIII, 1630–31, 1773). The House voted to recommit the bill on May 23, and on June 8 Sewall reported a modified bill (*Annals of Congress*, VIII, 1796, 1896). The House passed the bill on June 26 and the Senate passed it on July 3 with amendments (*Annals of Congress*, VII, 598; VIII, 2049). The House agreed to the Senate amendments on July 3 (*Annals of Congress*, VIII, 2088).

To Elizabeth Hamilton

[New York, June 8, 1798]

This is the third time [1] I have written to my love since her departure. I continue to enjoy good health and my spirits are as good as they can be in her absence. But I find as I grow older her presence becomes more necessary to me. In proportion as I discover the worthlessness of other pursuits, the value of my Eliza and of domestic happiness rises in my estimation.

Angelica [2] & her family are all well except that Mr. Church's [3] gout is not intirely gone. Peggy [4] has been as well as usual. Yesterday however she complained of a little gout in her hand. Cornelia [5] is well.

Tell your father that our affairs continue to mend & that there is every prospect that we shall not put on the French Yoke. Adieu My very dear wife.

Yrs. most affecty   *A H*

June 8. 1798

Mrs. H

ALS, Hamilton Papers, Library of Congress.
1. H to Elizabeth Hamilton, June 3, 5, 1798.

2. Angelica Schuyler Church.
3. John Barker Church.
4. Margaret Schuyler Van Rensselaer.
5. Cornelia Schuyler Morton.

From Rufus King [1]

London June 8. 1798.

My dear Sir

Since writing you a day or two past,[2] I have had the pleasure to receive your Letter by the Packet,[3] and am rejoiced to find my hopes confirmed by your Opinion that we shall not be wanting to ourselves in our Conduct towards France.

Immediately on hearing of the proceedings of the Admiralty Judge of st. Domingo,[4] I remonstrated to the Government against them, and was without delay answered that General Simcoe [5] had no power to erect the Court, that the appointment of Judge Cumbauld was illegal, and all his Decrees void and that those who had unfortunately suffered by them, must as in the Martinique Cases [6] apply for

ALS, Hamilton Papers, Library of Congress; copy, New-York Historical Society, New York City.
  1. The first four paragraphs of this letter are in a clerk's handwriting. King wrote the remainder of the letter.
  2. King to H, June 6, 1798.
  3. H to King, May 1, 1798.
  4. See H to King, May 1, 1798, note 3. See also H to King, June 6, 1798.
  5. John Graves Simcoe, Lieutenant Governor of Upper Canada, was granted a leave of absence from December, 1796, to July, 1797, to command the British part of Santo Domingo. See H to King, May 1, 1798, note 3.
  6. Early in 1794 American ships had been seized and condemned by an illegal prize court set up at Martinique by Admiral Sir John Jervis, later earl of St. Vincent, and General Sir Charles Grey. On August 8, 1794, Lord Grenville wrote to George Hammond that John Jay had presented to him a complaint entitled "A general Statement of the Captains of American Vessels Seized at Martinique." In the same letter he wrote: ". . . I have not hesitated to inform Mr. Jay, that, if the Allegations there made are true, the Proceedings therein mentioned are wholly Informal and void, there being no Vice Admiralty Court at Martinique constituted by His Majesty's Authority, nor any Power in His Majesty's Officers to erect such a Jurisdiction, so that the owners of all such Vessels will be entitled to their remedy in due course of Law, against all persons who may have acted under the sentences of a Tribunal not competent to hear or decide on those Causes, or indeed on any other" (Mayo, *Instructions to British Ministers*, 65). See also *ASP, Foreign Relations*, I, 495–96; Moore, *International Adjudications*, IV, 48–62.

Satisfaction to the High Court of Admiralty in England. I expected, and so it was determined, that orders Should have been instantly dispatched to suppress the Court: this was omitted from the negligence of the officer to whom the duty belonged in the Admiralty—hence the continuation of the Court of St. Domingo. Orders have however at length been Sent to suppress the Court.[7]

The Instructions of the 25. of Jany. 1798,[8] a copy of which was on the 7. Feby sent to the secretary of State,[9] have been misrepresented or not understood; instead of enlarging the effect of them will, as it was intended it should be, to contract the Description of Cases in which the trade of neutrals will be liable to interruption. The order as it is called of the 6. Novr. 1793 [10] authorized the Capture of all vessels carrying Supplies to, or laden with the produce of the French West Indies. The Instruction of the 8. of Jany 1794 [11] revoked this order, and Substituted another in which the bona fide neutral Trade between the united States and the french west Indies was considered as legal, while that between the French west Indies and Europe was liable to interruption by the vessels being sent in for adjudication. The late Instruction of the 25. of January, which I have thought a point gained enlarges the rights and security of the Trade of Neutrals; for instead of former restraints, it is now admitted that a direct Trade by neutrals between their respective Countries and the *French, Dutch* and *spanish* West Indies, out and home, and

7. Evan Nepean, Secretary of the Admiralty, to Simcoe, June 8, 1798 (PRO: Adm. [Great Britain] 2/1066).

On June 8, 1798, King wrote to Timothy Pickering: ". . . You will long since have been informed that the appointment of Judge Cambauld was illegal, and that his decrees are void. It was natural to have expected, after the answer that I received from Lord Grenville on this Subject, that orders would have been immediately despatched to St Domingo to Suppress the Admiralty Court. . . . Altho' I had repeatedly inquired, whether this order had been Sent, it is only a day or two Since I was informed that it had not been transmitted from a neglect in the officer of the Admiralty whose duty it was to have sent it; but that it Should be immediately dispatched" (LS, RG 59, Despatches from United States Ministers to Great Britain, 1792–1870, Vol. 7, January 9–December 22, 1798, National Archives).

8. See H to King, May 1, 1798, note 2.

9. King to Pickering, February 7, 1798 (LS, RG 59, Despatches from United States Ministers to Great Britain, 1792–1870, Vol. 7, January 9–December 22, 1798, National Archives). Pickering enclosed an extract of this letter in Pickering to H, June 9, 1798.

10. For this order, see *ASP, Foreign Relations*, III, 264.

11. For this "Instruction," see *ASP, Foreign Relations*, III, 264.

likewise the direct voyage from those Colonies to any port in Great Britain, are lawful and not liable to interruption.

That the naval officers will often exercise their authority however limited in abuse, will continue to be the case so long as the military profession is disgraced by a sordid love of Gain, and so long as the System of the Admiralty Courts of England shall be so little satisfactory as they really are.

We are as you will naturally suppose extremely impatient to receive information from the medituranean. It appears certain that the Toulon Expedition sailed about the 19th. May.[12] The force is variously reported. Buonaparte is supposed to be with the fleet, which is said to be 13 Ships of the Line as many frigates and nearly 400 Transports. All the naval characters agree that it is next to impossible that they can reach Ireland without Discovery. Indeed from the prevalence of the winds from the coast, a single ship would it is said be at this season, perhaps two months, in making her voyage from Toulon to Ireland. The Opinion that has most advocates is that the Expedition is against Portugal—that the Troops will be disembarked at Carthagina or Malaga in Spain, & that they will cross the mountains to Portugal. It is well understood that from the want of Subsistence they could not have marched thro Spain. But Portugal has no money, and all the Plunder that could be obtained wd. not defray the Expence of the Expedition! The enterprize would reduce Spain under the more complete controul of france: Cadiz wd. become a french Port, the English wd. be expelled from the Tagus, the spanish fleet wd. be relieved as soon as the windy season arrives, and from the Tagus and Cadiz, the Expedition may go against the Brasils and the Treasure of So Amer. may be at the Disposal of the Directory. Besides that Country may be revolutionized on the french model, and this may prepare the way for the measures to be adopted towards us. Letters from Lord St. Vincents[13] of the 19. May (when his fleet off Cadiz consisted of 25 sail of the Line in excellent condition) in-

12. See King to H, June 6, 1798, notes 1 and 2.
13. On May 19, 1798, Admiral the Earl of St. Vincent wrote to Nepean: "By His Majesty's hired Lugger the Valiant, which joined me this afternoon, I have received your letter of the 2d instant, enclosing Copy of the Orders of the Lords Commissioners of the Admiralty marked 'Most Secret,' to Rear Admiral Sir Roger Curtis, for proceeding with his squadron to join me, with their Lordships' instructions to me on this head" (PRO: Adm. [Great Britain] 1/397).

duce the belief that Sr. Roger Curtis would join him from the Greek Station by the 22. or 23d with 10 sail of the line. His orders are to leave a force to block up Cadiz and watch the Gut,[14] and to proceed with the residue of the fleet to search for and fight the Toulon Fleet, and according to every thing that we know, there is great reason to expect that he will be in season to intercept them even shd. their object be Carthagina or Malaga.

Adieu!   R K

It is agt. every probability that the Toulon Expedition can pass the Gut without discovery.[15]

From Rufus King

[London, June 8, 1798. Second letter of June 8 not found.[1]]

1. In the "List of Letters from . . . Mr. King" to H, Columbia University Libraries, two letters from King for June 8, 1798, are listed.

To Timothy Pickering

[New York, June 8, 1798]

My Dear Sir

Though I scarcely think it possible that the British Administration can have given the orders which accounts from various quarters attribute to them [1]—yet the circumstance of these accounts coming from different quarters and the conduct of so correct a man as Capt Cochran [2] make me apprehensive. I take the liberty to express to you

14. This is a reference to the Straits of Gibraltar.
15. On August 18, 1798, Pickering wrote to John Adams: "The Toulon fleet, consisting of 400 transports, convoyed by 13 sail of the line and as many frigates departed from Toulon the 19th of May: Lord St. Vincents was then off Cadiz with 25 sail of the line: Secret orders had been dispatched to Sir Roger Curtis to quit the Irish Station and join Lord St. Vincent with 10 sail of the line. This reinforcement probably joined Lord St. Vincent by the 22d. of May. And immediately after the junction Lord St. Vincents, leaving a sufficient force to block up Cadiz and watch the Gut of Gibraltar, was to enter the Mediterranean, to look for and fight the Toulon fleet which had Buonaparte on board" (*Naval Documents. Quasi-War, February, 1797–October, 1798,* 321–22).

my opinion that it is of the true policy as well as of the dignity of our
Government to act with spirit and energy as well towards G Britain
as France. I would *meet* the same measure to both of them, though
it should ever furnish the extraordinary spectacle of a nation at war
with two nations at war with each other. One of them will quickly
court us—and by this course of conduct Our Citizens will be enthu-
siastically united to the Government. It will evince that we are
neither *Greeks* nor *Trojans*. In very critical cases bold expedients are
often necessary. Will not a pointed call on the British Minister here
to declare whether he has any knowlege of the instructions alleged
be proper? The making this call & the answer public may have a
good effect.

No one, who does not see all the cards, can judge accurately. But
I am sure the general course I indicate cannot but be well.

Yours truly   A Hamilton
                                                          June 8. 1798

T Pickering Esq

ALS, Massachusetts Historical Society, Boston.
1. See H to Rufus King, May 1, 1798, note 2.
2. See H to King, June 6, 1798, note 2.

From Timothy Pickering

[*Philadelphia, June 9, 1798.* On June 9, 1798, Pickering wrote to
Hamilton: "I dropped you a hasty line to-day." *Letter not found.*]

From Timothy Pickering

Philadelphia June 9. 1798.

Dr. Sir,

I dropped you a hasty line to-day,[1] acknowledging the receipt of
your letters of the 7th. & 8th. I now inclose a copy of the new

ALS, Hamilton Papers, Library of Congress; ALS, letterpress copy, Massachusetts Historical Society, Boston.
1. Letter not found.

British Instructions,[2] with Mr. King's remark upon them.[3] These, I have not the least doubt, are the instructions which the American captains from the West Indies, by misconceptions, have represented to be so injurious to our commerce. Mr. Liston [4] knows of no other; nor has Mr. King mentioned any besides these. And you will observe that Mr. King considers them as extending the right, or the privilege, of neutral commerce, beyond the former instructions, and the long avowed claim of a right on her part (Britain) to interrupt and prevent any commerce of neutrals with the colonies of her enemies which was not permitted in time of peace.

The alien bills introduced into both houses of Congress [5] have undergone such alterations, I do not know, their present form; of one thing however you may rest assured, that they will not err on the side of severity, much less of cruelty. I wish they may really provide for the public safety.

Mr. Stoddert has accepted the office of Secretary of the Navy; [6] and I expected him to arrive by this day at farthest; as soon as he comes to town, I will communicate what you say of Captain Van Renselaer.[7]

In your letter of the 8th you renew the subject of the captures by the Thetis, Capt. Cochran. Suspecting that the Charleston complaints were the clamours of interested men engaged in illicit commerce, I mean with contraband goods, or covering the property of enemies

2. For the "new British Instructions," see H to Rufus King, May 1, 1798, note 2.

3. "Mr. King's remark upon them" is an extract from King to Pickering, February 7, 1798 (LS, RG 59, Despatches from United States Ministers to Great Britain, 1792–1870, Vol. 7, January 9–December 22, 1798, National Archives). This extract reads: "A new instruction dated the 25th of January last has been issued by the King in Council, respecting the trade of neutrals. The direct trade between the West Indies and us had before been acceeded to be legal under the old orders. This declares the Trade from the West Indies to the British ports in Europe legal. Neutrals carrying West India productions directly from the place of their growth to other European ports are liable to be sent in for lawful adjudication, upon the *presumption* that the property is enemy; but if on trial it turns out to be neutral, I think it must and will be restored" (copy, in Pickering's handwriting, Hamilton Papers, Library of Congress).

4. Robert Liston, British Minister to the United States.

5. See H to Pickering, June 7, 1798, note 6.

6. Although the Senate approved Benjamin Stoddert's nomination as Secretary of the Navy on May 21, 1798 (*Executive Journal*, I, 276), he did not assume office until June 18, 1798.

7. See H to Pickering, June 7, 1798.

to Great Britain, I mentioned the matter to Mr. Reed of the Senate,[8] who confirmed my suspicions. In short, in order to favour the French, and acquire great profits in trade, many American merchants have prostituted every fair principle of commerce, and put their captains on taking such deceitful oaths, as to render suspicious the papers of innocent merchants to their vast injury. Nobody has been more noisy about British depredations than Genl. Smith of Baltimore.[9] He particularly complained to me, ten months ago, of the loss of several of his vessels captured and sent into Mole St. Nicholas.[10] I represented his complaints to Mr. Liston, who wrote to the Admiral or Commanding officer at St. Domingo. The answer returned showed that one of Smith's vessels, on her voyage *outward*, had carried, and delivered to the French administration, eighteen hogsheads of *gunpowder;* cleared out as merchandize of *callicoes* &c. I communicated this to Genl. Smith who wrote me a long letter upon the subject; but without denying the fact as to the gun-powder. I do not mention this as tho' it justified the judge, one Cambauld, a corrupt villain, in condemning the vessel captured on her *return* voyage; but the gunpowder having been delivered to the French *govt.* the Judge was disposed to suspect the produce received in return also belonged to the French; and that judge is so utterly unprincipled, a suspicion alone would induce him to condemn, unless handsomely bribed to acquit. His character and conduct I have long since described to Mr. King, Who has conferred with Ld. Grenville, who pronounces the Court itself (appointed by Simcoe) illegal, like that erected by Admiral Jervis, formerly at Martinico. In the mean

8. Jacob Read of South Carolina.
9. Samuel Smith, a Baltimore merchant, was a member of the House of Representatives.
10. For an explanation of this sentence and the remainder of this paragraph, see Smith to Pickering, October 28, 1797 (copy, Massachusetts Historical Society, Boston); Pickering to Smith, December 30, 1797 (LS, Massachusetts Historical Society, Boston; LC, RG 59, Domestic Letters of the Department of State, Vol. 10, March 1, 1797–June 29, 1798, National Archives), January 29, 1798 (copy, Massachusetts Historical Society, Boston), April 21, 1798 (LS, Massachusetts Historical Society, Boston; LC, RG 59, Domestic Letters of the Department of State, Vol. 10, March 1, 1797–June 29, 1798, National Archives); Pickering to Liston, November 1, 1798 (LC, RG 59, Domestic Letters of the Department of State, Vol. 10, March 1, 1797–June 29, 1798, National Archives); Liston to Pickering, March 5, 1798 (copy, RG 59, Notes from the British Legation in the United States to the Department of State, 1791–1906, Vol. 2, January 10, 1796–November 19, 1803, National Archives).

time our fair merchants are suffering by its illegal acts. It is the shameful and often detected frauds in the documents furnished to our merchant vessels, that have induced the British naval officers to disregard their papers, and to rest satisfied with nothing short of an actual examination of their cargoes; and this vexation will doubtless continue, more or less, until the *honest* merchants come forward and expose their fraudulent neighbours.

I do not like the provisional army act: [11] I do not believe gentlemens' expectations from volunteers will be verefied: many small corps will be formed: but not in numbers to supply the place of an army; especially as the bill was so altered as to subject them to march not only to an adjoining state, but to the remotest state in the Union. It is true the President will not thus harass them: but they will be under apprehensions of it, and many will be discouraged. If they have spirit enough to disregard this; so would they march, when *requested* in time of invasion, into any state, altho' by *law* they might remain in their own or an adjoining state. Instead of waiting an actual invasion, I think the raising of the army ought *now* to be commenced. It would take many months to form & bring it into a state of discipline in which we could place any confidence. Small, predatory incursions of the French, tho' they might occasion great destruction of property, would not be *dangerous*, and the militia might be sufficient to repel them; but what we have to guard against is an invasion by a powerful army of veterans: and I do not know any body of *militia* adequate to stop their progress; and a fatal pannic might be the consequence. They would hold out their lives to entice, and they would entice multitudes, not to resist, at least, if they did not join their standard, as has happened in every republic in Europe which they have fraternized. I have indeed a confidence in the populous, well-armed, and unanimous northern states: but is there any 40,000 of that militia who could incounter, with any chance of success, 20,000 veterans? You know the militia cannot be moved at the order of the ablest commander—they are unmanageable; and the greater the number, the greater the mass of confusion. Gentlemen in Congress boast of the exploits of the militia in the American war: but where did they fight in a body of even five thousand men? where

11. "An Act authorizing the President of the United States to raise a Provisional Army" (1 *Stat.* 558–61 [May 28, 1798]).

did they fight successfully alone, without regular troops, except in small corps of a few hundred men, which might be put in motion without much hazard of disorder? And excepting at Bunker Hill (which was a wonderful action) the militia victories against regulars were after the war had raged several years, during which the men had been frequently called into actual service, and their minds and bodies were gradually prepared to meet dangers and hardships; and in the southern states, the militia men whose prowess is now pane-gyrized (not unjustly) were rendered desperate by their situation. But all these advantageous circumstances would be wanting in case of such an invasion as that against which we have to provide. Why is a provisional army thought of, if an invasion is not to be appre-hended? To propose a *provisional* army, to depend for its formation on an *actual invasion*, is to me the height of absurdity. Multitudes who would now enroll themselves, would at the moment when an invasion should find them unarmed and defenceless, shrink into ab-ject submission to the foe. But the president may also commence the raising this army in case of "imminent danger of invasion, discovered in his opinion to exist:" at the same time it is understood such dan-ger does not now exist. And what circumstances will render the danger imminent? The successful invasion of England—or even of Ireland (for in either case, if not wholly subdued, England would be fully employed) would put us in jeopardy. If England still struggled, France might be induced to keep all her force in Europe until the conquest was complete: but considering that she has a redundancy of soldiers, and a natural expectation would be presented of an easy conquest and submission here if she made a sudden and unlooked for invasion—I own that the danger would then appear to me imminent —and I think it so imminent even now, that the army ought forth-with to be raised. But admitting that she fails in her projects against England, she may be induced to make peace with her—and her alone; for such has been the uniform policy of the French Rulers, in all their successions. They will then renew their demands upon us, and we must yield, or make war alone. Britain certainly will not re-commence the war for our sakes: and tho' she would regret our submission to France, and therefore might be willing, in her negocia-tions of peace with France, to stipulate for us also, yet have we any right to expect it? With so many marks of aversion and repulsion towards her, could we have the face to ask it? I know there are some who deem her profligate enough, if France should propose a division of the states between herself & England, that the latter would agree to it: but I am not disposed to believe it. I think the animosities and hatreds engendered in the American revolution towards England exist yet in some breasts in greater force than our interest or our safety admit: and these passions will keep us aloof till any cooperation may become impracticable. We cannot expect overtures from England: I very much suspect she is waiting to receive them from us. I wish you were in a situation not only "to see all the cards," [12] but to play them; with all my soul I would give you my *hand;* and engage in any other *game* in which I might best co-operate, on the same side, *to win the stakes.*

I remain truly & respectfully yours,   Timothy Pickering.

Alexander Hamilton Esqr.

12. This is a quotation from H to Pickering, June 8, 1798.

For the Gazette of the United States

[Philadelphia, June 13, 1798]

Every day brings fresh confirmations of the truth of the prediction to our Envoys, that the French Faction in America would go all lengths with their imperious & unprincipled Masters. It is more and more evident, that as many of them as may dare will join the standard of France, if once erected in this Country. After all that has happened, there is no other solution of the indefatigable and malignant exertions which they are making to propagate disaffection to our own government and to justify or extenuate the conduct of France. The authors of these exertions understand too well the human heart not to know, that ideas which have once taken deep root in a community and have inlisted its passions against one object and in favour of another cannot suddenly be changed; and that in the event of an invasion they could not if so disposed prevent their followers from

ADf, Hamilton Papers, Library of Congress; *Gazette of the United States, and Philadelphia Daily Advertiser,* June 13, 1798.

acting in conformity with the strong byass which had been previously given to their feelings. They know this so well, that if they were not in their hearts more *Frenchmen* than *Americans:* if they were not ready in the gratification of ambition vanity or revenge, or in compliance with the wages of corruption, to immolate the independence and welfare of their country at the shrine of France— they would not as they do pursue a conduct which they cannot be insensible leads to that fatal result. Their pride, if not their patriotism, would prevent them. Openly claimed by a foreign Government as its obsequious tools, the jealousy of their own honor would prompt them to be forward in giving the lie to a claim to them so pregnant with ignominy. That this has not been the effect is a convincing proof that they have embarked beyond the power of retreat. It affords a presumption that they are in a situation which leaves them no longer wills of their own. It is astonishing to observe, that they not only do not contradict the charge by their actions; but seem little if at all solicitous to disavow it in their language; And in the measures which they advocate with an effrontery unequalled under similar circumstances in the history of any nation they display unequivocally their prostitute devotion to the enemies of their country.

A principal expedient employed by these men to second the views of the French Government and counteract the salutary impressions on the public mind, which its abominable treatment of us is calculated to produce, is to inculcate that our envoys in the conferences they have communicated have been the dupes of unauthorized and swindling impostors, and that our Government in publishing their dispatches has been actuated by a desire to make the circumstance subservient to a long premeditated design of rupture with France.

The French account of a transaction in which the Despots of France have violated a right of nations sacred among savage as well as civilized men, by imprisonning the ambassador of Portugal,[1] is pressed into the service of the infamous scheme of defaming our own government and vindicating those Despots. This account represents the Portugese minister as having been deceived into the advance of a large sum of money as a bribe to three of the Directory, by pretended agents of the French Government; which coming to light through the channel of the French Minister at the Court of Portugal

1. See Timothy Pickering to H, first letter of March 25, 1798, note 9.

occasionned the imprisonment of the Portugese ambassador and several of the pretended agents. And it is alleged that a like imposition has in all probability been practiced upon our envoys.

What may appear to be the real nature of the transaction in question can only be judged of when the Portugese Government free from the dread of France shall have told its story; when, if ever, the imprisonned Minister shall be at liberty to explain the grounds of the confidence which he reposes in the Agents to whom the money was advanced. Till then all judgment of the true complexion of the affair must be suspended.

In the mean time the character of bold inequity which the Directory have so eminently earned authorises the supposition that the Agents now disavowed were really Agents of the Government— that they actually received the bribe for the Directory; that these deeming it expedient afterwards to disappoint the expectation given to Portugal found it necessary to disclaim the inducement and as a color to their ill faith and as a shield against the infamy of the proceeding to imprison the Minister and the inferior agents. The present Rulers of France have soared to so stupendous a height of profligacy that the diminutive vices of other men afford no standard by which to judge of their conduct; no clue to the mysterious labyrinth of their complicated crimes.

There are even circumstances to countenance the supposition of this double plot. It is stated that *Wascovich*[2] one of the persons disavowed and seized was apparently in close connection with *Beau-*

2. Wiscovich (not Wascovich), a native of Dalmatia, had moved to Paris and was closely associated with Paul François Jean Nicolas Barras, a member of the Directory. On two different occasions he was involved as Barras's representative in attempts to offer bribes to diplomatic representatives in France. One such instance occurred in the summer of 1797 when he demanded money from Antonio D'Araujo D'Azevedo, the Portuguese minister to France, in the negotiations over the Portuguese–French treaty, which was signed on August 10, 1797, but was not ratified by Portugal. See Rufus King to H, June 27, 1797, note 5; Pickering to H, first letter of March 25, 1798, note 9. The second instance concerned negotiations with the Venetian ambassador. The Treaty of Campo Formio, October 17, 1797, provided among other things for the transfer of the territory of Venice to Austria. The Venetians were strongly opposed to this provision of the treaty and attempted to have it abrogated. At about the same time that Talleyrand's representatives were demanding bribes from the United States commissioners to France in the XYZ affair, Wiscovich was attempting to secure a bribe from Alvise Querini, the Venetian ambassador. In December, 1797, both the Portuguese ambassador and Wiscovich were imprisoned in the Temple. Wiscovich was released on May 20, 1798, and expelled from France.

marchais: was in "*ostensible familiarity with government-men*" and had actually had communication with a *real agent* of Government *for the purpose of discovering* the views of newly arrived foreign *envoys:* And it appears that *Beaumarchais* is not among the persons seized.

It may serve as an index to the affair to understand, that *Beaumarchais* is one of the most cunning and intriguing men of Europe—that he was employed under the royal government as a secret confidential Agent, in which capacity he acted between the UStates and France before the acknowlegement of our Independence, and that he is known to be in intimate connection with the present French Minister for foreign relations.[3]

In the capacity of confidential Agent a considerable part of the monies advanced by France for the use of the U States passed through his hands.[4] There was a sum of a million of livres which Doctor Franklin in the carelessness of confidence acknowleged to have been received of which the application could not be traced. When inquiry on behalf of our Government was made of the French Minister concerning the appropriation of this million the only answer to be obtained was that it was a "*secret du cabinet*".* But the Revolution has unravelled the secret. During the reign of Robespierre, *Beaumarchais* was in disgrace and a fugitive. The Ministry of that period not scrupling to unveil the corruptions of the old Government, charged the receipt of the missing million upon *Beaumarchais;* & furnished a copy of the *receipt which he is alleged to have* given for it.

This transaction proves that *Beaumarchais,* was besides being the confidential political Agent of the then Administration of France was the instrument or accomplice of its cupidity. What but the participation of the Minister in a scheme of embezzlement could have induced him to make a *cabinet-secret* of the application of this Million?

Who a more likely, a more fit instrument of the avidity of the

---

* *a secret of the Cabinet*

3. Charles Maurice de Talleyrand-Périgord.

4. This is a reference to the so-called "lost million." For an explanation and the subsequent negotiations concerning the "lost million," see the introductory note to Oliver Wolcott, Jr., to H, March 29, 1792. See also H to Thomas Jefferson, June 10, 1793; Pierre Augustin Caron de Beaumarchais to H, October 29, 1796; Talleyrand to H, November 12, 1796; Mathieu Dumas to H, December 8, 1797; Marquis de Lafayette to H, December 8, 1797; H to Wolcott, November 20, 1797; H to Lafayette, April 28, 1798.

present Government than this same *Beaumarchais?* When men apparently in close connection with him take bribes from foreign ministers professedly for the use of the Directory, what more probable than that they are truly for that use; that Beaumarchais is the link between the Directory and the ostensible Agents?

If afterwards—expedient or necessary to disavow, what more easy to be managed! *Beaumarchais* is no doubt too adroit to transact such business in a manner that can admit of proof of his Agency. If inculpated by his agents he has only boldly to deny the charge and to treat it as a part of the imposture. The all sufficient patronage of the Directory could not fail to insure credit to his denial and to shield him from detection.

In such a case the appearances to be expected are exactly such as occur in the present affair. The immediate and chief Agent goes untouched. The subalterns are consigned to punishment real or *seeming*. The semblance of punishment may even be a thing understood all round. As yet nothing more than imprisonment is known to have taken place; and it is very possible that final impunity may attend *Wascowick* and his colleagues; though from the character of the Directory, if necessary to their purposes, they would find no difficulty in the sacrifice of these men; by hurrying them to the guillotine after a mock-trial, or by giving them like *Carnot* [5] a secret passport to the other world. [6]

5. Lazare Nicolas Marguerite Carnot.
6. At this point in the draft H wrote and then crossed out three paragraphs which read: "If it be true as we are told that France has suspended the project of invading Portugal and is in negotiation with her under the auspices of Spain —it is very possible that the precautions of the Portuguese minister to establish the par[ti]cipation of the Directory were better than was at first suspected & that the apprehension of having the affair seriously probed may obtain for Portuga⟨l⟩ a suspension from Ruin.

"This comment upon the tra⟨nsact⟩ion is justified by the facts which ascertain⟨ed i⟩n our case. The informal Agents who presented ⟨them⟩selves to our envoys acted as it may be presumed those ⟨did⟩ who negotiated with the Portuguese Minister (See Exhibit C Decr. 13). The objects which they avowed were a bribe to the Directory and a contribution to the Republic (See Dispatch commencing the 27 of October 1797). Professing to have been sent on the errand they had undertaken by the Minister, Talleyrand they yet frequently pretend to offer only suggestions and opinions of their own; the better to manage an escape for the Government. But they sufficiently evince that a *bribe* and *contribution* are indispensable conditions of accomodation. And in our case their agency for the French Government is clearly ascertained. Obliged by the backwardness of our Envoys to speak out they expressly cite *Talleyrand* as the source of both propositions. And the conferences between one of

This comment upon the affair is justified by the facts *ascertained* in our case. The participation of the French Minister for foreign relations in the propositions of the secret Agents to our Envoys admits of no question. To be convinced of this we have only to compare the declarations and proposals of the Agents with those of the Minister himself.[7]

In the communications of those Agents the leading ideas are— that the Directory were greatly incensed at some passages in the *Presidents speech;* that *reparation* must be made for them, that money might be a *substitute* for other reparation; that this money was *to be offered* by our envoys, and to serve as *pocket money*, as a *gratuity* for the Directory; and that in addition to it there must be a loan to *the Republic* in the shape of a purchase of Dutch *Rescriptions* or in some other shape. The gratuity to be about 50000 £ Sterling.

The same ideas substantially appear in the Conference with Talleyrand him self.[8] In that of the 28th of October he begins by stating that the Directory has passed *an arrete* in which they had demanded of the envoys *an explanation* of some parts and *reparation* for other parts of the Presidents Speech to Congress; that he was sensible difficulties would exist on the part of the envoys relative to this demand, but that *by their offering money* he thought he could prevent the effect of the *arrete.*

The characteristic features in both cases are—*offence* given by the speech—*reparation* to be demanded by the Directory and a *commutation* of the required reparation for *money*. The only difference is that the Agents call this *pocket money* for the Directory, a *gratuity*

---

our Envoys and that Minister put it out of all doubt that the Agents had his authority for both.

"As a criterion of this it is to be observed that these Agents originally suggested the *bribe* or *gratuity*, contradistinguished from the *loan*, as a substitute for other *reparation* to the Directory for a pretended insult in the Presidents speech. In the conference between the Minister *Talleyrand* and one of our envoys of the 28. of October the same idea is distinctly marked, so as to e‹vin›ce a concert not only in substance but in circumstance between the Minister & the Agents. They began their conferences by stating the umbrage taken by the Directory at the Presidents Speech, the necessity of reparation for it, and the possibility of commuting that reparation for money *to be offered* by our Envoys. The Minister treading in their steps."

In the margin opposite these paragraphs H wrote: "Stand."

7. H is referring to the XYZ affair. For the dispatches, see *ASP, Foreign Relations*, II, 150–82. See also "The Stand No. V," April 16, 1798, note 28.

8. This sentence is not in H's handwriting.

&c, while the Minister gives it no specific name or destination. But we discover still more clearly from what follows that he means the same thing with the Agents. The envoy having answered that he and his colleagues had no power to make a loan, but could send one of their number for instructions on the proposition, if deemed expedient, provided that the other objects of the negotiation could be discussed & adjusted. *Talleyrand* replied that this matter *about the money* must be settled *directly without sending to America;* that he would not communicate the *arrete* for a week, and that if the envoys could adjust the difficulty with respect to the *Speech* an application would nevertheless go to the U States for a *loan.* The loan is here manifestly a different thing from the money to be advanced for reparation. The last must be arranged immediately though the first might wait the issue of an application to the Government of this Country. The first is plainly the 50000 Sterling for *pocket money;* the last is the contribution by way of loan to the Republic. This coincidence fixes definitively the concert between the Minister and the Agents and traces unequivocally to the former the double demand of a bribe and a *loan.* The conclusion is inevitable.

It is also confirmed by what took place on the 17 of December. When one of our envoys mentioned to the Minister that the person designated as *Y* had that morning made him *propositions* (alluding to those for the *gratuity* and *loan*) the Minister replied, that the *information which Y had given was just and might always be relied upon.* This was explicitly to recognize *Y* as his Agent and to authorize the giving of credit to his propositions. A quibble has been started on his point. It is pretended that the declaration that the *information* given by Y was just did not import that the *propositions* he had made was authorised. But besides that it was natural to look for vagueness of expression in so mysterious and so foul a transaction; as the term *information* was used in reply to the suggestion that *propositions* had been made, it must necessarily be understood to intend that the *information* which *Y* had given in reference to the *propositions* spoken of by the envoy was just and might be relied upon. Again *information* was the most apt term that could have been employed. *Y* and the other Agents professed not to *make propositions* but to *inform* our envoys what *propositions made by them* were likely to be acceptable.

Such are the wretched shifts to which the factious adherents of France are driven in the attempt to obscure the truth and to mislead their Countrymen. Their futility is evident. It is evident that the Agents who conferred with our Envoys were not impostors but were truly the emissaries of the French Minister, and that their most odious propositions were not only sanctionned but even *reiterated* by him. The connection between the Minister & the Directory from the nature of the thing can only be inferred from his Office and from his personal character. The most circumspect man in the world, it is utterly incredible that he would hazard himself in such a way, unless acting for the Directory he was assured of their omnipotent support. Whether he be himself a mercenary partaker of the bribes, which are extorted, or only the instrument of the Directory to maintain his influence with them for the accomplishment of some great ulterior design must be referred to time, and is of little moment to the United States.

Whatever then may have been the case with respect to the Portugese Minister, 'tis demonstrated that our Envoys have not been as alleged the dupes of unauthorised Agents; but have had the dexterity to ascertain the corruption & oppression from the mouth of the Minister himself. The probability is that in the other instance likewise the corruption which is now denied did really exist; as it most certainly does in our case, though it is to be looked for that here also it will be denied and our envoys if within the grasp of the Monsters made the victims of their fraudalent tyranny. The abject partisans of France anticipating this result are preparing the way for its justification.   *Detector*

James McHenry to the Military Committee of New York City [1]

New York 13 June 1798.

The Secretary of war, requests the opinion of the gentlemen composing the military committee of New York on the following particulars, with such observations, as they may think proper to favour him with, relative to the defence of the harbour and City.

Supposing batteries & block houses to be established at the following points vz. a battery at Sandy Hook, opposite the middle ground; three block houses, on the East and West bank, within the Hook, each to contain five 18 or five 24 pounders, two 12 pounders, and one 8 or 10 inch howitzer, and to command the ship channel, a battery of 6, 18 or 24 pounders on each side of the narrows; a small battery at Red Hook, another small one opposite to Governors Island on Long Island, and a battery on the opposite sides of Governors Island to co operate with the batteries on Long Island and Bedlows Island.

It is presumed, that these batteries and block houses, may be completed for about 70,000 dollars; and that the batteries at Sandy Hook, the narrows &c, could be maintained against the landing of an enemy, by the adjacent militia, and that a system of regulations and signals may be devised which would instantly procure to them their cooperation.

Assuming these data, the Committee will be so obliging as to consider, whether the commander of any naval force, unaided by a land army, ought to venture all the risks, to which his ships would be exposed, in passing and returning, through the fire of such a succession of batteries, with a view, merely to lay the City under contribution?

If the Committee should conclude, that such a chain of defences, would be calculated to deter from any naval enterprise, against the City, or render it so extremely hazardous, as to prevent most commanders, from venturing upon the experiment, they will be pleased to deliberate and give their opinion, whether (without abandoning the idea of works, upon and contiguous to the Island of New York, calculated for a last stand, or to drive any vessel from her moorings, that might attempt to lay within cannon reach of the City) it will not be advisable and proper, that the said works be undertaken, in preference to finishing or adding to the fortifications on Governor, Bedlow and Oyster Islands, further or other works than what may appear indispensible to the efficiency of the said system of defence?

The Secretary has subjoined the following maps and draughts, connected with the objects in reference, which the committee are requested to return to him, with the result of their deliberations.

James McHenry

No. 1. Postion of certain batteries at Sandy Hook & block houses for the East & West banks.

No. 2. The narrows, batteries &c.

No. 3. Plans &c of a block house &c.

No. 4. Explanations of the different parts of the block house &c.

No. 5. Chart from Sandy Hook &c. &c.

To the honorable Committee of the City of New York
for the defence of the harbour &c.

ALS, Hamilton Papers, Library of Congress; copy, George Washington Papers, Library of Congress.

1. This committee consisted of H, Aaron Burr, and Ebenezer Stevens. See "Call for a Meeting," June 4, 1798, note 2. See also the introductory note to H to McHenry, June 1, 1798; McHenry to H, June 4, 6, 1798.

On June 13, 1798, the [New York] *Argus. Greenleaf's New Daily Advertiser* reported: "Yesterday James M'Henry, Secretary of war, arrived in town from Philadelphia. The object of his journey . . . is to take a survey of the port and harbor of New-York."

Alexander Hamilton, Aaron Burr, and Ebenezer Stevens to James McHenry [1]

[New York, June 14, 1798]

Sir

We have carefully attended to the subjects presented to our consideration, by your note of yesterday and now offer to you the result of our reflections.

The idea of a succession of batteries from the Hook, to the City, very naturally occurs in contemplating the defence of this port, and doubtless has advantages. It would present dangers in the approach which may be expected to have considerable influence in dissuading from an enterprise which should have no other object than to lay this City under contribution, but it does not appear to us that its efficacy could be sufficiently relied upon when it is considered how adventurous an Enemy we have to encounter. The mere passage to batteries by ships with leading breezes has so often been proved to be matter of little difficulty, that it cannot be hoped that it would not be effected, if attempted—and the booty of this place may fairly be considered as an adequate temptation to run the risque, to say nothing of the political consequences (as a mean of distressing and disabling us) which might enter into the calculation.

We submit that a plan, the success of which must entirely depend on the degree of enterprise of an enemy, which again depends on national and *individual* character, cannot safely be relied upon, and that it would be inexpedient to exhaust the slender pecuniary means which are hinted at in the execution of such a plan. If great and efficacious obstacles could be opposed to the passage of a fleet to the City, it would be of the greatest importance, and as an ulterior measure, is to be contemplated. But for this, we conceive, much greater means are requisite than seem to be at command and considerable time must be employed in the execution, more than it is imagined we ought to count upon having. The measure as an ulterior one engages our enquiries, and the result if deferred will be communicated. But for the present it has appeared to us on mature reflection, that the best thing to be done with the means already provided is to establish such defences as promise to be effectual to prevent ships from taking and keeping stations near the City, from which they can cannonade and bombard it with effect. To this end it seems to us of primary importance to put the works already begun on *Governor's, Bedlow's* and *Oyster Islands* in a condition to be defended, and to annoy—to occupy with small works *Red Hook*, and *Powles Hook*, and to erect four batteries on New-York Island at points which can be indicated.

We beg leave to add, that if the General Government will take the necessary measures in relation to the three first mentioned Islands, and to Red Hook, and Powles Hook, means will be found on the part of this City, provisionally, and in confidence of reimbursement by the General Government, to establish the batteries on New-York Island with the necessary cannon and apparatus.

A few gun-boats may likewise be useful auxiliaries, and it will deserve examination whether the channel between Governor's, and Long Islands, cannot be stopped without too great expence.

It is our opinion that in respect to those points which have been mentioned as for the immediate care of the General Government, such expedients ought to be adopted as will quickly place them in a tolerable state of preparation, leaving more substantial ameliorations to a progressive effort.

Any battery on Long Island, other than at Red Hook, seems to us not immediately essential, and best to be defined to the other objects.   Alexander Hamilton
                                          Aaron Burr
                                          Eben. Stevens [2]

Copy, George Washington Papers, Library of Congress.
    1. H, Burr, and Stevens wrote this letter in their capacity as members of the Military Committee of New York City. See "Call for a Meeting," June 4, 1798, note 2. See also the introductory note to H to McHenry, June 1, 1798.
    2. The signatures are in McHenry's handwriting.

Simeon DeWitt to Aaron Burr, Alexander Hamilton, and Ebenezer Stevens [1]

Albany, June 18, 1798. "Mr. Abraham Bloodgood [2] will . . . exhibit to you a model of a floating battery of his own invention. . . ."

ALS, Hamilton Papers, Library of Congress.
    1. DeWitt was surveyor general of New York State. He addressed this letter to H, Burr, and Stevens in their capacity as members of the Military Committee of New York City. See "Call for a Meeting," June 4, 1798, note 2. See also the introductory note to H to James McHenry, June 1, 1798.
    2. Bloodgood was an Albany merchant.

Memorandum from Joseph F. Mangin to the Military Committee of New York City [1]

New York, June 18, 1798. "J'aurais desiré pouvoir presenter aujourd'hui à Messieurs du Comité Militaire, les plans des quatres batteries, conformement à leur demand; le tems qu'il m'a été donné est Si court, que je n'ai pû m'occuper que de la grande batterie. . . ." [2]

ADS, Hamilton Papers, Library of Congress.
    1. The title of this document is "Memoir relatif à la construction des batteries qu'on Se propose d'elever pour La deffense de Newyork."
    The Military Committee of New York City consisted of Aaron Burr, H, and Ebenezer Stevens. See "Call for a Meeting," June 4, 1798, note 2. See also the introductory note to H to James McHenry, June 1, 1798.
    In 1795 Mangin, an engineer born in France, succeeded his superior, Charles

Vincent, as engineer-in-chief of the fortifications of the port and harbor of New York. On May 9, 1796, Mangin was "admitted & sworn a Free Man of . . . [New York] City" and on May 18, 1796, was appointed "a Surveyor of this City" (*Minutes of the Common Council*, II, 236, 238). For Mangin's citizenship, see also the MS Minutes of the New York Supreme Court, under the date of May 7, 1796, January 19–November 5, 1796 (Hall of Records, New York City). On June 18, 1798, Ebenezer Stevens appointed Mangin to work with John Hills and George Flemming to draw up plans for fortifying the harbor of New York. These plans were completed on August 10, and on September 11, 1798, Stevens placed Mangin in charge of completing the fortification of Fort Jay on Governors Island (Stevens to H, February 28, April 4, 1799). Mangin was also the architect for several important buildings erected in New York City in the late seventeen-nineties and with John McComb, Jr., won a competition in 1802 for the plans for New York City Hall.

2. In the remainder of this document Mangin discusses in detail the measures he proposes for the defense of New York City.

From Justus Erich Bollmann [1]

Philadelphia, June 22, 1798. "When I had the Pleasure of seeing you last in this City, I informed you of my having established a commercial House in Partnership with my Brother. . . .[2] The Circumstances of the Times, I believe, will make it necessary for the United States to provide a Supply of arms and other military Implements from Europe, and it appears to me that a Part of them might be advantageously imported from Germany. I should like therefore to come to some Arrangement with Government on this Subject . . . and I drop you these few Lines in order to request you to mention me favorably to mr. Wolcott. . . ."

ALS, Hamilton Papers, Library of Congress.
1. Bollman, a physician and adventurer, was a native of Hanover. See H to George Washington, January 19, 1796.
2. Lewis Bollmann.

To Elizabeth Hamilton

[New York] June 22d. 1798

I believe my beloved that I omitted to write by the last Post thinking it would not find you at Albany; but as it seems possible from what Mr. Schuyler tells me that your stay may be prolonged [1] I write this to say to my darling that I begin to [be] *very anxious* for her return & hope it will be accelerated. I was very glad to receive a favourable account of her health & spirits.

AL[S], Hamilton Papers, Library of Congress.
1. Elizabeth Hamilton had left Albany before this letter reached her, for the envelope indicates that the letter was returned to New York City.

To Oliver Wolcott, Junior

[New York, June 25, 1798]

Dear Sir

I understand that the Collector of Philadelphia ¹ will speedily offer his resignation & that McPherson ² does not incline to be the successor—but that Major Jackson ³ is desirous of it.

If all this be so—and if your experience of his conduct in his present station gives you a confidence that he would execute the Office of Collector well, it would gratify me to see him appointed. Jackson has more than once given me marks of personal regard,⁴ that claim a reciprocal sentiment from me & a disposition to promote efficaciously his interest as far as it can be done consistently with the public Interest.

Should it coincide with your views you may make any use of my wishes that you can imagine may be serviceable to the Major.⁵

Yrs. Affecty

A Hamilton

June 25. 1798

O. Wolcott Esq

ALS, RG 59, General Records of the State Department, Applications and Recommendations, 1792–1801, National Archives.
1. Sharp Delany.
2. William Macpherson, a veteran of the American Revolution, had been an aide-de-camp to Benjamin Lincoln. He was appointed surveyor of the port of Philadelphia on September 11, 1789, inspector of the port of Philadelphia on March 8, 1792, and naval officer for the District of Philadelphia on December 30, 1793 (*Executive Journal*, I, 25, 111, 144).
3. William Jackson was appointed surveyor and inspector of the revenue for the port of Philadelphia on January 14, 1796 (*Executive Journal*, I, 197–98).
4. In July and August, 1797, Jackson had served as H's second when H and James Monroe had come close to fighting a duel. See Jackson to H, August 5, 1797.

5. On June 28, 1798, John Adams nominated George Latimer, a Philadelphia merchant, to be collector of customs for the District of Pennsylvania, and the Senate agreed to his appointment on the following day (*Executive Journal*, I, 282).

From Rufus King [1]

[*London, June 27, 1798. Letter not found.*]

1. "List of Letters from . . . Mr. King" to H, Columbia University Libraries.

From William Child [1]

New York, June 28, 1798. "William Child who some days since had the opportunity of offering his services to the Military Committee of New York (relative to the erection of a Telegraph) from which he has had no application or opportunity of explaining his plan respectfully requests the attention of Colonel Hamilton to his proposals with the advantages likely to accrue from such an Establishment. He would propose to have an Observatory at the Light House on Sandy Hook in which he would fix his large Telescope which is sufficient as soon as a Vessell appears in the Horizon at 40 or 50 Miles distant to ascertain her Size &c. . . ."

AL, Hamilton Papers, Library of Congress.
1. This letter was written to H in his capacity as a member of the Military Committee of New York City. See "Call for a Meeting," June 4, 1798. See also the introductory note to H to James McHenry, June 1, 1798.
Child, who lived at 219 William Street, New York City, submitted the same proposal to the Common Council of the City of New York on August 6, 1798 (*Minutes of the Common Council*, II, 460).

From Thomas Palmer [1]

New York, June 28, 1798. "Thomas Palmer one of the persons who had the honour to submit an Invention of a Spring Star Shot to Colonel Hamilton respectfully requests leave to trouble him again on that subject.[2] In consequence of some objections stated by Colo-

nel Stevens to the plan the projectors have studied the means of
obviating them previous to their sending it up as requested by the
Secretary at War to Philadelphia. Having one Shot now finish'd
which may do for the trial of the plan & pecuniary circumstances
not allowing them the means of trying it themselves T. Palmer
presumes on Colonel Hamiltons known encouragement to Ingenuity
& Industry to solicit his recommendation to the Secretary of War
for encouragement to this Invention or any other that he may be
found capable of & likewise for a recommendation to the Commandant at Governors Island for a trial of the Invention. . . ."

AL, Hamilton Papers, Library of Congress.
    1. Palmer was a tavern owner at 44 Cortlandt Street, New York City.
    2. This proposal was submitted to H in his capacity as a member of the
Military Committee of New York City. See "Call for a Meeting," June 4, 1798,
note 2. See also the introductory note to H to James McHenry, June 1, 1798.

From Henry Rutgers [1]

New York, June 28, 1798. "Immediately upon receipt of your
Note [2] I . . . found that 940 . . . are Enrolled, which I suppose is
the better half of the Ward."

ALS, Hamilton Papers, Library of Congress.
    1. Rutgers was a large landholder in New York City and a well-known phi-
lanthropist. He was also the assessor of the seventh ward of New York City.
Rutgers signed this letter: "in behalf of the Committee of the 7th Ward."
    This note was written to H in his capacity as a member of the Military
Committee of New York City. See "Call for a Meeting," June 4, 1798, note 2.
See also the introductory note to H to James McHenry, June 1, 1798.
    2. Letter not found.

To Oliver Wolcott, Junior

[New York, June 28, 1798]

Dear Sir
    Col Burr sets out today for Philadelphia. I have some reasons for
wishing that the administration may manifest a cordiality to him.[1] It
is not impossible he will be found a useful cooperator. I am aware

there are different sides but the case is worth the experiment. He will call on McHenry upon going to the City.

Yrs. truly   A Hamilton

June 28. 1798

O Wolcott Esqr

ALS, Connecticut Historical Society, Hartford.
    1. H and Aaron Burr were both members of the Military Committee of New York City. See "Call for a Meeting," June 4, 1798, note 2. See also the introductory note to H to James McHenry, June 1, 1798.

To Oliver Wolcott, Junior

[New York, June 29, 1798]

Dear Sir

I have this moment seen a Bill brought into the Senate intitled a Bill to define more particularly the crime of Treason &c.[1] There are provisions in this Bill which according to a cursory view appear to me highly exceptionable & such as more than any thing else may endanger civil War. I have not time to point out my objections by this post but I will do it tomorrow. I hope sincerely the thing may not be hurried through. Let us not establish a tyranny. Energy is a very different thing from violence. If we make no false step we shall be essentially united; but if we push things to an extreme we shall then give to faction *body* & solidarity.

Yrs. truly   A Hamilton

June 29. 1798

O Wolcott Esq

ALS, Connecticut Historical Society, Hartford; copy, Hamilton Papers, Library of Congress.
    1. On June 26, 1798, James Lloyd of Maryland reported to the Senate "a bill to define more particularly, the crime of treason, and to define and punish the crime of sedition" (*Annals of Congress*, VII, 589-90). Section 1 of this bill in its original version reads: "*Be it enacted by the Senate and House of Representatives of the United States of America in Congress assembled,* That the government and people of France and its colonies and dependencies, in consequence of their hostile conduct towards the United States, shall be, and they hereby are, declared to be enemies to the United States and the people thereof; and any person or persons owing allegiance to the United States, who shall

adhere to the aforesaid enemies of the United States, giving them aid and comfort, within the United States or elsewhere, and shall be thereof convicted, in the manner prescribed by the first section of a statute law of the United States, entitled, 'An act for the punishment of certain crimes against the United States,' shall suffer death" (copy, RG 46, Records of the United States Senate, Original Senate Bills, National Archives). An altered version of this bill passed the Senate on July 4, 1798 (*Annals of Congress*, VII, 599). For the final version of this measure, see "An Act in addition to the act, entitled 'An Act for the punishment of certain crimes against the United States'" (1 *Stat.* 596–97 [July 14, 1798]).

From Pierre Charles L'Enfant

Philadelphia July 1st 1798

Dr Sir

Being Just this moment told of a conversation you have had with Mr Soderestrom[1] in reply to a note which he handed to you from me,[2] am not perfectly comprehending what he related, he himself seeming to have but a Confuse recollection. While at the same time, as far as he has explained, it appear to me to be all Important well to understand you. I cannot esitate nor do I delay one Instant, requesting your own Explanation in what way has any political principles or connections, and the Conduct in my former public employment become matter for your animadversion!—and how, and upon what authority you asserted that I had been *paid a good price* by the french minister Adet,[3] or other—from which I ought to be well satisfied with my actual situation.

Whether, Sir, these were your private Sentiments or those of other people you delivered, you may well imagine is not Indifferent to me to Know.—and Beliving in the veracity of Mr Soderestrom who stated those points as being the principal he recollected of the conversation with you, you can Surrely not be Surprised if I feel alive at the Injurious ⟨–⟩ and in this direct manner ask you to Explaine and to trace out to me whence came those Ideas. Ideas which I must Say I held in too contemptible a light to belive orriginated with you. They are Sugestive indeed too vilainous and of an Ingenuity and base malice as I would hardly have suspected possible in any one man. well sensible however how generally them who would have done a man an Injury become the ⟨–⟩ Enemies of him that his Injuried. I should not much wonder but thus at once the Schem be to Cut short all my claims to the gratitude of the country. as this way of Exonerating the public of all debt to me,[4] may well compleat the vilany of those swindling Individuals who have robed me of all my property the small saving from the ⟨–⟩ by laborious pursuits of twenty two years services to the united States.

With the hope this will find you ready either to substantiate those charges you have advanced as above—or to point out the author, clearing in this way the Stigma that naturally must attack in all those whose mistaken policy it may be to slander honesty I shall beg you to believe I remain

Dr Sir   Your obedient hubl Servant   P. charles L'Enfant

Colo Alr Amilton

ALS, Columbia University Libraries.
  1. Richard Soderstrom was Swedish consul general at Philadelphia.
  2. Letter not found.
  3. Pierre Auguste Adet.
  4. On December 11, 1800, the House of Representatives received "a petition of Pierre Charles L'Enfant, praying for a due recompense for his services, while he was employed under the direction of the late General Washington, in planning and conducting the public buildings at the city of Washington, for which services the petitioner conceives he has not been sufficiently remunerated." This petition was rejected (*Journal of the House*, III, 738–39, 741). Subsequently, L'Enfant petitioned Congress eight times (*House List of Private Claims*, II, 309). On May 1, 1810, "An Act for the relief of P. C. L'Enfant" granted him "six hundred and sixty-six dollars and two thirds, with legal interest" from March 1, 1792 (6 *Stat.* 94).

From Rufus King

London July 2. 1798

Dear sir

France will pursue with us the Plan that she has elsewhere found successful. She will endeavour to overthrow us by the Divisions among ourselves which she will excite and support by all the means of which she is mistress. The Paris Papers of the 18. ulto. say le Citoyen Roziers est nommé Consul Genl. aux Etats unis. Garnier (en convenl. de Saintes) consul, & Boscq vice consul à Wilmington, Quillet, consul à Tanger, passe à Norfolk, Bosc à New York, et le Citoyen Sottin, ambassadeur pres la Republique Ligurienne, (& I presume the former Minister of Police) *vient d'etre nommé Consul a New York.*[1]

If anything could exceed the past insolence of France, it would be this Attempt to plant in our chief Towns a corps of revolutionary agents under the mark of pub. Characters, and whom she expects, I hope falsely, that our Govt. will receive and permit to reside among us, after having herself repeatedly refused and expelled from her territories our pub. Ministers.

Another arreté of the Directory has added Havre to the Ports into which our vessels are forbid an Entry—so that we cannot now enter the Ports of Toulon, Rochefort, L'Orient, Brest, Dunkerque or Harve.[2] Cadiz and the Texel are closed by the Br. Squadrons, and I apprehend that the Meuse will likewise be blockaded as the Br. north Sea fleet is by this time reinforced by the Russian Squadron.

We are still at a loss where Buena parte is bound—he sailed from Toulon the 19. of May.[3] My opinion has been that Ireland was his object. At present it seems to be the general Opinion that he never intended to leave the Mediterranean. In a few Days we must hear of him. The Eng. confidently believe that he will fall into the Hands of Ad. Neilson who is in pursuit of him.[4] In Ireland tho for some months there will be partial and unimportant Risings, the force of the Insurrection is broken and the Danger nearly over.[5] The chief's have been without much character and without any intellect. There is no indication that they have recd. a single musket from france, and in general they are without arms except Pikes. There is but one remedy for Ireland, and it is that which has proved so successful with Scotland. Ireland like Scotland must become an integral part of the Br. Empire, or she will continue ignorant, ill governed, oppressed, and wretched.

Yrs. &c   R K

Col Hamilton

ALS, Hamilton Papers, Library of Congress; copy, New-York Historical Society, New York City.

1. This sentence, except for the words in English within parentheses, is a quotation from a decree issued by the Directory on June 18, 1798. King enclosed a copy of this decree to Secretary of State Timothy Pickering in a letter dated July 2, 1798 (LS, RG 59, Despatches from United States Ministers to Great Britain, 1792–1870, Vol. 7, January 9–December 22, 1798, National Archives).

The individuals mentioned in this sentence were Jean Antoine Bernard Rozier, Jacques Garnier de Saintes, Louis Augustin Guillaume Bosc, Pierre Quillet,
and Pierre Jean Marie Sotin de la Coindière. When this letter was written,
two of these men were in the French consular service in the United States.
Rozier was vice consul at New York City. Bosc, who had been named as
vice consul at Wilmington, North Carolina, on May 15, 1797, was appointed
consul at New York on June 8, 1798. His commission is dated June 30, 1798.
Quillet, who resigned as vice consul at Alicante on February 20, 1797, was
named as consul to Sebenico, Dalmatia, on November 22, 1797. King's assumption concerning Sotin was correct, for he had been Minister of Police until
the end of 1797. The information in this paragraph has been supplied by Mr. F.
Dousset, Adjoint au Directeur Général des Archives de France.

On June 29, 1798, William Vans Murray, United States Minister to the
Netherlands, wrote to Pickering: "I find that John Sotin—late French minister
at Genoa—is recalled from thence, and is to go as Consul to New York. This,
be assured, Sir, is a very important event. He it is who has been the active
agent there is embroiling the insurgents against the King of Sardinia. He is a
dangerous man—subtle & contriving & will do every mischief in the power of
a wicked intriguer with an experience ripe & fresh from successful practice.
There can be but one design in sending such an incendiary from the rank of
minister to that of consul—at such a time, & to such a place!

"Garnier—a member of the tumultuary convention, is destined as consul at
Wilmington; which, whether in D. or N.C. I know not—both these indicate
probably the last effort at insurrection." (ALS [deciphered], Massachusetts
Historical Society, Boston.)

Long before H received King's letter, any possible problems arising from
consular appointments mentioned by King had become an academic matter.
On July 7, 1798, "An Act to declare the treaties heretofore concluded with
France, no longer obligatory on the United States" was approved (1 *Stat.* 578).
This act provided "That the United States are of right freed and exonerated
from the stipulations of the treaties, and of the consular convention, heretofore
concluded between the United States and France; and that the same shall not
be legally obligatory on the government or citizens of the United States." On
July 13, 1798, President John Adams issued a proclamation revoking the ex-
equaturs of all French consular agents in the United States (Adams, *Works of
John Adams*, IX, 170–72).

2. The arrêt to which King is referring reads: "Le directoire executif
considerant que chaque jour on acquiert des nouveaux indices des coupables
intelligences qu'intretiennent les ennemis de la Republique avec les malveillans
de l'intérieure; considérant que les motifs qui ont fait interdue aux americains
l'entrée des Ports de Brest, l'Orient, Rochefort, Toulon & Dunkerque sont
applicables au Port de Harve, contre lequel il y a lieu de craindre que la
perfidie Anglaise ne dirige spécialement ses funestes intrigues; oui le Rapport
du ministre de la marine & des Colonies, arrete 1. L'entrée du port de Harve
est interdit aux Bâtimens Americains. 2. Ceux des Bâtimens de cette nation qui
se trouveront maintenant au Havre, seront tenus d'en sortir sous le plus bref
delai; 3. Le ministre de la marine est chargé de l'Execution &c" (copy, in
King's handwriting, enclosed in King to Pickering, July 2, 1798 [LS, RG 59,
Despatches from United States Ministers to Great Britain, 1792–1870, Vol. 7,
January 9–December 22, 1798, National Archives]). See also *Réimpression de
L'Ancien Moniteur*, XXIX, 292.

3. See King to H, June 6, 1798, note 1.
4. See King to H, June 6, 1798, note 2.
5. See King to H, June 6, 1798, note 3.

To Pierre Charles L'Enfant [1]

[New York, July 3, 1798]

Dear Sir

I lose no time in answering your letter of the first instant. I am altogether at a loss to imagine how Mr Soderstrom could have so extremely misconceived me. You may be assured that he has done it— that it was not said that you received *a good price from Adet* or any other person or any thing like it.

The substance of what I observed was this—"that an opinion was entertained that your political opinions for a considerable time past had corresponded with the course of things in France—that there had been observed to be a great intimacy between you and some of the Diplomatic Agents of France in this Country (probably Mr Adet's name was mentioned in this sense) and that it had been expected it would have led you to some employment under the French Government." You will perceive that there is nothing in all this to impeach your honour—There was nothing intended to look to any questions between France and the United States—to imply that you had received money or any other compensation for any purpose, still less for any improper purpose.

It is very likely that it may have been also intimated that the supposed conformity of your opinions with the course of things in France, and your intimacy with the Diplomatic Agents had excited a jealousy concerning your way of thinking which might interfere with your prospect of employment under our Government.

The impressions I mentioned were not spoken of as my own but as existing in another quarter. The observations were made to a person who appeared in the character of your friend ⟨and⟩ certainly contained nothing intended to injure you or that ⟨would⟩ impeach your integrity. As to myself, as you very ju ⟨– –⟩ to be aware, I could not wish to wound you but have uniformly desired and endeavoured to serve you.

I remain Dr Sir   Your obedt Servt

Major L'Enfant   New York July 3rd 1798

Df, Columbia University Libraries.
1. For background to this letter, see L'Enfant to H, July 1, 1798.
This letter was written on the back of L'Enfant to H, July 1, 1798.

From Gaspard Joseph Amand Ducher [1]

paris 4 juillet 1798

J'espere, Monsieur, que Cette Lettre vous trouvera ainsi que Mde. hamilton dans l'état de Bonheur que vous merités L'un et L'autre.

J'ai un très grand besoin de mes fonds; vous me devez jusqu'a *aujourdhuy*, deux mille neuf cents quatre vingt dix huit piastres. Cette somme comprend l'intérze de l'intéret Échu chaque année; votre délicatesse ne peut pas S'y réfuser; autrement je perdrois sur L'intéret, Le Bénéfice que vous feriez sur L'intéret de L'intéret, avec lequel vous vous L'èléveries d'une partie du principal.[2]

Pour M'envoyer mes fonds, je vous prie de faire comme pour vous même.

Je vous ai voué estime et amitié pour la vie.   Ducher

Chez Le Citoyen *Boileau* notaire, *Rue de Laloi* près La fontaine.

ALS (marked "Duplicate"), Hamilton Papers, Library of Congress.
1. In 1786 Ducher was appointed vice consul *ad interim* at Portsmouth, New Hampshire, and in 1788 was transferred to Wilmington, North Carolina. He returned to Paris in 1790, and for the next three years he sought to induce the French government to adopt a policy of encouraging trade through navigation laws (Frederick L. Nussbaum, *Commercial Policy in the French Revolution* [Washington, 1923], 14, 17, 35, 271–304).
2. See H to Robert Troup, July 25, 1795. See also H's Cash Book, March 1, 1782–1791.

Plan for a Legion

[July 5–15, 1798] [1]

To determine what is proper to be done it is necessary preliminarily to contemplate a fundamental or elementary organisation the aggregate of which constitutes the army.

This element ought to be a legion consisting of

> Four Regiments of Infantry
> One Squadron of Dragoons
> one Batalion of Artillery

A Regiment of Infantry to consist of two Batalions each batalion of five companies (of which one a company of Grenadiers) each company of

> 1 Captain
> 2 Lieutenants
> 8 Sergeants
> 96 Rank & file

Each batalion to be commanded by a Major and a Regiment by a Colonel.

Each Regiment to have attached to it

> one Troop of Dragoons
> one Company of Artillery

Each batalion to have two six pounders and One Twelve pounder.

The Squadron of Dragoons of Legion composed of 4 Troops to be commanded by a Major & the batalion of Artillery composed of 4 Companies by a Major also. Every two batalions of Artillery a Regiment commanded by a Colonel. The Artillery aggregately to be commanded by a Major General. The Dragoons aggregately by a Major General.

The army will be the aggregate of these Corps with an additional quantity of Artillery men for Garrisons & the Park & with an additional number of heavy cavalry.

It is not to be understood that the Dragoons attached to the batalions are always to act with them—on the contrary they are to be combined & subdivided according to circumstances—but when a batalion a Regiment a brigade or a legion is to be detached it carries with it its appendages and the service is always performed by entire corps. So always the twelve pounders may be combined and transported from point to point as the service may require.

These corps to be thus further organized. Two Regiments with their appurtenances to form a brigade commanded by a Brigadier. The legion to constitute a division commanded by a Major General.

Two legions to constitute a grand Division commanded by a Lieutenant General.

The army itself to be commanded by a "General in Chief" or "General."

The Army to have an Inspector General with the Rank of Major General—A Quarter Master General with the like rank—An "Intendant" without rank to to charged with the whole business of supplies—Deputies of course—The Adjutant General should be Deputy Inspector General.

It is understood that the existing establishment consists of four Regiments of Infantry [2]

2 Corps of Artillery & Engineers [3]   about 1600
2 Companies of Dragoons [4]

And it is probable 12 Regiments of Infantry will be added.[5]

On the principles of the foregoing plan These corps may be considered as forming 4 Legions & Eight brigades.

The appointments of Officers will correspond & there may be immediately a

Major General of Artillery & Qr. Master General. But the provision yet made permits only a Qr. Master General of the rank of Lieutenant Col.[6]

There being already One Major General [7] there would remain to be appointed three more besides the Major General of Artillery.[8]

AD, Hamilton Papers, Library of Congress; copy, in the handwriting of Philip Church, Hamilton Papers, Library of Congress.

1. H prepared this document after July 5, 1798, when the House of Representatives began to debate the resolutions which became "An Act to augment the Army of the United States, and for other purposes" and before July 16, 1798, when the act became law (*Annals of Congress*, VIII, 2088–93; 1 *Stat.* 604–05).

2. "An Act to ascertain and fix the Military Establishment of the United States" (1 *Stat.* 483–86 [May 30, 1796]) established the strength of the Army at four regiments of infantry.

3. "An Act providing for raising and organizing a Corps of Artillerists and Engineers" (1 *Stat.* 366–67 [May 9, 1794]) established the first regiment, and "An Act to provide an additional regiment of Artillerists and Engineers" (1 *Stat.* 552–53 [April 27, 1798]) established a second regiment.

4. "An Act to ascertain and fix the Military Establishment of the United States" (1 *Stat.* 483–86) set the number of companies of Dragoons at two.

5. This is a reference to "An Act to augment the Army of the United States, and for other purposes" (1 *Stat.* 604–05).

6. This is a reference to the quartermaster general provided for by Section 7 of "An Act authorizing the President of the United States to raise a Provisional Army" (1 *Stat.* 558–61 [May 28, 1798]).

7. This is a reference to the major general provided for by Section 6 of "An Act authorizing the President of the United States to raise a Provisional Army" (1 *Stat.* 558–61).

8. H wrote on the cover of the copy of this document: "Plan for a Legion not well digested."

From George Washington [1]

[*Mount Vernon, July 5, 1798. Letter not found.*]

1. "List of Letters from G—— Washington to General Hamilton," Columbia University Libraries.

From Pierre Charles L'Enfant [1]

philadelphia July 6. 1798

Dr Sir

Perceiving from your letter of the 3d instant that there must have been some misconception of misrepresentation of what you mentioned, respecting me, to M. Soderestrom,[2] and your explanation upon the whole shewing there was nothing contained in your conversation with that gentleman to Injure me nor *that could* impeach my Integrity or honor—I here testify this to be satisfactory.

only as you remark those Impressions mentioned were not Spoken as your own. I had wished and must repeat the request for information in what quarter these first Existed—for although such impressions Should not impeach my honor—Still you Intimate as likely it will interfere with my prospect of employement under Government and this, you will admit, leave it as important for me to trace out who are the persons whose cavils and machinations So Injuriously influence against me. To those who observed to be a great Intimacy between me and Some diplomatique agents of france in this Country and that such as to have Existed a jalousie of my way of thinking—I could Said I believe those agents themselves would be much surprised at hearing the charge—but I would only ask—if *opinions* of my good wish to france are reasons Conclusive of a deffection of my attachement to the United States ranking as I do amongst the first who have fought and bled for the attainment of American liberty and Independence and having never been behind since when occasions offered to Render myself usfull to the United States I truely had not imagined possible my principle would be at this time mistrusted—and that upon the insidious surmisses of malice and Jalousie

I thus Should be left out of a merited prefferement without a near anquiry being of the circumstances that may have give room for Injurious Sugestions.

Should you not wish to give the Intelligence I want for an Investigation heighly Interesting to me, I Shall at least hope—from what you assure me that you have *uniformly desired and Endeavoured* to serve me in that you will not rest then, but will endeavour a new and by Every means in your power Exert to procure a redress of the wrong done.

I have the honor to be   Dr Sir.   your obedient Humb servant

P. charles L Enfant

Coll. A. Amilton

ALS, Hamilton Papers, Library of Congress; ALS (marked "duplicate"), Hamilton Papers, Library of Congress.
    1. For background to this letter, see L'Enfant to H, July 1, 1798; H to L'Enfant, July 3, 1798.
    2. Richard Soderstrom.

From Rufus King

London July 7. 98

Buena parte has made the Debut of the campaigne by the easy tho important conquest of Malta.[1] This Island has been supposed impregnable and therefore was the Depositary of great wealth removed there from Italy. It contained likewise an excellent arensal, two or three ships of the Line, and as many as 6.000 excellent Seamen. It was the maltese Seamen who made the fine campaign under Suffrein in the E. Indies during the American war.[2] Sicily is near and from thence the french will obtain Provision shd. Ad. Neilson attempt to blockade the fleet in the Harbour of Malta.[3] Buena Parte may perhaps take possession of Sicily, after which Naples would almost fall of course. We are left to conjecture what are his ulterior Plans. I dont perceive that it is believed that the Eng. Squadron can owing to the tempests of those seas, maintain a long Blockade. At Rastadt procrastination is the game [4]—the french journalists amuse themselves with calling it "the Eternal Congress." I see no likeli-

hood of a concert upon the Continent agt. france. The struggle is
left to England, who certainly maintains it with increased zeal & Resolution for some months past. We hear not a word about peace, no
one appears to think that peace would bring safety. The affair of
Ireland is nearly finished.[5] Cornwallis [6] has requested that no more
troops shd. be sent him, and that those on their way shd. be counter-
manded. In this state of things we are (for so I consider our Situation) forced into the war—a war of Defense. Have you recd. a
former letter of mine on this subject.[7] It is of infinite importance that
we are not deceived by ourselves or others. We must do more than
merely defend. I still think the object that I have before suggested
demands all our consideration, wisdom and Energy. Dont suppose
that I would combine our fortunes with those of others; on the contrary whatever our interest may require in regard to a cooperation
with others I am averse to indissoluble engagements with any one.
The Continent of Europe cannot be saved—but this is no reason
why America shd. likewise perish. France is the only nation that
projects enterprizes or succeeds in putting them in Execution—all
others are puzzled in a perpetual Effort to find out & defeat the
Plans of France without concerting and attempting to execute one
that might give to france the Disadvantage of Defence. If we follow
this course I dread the issue.

   farewell yrs. &c

I am mortified with the probable result of the Elections of New
york. Mr. Jay according to probabilities is reelected,[8] but how very
considerable has been the Opposition. Besides what is to become of
us if we return such Members to Congress as I think it likely will
compose a majority of our next Delegation? [9]

AL, Hamilton Papers, Library of Congress.
   1. See King to H, June 6, 1798, note 1. See also King to H, June 8, July
2, 1798.
   2. Pierre André de Suffren de Saint-Tropez, a French naval commander and
a member of the Maltese order, accompanied Charles Henri Hector, comte
d'Estaing to America in 1778. In 1780 his naval command captured twelve British ships and in 1781 defeated the British in a naval battle near the Cape Verde
Islands. In 1782 in the East Indies he conducted a successful campaign against
Admiral Sir Edward Hughes.
   3. See King to H, June 6, 1798, note 2.
   4. The Treaty of Campo Formio, concluded between France and Austria
on October 17, 1797, provided for a congress at Rastatt to make peace with

the German empire. The congress which met in December, 1797, lasted—despite the lack of accomplishment—until April, 1799.

5. See King to H, June 6, 1798, note 3.

6. On June 12, 1798, ". . . Marquis CORNWALLIS was appointed LORD LIEU-TENANT and COMMANDER IN CHIEF in Ireland" (*The* [London] *Times,* June 14, 1798). On July 1, 1798, Cornwallis wrote to Major General Robert Ross: "[Henry] Dundas wrote to me to know whether we wanted all the regiments they were sending to us, and I have in answer assured him that in my opinion we had not the least occasion for them . . ." (Charles Ross, ed., *Correspondence of Charles, First Marquis Cornwallis* [London: John Murray, 1859], II, 355). On July 14, 1798, *The* [London] *Times* reported: "He [Cornwallis] is Governor-General *in* Council, as well as Commander in Chief. His authority is paramount. . . ."

7. See King to H, May 12, June 6, 1798.

8. Although New York's gubernatorial election was held in the first week of May, 1798, the canvass was not completed until the middle of the following June ([New York] *Argus. Greenleaf's New Daily Advertiser,* June 12, 13, 1798). John Jay was re-elected over Robert R. Livingston by a vote of 16,012 to 13,632 (Werner, *New York Civil List,* 207).

9. The New York delegation to the Fifth Congress had consisted of six Republicans and four Federalists. This ratio was changed in the Sixth Congress to seven Republicans and three Federalists. See also H to Jay, April 24, 1798, note 2.

To George Washington

[Philadelphia, July 8, 1798]

Dear Sir

I was much surprized on my arrival here to discover that your nomination had been without any previous consultation of you.[1] Convinced of the goodness of the motives it would be useless to scan the propriety of the step. It is taken and the question is—what under the circumstances ought to be done? I use the liberty which my attachment to you and to the public authorises to offer my opinion that you should not decline the appointment. It is evident that the public satisfaction at it is lively and universal. It is not to be doubted that the circumstance will give an additional spring to the public mind—will tend much to unite and will facilitate the measures which the conjuncture requires—on the other hand, your declining would certainly produce the opposite effects, would throw a great damp upon the ardor of the Country inspiring the idea that the Crisis was not really serious or alarming. At least then, Let me entreat you & in this all your friends indeed all good citizens will unite, that if you do not give an unqualified acceptance that you accept provisionally—making your entering upon the duties to depend on future events so that the Community may look up to you as their certain Commander. But I prefer a simple acceptance.

It may be well however to apprise you that the arrangement of the army may demand your particular attention. The President has no *relative* ideas & his prepossessions on military subjects in reference to such a point are of the wrong sort. It is easy for us to have a good army but the selection requires care—it is necessary to inspire confidence in the efficient part of those who may incline to military service. Much adherence to routine would do great harm. Men of capacity & exertion in the higher stations are indispensable. It deserves consideration whether your presence at the seat of Government is not necessary. If you accept it will be conceived that the arrangement is yours & you will be responsible for it in reputaton. This & the influence of a right arrangement upon future success seem to require that you should in one mode or another see efficaciously that the arrangement is such as you would approve.

I remain Dr Sir   Yr. Affect & obedt servant   A Hamilton
                                                       July 8. 1798

General Washington

ALS, George Washington Papers, Library of Congress; copy, Hamilton Papers, Library of Congress.

1. Because of the threat of war with France, Congress on May 28, 1798, passed "An Act authorizing the President of the United States to raise a Provisional Army," which was not to exceed ten thousand men (1 *Stat.* 558–61). This act also provided "That whenever the President shall deem it expedient, he is hereby empowered to appoint, by and with the advice and consent of the Senate, a commander of the army which may be raised by virtue of this act, and who being commissioned as lieutenant-general may be authorized to command the armies of the United States. . . ."

On June 22, 1798, John Adams wrote to Washington: "In forming an Army, whenever I must come to that Extremity, I am at an immense Loss whether to call out the old Generals or to appoint a young Sett. If the French come here we must learn to march with a quick Step, and to Attack, for in that way only they are Said to be vulnerable. I must tax you, Sometimes for Advice. We must have your Name, if you, in any case permit Us to Use it. There will be more efficacy in it, than in many an Army" (ALS, George Washington Papers, Library of Congress; LC, Adams Family Papers, deposited in the Massachusetts Historical Society, Boston). On July 2, before Washington had replied to this letter, Adams nominated Washington "Lieutenant General and Commander in Chief of all the armies raised, or to be raised, in the United States," and on the following day the Senate unanimously confirmed the nomination (*Executive Journal*, I, 284). On July 4 Washington replied to Adams's letter of June 2 and stated: ". . . In case of *actual* Invasion by a formidable force, I certainly should not Intrench myself under the cover of Age & retirement, if my services should be required by my Country, to assist in repelling it" (ALS, Adams Family Papers, deposited in the Massachusetts Historical Society, Boston; ALS, letterpress copy, George Washington Papers, Library of Congress). On July 7 Adams wrote to Washington informing him of his appointment (ALS, Adams Family Papers, deposited in the Massachusetts Historical Society, Boston; copy, George Washington Papers, Library of Congress) and entrusted the letter to James McHenry to deliver to Washington (Adams to McHenry, July 6, 1798 [LC, Adams Family Papers, deposited in the Massachusetts Historical Society, Boston; copy, George Washington Papers, Library of Congress]). McHenry delivered Adams's letter to Washington on July 11 (McHenry to Adams, July 10, 1798 [ALS, Adams Family Papers, deposited in the Massachusetts Historical Society, Boston]), and on July 13 Washington wrote to Adams accepting the appointment (ALS, Adams Family Papers, deposited in the Massachusetts Historical Society, Boston; ALS, letterpress copy, George Washington Papers, Library of Congress.

For earlier correspondence concerning the possibility of Washington's serving as commander in chief, see H to Washington, May 19, June 2, 1798; Washington to H, May 27, 1798.

To Elizabeth Hamilton

Philadelphia 9th July 1798

I arrived here, My Dear Betsey, on Saturday in good health & not much fatigued. But I was immediately surrounded by a number of persons who engaged me till the hour of the Post had past by; so that I did not write as I intended. I cannot lose the opportunity of today; though I intend certainly to leave this place tomorrow in the Mail stage which arrives on Wednesday Morning. Mean time I command you as you love me to take care of yourself, to keep up your spirits, and to remember always that my happiness is inseparable from yours.

You wil be glad to know that *Decatur* in one of our vessels of War has captured & brought in a French Privateer of Twelve Guns.[1] It gives general satisfaction.

God bless My beloved   A Hamilton

Mrs. H.

ALS, Hamilton Papers, Library of Congress; copy, Columbia University Libraries.

1. On July 9, 1798, the *Gazette of the United States, and Philadelphia Daily*

Advertiser reported: "We have the satisfaction to announce to our readers that the Delaware sloop of war, capt. [Stephen] Decatur (who only went out to sea on Friday [July 6]) on Saturday evening captured a French privateer schooner of 12 guns and 70 men, close in with Egg-Harbour, and last evening the prize was brought to Fort Mifflin. Captain Decatur left his ship at New-Castle, and brought this intelligence to town. Capt. D. after he got to sea on Saturday morning, met with the ship Alexander Hamilton, from New York to Baltimore, the captain of which informed him that he had been plundered by a French privateer, and gave him directions what course he had steered. Capt. D. immediately went in search of her, and soon got in sight of four schooners; but not knowing which was the armed schooner that he had received information of, he thought it best to stand off as if he were a merchantman and alarmed at what might be armed vessels.

"The manœuvre had the intended effect, for the armed schooner gave her chace, until she discovered the Delaware to be a vessel of force, when she attempted to sheer off and get in land (where she supposed she should be safe, taking the Delaware for an English vessel of war) but she was obliged to surrender after a pretty long chace to the Delaware, and several shot being fired at her. This privateer is a new vessel said to have been built at Baltimore. She sailed from Cape Francois on the 19th of June, and has been on our coast only two days, during which time she has captured the ship Liberty Capt. Vredenberg, which sailed a few days from this port for Liverpool The vessel was sent to the West Indies, and the Captain and Crew of the Liberty were put on board a vessel bound for Boston. This privateer had also taken an English brig."

On July 10, 1798, the same paper reported: "The name of the French privateer taken by the Delaware is *Le Croyable,* she was commanded by a Capt. Sylvester, who has been an old Offender against our trade. When he was taken on board the Delaware, he expressed much surprize to Capt. Decatur at being taken by an American Vessel, observing *he had a commission from the French Government and wished to know how long France and America had been at war, as he said this was the first time he had heard of it?* We are happy to say, that he had not a single American in his crew; they were wholly French, and were yesterday landed at the Fort, where they will be kept under guard until they are otherwise disposed of. The Delaware returns immediately to her cruizing ground."

INDEX

COMPILED BY JEAN G. COOKE